A History of Western
Choral Music

A History of Western Choral Music

ROMANTICISM THROUGH THE AVANT-GARDE

Volume 2

CHESTER L. ALWES

OXFORD
UNIVERSITY PRESS

OXFORD
UNIVERSITY PRESS

Oxford University Press is a department of the University of Oxford. It furthers
the University's objective of excellence in research, scholarship, and education
by publishing worldwide. Oxford is a registered trade mark of Oxford University
Press in the UK and certain other countries.

Published in the United States of America by Oxford University Press
198 Madison Avenue, New York, NY 10016, United States of America.

© Oxford University Press 2016

Library of Congress Cataloging-in-Publication Data
Alwes, Chester Lee, 1947– author.
A history of Western choral music / Chester L. Alwes. volumes cm
Includes bibliographical references and index.
ISBN 978–0–19–517742–8 (v. 1, hardback : alk. paper) — ISBN 978–0–19–936193–9 (v. 1, pbk. : alk. paper) —
ISBN 978–0–19–937699–5 (v. 2, hardback : alk. paper) — ISBN 978–0–19–937700–8 (v. 2, pbk. : alk. paper)
1. Choral music.   I. Title.
ML1500.A46 2014
782.509—dc23

Hardback printed by Bridgeport National Bindery, Inc., United States of America

IN MEMORIAM

RICHARD F. FRENCH

(1915–2001)

Contents

Preface

Volume 2 picks up where volume 1 left off, completing the major genres common to both the Classical and Romantic periods: oratorio (chap. 1), part song (chap. 2), dramatic music (chap. 3), and the phenomenon of the choral symphony (chap. 4), which starts with Beethoven's Ninth Symphony and continues to the present. This music can, with varying degrees of success, be put into categories that provide the illusion of control or taxonomy.

However, categorizing the music of our own time is a difficult and elusive task because it has, as yet, no history. The discipline of history requires some degree of temporal separation in order to recognize larger trends that may not be visible to contemporaneous musical activity. Moreover, in its disparity, the music of the twentieth and early twenty-first centuries defies easy categorization by genre, compositional lineage, or chronology, resisting efforts to discuss it systematically. Ultimately, the most efficient way to proceed was to retain those aesthetic labels already in general use. Each of the first six chapters in volume 2 is devoted to a particular genre or to a compositional approach. Chapters 5 through 8 examine different "-isms," one per chapter: French Impressionism and Avant-gardism; Schoenberg's serialism, nationalism's use of indigenous ethnic materials as the basis for a new type of composition and, finally, the neoclassicism of Stravinsky and Hindemith. After that, we turn to the radical experiments of the avant-garde after World War II, music of such difficulty that it required a new type of specialized vocal ensemble that bore little resemblance to the choral groups of the past. Chapter 10 surveys the response of a diverse group of composers whose response to the avant-garde involved the conscious preservation of the inherited choral tradition, even if they added to it their own modernisms. Chapters 11 and 12 focus on the choral music of the United States and the British Isles, nations that have not only produced a wealth of choral music but also share in common so much history. The final chapter documents a new type of opposition to modernism, the return to a kind of musical simplicity that is simultaneously contemporary and accessible.

As this book progressed, the difficulty of writing a book of "history" became increasingly problematic. The technological revolutions of the past fifty years have radically changed the ways we access information, interact with one another, and do research. The shrinking of the physical and temporal distances that once divided us now presents us with unprecedented access to literally any kind of music; but such easy access challenges the traditional notion of a choral canon. The music discussed in volume 1 and the first four chapters of volume 2 once constituted a consensus common core of choral literature, but technology's impact on the recording industry, the music-publishing business, and the marketing of choral music and performance calls into question even the validity of such a canon. In this author's lifetime, recording has progressed from vinyl records to cassette tape to compact discs and now to digital streaming of both live and recorded music. The gradual impact of the innovations of such printers of music as Gutenberg, Petrucci, Breitkopf, and Novello that once shaped music's history now takes place in a continuous virtual present that makes any kind of music from any culture instantly available. All that this book can do is make the most sense of what historical certainty we think we have, then try to acknowledge current trends that are changing day by day. At this point, it is impossible to put the recent past into any meaningful or lasting historical context; that task belongs to another author and another time.

I must acknowledge the lack of a thorough discussion of the important contributions made by contemporary Canadian and Latin American choral composers. In the case of Canada, I found no logical place to put such a discussion; the diverse and vibrant choral music of Latin America is such that we don't yet know whether it constitutes art music in the traditional Western sense or is merely a novelty that gives our performances the appearance of being inclusive.

In the time of Palestrina or Bach, all composition was contemporary. Today, conductors have to contend with both historical repertory and an overabundance of new music tailored to meet the needs of the market. As conductors, the task of balancing these competing repertories and their respective values makes it increasingly difficult for us to be what Eric Leinsdorf called us to be, "the composer's advocate."

Chester L. Alwes
Mahomet, IL

Acknowledgments

In volume 1, I appropriately acknowledged the many musicians and scholars who have directly influenced me. In this second volume, I realize how indebted I am to the generations of students who have forced me to expand my horizons to deal with their changing priorities and expertise. I have had to acknowledge (often grudgingly) the changing realities of how information is accessed, research is done, and education takes place. In the course of compiling this volume, I have increasingly realized my dependence on a new generation of choral scholars and conductors like Andrew Megill, Donald Nally, Kristina Boerger, Craig Johnson, and Dominick DiOrio (to name only a few). As my reliance on the seers who shaped my own development has lessened, this new generation has emerged to add a much needed, fresh perspective.

I have gained a new appreciation of the quality of the Music and Performing Arts Library at the University of Illinois. I am especially indebted to John Wagstaff, Head Music Librarian and the members of his wonderful staff. In the world of publishing that is changing at a dizzying pace, I thank the assistance of the staff at Oxford University Press, especially Suzanne Ryan, for undertaking the physical production of this volume and its predecessor. There is a small group of people to whom I am indebted on a more personal, direct basis: Toby Greenberg, who secured the wonderful art and all the necessary licenses; Jean Jesensky, who tackled the task of making an index of the book's contents that allows greater ease of access for those who use it; Derryl Singley, whose expertise is responsible for the quality of the musical examples that illuminate my narrative; Molly Morrison of Newgen, who, once again, guided the book through all the pitfalls of production; and colleagues who have generously given their time to engage with me in philosophical discussions and the nitty-gritty task of helping clarify ideas and check facts. I am especially grateful to Leonard Rumery for his careful reading of the entire book and many valuable suggestions. Thanks, too, to Bill Brooks, Bob Demaree, Steve Taylor, Tom Ward, and others too numerous to mention who helped flesh out the skeleton of this volume and were generally supportive in ways they did not even understand at the time.

But there is one person who, more than all the others, is directly responsible for this book becoming a reality, my editor, Mary L. Sutherland. Her wise counsel, firm hand, devotion to music, and infinite patience have made this book a reality and, in the process, taught me a great deal about music, teaching, and scholarship. Her contribution has far exceeded the normal task of a line editor, producing benefits that will never be known by the readers but which must be acknowledged. Her importance to me and this book is outdistanced only by that of my wife, Marlys Scarbrough, who has had to live through my trauma as a "book virgin." Without her steadfast support and encouragement, I doubt this book would have ever seen the light of day.

Abbreviations

BB	Belá Bartók Thematic Catalogue
BL	*Benjamin Britten: Letters from a Life*
BWV	*Bach-Werke-Verzeichnis*
CM	Choral Music: A Norton Historical Anthology
CRM	*Classic and Romantic Music: A Comprehensive Survey*
DDT	*Denkmäler der Deutscher Tonkunst*
DGG	*Deutsche Grammophon Gesellschaft*
DTB	*Denkmäler der Tonkunst in Bayern*
DTÖ	*Denkmäler der Tonkunst in Österreich*
DTV	*Deutscher Taschenbuch Verlag*
ESM	*European Sacred Music*
FP	Francis Poulenc Thematic Catalogue
GH	*Gustav Holst: The Man and his Music*
GHM	Gustav Holst Thematic Catalogue
H	Bohuslav Martinů Thematic Catalogue
HCRL	*Haydn: Chronicle and Works*
HWCM I	*History of Western Choral Music*, vol. 1
JB	*Johannes Brahms: A Biography*
K.	Köchel (Mozart)
LU	*Liber Usualis*. Benedictines of Solesmes.
MGG	*Musik in Geschichte und Gegenwart*
MQ	*Musical Quarterly*
MT	*Musical Times*
NAWM	*Norton Anthology of Western Music*, 3rd ed. (1996)
NBA	*Neue Ausgabe sämtlicher Werke* (Bach)
Neoclassicism	*Neoclassicism in Music: From the Genesis of the Concept through the Schoenberg/ Stravinsky Polemic*
NG	*The New Grove Dictionary of Music and Musicians* (1980)
NG2	*The New Grove Dictionary of Music and Musicians*, 2nd ed. (2001)
OHWM	*Oxford History of Western Music*
OUP	Oxford University Press
SW	*Sämtliche Werke* (Arnold Schoenberg)
WAB	*Werkverzeichnis Anton Bruckners*
A	Alto (solo)
a	alto (chorus)
acc.	accompaniment, accompanied by
+	augmented chord
B	Bass (solo)
b	bass (chorus)
Bar	Baritone solo
bn	bassoon
C	Contralto solo
cel	celesta
chbr	chamber

cl	clarinet
db	double bass
dbn	double (contra) bassoon
°	diminished chord
eng hn	English horn
fl	flute
hmn	harmonium
hp	harp
hpd	harpsichord
inst(s)	instrument(s)
It.	Italian
Lat.	Latin
LH	Left hand
Mez	mezzo-soprano solo
mic	microphone
nar(s)	narrator(s)
ob	oboe
orat(s)	oratorio(s)
org	organ
perc	percussion
pf	piano
pic	piccolo
qnt(s)	quintet(s)
qrt(s)	quartet(s)
recit(s)	Recitative(s)
rev(s)	revision(s), revised (by/for)
RH	Right hand
S	Soprano (solo)
SATB	soprano, alto, tenor, bass
s	soprano (chorus)
SO	Symphony orchestra
spkr(s)	speaker(s)
str	strings
br	brass
synth	synthesizer
T	Tenor (solo)
t	tenor (chorus)
timp	timpani
tpt	trumpet
tbn	trombone
va	viola
vc	cello
vib	vibraphone
vle	violone
vn	violin
v/vv	voice/voices
v./vv.	Verse (s)
ww	woodwind
xyl	xylophone

A History of Western
Choral Music

1

The Oratorio from Haydn to Elgar

During Joseph Haydn's first visit to England (1791–92), he attended one of the series of annual Handel Commemoration concerts in Westminster Abbey where he heard complete performances of *Messiah* and *Israel in Egypt*, as well as excerpts from *Saul, Esther, Judas Maccabeus*, and *Deborah*. While in England, Haydn received the libretto for his oratorio *The Creation*, after having decided to compose an oratorio at the instigation of the impresario Salomon, who organized Haydn's concert appearances. The strength of this work and its successors (notably Mendelssohn's *Elijah*) tends to obscure the fairly large body of late eighteenth-century oratorios tied to neither Handel nor England.

THE ENGLISH ORATORIO AFTER HANDEL

There were, of course, English composers who eagerly took up Handel's mantle: Thomas Augustine Arne (1710–78); John Christopher Smith, the younger; John Stanley (1712–86); Charles Avison (1709–70); and Johann Christian Bach (1735–82).[1] Handel's popularity was so great that these compositions were largely regarded as alternatives to his music rather than successors. Indeed, pasticcios using Handel's music set to completely different texts (e.g., Samuel Arnold's *Redemption* [1770?]) were often preferable alternatives to mere imitations.

Across the Channel, oratorios employed either the Italian *oratorio volgare* or various Protestant models. Throughout the second half of the eighteenth century, Italian composers wrote oratorios that were essentially *opera seria* based on sacred stories, which is precisely how J. G. Walther defined the genre in his 1732 *Musikalisches Lexikon*.[2] Italian oratorio composers include Leonardo Vinci, Leonardo Leo, Nicola Porpora, Niccolò Jomelli, Giovanni Paisiello, Baldassare Galuppi, and, at the Catholic court in Dresden, Johann Adolf Hasse, the Czech composer Jan Dysmas Zelenka (1679–1745), and Johann David Heinichen (1683–1729). The best known of Hasse's oratorios, according to Howard Smither, is *La Conversione dell' Santo Agostino* (1750).[3]

Italian influence dominated oratorio production at the Viennese court, beginning with Antonio Caldara. Along with Antonio Draghi and Marc'Antonio Ziani, Caldara introduced this style to native Austrian composers: J. J. Fux, J. G. Reutter, and Florian Gassmann. The death of Emperor Charles VI (1740) led to a decline in oratorio performances, but the genre resurfaced in occasional performances (most often during Lent) of works by Giuseppe Bonno (1711–88) and Antonio Salieri (1750–1825).

In Vienna, the founding of the *Tonkünstler-Sozietät* in 1771 led to a resurgence of the oratorio. This society provided another important link between Handel and Haydn: the influence of Baron Gottfried van Swieten. In 1779 the *Tonkünstler-Sozietät*'s Lenten oratorio performances included Handel's *Judas Maccabeus*, with a German translation by van Swieten. Beginning in 1786, van Swieten and a group of his peers arranged private performances of Handel's oratorios at the Imperial Court Library. This group, the *Gesellschaft der Associerten*, commissioned a choral version of Haydn's *Seven Last Words*, both oratorios, and Mozart's orchestrations of Handel's oratorios (most notably *Messiah*). According to Georg Griesinger, an early Haydn biographer, Haydn and Mozart alternated as musical directors for these performances.[4]

FRANZ JOSEPH HAYDN (1732–1809)

Largely overlooked in Haydn's career is his Italian oratorio *Il ritorno di Tobia* (1775), composed for the *Tonkünstler-Sozietät*. The libretto by Giovanni Boccherini is based on a story from the book of Tobit in the Apocrypha. Howard Smither states that "this is essentially a Metastasian libretto: Boccherini observes the unities of time, place, and action; events which occurred in another time and place are narrated in past tense; the libretto proceedes [sic] mainly by alternation between recitatives and arias; the only ensemble is a duet; and each part closes with a chorus."[5] This description, a common template, fits any number of oratorios written at that time.

Both Pietro Metastasio (1698–1782) and Apostolo Zeno (1668–1750) were the leading opera and oratorio librettists at the Viennese court. In 1729, Metastasio replaced Zeno as court poet, holding that post until his death. His work was so popular that those fifty years (1729–82) became known as the "Metastasian era." The primary influences on Metastasio were Petrarch and his sixteenth-century imitators and the moral philosophy of René Descartes (*Les passions de l'âme*). Metastasio's libretti frequently combined plot lines from antiquity (including the Bible for oratorios) with the Cartesian notion that virtue was best embodied in an individual's ability to control human passion.

The typical Metastasian libretto assumed some basic musical and structural needs such as: (1) scene changes (in the operas) associated with the entrance or exit of a character; action depicted primarily through dialogue (recitative) leading to a concluding aria; (2) arias with two contrasting texts using the *da capo* aria form; and (3) ensembles or choruses (in nonoperatic formats) that conclude an act (of which there are typically three in operas and two in oratorios). Accordingly, Haydn's oratorio *Il ritorno di Tobia* has two acts, each concluded by a chorus.

Another important feature of Metastasio's libretti was the preservation of the ancient unities of time, place, and action. Taken to their most extreme form, use of these unities limited the action to a single day and place. For example, in one of Metastasio's more popular libretti, *Betulia liberata*, which served as the bases of oratorios by Gassmann, Holzbauer, Jommelli, Reutter, and Mozart, the deeds of Judith in the camp of the Assyrians (including the beheading of Holofernes) are told in the past tense because they took place outside the city (Bethulia). These limitations become more evident as we explore later oratorios.

DIE SCHÖPFUNG ("THE CREATION")

Haydn's two late oratorios, *The Creation* and *The Seasons*, are generally more highly regarded than his earlier Italian work. These two oratorios are significant departures from typical Austrian oratorios of the time. Most obvious is the enhanced role of the chorus, a change likely prompted by Haydn's exposure to Handel's music.[6] Haydn received the libretto in England and had it translated into German by van Swieten, who elaborated on his role as translator in a letter printed in the *Allgemeine Musikalische Zeitung* of 1798.[7] Haydn's work on the oratorio occupied him for about a year (1796–97), and the premiere took place in the Schwarzenberg Palace in Vienna on April 30, 1798. According to contemporary accounts, Haydn himself supervised from the keyboard the large chorus and orchestra, which consisted of around 180 performing forces.[8] One of the controversies surrounding this initial version of the oratorio involved the thorny question of how van Swieten's translation compared with the English text of the bilingual publication (1800).[9]

The layout of the libretto clearly departed from the Metastasian model, having three (rather than two) parts and the action taking place over six days. The adoption of three parts was another bow to Handel, whose oratorios typically had three parts. The English libretto drew on three principal literary sources: (1) The biblical account of the Creation (Genesis 1 and 2); (2) John Milton's poem *Paradise Lost* (especially Bk. 7); and (3) Psalm 19:1–5 and Psalm 104:27–30.

The libretto unfolds logically: Part 1 covers the first four days of Creation, Part 2 the fifth and sixth days, and Part 3 describes Adam and Eve in the Garden of Eden. Nicholas Temperley points out that each day contains the following elements: prose (past tense) from Genesis and set as recitative; poetic commentary (present tense) scored for either ensemble or chorus; prose (past tense) set as recitative, which leads to a choral hymn of praise.[10] For days one, two, and four, Haydn used this pattern literally; for days three, five, and six he expanded it by repeating the first two elements before proceeding to the final two.

Table 1.1 confirms the alternation of the literary elements posited by Temperley: recitative (from Genesis) and solo/ensemble/chorus, generally poetic, except for the texts of no. 13 "The Heavens are telling" and no. 27 "Achieved is the glorious work," both of which are taken from the book of Psalms. The text column reveals that the libretto did not set all of the texts of Genesis 1, omitting vv. 5, 8, 12–13, 17–19, 23, 25, and 27–30. Many of these omissions result from the librettist's decision to abandon the Genesis formula of ending each day with "And there was evening and there was morning, a (insert number) day." The exclusive use of Miltonian poetic texts for Part 3 represents an even more notable departure from the alternating text types of Parts 1 and 2.

There are five vocal soloists, representing only three of the voice parts (S, T, and B).[11] The first three, appearing exclusively in Parts 1 and 2, have angelic names—Gabriel (S), Uriel (T), and Raphael (B). Gabriel ("mighty one of God") is believed to be the angel who delivered the Koran to the Prophet Mohammed. Uriel ("my light is God") is the archangel of the Apocrypha,

Table 1.1 Haydn, *The Creation*, formal structure

Movements		Text	Key
Day 1:	Accompanied Recitative (Raphael)	Gen 1:1–4	
	Chorus	Gen 1:1–4	E♭ major
	Accompanied Recitative (Uriel)	Gen 1:1–4	E♭ major–C major
	Aria (Uriel) with chorus	Poetic	A major–C minor–A major
Day 2:	Accompanied Recitative (Raphael)	Gen 1:6–7	
	Aria (Gabriel) with chorus	Poetic	C major
Day 3:	Secco Recitative (Raphael)	Gen 1:9–10	
	Aria (Raphael)	Poetic	D minor/D major
	Secco Recitative (Gabriel)	Gen 1:11	
	Aria (Gabriel)	Poetic	B♭ major
	Secco Recitative (Uriel)	(Quasi–biblical)	
	Chorus	Poetic	D major
Day 4:	Secco Recitative (Uriel)	Gen 1:14–16	
	Accompanied Recitative (Uriel)	Poetic	D major–C major
	Chorus and Trio	Ps 19	C major
Day 5:	Accompanied Recitative (Gabriel)	Gen 1: 20	
	Aria (Gabriel)	Poetic	F major
	Recitative secco/Acc. (Raphael)	Gen 1:21–22	D minor
	Trio	Poetic	A major
	Chorus with trio	Poetic	A major
Day 6:	Secco recitative (Raphael)	Gen 1:24	
	Accompanied Recitative	(Poetic)	
	Aria (Raphael)	Poetic	D major
	Secco recitative (Uriel)	Gen 1:26	
	Aria (Uriel)	Poetic	C minor
	Secco recitative (Raphael)	Gens 1:31	
	Chorus	Poetic	B♭ major
	Trio (Gabriel, Uriel, Raphael)	Ps 104:27–30	E♭ major/minor
	Chorus (reprise)		B♭ major
Part 3			
	Accompanied Recitative (Uriel)	Poetic	E major–C major
	Duet (Adam and Eve) + chorus	Poetic	C major
	Secco Recitative (Adam)		Poetic
	Duet (Eve and Adam)	Poetic	E♭ major
	Secco Recitative (Uriel)		Poetic
	Chorus (with SATB soli)	Poetic	B♭ major

mentioned in Esdras 2; this angel also appears as a character in Milton's *Paradise Lost* and in Longfellow's poem *The Golden Legend*. Raphael, another of the seven archangels, means "God heals." The other two soloists are Adam and Eve, who, understandably, sing only in Part 2. Often, for reasons of economy, the same soloists sing Gabriel/Eve (S) and Raphael (B)/Adam (Bar).

The three angelic soloists of Parts 1 and 2 do not interact dramatically nor do Adam and Eve engage in dialogue. These restrictions were not viewed as defects but as part of the essential difference between opera and oratorio. To compensate for the absence of dialogue, costumes, and scenery, oratorio composers had historically used a narrator (*historicus, testo*). In *The Creation*, the three angelic soloists fulfill this function, introducing the Creation events. But even here they are not *dramatis personae* because the idiom itself precludes drama: How could there be drama when no people yet exist? The angels are passive reporters, a quality unique to this particular libretto.

In addition to providing the impetus for Haydn to write an oratorio, Handel's influence also furnished a specific musical model that Haydn felt bound to follow. The complete Handel oratorios that Haydn heard in 1791 were *Messiah*, which had already attained great popularity, and *Israel in Egypt*; both are exclusively biblical and lack any action. Like *Messiah*, *The Creation* is biblical (but not exclusively so), contemplative rather than overtly dramatic, dominated by powerful choral writing, and devoid of the clearly defined presence of a *historicus*. We can extend this comparison to include the substantial role that accompanied recitatives play in both works. Haydn's understanding of and attempt to emulate the Handelian oratorio simultaneously defines his aesthetic orientation as well as the path that the nineteenth-century oratorio took.

But Handel's music was not the only influence that shaped Haydn's *The Creation*. The original librettist imbued the text with numerous markers of contemporary cosmology: the text celebrated nature; in part, this resulted from the decision to use the text from Genesis 1 rather than the parallel account in Genesis 2. This emphasis also reflected the influence of the Deists, a group whose belief in reason led them to question literal truth of the Bible. And too, Enlightenment philosophy intersected with traditional Christianity, a meeting marked by many clashes, but the Deists and the Christians agreed that God's creation was an orderly process, moving logically from simple (or macrocosmic) to complex (microcosmic).

Another group whose ideals affected the structure of Haydn's oratorio was that of the Freemasons, a movement begun in England in 1717 and which embodied the principles of the Enlightenment. Nicholas Temperley suggests that the anonymous librettist of *The Creation* may have been a Freemason.[12] Haydn himself was a Mason, as was Mozart, and the symbolism of Masonic ritual was as vital to his oratorio as it was to Mozart's *Die Zauberflöte*. The oratorio envisions a Master Architect, one whose supreme knowledge brings order out of chaos, and this orderliness also colors the oratorio's structure. Although tripartite structure is also Handel's preference, the number 3 plays a prominent role in Masonic symbolism, manifested in the libretto's use of three angelic soloists.[13] Furthermore, the libretto divides the tasks of these soloists in a rational way: Uriel sings of light (no. 2, nos. 11–12); Gabriel's arias focus on the creation of plants (nos. 8–9) and birds (nos. 14–15); Raphael's texts detail the separation of land and sea (and its inhabitants) and the creation of the other animals up to but not including man (nos. 21–22). Haydn's careful distribution of the arias (two for each soloist) was yet another manifestation of such Enlightenment planning.

The tonalities presented at the beginning of the work become archetypes for the entire oratorio and musical symbols of the Enlightenment. Haydn set the "Depiction of Chaos" in C minor, reserving C major for the creation of light. Even more striking is the juxtaposition in Uriel's aria ("Now vanish before the holy beams the gloomy shades of night") of A major and C minor ("Despairing cursing Rage" as the remnant of chaos); the return to A major coincides with the text "a new created world," in which order and reason prevail.[14]

All of this juxtapositioning suggests a structure for the oratorio in which tonality plays a significant role. If C minor represents chaos, its parallel mode, C major, embodies reason or God, who divided darkness from light. This tonal dichotomy might well explain the libretto's omission in Genesis 1:5 where the archetypes of darkness and light are explained as night and day. The extended movements of Parts 1 and 2 tend toward keys closely related to the C minor/major orbit.

The tonalities that mark the end of each day of creation form this sequence:

Part 1:
A major (day 1); C major (day 2); D major (day 3); C major (day 4)

Part 2:
A major (day 5); B♭ (day 6)

Part 1 favors C major. Beginning with Part 2, however, there is a pronounced shift toward flat keys, beginning with no. 15 (F) and ending with the triptych that concludes Part 2 (B♭–E♭–B♭). The intervening nonrecitative items reprise the three central tonalities of Part 1: A (no. 19), D (no. 22), and C (no. 24). The overall harmonic plan of the oratorio features a descent from C to B♭ within Parts 1 and 2, and again in Part 3.[15] The result is the unprecedented phenomenon of a classical composition that begins in one key and ends in another.[16] First, C major replaces C minor as God brings order out of chaos.[17] This same tonality dominates Part 1, ending the second day (no. 5, "The marv'lous work beholds amazed") and the fourth day (no. 13, "The heavens are telling"). Haydn reserves the most important appearance of C major for the aria "In native worth and honor clad," highlighting that God created man "in his own image."

The ensuing descent to B♭ represents the Fall of Adam, a view reinforced by two subsequent events. When Raphael joins the trio in no. 26, he sings "But as to them thy face is hid, with sudden terror they are struck. Thou tak'st their breath away; they vanish into dust." Haydn illustrates mankind's isolation from God by moving dramatically from E♭ major to E♭ minor. The lengthy, descriptive orchestral introduction that opens Part 3 is in E major, a key removed from the B♭ conclusion of Part 2 by the interval of a tritone. Haydn uses this tonal remove—the dreaded tritone—to contrast the tranquil portrayal of dawn on the first day of humanity in the Garden of Eden with the impending disruption of the relationship between God and his creation fomented by Satan.

Haydn's music is so well known and beautifully written that it scarcely requires more adulation. There is one piece, however, that stands out for its innovative, audacious approach to form, orchestration, and pictorialism—the oratorio's overture "Representation of Chaos." Theorists and commentators have long recognized the special qualities of this extraordinary movement. Nothing in Haydn's earlier music prepared his audience for the powerful overture depicting chaos by negating its obverse, order. In eighteenth-century music, order is manifest in the use of periodic phrasing based on accepted tonal hierarchies. A well-known classical melody, not unlike Mozart's *Eine kleine Nachtmusik*, features phrases that combine to form short periods. For example, *Nachtmusik*'s opening phrase has two four-bar periods that use the same rhythm to arpeggiate first an ascending tonic chord (C) and then a descending dominant (G⁷). Together, these periods comprise an antecedent phrase to which Mozart provides the necessary consequent phrase and then repeats (and varies) the process to grow the form. What makes the music work is the predictability and regularity (four-bar phrases using alternation of tonic and dominant seventh chords and identical rhythmic construction) of its construction.

Haydn, on the other hand, posits that chaos is expectation denied but achieved, in this case, by avoiding any cadence that might establish a key. After an initial unison C, marked *forte* and spread over four octaves, the first harmony is a quiet, tentative, first-inversion A♭ major chord (ex. 1.1a).

Example 1.1 a/b: Haydn, *The Creation*

a. mm. 1-6

b. m. 35

Haydn did not create a cadence until mm. 20–21, and this is to D♭, the Neapolitan of the presumptive tonic. The half-step motion implicit in this unexpected cadence (C–D♭) becomes a unifying motive for the overture; the same melodic half step, everywhere present, also facilitates his denial of harmonic expectation. A prominent rhythmic motive (ex. 1.1b) adds another layer of chaos: because it appears in so many different orchestral voices, it produces a texture of multiple obbligato parts as opposed to the melodic/thematic dominance of the strings (especially vln 1)—the hallmark of previous classical orchestration.

Haydn sustains this mysterious harmonic flux and unusual orchestral texture for thirty-nine measures before cadencing to another unison C in m. 40. We hear this accented repetition of the movement's tonic as a recapitulation; the next six measures literally reprise mm. 3–8. But the insecure harmonies of the opening reappear nine measures later (mm. 51–55), created by an extended chromatic bass line (F–E–E♭–D–D♭–C–B–C), which sets up the long-anticipated cadence to C minor and Raphael's solemn intonation of the first verse of Genesis 1.[18]

Van Swieten's musical suggestions to Haydn concerning this passage are interesting: "In this chorus, the darkness should disappear little by little, but enough of the darkness should remain so that the instantaneous transition to light is felt quite strongly. 'Let there be light,' etc. ought to be said only once."[19] Haydn followed van Swieten's advice by indeed stating the text only once and making it strongly felt. Nonetheless, no one in the audience could possibly have anticipated the now famous creation-of-light cadence. According to Frederik Silverstolpe, Haydn kept the use of this device secret from even his closest friends:

> That was the only passage of the work which Haydn had kept hidden. I think I see his face even now, as this part sounded in the orchestra. Haydn had the expression of someone who is thinking of biting his lips, either to hide his embarrassment or to conceal a secret. And in that moment when light broke out for the first time, one would have said that rays darted from the compos-er's burning eyes. The enchantment of the electrified Viennese was so general that the orchestra could not proceed for some minutes.[20]

The musical effect of this moment is as profound today as it undoubtedly was in 1798.

Of all the choruses in *The Creation*, none is more famous than "The Heavens are tell-ing," the text of which paraphrases Psalm 19:

> The heavens are telling the glory of God;
> The wonder of his works displays the firmament.
> Today, that is coming, speaks it the day;
> The night that is gone, to following night.
> In all the lands resounds the word,
> Never unperceived, Ever understood.

The chorus sings only the first sentence, the final two being the province of the solo trio. The alternation of choral and solo textures creates a rondo-like form. The chorus begins *attacca* from the conclusion of Uriel's preceding recitative, which ends on a half-cadence to G. Although not nearly as dramatic as the creation of light in the first movement, the cadence from the recita-tive's conclusion—this one to C—alludes to the creation of all the lights in the firmament. Bruce MacIntyre has convincingly shown that the melodic curve of this chorus reappears in melodies heard throughout the oratorio (ex. 1.2).[21]

Example 1.2 Haydn, *The Creation*, no. 14, mm. 1–4

What makes this chorus so amazingly effective are the subtle variations of texture and tempo that Haydn introduces with each return of the chorus. Each new entrance ratchets up the tempo, creating exuberance in both this chorus and the first part of the oratorio.

The end of Part 2 succeeds in at least matching this impressive conclusion. To some extent, its weight results from the sheer mass of the triptych—a solo trio flanked by two choruses that function as theme and enhanced variation. This chorus shares with "The Heavens are telling" a use of paraphrases from Psalm 19 and Psalm 104:27–30. The two choruses use the same key (B♭), tempo (*Vivace*), and text (lines 1 and 4 of the opening become lines 1 and 2 of the reprise). But the second chorus is three times as long as the first, due to Haydn's inclusion of a fugal texture, which provides further evidence of Handel's influence. Haydn sets this Trio in E♭ and in triple meter (*Poco adagio*), apportioning the text in an appropriately orderly fashion. Gabriel (S) and Uriel (T) sing v. 1; Raphael (B) sings v. 2; and all three soloists unite for v. 3, creating a modified recapitulation of the opening music. If there were any doubts concerning Handel's influence, the resemblances between Haydn's fugue subjects and the "Hallelujah Chorus" surely dispel them (ex. 1.3).

Example 1.3 Haydn, *The Creation*, no. 27, mm. 9–13

DIE JAHRESZEITEN ("THE SEASONS")

Within a year of the premiere of *The Creation*, Haydn set to work on another oratorio, *The Seasons*, the libretto of which was based on the Scottish poet James Thomson's (1700–1748) poem celebrating the four seasons. As he had for *The Creation*, Gottfried van Swieten translated Thomson's English poem into German. In some instances, van Swieten's German relied on an earlier translation (1745) by Barthold Heinrich Brockes (1680–1747), who was principally known for his Passion oratorio texts set by Bach, Handel, Telemann, Stölzel, and Mattheson. Van Swieten not only translated Thomson's poetry but also crafted it to function as choruses, recitatives, and arias. In the process, van Swieten drastically shortened the original poem, recasting it to fit the traditional musical forms associated with the oratorio and, in the process, establishing new precedents for what constituted an oratorio. The clearest problem concerning this text is its lack of a structural template like the one successfully employed in *The Creation*. In *The Seasons* there is no orderly progression toward a satisfying and logical dramatic conclusion but rather a pictorial representation of events typical of all four seasons. For example, the program of Spring (*Der Frühling*) unfolds as the transition from "surly winter" to spring (both instrumental and vocal); followed by a pastoral chorus welcoming the arrival of spring; then a recitative and aria for Simon (bass) celebrating the farmer's fieldwork; next the farmer's prayer for "propitious" weather (recitative and aria for tenor); an impromptu interlude follows in which Hanne (soprano) and Lukas (tenor) invite their companions to "wander 'mid the sweets of May," where all is "lovely, all delightful, all replete with joy"; and finally, a concluding hymn of gratitude and praise in "God of light! God of life! Hail gracious Lord," to which the addition of a fugue on "Endless praise to thee we'll sing" seems a pro forma, obligatory response.

While the texts of mvts. 2 through 5 proceed logically, the concluding chorus seems somewhat contrived. At the end of the duet and chorus, Simon injects a totally new thought: "Every feeling, every longing from our Maker flows." This awkward textual transition allows Haydn to compose an ersatz sacred chorus. Although this chorus is beautiful and well crafted, it lacks textual and formal coherence and ends in a different key than the one in which it began.

The text of Simon's aria, *Schon eilet froh der Ackermann* ("With joy the impatient husbandman") illustrates this problem (Table 1.2); both van Swieten's German text and a modern translation reveal a somewhat consistent scansion but the lack of a rhyme scheme. While the scansion of the two verses is quantitatively the same, they occur in different configurations (8-6-8-6 and 8-6-6-8); the only rhyme is in the German text, and it is limited to the opening line of each strophe.

Haydn sets the robust opening text in C major, with an appropriately muscular theme (ex. 1.4).

Example 1.4 Haydn, *The Seasons*, part 1 (Spring), no. 3b, mm. 9–12

But the strong cadence to C that ends v. 1 is immediately followed by A♭ major (ex. 1.5), hinting at C minor, the key in which v. 2 begins.

Table 1.2 Haydn, *The Seasons*, part 1, 3b, Text

German	English	Syllable Count	Rhyme
Schon eilet froh der Ackermann	With joy the impatient husbandman	8	a
Zur Arbeit auf das Feld;	Drives forth his lusty team,	6	b
Im langen Furchen schreitet er	To where the well-used plow remains,	8	c
Dem Pfluge flötend nach.	Now loosened from the frost.	6	d
Im abgemessnem Gange dann	With measured step he throws the grain	8	a
Wirft er den Samen aus,	Within the bounteous earth.	6	f
Den birgt der Acker treu	O sun, soft show'rs and dews!	6	g
Und reift ihn bald zur goldnen Frucht.	The golden ears in plenty bring!	8	h

Example 1.5 Haydn, *The Seasons*, part 1 (Spring), no. 3b, mm. 48–58

After repetitions of the text in various tonal areas (E♭ and C minor), Haydn reprises the opening text and music to create a ternary form. This recapitulation omits most of the original first half, concentrating on presenting lines 3 and 4 of the text in C major.

One specific musical detail reveals Haydn's characteristic sense of humor. The happy plowman whistles while he works; Haydn suggests that the farmer (and perhaps the listener) is musically literate by placing the theme of his "Surprise" Symphony No. 94 in the piccolo part (ex. 1.6).

Example 1.6 Haydn, *The Seasons*, part 1 (Spring), no. 3b, mm. 17–20

Haydn's aria also captures the rustic quality of the Austrian countryside and peasantry. His fascination with this topic is not limited to this aria or even this segment of the oratorio. Giorgio Pestelli twice alludes to this rural quality, noting that

> [t]he Mozartean accent that was noticeable in the best "London" symphonies became more apparent in the works written during the early years of Mozart's posthumous fame. Many arias, especially in *The Seasons*, begin in a manner fit for Papageno ... there is a note of the kind of bourgeois morality that occurs in Goethe's contemporary elegy *Hermann und Dorothea* (1797). Hermann's mother could easily live in the countryside of *The Seasons*, so neat and tidy, as, worried about her son, she crosses the garden in a hurry, but

not enough of a hurry to prevent her from tidying up a stake or removing a caterpillar from a cabbage, "since an industrious woman never takes a step without purpose."[22]

Pestelli suggests an attitude more romantic than classical. If Simon sings in a manner "fit for Papageno," he possesses, by inference, that sense of nobility that many authors (from Jean-Jacques Rousseau on) attribute to such rural people. The naïve bourgeois morality and sensitivity that *The Seasons* projects, while perfectly amenable to Austrians, proved somewhat at odds with perceptions elsewhere, which perhaps accounts for the work's relative lack of popularity outside of Austria.

In *The Seasons*, Haydn's central problem is the libretto's lack of drama. Unlike *The Creation*, in which both soloists and chorus had clearly defined roles within a consistent formal plan, the texts of this oratorio (Thomson's and van Swieten's) are descriptive and contemplative. The lack of drama that was understandable and forgivable in *Creation* becomes a problem here in *Jahreszeiten*, and this forced Haydn to adopt a wider array of vocal textures to compensate for the libretto's bland, predictable poetry.

This is not to say that the work lacks wonderful choruses. In Part 3, Autumn (*Herbst*), there are two—"Hört das laute Getön" (no. 26) and "Juchhe! Juchhe! Der Wein ist da" (no. 28)— filled with vivid musical effects summoned forth by the archetypal activities they describe (hunting, drinking, dancing). Although apt and colorful, the musical conceits of these choruses are hardly those typically found in an oratorio. Despite the resulting palette of choral and orchestral color, in these choruses Haydn seems to lack the inspiration evident in the choruses of *Creation*. In the hunting chorus, for example, this traditionally male activity restricts the women of the chorus to rather inane comments or repetition of text already sung by the male chorus.

More impressive is the drinking chorus "Juchhe! Juchhe! Der Wein ist da," which features frequent antiphonal exchanges between the male and female singers. While hardly dramatic, this dialogue at least seems plausible given the existing social fabric. Haydn utilizes interjections of the word "Juchhe!" (hurrah!) to move to increasingly remote tonal areas: to G (m. 37), A minor (m. 43), E minor (m. 48), and, ultimately, F♯ minor (m. 53). The "Juchhe!" chords (ex. 1.7) typically initiate a cadential progression, often to unexpected keys.

Example 1.7 Haydn, *The Seasons*, part 3 (Autumn), no. 16b, mm. 35–39

Another masterful touch is his change of meter (to 6/8) and tempo (to *Allegro Assai*) to signal the textual transition from a generic praise of wine to the activities associated with making it. With typical humor, Haydn succumbs to tone painting implicit in the text (e.g., fife and drum and drones with chromatic *appoggiatura* for the bagpipe). The music whirls and spins through a series of keys to suggest the increasing inebriation of the peasants, a state humorously portrayed by Haydn's skewed rhythmic treatment of the choral fugue's subject (ex. 1.8).

Example 1.8 a/b: Haydn, *The Seasons*, part 3 (Autumn), no. 16b

The vocal bass's errant presentation of the theme is proof positive that things are getting out of hand.

Despite the problems of textual and formal coherence presented by its libretto, *The Seasons* is the first significant oratorio based on a secular, nonbiblical text. As such, it becomes the precedent for other nineteenth-century secular and/or nonbiblical oratorio-like works to meet the demands of the increasingly large and diverse body of choral societies, which depended on works with symphonic accompaniment (e.g., the Berlin *Sing-Akademie* [1791] and Vienna's *Gesellschaft der Musikfreunde* [1812]). Far from supplanting the traditional biblical oratorio, these newer oratorios accommodate the increasingly secular literary tastes of the romantic era; they provided an alternative to biblical texts that were less appealing to some or for whom Nature itself was the new, enlightened religion.

FELIX MENDELSSOHN (1809–47)

Haydn's successor in the English oratorio market was Felix Mendelssohn, whose rationale for composing oratorios had less initially to do with Handel and England than his fascination with Johann Sebastian Bach. Haydn's enormous popularity in England predestined the success of his oratorios in that country. It also seems to have engaged the English to look to the Continent for his and Handel's successors in the burgeoning oratorio and cantata market. In *The Mirror of Music*, Percy Scholes documents the growth of English choral festivals, choral societies, and newer denominations like Methodism whose volunteer choirs lacked the resources of Anglican cathedrals. All of these things created a demand for new choral music.[23] Not surprisingly, this rapid growth prompted advances in the new field of "music education," as people like Joseph Novello, John Curwen, John Hullah Pike, and others designed pedagogical materials to increase the musical ability of these largely amateur choruses.

PAULUS, OP.36

In 1829 Mendelssohn lobbied his teacher, Karl Friedrich Zelter, to allow the *Sing-Akademie* to perform Mendelssohn's new orchestration of Bach's *St. Matthew Passion*. Zelter himself was acquainted with Bach's music through his composition study with C. F. C. Fasch (1736–1800), the harpsichordist at the Berlin court of Frederick the Great during C. P. E. Bach's tenure there, and J. P. Kirnberger. All were familiar to some extent with J. S. Bach's works. Mendelssohn's motivations for pursuing this project are complex and numerous, and not unlike Mozart's various Handelian projects undertaken at van Swieten's instigation. Old Bach represented a German prototype for romantic composers following Austrian dominance in the Classical period.

Mendelssohn's family background was German-Jewish aristocracy; his father, Abraham Mendelssohn, had had his children baptized in 1816, most likely to ensure their assimilation into German society. Felix's interest in the music of J. S. Bach sparked an in-depth examination of that music as a model for Lutheran compositions (choral and organ) and gave rise to an increasing awareness among both Protestants and Catholics in seventeenth- and eighteenth-century music. Mendelssohn's early successes in composing and conducting led him to the prestigious posts of director of the Leipzig Gewandhaus, the Leipzig Conservatory, the *Staats- und Domchor Berlin*, and the Berlin Opera Orchestra. He singlehandedly brought the German chorale back into the spotlight by its inclusion in symphonic, organ, and choral compositions. Richard Taruskin states that "he did more than any other single musician to reinvent not only German, but all of modern concert life in the form that we now know it."[24] Felix Mendelssohn died at the ripe young age of thirty-eight, no doubt due to overwork.

Returning from Italy in 1831, Mendelssohn visited Johann Schelble, the founder and conductor of the Frankfurt *Cäcilienverein*, who first broached the idea of an oratorio based on the life of St. Paul. This meeting was tantamount to a commission as Mendelssohn then began corresponding with Julius Schubring, a Lutheran pastor in Dessau, about drafting a libretto.[25] The composition of the oratorio occupied Mendelssohn from March 1834 through 1835; he completed the autograph score early in 1836 and sent it to the publisher Simrock, who printed choral scores in time for the work's premiere at the eighteenth Lower Rhein Music Festival in Düsseldorf on May 22, 1836. Mendelssohn conducted, leading an enormous contingent of 356 singers and 172 orchestral musicians in that performance, which prompted the organizers of the 1837 Birmingham Festival to invite Mendelssohn to conduct the oratorio in England.[26]

Paulus is scored for SATB soli, large mixed chorus, and a huge orchestra of paired winds (plus contrabassoon and ophicleide), four horns, two trumpets, three trombones, timpani, strings, and organ. Schubring's libretto has two parts: the first recounts the martyrdom of Stephen (nos. 1–11) and Paul's dramatic conversion (nos. 12–22); the second part details the missionary journeys of Paul and Barnabas (nos. 23–45). Schubring drew the essential narrative from the book of Acts, to which he added texts from the Hebrew Bible (Leviticus, Isaiah, and various psalms), the New Testament (Matthew, Romans, James, and 2 Timothy,) and several well-known Lutheran chorales.

Since the seventeenth century, oratorio had been distinguished from the *historia* by its use of a text not limited exclusively to the Bible. Given the many textual omissions, conflations, and insertion of texts other than those found in Acts, *St. Paul* definitely qualifies as an oratorio. A particularly complex textual construction appears in no. 6, which contains recitatives for soprano and tenor, a chorus, and a concluding recitative.

By stitching together separate, unrelated verses from Acts 7, the recitative employs texts that recount Israel's relationship with God's appointed prophets. Even more radical is the textual construction of the chorus's text, which contains three words from Acts 21:36 ("Weg mit ihm!") in addition to the proscription from Leviticus 24:16. The first text describes Paul's possible fate at the hands of the angry residents of Jerusalem; the second the punishment for blasphemy.

Mendelssohn's musical setting is both interesting and informative. The soprano recitative, though accompanied by strings, resembles the Evangelist's recitatives in Bach's Passions. The textual prompt "Stephanus sprach" (m. 8) leads to a brief instrumental passage, notable for the addition of the bassoon's color as it doubles the violin. This brief interlude appears three times in the course of the recitative suggesting that it is a "recognition" motive associated with Stephen (ex. 1.9).[27]

Example 1.9 Mendelssohn, *St. Paul*, op. 36, no. 6, mm. 9–10

Mendelssohn's rubric above Stephen's initial music indicates that the recitative should gradually get faster and louder to mimic Stephen's increasingly animated discourse.[28] The *Allegro molto* at m. 38 coincides with a meter shift and a dynamic increase to *fortissimo*, mirroring Stephen's diatribe that culminates with the denunciation: "You have received the law through the intervention of angels, and have not upheld it." This stinging indictment provokes a brief chorus (D minor, *presto*), the text ("*Weg mit dem, er lästert Gott, und wer Gott lästert, der soll sterben!*") and the music of which are clear relatives of the *turba* choruses in Bach's Passions.

Most of the choral texts do not come from Acts, indicating a lack of texts suitable for grand, oratorio-style choruses. Examples include such choruses as *Siehe, wir preisen selig* (James 1:12), *Mache dich auf! Werde Licht!* (Isaiah 60:1–2), and *O, welch eine Tiefe des Reichtums* (Romans 11:33, 36b). The bass arias *Vertilge sie, Herr Zebaoth* (no. 13), *Ich danke dir, Herr* (no. 19), and *Gott, sei mir gnädig* (no. 17) all employ texts from the Psalms, the last an interesting appropriation of Psalm 51 to express Saul's misery prior to Ananias's arrival.

The most intriguing additions are the Lutheran hymns interpolated at key points in the narrative, suggesting yet another Bach reference. Some of the chorales—*Allein Gott in der Höh sei Ehr* (no. 3) and *Wachet auf, ruft uns die Stimme* (no. 16)—are entire movements. The first comes immediately after the opening chorus, while *Wachet auf* follows the "conversion" scene, which in turn leads to another grand chorus (*Mache dich auf, werde Licht!*) with brass fanfares placed between the phrases of the chorale. Curiously, Mendelssohn omits the repeat of the chorale's initial melodic section, perhaps because its text (*Mitternacht heisst diese Stunde*) is even less relevant to the oratorio's story than the part he chose to use.

More typically, Mendelssohn uses chorales as part of a larger musical complex, two examples of which are found in Part 2. Two verses of the chorale *O Jesu Christe, wahres Licht* (see ex. 1.10) follow the chorus *Ist das nicht, der zu Jerusalem verstörte* (no. 29).

Example 1.10 Mendelssohn, *St. Paul*, op. 36, no. 29, mm. 78–82

Within the musical complex (no. 36) that consists of the concluding fugal chorus, preceded by recitatives for tenor (Barnabas) and bass (Paul), the bass aria (*Wisset ihr nicht, dass ihr Gottes Tempel seid*) Mendelssohn inserts phrases of Luther's paraphrase of the Nicene Creed, *Wir glauben all' an einem Gott* as a cantus firmus (ex. 1.11).

The most intriguing chorale usage involves the oratorio's overture, which opens with a fantasia on *Wachet auf*, followed by a fugue (m. 43f.) in which the hymn's opening phrase appears numerous times in different keys. Mendelssohn's choice of *Wachet auf*, the prominent placement he gave it, and his omissions of text and melody imply that Mendelssohn used it less as a specific textual commentary than yet another generic reference to J. S. Bach.[29]

St. Paul contains wonderful music, hardly any of which is known or performed today. Part 2, however, contains two interesting choruses—the well-known "How lovely are the messengers" (*Wie lieblich sind die Boten*, no. 26) and the less familiar, penultimate chorus, "See what love hath the Father bestowed on us" (*Sehet welch eine Liebe hat uns der Vater erzeiget*, no. 43). *St. Paul* remains less popular than *Elijah* at least partially because Mendelssohn chose to re-create Bach's Passion music within a story that presented no plausible need for it.

Example 1.11 Mendelssohn, *St. Paul*, op. 36, no. 36, mm. 141–49

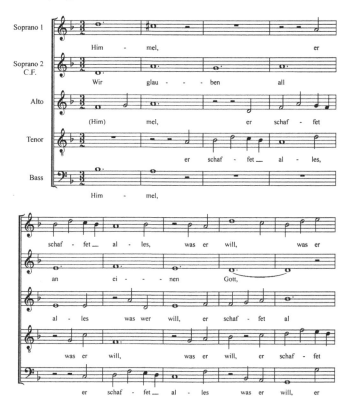

ELIJAH, OP. 70

The success *St. Paul* enjoyed at the Birmingham Festival in 1837 provided Mendelssohn with a commission for yet another oratorio. Again, he turned to Julius Schubring to create the libretto, a task that presented problems different from those encountered in *St. Paul*. As a Hebrew Bible figure, Elijah conformed to the Handelian tradition, but the story in 1 Kings 17–19 itself was not that well known. Chapter 17 focuses on Elijah's healing of the widow's son, but the first fifteen verses of chapter 18 recount an interaction between Elijah and Obadiah and do not figure prominently in the oratorio. The remainder of chapter (18:16–46) provides the principal drama of the oratorio—Elijah's confrontation with the Baalites. In chapter 19:1–15a, Queen Jezebel attempts first to discredit, then to destroy Elijah. The scarcity of usable dramatic text forced Schubring to draw on other biblical texts—Deuteronomy, Exodus, 1 and 2 Samuel, 1 Chronicles, Psalms, Malachi, and Matthew—to an even greater extent than he did in *St. Paul*. The text from Matthew was the result of Schubring's insistence that Elijah was more compelling and acceptable as a precursor of the Messiah than as a character in his own right. Therefore, the oratorio was extended past its original conclusion (no. 38) to include Schubring's "Christian" additions (nos. 39–41), which, in turn, required a new concluding chorus (no. 42).

Schubring's libretto recounts the story from 1 Kings as a series of discrete scenes (Table 1.3).

Table 1.3 Mendelssohn, *Elijah*, op. 70, scenic construction

Part 1	
God's Curse—Famine:	Introduction, Overture, and mvts. 1–5
"Widow's Scene":	mvts. 6–9
"Baal Scene":	mvts. 10–18
"Miracle of Rain"	mvts. 19–21
Part 2	
"Queen's Scene"	mvts. 22–24
Elijah's exile	mvts. 25–32
God's appearance	mvts. 33–35
Elijah's Transfiguration and Ascension	mvts. 36–38
Christian Addendum	mvts. 39–41
Final Chorus	mvt. 42

The libretto illustrates the lack of temporal coherence increasingly found in nine-teenth-century oratorio libretti in sharp contrast to the earlier adherence to the Metastasian unities of time, place, and action, mostly seen and heard in *opera seria*. Mendelssohn's solution to these often abrupt shifts of time and place is to provide a web of motives to provide dramatic coherence. The most important of these appear in the oratorio's introduction.

The first motive (see ex. 1.12), a solemn fanfare for winds and brass, announces Elijah's appearance.[30]

Example 1.12 Mendelssohn, *Elijah*, op. 70, Introduction

The prophet's first words are sung to an ascending octave arpeggio signifying the "strength of God."[31] But the most dramatic motive is Elijah's pronouncement of God's curse (famine) upon Israel realized musically as three descending tritones (sung and played). Finally, the recitative concludes as it began, with the fanfare for Elijah, God's prophet, who pronounced this judg-ment. The reappearance of these motives (and several others) throughout the oratorio mitigate the story's lack of dramatic cohesion.

Fig. 1.1 Facsimile of the score of Felix Mendelssohn's oratorio *Elijah*

While the motive depicting God's strength occurs more frequently (it is also used for the god of the Baalites), the curse motive is more dramatically and formally significant. Its return in mvt. 5 ("His curse hath fallen down upon us") highlights the children of Israel's indifference to Obadiah's pleas to repent. It also figures prominently in the Baal scene (mvts. 10–17), identifying idolatry as the curse's genesis. But the tour de force is Mendelssohn's bold presentation of that motive in the basses of the chorus and orchestra on the ultimate page of the score (ex. 1.13).

Example 1.13 Mendelssohn, *Elijah*, op. 70, no. 42, mm. 113–19

Amid the jubilant "Amens," the reappearance of the curse motive seems odd, unless Mendelssohn intended to suggest that a similar fate awaits the Israelites should they abandon Yahweh in the future.[32]

Ultimately, Mendelssohn's use of a tonal symbolism reminiscent of Haydn's *The Creation* is more important than these several motives. There is no evidence to suggest that Mendelssohn was aware of Haydn's tonal scheme; nonetheless, it is interesting that he chose C major to represent God and C minor to portray his curse. A whole array of tonal symbolism derives from the functional relationship of other tonalities to the "God/curse" duality. A minor, the relative minor of C, represents God's anger (nos. 2, 17, 24, 30, and 33), while its parallel mode, A major, symbolizes the people's growing trust in God in Part 2 (nos. 25, 27, and 40). Conversely, the relative major of the curse motive (E♭) symbolizes the trust in God required to end the curse (4, 10, 14–15, 19–20) (see Fig. 1.1).

Following the classical hierarchy, the tonality next in significance after C is its dominant (G), which Mendelssohn uses to represent the people's trust in God (Part 1, nos. 7, 9, and Part 2, no. 22). The subdominant of C (F) comes to represent trust in Jehovah (Part 2, nos. 32–33) or, alternatively, in Baal (Part 1, no. 11). Mendelssohn seems to have used D minor (relative minor of F major) at the beginning of the oratorio to represent man's lack of trust in God (introduction; overture, and no. 1). Conversely, D major, Handel's "God" key, plays a similar role in Mendelssohn's tonal cosmology, reserved for choruses in Part 2 (nos. 28–29 and 41–42) that praise God's name and power.

The tonality of F♯ minor conveys the despair resulting from misplaced trust either in Baal (Part 1, nos. 12–13) or Queen Jezebel (Part 2, no. 26), as well as Elijah's depression, "It is enough" (no. 26). That same key also provides a link (via the circle of fifths) to two other significant tonalities—B minor and E major. Part 2 begins in B minor with "Hear Ye, Israel" symbolizing Jezebel's attempt to placate the people. In the circle of fifths, that key comes between F♯ (the key signifying the people's rebellion against Yahweh) and E (the key representing God's appearance to Elijah [Part 2, no. 34]).[33] Three brief premonitions of this key acknowledge God's power and mercy. The first occurs in the opening chorus ("Will then the Lord be no more God in Zion?" mm. 35–41), the second as Elijah prays for mercy for the widow's son (Part 1, no. 8, mm. 66–84), and the last in the Baal scene (Part 1, no. 16, mm. 83–93) when the Israelites acknowledge that "Our God is one God and we will have no other Gods before the Lord."

Save for the absence of the Lutheran chorale, the musical genres used by Mendelssohn in *Elijah* are similar to those found in *St. Paul*; they become more dramatic in *Elijah* because the story from the Hebrew Bible precluded any imitation of Bach's Passions. That said, *Elijah* is not a flawless work. Despite its dramatic music, the work possesses an aimless story articulated in an antiquated English text that in itself demands more familiarity with the Bible than a modern secular audience might have. Finally, the length of the work (approximately two hours and fifteen minutes) frequently requires cuts that inevitably impact the drama. In reality, *Elijah* should never have become a modern success. Yet, *Elijah* is surpassed only by *Messiah* in terms of its popularity among singers and audiences. If the most famous chorus is "He watching over Israel" (with the charming trio "Lift thine eyes" that precedes it), the chorus's role as protagonist in the Baal scene is often referred to as one of the great moments in history of oratorio. No less wonderful is the solo writing, as *Elijah* constitutes the premier bass-baritone role in the canon. Mendelssohn hardly neglects the other soloists, providing each with at least one great aria: "If with all your hearts" (T), "O rest in the Lord" (A), and "Hear ye, Israel" (originally written for the soprano Jenny Lind, the "Swedish nightingale").

BEETHOVEN AND BERLIOZ

Mendelssohn's death in 1847 broke the oratorio's direct line of descent from Handel. In the first half of the nineteenth century, oratorios began to appear that transcended the traditional definitions of the genre. These included singular oratorios produced by two of the most prominent composers of early romanticism—Ludwig van Beethoven (1770–1827) and Hector Berlioz (1803–69). Beethoven's oratorio, *Christus am Ölberge*, op. 85 (*Christ on the Mount of Olives*), was composed hastily (1803, rev. 1804) in response to a request for an opera for the *Theater-an-der-Wien*. Franz Xavier Huber's libretto consisted of only six numbers, all of which emulate the template used in Haydn's *The Creation*. Like that work, there are only three named characters, Jesus (T [instead of a bass as was common in the German Passion/oratorio tradition]), Peter (B), and the Seraph (S). Most of the oratorio's music has been forgotten, save the powerful "Hallelujah" chorus that closes the work.

Berlioz's oratorio *L'Enfance du Christ* op. 25 (*The Childhood of Christ*) stretched even farther the notion of what an oratorio can be. Like later exponents of the genre, Berlioz struggled with what to call the work, eventually settling on the accurate, if somewhat generic, description "*trilogie sacré*," the three components of which are "Herod's Dream," "The Flight into Egypt," and "The Arrival at Sais." The well-known "Shepherds' Farewell" that closes the second portion of the oratorio played a seminal role in the work's genesis. If Berlioz's veracity can be trusted, he originally sketched this music as an "Andantino for organ" during a somewhat dull social evening in 1850. He eventually added words appropriate to a group of shepherds serenading the departure of the Holy Family. A little ritornello for winds imitating the shepherds' pipes promotes this pastoral impression. To create interest in his piece, Berlioz passed it off as the work of an obscure seventeenth-century composer, Pierre Ducré, but Berlioz's supposed discovery was pure fabrication. When Berlioz realized that people genuinely liked this little chorus, he expanded it by adding an overture and a tenor solo. This *scena*, in turn, became the cornerstone of what is perhaps an odd example of a nineteenth-century oratorio. The completed "oratorio" received its premiere in 1853.

ROBERT SCHUMANN, *DAS PARADIES UND DIE PERI*, OP. 50

The evolution begun by Beethoven and Berlioz continued in two well-known composers not usually associated with the genre: Robert Schumann (1810–56) and Franz Liszt (1811–86). Both produced large works for chorus and orchestra that expanded the notion of just what an oratorio was. In a review written in 1841, Robert Schumann expressed his fear that with a few notable exceptions (Mendelssohn's *St. Paul* being one), the oratorio was in danger of becoming extinct.[34] John Daverio dubs 1843 as Schumann's "Oratorio Year," alluding to the scholarly tendency to view Schumann's output in terms of his focus on a particular genre (e.g., *Lieder*, symphony, chamber music, and the like, in a particular year). At about the same time Mendelssohn was composing *Elijah*, Schumann completed *Das Paradies und die Peri*, op. 50, a project that dates back to at least 1840. In December of that year, Schumann listed in his book of future compositional projects three of the four tales contained in Thomas Moore's epic poem *Lalla Rookh* (pub. 1817).[35] Schumann was ambivalent about the precise compositional treatment the texts

Fig. 1.2 Illustration from the 1861 edition of Thomas Moore's *Lalla Rookh*

would require: "concert piece," "opera," and "oratorio" were among the options he considered. Like Mendelssohn, Schumann was obsessed with composing an opera; he declared in his diary that "An opera will be my next work, and I'm fired up to proceed."[36] But Schumann ultimately concluded that the tale of the *Peri* was not suitable for operatic treatment, as he makes clear in a letter written prior to the completion of its sketches: "At the moment, I am involved in a large project, the largest I've yet undertaken—it's not an opera—I believe it well-nigh a new genre for the concert hall. I plan to put all my energy into it and hope to have finished it within the year."[37] In retrospect, one wonders why a work so highly valued by Schumann remains virtually unknown and unperformed by contemporary critics and audiences.

In part, this neglect derives from Schumann's uncertainty regarding the nature of the work. Based on a poem rooted in Persian mythology, the text had no connection to the Bible or to the sacred stories that formed the foundations of the oratorio. Thus Schumann decided that the work was unsuitable for operatic treatment. So what kind of piece did Schumann believe he was creating?

On the title page of the published score, Schumann called the work "Dichtung" (poetry). Although Clara Schumann referred to it as an oratorio, Robert himself, while affirming the work's novelty, saw its only precedent in several didactic oratorios of Carl Loewe, an eighteenth-century composer, conductor, and singer.[38] Franz Liszt viewed it as a "secular oratorio," which he regarded (along with the keyboard miniature) as one of the central contributions of Schumann's *oeuvre*.[39] In a letter written in June 1843, Schumann states that the work is "an oratorio, though not for the chapel, but rather for 'cheerful' folk."[40] Carl Dahlhaus has argued that such genres as the dramatic cantata, the choral ballad and ode, and the secular oratorio are primarily achievements of the nineteenth century.[41] If the work is not one of these, the fact that it is based on a lengthy English poem might suggest Haydn's *The Seasons* as a possible model. As far as we know, though, Schumann neither espoused such a view nor acknowledged any awareness of Haydn's work.

The safest path is to place *Paradise and the Peri* among that rather amorphous body of nineteenth-century choral/orchestra music: dramatic in nature and intended for the concert hall. Nonetheless, the story of the *Peri* resonates with such typical romantic notions as redemption and exoticism, particularly as expressed in stories drawn from non-Western culture.[42] John Daverio said it best:

> Indeed, the theological scheme of the Peri tale—Originary bliss-Fall-Paradise regained—readily maps onto the historical scheme—classical antiquity–contemporary critique–redemptive future—articulated in the fragments and essays of the early framers of Romanticism, Novalis and the Schlegel brothers among them. Schumann too subscribed to this tripartite philosophy of history ... the *Neue Zeitschrift für Musik* rested on a critical foundation in which preservation of the past, recognition of the deficiencies of the present, and hope in the future interlock and mutually support one another.[43]

The libretto of *Paradise and the Peri* has three parts, each with two large scenes. The "heroine" (the Peri) is the offspring of a fallen angel and a mortal, a lineage that bars her entry to Paradise (Fig. 1.2). In Moore's poem the Peri is promised admission by the gatekeeper upon the presentation of a suitable gift. Her three attempts to find such a gift provides the structure of the libretto. The story itself exemplifies an ultimate romantic archetype—the visionary quest, here given a somewhat religious slant (original bliss, "Eden" in *The Creation*, the "fall" from perfection, and ultimate redemption through an act of selfless love). Such an interpretation is the only pretext for viewing Schumann's work as an "oratorio."

Musically, Schumann likely wanted to demonstrate his ability to create a large-scale work in which elegant detail and structural integrity found a satisfying balance, and, to judge from the unanimous praise of contemporary critics, he succeeded. Schumann eschewed the motivic complexity Mendelssohn had used in *Elijah* by seeking a "new path," one that synthesized numerous contemporary trends.[44] John Daverio specifically cites the influence of H. A. Marschner (specifically, his *Klänge aus Osten*); Carl Loewe's attempted synthesis of opera and oratorio (in *Johannes Huss*[45]); Berlioz (who visited Schumann early in 1843); Carl Maria von Weber (especially *Oberon* and *Euryanthe*); and Mendelssohn's secular cantata/ballad *Die erste Walpurgisnacht*, the final rehearsal and premiere of which Schumann attended in early 1843. While these diverse compositions may have indeed influenced the genesis of *Paradise and the Peri*, all were trumped by Schumann's desire to create a new musical continuity based on harmonic and metric relationships that bound one movement to another. It is this technique that has marked *Paradise and the Peri* as one of Schumann's truly innovative works.

Schumann deliberately identified the Peri and other named characters with specific soloists (the alto and tenor soloists as the principal narrators), countering that constancy with the changing identity of the chorus (warriors, spirits, etc.) and precise attention to details of orchestral color. Schumann's successful balancing of these elements of structure led Daverio to assert that "of the nineteenth century's larger creations for vocal and orchestral forces, only Wagner's *Parsifal* equals the *Peri* in dispositional logic and symmetry."[46]

Despite its variety of harmony, texture, meter, and orchestration, *Paradise and the Peri* remains a series of miniatures fused into an aural unity, which the listener either accepts or denies. It was this formal fusion that Schumann regarded as innovative, though, as he told Franz Brendel, the resulting continuity occasioned critical disapproval.[47] Instrumental transitions (reminiscent of Beethoven) or certain harmonic connections, which become apparent only when repeated in a new movement, mold the sections into a seamless continuity, as the layout of Part 3 of the "oratorio" illustrated in Table 1.4.

This information, while useful, fails to convey the novelty of Schumann's fusion of multiple musical segments because the music itself resists traditional labels. The simplest movements, like *O heil'ge Tränen, inn'ger Reue* (no. 24) use a single meter, tonality, and scoring throughout. Movements for solo voice, however, defy such conventional labels as recitative, aria, and the like. Initially, Schumann tried many different labels to describe the solo movements, but the only term used in the full score is *Rezitativ*; all the other movements bear the generic rubric of "solo." Daverio comments that "Still, the notion of the 'Rezitativischer Gesang,' a syntactically flexible vocal line supported by a motivically rich orchestral texture, appropriately describes the writing in a large number of the oratorio's movements (e.g., sections of nos. 1, 3–5, 7, 9–12, 14, 16, 19, 20, and 25)."[48] It is in precisely such movements as these that Schumann employs instrumental themes to unify disjunct segments.

An example of this flexible vocal style is mvt. 20, which Daverio classifies as a recitative-and-aria.[49] The movement's beginning and end are the locus of Schumann's innovative continuity. Its initial tempo indication, *noch langsamer* (even slower), presumes a proportional relation to the tempo of the preceding movement, a blend of recitative and aria (itself marked *etwas langsamer*), which, after describing the Peri's anticipation of the beauties of paradise, takes a foreboding turn, as the angel (alto solo, m. 45) announces the insufficiency of the Peri's second gift. The Peri's realization that her second gift has been deemed inadequate explains the ambivalent tonality of mvt. 19 with its prominent use of semitone inflections and a motive built on the Baroque "sigh" motive (ex. 1.14b), as well as the reprise (ex. 1.14c) in mvt. 20 of an orchestral motive portraying her dejection, first heard in the opening measures of the oratorio (1.14a).

Table 1.4 Schumann, *Das Paradies und die Peri*, op. 50, 18–26, overview

Movement	Text	Key	Meter	Scoring
18. *Chor der Houris*	*Schmücket die Stufen zu Allahs Thron*	G–V/G	2/4	S, A, ssaaww, br, str
19. T1 and A (Engel) soli	*Dem Sang von ferne lauschend*	G–D	4/4	T, A + str, ww, hn and tbns
20. S 1 (Peri)	*Verstossen! Verschlossen auf's neu' das Goldportal!*	B–D	4/4 2/2	S, ww, hn and str
21. Bar	*Jetzt sank des Abends gold'ner Schein*	F♯ minor	3/4	Bar, ww, hn, str
22. T, *Chor des Peris*, Bar	*Und wie sie niederwärts sich schwingt*	B minor	4/4	T, Br, ssaa, WW, hn, str
23. Soprano (Peri), Tenor, Mezzo, Tenor, Baritone	*Hinab zu jenem Sonnentempel!*	E minor–A–E minor– E major–G–B minor	4/4 2/2	S, T, MS, Bar, ww, br & str
24. Chor	*O heil'ge Tränen, inn'ger Reue*	G	2/2	SATB satb, ww, hn, str
25. S (Peri), T, satb	*Es fällt ein Tropfen aufs Land Ägypten*	E minor–V/G	4/4	S, T, satb, hn, ww, str
26. Finale	*Freud, ew'ge Freude, mein Werk ist getan!*	A7–D–G	2/2	S, satb, Full orchestra

Example 1.14 a–c Schumann, *Das Paradies und die Peri*, op. 50

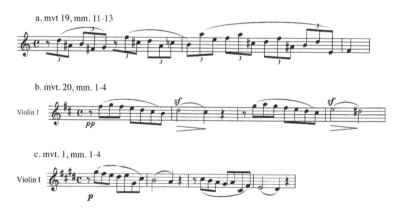

a. mvt 19, mm. 11-13

b. mvt. 20, mm. 1-4

c. mvt. 1, mm. 1-4

For the aria portion of mvt. 20, a D major Allegro (*alla breve*), Schumann contrives a quasi-rondo form, the ebullience of which is reminiscent of his "Spring" Symphony No. 1, op. 38. The audible thematic repetition (see ex. 1.15) provides the movement's loose form but in no way impedes Schumann's seemingly effortless depiction of the Peri's indefatigable optimism.

Example 1.15 Schumann, *Das Paradies und die Peri*, op. 50, mvt. 20, mm. 22–29

doch will ich nicht ruh'n, will oh - ne Rast von ei - nem Po - le zu an - dern schrei - ten,

This strong expression of the Peri's optimism ends, obviously inconclusively due to a deceptive cadence to B minor (m. 158). This prompts an orchestral "postlude" based on stretto entries of a melody, which incorporates the movement's two principal tonalities—B minor (recitative) and D major (aria), and resembles the lachrymose motive seen in example 1.16.[50]

Example **1.16** Schumann, *Das Paradies und die Peri*, op. 50, mvt. 20, mm. 158–70

Schumann uses A as a common-tone connection of the aria's D major and the F♯ minor of the next movement, no. 21. Once again, Schumann indicates a temporal relationship, suggesting that the half note of no. 20 (slowed via *ritardando*) should become the quarter note of no. 21.

Choruses comprise ten of the twenty-six movements of this oratorio; in addition to its three main parts, the chorus takes the part of the dramatis personae as warriors, Nile spirits, Peris, and the like, as needed. Even if none of these choruses ranks among the pantheon of oratorio choruses, Schumann demonstrates considerable craft as a choral composer. Particularly affecting is the chorus *Weh, weh, er fehlte das Ziel* (no. 8), a lament on the death of the youth who challenges the oppressor Gazna in Part 1 (ex. 1.17) and *O heil'ge Tränen, inn'ge Reue* (no. 24), in which the chorus marks the tears of the repentant criminal that provide the Peri entry into paradise (ex. 1.18).

Example **1.17** Schumann, *Das Paradies und die Peri*, op. 50, mvt. 8, mm. 1–11

Example 1.18 Schumann, *Das Paradies und die Peri*, op. 50, mvt. 24, mm. 1–9

Schumann's indebtedness to Handel-via-Haydn is evident in the fugal chorus that ends Part 1. What begins as the choral equivalent of a symphonic finale becomes an immense fugue (m. 115), which looks backward to those of Handel and Haydn and forward to those of Brahms.[51] The esoteric story and unabashed lyricism of *Paradise and the Peri* may prevent it from joining the "canon" of the Romantic-era oratorio repertory, but this music (despite its resistance to being excerpted as concert pieces) deserves the attention of contemporary choral societies.

FRANZ LISZT (1822–86)

Discussions of Masses (chap. 12) and liturgical choral music (chap. 14) in vol. 1 showed Franz Liszt to be an unexpectedly prolific composer of choral music. During his years in Rome (1861–69), Liszt composed two oratorios, *Die Legende von der heiligen Elisabeth* (1857–62) and *Christus* (1866–72). Liszt's first oratorio—his nod to the burgeoning growth of nationalism—venerated his county's patron saint, Elizabeth (1207–31). Otto Roquette, a professor at the Darmstadt Polytechnikum, wrote the text, but Liszt had some difficulty deciding precisely what kind of work this would eventually be. He proffered his thoughts on the essence of oratorio in a discussion of Adolph Bernhard Marx's oratorio *Moses*: "Why call it an 'oratorio?' Is its nature not something entirely different? . . . For this work has little to do with worship, as do former works with such a title; it revolves around fantasy rather than a belief. . . . The character of oratorio is markedly epic; accordingly, lyric and dramatic elements only appear episodically."[52]

Here Liszt elucidated the central problem surrounding the nineteenth-century oratorio. For him, it resided in a certain mixture of lyric, dramatic, and epic qualities. His criticism of Marx's oratorio could have been applied just as easily to his own work since lyric elements predominate. Liszt's notion that an oratorio had "little to do with worship" reflected how far contemporary reality had diverged from historical tradition. Determining what "oratorio" meant had become increasingly problematic. From its inception in the late sixteenth century, the oratorio had been differentiated from opera, becoming, in the nineteenth century, more reliant on those qualities Liszt called "lyric" and "epic." As the narrator became less important, the genre placed new emphasis on orchestral color, recognition motives, and other purely musical devices to compensate for the absence of those elements essential to opera—dialogue, action, costumes, scenery, and staging.

More than any work discussed thus far, *The Legend of St. Elizabeth* abandoned the tried-and-true Metastasian unities of time, place, and action. To fashion a musical composition out of six paintings chronicling events that were literally years apart required Liszt to conjure up a new type of musical unity.[53] Liszt's acknowledgments to those who helped him assemble the various musical materials describe the collection of melodies that became the thematic underpinning of his entire oratorio. First, Liszt became familiar with liturgical music for the feast of

St. Elizabeth, specifically citing items from sixteenth- and seventeenth-century breviaries and choral books.[54]

> I have used from these liturgical treasures two chief motives in particular, which from ancient times have had religious and historical relationship with St. Elizabeth. For the exact statement of both motives, besides their use in my composition... I hereby proffer my sincere thanks to the same sources.
>   Likewise I owe similar thanks to Edward Remenyi (of Pest) and Mr. Gottschalk (Cantor of Tieffurth in Weimar), for the kind delivery of two folk-melodies which I have employed in my work.[55]

Example 1.19 a–e Liszt, *Die Legende von der heiligen Elisabeth*

a. *Quasi Stella matutina* (Elizabeth's motive)

b. "Cross" motive

c. Crusader's Hymn (*Schoenster Herr Jesu*)

d. Hungarian folk tune

e. Hungarian hymn melody

The Gregorian antiphon proper to the feast of St. Elizabeth becomes the saint's musical signature (ex. 1.19a) wherever she is the focus of the story or mentioned by someone else. The second motive is a generic Gregorian incipit (ex. 1.19b) that Liszt used in other compositions (the *Graner Festmesse*, the final chorus of the "Dante" Symphony, the tone poem *Die Hunnenschlacht*, and, especially, *Via Crucis*) to symbolize the cross. In Part 3 it represents the Crusaders, which Elizabeth's husband, Ludwig, joined. This association generates another melodic reference—the "Crusader's Hymn" (ex. 1.19c) *Schönster Herr Jesu*, the hymn tune of which is, in this case, *St. Elizabeth* (*Schlesische Volkslieder*, 1842). One of the folk tunes (for which Liszt thanked Remenyi) symbolizes Elizabeth's (and Liszt's) Hungarian nationalism (ex. 1.19d) The other melody (ex. 1.19e) is an old hymn that Liszt uses in the fifth and sixth scenes to recount Elisabeth's deeds of charity. Although Liszt does not use these motives (and subsidiary themes like the one representing Landgrafin Sophie) as *Leitmotiven* in the Wagnerian sense, he fashions them into a melodic narrative that guides the listener through the story. As in Mendelssohn's *Elijah*, motives such as these are attached to significant actors in the drama and religious archetypes, and help compensate for the libretto's disjunct nature.

These kinds of problems became even more acute in *Christus* because Liszt had to compile his own libretto; he also had the mistaken assumption that his audience would know and recognize the plainsong themes that were to create the form. If anything, *Christus* is less amenable to modern performance than *St. Elizabeth* given its duration (ca. 3 1/2 hours without cuts), enormous forces, and self-sufficient nature of mvts. 6 (the "Beatitudes") and 12 ("Stabat Mater").[56]

ORATORIO IN NINETEENTH-CENTURY ENGLAND

The oratorio flourished in nineteenth-century England due in great part to the growth of amateur choral societies and festivals, and the demand for new music for them to sing. The most famous of these festivals were the triennial Three Choirs' Festival (est. 1767) and the Birmingham Festival (est. 1784). After Mendelssohn, the English oratorio market was dominated by foreign composers like Charles Gounod, Antonin Dvořák, and the other composers in this selective list of popular oratorios in nineteenth-century England (Table 1.5):

Table 1.5 Oratorios performed in nineteenth-century England

Continental Composers	
Louis Spohr	*Calvary* 1839; *The Fall of Babylon*, 1842
Gioacchino Rossini	*Mosè in Egitto*, 1855
Lorenzo Perosi	*La Trasfigurazione di Cristo*, 1898
Anton Rubinstein	*Paradise Lost*, 1870
César Franck	*The Beatitudes*, 1879
Camille Saint-Saëns	*The Deluge*, 1879; *The Promised Land*, 1913
Horatio Parker	*Hora Novissima*, 1893
English Composers	
William Crotch	*Palestine*, 1839
Michael Costa	*Naaman*, 1864
W. Sterndale Bennett	*The Woman of Samaria*, 1867
John Frederick Bridge	*Mt. Moriah*, 1874
George Macfarren	*The Resurrection*, 1876; *St. John the Baptist*, 1880
Alexander Mackenzie	*The Rose of Sharon*, 1884
Alfred R. Gaul	*The Holy City*, 1882
Arthur Sullivan	*The Golden Legend*, 1886; *The Light of the World*, 1873
John Stainer	*The Crucifixion*, 1887
Frederic H. Cowen	*Ruth*, 1887
Samuel Coleridge-Taylor	*The Atonement*, 1903; *The Song of Hiawatha*, 1898
C. Hubert H. Parry	*Job*, 1892; *King Saul*, 1894; *The Soul's Ransom*, 1906
Edward Elgar	*The Dream of Gerontius*, 1900
H. Walford Davies	*The Temple*, 1902
Granville Bantock	*Gethsemane*, 1910; *King Solomon*, 1937

EDWARD ELGAR (1857–1934)

Another important figure in the evolution of the English oratorio is Edward Elgar. That he composed oratorios at all resulted from his participation (as violinist) in the Three Choirs Festival. From the pit he had ample opportunity to see what worked and what didn't; consequently, his oratorios possessed an innate sense of dramatic pacing and provided the *desiderata* of both audiences and performers. In 1890 Elgar conducted his *Froissart Overture* at the Three Choirs Festival in Worcester. This success led to additional conducting opportunities and, more importantly, to a series of "festival" compositions, including the *Serenade for Strings* (1892), *The Black Knight* (1893), *Scenes of the Bavarian Highlands* (1896), *Lux Christi* (1896; revised in 1899 as *The Light of Life*), *King Olaf, Te Deum,* and *Benedictus* (1897), and *Caractacus* (1898). The premiere of the orchestral *Enigma Variations,* op. 36 (1899), established Elgar as an English composer worthy of Continental notice; it also resulted in a commission tendered by the Birmingham Festival for a new oratorio to be the centerpiece of its 1900 festival. Elgar began setting a poem that had haunted him for a decade—John Henry Newman's poem *The Dream of Gerontius* (Fig. 1.3). Initially, his choice did not prove popular. In early March, the *Leeds Mercury* reacted to the forthcoming work with what must have been typical distaste: "Newman's poem does not exactly 'yearn' for musical treatment, but there are many possibilities about it and Mr. Elgar, who may be described as in thorough sympathy with the poet and his views, can be trusted to make the utmost of them."[57]

Fig. 1.3 John Henry Newman (1801–90)

If today *The Dream of Gerontius* is considered Elgar's masterpiece, such approbation did not result from its first performance. Even before its composition, controversy surrounded the text, which was both unconventional and contrary to the staunchly anti-Catholic sentiment of nearly everyone involved in its premiere. Percy Young commented that

> in retrospect, it is remarkable that the Birmingham Festival Committee approved the choice of *The Dream of Gerontius* for the 1900 Festival. The com- poser was, in their view, well qualified to write the music for a work which, if not an oratorio, would give some appearance of belonging to that genre. As with opera in the eighteenth century, the nature of a libretto, more often than not, was a matter of indifference. But Newman's poem had within it the seeds of politico-religious divisiveness.[58]

From the outset, problems plagued the work's path to performance, most of which resulted from Elgar's overly optimistic assessment of the chorus's ability. Difficulties in the printing and distribution of the parts, as well as the untimely death of the chorus master (an ardent admirer of Elgar and well acquainted with his style) only made matters worse. The first performance (October 3, 1900) was a catastrophe. As the *Observer* noted in its review: "The shortcomings of the choir were especially to be regretted, because Mr. Edward Elgar's sacred cantata, *The Dream of Gerontius*, the outcome of eight years' thought, and a choral masterpiece, was presented in so faulty and pointless a manner as to seriously jeopardize its success."[59]

In retrospect, it is amazing that the oratorio survived its premiere to become as highly esteemed among English choral singers as Handel's *Messiah*. Its theology notwithstanding, the sheer novelty of Elgar's approach to drama and form, coupled with such difficult choral pas- sages as the fugue on "Dispossessed, Aside thrust" conspired to make the oratorio's reception less than auspicious. The work's ultimate success is a testament to Elgar's masterful manage- ment of the large choral and orchestral forces along with the ingenious way he manipulates the handful of themes, the successive presentations of which are skillfully disguised or varied enough to avoid monotony.

THE DREAM OF GERONTIUS, TEXT

Newman wrote his lengthy *The Dream of Gerontius* while convalescing from a serious illness, one that caused him to consider his own mortality. The poem first appeared in the May and June 1865 issues of *The Month*, a Jesuit magazine published in London. The original poem contained nine hundred lines arranged in seven sections. The first, describing Gerontius's last hours on earth, became the first part of Elgar's oratorio. Charles Edward McGuire offers this synopsis of the remainder of the poem:

> Paragraphs 2–5 introduce Gerontius' Soul to various aspects of the afterlife in succession: his Guardian Angel, the Soul's purpose in Heaven (to be judged), Demons and Angels.... These paragraphs are extremely descriptive, but mostly static. Real action does not occur until the sixth paragraph, where the Angel of the Agony (the Angelic Witness to Christ's trial in the Garden of Gethsemane) pleads for Gerontius' Soul and the Soul is judged by God. After the Judgment, the Soul is "consumed, yet quickened by the glance of God" and

cries for release to Purgatory. The Angel places the Soul in Purgatory in the seventh paragraph, and then bids it farewell, though promising a quick return to bear it to Heaven.[60]

The poem's first section presents Gerontius as an aged Everyman, ignorant and fearful of what will happen to him after death.[61] Because of its reliance on Newman's poem, Part 1 of the oratorio gives the impression of greater drama and unity than does the second part. The radical excisions made for Part 2 shifted the textual focus from the beauty and wonder of heaven to a contemplation of death and judgment, topics whose universality transcends the poem's dogma.

THE DREAM OF GERONTIUS, MUSIC

Percy Young notes that in *Gerontius*, Elgar "broke away from the conventions and, following the principle of Wagnerian music drama, constructed a completely unified whole, in which no single section was independent."[62] There are many points of similarity between Elgar's oratorio and Wagner's music dramas: the presence of a thematically essential prelude; the frequent use of recognition motives; music that unfolds continuously in avoidance of traditional set pieces (recitative, aria, chorus, etc.); and the prominent role that chromatic harmony plays in the musical design. McGuire again notes the presence of several "set-pieces"—music conceived with independent performance in mind.[63] Specifically, he cites the "Prelude and Angel's Farewell" performed in 1901, published in 1902, and recorded by Elgar in 1917:

> Even with the relatively large number of music festivals and other performing organizations in existence at the time, most composer and publisher profits came from the publication of vocal scores and smaller, excerpted selections for church services, amateur choral societies and household consumption. Publishers bought oratorios with this sort of segmentation in mind. A prime example is John Stainer's *Crucifixion*. For this composition, two contracts exist, signed the same day: one for the oratorio itself, and one for the rights to publish a hymn from it separately.[64]

Subsequent publication of several excerpts from *Gerontius*—"The Angel's Song" (1900), *Sanctus Fortis* (1902), and the chorus "Praise to the Holiest in the Height" (1954)—suggest that Novello had such plans in mind from the outset. This assumption, if true, forces a radical rethinking of the oratorio's musical structure, specifically the role played by the motives presented in the prelude and reprised throughout the work. Whatever musical coherence these themes may create, the possible extractions of portions of the oratorio undercuts their significance as reminiscence motives. Alternatively, McGuire suggests that the motives provided a foundation over which the vocal melody could freely unfold; to that end, he refers to them as "accompaniment" motives."[65] Still, the return of various motives first heard in the prelude supports their structural role. There are no fewer than nine distinct motives in the prelude (ex. 1.20).

Example 1.20a–i Elgar, *The Dream of Gerontius*, op. 38, Prelude

a. mm. 1-10

b. mm. 18-20

c. mm. 20-23

d. mm. 29-34

e. mm. 60-66

f. mm. 66-74

Example 1.20 Continued

g. mm. 98-105

h. m. 144

i. mm. 176-179

This piece is actually a series of episodes, each based on the presentation and development of a motive. Beginning with A. J. Jaeger's analysis in the program book for *Gerontius*'s premiere, there has been a tradition of giving these motives descriptive titles, such as "Judgment," "Fear," "Go Forth," and "Devil's Chord." The following list by Ernst Newman coordinates with the nine themes (ex. 1.20).[66] While the final motive is technically not part of the prelude, it functions in a manner similar to those contained within the movement itself.

The periodicity of Elgar's solo melodies, central to McGuire's conception of the oratorio's structure, is clearly evident in the tenor aria "Sanctus Fortis". Even though the aria as a whole gives the impression of being a typical Wagnerian "continuous melody," it is, in fact, compounded from a remarkably periodic series of melodies (Table 1.6).

Table 1.6 Elgar, *The Dream of Gerontius*, "Sanctus Fortis," form

Aria segment	Location	Periodic structure
1. *Sanctus fortis, Sanctus Deus*	mm. 331–46	16 mm. 4 + 4 + 4 + 4
2. Firmly, I believe	mm. 346–63	18 mm. 4 + 4 + 4 + 4 (+2)
3. And I trust and hope most fully	mm. 366–84	19 mm. 4 + 6 + 4 + 5
4. Simply to his grace	mm. 386–406	18 mm. 9 (1+8)+ 9 (1+8)
5. *Sanctus fortis, Sanctus Deus*	mm. 407–23	16 mm. 4 + 4 + 4 + 4
6. And I hold in veneration	mm. 427–43	20 mm. 4 + 4 + 4 + 4 + 4
7. And I take with joy	mm. 444–61	16 mm. 4 + 4 + 4 + 4
8. Adoration aye be given	mm. 462–76	16 mm. 4 + 4 + 4 + 4
9. *Sanctus fortis, Sanctus Deus*	mm. 477–92	16 mm. 4 + 4 + 4 + 4

Apart from this macrostructure, Elgar's unfolding melodies rely on antecedent-consequent components (ex. 1.21a), sequential restatement and the return of similar melodic shapes for different texts (ex. 1.21b). The preponderant use of four-measure phrases and frequent recasting of material (literal, transposed, and modified) separate Elgar's approach from Wagner's.

Example 1.21 a/b Elgar, *The Dream of Gerontius*, part 1

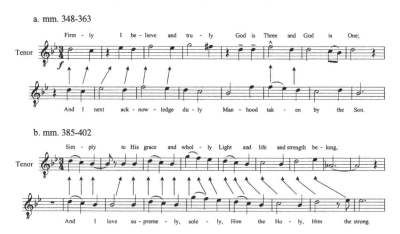

Charles McGuire points to the importance of three extended tableaux in Part 2, which operate *narratively* on three distinct levels: (1) the audience listens to the other two levels; (2) Soul and Angel experience level three; (3) the *tableau entendu*: Soul and Angel view various auxiliary characters that comprise heaven. These are, musically, in Part 2, the "Demon's tableau" (199–404); the "Angelicals tableau" (mm. 405–855), and the "Judgment tableau" (mm. 855–1154).[67]

The most extensive structure is the Angelicals tableau, eventually published separately by Novello. The scene opens with a dialogue (level 2) between the Soul and the Angel discussing judgment before God. This is Elgar's first use of music representing the Angelicals ("Praise to the Holiest in the Heights")—quiet yet agitated triadic arpeggios (strings and harps) on G♯ minor, E major, and C major. Elgar continues to a solo monologue to highlight the principle sections of this large scene (mm. 542 and 567). Each of these monologues prompts a reprise of the "Angelicals" music first heard at m. 450. Recurring use of this music allows for a fluid drama (almost Wagnerian) that is nonetheless musically unified. The second monologue (m. 567f.) ushers in the chorus's C-major reprise of "Praise to the Holiest in the Height."

Elgar then introduces a new meter (6/4) and "Brahmsian" harmony based on parallel sixths to set the text "O loving wisdom of our God!" (m. 587). This new musical idea propels the next hundred measures, occasionally punctuated by an orchestral motive first heard in Part 1 accompanying the priest's proclamation "Proficiscere anima Christiana" (ex. 1.22, Part 1).

Example 1.22 Elgar, *The Dream of Gerontius*, part 1, mm. 667–72

This music is both a new episode in the larger tableau (mm. 588–712) and a complementary theme that Elgar combines effortlessly with "Praise to the Holiest."

The remainder of the Angelicals tableau (mm. 717–1154) is a choral paean that reveals the glory of heaven in its expanded choral forces (double chorus) and carefully controlled acceleration of tempo. Soloists and any reminiscence motives are conspicuously absent during this entire section. The heavenly hymn complete, Elgar effects a transition to the "Judgment tableau" (m. 845) through a sudden change of tempo (to *Larghetto*) and alternate presentations of the fear motive (Part 1, m. 18) and the orchestral theme that has dominated since the *Più mosso* at m. 541.

The judgment tableau begins with the Angel's pronouncement "Thy judgment is near, for we have come to the veiled presence of God." In this segment many of the earlier reminiscence motives return, combined with new material (notably the aria for the Angel of the Agony, m. 876, the construction of which closely resembles *Sanctus fortis*). The semichorus returns (Part 2, m. 967) singing the music of the Kyrie (Part 1, m. 238), which merges seamlessly into the prayer, "Lord, be merciful," crafted from the "Go Forth upon thy journey" music (Part 1, m. 698). Another orchestral transition (Part 2, m. 992) produces an intensely loud and dissonant crash, from which the Soul's plaint "Take me away" (sung to the "Miserere" motive) emerges. The Soul's ensuing soliloquy leans heavily on the music of *Sanctus fortis, Sanctus Deus* (Part 1, m. 331). After a brief choral passage based on Psalm 90 (m. 1047), Elgar gives the Angel her last and most beautiful melody, "Softly and gently" (ex. 1.23).

Example 1.23 Elgar, *The Dream of Gerontius*, part 2, mm. 1073–78

Elgar's *The Dream of Gerontius* is an amazing compositional feat. Careful listening and score reading can indeed highlight the most important musical moments and a deeper understanding and appreciation for this sprawling composition.

CONCLUSION

The oratorios of the nineteenth century are clearly built on the foundations and traditions of the Baroque era, most notably those by Handel. To that extent, Alfred Einstein's contention that in the nineteenth century the "big oratorio still lived because Handel had once lived and created an influential model" is true.[68] Could or would Haydn have composed *The Creation* had he not experienced the Handel Celebration at Westminster Abbey in 1791? From that work forward, the impetus to compose large choral-orchestral works, and the literary and dramatic conventions that governed them, underwent a profound change with the advent of romanticism. Handel's real contribution to the new oratorio was the essential role played by the chorus; in that sense, all of the nineteenth-century compositions that bear that label (whether from the composer or others) participate in the Handelian legacy.

What begins to change, as early as Haydn's *Die Jahreszeiten*, is the absence of any connection to sacred stories or the traditional dramatic unities of time, place, and action. Whether sacred (as in Mendelssohn's *Paulus* and *Elijah*), secular (Schumann's *Das Paradies und die Peri* or his *Szenen aus Goethes Faust*), or poetic (Elgar's *The Dream of Gerontius*), one becomes increasingly aware of a break between the text as drama and the way a given composer chooses to present it. Increasingly, the term "oratorio" comes to stand less for a historically defined musical genre than for a choral-orchestral work, the drama of which represents constituencies unique to the nineteenth century. This trend is clearly manifested in the increasing diversity of subjects and what we perceive as less universal, more consumer-oriented musical sentiments. If in the operas of the nineteenth century the chorus increasingly emerged as a *vox populi* or a symbol of nationalistic striving, then grand and powerful choral-orchestral music—whether sacred or secular—came to fill the same role in popular concerts that no longer depended on the church either as a venue or ambience.

2

Part Song in Nineteenth-Century Germany and England

Alfred Einstein's view of the role of choral music in the history of nineteenth-century music is fairly typical of general histories of music:

> The Romantic period was no longer a century of great vocal composition. There was still a succession of delicate and refined *a cappella* composers, such as Mendelssohn and Brahms, who achieved effects of harmony and color inconceivable to the sixteenth century, the time when the classical *a cappella* style was in flower. The means of achieving this refinement became, especially in Germany, the composition for men's chorus, which owed its impetus, however, not to purely artistic reasons, as it became more and more an expression of nationalistic or party activity.[1]

A paradigm shift took place in the nineteenth century in terms of where concerts happened, who was in attendance, and how many performers were involved. The correlation between public concerts and the decline of patronage was already underway in the twilight of the Baroque, despite Haydn's fealty to the Esterhazy family. Mozart forsook a comfortable life at the Salzburg chapel to become a free agent in Vienna, while Beethoven was never attached to any institution or person for long. The scientific, political, and industrial revolutions of the eighteenth century created a new social order in which composers were forced to reinvent themselves in order to keep pace with the rapidly changing world.

Nowhere is this dynamic clearer than in the genre we call the part song. Vocal chamber music was hardly new, but the part song was novel in that it was the provenance of amateur performers, created for their own enjoyment. Einstein correctly views *a cappella* singing as an essential by-product of the emerging *Männerchorvereine* (male choir associations). These organizations grew out of the informal *Liedertafel* (literally, "song table") groups, the model for which was a small group of amateur male singers from C. F. Zelter's Berlin *Singakademie* who gathered for evenings of singing and refreshment. Franz Gehringer defines *Liedertafel* as "a society of men who met together on fixed evenings for the practice of vocal music in four parts, drinking forming part of the entertainment." These began to appear in response to an economic depression in Germany caused by Napoleon's rule. The original *Liedertafel* had twenty-four members and met for the first time on December 28, 1808; others soon followed in Frankfurt am Main, Leipzig (1815), Magdeburg (1818), and other German cities, and as the movement spread the groups became larger.[2]

Members of each individual club arranged the vocal music, but the *Liedertafel*'s rapid expansion to other cities not only required greater organization but also tapped into professional musicians to create the new repertory. The inevitable element of competition led choruses to seek out professional composers to serve as conductors. This development accounts for the part songs composed by Schubert, Schumann, and Mendelssohn that contain both *Liedertafel* pieces and works requiring a higher level of artistry in both composition and performance.

FRANZ SCHUBERT (1787–1828)

Fig. 2.1 Franz Schubert performing at the home of Joseph von Spaun (Moritz von Schwind)

The first composer to create a substantial body of music for male chorus in the nineteenth century was Franz Schubert (Fig. 2.1). Compositions like his *Trinklied aus dem 16. Jahrhundert* (D. 847), with its satirical Latin text and celebration of wine drinking, appealed to the membership of most *Liedertafeln*. Schubert's music is redolent of the lighthearted, masculine camaraderie of the singing groups (ex. 2.1).

Example 2.1 Schubert, *Trinklied aus dem 16. Jahrhundert*, mm. 1–8

His *Trinklied* is the exception; the majority of Schubert's part songs for male chorus aspire to loftier sentiments such as the love of nature, freedom from the constraints of modern society, romantic love, and mystical pictures of the night, and also to music of a more sophisticated and intimate nature.

A mixture of sophisticated poetry and *Liedertafel*-style music aptly describes Schubert's *Widerspruch* (D. 865), the march-like rhythm, tempo, and strong tonal harmonies, all of which somehow evoke the joys of nature. But Schubert's introduction of the song's parallel mode (D minor) and unison writing in the middle section (mm. 55–88) contrast with the earlier vigor. From the mountaintop, the poet peers down at the valley far below and exclaims, "O, how constricted and narrow the town seems," words that led Schubert to write a descending chromatic line that magically reaches the key of F♯ major (the sharp mediant) when the text says "and my heart yearns to withdraw into its little chamber." Despite the desire to remain in this wonderful place, Schubert forces the music back to a D major reprise of the opening music and becomes the ultimate expression of the poem's title "Contradiction" (ex. 2.2).

The best of Schubert's part-song output is his setting of J. G. Seidl's poem *Nachthelle* (D. 892) for tenor solo, male chorus, and piano. The poem evokes a romantic archetype—night illuminated by moonlight and twinkling stars as captured in the piano's incessant repetition of a chord so spaced as to "twinkle" (ex. 2.3). Schubert's music masks the poem's simple strophic design in the accompaniment's persistent rhythm and his use of a different tonal center for each verse: B♭–F, D♭–D, D–E♭.

At the end of Seidl's poem in the subdominant, Schubert then resorts to a twofold repetition of v. 1 to get back to B♭, a move that effectively doubles the piece's length. Given the harmonic digressions in the first three verses, the return of v. 1 and its music (m. 79) sounds like a recapitulation, even though it begins in E♭. An abrupt chromatic alteration replaces the earlier modulation to the dominant (mm. 17–39) to arrive via the circle of fifths at F major (m. 98), from which point Schubert can reprise music originally heard in the dominant and now heard in the tonic. The piece could well have ended here (m. 117), but Schubert repeats the first chromatic shift (from E♭ to C) moving from B♭ to G, the B♮ of which functions enharmonically as C♭, the Neapolitan of the tonic. After another variant of this progression (m. 136), the music remains firmly in the tonic key of B♭.

Example 2.2 Schubert, *Widerspruch*, D. 865, mm. 63–82

Example 2.3 Schubert, *Nachthelle*, D. 892, mm. 1–3

The well-known, tuneful *Ständchen*, op. 135, exists in versions for both male and female chorus.[3] Other noteworthy pieces for male chorus are *Der Gondelfahrer* (D. 809), *Gesang der Geister über den Wassern* (D. 714, scored for eight-part male choir, and five-part strings), *Grab und Mond* (D. 893), and the lyrical setting of Goldoni's *La Pastorella* (D. 513). In *Grab und Mond*, Schubert realizes the implicit drama of Seidl's poem by setting its two contrasting parts to the same music, the second version a half step lower than the first.

By comparison, Schubert's output for women's voices is relatively small. The most notable works for female choir are *Gott in der Natur* (D. 757), the SSAA version of *Ständchen* (D. 920), and Psalm 23 (D. 706). The part songs for mixed voices form a slightly larger group with an accompanying expansion of style, length, and difficulty. (Schubert is thought to have originally scored many of these songs for solo voices.) The simpler, more accessible songs include *Der Tanz* (D. 826) and *Lebenslust*. Such works as *Des Tages Weihe* (D. 763), *Gott im Ungewitter* (D. 985), and the cantata *Mirjams Siegesgesang* (D. 942) are somewhat more complex. The cantata is not a part song but an attractive, extended work for soprano solo, SATB chorus, and piano based on Grillparzer's poetic version of the "Song of Miriam."

ROBERT SCHUMANN (1810–56)

Perhaps no romantic composer of choral music has been more overlooked by historians and conductors than Robert Schumann.[4] His part songs for mixed, women, and male chorus exhibit enormous range. Best known, but somewhat atypical, is *Zigeunerleben*, the third of a set of three settings of Emmanuel Geibel's poems in *Drei Gedichte*, op. 29. Neither the *New Grove Dictionary* nor John Daverio's Schumann biography classify these pieces as part songs but refer to them instead as vocal quartets with piano accompaniment. The same definition holds true of Schumann's four pieces for women's chorus with piano op. 114.[5] Schumann even provides ad-lib parts for triangle and tambourine to evoke the exoticism of Gypsy life. The persistent repetition of the poem's dactylic (long-short-short) rhythm is the primary means by which Schumann unifies his setting of this lengthy, narrative poem. General observations regarding Schumann's part songs show that many of them were composed in 1849: there are more mixed-chorus pieces than ones for male or female choir; Schumann often uses the descriptive title *Romanzen und Balladen*; and the poetry he draws on comes from such notable poets as Friedrich Rückert, Heinrich Eichendorf, Robert Burns, Eduard Mörike, and others.

The year 1849 seems to have been Schumann's watershed year. He wrote to Ferdinand Hiller, then the municipal music director in Düsseldorf: "For some time now I've been very busy—it's been my most fruitful year—it seems as if the outer storms impelled people to turn inward, and only therein did I find a counterforce against the forces breaking in so frightfully from without."[6] Schumann's new interest in choral music began with his appointment as conductor of the Dresden *Liedertafel*, succeeding Hiller in October of 1847, closely followed by his organization of the *Verein für Chorgesang*. In the latter part of 1847, Schumann composed the songs of his opp. 62 and 65 for the *Liedertafel*. Even though he resigned his directorship the following year, he dedicated his last two sets of male chorus music—the *Fünf Gesänge aus H. Laubes Jagdbrevier*, op. 135 (four horns ad lib) and the "motet" *Verzweifle nicht im Schmerzenstal* (for double male chorus and organ, orchestrated in 1852) to this group.

Schumann also used his new choral society to try out portions of such larger choral works as the *Schlussszene* from *Faust* and the *Requiem für Mignon*; he also programmed the music of earlier part-song collections (opp. 55 and 59). Then, in 1849 Schumann composed all four volumes of the *Romanzen und Balladen für gemischten Chor* (opp. 67, 75, 145, 146); the two volumes of *Romanzen* for women's voices (opp. 69 and 91); and the *Vier doppelchörige Gesänge für grössere Chorvereine*, op. 141, this one specifically intended to show off the improvement of his new choral society.[7]

The part songs for mixed chorus range from strophic choral songs (often with an element of "folk style") to the elaborate double choir pieces of op. 141. Schumann's first setting of Robert Burns's "John Anderson" (op. 67, no. 5) typifies the first style (ex. 2.4).

Example 2.4 Schumann, *John Anderson*, op. 67, no. 5, mm. 1–8

Schumann uses the same declamatory homophonic style, conventional vocal ranges, harmony, and rhythm for both verses, illustrating the closest connection between the strophic *Lied* and the part song.

Der traurige Jäger (op. 75, no. 3) also begins with identical strophes, the soprano melody doubled by the second alto. The harmony, which seems to hover between A minor and F major, contains some interesting chromaticism, apparently prompted by the words "Die Wälder rauschten leise, sein Jagen war vorbei; der blies so irrer Weise, als müsst' das Herz entzwei" ("The woods sighed lightly, his hunting was over; who blesses such a strange path risks having a broken heart") (ex. 2.5).

Example 2.5 Schumann, *Der traurige Jäger*, op. 75, no. 3, mm. 17–24

The music for the poem's conclusion combines the opening diatonic style with the chromatically inflected melody of the third (cf. mm. 20–21 and 28–29 of the soprano part).

By the time Schumann composed his op. 141, the competence of his choir and his conducting skills had improved considerably. All four strophes of Rückert's poem begin with the phrase *Sterne, in des Himmelsferne*, and Schumann initially follows suit, setting that text in vv. 1 and 2 to the same melody (mm. 1–21 = 22–42). This repetition is missing in the final two strophes and indicates that this piece is neither strophic nor simple in texture or harmony. The first noticeable change comes early in the third verse (m. 44), when Schumann diverges from G to E major at *Himmelsferne* (m. 44).

Example 2.6 Schumann, *An die Sterne*, op. 141, no. 1, mm. 46–54

This harmonic change also triggers different choral textures, accents, and vocal combinations (ex. 2.6). While v. 4 follows the same textual pattern, its reference to the "spirit taking wing" prompts Schumann to adopt a faster tempo with accelerated antiphonal exchanges. Schumann abruptly interrupts these by introducing soloists who sing lustrous C-major harmonies ("hoffend, glaubevoll!"), which the chorus repeats.

Given the similarly significant size of Schumann's part songs for male and female voices requires that we examine at least one representative of each type. "Die Rose stand im Tau" (op. 65, no. 1) immediately reflects the collection's generic title "Ritornelli [Refrains] in Canonic Style," by using canon.[8] To the normal complement of four voices (TTBB) Schumann adds another baritone part that sings in strict canon with the first tenor. The one-measure delay and different pitch level (a fifth below) add considerable harmonic and contrapuntal depth this setting of Rückert's brief, epigrammatic text (ex. 2.7).[9]

Example 2.7 Schumann, *Die Rose stand im Tau*, op. 65, no. 1, mm. 1–11

Schumann's part songs for women's chorus match those for men in terms of harmonic color, richness of scoring, and contrapuntal construction. The twelve songs of opp. 69 and 91 all employ at least four parts. With one exception (*In Meeres Mitten*, op. 91, no.6) Schumann provides ad-lib piano parts to compensate for the absence of the vocal bass.[10] Schumann's evocative setting of *Der Wassermann* (op. 91, no.3) reveals the beauty and expressivity of these compositions (ex. 2.8). Kerner's irregular poetic rhythm (lines of four feet that alternate irregularly between dactyls and iambs) gives this "volkstümlich" scena a somewhat dark, romantic twist, reflected in Schumann's choice of G minor for the first two verses. The dialogue between the maiden and the stranger (stanza 3) occasions a key change (to E♭ major) and a revoicing of the vocal ensemble to represent the characters. Given no male voices, Schumann allots the words of the "water sprite" to a low unison alto line doubled by the left hand in the piano.

Example 2.8 Schumann, *Der Wassermann*, op. 91, no. 3, mm. 16–22

Schumann's part songs presage those of his protégé, Johannes Brahms. The lush four-part writing and ad-lib piano accompaniment of *Der Wassermann* find a counterpart in Brahms's op. 44, while the canonic writing in *Die Rose stand im Tau* and use of double chorus in *An die Sterne* foreshadow aspects of Brahms's music, which are often attributed to his study of historical music.

FELIX MENDELSSOHN (1809–47)

Mendelssohn's association with the Berlin *Singakademie* and its conductor, C. F. Zelter, made his composition of light, convivial music inevitable. Mendelssohn's part-song output equally divides between mixed and male ensembles. The mixed-chorus part songs appear in five collections composed between 1839 and 1844; in some cases, dates on the manuscripts show that one or more were written in the same day. No single factor determines the contents or order of a given collection, all five of which share the title *Lieder im Freien zu singen*.[11] Nor is it likely coincidental that the first piece of op. 41 and the last of op. 100 share the same title (*Im Walde*). It might be that this shared reference to the forest, that most sacred temple of nineteenth-century German romanticism, constitutes Mendelssohn's deliberate attempt to provide his part songs with a thematic frame.

Mendelssohn's use of the term *Lieder* probably indicates soloistic performance as opposed to the rubric *für vierstimmigen Männerchor* for the male chorus pieces.[12] The genesis of Mendelssohn's part songs within a relatively narrow time frame explains the greater stylistic consistency of his output compared to those of other composers. All of the *Lieder* for mixed chorus, for example, use four voices without *divisi*. Mendelssohn tends to favor major tonalities: four begin in minor but end in major, and only one (op. 41, no. 3) remains minor throughout. Mendelssohn avoids the strict counterpoint used by Schumann (especially op. 65), substituting instead variations in vocal texture in its place. This process frequently involves the seamless alternation of homophony and a motivic interaction between the voices by often using vocal pairs (especially SA and TB). The resulting variety also obscures Mendelssohn's predilection for strophic texts.

The locus classicus of Mendelssohn's output is his setting of Goethe's *Die Nachtigall*. Mendelssohn sets this brief poem three times, using the same melody for each strophe (ex. 2.9).

Example 2.9 Mendelssohn, *Die Nachtigall*, op. 59, no. 4, mm.1–12

The melody appears first in the soprano, then the tenor, and then again in the soprano. Mendelssohn counters this melodic sameness by varying the textures in these repetitions. The opening duet for soprano and alto, for example, appears verbatim in the male voices (v. 2) with the addition of a treble descant. In v. 3, he simply uses the lower three voices to harmonize the soprano melody. Perhaps in order to create a composition of adequate length Mendelssohn decided to repeat the same text and melody three times. But a more intriguing explanation may lie in the enigmatic third line of Goethe's text—*"was Neues hat sie nicht gelernt?"* Goethe asks why we should expect the nightingale to return in the spring having learned a new song; if this supposition is so, Mendelssohn's repetition of the same melody reflects the bird's preference (and his own) for the simple, "old, dear songs," or even, perhaps, to make the obvious statement that it would be impossible for the nightingale to learn a new song.

The rest of op. 59 affords an excellent overview of Mendelssohn's part songs. Directly preceding *Die Nachtigall* is *Abschied vom Walde* (op. 59, no.3), a secular hymn to the forest. And its predecessor, the setting of Goethe's *Frühzeitiger Frühling*, is one of this opus's longer part songs. Here Mendelssohn disguises the poem's strophic regularity first by varying the choral texture of the first two verses, then by changing meter (from triple to duple) and writing new music to portray the "buzzing bees" described in v. 3 (ex. 2.10).

Example 2.10 Mendelssohn, *Frühzeitiger Frühling*, op. 59, no. 2, mm. 81–6

Like Schubert, Mendelssohn often avoids female choral songs, preferring to compose chamber duets in lieu of part songs. *Herbstlied* (1844) is one of six duets that comprise op. 63; it combines simple lyricism and 6/8 meter to lament the impending end of summer and all the things associated with it—plants, social interaction, and, of course, love. The virtual absence of female part songs from his *oeuvre* makes Mendelssohn's songs for male chorus even more historically significant, reinforcing the link between the composer and Zelter's *Liedertafel*. Compared with the part songs for mixed voices, those for male chorus rely more on homophony, often alternating between solo voices and full chorus. The commonplace *Liedertafel* themes of drinking, love, the forest, and nature dominate these titles. Mendelssohn's finest male chorus work is undoubtedly *Der Jäger Abschied* (op. 50, no. 2), a paean of nearly religious fervor to the forest and a bit of romantic flavor takes the form of ad-lib accompaniment with hunting horns and trombone. The idiomatic color of the horns even permeates the voice parts, as seen in the use of horn fifths to set the text "Lebe wohl" (farewell), as perhaps a nod to Beethoven (ex. 2.11). The increasing importance of the French horn in nineteenth-century orchestras began by deliberately including such idiomatic and rustic gestures. One frequently finds the use of the device any time there is an allusion to hunting (both in texted works such as Haydn's oratorio *Die Jahreszeiten* or operas like Weber's *Der Freischütz* [1821] and Rossini's *Guillaume Tell* [1829]) and even symphonic music from Haydn through Mahler.[13]

Example 2.11 Mendelssohn, *Der Jäger Abschied*, op. 50, no. 2, mm. 12–23

Liebe und Wein (op. 50, no.5) assays other standard *Liedertafel* topics. Given the rubric *Im betrunkenen Ton zu singen* ("In a drunken manner . . ."), this song counters Mendelssohn's ubiquitous 6/8 meter with changes of mode (G minor to G major) and tempo (*Maestoso/Allegro molto*) that portray the pain associated with love and at least one remedy for it.

JOHANNES BRAHMS (1833–97)

Quantitatively and qualitatively, the part songs of Johannes Brahms are the consummate achievement of the romantic part song. Here there are no traces of the *Liedertafel* tradition, an absence due less to his preoccupation with a more professional or more socially circumscribed audience than to the increasing popularity and sophistication of amateur and coed choral singing. Brahms composed only one set of songs for male chorus (op. 41, 1867), which underscores the waning significance of the *Männerchor*. Like Schumann, Brahms concentrates on part songs for mixed and female choruses (with and without accompaniment), suggesting an intermingling of sacred with secular, folk song, and art music, and the simple with the complex. Brahms's music for women's chorus reflects this diversification. Only the *Zwölf Lieder und Romanzen* (op. 44) are really part songs, since this title reveals the continued influence of Schumann. Like Schumann again, Brahms favors four-part women's chorus with ad-lib piano accompaniment to reinforce the lowest voice.

But it is the songs for *a cappella* mixed chorus that are the summit of his part-song output. In the *Drei Gesänge*, op. 42, Brahms sets poems by Clemens Brentano, Wilhelm Müller, and Ossian (translated by Herder). As an exemplar, take the second of these pieces, Müller's *Vineta*. Brahms uses his signature choral texture, a six-part ensemble with divided alto and bass, to impart a rich, burnished color appropriate to Müller's sentimental poem. Brahms's setting reveals the ingenuity of Müller's typically romantic poetic conceit—a juxtaposition of the outer world of nature and mythology (vv. 1–3) with the parallel, inner world of dreams and the human heart (vv. 4–6). The first three verses describe a sailor who returns, again and again at sunset, to the spot where he once saw a beautiful city beneath the waves. In the last three verses of the poem, Müller's metaphor changes from nature and the depths of the sea to the recesses of the human heart.

Brahms's music reinforces this textual dualism. While confirming the poem's strophic regularity by using the same music for vv. 1, 2, and 5 (and parts of it in vv. 3 and 6), his change of mode and vocal texture for v. 4 adds a new level of sophistication to the part song. A descending B-minor melody sung by the unison lower voices (A/B) signals the poem's metaphoric shift (ex. 2.12). The basses transgress the limits of the new mode, continuing their descent through A to G major to depict the "soft, muted" sound of bells in a harmonic palindrome anchored in the circle of fifths.

Example 2.12 Brahms, *Vineta*, op. 42, no. 2, mm. 42–52

Brahms returns to B major by turning G major into a dominant-seventh chord, the F♮ of which is enharmonically the equivalent of E♯. Although the resulting chord sounds like a G V⁷, it functions as a German sixth chord, which resolves first to B major (2nd inversion) and then E major before closing the verse with a half-cadence to B.

The *Sieben Lieder*, op. 62 (1872), is a larger collection with a commensurately greater variety of poetry and vocal scoring. The texts of *Rosmarin* and *Von alten Liebesliedern* come from that uniquely romantic anthology *Des Knaben Wunderhorn* (1805), assembled by Clemens Brentano and Achim von Arnim. The next four poems all are taken from Paul Heyse's *Jungbrunnen* ("Springs of Youth"), a collection Brahms had already used in op. 44. The last text is an "old German" poem, *Vergangen ist mir Glück und Heil*, set to music that looks and sounds appropriately antiquated. With the exception of no. 5, *All' meine Herzgedanken* (SAATBB), Brahms scores all of these *Lieder* for four voices and adheres to the poetry's strophic design.

The most popular piece in this opus is *Waldesnacht*, op. 62, no. 3, whose three verses atypically adopt the most rigid aspect of the strophic song, using exactly the same music, dynamics, and expression marks for all three verses—but is it really the same music? Strophic compositions pose a problem often unperceived by performers, namely, how to realize the subtle changes of textual nuance when seeing the same music. In *Vineta* Brahms changes the music to mirror changes in text and mood; *Waldesnacht* has no such changes. Should we then conclude that Brahms intends no differences in the performance of each verse? If the similar tone of these verses prompts a single musical interpretation, the retention of a D-major key signature hardly explains Brahms's subtle shift to the parallel mode (mm. 5–7) or the canonically generated seventh chords at "Träumerisch" (ex. 2.13).

Example 2.13 Brahms, *Waldesnacht*, op. 62, no. 3, mm. 12–16

Some of the other compositions of op. 62 deserve a passing mention. In *Von alten Liebesliedern*, Brahms uses antiphonal choirs of women and men's voices to re-create the poetic dialogue. His setting of *Dein Herzlein mild* is elegant and graceful, an eight-bar period effortlessly extends contrapuntally to eleven measures. *All' meine Herzgedanken* (op. 62, no.5) features one of Brahms's most endearing melodies, made lovelier by antiphonal echoes. Then there is the wistful, mysterious passage of the breeze through the forest in *Es geht ein Wehen* (op. 62, no.6), achieved by using parallel sixth chords in the three upper parts over a static bass pedal. Here, the antiquated text of *Vergangen ist mir Glück und Heil* prompts Brahms to employ 4/2 meter ("white" notes à la Palestrina) and a modal melody.

The *Lieder und Romanzen*, op. 93a, is a collection of multicolored jewels that defy easy classification. Although many use strophic texts, Brahms suppresses this feature through unpredictable changes of meter and key. While the first two verses of the *Der bucklichte Fiedler* are strophic, Brahms writes out the repetition down to the insertion of a single 5/4 measure to conclude the second phrase. In v. 3, the poem's reference to the fiddler (*bucklichte Fiedler*) leads Brahms to use the pitches of the violin's open strings (ex. 2.14). The irregular scansion of the Serbian folk poem *Das Mädchen* induced Brahms to alternate between 3/4 and 4/4, use a solo soprano to portray the maiden, and change mode (B minor to B major) to represent the difference of her reaction to kissing an old man and a young man.[14] Such romantic topics also dominate opp. 92–94, but the texts used here deal more with love lost than love found.[15]

More straightforward is the combination of Achim von Arnim's text and Brahms's musical setting of *O süsser Mai* (ex. 2.15). Brahms's music is sweetly luminous, yet darkly shaded. The central tonality, C major, informs every important cadence. Brahms paints the poem's wistful ambivalence by vacillating between major and minor mode, and setting the text in a "stop-and-go" manner.

Example 2.14 Brahms, *Der bucklichte Fiedler*, op. 93a, no. 1, mm. 22–36

Example 2.15 Brahms, *O süsser Mai*, op. 93a, no. 3, mm. 1–11

The poem's shift to first person in the third phrase summons the insertion of three flats (B♭, E♭, and A♭) effectively creating C minor. The maiden's self-reproachful indifference to nature's beauty is heard in the restless, offset rhythmic motion, now exacerbated by the collusion of the lower three voices against the soprano (ex. 2.16).

Example 2.16 Brahms, *O süsser Mai*, op. 93a, no. 3, mm. 12–16

Brahms adds even more *Angst* by returning (m. 16) to the chromaticism that concludes the opening section. The poem's modified textual reprise minimizes this *chiaroscuro* (mm. 22), replacing the first phrase's chromatic inflections (m. 5–11) with seventh-chord arpeggios that are purely C major.

The final set of part songs for mixed chorus is arguably Brahms's masterpiece. The *Fünf Gesänge*, op. 104, began to gestate in 1888 during Brahms's third summer in the Swiss town of Thun, a period during which he also composed the songs of opp. 106 and 107, vocal quartets (op. 112), the solo version of *Zigeunerlieder* (op. 103), and his initial sketching of the *Fest- und Gedenksprüche* (op. 109). The texts of the *Fünf Gesänge* all have the bittersweet, resigned character associated with Brahms toward the end of his life (e.g., *Vier ernste Gesänge*, op. 121). The five poems he sets are *Nachtwache I* and *II* (Friedrich Rückert), *Letztes Glück* (Max Kalbeck), *Verlorene Jugend* (Bohemian, trans. by Josef Wenzig), and *Im Herbst* (Klaus Groth), but not all of these pieces date from 1888. Brahms sent *Im Herbst* to his physician friend Theodor Billroth on August 16, 1886.[16] Two years later (August 15, 1888), Brahms sent *Letztes Glück* to another close friend, the poet, Max Kalbeck.[17] According to Siegfried Kross, *Verlorene Jugend* probably came into being that same summer, but the two Rückert settings were not written until 1889, the year of publication.[18]

What distinguishes these pieces from their forebears is less a relaxation of textual focus or change of musical style than the emergence of contrapuntal technique. If *Verlorene Jugend*'s use of canon provides the clearer example of this trend, Brahms's use of intricate counterpoint is more nuanced and diverse in *Leise Töne der Brust*, op. 104, no. 1. Brahms subdivides his favorite six-voice texture into female and male choirs, the upper voices of each choir presenting a sequential melody (ex. 2.17).

Example 2.17 Brahms, *Nachtwache I*, op. 104, no. 1, mm. 1–9

At "hauchet zitternd hinaus" Brahms writes strict canons between the outer voices of each choir, but he returns to antiphonal texture for "öffen ein liebendes Herz," creating a ternary design based on texture. Another example of such texturally derived form is his use of imitation between the male and female voices in mm. 1–15. Rückert's last text phrase—"trag ein Nachtwind euch seufzend, in meines zurück"—prompts Brahms to use three different textures: a homophonic, *portato* passage (slurred staccato notes) used earlier (mm. 5–8) with the same melody (ex. 2.18); two antiphonal presentations of "seufzend" ("sighing") that traverse the circle of fifths (F#°, B7, E7, A7, D major), and yet another antiphonal passage that sets "in meines zurück" as a kind of textural imitation.

Example 2.18 a/b Brahms, *Nachtwache I*,
op. 104, no. 1
Clifford Bartlett, ed. *Madrigals and Partsongs*
© Oxford University Press 2001. Used by permission.
All rights reserved. Photocopying this copyright material
is ILLEGAL

Nachtwache I differs from all its predecessors in that, absent a strophic poem, Brahms must use sequence and antiphony to create a convincing formal structure. While he carefully attends to syntax and word expression in all of these works, his use of counterpoint in op. 104 provides unequivocal proof that we are no longer in the world of the *Liedertafel*.

Brahms also published a number of collections of secular vocal music with piano accompaniment: *Drei Quartetten*, op. 31, (1864); *Liebeslieder Walzer*, op. 52; *Vier Quartetten*, op. 64; *Neue Liebeslieder Walzer*, op. 65; *Vier Quartetten*, op. 92; *Tafellied*, op. 93b; *Zigeunerlieder*, op. 103; and *Quartetten und Vier Zigeunerlieder*, op. 112. With the possible exception of op. 103, Brahms did not conceive of these compositions as choral; nowhere is his intent clearer than in the *Liebeslieder Walzer*, op. 52. Attempting to capitalize on the success of his waltzes for piano four-hands (op. 39), Brahms's specification "for piano four-hands, voices ad lib" indicates that the vocal parts were hardly obligatory. Performance of these waltzes as four-hand piano music may bear the composer's imprimatur, but it is an option unthinkable to anyone who has ever sung them. Performance by a vocal quartet may eliminate ensemble issues, but it also dispenses with the textural distinction implicit in his creation of movements for one or two voices and those featuring all four parts. In the case of the quartets (opp. 31, 64, 92, and 112), long-breathed vocal lines like the following excerpt from *Der Abend*, op. 64, no.2, seem to suggest soloistic performance (ex. 2.19).

Accompanied part songs gained great popularity in the nineteenth century, as the presence of wonderful examples in the works of Schubert, Schumann, Berlioz, Rossini, Cornelius and Reger attest. Aside from Brahms, the only extended cycles are Robert Schumann's *Spanisches Liederspiel*, op. 74; *Minnespiel*, op. 101; and *Spanische Liebeslieder*, op. 138, all virtually ignored today.

Example 2.19 Brahms, *Der Abend*, op. 64, no. 2, mm. 31–42

OTHER GERMAN PART-SONG COMPOSERS

The part-song genre flourished with composers like Anton Bruckner, Peter Cornelius, Max Reger, Josef Rheinberger, Fanny Mendelssohn Hensel, and Clara Schumann. This repertory led to cultivation of the genre in England and, to lesser degrees, in France (Berlioz), Italy (Rossini), eastern Europe (Dvořák), and Scandinavia (Grieg). In the less established of these musical traditions, part songs became nearly inseparable from the issue of nationalism.

Anton Bruckner (1824–96) joined the *Liedertafel Frohsinn* in 1856 and eventually became the group's conductor (1860–61).[19] Only later did he compose music for this group and a larger male chorus, the *Niederösterreichischer Sängerbund*, in Linz. His secular choral music comprises twenty-four part songs for unaccompanied male voices, another ten with accompaniment (piano, organ, or winds), two works designated for male quartet, and four pieces for mixed chorus/quartet. The first group comprises simple strophic songs or brief, robust settings of the mottos of various choral organizations. Typical *Liedertafel* settings, like *Am Grabe* and *Trösterin Musik* (1877) are slightly more complex (see ex. 2.20).[20] Bruckner's indication of an optional organ part hardly disqualifies the latter work's inclusion in the repertory of amateur male choruses.

Example 2.20 Bruckner, *Trösterin Musik*, WAB 88, mm. 1–8

Bruckner's use of vocal soli, idiomatic instrumental accompaniment, and poems of greater literary quality signal his progression beyond typical *Liedertafel* fare. Two examples of such music are his *Vaterlandslied,* WAB 92 (scored for tenor and baritone soli and four-part male chorus *a cappella*) and *Um Mitternacht,* WAB 89 (for alto solo, male chorus and piano). In *Das hohe Lied,* WAB 74, Bruckner experiments with a "hummed" (*Brummstimme*) accompaniment for three vocal soloists.[21] This novel sonority and eight vocal parts proved unsuccessful, leading Bruckner to orchestrate the work for strings and brass (four horns, three trombones, and tuba).

Among the minor masters of *Chorlieder* Peter Cornelius (1824–74) is singularly interesting. Initially a pupil of Liszt, Cornelius fell under the mesmerizing influence of Richard Wagner after 1861. Although his operas are relatively unimportant, Cornelius achieved notable success in his songs for solo voice and ensemble. His twenty-four works for male chorus include four sacred pieces (his *Requiem aeternam* is the most interesting) and three collections with assigned opus numbers: *Trauerchöre,* op. 9 (1869); *Drei Männerchöre,* op. 12 (1873); and *Reiterlied,* op. 17 (1783). The first of the four *Trauerchöre, Ach wie nichtig, ach, wie flüchtig,* is the only one that is not strophic. Two others make historical references: *Mitten wir im Leben sind* uses Notkus Balbulus's sequence *Media vita in morte sumus* (Martin Luther's translation); *Grablied* sets an original poem to the music of Schubert's *Der Tod und das Mädchen* (ex. 2.21).

Example 2.21 Cornelius, *Grablied,* op. 9, no. 4, mm. 1–16

Cornelius's catalogue also contains four cycles for mixed chorus: *Drei Chorgesänge,* op. 11 (1871); *Drei Psalmenlieder,* op. 13 (1872); *Liebe: ein Zyklus von 3 Chorliedern* (nach Angelus Silesius), op. 18 (1872); and *Vier Italienische Chorlieder,* op. 20 (1872). Like *Grablied,* Cornelius uses earlier music to set poetry by Rückert (op. 11) and Silesius (op. 18) along with Cornelius's own poetry (opp. 13 and 20). All three of his *Psalmenlieder* are based on keyboard music by J. S. Bach: *Busslied* (after Psalm 88) on the Sarabande of Bach's French Suite No. 1 (BWV 812); *An Babels Wasserflüssen* (Ps. 137) on the Sarabande of Bach's English Suite No. 3

(BWV 808); and *Jerusalem* (after Ps. 122) on Minuet 2 of Bach's Partita in B♭ (BWV 825). In op. 20 Cornelius used music by the late-sixteenth-century composers (Gastoldi, Vecchi, and Donato) to set his own poetry: (1) *Das Tanzlied* (Donato: *Chi la gagliarda* in *Il primo libro di Canzon Villanesche alla Napolitana*, 1550); (2) *Amor im Nachen* (G. G. Gastoldi: *Amor Vittorioso: Balletti a cinque voci*, 1591); (3) *Liebeslied* (G. G. Gastoldi: *A lieta vita: Balletti*, 1591); and (4) *Zug der Juden nach Babylon* (Orazio Vecchi: *Il Convito musicale*, 1595). Already the musical source of Thomas Morley's "Sing we and chant it," Gastoldi's "A lieta vita" was updated by Cornelius, who added modern dynamic and tempo marks (ex. 2.22).

Example 2.22 Cornelius, *Liebeslied*, op. 20, no. 3, mm. 1–8

Cornelius even turned to instrumental music from Arbeau's *Orchésographie* (1588) for *Blaue Augen* and based *Freund Hein* on the *Molto adagio* movement of Beethoven's String Quartet, op. 132.[22]

Among nineteenth-century composers, Max Reger (1873–1916) is known for his extremely chromatic music, especially his organ compositions, but he also produced a large and diverse corpus of secular choral music. The voicing (SAATBB) and harmony of *Drei Sechsstimmige Chöre*, op. 39, are reminiscent of Brahms, but despite its dedication to various *Liedertafeln* and male choirs, the complex rhythm and chromatic harmony in the opening of *Über die Berge!* belie its use by such organizations (ex. 2.23).[23]

Example 2.23 Reger, *Über die Berge*, op. 38, no. 3, mm. 1–3

The textural density, chromaticism, and extreme vocal ranges exhibited in those pieces seem far removed from the *Liedertafeln*, but they pale in comparison with op. 83, the first eight pieces of which are dedicated to the *Wiener Männergesangverein*. The first composition, *An das Meer*, routinely uses eight parts, exploiting extremes of ambitus (E to B′) and dynamics (*ppp* to *ff*)

not routinely found in such music. While such complexity and density are not present throughout this collection, it is just such music that has shaped most musicians' opinions about Reger's music. Conversely, the *Drei Chöre*, op. 6 (mixed chorus and piano), and many of the *a cappella* works for mixed voices have proved reasonably accessible.

The part-song genre included contributions from composers as diverse as Joseph Haydn, Hector Berlioz, Franz Liszt, and Hugo Wolf (1860–1903). Though relatively small in number, Haydn's part songs and folk songs were among the first pieces in this genre to appear. Berlioz composed a surprisingly varied array of smaller, accompanied choral works ranging from the early *Ballet des Ombres*, op. 2, to *Sara la baigneuse*, op. 11. And although Liszt did not compose what could be described as part songs, his wide array of *a cappella* sacred and secular music merits more attention than it has received. Wolf's *oeuvre* included both sacred/spiritual (*Sechs Geistliche Chöre*, 1881) and secular works (e.g., his electrifying setting of Mörike's poem *Der Feuerreiter*, composed in 1888, arranged for chorus in 1892).

In the nineteenth century, women took on increasing roles as performers, as the compositions for women's chorus by Mendelssohn, Schumann, and Brahms attest. That most of this repertory was sacred provides a significant insight into the status of female choirs in the nineteenth century: denied access to the venues and themes of their male counterparts, female choruses tended to perform sacred repertory in both private and public concerts. Nor should the role of women as composers in their own right be overlooked. The foremost examples were Clara Schumann (1819–96)[24] and Fanny Mendelssohn Hensel (1805–47),[25] both of whom had obvious connection to established male composers of the era.

PART SONG IN ENGLAND

By the time the first *Liedertafel* in Germany was formed, part-song singing was already a well-established tradition in England. In 1761 the Nobleman and Gentleman's Catch Club provided the same opportunities for singing and socializing as did those by the German singing societies. By 1763, the Catch Club established a yearly composition prize, a competition dominated by Samuel Webbe (1740–1816) who, from 1784 until his death, served as the club's secretary. Essentially a hymnodist, he became a central figure in the foundation of the Glee Club (1763), an organization similar to the Catch Club but without membership limitations based on social class. From 1790 on, Webbe's glee, *Glorious Apollo*, opened every meeting of the club. Other composers associated with the Glee and Catch Clubs at the beginning of the nineteenth century included William Horsley (1774–1858), John Goss (1800–1880), Thomas F. Walmisley (1783–1866), and Samuel Sebastian Wesley (1810–76).[26] Changes in the social fabric of England, precipitated by the Industrial Revolution and the rise of a significant middle class, led to the demise of the Catch Club, which awarded no prizes between 1784 and 1811. Another contributing factor was the success of the Glee Club and its various offspring. Ironically, these organizations suffered a similar fate in the early nineteenth century due to the increasing influx of foreign music and musicians (notably Felix Mendelssohn). The Continental influence reached its apex in 1836 with the publication of *Orpheus, A Collection of Glees by the Most Admired German Composers with English Poetry*. This nineteenth-century equivalent of *Musica Transalpina* presented short pieces by Weber, Spohr, and others in its first issue. The use of the term "glee" in the title revealed more about the publication's market than the music's style. Contemporary journals were quick to point out that these songs exhibited "nothing of the design of the English glee."[27] The publication of *Orpheus* effectively signaled the arrival of the *Liedertafel* repertory in England; such was its popularity that following its initial publication run (1836–58), Novello expanded it in 1878 to include more modern German part songs.

Another consequence of the Industrial Revolution was the foundation of institutes to train workers to meet the demands of the new industrial technology. Singing was seen as an ideal vehicle to promote social interaction and a heightened sense of morality among the working class. This emphasis on education led to the introduction (ca. 1830) of singing classes and performances as a means of enriching the lives of the working class (and perhaps salving the conscience of those who employed them in often deplorable conditions). Two names prominently associated with this new movement are John Pyke Hullah (1812–84) and the Reverend John Curwen (1816–80), both of whom published manuals promulgating the teaching of sight-singing. Curwen is remembered for his advocacy of the Tonic Sol-Fa method eventually adopted by Joseph Novello.[28] The first public concert of Hullah's ensemble (April 13, 1842) and the critical approval it garnered assured the popularity of his arrangements, which the *Musical World* believed should be on "every cottage book-shelf in the Kingdom."[29] The volume contained thirty-seven pieces of varying difficulty, including thirteen Renaissance works by Elizabethan and Italian composers, ten English glees, choruses by Gluck, Cherubini, and Purcell, a *solfeggio* based on Scarlatti, madrigals by William Horsley (1774–1858) and George Macfarren (1813–87), national songs by Thomas Arne (1710–78) and Robert Lucas de Pearsall (1795–1856), and a part song composed for Hullah's Upper Singing School by Ignaz Moscheles (1794–1870). In 1844 Novello's new publication, the *Musical Times*, undertook the dissemination of musical news throughout England and included as an added feature new compositions—the first choral "octavos."

Joseph Novello ardently championed the compositions of Felix Mendelssohn, republishing his part songs that had originally appeared in *Orpheus*. Greeted with delight by critics and performers alike, these simple songs in four parts were ideally suited to the burgeoning English market. Typical of these English adaptations was William Bartholomew's translation of Mendelssohn's *Abschied vom Walde* (op. 59, no. 3) as "Departure." But despite Novello's success, English translations of German part songs did not provide a viable solution to the needs of fledgling English choral groups. That solution came in 1850 when E. G. Monk (1819–1900) approached Joseph Novello to suggest commissioning works by English composers in order to meet the needs and match the abilities of modern choristers. The result, *Novello's Part Song Book*, began under Monk's editorship in May 1850. This promising enterprise lasted only twelve months, its fate sealed by perceptions that the music was inadequate artistically, even if it did recognize and cater to the technical limitations of contemporary choirs.

A more positive, enduring solution was the founding of the English Glee and Madrigal Union (ca. 1850) to "preserve from oblivion the masterpieces of our English school of vocal part-songs—madrigals, glees, rounds and catches."[30] More important still was the choir established by Henry Leslie (1822–96) in response to the successful tours by German choirs. This group's unprecedented attention to detail and insistence on excellence rapidly became the model for English *a cappella* choral performance. Adroit businessman that he was, Joseph Novello published a new version of *Novello's Part-Song Book* (1863) to capitalize on the success of Leslie. This new repertory relied on distinguished English poetry, ranging from Shakespeare to contemporary poets like Alfred Tennyson.

RISE OF THE MUSICAL COMPETITION

After winning the Paris choral competition in 1878, Leslie announced plans to disband his choir following the 1880 season. A member of Leslie's choir, Lionel Benson, founded the Magpie Madrigal Society in 1885 and recruited former members of Leslie's choir. The numerous choirs formed in the wake of Leslie's withdrawal gained additional impetus from the rise of English choral competitions, instigated by the contralto Mary Wakefield (1853–1910). In 1886 she sponsored a competition in her hometown of Kendal, which led to the phenomenon of "test pieces," works by contemporary composers that were obligatory for choirs participating at a given level. Among the earliest composers of such pieces were Charles Villiers Stanford (1852–1924) and C. Hubert H. Parry (1848–1918) (see Fig. 2.2). In addition to the Welsh *Eisteddfod* (which stressed performance of oratorio excerpts) and the Wakefield competitions, the Morecambe Festival (1891) created an open division designed to attract the best choirs in England. The published test pieces for the 1898 festival included pieces by Henry Leslie, John Hatton, Henry Smart, Mendelssohn, Pinsuti, Pearsall, and Stanford.[31]

The *Musical Times* hailed Stanford's first published collection of part songs (op. 47, 1892) as "amongst the most artistic of their kind."[32] These works added imitation and independent part-writing to the existing part-song model. Stanford's output began with three sets of "Elizabethan" part songs, followed by arrangements of folk songs from his native Ireland. While Stanford generally set strophic poems, his musical settings often expanded the final verse to create a sense of musical climax. On the whole, the style of the Irish songs was more conservative, mainly because Stanford closely followed the tunes traditionally associated with certain texts. These folk song arrangements differ from his Elizabethan part songs, which were freely composed. The most popular of Stanford's part songs ("The Blue Bird") comes from the first of two publications (opp. 119 and 127) devoted to the poetry of Mary Coleridge (1861–1907), a great-grandniece of the more famous Samuel Taylor Coleridge. Paul Rodmell believes that the majority of these part songs are inconsequential, as even the titles might tend to suggest.[33] The exception is "The Blue Bird," of which Rodmell writes, "Deserving of its renown, Stanford's skill here led to a piece little short of perfection. The slow-moving choral parts, replete again with secondary sevenths, create a perfect picture of a still, hot day, while the solo soprano soars above playing the role of the bluebird" (ex. 2.24).[34]

Example 2.24 Stanford, *The Blue Bird*, op. 119, no. 3, mm. 1–13
Clifford Bartlett, ed. Madrigals and Partsongs © Oxford University
Press 2001. Used by permission. All rights reserved. Photocopying this
copyright material is ILLEGAL.

In the 1890s, C. Hubert H. Parry followed Stanford's lead, with his "Six Lyrics from an Elizabethan Song Book" followed by "Six Modern Lyrics." Parry's belief in the primacy of the text accorded perfectly with Stanford's view:

> In music associated with words it is absolutely inevitable that the mood and expression of phrase and figure and melody and harmony, and even of form must be in close and intimate relation with the words. The more perfect the instinct of the composer for the musical equivalents of the sentiments expressed by the words, the more perfect will be the style; and the more perfect the invention which can dispose of the ingredients in an effective and original manner, the more complete the work of art. The composer has the moods and details of expression supplied him, and the hearers understand the music through its relation to the words.[35]

Despite its somewhat stilted syntax, Parry's setting of Percy Bysshe Shelley's poem "Music, when Soft Voices Die" (1897) confirms his adherence to these precepts (ex. 2.25).

Example 2.25 Parry, *Music, when Soft Voices Die*, mm. 1–4
Clifford Bartlett, ed. *Madrigals and Partsongs* © Oxford University Press 2001.
Used by permission. All rights reserved. Photocopying this copyright
material is ILLEGAL.

Stanford and Parry provide a logical point of connection to the next generation of English composers, Gustav Holst (1874–1934), Ralph Vaughan Williams (1872–1958), and Edward Elgar (1857–1934). Strictly speaking, Elgar's part songs surpass conventional notions of that genre as "commonplace part-music."[36] His earliest part song "My Love Dwelt in a Northern Land" (1890) was constructed on two contrasting sections and contains an unexpected textual twist because the song itself is actually a dirge. "Weary Wind of the West," written as a test piece for the 1903 Morecambe Festival, presented significant new challenges for each voice part. But the crowning glory of Elgar's work are the four part songs published in 1907 as his opus 53: "There Is Sweet Music" (Alfred, Lord Tennyson), "Deep in My Soul" (Lord Byron), "O Wild West Wind" (Percy Bysshe Shelley), and "Owls" (Anonymous).

These extraordinary pieces relate to the typical English part song in roughly the same way that Brahms's compositions did to those of his predecessors. One is immediately aware of the quality of the texts Elgar chose to set. Of the four, the best known and certainly the most unusual, was the first—"There Is Sweet Music," which at first glance appears to be bitonal. The key signature of the women's voices is four flats (A♭ major), while the male voices have one sharp (G major). This polytonality is illusory, as Elgar uses antiphonal male and female "choirs" to avoid any possible tonal conflict. He takes consistent advantage of the enharmonic relationships that these two keys presented—the G-major tonic of the male chorus easily becomes E minor, which, in major, provides G♯, the enharmonic tonic of the female voices. Similarly, the use of incidental flats (C♭, B♭♭, etc.) in the women's parts allow their music to enter the harmonic realm of the men. Since one tonality ultimately had to emerge victorious, Elgar ends the song with alternating A♭ and G-major triads that finally settle on G (ex. 2.26).

Fig. 2.2 Photo of Edward Elgar (*left*) with fellow composers at the Bournemouth Festival (July, 1910)
(*Back row, l–r:* Hubert Parry, Edward German; *Front row, l–r:* Elgar, Dan Godfrey, Alex Mackenzie, Charles Stanford)

Example 2.26 Elgar, *There is Sweet Music,* op. 53, no. 1, mm. 44–46

By comparison, the two middle pieces are harmonically straightforward; both employ an E♭-major key signature and hew closely to that tonality. As the melody of "Deep in My Soul" illustrates (ex. 2.27), these traditional markers are stretched by some ingenious enharmonicism.

Example 2.27 a–c Elgar, *Deep in My Soul*, op. 53, no. 2

Elgar reprises the opening music, now in A♭ minor, to create a closed musical form.

The anonymous poem "Owls" is neither fast nor conclusive, using the dark key of C minor that becomes C♯ minor in the middle section only to return to C minor, a somewhat bizarre twist on strophic design and quiet, furtive declamation. The poem's three strophes exhibit striking textual similarities. Thus, Elgar plays the text's game of seeming similitude, setting the "nearly identical" strophes to nearly identical music. If each verse's music is almost the same, their tonalities are as different as one can imagine—the first strophe is in C minor, the second is transposed up a semitone, the third returns to C minor. Elgar also plays rhythmic games designed to highlight the unexpected words "bier" and "pall." And the final exchange is as different harmonically as its text is from the two preceding strophes (ex. 2.28).

Example 2.28 a/b Elgar, *Owls*, op. 53, no. 4

At this point we have crossed the invisible barrier separating the nineteenth century from the twentieth, but the different stances taken by composers like Sullivan, Parry, Stanford, Finzi, and Holst make it difficult to tell on which side of that line they fall, both stylistically, individually, and in relation to one another. It remained for Benjamin Britten (1913–76) to make the "crooked" line separating these different stylistic positions into a "straight," visible meridian.

CONCLUSION

The part song was perhaps the prime contribution of romantic composers to the choral art. Although it began as decidedly an amateur enterprise, the rapid growth of small choral groups and the amazingly prolific output by poets of the time (not to mention the increasing availability of folk music) helped boost the prestige of such music making. Even if a few general histories have underestimated the role of choral singing (and the music produced to satisfy the demands of choirs for popular, new music), the quality of the composers and the volume of their outputs clearly illustrate the significance of this genre. It was the decline of large-scale choral works that Alfred Einstein found so troubling. Much of the secular chamber music was intended less for concert performance than as entertainment for convivial occasions in private homes. Like the song cycle, with which they shared a similar social function, these choral collections possessed substantial musical integrity, color, and quality. The ability not merely to entertain but to move the very soul of the listener assures such compositions a continued presence in contemporary choral performances.

3

Choral Music in Nineteenth-Century Drama

There is a significant body of nineteenth-century choral music that resists classification within any preexisting choral genre. The rise of public concerts and the growth of choral societies led to increased demand for choral pieces based on secular literature and accompanied by orchestra. This type of dramatic music might ultimately have owed its existence to the increasingly prominent role of the chorus in the rapidly evolving world of opera. In this chapter we examine the new and important place of the chorus in nineteenth-century opera as prelude to a survey of selected dramatic works for the concert hall.

CHORAL MUSIC IN NINETEENTH-CENTURY OPERA

Any discussion of nineteenth-century operatic choral music must begin with Mozart, who, despite his death almost a decade before the century began, was already proclaimed (along with Haydn and Beethoven) by E. T. A. Hoffmann as a "romantic" composer.[1] The chorus's role varies greatly in Mozart's opera, hardly a surprising development given the range of styles they embraced. In his last five operas, Mozart shifted from the *opera buffa* trilogy based on libretti by Da Ponte (*Le nozze di Figaro, Così fan tutte, Don Giovanni*) to *Singspiel* (*Die Zauberflöte*) to *opera seria* (*La Clemenza di Tito*). His earlier work, *Idomeneo* (1781), contained an exceptional array of choruses both dramatic (*Corriamo, fuggiamo quel mostro spietato*, a possible prototype for the Lachrymosa of Mozart's Requiem) and pictorial (*Placido il mar, andiamo*).[2]

The prominence of choruses in this opera is the result of the so-called reform operas of Christoph Willibald von Gluck (1714–87) and his librettist, Ranieri de' Calzabigi (1714–95). During the preceding era dominated by Pietro Metastasio (1698–1782), the use of chorus or even ensemble was typically relegated to a short concluding chorus of praise or judgment.[3] The Metastasian emphasis on vocal display and mythological stories, sometimes allegorically arranged to flatter wealthy patrons, left the presentation of conflict and drama to individual characters, the chorus being "decorative, subsidiary, musically neutral, with a function analogous to the stage set."[4] Gluck's reforms, based upon the model of the French *tragédies lyriques*, elevated the role of both chorus and ballet. Especially noteworthy for its multiplicity of textures and forms was Gluck's *Orfeo ed Euridice*, in which the chorus asserted a new prominence, especially in act 2.

It was hardly predictable that the structural rigidities of Italian *opera seria* failed to survive the new ideals put forward after the French Revolution. In the wake of this tumultuous event, the chorus emerged as a powerful metaphorical force, poised to participate more fully in evolving forms of more democratic and inclusive artistic expression. Themes of tyranny or humanitarianism were particularly prominent in such French-derived operas as Beethoven's *Fidelio* (1805). *Fidelio*, based on a French libretto by Jean-Nicolas Bouilly (*Léonore, ou L'amour conjugal*), gave the chorus an identity and dramatic purpose. Florestan, a political prisoner, marked for death, came to symbolize the political repression of a people, represented by the chorus. At the end of the opera, the same chorus was then available to lend depth and breadth to this celebration of freedom and human dignity.

The French Revolution changed more than the ruler of France or even the reality of dynastic rule; it established a new political modus operandi in which all parties, regardless of their philosophies, came to identify the "people" as their ultimate source of political power. Consequently, the individual good was inextricably bound to the larger good of the nation, whether that involved freedom from tyranny, economic success, a victory in battle, or anything that might be construed to represent the commonwealth. Within a discussion of evolving concepts of dramaturgy and the need for verisimilitude in opera, Hervé Lacombe points out that ensembles and choruses allowed several individuals to speak at once, something not possible in eighteenth-century opera.[5] Initially, this trend involved an ensemble of characters, but gradually the chorus became one of the more realistic elements of the drama, appearing in situations that in real life logically required a group of people. As a result, almost all nineteenth-century operas featured a real chorus as an essential part of the scenic and moral dimensions of the story.

This trend was especially clear in the French Grand Opera of the 1820s. Recent scholarship points to the pivotal roles played by Daniel-François-Esprit Auber (1782–1871) and the librettist Eugène Scribe (1791–1861). Discussing Scribe's contribution, Louis Véron, director of the Opéra from 1831 to 1835, emphasized the essential role of the chorus, noting:

> An opera in five acts can live only with a very dramatic action, putting into play the grand passions of the human heart and powerful historical interests. This dramatic action, moreover, ought to be intelligible to the eyes, like the action of a ballet. The choruses must play an impassioned role and be, so to speak, one of the interesting characters of the piece. Each act ought to offer contrasts in sets, in costumes, and especially in skillfully prepared situations.... *La Muette de Portici, Robert le Diable, Gustave III, La Juive, Les Huguenots, Le Prophète* by M. Scribe offer that fertility of ideas, those grand dramatic situations, and fulfill all conditions for variety in staging required of the poetics of an opera in five acts.[6]

The assumption of five acts required a new array of devices and artists. Beyond the composer and librettist, this format placed increased importance on the visual elements produced by the stage designer, choreographer, machinist, and the artist responsible for creating the mise-en-scène. Each strove to reproduce the physical setting and atmosphere of a story with scrupulous attention to historical detail.

No less a figure than Victor Hugo emphasized the importance of attention to historical and pictorial detail in the setting of a drama, what he called the *couleur du temps*. The formation of a *Comité de Mise en Scène* at the Opéra and the appointment of a director, or the *metteur en scène*, were essential prerequisites to the success of what is generally conceded to be the first "grand" opera, Auber's *La Muette de Portici* (1828). Today, we take the visual components of opera for granted (realistic stage action, elaborate sets and costumes), but this expectation sprang from the innovations required by the extension of the drama from three to four to five acts. Richard Wagner, always an acute observer of dramatic music, described the chorus's new role "as a crowd playing a real part in the action and of serious interest to the audience."[7]

From the beginning of *La Muette de Portici*, the chorus plays an essential dramatic and musical role, appearing in all but one of the numbers that comprise act 1. If the chorus's presence in the "Introduzione" seems traditional, Auber's division of the chorus into two parts—one onstage and one offstage—signaled the chorus's new importance. In the *Scène et Choeur* (mvt. 4), the chorus participates directly in the drama, singing "Dieu puissant! Dieu tutélaire!" as they crowd the front of the church. And when they kneel ("Nous t'implorons à genoux"), the heroine, Fenella, is able to see that the groom is the same man who had earlier seduced her. The drama, thus joined, continues into the Finale, heightened by the dramatic conceit of a mute girl trying to convey the details of her dilemma to those surrounding her. The emergence of the newly married couple from the church provokes a confrontation between Alphonse and Fenella mirrored by choruses representing the townspeople and soldiers. With the exception of act 4, the chorus is a constant dramatic presence, assisting the plot's development toward its unexpected and tragic resolution in the suicide of Fenella.

Auber's innovations not only impressed Parisian audiences but also laid the groundwork for Rossini's final opera, *Guillaume Tell* (1829), specifically composed for the Paris Opéra. The chorus represented factions of the Swiss whose political destiny lay at the heart of the drama. Though significant in terms of its presence, the chorus in Auber's opera was, for the most part, restricted to self-contained scenes or to supporting solo arias or ensembles (as in act 2, scene 1 of *La Muette*). Initially, the chorus in *Guillaume Tell* operates in the same way, providing a realistic picture of the Swiss in their native environment going about their daily lives (e.g., "Quel jour serein le ciel présage," act 1, scene 1).[8] Later, however, the chorus emerged as a protagonist equal, if not greater, in significance than any individual character. From the finale of act 1 through act 2, the chorus is "emancipated."[9] The murder of a retainer of the hated Austrian governor (Gesler) by Leuthold and his escape (facilitated by Tell) places the local populace in direct conflict with troops led by Rudolph, the chief of Gesler's archers. Musically, this confrontation involves the soldiers (male chorus), the Swiss people (mixed chorus), and Tell's wife and son. Exchanges between these choral factions escalate through the Finale culminating in the seizure of the patriarch, Melchtal.

Act 2 opens with another choral complex—a chorus of huntsmen (accompanied by horns) interrupted by the distant sounds of shepherds singing a *Nachtgesang*. At first, Rossini seems to have returned to using the chorus as scenery, as they sing two archetypes of nineteenth-century male choral music (hunting songs and pastoral music). But Gesler looms ominously, eventually galvanizing the three separate cantons (Unterwald, Schwitz, and Uri) to make a unified response to Melchtal's assassination. This coalition is formalized by the chorus of solidarity,

"Jurons par nos dangers" ("We swear by all our wrongs") as all three groups pledge allegiance to Tell (ex. 3.1).

Example 3.1 Rossini, *Guillaume Tell*, act 2, Finale, mm. 365–70

The need for three male choruses on stage (each representing one of the cantons) required an ensemble of unprecedented size as the space and scenery necessary to make their presence realistic became an indispensable part of the opera's dramatic fabric (see Fig. 3.1). Nestor Roqueplan, director of the Opéra from 1847 to 1854, inferred that forces of such size and the resources were unprecedented:

> Previously, the chorus used to line up in two blocks, to the left and right, and stood still, both men and women, without participating at all in the action taking place within the circle of singing tailor's dummies. The new styles of production gave movement to each and every one of them, swords to draw from scabbards, daggers to flourish in the air, arms to throttle the first person to cross their paths, legs to carry them at the run to liberate Naples [where Auber's *La Muette di Portici* takes place] or Switzerland [where Rossini sets *Guillaume Tell*].[10]

Fig. 3.1 Halévy's *La Juive* (1835), act 2, Paris Opéra

Rossini wrote this opera in French not only because he was in Paris at the time but also because the theme of Austrian domination was one with which the French could identify. For later performances in Italy, Rossini changed the opera's title to *Rodolpho di Sterlinge* and relocated it to Scotland to avoid Austrian censorship.[11] Performance in Italian required a translation, which softened the libretto's political agenda. The new necessity most affected the final chorus, when the free and unified Swiss sing, "Liberté, redescends des cieux! Et que ton règne recommence, Liberté, redescends des cieux!" ("Liberty, descend again from heaven / And may your reign begin anew!"). This text is already considerably less inflammatory than the three-act version (1831), in which the chorus sang: "Des bois, des monts, de la cité, Aux cieux où Melchtal est monté, Qu'un cri, qu'un seul soit répété: Victoire et liberté!" ("From the woods, from the peaks, from the city to the heavens where Melchtal has gone, let one cry and only one cry be repeated: Victory and liberty!"). In the revised version, the word "victory" is nowhere to be found, reference to it muted to prayerful hopes rather than boisterous clamor.[12] The Italian translation ("Such contentment I feel inside, my spirit cannot express") retained none of the original's republican sentiments.

Less easily translated was the pivotal role of the traditional Alpine melodies used by Rossini to set the geography of his drama. These melodies represented neither folk music nor misplaced nationalism but a particularly French personification of the Swiss, established as early as Jean-Jacques Rousseau (1712–78), who coined the term *ranz des vaches* ("call to the cows") to describe these uniquely Swiss tunes. For Anselm Gerhard, the quotation of one particular melody (ex. 3.2e) in the opera's final chorus is a direct result of what the concluding text signifies.[13] But more explicit are the three different *ranz des vaches* (played on French horn and bassoon) that signaled the arrival of each canton at the end of act 2 (ex. 3.2 b–d).

Example 3.2 a–e Rossini, *Guillaume Tell*, "Ranz des vaches"

a. act 1, scene 4, mm. 5-8

b. act 1, scene 4, mm. 14-19

c. act 2, no. 22, mm. 3-5

d. act 2, no. 23, mm. 88-90

e. act 2, no. 24, mm. 3-6

These quotations legitimize the "pledge chorus," *Jurons par nos dangers*, as surely as they herald the canton's pledge to rid Switzerland of the oppressive Austrian regime.

OPERA IN ITALY AND GERMANY—GIUSEPPE VERDI AND RICHARD WAGNER

The revolution that Auber, Rossini, and Meyerbeer created in Paris had implications for the development of opera elsewhere in Europe. Table 3.1 shows the relative chronology of the operas produced in Paris with those composed in Germany and Italy. The list for the Paris Opéra features works by Giacomo Meyerbeer (1791–1864) and J. F. Halévy (1799–1862). More important are the early works of the two emerging giants of romantic opera, Richard Wagner (1813–83) and Giuseppe Verdi (1813–1901).

Choral representation of political oppression was a theme also found in the grand operas of Giacomo Meyerbeer (notably *Les Huguenots*, 1836) and the early operas of both Verdi (*Nabucco*) and Wagner (*Rienzi*). *Nabucco*, a political drama transported back in time to the Babylonian exile of Israel, contains perhaps the most beloved of all opera choruses, *Va pensiero*. Allegedly a de facto anthem of the Italian *Risorgimento*, Mary Ann Smart argues that for a purported celebration of patriotism, the chorus's text and music are full of "incongruous calm and repose."[14] Indeed, Verdi's setting in F♯ major is pastoral (triplets within 4/4) and wistful, with no obvious revolutionary fervor.

In addition to this legendary chorus, *Nabucco* has a considerable volume of other choruses innately linked to its dramatic and musical structure. Scored in the French manner, the chorus appears in three of the four musical numbers in act 1. A hint of the chorus's new dramatic prominence is its intrusion into the Largo and Cavatina of Zaccaria's aria ("Sperate, O figli!"). Both acts 2 and 4 contain at least one purely choral movement; act 3 begins with a substantial chorus (*È l'Assiria una regina*) that matches *Va pensiero* in length, foreshadowing the defining choral unison of its more famous predecessor (ex. 3.3).

Table 3.1 Nineteenth-century French, German, and Italian opera

Paris

1828	Auber: *La Muette de Portici*
1829	Rossini: *Guillaume Tell*
1830	Auber: *Fra Diavolo*
1831	Meyerbeer: *Robert le Diable*
1835	Halévy: *La Juive*
1836	Meyerbeer: *Les Huguenots*
1849	Meyerbeer: *Le Prophète*

Germany/Italy

1820	Weber: *Der Freischütz*
1842	Wagner: *Rienzi*; Verdi: *Nabucco*
1843	Wagner: *Der fliegende Holländer*
1844	Verdi: *Ernani*
1845	Wagner: *Tannhäuser*
1847	Verdi: *Macbeth*
1849	Verdi: *Luisa Miller*
1850	Wagner: *Lohengrin*
1851	Verdi: *Rigoletto*
1853	Verdi: *Il Trovatore, La Traviata*
1855	Verdi: *Les Vêpres siciliennes*
1857	Verdi: *Simon Boccanegra*

Example 3.3 Verdi, *Nabucco*, *È l'Assiria una regina*, act 3, scene 1, mm. 39–47
John Rutter, ed. *Opera Choruses* © Oxford University Press 1995. Used by permission. All rights reserved. Photocopying of this copyright material is ILLEGAL.

As memorable as the melodic curve of *Va pensiero* is, Verdi's decision to have it sung by a mixed chorus in unison makes this chorus the embodiment of a people's unity. The simple

texture stands in stark contrast to more traditional representations of a politically mobilized group, that is, hymnic or national anthems. This new texture also marks the full emergence of the chorus as a group of operatic singers, now required to execute the same stylistic devices so frequently found in solo arias. Hymnic choruses in opera had a long-standing presence in opera, going back to *O Isis und Osiris* from Mozart's *Die Zauberflöte* (1791). The solemnity of this scene established a precedent for the hymnic (if not overtly religious) choruses found in other Verdi operas: *Ernani* (*O Signore, dal tetto natìo*), *Macbeth* (*Patria oppressa*), *Il trovatore*, *La forza del destino,* and especially *Aida.*

The chorus in nineteenth-century opera found its most natural and logical placement in the church (thanks to Hugo's *couleur du temps*). Beginning with Auber's *La Muette de Portici* and in the grand operas of Meyerbeer, notably *Le Prophète*, religious conflict now becomes an alternative to political strife as is clear from its role in the plots of Halévy's *La Juive,* Meyerbeer's *Les Huguenots,* and Verdi's *Simon Boccanegra.* Conversely, while Verdi's *Aida* (1871) stresses religious tolerance, it also manages to include another famous hymnic chorus from the *Papa dei cori* (an affectionate nickname for Verdi)—the triumphal chorus, *Gloria all' Egitto.*[15]

Another combination of religion and the people as proletariat is central to Modest Mussorgsky's masterpiece, *Boris Godunov* (1874). Chorally speaking, the centerpiece is the "Coronation Scene" that serves as prologue to the opera. Mussorgsky initially presents a fearful populace: one moment they pray to God for deliverance, the next they are abused by the police who regard them as a threat. It is out of this tension that the musical triptych generally known as the "Coronation Scene" emerges. David Brown sees this tripartite design as a possible borrowing from Glinka's *A Life for the Tsar,* which uses two choruses to flank a central solo movement in its epilogue.[16]

Mussorgsky's "Coronation" begins with an instrumental introduction built around two dominant-seventh chords that share two common tones: C (the tonality of the movement) and F♯/G♭. And again, the dreaded tritone separation of these tonal centers is perhaps an ominous portent of things to come (ex. 3.4).

Example 3.4 Mussorgsky, *Boris Godunov*, act 1, scene 2, mm. 3–6
John Rutter, ed. *Opera Choruses* © Oxford University Press 1995.
Used by permission. All rights reserved. Photocopying of this copyright material is ILLEGAL.

After an initial acclamation, the chorus sings of their optimism for Boris's reign; the chorus, *Uzh kak na nyebye soln,* has its melodic basis in Russian folksong and harmony from traditional Russian church music (ex. 3.5).[17]

Example 3.5 Mussorgsky, *Boris Godunov*, act 1, scene 2, mm. 399–410
John Rutter, ed. *Opera Choruses* © Oxford University Press 1995. Used by
permission. All rights reserved. Photocopying of this copyright material
is ILLEGAL.

Vladimir Morosan points out that this melody is a folk song (*Slava Bogu na nyebye*), and that
Mussorgsky's varied settings of it exemplify the heterophonic process of "harmonization"
common to both folk music and Orthodox church music.[18] In the opera, the crowd's joyous
shouts of *Slava!* have hardly subsided when Boris's appearance is announced by the music's
sudden shift to C minor, followed by the intonation of a foreboding motive, which Robert
Oldani has labeled the "anxiety theme."[19] After Boris's prayers for knowledge regarding the
source of his distress, the church bells summon a resumption of the crowd's acclamation to
conclude the prologue.

As important as these "political" choruses are in advancing the role of the chorus as
a dramatic force, they are dwarfed by the numerous, essentially pictorial, choruses such as the
opening chorus of *Richard Cœur de Lion* (1784) by André Grétry; the "Huntsmen's Chorus" in
Carl Maria von Weber's *Freischütz* (1821); the "Chorus of Wedding Guests" from Donizetti's
Lucia di Lammermoor (1835); the "Chorus of Villagers" in Smetana's *Prodaná nevěsta* (*The
Bartered Bride*, 1866); the *Tanz der Lehrbuben* (act 2, scene 1) in Wagner's *Die Meistersinger von
Nürnberg* (1868); the "Pilgrim's Chorus" from *Tannhäuser* (1845); the famous "Anvil Chorus"
from Verdi's *Il Trovatore* (1853); the opening chorus of *Don Carlo* (1867); and the choruses of
the cigarette girls (*Dans l'air nous suivons des yeux*) and bullfighters (*Les voici! Voici la quadrille
des Toreros!*) in Bizet's *Carmen* (1875).

Another standard ploy to legitimize the chorus's presence on stage is the inclusion
of a party scene. Although such choruses are numerous, three examples are outstanding: the
Brindisi in act 1 of Verdi's *La Traviata* (1853); the "Ballroom Scene" from Johann Strauss's
Die Fledermaus (1874); and the "Waltz Scene" from Tchaikovsky's *Eugene Onegin*. All blend
pageantry, choreography, and elaborate costumes into a synergy, which is an essential but
rarely memorable element of the plot. In Verdi's *Brindisi*, for example, the chorus, made up of
guests attending a party at the home of Violetta Valery, is caught up in the flirtation between
Alfredo Germont and Violetta. Asked to make a toast, Alfredo complies, improvising one of
Verdi's more popular melodies, *Libiamo ne' lieti calici* (ex. 3.6).

Example 3.6 Verdi, *La Traviata*, act 1, "Brindisi," mm. 249–57
John Rutter, ed. *Opera Choruses* © Oxford University Press 1995. Used by
permission. All rights reserved. Photocopying of this copyright material is ILLEGAL.

The chorus here provides background and support, concluding Alfredo's toast with a brief tag and Violetta's with a unison rendition of the tune in the subdominant (E♭). The toast proper ends with a choral accompaniment to Alfredo and Violetta's duet. Dance music from the next room provides the pretext for the chorus's exit; they eventually return (after the lovers' duet) to sing a *stretta* of the opening orchestral music as their polite thank-you-and-farewell. The chorus here is window dressing, without clear, dramatic function or real musical substance. Nonetheless, their presence (and subsequent absence) transports the audience to a specific time and place; by assuming the dress, actions, and decorum of that place, the chorus assumes an identity integral to the dramatic success of the opera.

More often than not, these choruses function more as "costume" (*couleur du temps*) than as dramatic conflict. The pair of choruses in act 2 of *La Traviata* illustrates this function; both *Noi siamo zingarella* and *Di Madride noi siamo matadori* inject the chorus into the evolving drama between Flora and the Marquis (eventually joined by the Doctor and Gastone) as spectators rather than actors. Verdi's use of female and male choruses seems motivated by the need for spectacle and variety; ultimately, the famous Triumphal March from *Aida* fulfills roughly the same role.

Sometimes, the chorus transcends mere visual spectacle to become an indispensable element in the escalating drama. This is true in Richard Wagner's *Der fliegende Holländer*, in which the chorus consists of male (Norwegian sailors) and female (young ladies involved in domestic activity) ensembles. Such gender-based ensembles make perfect sense in a small seaside village where men and women are often separated for long periods. Thus the separation of male and female choral singers becomes social commentary, reflecting not only the dichotomy of landscape (aboard ship and on land) but also the social roles that separate the two groups. In act 1, the men represent the crews of two separate ships (and worlds). If the men dominate act 1, act 2 belongs to the women, who open with the spinning song *Summ' und Brumm, du gutes Rädchen*. The social conflict that remains relatively hidden in act 1 boils to the surface as this rather mindless, innocuous song is interrupted on an increasingly frequent basis by Senta's macabre fascination with the Dutchman, represented by the gradual incursion of the fourths and fifths associated with him (first heard in the opera's overture) in her ballad *Johohoe! Traft ihr das Schiff im Meere an*. Concerning this scene, Joachim Köhler writes: "In the petty bourgeois spinning room in which we have just heard a chorus of well-mannered young ladies, the daughter of the house reveals herself to be a somnambulist with a penchant for summoning up ghosts, while the demon whom she summons into life appears wearing an old-fashioned costume and singing a sentimental aria. Nothing is what it seems to be when a painted piece of lifeless canvas can suddenly become the most terrifying reality."[20]

This conflict is completely missing in the version published in John Rutter's anthology, *Opera Choruses*, because the dialogue separating vv. 1 and 2 of the song is omitted.[21] The apparent simplicity of this editorial decision underscores the problem inherent in excerpting the choral portion of any opera from its original context. In the opera itself, the situation becomes even worse, for, after the eighty-nine measures of music that concludes with Senta's derisive comment, "Are you really trying to make me seriously angry with your frivolous laughter?" the spinning song resumes in a frantic and ultimately futile effort to forestall Senta's scorn and her morose love ballad. Performed outside this dramatic context, Wagner's chorus has a totally different dramatic impact. Lost is the trite counterpoint the "Spinning Chorus" provides to Senta's gradual, yet inevitable acquiescence to retelling the story of the Dutchman with whom she is obsessed.

The same critique may be applied to the version of the "Sailor's Chorus" from act 3 (*Steuermann! Lass die Wacht!*).[22] As presented in Rutter's anthology, this chorus (the first 106 measures of act 3) makes for a rousing (though difficult) sea chantey. Within the opera, however, Wagner's portrayal of the naive frivolity of the Norwegian seamen is a much longer (700 measures) and more complex dramatic scene, which occupies more than half of the final act. The complete scene involves first the flirtation between the sailors and the women, then a kind of "whistling-in-the-graveyard" bravado that leads the women to awaken the Dutchmen's crew. Considerably later (417 measures), Wagner adds a second strophe. Even though the choral music is identical, Wagner has managed gradually to inject the chromatic storm music and the Dutchman's signature motive into its orchestral accompaniment (ex. 3.7).

Example 3.7 Wagner, *Der fliegende Holländer*, act 3,
scene 1, mm. 551–62
John Rutter, ed. *Opera Choruses* © Oxford University Press 1995. Used by
permission. All rights reserved. Photocopying of this copyright material is ILLEGAL.

Choruses in Wagner's subsequent operas did maintain the traditional functions of the opera chorus described earlier. One immediately thinks of the "Pilgrim's Chorus" from act 3 of *Tannhäuser* (1845), the famous "Bridal Chorus" that opens act 3 of *Lohengrin* (1850), and "Procession and Chorale" from *Die Meistersinger von Nürnberg* (1863). After *Lohengrin*, however, Wagner is less engaged with the chorus as an element of drama, as we see the relatively low profile of the chorus throughout the Ring cycle. In *Parsifal* (1882), the chorus is significant less for its dramatic presence than for the sense of ritual and color it provides. Positioned at the end of Wagner's operatic output, *Parsifal* nonetheless reveals its connection to his earlier operas and to the little-known oratorio *Das Liebesmahl der Apostel*, which, like *Parsifal*, is intimately connected to Dresden, the Holy Grail, and male chorus. The clearest manifestation of this connection is the omnipresence (both vocal and instrumental) of the now clichéd "Dresden Amen" (ex. 3.8).

Example 3.8 Wagner, *Parsifal*, Overture, mm. 56–59

Strikingly, Wagner uses the female choral voices only as sound, never as a physically present, dramatically significant group. In the Grail scenes (acts 1 and 3), the women's voices sound from the middle and upper levels of the vaulted dome, transforming the operatic stage into Dresden's Frauenkirche.[23] The invisible female choir convincingly projects an angelic presence in the heights of heaven. Perhaps the most remarkable use of the women's voices, the first statement of Parsifal's emblem, *Durch Mitleid wissend* ("Enlightened by compassion"), is also the subtlest (ex. 3.9).

Example 3.9 Wagner, *Parsifal*, act 1, scene 2, "Grail scene," mm. 1405–11

Wagner combines the voices of the *Jünglinge* (tenors) and *Knaben* (altos, singing from the "middle heights" (*mittleren Höhe*) to produce a blended, androgynous vocal tone. Significantly, their melody features the same fifths (the musical personification of *Parsifal*) heard even before Parsifal appears, when Gurnemanz refers to the One who alone can heal the wound of Amfortas, the keeper of the Grail. Katharine Syer cites evidence from the diaries of Cosima Wagner indicating the precision and symbolism of Wagner's calculation: "He [Wagner] then plays the first theme of *Parsifal* to himself and, returning, says that he gave the words to a chorus so that the effect would be neither masculine nor feminine; Christ must be entirely sexless, neither man nor woman."[24]

The role of the chorus in Wagner's operas is less doctrinaire than the other works sampled in this chapter. Unlike the composers of French Grand Opera (a tradition to which even Verdi more or less adheres), Wagner used the chorus to further a dramatic concept or sound without recourse to the traditional roles that the chorus had assumed throughout the century. It is no surprise that the author of *Oper und Drama* (1850/51) is not bound to past traditions regarding use of the chorus. As Wagner's libretti are concerned with ideas and archetypes than specific characters, so too does his music adopt an array of devices that redefined nearly every aspect of opera in the second half of the nineteenth century. To a large extent, Wagner's intimidating presence may explain why some of the composers discussed in the second half of this chapter avoided the composition of opera altogether, opting for different kinds of choral drama.

JOHANN WOLFGANG VON GOETHE
AND DRAMATIC CHORAL MUSIC

The dominant literary figure of the late eighteenth and early nineteenth centuries is Johann Wolfgang von Goethe (1749–1832) (Fig. 3.2); his body of poetry and drama has become a primary text source for composers interested in producing dramatic music. Goethe's most important work is *Faust*, the two parts of which were published in 1808 and posthumously in 1832. Table 3.2 outlines a brief, selective list of dramatic musical works based on this play.

The fascination of composers with this story has been partly explained by the literary critic Dieter Borchmeyer: "In the literature of the world, there is scarcely any dramatic poem that is so filled with 'inaudible music,' and yet, in spite of the numberless compositional attempts to imitate it and the clearly operatic structure of the end of the second part, [there is no work] so inimical to composition as Faust."[25]

The problem for composers, irrespective of their chosen format, was to create music for a text that Goethe himself thought was beyond anyone's ability. In a conversation with Goethe in 1829, Johann Peter Eckermann said, "But I haven't given up hope of seeing suitable music

Fig. 3.2 Johann Wolfgang von Goethe (ca. 1790),
J. H. W. Tischbein

Table 3.2 Compositions based on Goethe's *Faust*

Opera:

Louis Spohr	*Faust* (1816)
Charles Gounod	*Faust* (1859)
Arrigo Boito	*Mefistofele* (1868)
Ferruccio Busoni	*Doktor Faust* (unfinished)

Cantata:

Hector Berlioz	*Huit scènes de Faust* (1829)
	La Damnation de Faust (1846)
Felix Mendelssohn	*Die Erste Walpurgisnacht*, op. 60 (1833)
Robert Schumann	*Szenen aus Goethes "Faust,"* WoO 3 (1844–53)

for Faust," to which the poet replied, "That's quite impossible."[26] In spite of Goethe's opinion, composers struggled to produce a varied array of dramatic music based on this timeless story.

HECTOR BERLIOZ, *LE DAMNATION DE FAUST*, OP. 24.

The first and one of the more notable contributions to the body of nonoperatic compositions inspired by *Faust* are those of Hector Berlioz. His initial sojourn into the *Faust* legend is the dramatic cantata *Huit scènes de Faust* (1828–29), composed during his days at the Paris Conservatoire; here he uses eight scenes chosen from the French prose translation by Gérard de Nerval (Paris, 1828). Daniel Albright notes that Berlioz's instincts "led him to ignore the main character."[27] Accordingly, the principal character is totally absent from his original op. 1, a work Berlioz withdrew almost immediately, perhaps realizing his failure to fully tap the story's literary wealth. When Berlioz returned to Goethe's masterpiece in 1844, he used the earlier music as a point of departure for his "dramatic legend" *La Damnation de Faust* (1846) (see Fig. 3.3).

Despite attempts to stage this work, Berlioz's *La Damnation de Faust* is neither an opera nor a symphony like *Roméo et Juliette*. This new dramatic composition uses primarily instrumental music to realize Goethe's drama as well as its loose adherence to the story.[28] The titles that appear in Table 3.3 suggest that Berlioz began the new work using those movements of the earlier *Huit scènes*, whose texts explicitly suggest musical forms. While the four large parts of *La Damnation* present Faust as a character, the texts Berlioz employs are less than directly linked to Goethe's original; Berlioz expects his audience to rely more on their imagination than their eyes and ears to grasp the unfolding dramatic flow.

Table 3.3 Berlioz's use of *Huit Scènes de Faust* (1829) in *La Damnation de Faust* (1846)

Première Partie:	1. *Ronde de paysans*
Deuxième Partie:	2. *Chant de la fête de Pâques*
	3. *Chanson de Brander*
	4. *Chanson de Méphistophélès*
Troisième Partie:	5. *Le Roi de Thulé*
	6. *Sérénade de Méphistophélès*
Quatrième Partie:	7. *Romance de Marguerite*

Fig. 3.3 Goethe's Faust: *Satan Flying over the City at Night* (Engraving by Eugène Delacroix, 1861)

Berlioz sets Part 1 in Hungary, ostensibly so that he could, as his critics claimed, include his brilliant version of the Rákóczy March; its instrumental music clearly depends on a literary program to guide the listeners through the unfolding spectacle. The new music provides the first of the original eight scenes, the *Ronde de paysans*, with a musical rationale of a pastoral chorus depicting the rustic life of the peasants. Immediately following this bucolic scene, Berlioz inserts his *Marche hongroise* (a "chant de guerre des Hongrois") to signal the arrival of an unidentified military force.

In act 2 Faust is back in Germany; sitting alone in his study, he hears an Easter Hymn (*Chant de la fêtes de Pâques*), which reminds him of happier times. Like the Ghost of Christmas Past in Dickens's *A Christmas Carol*, Mephistopheles forces Faust to relive his past, an odyssey that begins in Auerbach's cellar with a drinking chorus that closes with an elaborate "Amen" fugue on the theme of the *Chanson de Brander* (ex. 3.10).

Not to be outdone, Mephistopheles sings his own song (*Chanson de Méphistophélès*), but Faust, revolted by the debauchery, insists that they leave the cellar. Mephistopheles next takes Faust to the banks of the Elbe where another set piece—a pastoral song sung by a chorus of gnomes and sylphs—hypnotizes Faust, inducing a dream in which he sees Gretchen (Marguerite). The ensuing *Ballets de Sylphes* emphasizes the important role that dance historically plays in French dramatic music. Not realizing that he has seen Marguerite in a dream, Faust asks Mephistopheles to take him to her, prompting the choral scene (*Chor de Soldats et chanson d'Étudiants*) that concludes Part 2. Those portions of the *Huits scènes* used in parts 3 and 4 are similarly joined with new music that creates a plausible framework for their use. If the result is a flawed, rather genreless work, whose cautionary tale of a genius that creates catastrophe is presaged by Berlioz's *La mort d'Orphée* (1827) and the *Symphonie fantastique* (1830), it is nonetheless a wonderfully colorful, choral-orchestral work for the concert hall.

Example 3.10 Berlioz, *La Damnation de Faust*, op. 24, act 2, scene 6, mm. 184–9

FELIX MENDELSSOHN, *DIE ERSTE WALPURGISNACHT*, OP. 60.

In his "grand cantata," *Die erste Walpurgisnacht*, Felix Mendelssohn set a poem that Goethe had sent to Karl Friedrich Zelter, Mendelssohn's mentor.[29] Goethe considered this the first draft of an operatic libretto (in the manner of Mozart's *Die Zauberflöte*) based on the Faust legend. Zelter introduced Mendelssohn to Goethe in 1821, beginning a friendship that lasted until the poet's death. At the conclusion of their last meeting in 1830, Goethe gave Mendelssohn a personally inscribed sheet of the autograph of *Faust*.

Goethe includes the *Walpurgisnacht* legend in three separate works: twice in *Faust*—Part 1 (the "German" *Walpurgisnacht* followed by the *Walpurgisnachtstraum*), once in Part 2 (the "classical" *Walpurgisnacht*), and as the poem Zelter ultimately gave to Mendelssohn after trying unsuccessfully to set it himself. This poem recounts the ancient legend of *Walpurgisnacht*, the night before the first day of May, on which the ancient Druids gather to worship despite the threat of Christian persecution. Despite numerous reprints of Goethe's works, this poem remains essentially unchanged. Mendelssohn's interest in setting this poem sprang from an encounter with Berlioz in Rome in the spring of 1831. Berlioz had showed Mendelssohn the score of his *Symphonie Fantastique*, causing Mendelssohn to feel fascinated and alarmed—first by Berlioz's romantic imagination and then at the orchestration and the lurid details of the symphony's literary program.

Mendelssohn's first sketches of *Die erste Walpurgisnacht* (1830–31) languished for more than a decade before the work's completion and premiere at Leipzig's Gewandhaus on February 2, 1843. In its final form, the composition consists of ten movements (Table 3.4). The structural integrity and power of expression are this composition's primary strengths. Mendelssohn achieves this "structural integrity" by using thematic transformation to mitigate the music's through-composed, dramatic continuity. Most of these themes derive from a basic cell, which first appears in the *Overture* (ex. 3.11a–e).

Table 3.4 Mendelssohn, *Die erste Walpurgisnacht*, op. 60, form

Movement	Key	Meter	Tempo	Scoring	Length (mm.)
Overture	A minor	3/4 4/4	Allegro con fuoco Allegro vivace non troppo	Orchestra	409
1. Aria with Chorus	A major	4/4 2/2	Allegro vivace non troppo Allegro assai vivace	T, satb, orch	220
2. Aria with Chorus	D minor	3/4	Allegretto non troppo	A, ssa, ob, str	83
3. Aria + Chorus Recitative + Chorus	A minor	4/4	Andante maestoso Più animato	B, ttbb, ww, str satb,ww, str	44
4. Chorus	E major	2/2	Allegro leggiero	B, str satb, orch	73
5. Recitative + Chorus	A minor–G minor/major	3/4 4/4	Allegro moderato	satb, orch	13 63
6. Chorus	E minor–A minor	6/4	Allegro molto	B, satb, orch	306
7. Chorus + Aria	A minor–V/C minor	2/4 4/4	L'istesso Tempo Andante maestoso	T, satb, ww, str	20 51
8. Aria + Chorus	C minor	4/4	Allegro non troppo	B, satb, orch	47
9. Aria + Chorus	C major	4/4	Andante maestoso		42

Example 3.11 a–e Mendelssohn, *Die erste Walpurgisnacht*, op. 60, Thematic transformations

a. Overture, mm. 3-5

b. mvt. 1, mm. 8-9

Es lacht der Mai

c. mvt 4, mm. 14-15

Ver - theilt euch hier,

d. mvt. 7, mm. 29-30

Doch ist es Tag so - bald man mag

Example 3.11 a–e Continued

e. mvt. 9, mm. 5-8

Die Flam-me   rei-nigt sich vom Rauch: so rei-nig'   un-sern - Glau - ben!

The operatic nature of this grand cantata is evident in the instrumental music that connects mvts. 6 and 7: mvt. 6 is a lengthy chorus, which reaches its dynamic climax marked by a deceptive cadence (V/A to F) and change to 2/4 meter only to merge seamlessly with mvt. 7 by virtue of music best described as scene-change music. Given the lack of staging and scenery this transition lacks an obvious raison d'être; in the first twenty measures Mendelssohn gradually diminishes and slows the orchestra's music preparing for the entry of the Priest and the Druid Chorus (*Andante maestoso*) whose music occupies the next seventy-one measures.

Despite the work's sense of dramatic continuity, two musical movements dominate. The first is a long, typically picturesque overture (409 mm.), in which Mendelssohn depicts winter (*Das schlechte Wetter*) and the transition to spring (*Der Übergang zum Frühling*).[30] The other large movement is the aforementioned complex of mvts. 6 and 7. At its outset, a recitative reveals the Druid's plan for keeping the Christians from disturbing their ceremony. An expansive chorus follows, describing the way they plan to accomplish this task. This chorus reminds one of *The Sorcerer's Apprentice* by Paul Dukas—a simple yet foreboding melody, barely audible at the outset that expands through a series of variations marked by increasing instrumentation and dynamics (ex. 3.12a). A sudden change of key (G minor to E major), tempo (*Allegro moderato* to *Allegro molto*), and meter (6/8 to 2/4) launches an even more intense chorus that ends with an orchestral interlude that functions as scene change music.

Example 3.12 a–b Mendelssohn, *Die erste Walpurgisnacht*, op. 60

a. mvt. 6, mm. 19-22

b. mvt. 7, mm 1-9

Mendelssohn specifies three solo voices: alto, tenor, and bass, but the alto only appears briefly in mvt. 3, while the tenor and bass both have extensive roles. Mendelssohn carefully divides his chorus into ensembles of male and female voices to create sonic variety and different characters. In the first vocal movement the tenor heralds spring's arrival, and the women of the chorus take up his happy song (ex. 3.13a). In mvt. 3, the male chorus joins the bass soloist (the Druid Priest) in a rousing chorus of defiance.

Example 3.13 a–b Mendelssohn, *Die erste Walpurgisnacht*, op. 60

a. mvt. 1, mm. 8-13

Soprano   Es lacht der Mai!   der Wald ist frei   von   Eis und Reif - ge - hän - ge.

Alto   Es lacht der Mai!   der Wald ist frei   von   Eis und Reif - ge - hän - ge.

Example 3.13 a–b Continued

b. mvt. 3, mm. 31-37

Example 3.14 Mendelssohn, *Die erste Walpurgisnacht,*
op. 60, mvt. 4, mm. 14–22

By far the most charming choral music is the chorus *Verteilt euch, wackre Männer hier*, describing the Priest's ordering watchmen to disperse and hide; their furtive movement allows Mendelssohn to create one of his distinctive, elfin-type scherzos (ex. 3.14).

Lamentably, this colorful, dramatic concert piece is neither well known nor frequently performed. The relative brevity and lack of a resonant story may explain the rare performance of this transparent (though colorful) music. The choral writing is vintage Mendelssohn, comparable in style, craftsmanship, and accessibility with far more popular oratorios. But unlike these works, *Die erste Walpurgisnacht* is not substantial enough to stand alone. Finding the right composition(s)—choral and/or orchestral—with which to pair it may be the most formidable impediment to its performance today.

ROBERT SCHUMANN, *FAUSTSZENEN*, WoO. 3

The final work in this *Faust* triptych is Robert Schumann's *Szenen aus Goethes Faust*. Even its title evokes memories of Berlioz's *Huit scènes de Faust*. Like Berlioz, Schumann was torn with indecision concerning how best to realize the operatic nature of the play (especially Part 2). At about the same time Felix Mendelssohn was composing *Elijah*, Schumann set the finale of Part 2, initially believing that he had embarked on the composition of a "*Faust* opera." He wrote to Alfred Brendel that "for as long as I have known this scene [finale to Part 3], I have felt its effectiveness could be enhanced precisely through the medium of music."[31] Nonetheless, Schumann's setting of Goethe's *Faust* occupied him from 1844 to 1853, evolving less along operatic lines than as a work for the "power and masses of the choir and orchestra," the same forces he urged Brahms to use in the essay *Neue Bahnen*, published in the *Neue Zeitschrift für Musik* of 1853.[32] The initial result was an oratorio based on the finale of Part 2, which Peter Horst Neumann argues was never considered for operatic performance: "Schumann never considered a theatrical, somewhat operatic performance of his *Faust*-Scenes; they are intended for the concert hall. This must have been the case because the inspiration for his *Faust* project sprang from the 'Mountain-Glen Scene' at the end of the second part, the portion of the work that is least compatible to the stage. He had already composed it in 1847–48, ending with the 'Chorus Mysticus' and it gives the appearance that, from the outset, it had been his intention to compose only this oratorio-like apotheosis."[33]

Additional confirmation of the belief of Neumann and others that Schumann considered his setting of *Fausts Verklärung* a self-sufficient composition are the simultaneous performances on August 29, 1849, in Weimar (conducted by Liszt), Dresden (under Schumann), and Leipzig to commemorate the centennial of Goethe's birth. But if, as Neumann would have us believe, Schumann viewed the end of Part 2 as "that portion of the work that is least compatible to the stage," why did Schumann, unlike Mahler, set the scene in its entirety and provide stage directions regarding the placement of the various characters?[34] Such instructions seem to argue against Schumann's proclaimed intention that this piece was already an oratorio or would become part of a larger oratorio at some future time. Table 3.5 provides a formal outline of the original music (the eventual Part 3) for *Fausts Verklärung*.

Schumann retains a common tempo and tonality only in the first two movements; the remaining five all involve shifts of both meter and key designed to facilitate the flow of the drama. In a number of cases, Schumann indicates proportional tempo relationships (e.g., in mvt. 3, the rubric *Die Viertel etwas schneller als vorher die Halben* ["The quarter note is somewhat faster than the previous movement's half-note"]) that hint at an evolving musical structure quite different from the closed forms of the past.

Table 3.5 Schumann—*Faustszenen*, part 3

1. Chorus	9/8	FM
2. Tenor Solo	4/4	D minor
3. Bass solo	4/4–2/2	B♭
Bass solo/SSA soli	4/4	B♭–G minor–B♭
4. Angel Chorus (ssaa)	3/4	A♭–C♯ minor–G♭– B♭
5. Baritone solo	4/4	G–G minor
6. Chorus/Soli	2/4	B♭–C–A minor–A–V/A
7. Chorus	2/2–2/2	F major

After the 1849 performances of *Fausts Verklärung* Schumann decided to expand the work to include earlier portions of Goethe's drama. In so doing, Schumann ignored the Cellar Scene, the Easter Procession, and the *Walpurgisnacht*. Ultimately, the completed *Faust Scenes* include the movements as set out in Table 3.6.

There are a number of interesting facts that bear upon the genesis and form of Schumann's composition. The first is the textual unity of Part 3, which premiered in 1849; all seven movements of Part 3 set continuous texts taken from act 5 of the second portion of Goethe's work. Compared to this wholeness, the texts of the first two parts are far more piecemeal; the three scenes in Part 1 all use noncontiguous texts from *Faust 1*, while four entire acts are missing between the first scene of Part 2 (*Faust 2, Erster Akt*) and the two concluding scenes (*Faust 2, Fünfter Akt*). Textual omissions eliminate the character of Mephistopheles (as in Berlioz's elimination of Faust in his *Huit scènes*), focusing instead on Gretchen (Part 1) and Faust (Part 2).

Table 3.6 Schumann—*Szenen aus Goethes Faust*, WoO, 3, form

Overture (1853)

Erste Abtheilung (Part 1):
1. *Scene im Garten* (Garden Scene) = *Faust 1*, vv. 3163–92 and 3207–10
2. *Gretchen vor dem Bild der Mater dolorosa* = *Faust 1*, vv. 3587–834
(Gretchen before a picture of the Sorrowful Virgin Mary)
3. *Scene im Dom* (Cathedral Scene) = *Faust 1*, vv. 3776–834

Zweite Abtheilung (Part 2):
4. *Sonnenaufgang* (Sunrise) = *Faust 2, Erster Akt*, vv. 4621–685 and 4695–727
5. *Mitternacht* (Midnight) = *Faust 2, Fünfter Akt*, vv. 11384–411, 11416–440, 11453–466 and 11487–510
6. *Fausts Tod* (The Death of Faust) = *Faust 2, Fünfter Akt*, vv. 11511–594

Dritte Abtheilung (Part 3):
7. *Fausts Erklärung* (Faust's Transfiguration), No. 1 = *Faust 2, Fünfter Akt*, vv. 11844–853;
   No. 2 = *Faust 2, Fünfter Akt*, vv. 11854–865
8. No. 3 = *Faust 2, Fünfter Akt*, vv. 11866–933
9. No. 4 = *Faust 2, Fünfter Akt*, vv. 11934–988
10. No. 5 = *Faust 2, Fünfter Akt*, vv. 11989–12019
11. No. 6 = *Faust 2, Fünfter Akt*, vv. 12020–103
12. No. 7 = *Faust 2, Fünfter Akt*, vv. 12104–111

Parts 1 and 2 occupied Schumann from 1849 to 1850. Given the prior existence of Part 3, Schumann had to compose the work backwards, interweaving motives and tonalities from that earliest portion of the whole into the new music that was now to precede it aurally. The main key center of the entire work is D minor, which appears in Part 3 only in the second movement (*Pater ecstaticus*) and in the finale (no. 7, m. 30). Schumann took pains to utilize D minor as the key of the overture (the final portion of the composition, 1853) and also in the concluding scenes of Parts 1 (the "Cathedral Scene") and 2 ("Faust's Death"). It is significant that the music of "Sorrow" (*Sorge*) in the "Midnight Scene" (Part 2, scene 2 is also in D minor). Schumann attempted to reinforce this tonality by inserting a melodic motive, originally found twice in Part 3 (mvt. 2 and the second version of mvt. 7) into the overture, the music associated with the Evil Spirit in the Cathedral Scene (Part 1, scene 3), the second half of the "Ariel scene," and the opening music of "Midnight." The intended association of this motive with evil is most evident in Part 1, no. 3, and Part 2, no. 2 (ex. 3.15).

Example 3.15 a-d Schumann, *Szenen aus Goethes Faust*, WoO 3

a. part 3, no. 2, mm. 1-5

b. Overture, mm. 31-36

c. part 1, mvt. 3, mm. 1-3

d. part 2 no. 5, mm. 14-17 ("Mitternacht")

Arnfried Edler has suggested the following constellation of tonalities as further evidence of Schumann's attempts to retrofit the music of Parts 1 and 2 into the overall tonal planning dictated by Part 3:

> F major stands as the putative tonic of the whole, given its appearance in the first vocal movement and as the key in which the final part both begins and ends. At the furthest remove from this key is the B-minor tonality of "Midnight" during which Faust is blinded by the breath of "Sorrow"; the ending in B major represents Faust's triumph over this adversity (*Lass glücklich schauen, was ich kühn ersann*). B♭ major is a "seraphic" tonality, used for the Ariel scene (fairies not angels) and the music of *Pater seraphicus* in Part 3, mvt. 3. G major and E major represent Faust's joy in life in the second half of Part 2, mvt. 4

(*Des Lebens Pulse schlagen frisch, lebendig* in G and the conclusion in E major) and his ecstasy when Dr. Marianus glimpses the "Queen of Heaven," Part 3, mvt. 5.[35]

Despite his attempts to create a musical connection between the chronological disconnect of the entire composition, Part 3 appears to be far more successful than the work as a whole. As was the case in his earlier choral-orchestral work, *Das Paradies und die Peri*, Schumann was able to weld these seven movements together into a seamless whole, the conclusion of one movement frequently dovetailing into the onset of the next.[36] Such continuity of music and drama is noticeably absent from the work's newly composed completion, which raises the question posed by Hermann Jung in his discussion of this composition: "Wozu Musik zu solch vollendeter Poesie?" ("From whence comes music for such perfect poetry?")

JOHANNES BRAHMS

After his completion of *Ein Deutsches Requiem*, op. 45, in 1867, Brahms never again composed an extended work for chorus and orchestra. He did, however, compose an impressive series of pieces that form a more significant (with one exception) part of standard choral-orchestral repertory than any of the previously assayed works based on *Faust*. Three dramatic compositions by Brahms use texts by Goethe:

Op. 50	*Rinaldo*	Goethe (after Tasso)
Op. 53	*Alto Rhapsodie*	Goethe, *Harzreise im Winter*
Op. 54	*Schicksalslied*	Friedrich Hölderlin
Op. 55	*Triumphlied*	biblical
Op. 82	*Nänie*	Friedrich Schiller
Op. 89	*Gesang der Parzen*	Goethe, *Iphigenie auf Tauris*

Considerable debate exists concerning the genesis of *Rinaldo*; completed in the summer of 1868 it lies perilously close to the German Requiem, a placement noted by Clara Schumann, "Ist das Werk nach dem Requiem bedeutend genug?"[37] Her question ("Following the Requiem, is the work significant enough?") is certainly reasonable, given the two starkly different texts that Brahms utilized at separate times. In a letter to Joseph Joachim (June 1863), Brahms writes that he is sending "his melodies for Goethe's *Rinaldo*" and reminding Joachim about the three hundred thaler he received from the *Liedertafel* in Aachen as the prize money for a "large composition for male chorus."[38] The story of Goethe's cantata text first appeared in Torquato Tasso's epic poem, *Gerusalemme liberata*; Goethe wrote his adaptation of the story in 1811 in the form of a dramatic cantata. Brahms's initial work on the score was interrupted by his appointment as director of the Vienna *Singakademie* in 1867, so not until the summer of 1868 did Brahms compose the final chorus, *Auf dem Meere*, completing the piece for the Aachen *Liedertafel*.

Brahms scores Goethe's dramatic cantata for tenor soloist, male chorus, and large orchestra, arranging Goethe's text as a series of solo movements in dialogue with a chorus. These are separate, numbered movements, realized only by changes of key, meter, and texture. Despite the intense drama inherent in Goethe's text, Brahms creates a cantata with two disproportionate parts—the extended cantata (1,144 mm.!) and the finale, *Auf dem Meere* (346 mm.), originally with a separate pagination. In the introductory notes to his new edition, J. Bradford Robinson gives this assessment of the composition: "With its clear stage setting and its 'unity of time, place and action,' it is as close as Brahms ever came to opera. Nor is there any overlooking the influence of *Fidelio, Der fliegende Holländer*, and Carl Maria von Weber—strains not otherwise heard in Brahms's music—and perhaps even Schubert's religious cantata *Lazarus*, which Brahms examined in manuscript shortly after its rediscovery."[39] Despite this approbation and the generally high quality of the composition, *Rinaldo* has failed to garner contemporary performances, perhaps owing to its length and scoring.

The same is hardly true of Brahms's principal composition project from the early summer of 1869, the *Alto Rhapsody*, which also uses a Goethe text. In a letter to Hermann Dieters, a pedagogue and author of musical books, Brahms inquires about an excerpt from Goethe's *Harzreise im Winter (Aber abseits, wer ist's?)*; he remembers hearing Johann Friedrich Reichardt's (1752–1814) song performed at Dieters's house. He asks to borrow that score for a brief time so that he can write a composition in recognition of his famous predecessor (Reichardt). According to Jan Swafford, the true motivation for writing the *Alto Rhapsody* has more to do with Brahms's learning of Julie Schumann's engagement, which dashed forever his unfounded hopes of a life with her. "To everyone he called it—whether wrathfully, sentimentally, or jokingly—a bridal song. It is an evocation of despair and a prayer for peace, addressed to a God who may not be capable of hearing it. When he sent the Rhapsody to the publisher Simrock, Brahms snarled, 'Here, I've written a bridal song for the Schumann countess—but I wrote it with anger, with wrath! What do you expect!'"[40]

Goethe wrote his poem after a visit to the Harz Mountains in 1777, at which time he encountered a young misanthrope named Plessing, who had, in true romantic fashion, withdrawn from the world to live surrounded only by books and nature. Plessing was the kind of person who, in Goethe's words, "goes off by himself, who has drunk misanthropy from the fullness of love." Can there be any doubt that Brahms saw himself as the object of Goethe's poem? Swafford recounts a visit by Brahms a week after Julie's wedding when he played the *Alto Rhapsody* for Clara. Clara wrote in her journal, "It is long since I remember being so moved by a depth of pain in words and music. . . . This piece seems to me neither more nor less than the expression of his own heart's anguish. If only he would for once speak as tenderly!"[41] Of Goethe's eighty-eight lines of poetry, Brahms sets only twenty-two. Taken from the center of the poem, their meaning provides solace to his own heart. Goethe may have written these lines to give hope to a desperately lonely hermit, but they resonate in the heart of anyone who has known such sadness and seeks comfort—the same comfort that lies at the core of the German Requiem, the same searching that permeates the searing questions of Brahms's motet *Warum ist das Licht gegeben dem Mühseligen?* (op. 74, no.1). Analysis of Brahms's *Alto Rhapsody* is unnecessary, for no amount of academic speculation can explain the affect of this music, the incredible gulf that lies between its tortuous opening in C minor and the lustrous C major of the final stanza. While perhaps not as overtly dramatic as music examined earlier in this chapter, one need only see the opening measures of the concluding prayer to understand the profundity of Brahms's achievement (ex. 3.16).[42]

Brahms's third and final setting of a Goethe text is his last choral-orchestral work, *Gesang der Parzen*, op. 89 (1882). Brahms was notorious for his near-ominous obsession with fate, which plays out in the opening of his Symphony No. 1 in C minor, the C-minor portion of the *Alto Rhapsody*, and the central Allegro of *Schicksalslied*, op. 54 (also in C minor). We might conclude that Brahms associates the key of C minor with fate (another example is the sixth movement of the German Requiem). Despite the mood that C minor connotes, each of the aforementioned works ends with some expression of hope—the *Alto Rhapsody* ends with a sublime prayer in C major; the C-minor section (*Doch uns ist gegeben auf keiner Stätte zu ruh'n*) of *Schicksalslied* contrasts with the work's opening in E♭ major, ingeniously transposed to C major to make a satisfying, if wordless, conclusion.

Example 3.16 Brahms, *Alto Rhapsody*, op. 53, mm. 116–27

If these fate-filled pieces conclude hopefully, the same cannot be said of *Gesang der Parzen*, which Brahms often called simply *Parzenlied*, the implication being it was the antipode (tonally and emotionally) to his other choral-orchestral Lied, the *Triumphlied*, op. 53, whose D-major brilliance may be traced to Handel (who also wrote occasional music celebrating military victories).[43] *Gesang der Parzen*'s pervasive D minor allows no ray of hope to pierce the eternal pessimism of Goethe's cynical text. In Goethe's *Iphigenie auf Tauris*, Iphigenia, faced with two equally unthinkable choices, remembers a song from her youth that gives voice to mankind's impotence concerning the decisions of the Fates. It is this text (from act 4 of Goethe's play) that Brahms sets in its entirety.

The opening orchestral introduction stirred controversy and became the subject of much discussion by supporters and critics alike. Theodor Billroth wrote: "Hanslick ... will probably get a shock in the first few bars.... You will, of course, have your conscious and unconscious grounds ... to emphasize these abnormal hardnesses of the *Parzen*, but our modern ears are sometimes pained by it."[44] Even more startling than its dynamic and dissonance is its initial avoidance of the tonic (D minor), which is not heard until m. 3. Brahms writes of this passage, "Think back for a moment to the minor chord [in the third bar]. Think of how the modulation from then on would be without any effect, and also quite restless, as if one were searching for something, unless one had heard this progression before and very much emphasized!"[45] Brahms alludes to his "grounds" for using such vague, unpredictable language: How could a composition about the inscrutable working of fate begin in anything approaching a stable tonality? At the core of this composition lies harmonic ambiguity, sudden and unexpected diversions of the harmonic stream, and the use of Brahms's signature six-part choral divisi (SAATBB) that emphasizes the dark color of the choral ensemble's lower voices.

If harmonically daring, Brahms's use of rhythm is more straightforward; he unfailingly realizes Goethe's dactylic meter as a quarter and two eighth notes. Of this almost obsessive rhythm, Siegfried Kross writes:

> While the language of the metric construction of the "Song of the Fates" recognizes only the unbending scheme of four dactyls with the major emphasis on the second, other, Brahms has at his disposal different possibilities of text setting in his musical setting that would not require breaking this metrical scheme. But Brahms steadfastly foregoes these. His setting is dominated through and through by the simplest rhythmic realization of the scansion—quarter and two eighths. Consequently, there can be no doubt that the composer uses this simple rhythm as a means of expression, just as he had restrained himself to use the same intervals as the compositional style in *Nänie*. Even the semantic connotation is the same—the supernatural constraint of the fate of mortals. The avoidance of any rhythmic differentiation clearly stems from the same purpose, to increase the psychological dynamic of the composition.[46]

Kross would likely agree that Brahms's obstinate repetition of this dactylic rhythm has an effect akin to the principal motive of Beethoven's Fifth Symphony, except that, in this case, the incessant pounding of that rhythm is intended to make the listener aware of the inevitability and the inhumanity of the Fates' decree. Opportunity to avoid this monotonous repetition resides in the irregular composition of Goethe's verses, no two of which arrange their number of feet in the same grouping. Goethe's stanzas have different numbers of lines (6, 5, 7, 5, 5, 7, and 6) comprising the same number of two dactyls. Brahms's handling of the persistent dactyls is even more diverse than Kross would have one believe. The first variation he makes affects the length of the dactyl unit. The first two lines of text and music adopt the poem's dactylic rhythm (ex. 3.17a), which Brahms augments (m. 39), while retaining its antiphony intact.

Example 3.17 a–b Brahms, *Gesang der Parzen*, op. 89

Brahms disguises this deceleration of the rhythmic pulse by simultaneously increasing the speed and activity of the orchestral accompaniment (eighths give way to dotted-eighth-sixteenth figures). This slower dactyl is kept through the beginning of the third strophe ("Erhebet ein Zwist sich"), but reverts to the original, faster rhythm at the words "so stürzen die Gäste" in m. 51 (now accompanied by triplets in the orchestra). Despite using the same rhythm at the

Table 3.7 Brahms, *Gesang der Parzen*, op. 89, meter, key, and text

Measures	Meter	Tonality	Text
1–19	$\frac{4}{4}$	D minor	
19–31			v. 1
31–35			
35–47		B♭/F major– C major	v. 2
47–70		F minor–C	v. 3
71–83		F–A	v. 4
84–99		C♯ minor–A	v. 5
100–115	$\frac{3}{4}$	D minor	v. 1
111–61	$\frac{4}{4}$	D major	v. 6
162–76		D minor	v. 7

same tempo, the whole character of the gesture changes (in keeping with the text) because of the interpolated augmentation.

The most obvious formal marker is key change: D minor dominates three large chunks of the piece (mm. 1–82, 100–115, and 162–end). Between the sections in D minor there are two sections governed by key signatures with sharps (Table 3.7). The first section (mm. 83–100) is nominally in C♯ minor, but, in truth, key is difficult to discern for the music is turbulent and chromatic, befitting the text of strophe 5 ("From the gorges of the deep"). As if assuaging this rather drastic departure of key, Brahms inserts the text and music of the opening (mm. 100–115) as both a recapitulation and also a preparation for the change to the signature of D major. The setting of v. 6 is unique because it uses the major mode and introduces a new meter (3/4). Brahms's new music reflects the text (v. 6, "The rulers turn their benevolent eyes"), giving the listener the only hopeful, radiant music in the entire work. There is irony in this change because the eyes of the mythical gods are actually turning away from mankind, not toward them. But perhaps, as in *Schicksalslied*, Brahms finds the prospect of ending the composition without any hint of warmth or redemption, thus the change to D major despite the text's hidden irony. All that is left is to return one last time to D minor for the bleak textual and musical coda. But within this key-driven formal design are some subtle musical repetitions that render the music's form elusive. The most obvious of these musical repetitions involves vv. 2 and 4. The music of v. 2 begins in D minor but changes to major-sounding music for the text "Auf Klippen und Wolken" ("On cliffs and clouds"). That same music reappears (mm. 71–80) with nominal changes of rhythmic detail because Brahms determines that there is a textual parallelism between the second and fourth strophes; indeed, each verse contains the phrase *goldene[n] Tische[n]* (golden tables) (ex. 3.18).

Example 3.18 a–b Brahms, *Gesang der Parzen*, op. 89

a. mm. 51-54

b. mm. 83-88

Another textual and musical parallel exists between the conclusion of strophe 3: "*Und harren vergebens, Im Finstern gebunden, Gerechten Gerichtes*" ("and they wait futilely, bound in the dark, for justice to be served") and the conclusion of strophe 5: "*Gleich Opfergerüchen, Ein leichtes Gewölke*" ("like burnt offerings, a light mist"); here Brahms acknowledges the similarity musically (compare mm. 60–68 and 90–100).

As stated earlier, the music for v. 6 dispenses with Fate's insistent dactyls and minor tonality because this one text contains something other than complete despair. The final strophe, returns to the minor music of the opening, over which Brahms sets the final six lines as a muttered unison incantation broken only by the sequence of three descending triads, each approached chromatically from above:

mm. 164–65:   F♯ minor   [D](C♯, A, F♯)
mm. 168–69:   B♭ minor   [G♭](F, D♭, B♭)
mm. 172–74:   D minor   [B♭](A, F, D)

The inevitability of this tonal descent dashes all hope as inevitably as does the final strophe of Goethe's poem *Gesang der Parzen*: "Thus sang the fates / the old, vanished one / listens to the old songs / in nocturnal caves / thinks of his children and grandchildren / and shakes his head."

CONCLUSION

Choral music as drama took many forms in the nineteenth century, especially in the area of opera and particularly in Parisian Grand Opera, where changes in dramaturgy led to the more active participation of the chorus. Of the other types of choral drama, many found a common denominator in the poetry of Johann Wolfgang von Goethe. Specifically, such leading composers as Berlioz, Mendelssohn, Schumann, and Brahms created unique works based on Goethe's texts, none of which quite succeeded in bending the poet's words to fit the supreme dramatic form of the age—that of opera. Perhaps this has something to tell us about the nature of operatic libretti and the kinds of stories that lend themselves to dramatic treatment. That Goethe resisted translation onto the operatic stage is perhaps the ultimate validation of his own judgment that poetry was most important and, therefore, inimical to any musical setting. It may indicate that the greatest works of art, irrespective of their medium, are those that are complete in themselves, the product of an artist engaged in a single exercise of one's craft. Certainly in the case of Robert Schumann's *Szenen aus Goethes Faust*, the question could be raised as to the artistic validity of the whole, considering that Schumann himself regarded his *Fausts Verklärung* (1849) as a finished work before deciding on the work's final form in 1853.

4

Choral Symphony from Beethoven to Berio

The dominance that symphonic thinking and formal procedures exercised on Mass composition between 1750 and 1900, especially in the sacred works of Haydn, Mozart, and Beethoven, led to the invention of the term "symphonic Mass." This statement effectively implies the dominance of form over expression, of "celebrative" music over "expressive." Beethoven's Symphony No. 9 in D minor, op. 125 (1824), initiated a complete reversal of this trend: purely symphonic works increasingly began to include sung text(s). The following list of such symphonies includes a heterogeneous group of nineteenth- and twentieth-century works (Table 4.1).

Table 4.1 A chronological list of choral symphonies

Beethoven	Symphony No. 9 in D minor, op. 125	1824
Mendelssohn	Symphony No. 2 in B♭, op. 52 (*Lobgesang*)	1840
Berlioz	*Roméo et Juliette* (*Symphonie Dramatique*), op. 17	1838–39
	La Damnation de Faust (*Légende Dramatique*), op. 24	1845–46
Liszt:	"Faust" Symphony	1854–57 rev. 1861
	"Dante" Symphony	1855–56
Mahler:	Symphony No. 2 ("Resurrection")	1888–94
	Symphony No. 3	1893–96
	Symphony No. 8 ("Symphony of a Thousand")	1906–7

Table 4.1 Continued

Vaughan Williams	Symphony No. 1 ("Sea Symphony")	1910
Ives	Symphony No. 4	1910–16
	Symphony (New England Holidays)	1919
Rachmaninoff	The Bells (*Kolokola*), op. 35	1913
Szymanowski	Symphony No. 3, op. 27 (*The Song of the Night*)	1914–16
Brian	"Gothic" Symphony	1922–28
Holst	First Choral Symphony, op. 41	1922–34
Shostakovich	Symphony No. 2, op. 14 (*Oktyabryua*)	1927
	Symphony No. 3, op. 20 (*Pervomaskaya*)	1929
Stravinsky	Symphony of Psalms	1930
Harris	Folksong Symphony	1940
Hilding Rosenberg	Symphony No. 4 (*The Revelation of St. John*)	1940
	Symphony No. 5 (*The Keeper of the Garden*)	1944
Milhaud	Symphony No. 3, op. 271 (*Te Deum*)	1946
Cuclin	Symphony No. 5	1947
	Symphony No. 10	1949
	Symphony No. 12	1951
Mennin	Symphony No. 4 (*The Cycle*)	1949
Britten	Spring Symphony, op. 44	1950
Hovhaness	Symphony No. 12, op. 188, "Choral"	1960
Shostakovich	Symphony No. 13, op. 113 (*Babi Yar*)	1962
Bernstein	Symphony 3 (*Kaddish*)	1963
Berio	Sinfonia	1969
Górecki	Symphony No. 2 (*Copernicus*)	1972
	Symphony No. 3 ("Symphony of Sorrowful Songs)	1976
Williamson	Symphony No. 3 (*The Icy Mirror*)	1972
Leighton	Symphony No. 2, op. 68 (*Sinfonia mistica*)	1974
Hanson	A Sea Symphony	1977
Schnittke	Symphony No. 2 (*St. Florians*)	1979
	Symphony No. 4	1983
Soproni	Symphony No. 3 (*Sinfonia da Requiem*)	1983
Hovhaness	Symphony No. 59, op. 398 (*Sinfonia sacra*)	
Tur	Symphony No. 2	1987
Hanuš	Symphony No. 7, op. 116 (*The Keys of the Kingdom*)	1989–90
Penderecki	Symphony No, 7 "Seven Gates of Jerusalem"	1996
Henze	Symphony No. 9	1997
Dun	Symphony 1997 *Heaven Earth Mankind*	1997
Glass	Symphony No. 5 (*Requiem, Bardo,* and *Nirmanakaya*)	1999
Zwillich	Symphony No. 4 "The Gardens"	1999
Glass	Symphony No. 7 "Toltec"	2005
Kyr	Symphony No. 9 (*The Spirit of Time*)	2000
Penderecki	Symphony No. 8 "Songs of Transitoriness"	2005

This list raises the inevitable question of how the inclusion of a chorus changed the essence of heretofore instrumental works called "symphony." Beethoven's Ninth Symphony, while conforming to the four-movement shape of contemporary works, was substantially longer and more complex than any of its predecessors.

LUDWIG VAN BEETHOVEN, SYMPHONY NO. 9 IN D MINOR, OP. 125

The first symphony to use chorus, Beethoven's op. 125 concludes with a setting of Schiller's *An die Freude*, for soloists and chorus. His decision interrupted the increasingly dominant role that instrumental music had played since the rise of public concerts in the eighteenth century.[1] Symphonies written in the eighteenth century showed no inclination to include any sort of vocal music, making Beethoven's decision all the more dramatic. This unexpected change in aesthetic and symphonic thinking is heralded in the opening of its final movement.

The opening ninety-one measures present stormy music, which is periodically interrupted by a recitative-like line for the cellos and basses. They foreshadow the theme that the baritone ultimately sings. In between these episodes Beethoven recalls the principal themes of the first three movements, each interrupted by the cello-bass recitative. Finally, in m. 92 we hear the well-known "Ode to Joy" theme, which Beethoven develops as a set of increasingly complex orchestral variations. Beethoven reprises the movement's first seven measures (mm. 208–14) as a final renunciation of the purely instrumental process. The baritone soloist's appearance in the next measure dramatically and prophetically defines Beethoven's new agenda:

> *O Freunde, nicht diese Töne! Sondern lasst uns angenehmere anstimmen, und freudenvollere.*
> (O Friends, not these sounds! Rather, let us sing ones that are more agreeable and joyful.)

These words, however, do not appear in Schiller's ode; Beethoven himself may have been the author.[2] These words emphatically reject the three preceding movements by the "nicht diese Töne" statement, meaning that instrumental music was incapable of saying what Beethoven wanted to say: Beethoven replaces the instruments with the human voice, music that is more "agreeable and joyful."

After this lengthy preface, the true finale commences in m. 236, a division marked by changes of meter (3/4 to 4/4), key (D minor to D major), and tempo (*Allegro assai*) as well as the resumption of the theme first annunciated by the low strings in m. 92. Beethoven's process becomes clear as the chorus sings Schiller's strophic text, expanding on the orchestra's earlier theme-and-variation process. The first three strophes of Beethoven's text are sung by soloists; the chorus's role is to repeat the final couplet of each verse:

> (1–2) *Freude, schöne Götterfunken, Tochter aus Elysium,*
> (3–4) *Wir betreten feuertrunken, Himmlische, dein Heiligtum!*
> (5–6) *Deine Zauber binden wieder was die Mode streng geteilt;*
> (8) *Alle Mensche werden Brüder wo dein sanfter Flügel weilt.*
> (13–14) *Wem der grosse Wurf gelungen, eines Freundes Freund zu sein,*
> (15–16) *Wer ein holdes Weib errungen, mische seinen Jubel ein!*
> (17–18) *Ja, wer auch nur eine Seele sein nennt auf dem Erdenrund!*
> (19–20) *Und wer's nie gekonnt, der stehle weinend sich aus diesem Bund.*
> (25–26) *Freude trinken alle Wesen, an den Brüsten der Natur;*
> (27–28) *Alle Guten, alle Bösen folgen ihrer Rosenspur.*
> (29–30) *Küsse gab sie uns und Reben, einen Freund geprüft im Tod;*
> (31–32) *Wollust ward dem Wurm gegeben und der Cherub steht vor Gott!*

The numbers refer to the lines of Schiller's poem. Text in bold was either changed or added by Beethoven.

Instead of an expected modulation to the dominant (A), Beethoven dramatically turns to F major (the dominant of B♭ major), the tonality for a new series of variations in the form of a Turkish march (complete with triangle, cymbals, and bass drum). This new "movement" (in B♭ major, 6/8, marked *Allegro assai vivace*) presents a single verse of text, sung by solo tenor and male chorus, then developed fugally (ex. 4.1).

Example 4.1 a/b Beethoven, Symphony No. 9 in D minor, op. 125, mvt. 4

This development ultimately reaches F♯ (m. 190), the farthest possible remove tonally from the original tonic; retaining this unlikely pedal point in the unison horns, Beethoven pivots to D major and a recapitulation of the initial text and music.

As is common in his later period works, Beethoven frequently changes key and tempo in setting his next strophe, a composite of disjunct yet clearly paired lines:

(9–10) *Seid umschlungen Millionen! Diesen Kuss der ganzen Welt!*
(11–12) *Brüder, über'm Sternenzelt muss ein lieber Vater wohnen.*
(33–34) *Ihr stürzt nieder, Millionen? Ahnest du den Schöpfer, Welt?*
(35–36) *Such' ihn über'm Sternenzelt, Über Sternen muss er wohnen.*

This is the last of Schiller's text that Beethoven used;[3] the remainder of the work consists of textual restatements of the preceding verses in a lengthy multipartite closing section that remains steadfastly in D major, despite many changes of dynamic, tempo, mode, scoring, and meter.

The finale of the Ninth Symphony features the same formal syncretism that permeates all of Beethoven's late works, most notably the original Finale of the String Quartet, op. 130. When his publisher refused to publish the quartet with this Finale, Beethoven promptly wrote a new one, publishing his mind-bending *Grosse Fuge* separately as op. 133. Like the symphony, the fugue telescopes the four traditional symphonic movements into a single complex structure of interlocking, thematically related parts. Both Finales can be viewed as four-movement symphonies bound together by a common theme that undergoes continuous development or variation.

FELIX MENDELSSOHN, SYMPHONY NO. 2 IN B♭, OP. 52

The first successor to Beethoven's Ninth was Mendelssohn's Symphony No. 2, op. 52, more popularly known as the *Lobgesang* ("Hymn of Praise"). The composition Mendelssohn called a "Symphony-Cantata" had been commissioned and performed for a festival celebrating the quadricentennial of Johannes Gutenberg's invention of movable-type printing.[4] The clearest similarity between Mendelssohn's and Beethoven's symphonies lies in their shared use of three instrumental movements and a choral Finale. The similarity is, however, superficial, for Mendelssohn's instrumental movements are more a prelude to the choral Finale than independent, symphonic compositions. Indeed, many early vocal scores combine the instrumental movements together as a "Sinfonia." Mendelssohn also assigns his Finale a separate title and opus number, which do not appear on the symphony's title page.[5] This separation undercuts Mendelssohn's attempt to unify the movements by use of a recurring motive.

Example 4.2 Mendelssohn, Symphony No. 2
in B♭ Major, *Lobgesang*, op. 52, mvt. 1

(Al - es was O - dem hat   lo - bet den Herrn.)

This motive (ex. 4.2) appears prominently in the first movement of the symphony and returns as an oboe counterpoint to the chorale-like middle theme of the second movement (G minor, Allegretto). The third movement, an *Adagio religioso* in D major with a contrasting middle section in D minor, does not use the motive.

The Finale (mvt. 4) is a cantata comprising ten sections. Like most non-oratorio works of this period, Mendelssohn adopts a fluid approach to the traditional elements of form. In the opening chorus of mvt. 4, for example, Mendelssohn uses three tempo changes to gradually ratchet up the drama. The "Alles was odem hat" theme of the symphony's first movement appears first in the orchestra, then as a subject of a fugato in section 2, *Allegro moderato*, and then after completely new musical material in the final ten bars of the chorus. This theme is not heard again until the last eleven measures of section 10, the so-called *Schluss Chor*, as a tonal reminder of the symphony's opening theme.

The first five sections of the Finale flow together without discernible pause, as do sections 6–8. Mendelssohn facilitates this seamlessness by pairing sections with related tonalities, most notably the double pair of sections (nos. 1 and 2, 9 and 10) in B♭. Within this frame, pairs of numbered sections in the relative minor (nos. 3 and 4), the subdominant (no. 5) and its relative key C minor (no. 6), and G major and its dominant (nos. 7 and 8) round out the larger harmonic plan. Although the symphony's unifying motive (ex. 4.2) figures prominently in the first and last choruses of the the fourth movement, the duet with chorus, "I Waited for the Lord" remains the best known part of the cantata (no. 5).[6] This melody is pure Mendelssohn—lyric, syllabic, and compatible with the other counterthemes (ex. 4.3). Short though the first three movements are, Mendelssohn seems to have added his fourth movement in emulation of Beethoven's Ninth.

Example 4.3 Mendelssohn, Symphony No. 2 in B♭ Major,
Lobgesang, op. 52, mvt. 4, no. 5, mm. 32–39

Ich har - re - te des Herrn und er neig - te sich zu mir,   und hör - te mein Fleh'n,   er hör - te mein Flehn,

HECTOR BERLIOZ, *ROMÉO ET JULIETTE*, OP. 17

Hector Berlioz composed two works in the 1840s that challenge traditional notions regarding the interaction of symphony orchestra and chorus. The first is *Roméo et Juliette* (1839), which he dubbed a "dramatic symphony," stating, "The genre of this work will surely not be misunderstood. Although voices are frequently used, it is neither a concert opera nor a cantata but a choral symphony [*Symphonie avec chœurs*]."[7] The composer's words notwithstanding, the nature of the work has elicited controversy since Berlioz himself often performed the instrumental portions separately, especially the conclusion of no. 2—the *Grande Fête chez Capulet*. He also endorsed performance of mvts. 2–4 as an orchestral suite, tacitly acknowledging the logistical and financial difficulties posed by the added vocal or choral movements that follow. Contemporary critics connected this work to Beethoven's famous choral symphony, but this comparison is viable only if mvts. 1, 5, and 6 are omitted (Table 4.2).[8] Julian Rushton has suggested that the work is best understood as a "covert opera," in which Berlioz used his expressive instrumental language as a substitute for the actors and singers normally entrusted with conveying the dramatic action.[9] Daniel Albright concludes that despite the work's extensive vocal material, it is a indeed genuine symphony.[10]

Movements 2, 3, and 4 are purely orchestral (save for a brief offstage choral passage in "Roméo seul"), clearly corresponding to the first three movements of a typical symphony. Berlioz's choral writing in the Prologue and Finale reflects the traditional French choral scoring (STB with *divisi*). Berlioz employs a narrative *petite chœur* in the first and last movements, merging with two large choirs that represent the entire Montague and Capulet families. Berlioz specifies that the *petite choeur* should consist of only twelve voices (four each of sopranos, tenors, and basses). He kept their music simple and syllabic, reflecting their narrative function.

Berlioz reserves the female choral voices for the first and last movements, save for a contingent of sopranos from the "Capulet choir" who join their male counterparts in mvt. 5, *Convoi funèbre de Juliette*. Berlioz subtitles the movement a "fugal march" in which the voices and instruments alternately present imitative counterpoint and unison psalmody.[11] For the first sixty-four measures, Berlioz limits the sopranos and tenors to an intermittent monotone within the evolving orchestra fugue (indicating a procession); the text is similarly repetitive—*Jetez des fleurs pour la vierge expirée!* ("Throw flowers on the dead virgin!") (ex. 4.4).

Table 4.2 Berlioz, *Roméo et Juliette*, op. 17

1. *Introduction: Combats—Tumulte—Intervention du Prince*
    Prologue (A, T, stb)
    Strophes (A, stb)
    Scherzetto (T)
2. *Romeo seul—Tristesse—Bruit lointain de bal et de concert—Grande fête chez Capulet*
3. *Scène d'amour*
4. *Le Reine Mab, ou la Fée des Songes: Scherzo*
5. *Convoi funèbre de Juliette*
6. *Roméo au tombeau des Capulets*
    Invocation
7. *Final*
    Air
    Serment

Example 4.4 Berlioz, *Roméo et Juliette*, op. 17, no. 5, mm. 1–4

For the remainder of the movement, the chorus assumes a primarily melodic role (in E major, eventually doubled by the winds), relegating their psalm tone to the unison strings. To the previous text, the chorus now sings "Jusqu'au tombeau suivez notre soeur adorée" ("We now follow our adored sister to the tomb"), developed over the course of mm. 65–112.

Encompassing 462 measures of mostly vocal music, the Finale is truly grand. Berlioz prescribes the overall form in his three principal subdivisions: Introduction, mm. 1–130; *Air* (Fr. Laurence), mm. 131–374; and *Serment de Reconciliation* (Reconciliation Oath), mm. 375–462. As the mediating force between the contentious families, each of whom blames the other for the tragic deaths of their children, Fr. Laurence dominates the movement.

The Introduction opens with antiphonal writing, which represents the conflict between the two families. Fr. Laurence's *Air* is bipartite, his entreaties to both families to forgive but not forget their dead children first falling on deaf ears (mm. 233–58), then finding acceptance (mm. 342–74) from the double choruses. The last section, Laurence's *Serment de Reconciliation*, provides the dramatic and musical dénouement of the work, as he unites the families in a solemn vow to uphold God's law, appropriately intoned as a choral hymn, *Jurez donc par l'auguste symbole* ("Swear then, by the high symbol of God."). It provides a fitting conclusion to this oddly symmetrical work, which commingles opera (mvts. 1, 5–7) and symphony (mvts. 2–4), ultimately affirming the operatic tonal center of B minor/major over the symphony's F-major center.

JOHANN WOLFGANG VON GOETHE (1739–1832)

After Shakespeare, it is generally understood that the most popular romantic author for composers of nineteenth-century dramatic music is Johann Wolfgang von Goethe. His masterpiece, *Faust*, was the basis for numerous dramatic choral works (see chap. 3). In addition to Gounod's famous opera, Hector Berlioz and Franz Liszt composed symphonic works based on the Faust legend. Although Berlioz's *La Damnation de Faust* uses the same principles as *Roméo et Juliette*, it is not truly symphonic. At first glance, though, Liszt's "Faust" Symphony (1854–57) seems to imitate the three symphonic movements and choral Finale of Beethoven's Ninth. But Liszt's three instrumental movements are actually symphonic portraits of Faust, Gretchen, and Mephistopheles. Three years after the work's premiere (1854) Liszt composed a setting of the *Chorus Mysticus* for tenor solo and male chorus; the text is the conclusion of Goethe's *Faust* "Alles Vergängliche" (*Chorus Mysticus*). While this provided a choral conclusion, it remained an optional ending, paling in comparison to what Mahler would later do with that same text.

Liszt also composed a symphony in two movements based on Dante's *Divine Comedy*. Planned as early as 1839, the work was composed in between 1847 and 1848, elaborated on in 1865/66, and dedicated, at along last, to Richard Wagner. The two movements present the *Inferno* and *Purgatorio and Vision*. As part of *Vision* Liszt introduced a two-part treble chorus (either women or boys), who sing the opening verse of the *Magnificat* combined with ecstatic shouts of "Hallelujah" and "Hosanna." Liszt gave explicit instructions that the choir and its accompanying harmonium should be separated from the orchestra, preferably located in a gallery above.

GUSTAV MAHLER (1860–1911)

One of the most important symphonic composers of the late-nineteenth century, Gustav Mahler also represents the high point of vocal influence in symphonic composition (Fig. 4.1). Mahler's second, third, and fourth symphonies drew on the orchestral songs based on texts from the German anthology *Des Knaben Wunderhorn*, compiled by Achim von Arnim and Clemens Brentano (1805–8) (Table 4.3).

Table 4.3 Mahler, *Des Knaben Wunderhorn* settings in symphonies 2–4

Symphony 2 (1888–94)
    Mvt. 3—*Des Antonius von Padua Fischpredigt*
    Mvt. 4—*Urlicht*
    Mvt. 5—*Aufersteh'n, ja aufersteh'n* (F. Klopstock)
Symphony 3 (1893–96)
    Mvt. 4—*Was spricht die tiefe Mitternacht* (Nietzsche)
    Mvt. 5—*Es sungen drei Engel* (*Knaben Wunderhorn*)
Symphony 4 (1899–1900)
    Mvt. 4—*Das himmlische Leben* (*Knaben Wunderhorn*)

SYMPHONY NO. 2 (1888–94)

In addition to the *Knaben Wunderhorn* songs, two of these symphonies include music for chorus. In the Third Symphony, the choral presence takes the form of a treble chorus singing *Es sungen drei Engel* (mvt. 5).[12] But the choral Finale of the Second Symphony, which directly follows the *Wunderhorn* song, "Urlicht," is far more substantive.

    Although Mahler eventually rejected the use of literary programs for his symphonies, at least three prose commentaries outline what the music of each movement of the Second Symphony represents.[13] None of these programs, however, accounts for the presence of a choral finale. In a letter to Arthur Seidl (1897), Mahler recounted his motivation for composing a choral Finale:

> I had long contemplated bringing in the choir in the last movement, and only the fear that it would be taken as a formal imitation of Beethoven made me hesitate again and again. Then Bülow died, and I went to the memorial service.—The mood in which I sat and pondered on the departed was utterly in the spirit of what I was working on at the time.—Then the choir, up in the organ-loft, intoned Klopstock's *Resurrection* chorale.—It flashed on me like lightning, and everything became plain and clear in my mind! It was the flash that all creative artists wait for—"conceiving by the Holy Ghost"![14]

Mahler's use of the chorus was less an imitation of Beethoven than a means of including the text he perceived as the only logical solution to issues raised in the preceding movements. More like Beethoven's model is Mahler's recollection of themes from preceding movements. After this thematic reprise, a series of themes, some new, some already heard, unfolds. The most notable of these is a theme from the first movement; that theme (ex. 4.5a), based on the Requiem sequence, *Dies irae*. The opening theme of the fifth movement of Symphony 2, inverts the well-known chant melody (ex. 4.5b).

Example 4.5 a–b Mahler, Symphony No. 2 in D minor
© 1917 by Universal Edition Vienna, London © Renewed. Used by permission of European American Music Distributors, LLC, U.S. and Canadian agent for Universal Edition, Vienna.

a. mvt. 1, mm. 270-277

b. mvt. 5, mm. 70-78

The complex of motives presented in mm. 26–193 functions as an exposition; following form, the next large section is developmental (mm. 194–417). In lieu of the traditional recapitulation, Mahler presents instead a transformation of the exposition's themes (mm. 418–71), which also serves as a prelude to the first choral entrance (m. 472).

Example 4.6 Mahler, Symphony No. 2 in D minor, mvt. 5, mm. 472–79
© 1917 by Universal Edition Vienna, London © Renewed. Used by permission of European American Music Distributors, LLC, U.S. and Canadian agent for Universal Edition, Vienna.

Example 4.6 shows that the vocal ranges for the chorus are quite low (especially the second bass). Mahler appends the following note to his score: "The second basses are not written an octave higher in order to achieve the impact intended by the author; what matters is not that these low pitches are heard throughout, but this way of writing should only prevent the deep basses from perhaps taking the upper bass's notes in order to reinforce the upper notes."[15]

The remainder of the movement unfolds as both choral and solo vocal music (SA), following the verse structure of Klopstock's ode and the text added by the composer. Although Klopstock's text is always referred to as an ode, it is instead a hymn text of five verses intended (as Klopstock noted) to be sung to the Lutheran chorale melody *Jesus Christus, unser Heiland, der den Tod überwand.* Mahler uses only the first two verses of Klopstock's hymn as the first two texts sung by the chorus.

The remainder of the text (sung by the soloists and chorus between mm. 560 and 712) is solely Mahler's creation, expanding on Klopstock's verse in a free manner that allows him to use the music already heard in the opening section of the movement "O Glauben" as sung by the alto (m. 560) begins as a literal repeat of music first played by the orchestra (mm. 97–113). Mahler's final text (mm. 712–31) borrows the basic syntax of the poet's first verse, changing the words only slightly to create the wanted choral apotheosis.

Despite Mahler's denial of Beethoven as a model, the presence of a choral Finale, the complex array of formal structures and motivic relationships, and the use of poetry conceived on an elevated, spiritual plane argue otherwise. Mahler's negation of the specifically Christian connotations of Klopstock's hymn and the song *Urlicht* provide further evidence that, like Beethoven, he sought universal sentiments.[16] Edward Reilly sums up this complex relationship succinctly:

> Clearly, in his use of the *Dies irae* motive and the *Wunderhorn* text, and in borrowing from Klopstock's hymn, Mahler was drawing from Christian tradition and established musical symbolism. But it also seems clear that he has attempted to remove these sources from any narrow form of dogmatic Christianity, and ultimately from any form of doctrinal religion.... The textual references are to "God," never explicitly to Christ. And where the variant of the "Urlicht" poem mentioned earlier does connect the symbol of the rose with Christ, the *Wunderhorn* version used by Mahler does not. Fundamentally, however, unlike either a Christian or a Jewish God, the God implied by Mahler's text does not judge. Mahler seems clearly to have drawn on the Christian concept of the Last Judgment, and even to have modelled the implied sequence of events in his final movement along the lines of

Fig. 4.1 Gustav Mahler (1909)

the Last Judgment as described in the *Dies irae* or other religious texts. Ultimately, however, he removed all the inscriptions in his score that spell out these connections, perhaps realizing that his message went beyond a single creed.[17]

Symphony No. 8 ("Symphony of a Thousand") is Mahler's "choral symphony."[18] By 1906 Mahler's notion of symphonic form could accommodate two large, texted movements, even though the earlier Seventh Symphony still followed his trend of using two massive outer movements to frame a variable series of inner movements (much like the format of Beethoven's late quartets). It is hard to imagine a more unlikely juxtaposition of texts and philosophy than the Latin hymn *Veni creator spiritus* and the end of act 2 of Goethe's *Faust*.[19] Only by viewing these texts as two commentaries on the same basic idea—love's power to effect salvation as incarnate in the love of God the Creator and the empowering creativity of the eternal feminine—are we able to explain this unprecedented symphonic format.

In her memoirs, Alma Mahler relates that Mahler composed the first movement relying solely on his memory of Goethe's text. A complete version of the text, later wired from Vienna, confirmed that he had indeed set the text without omissions.[20] The same cannot be said for Mahler's treatment of *Veni creator spiritus*. An interlinear comparison of the Latin text and Mahler's text reveals inconsistencies in word order and Latin prosody, the result of either an imperfect memory of the text or of a freedom of approach somewhat reminiscent of Berlioz's treatment of the *Dies irae* in his *Grande Messe de Morts*.[21] Mahler includes a verse (lines 25–28) not found in the hymn and reorders the first five verses (1, 2, 4, 5, 3).[22] Beginning with v. 2 Mahler deliberately rearranges the sequence of words to accommodate the distinctive rhythmic and melodic contour of *Veni creator spiritus* (ex. 4.7).

Example 4.7 a–c Mahler, Symphony No. 8 in E♭ Major, mvt. 1

a. mvt. 1, mm. 1-4, *Veni creator spiritus*

b. mvt. 1, mm. 31-34

c. mvt. 1, mm. 8-12

In m. 31, we find the first example of this reordering in the bass part of chorus 1, who sing "tuorum visita," (omitting "Mentes") to this important theme. Given the pervasive prominence of this motive throughout the entire movement, there are numerous examples where Mahler uses only the final two words of a line because they more closely fit this important theme's rhythm.

Many commentators have described the first movement broadly as a sonata-allegro design. The music may be construed in three large segments that correspond to the typical components of first-movement sonata form:

Exposition	Development	Recapitulation	Coda
mm. 1–168	mm. 169–413	mm. 413–519	mm. 519–80

The sheer size of the movement suggests the inadequacy of this traditional nomenclature to describe the symphony's musical content. Like the Credo of Beethoven's *Missa Solemnis*, one needs to look at three factors—text, theme, and tonality. While thematic content and tonality are commonplace for any instrumental work of the period, the addition of text is unique to symphonic construction.

Mahler's symphony begins and ends in the same key (E♭ major), yet conceals a world of complex, often contradictory tonal relationships. There are twenty-two changes of key signature, all of which involve flats, in just the first movement. The most intriguing and unexpected aspect of this section is the appearance of a signature of four sharps (m. 217). The true significance of this change of key becomes clear only at *Accende lumen sensibus* (m. 262) in the unexpected key of E major (ex. 4.8). The simplest theoretical explanation for this key's appearance is the enharmonic equivalence of A♭ (the subdominant of E♭) and G♯ (the mediant of E major); this relationship doesn't explain why Mahler chooses to juxtapose tonalities so close intervallically (a semitone apart) yet so far removed tonally (three flats to four sharps). The signature of four sharps appears four times in part 1 (mm. 217, 258, 366, and 494). Its first occurrence signals the use of C♯ minor to set the displaced text *Infirma nostri corporis* (line 15), while the last (m. 494) governs a brief orchestral passage just prior to the coda. The middle two occurrences both involve the text "Accende lumen sensibus" ("Kindle a light in our senses"), a phrase pivotal to understanding Mahler's larger concept of the work. Both passages occur within what would be the development section of the proposed sonata design (mm. 261–90 and 366–85); similarly, both present an important motive heard throughout the entire work (ex. 4.8).

Example 4.8 Mahler, Symphony No. 8 in E♭ Major, mvt. 1, mm. 261–5

If the formal coherence of *Veni creator spiritus* is difficult to discern in spite of the context of sonata design, the formal processes of the second part are even more problematic because this movement uses so much more text. All told, Mahler uses twenty-three separate texts from the second act of Goethe's *Faust*, all of which are connected to specific characters and the chorus. Goethe's poetry allows neither the kind of text manipulation seen in the first movement nor the imposition of an abstract formal design. Conversely, the length and structural complexity of this *scena* creates unique problems of both internal (within mvt. 2) and external musical unity. The resulting symphonic structure more closely resembles Mahler's orchestral song cycles (most notably *Das Lied von der Erde*) than his earlier symphonies.

The first movement leaves little to be resolved musically, but its impact continues in Mahler's insertion of its thematic material in the second movement.[23] These insertions are less formal repeats than remembrances of the first movement that take place within Goethe's secular drama. Such a reference occurs in the *Pater ecstaticus*'s opening solo "Ewiger Wonnebrand" (m. 219), the theme of which re-echoes mvt. 1 and foreshadows the concluding *Chorus Mysticus* (ex. 4.9).

Example 4.9 Mahler, Symphony No. 8 in E♭ Major, mvt. 2, mm. 219–25

a, mvt. 2, mm. 219-25

b. mvt. 2, mm. 1498-1509

The second movement, like the first, begins and ends in E♭ but prominently features sections in E major (ex. 4.10). The first of these, Dr. Marianus's aria (m. 638) "Höchste Herscherrin der Welt!" plays a significant role in the overall tonal design of the symphony. This one passage contains a remarkable series of events: the first appearance of E major (m. 638) and the harps; an orchestral modulation to E♭ for the horn's reprise of the *Accende* motive (m. 699) and then a chromatic return to E major set up by dominant seventh arpeggios in the harps and piano (mm. 771–74) representing the ascension of the *Mater Gloriosa*.[24] Then follows one of Mahler's signature Adagios (scored for hp, str, pf, cel, and harm), which produces some ecstatic music reminiscent of the heavenly music that concludes his Third Symphony. Subsequent reminiscences of this gesture are never in E major, suggesting the profound symbolism of these two conflicting tonalities—E major represents the unattainable in both this symphony and, by extension, in human experience. The persistence of E♭, though, is less a validation of classical tonal planning than a celebration of what *is* attainable—humanity's triumph over doubt and skepticism. This realization comes in the symphony's glorious apotheosis, the *Chorus Mysticus*, and this reveals a multilayered musical synthesis of themes. There is a notable similarity (particularly rhythmic) between Mahler's *Chorus Mysticus* and the alternate choral conclusion that Liszt composed for his *Faust Symphony*.[25] Only here does Mahler reconcile the symphony's disparate tonalities and welter of themes; this melody closely resembles the *Accende* motive in its original form (see again ex. 4.8). What we realize in hindsight is that these two movements are bound quite closely together in that the first theme heard in the second movement (ex. 4.10a) transforms Mahler's *Veni creator* motive of mvt. 1, as does the horn melody in example 4.10b.

Example 4.10 a–b Mahler, Symphony No. 8 in E♭ Major, mvt. 2

Mahler's Eighth Symphony comes closer to Beethoven's conception of a choral symphony than any other example of the genre.

THE CHORAL SYMPHONY AFTER MAHLER

If Mahler's "Symphony of a Thousand" represents the apogee of the genre, then there are many successors that lay claim to the designation "choral" symphony, the most notable of which is Igor Stravinsky's 1930 *Symphony of Psalms* (see chap. 8, this volume). In the twentieth century, choral symphonies found great popularity in England; composers like Ralph Vaughan Williams, Gustav Holst, Havergal Brian, Benjamin Britten, and Kenneth Leighton all made significant contributions. Brian (1876–1972), possibly one of the most prodigious symphonic composers since Haydn and Mozart, remains largely unknown outside a small group of devotees. Several of his thirty-plus symphonies use chorus, the best known of which is the *Gothic Symphony* (1919–27), comparable in size to Mahler's works (as are several equally unknown compositions of interminable length). Like his predecessors, Brian follows Beethoven's template, composing three purely orchestral movements and a choral Finale. And, like Mahler, Brian combines texts from Goethe's *Faust* (mvts. 1–3) with a *Te Deum laudamus* (mvt. 4). Brian's symphony differs from Liszt's *Faust* symphony in that his three orchestral movements are not character sketches but celebrations of Faust as the prototypical Gothic man, a mystic seeker of hidden knowledge. Together they form a prelude to the massive *Te Deum* that roughly doubles their combined length. Brian unifies his sprawling work by following a fairly simple tonal scheme and grouping melodies (rarely repeated) into families of themes.

Holst and Vaughan Williams are more familiar names, linked both chronologically and by their pioneering work in the collection of English folk songs (see chap. 7, this volume). In their choral symphonies, though, the focus is on poetic text. Vaughan Williams's *Sea Symphony* (1910) employs poetry by Walt Whitman, the poet who captured the imagination of early twentieth-century composers much as Goethe had in the nineteenth century.[26] The four movements of this symphony have separate titles and different characters: (1) *A Song for All Seas, All Ships*, principally in D major, 4/4, and *Andante maestoso*; (2) *On the Beach at Night Alone*, principally in E minor, 3/4, and *Largo sostenuto*; (3) Scherzo, *The Waves*, principally in G minor, 3/4, and *Allegro brillante*; and (4) *The Explorers*, principally in E♭ major, 4/4, and *Andante con moto* (m. 39).

These titles reference the "Sea Drift" section of Whitman's *Leaves of Grass* (1891–92). Vaughan Williams sets Whitman's poetry without alteration in mvts. 1 and 2, although the first movement combines two separate poems; the first is a single stanza from part 8 of Whitman's "Song of the Exposition," presumably chosen to provide the symphony with a grand beginning. The remainder of the text is the poem "Song for All Seas, All Ships." Movement 3, *The Waves*, quotes the final poem in "Sea Drift," "After the Sea Ship." Vaughan Williams pares the fourteen lines of *On the Beach at Night Alone* down to eleven, while the Finale contains carefully edited but largely intact portions of three different sections (6, 11, and 13) from "Passage to India."[27]

Although each movement begins and ends in a specific key, its range of harmonies is by no means restricted to those keys that form the traditional hierarchy of that tonality. Explaining the keys of these movements (D major–E minor; G minor–E♭) as pairs in sharp (mvts. 1 and 2) and flat keys (mvts. 3 and 4) does nothing to relate the work to any traditional symphonic pattern. The composer's only obvious bow to symphonic convention is his designation of "The Waves" as a *Scherzo*, that is, a movement in rapid triple meter, typically in rounded binary form (abab'), and containing a contrasting trio section. Because of the unusual relation of their tonal centers, ascribing traditional symphonic functions to the other movements is nearly impossible. These departures lead one to accept more readily the prominence of the chorus, which eclipses all its predecessors except Mahler's Eighth.

GUSTAV HOLST, *FIRST CHORAL SYMPHONY*, OP. 41

Holst's *First Choral Symphony*, so called despite the lack of successors, was sketched in 1923 and finished early in 1924. Holst's uses poetry by John Keats without regard for its original context, which drew the disapproval of several literary purists.[28] The introduction and first movement combine stanzas from two separate parts of Keats's *Endymion* (the "Chorus of the Shepherds" and the "Roundelay" in Book 4). The slow movement is unique in its use of the entirety of Keats's famous *Ode on a Grecian Urn*. In the Scherzo, Holst returns to a combinative approach, using the first seventy-six lines of Keat's "Fancy" and the first ten lines of "Folly's Song" from the larger poem *Extracts from an Opera* (1818). The Finale is the most complex construction of all, combining excerpts from the *Ode on Apollo* (February 1815) with another portion of *Endymion*.[29] While less popular than Vaughan Williams's *Sea Symphony*, Holst's work has a greater sense of individuality and modernity. Imogen Holst notes that the middle two movements were her father's favorites, perhaps because he struggled to stretch his musical ideas to the requisite breadth of a symphonic finale. Setting Keats's *Ode on a Grecian Urn* in any format is a daunting task due to its length, strophic design, and familiarity, but Holst rose to the challenge by using a motive comprising stacked perfect fifths, a sonority he evidently favored, given its frequent appearance in his music (ex. 4.11a–d).

Example 4.11 a–d Holst, arpeggiated fifth themes

a. Holst, *Hymns to the Rig Veda*, op. 26, no. 3/1, mm. 1-3

b. Holst, *Ode to Death*, op. 38, mm. 1-2

c. Holst, *Nunc Dimititis*, mm. 1-4

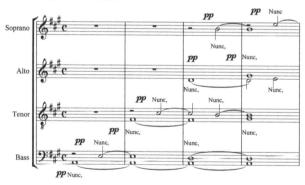

d. Holst, *First Choral Symphony*, op. 41, mvt. 2, mm. 1-4

At the beginning of the Adagio in his autograph score, Holst writes: "Not mysterious, but everything clear cut, like sun rising on frost." Holst uses these open fifths to conjure up the pristine iciness inspired by Keats's lines: "Cold Pastoral! When old age doth this generation waste, Thou shalt remain (ex. 4.12)."

Example 4.12 Holst, *First Choral Symphony*, op. 41, mvt. 2, mm. 132–37

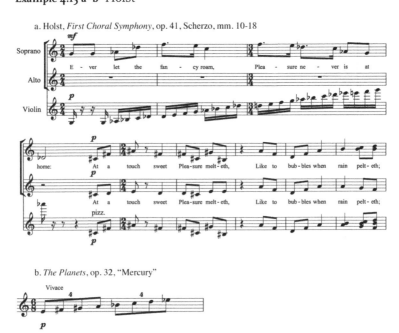

Another striking aspect of this movement is the ostinato for "Who are these coming to the sacrifice?" which is somewhat reminiscent of the ostinato found in the third movement of Stravinsky's *Symphony of Psalms*, except that Holst's pattern of pitches is metrically regular. Remarkable in a different way is the vibrant choral Scherzo, "Ever let the Fancy roam," in which the chorus faces the multiple challenges of wickedly quick declamation and bitonal harmonic progressions (4.13a). In this wispy music, one can hear echoes of "Mercury" from *The Planets*, op. 32, the popular orchestral suite that provides a synthesis of Holst's style (ex. 4.13b).

Example 4.13 a–b Holst

Holst drew his melody from the modal scales of English folk song, and from that source he created a uniquely modern harmony, as seen in his setting of "Beneath my palm trees" in mvt. 1.

Example 4.14 Holst, *First Choral Symphony*, op. 41, mvt. 1, mm. 14–21

Another prominent modal feature is the Lydian tritone between F' and B', employed especially to create musical suspensions. Perhaps Benjamin Britten's fondness for this piquant sonority derives from his affection not only for Holst's music but also for Elgar's *The Dream of Gerontius* (see chap. 1), works that Britten loved and recorded. If any music sounds Brittenesque then, it is contained in Holst's *Choral Symphony*.

BENJAMIN BRITTEN, *SPRING SYMPHONY*, OP. 44

Like the choral symphonies of Vaughan Williams and Holst, Britten uses the typical four-movement structure commonly found in symphonies; while both Vaughan Williams and Holst utilize poems by a single poet, Britten demonstrates his literary savoir faire by compiling a bold, even bizarre poetic anthology (Table 4.4).[30] The texts are drawn from centuries of English literary history, ranging from the medieval Reading Rota ("Sumer is icumen in," a thirteenth-century round or rota from Reading Abbey, Southampton) to the twentieth-century poetry of W. H. Auden.

Britten scores his symphony for large mixed chorus, boys chorus, and three soloists (SAT), using these forces with typical care and efficiency. The chorus begins and ends the symphony, and it appears at least once in each of those movements. Overall the impression is less that of a symphony than an orchestral song cycle like Mahler's *Das Lied von der Erde*. The closest analogues to traditional symphonic movements are parts 3 and 4. While Britten does not explicitly designate the three movements of Part 3 as a *Scherzo*, all are in quick tempos (*Allegro impetuoso*, *Allegretto grazioso*, and *Allegretto molto mosso*) and bustling rhythms reminiscent of the scherzo-like "Hymn" of the *Serenade for Tenor, Horn, and Strings*, op. 31. This segment of the symphony may well serve as an exemplar for Britten's approach as a whole. The three texts

Table 4.4 Britten, *Spring Symphony*, op. 44, texts

Mvt. 1:.	a. Introduction (Anon.)
	b. "The Merry Cuckoo" (Edmund Spenser)
	c. "Spring" (Thomas Nashe)
	d. "The Driving Boy" (George Peele and John Clare)
	e. "The Morning Star" (John Milton)
Mvt. 2:	f. "Welcome Maids of Honour" (Robert Herrick)
	g. "Waters Above" (Henry Vaughan)
	h. "Out on the Lawn I Lie in Bed" (W. H. Auden)
Mvt. 3:	i. "When will my May come?" (Richard Barnefield)
	j. "Fair and Fair" (George Peele)
	k. "Sound the Flute" (William Blake)
Mvt 4:	l. Finale: "London, to Thee I do present" (Beaumont and Fletcher)
	Reading Rota ("Sumer is icumen in")

are each given their own unique vocal and instrumental color. All are musically linked, the sustained A′ of the tenor that concludes Part 3, no. 1, defines the tonality of the ensuing duet, and the conclusion of that duet connects [*attaca*] to the opening sonority of the ending chorus (A–B–C♯). Despite a signature of two flats (implying G minor), the tenor melody never adopts that key and ends on a sustained A′. The primary accompaniment for the sung text is a bitonal harp accompaniment, prefaced and interrupted by similar music for the strings. Noteworthy is Britten's decision to set the first two sestinas as identical strophes dominated by periodic phrasing and the presence of palindromic perfect fourths.

Britten sets the two stanzas of "Fair and Fair" in an ABA form. In the first A section, the soprano and tenor sing lines 1–4 and 5–8 respectively to the same music, then they repeat the process, the soprano singing lines 9–15 to a new melody, only the last phrase of which is sung (transposed) by the tenor. For the second stanza, Britten has both voices sing the same music in close canon (one eighth-note separation) save for the final two lines of text, which are sung in unison. While there is a prominent string ostinato on a second inversion A-major triad, the music migrates far afield at the prompting of the obbligato woodwind parts.

The final poem, "Sound the Flute," is similarly ambiguous tonally, unified primarily by the persistent rhythmic ostinato of the orchestra (reminiscent of Holst's *The Planets* and *Hymn of Jesus*). The poem's three strophes are sung by separate choral groups: male voices (v. 1), female voices (v. 2), and boys' choir (v. 3); each of these vocal ensembles has its own separate instrumental color (brass, woodwinds, and strings respectively). The only tutti music comes as the female and then the male voices join the boys for the final line of their text, bringing with them their own orchestral ensembles.

The Finale lives up to its title and placement by bringing all of the forces together in a single large movement. Britten composes a strange little waltz (reminiscent of the *Ländler* in Mahler's Second Symphony), oddly accompanied by a cow horn, whose obstinately relentless C′ unites rural society with the sophisticated population of London and lends musical focus to the movement's diverse texts. With typical panache Britten makes this unusual blend of music and text work, only to reveal at the movement's end that everything heard to that point was preparation for the boys' choir's singing of the famous *Soomer is icoomin' in, Loode sing cuckoo*. This is Britten's orthography as found in the score; the text in the symphony's prefatory material uses the more traditional spelling (*Sumer is icumen in, Lhude sing cuccu*).

The specific reference to the cuckoo in this well-known tune may have provided Britten with the symphony's most prominent textual and musical image—the cuckoo's song. We find textual references to it in Spenser's sonnet (*The Merry Cuckoo*, mvt. 1, b), the refrain of *Spring* (mvt. 1, c), and the finale. Britten subsequently uses the descending third of the cuckoo's song in four other places that lack this textual prompt. Whether the result of conscious planning or not, this motive shows up in the conclusion of each movement of the symphony (ex. 4.15).

Example 4.15 a–i Britten, *Spring Symphony*, op. 44

a. part 1, no. 2, mm. 1-3

b. part 1, no. 3, m. 12

c. part 1, no. 4, mm. 42-43

d. part 5, no. 5, mm. 5-7

e. pt. 3, no. 3, m. 22

f. pt. 4, mm. 86-87

g. pt. 4, mm. 205-12

Example 4.15 a–i Continued

Britten uses this motive's distinctive minor third in both *rectus* and *inversus* forms, setting texts that, for the most part, lack any textual reason for doing so.

While generally consonant, Britten's music is not tonal in the traditional sense. It is no surprise, then, that individual movements often conclude in a different tonality than they began, despite the continuous presence of traditional key signatures. Britten's processes of thematic and harmonic development create a singular logic that mitigates differences of pitch center. In Parts 3 and 4, harmonic progression is dictated by the same interval (minor thirds: [G–E and A–C respectively]) used in the cuckoo motive. The movements of Part 2 encompass both major (D–B♭/A♯) and minor (B♭/G minor) versions of that interval. If one overlooks the introductory chorus, Part 1 moves from D to F and includes several third relationships between movements (e.g., F♯ [mvt. 1, part b] to A7 [mvt. 1, part c], A7 [mvt. 1, part c] to F [mvt. 1, part d] and F [mvt. 1, part e.] to D [the opening sonority of part 2]). With Britten, one never assumes that such occurrences are coincidental. Such tonal planning, whether representative of the cuckoo motive or not, reflects a larger symphonic design.

SHOSTAKOVICH, BERNSTEIN, AND BERIO

Although there are numerous symphonies that can be regarded as "choral" (such as Karol Szymanowski's "Song of the Night," op. 27), only the choral symphonies of Dmitri Shostakovich (1906–75), Leonard Bernstein (1918–90), and Luciano Berio (1925–2003) will be discussed here.

LEONARD BERNSTEIN

Bernstein's Third Symphony ("Kaddish") from 1963 clearly follows the Beethoven-Mahler model. As music director of the New York Philharmonic Orchestra from 1958 to 1969, Bernstein knew the symphonic repertory inside and out, including the choral symphonies of Beethoven and Mahler; in fact Bernstein played a major role in the rebirth of Mahler's music in the second half of the twentieth century (Fig. 4.2). Like Mahler, Bernstein uses the voice in several of his symphonic works. In first symphony, "Jeremiah" (1942), he uses a mezzo-soprano soloist. The human voice—whether as soloist in his First Symphony or both chorally and narratively in the Third—becomes a sub-text for all of Bernstein's symphonies: man's search for faith. As Bernstein remarked:

> Although everything I write seems to have literary or dramatic underpin-ning, it is, after all, music that I am writing. Whatever happens in the music happens because of what the music does, not because of the words or the extramusical ideas.... The work I have been writing all my life is about the struggle that is born of the crisis of our century, a crisis of faith. Even way back, when I wrote JEREMIAH, I was wrestling with that problem. The faith or peace that is found at the end of JEREMIAH is really more a kind of com-fort, not a solution. Comfort is one way of achieving peace, but it does not achieve the sense of a new beginning, as does the end of AGE OF ANXIETY (Symphony No. 2, 1947-9) or MASS [emphasis in all capitals is Bernstein's].[31]

Fig. 4.2 Leonard Bernstein (1970)

His quest for answers to the questions precipitated by a crisis of faith culminates in the Third Symphony, which takes its name and some of its textual content from the Jewish prayer for the dead that routinely closes the sabbath service. The word "Kaddish" means "exaltation," and this symphony's four movements explore how topics as diverse as crisis, faith, and death can become the basis of exaltation.

The traditional sequence of four movements obscures a deeper ternary design based on Bernstein's use of the "Mourner's Kaddish" (in mvts. 1, 2 and 3-4). Scored for speaker, boys' choir, mixed chorus, and large orchestra, the symphony features sonorities and devices found in more familiar works such as *Chichester Psalms* (1965) and *Mass* (1971). Of these, it is the speaker who talks with God, often in ways that are as untraditional (even heretical) as the "Un-Credo" of the *Mass*. Hints of *Chichester Psalms* are heard in the frequent use of 7/8 meter (in fast tempo) and the presence of four percussionists (plus timpani). Conspicuously different is the symphony's harmonic language, which at times involves twelve-tone rows. Even before the first appearance of a tone row, Bernstein makes a textual allusion to Arnold Schoenberg; the initiator of twelve-tone rows. Bernstein's symphony opens with nearly the same words that close Schoenberg's Modern Psalm, op. 50: "Lord, teach me how to pray."

The first motive of the symphony's opening movement features a distinctive pitch class set, which the first violins extend by adding minor sevenths (ex. 4.16a) prior to its combination with a violin countertheme (ex. 4.16b). The orchestra introduces the first of two tone rows (ex. 4.16c) precisely where the tempo changes to *Allegro molto* and the meter takes up the characteristic Bernstein 7/8 lilt; when repeated, Bernstein combines the row with a distinctive choral countermotive (ex. 4.16d).

Example 4.16 a–e Bernstein, Symphony No. 3, "Kaddish," mvt. 1
© Copyright 1963, 1965, 1977, 1980. Copyright assigned to Amberson Holdings LLC, Leonard Bernstein Music Publishing Co., LLC, Publisher.

Bernstein has laid out the principal motivic content of the first movement in this brief space; what follows is a process similar to that used in the *Chichester Psalms*—repetition (literal and transposed) and reworking of this basic material to grow the movement. Even Bernstein's tone row is treated with less than the pristine consistency advocated by Schoenberg, using only several of the forty-eight versions available within the standard twelve-tone matrix.

The second movement begins with a percussion riff, followed by a variant of counter-theme 1, followed at m. 25 by the nucleus of a second tone row (ex. 4.16e). As before, the exposition of this theme involves extensive development featuring inversion and fragmentation of the principal themes. Beginning in m. 45, Bernstein reprises this opening theme in a vocal stretto (ex. 4.17a) that establishes a new direction for development (ex. 4.17b).

Example 4.17 a/b Bernstein, Symphony No. 3, "Kaddish," mvt. 2
© Copyright 1963, 1965, 1977, 1980. Copyright assigned to Amberson Holdings LLC, Leonard Bernstein Music Publishing Co., LLC, Publisher.

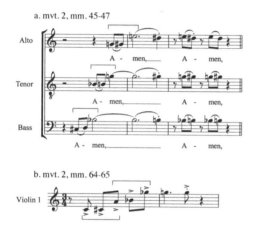

Bernstein titles the conclusion of this movement *Kaddish 2*. It is another of Bernstein's re-creations of the Mahler-like Adagios he knew so well and loved; scored for soprano solo, strings, and harp, it is both precursor to the middle movement of *Chichester Psalms* and his own take on the Adagietto of Mahler's *Fifth Symphony*, a work he revived and made popular in the 1970s.

The Scherzo of Bernstein's symphony, however, contains the richest thematic development. The principal motive of the first movement, row 1 (ex. 4.16c) and the consecutive sevenths of countertheme 1 (ex. 4.16d) all appear, tossed back and forth amid music whose unbending *pianissimo* bustle recalls the middle movement of Dallapiccola's *Canti di Prigionia*. Starting in m. 229, Bernstein gives us the final piece of his thematic puzzle, a broad Coplandesque melody that dominates the remainder of the movement even as it struggles against the return of fragments of earlier motives (once again, like the second movement of *Chichester Psalms*). Some daunting choral writing remains following the last words of the speaker (m. 322). Unlike Mahler, the vocal and instrumental components are equal partners in the presentation of the "message" of Bernstein's Third Symphony.

DMITRI SHOSTAKOVICH

Among Dmitri Shostakovich's fifteen symphonies are several that include voices. The composer was out of favor with the Soviet regime in the 1950s but underwent a transformation in the late fifties and early sixties. One of the works responsible for his change of status in the early 1960s was his Symphony No. 13 ("Babi Yar"), inspired by the poems of the young Russian poet Yevgeny Yevtushenko (b. 1933). In the article "How Music Is Born," Shostakovich discusses how art and literature contribute to creative thought: "Various kinds of art other than music can often prompt a subject for a work. We know, for instance, that *Pictures from an Exhibition* were inspired by Mussorgsky's impressions of painting. It is natural for a composer to look to literature, painting, cinema and theatre for ideas . . . my latest, Thirteenth Symphony and 'Execution of Stepan Razin' were inspired by Yevtushenko's poems."[32]

This symphony began as a discrete composition for bass solo, unison male chorus, and orchestra completed in April 1962; in Shostakovich's catalogue of new works, this one is listed simply as "Babi Yar." Shostakovich understandably set this one poem since Yevtushenko's reputation mirrored his own in many ways: both were antiestablishment types whose dissidence potentially placed them in harm's way. Yevtushenko's "Babi Yar" is probably his best-known poem; it protests the Soviet government's refusal to recognize the mass murder of 33,000 Jews in the city of Kiev at the end of September 1941. Given the subject, the music is appropriately dark and grim, dominated by brass and woodwind color with only a baritone soloist and a unison male chorus to declaim the text.

Eventually Shostakovich added four additional movements, all based on poems by Yevtushenko. Shostakovich amalgamated these four poems into a scherzo-like second movement and a large finale that involves three poems numbered separately in the score but performed without pause. The Moscow Philharmonic, bass soloist Vitaly Gromadsky, and the bass sections of the Republican State Choir and the Choir of the Gnessin Institute, conducted by Kiril Kondrashin, premiered the symphony on December 18, 1962. The work is scored for large orchestra and a unison chorus of 140 singers.

The added poems by Yevtushenko are "Humor" (mvt. 2), "In the Store," "Fear," and "Careers." All the settings have English titles, but the poems are in Russian. Particularly interesting is the second movement, "Humor"; although it is marked *Allegretto*, it has a more of a Scherzo-like character, the music aptly portraying the gallows humor in music reminiscent of the tenor and baritone duet, "Out there, we've walked quite friendly up to Death" from Britten's *War Requiem*. Shostakovich realizes "Humor" through a bitonal interplay between C major and other pitch collections that show signs of octatonic organization. The three continuous movements that make up the "finale" are tonally ambiguous but linked together by retained pitches that connect one to the next:

Title	Key Signature/Harmony	Starting pitch	Final pitch
3. "In the Store"	1 sharp (E minor/G major)	B	A♭
4. "Fear"	No sig. (G♯ pedal)	A♭/G♯	B♭
5. "A Career"	2 flats, 1 sharp	B♭	B♭
	(B♭/G minor)		+ G♭ and A♭

LUCIANO BERIO

Sinfonia, a singularly unique work by Luciano Berio (1925–2003), was commissioned in 1968 by the New York Philharmonic to celebrate their 125th anniversary; as part of the commission, Berio was asked to include vocal music for the Swingle Singers. To the original four movements, Berio added a fifth movement in 1969. He inferred the work's title did not imply any connection with the classical genre of the symphony. Rather, he meant "Sinfonia" to suggest the

Fig. 4.3 Luciano Berio (ca. 1990s)

etymological sense of the word, that is, the "sounding together" of voices (eight amplified soloists) and symphony orchestra. This conception extends the traditional understanding of both the
choral and symphonic elements to include both separate performance and simultaneous interaction between the two groups. The texts Berio chose are emblematic of what he called his "New
Vocalism," a recognition of his attachment to texts of high literary value and the virtuoso singing
necessary to render those texts audible. But textual audibility or a clear understanding of the text
was not his goal. Unlike all of the other works discussed in this chapter, Berio intends that there
will be moments when the texts are not necessarily heard or understandable (Fig. 4.3).

Berio draws the texts of his first three movements from three diverse sources, another
indication of his nontraditional approach to the genre. The first movement uses fragments of
Claude Lévi-Strauss's anthropology book *Le cru et le cuit* (1965), in which the author discusses
Brazilian myths about the origin of water. For the second movement Berio does a phonemic
deconstruction of "O Martin Luther King"; initially inchoate, the name of the celebrated civil
rights leader gradually emerges from the phonemic babble. David Osmond-Smith points out
that the simple, apostrophic text "O Martin Luther King":

> is gradually assembled from its phonetic components as the piece proceeds.
> Berio starts with all the vowels from this text, and assembles them in anti-
> clockwise order; he then separates them into two anticlockwise triangles of the
> sort discussed above in relation to *Sequenza III*, follows this with a clockwise

and anticlockwise triangle, and finally states the two clockwise triangles that form the correct vowel sequence of the text. . . . With the vowels in place, Berio starts to add the consonants, proceeding from the vowel-like voiced consonants to the more disruptive unvoiced ones.[33]

This complex, rather arcane technique can be understood only by reconstructing Berio's process. The first twenty-one measures of the first soprano part contain no consonants, only an inscrutable series of vowels. If, however, one assigns each vowel its IPA (International Phonetic Alphabet) symbol, then the series of phonemes becomes a kind of shorthand for the movement's text "O Martin Luther King." To some extent, a separate sequence of pitches, which rotate in a different cycle, acts to clarify the otherwise random phonemes. This description applies to only one of the eight voice parts; incomplete by itself, this part requires the content of the other voices to gain a semblance of meaning, taking no account of the separate layer of instrumental sonorities. Only now we can begin to have some sense of the complexity of the scheme.

For his third movement Berio uses a text from Samuel Beckett's *The Unnamable*. Here, phrases of text generate a series of reflections and semantic constructions reminiscent of James Joyce's *Ulysses*.[34] The fourth and fifth movements are content to draw their texts from two of the first three movements, which Berio distributes as random phonemic collages. In the fourth movement the orchestra does its own deconstruction, in this case using the minuet of Mahler's Second Symphony as its starting point. As the movement progresses, the audibility of Mahler's music is gradually overwhelmed by the intrusion of quotations from an array of landmark instrumental compositions. By juxtaposing Mahler's music with these in a kaleidoscopic manner, Berio creates a quasi-Cubist collage. These quotations interact with and are grafted onto Mahler's music, creating less a quodlibet of familiar and not-so-familiar themes than Berio's assessment of Mahler's symphonies within the history of symphonic music. Alfred Schnittke gives a complete list of these orchestral excerpts in one of the articles that comprise *The Alfred Schnittke Reader*.

CONCLUSION

This chapter's discussion of works for chorus and orchestra is titled "choral symphony," and so it is both an ironic twist of music history and a fitting evolutionary path for a century dominated by cyclic forms—the song cycle, "cycles" of programmatic piano music, and, ultimately, Friedrich Nietzsche's notion of *Ewiges Verkehr* ("Eternal Return"). We have already discussed the history and development of the Mass in the eighteenth and nineteenth centuries in vol. 1, chap. 12, of this book. The focus there was on the ways composers adapted symphonic thinking to setting the words of the Latin Mass. The hard-fought battles over the relative balance between what Charles Rosen described as "expressive" and "celebrative" text settings resulted in the emergence of symphonic music as the clear "winner."[35] With the advent of choral symphonies, it seems that the tables had been turned, for choral music exacted some measure of revenge for its earlier sublimation. By the time Beethoven composed his Ninth Symphony, he had reached the conclusion that the so-called absolute music was insufficient to express his "feelings," that only text and the human voice could elevate musical expression to the level of discourse he desired.

From that point on, the Ninth Symphony and the *Missa Solemnis*, its sister work, became benchmarks against which, most people agree, other choral-orchestral music is measured. The concert Masses by Schubert, Bruckner, Berlioz, and Liszt blend imperceptibly into the emerging body of music for chorus and orchestra that had the solemnity of the oratorio without being obliged to tell sacred stories. In the case of the choral symphony, each composer sought (usually in vain) to match Beethoven's achievement. Of the works that are nominally symphonic, the clearest pretender is Mendelssohn's Symphony in B♭, op. 52, while the choral symphonic works of both Berlioz and Liszt are consigned to some nether world that defies easy categorization. It is only with the symphonies of Mahler that Beethoven's grand concept was successfully taken up, but by this time the nature of the symphony itself had changedg dramatically due to the inclusion of words either tangentially (as a literary program) or directly (as texts sung by either vocal soloists and/or chorus).

The continuation of the choral symphony in the twentieth century is less a matter of aesthetic necessity than a testament to the increasingly diffuse meaning that the word "symphony" conjures up. The combination of voices with orchestral music is no longer a novelty; instead, it marks not only the increasing reality of the necessary coexistence of orchestras and choruses but also the continuing penchant for composers to provide music to celebrate this collaboration.

5

French Choral Music from Debussy to Messiaen

The twentieth century could not wait fifteen years for a round number; it was born, yelling, in 1885.

Roger Shattuck, *The Banquet Years*

France has witnessed several revolutions that reshaped, one way or another, Western culture. The French Revolution of the eighteenth century produced the Reign of Terror that sent shock waves through the royal houses of Europe. In the 1840s another revolution, immortalized by Victor Hugo in *Les Misérables*, pitted the "haves" against the "have-nots." This penchant for revolution took musical form in the renunciation of traditional culture and esthetic values by French artists of the late nineteenth century. Four traits define the French artistic movement commonly known as the avant-garde:

1. Rejection of "maturity" in favor of a childlike wonder, simplicity, and candor, personified in Arthur Rimbaud's synesthetic concept of the "child-man."

2. An ability, born as caricature and parody but transformed into absurdity, to laugh at the overly serious and poke fun at the establishment. Classical logic's "reductio ad absurdum" as a means of proving truth is replaced by the absence of *a priori* values that marks modern existence.

3. An alternative consciousness, encountered naturally in dreaming or the euphoria/hallucination induced by mind-altering substances increasingly encountered among avant-garde artists.

4. A deliberate ambiguity or equivocal interpretation of meanings for any given sound or symbol. Such ambiguity results from the convergence of the three preceding attitudes.[1]

Roger Shattuck aligns the role that ambiguity plays with several prominent artists working in different disciplines: "For the symbolists—Mallarmé above all—language was endowed with a mystery of meaning that increased with the number of different directions in which each word could point. Jarry ... [maintained] that all meanings that can be discovered in a text are equally legitimate. There is no single true meaning, banishing other faulty ones."[2]

CLAUDE DEBUSSY (1862–1918)

In music, ambiguity took the form of an increasing disinterest in traditional tonality. Shattuck found this attitude most clearly embodied in Erik Satie's preference for modal scales and imperfect cadences, attributes that also appeared in the music of Claude Debussy, even in such a relatively unrepresentative work as the *Trois Chansons de Charles d'Orléans* (1898). The first of these, *Dieu! Qu'il la fait bon regarder!*, epitomizes Debussy's neomodal style (ex. 5.1).

Example 5.1   Debussy, *Trois Chansons de Charles d'Orléans*, no. 1, mm. 1–5
Clifford Bartlett, ed. *Madrigals and Partsongs* © Oxford University Press 2001.
Used by permission. All rights reserved. Photocopying of this material is ILLEGAL.

The key signature of five sharps normally indicates either B major or G♯ minor, but Debussy's music is in neither key: his harmonies oscillate between F♯ major and C♯ minor. While F♯ is the dominant of B major (the putative tonic), there is no cadence to B. Despite the key signature, Debussy asserts that F♯ is the tonic and C♯ its minor dominant. The scale on which Debussy based his composition is neither major nor minor but the Mixolydian mode beginning on F♯:

F♯′–G♯′–A♯′–B′–C♯″–D♯″–E″–F♯″

Any sense of tonality is further weakened by parallel chord progressions that avoided the functional harmonies associated with tonality (ex. 5.2).

Example 5.2 Debussy, *Trois Chansons de Charles d'Orléans*, no. 1, mm. 17–19
Clifford Bartlett, ed. *Madrigals and Partsongs* © Oxford University Press 2001.

This melody, also seen in mm. 6–9 and mm. 23–25, embraces another ambiguity by its alternation between A♮ and A♯; depending on which pitch Debussy uses, the music fluctuates between F♯ Dorian (A♮) and F♯ Mixolydian (A♯).

Then there is the text—a poem by Charles D'Orléans (1394–1465), royally connected and one of the last great French courtly poets; he was captured at the Battle of Agincourt in 1415 and held captive (yet luxuriously) for twenty-five years in England.[3] Part of Debussy's fascination with the poems of D'Orléans was their antiquity, which, Debussy believed, made them strikingly contemporary. They were written in an earlier time when France was under the yoke of a foreign power (as she had been to Germany since the Franco-Prussian War of the early 1870s). The text's very antiquity provided a pretext for Debussy's use of modality, a harmonic system that had the added benefit of *not* being German.

Debussy employed another historical reference in the second chanson, *Quant j'ai ouy le tabourin sonner*, where the chorus accompanies the mezzo-soprano soloist with onomatopoeic imitations of drum sounds (*tabourin*). Debussy likely heard a performance of Janequin's program chanson *La Guerre* by the *Association chorale professionelle* in March 1914. Following that performance, Debussy wrote that Janequin's masterpiece "conveys all the hubbub and the rough way of life at an army camp. It is noted down shout by shout, noise by noise: the sound of the horses' hooves mingles with the fanfares of trumpets in a subtly ordered tumult. Its form is so direct that it would almost seem to be 'popular music,' so accurate and picturesque is the musical representation of these events."[4]

The opening measures of Debussy's *Quant j'ai ouy le tabourin sonner*, mimic Janequin's musical onomatopoeia. A similar type of rhythmic patter appeared in two of the *Trois Chansons* by Debussy's younger contemporary, Maurice Ravel (1875–1937).[5] Ravel's music, especially his keyboard music, shows more indebtedness to historic French composers like François Couperin and Jean-Philippe Rameau than Debussy's had.

Choral music is scarce in Ravel's output, but Debussy composed quite a bit of it, even if little is known today. These works include several orchestrally accompanied compositions for women's chorus, of which the largest is *La Damoiselle Élue* (1887), based on Dante Gabriel Rossetti's poem of the same name and scored for mezzo-soprano, women's chorus, and orchestra.[6] Two other works, *Salut Printemps* (1882) and the third of his *Nocturnes*, *Sirènes* (1897–99) follow, the latter using the same key signature and tonal center as the first of the *Trois Chansons*.

Debussy's least-known choral work is perhaps the most fascinating—*Le Martyre de Saint Sébastien*, composed in 1911 as incidental music for Gabriele d'Annunzio's play. The

Russian dancer Ida Rubenstein choreographed the work with Michel Fokine and Leon Bakst provided the sets. Both Fokine and Bakst were associates of Diaghilev's *Ballets Russes*, which produced Stravinsky's *The Rite of Spring* two years later. Like *The Rite*, its notorious successor, *Le Martyre* sparked controversy by blending a story of Christian martyrdom with tinges of neopaganism and Hellenistic secularism. When the bishop of Paris learned that the seductive Ida Rubinstein would dance the part of Sebastian as an androgynous, even blasphemous personification of the saint, he forbade Catholics to attend the performance. From this stage work Debussy crafted a kind of secular oratorio in five parts (following the five acts of the play). Each of these—*Le Cour de Lys* (The Court of Lilies), *La Chambre Magique* (The Magic Chamber), *Le Concile des Faux Dieux* (The Council of the False Gods), *Le Laurier Blessé* (The Wounded Laurel), and *Le Paradis* (Paradise)—is introduced by a narrator, who describes the action about to take place. If heard at all today, *Le Martyre* survives as an orchestral suite of tableaux.

DEBUSSY'S PREDECESSORS

Martin Cooper identifies five dominant composers active in France between 1918 and 1937: Charles Gounod (1818–93), César Franck (1822–90), Camille Saint-Saëns (1835–1921), Georges Bizet (1838–75), and Emmanuel Chabrier (1841–94).[7] Of these, Chabrier composed no choral works. His opposite was the prolific Charles Gounod, Mendelssohn's successor as the favored composer of English choral societies. To some extent, Gounod's experience as conductor of the choral society *Orphéon* between 1852 and 1860 accounted for his expertise as a choral composer. Among his best works were those written specifically for the Birmingham Festival—the sacred trilogies *La Rédemption* (1882) and *Mors et Vita* (1885). More popular were the *Messe Solennelle de Sainte Cécile* (1855) and the melody he wrote for *Ave Maria* (1859), accompanied by the flowing arpeggios of Bach's C-major prelude (BWV 846).

None of the other three composers match the size of Gounod's choral output. Bizet's most-recognized choral music appears in his opera *Carmen* (1875); Saint-Saëns's best-known piece is the *Oratorio de Noël* (1863), an accessible work dominated by operatic solo writing. Although more widely esteemed for his organ works than his choral output, César Franck produced several important pieces, including four oratorios; the foremost of these is *Les Béatitudes* (1869–79), a work that deserves contemporary performance. Franck's adept use of hymn-like melodies as the bases for his monumental organ trilogy *Trois Chorales* (1890), along with his Symphony in D minor, the violin sonata, and other motivically inspired works, gives insight into his masterful ability to compose "absolute" music in more than one genre. Richard Taruskin's succinct and possibly best description of Franck's fingerprint states: "These slithery harmonies, directing myriad recombinations of charged motivic particles on their trajectory through musical space, produce an effect even more like that of a Wagnerian music drama . . . thus supremely realizing the objective of 'absolute' music: to say what is unsayable, to speak the unspeakable."[8]

Perhaps Franck's most enduring legacy was the impressive body of students he attracted to the Paris Conservatoire (beginning in 1872). These included the song composers Ernst Chausson (1855–99) and Henri DuParc (1848–1933), the organists Alexandre Guilmant (1837–1911) and Charles Bordes (1863–1909), and Vincent d'Indy (1851–1931). These last two founded the *Schola Cantorum* (originally called the *École de Chant, Liturgique et de Musique Religieuse*) in 1894 to train a new generation of French church musicians. Bordes and d'Indy subsequently hired Franck away from the Conservatoire to become the teacher of Gabriele Pierné (1863–1937), Charles Tournemire (1870–1939), and Louis Vierne (1870–1937). D'Indy became the director of the *Schola* in 1900, counting among his pupils Albert Roussel (1869–1937) and Paul Dukas

(1865–1935). Despite its lofty ideals to raise music from polite entertainment to serious art, the *Schola* exerted a somewhat conservative influence on French music and fostered new performances in Paris of such forgotten masters as Charpentier, Rameau, Lully, and Gluck, all of whom had, at that time, been sorely neglected.

GABRIEL FAURÉ (1845–1924)

Another name linked with Debussy is Gabriel Fauré, whose music bridged the end of romanticism and the stylistic Babel of the early twentieth century. Born while Berlioz was still alive, Fauré lived well into the twentieth century, serving as a teacher at the Paris Conservatoire (succeeding Massenet in 1896) and as its director (in 1905, succeeding Théodore Dubois). His pupils included Maurice Ravel, Florent Schmitt (1870–1958), Charles Koechlin (1867–1950), Georges Enescu (1881–1955), Jean Roger-Ducasse (1873–1954), and Nadia Boulanger (1887–1979).

Fauré's choral works include two relatively early sacred compositions—the *Cantique de Jean Racine* (op. 11, 1873) and his well-known and lovely *Requiem* (op. 48, 1887). The *Cantique*, Jean Racine's translation of a medieval hymn of unknown authorship, dates from the end of Fauré's tenure at the *École Niedermeyer*.[9] Perhaps Racine's position as a literary classicist had something to do with the form of Fauré's composition. Here, sectional lengths (verses and interludes) are nearly identical, and Fauré's tonalities outline the tonic (D♭) triad. The main melody, first heard in the introduction, has a single accidental (A♮ in m. 9) which effects a temporary modulation B♭ minor, the harmony that the B section ends with just prior to the return of A. Fauré's melodic construction relies on the repetition of two basic motifs (see ex. 5.3). The middle section (B) is similarly classical in the periodicity of its phrase construction (three four-measure phrases). In all of these respects, this composition discloses a balance that looks very much like a classical form.

Example 5.3 Fauré, *Cantique de Jean Racine*, op. 11, mm. 1–13
John Rutter, ed. *European Sacred Music* © Oxford University Press 1996 Used by permission. All rights reserved. Photocopying this copyright material is ILLEGAL.

Not as well known is Fauré's *Madrigal*, op. 35 (1884), a setting of Armande Silvestre's poem for mixed chorus and piano. Its simple harmonies and lush melodic writing make it deserving of more frequent performance.

Among the multitude of settings of the Requiem Mass, Fauré's (op. 48) is notable for its omission of the entire *Dies irae* sequence. But within the "Libera me," Fauré quotes the opening words of the sequence itself appear in a short but forceful reminder of hell's terror. Overall, the "Libera me" presents a serene, beatific view of the afterlife designed entirely to comfort those who mourn, rather than creating spiritual angst. In a conversation with Louis Aguettant in 1902, Fauré made his beliefs concerning the nature of his Requiem completely clear: "My Requiem ... people said it did not express the terror of death, someone called it a berceuse of death. But that is how I feel death: as a happy deliverance, a yearning for the happiness of the beyond, rather than as a distressing transition. . . . Perhaps also my instincts have led me to side-step convention as I have been accompanying burial services on the organ for so long! I cannot stand it any longer. I wanted to do something else."[10] Fauré's nondramatic approach informs the work's original orchestration of the four movements that comprise Fauré's autograph: lower strings (no violins save for a violin solo in the Sanctus), harp, timpani, and organ. These four movements (Introit/Kyrie, Sanctus, Agnus Dei, and "In Paradisum") were first performed for a funeral on January 16, 1888. The similarity of textual mood throughout may account for the relatively simple orchestration, but a note in Fauré's hand, penciled on the title page of the manuscript of the Agnus Dei, indicates that the orchestration was incomplete.[11]

Subsequently, the composer added pairs of trumpets and horns in May 1888. And for its public performance on May 17, 1894, Fauré added the "Offertoire," "Pie Jesu," and "Libera me," and revised the orchestration. Even this version lacks the full orchestration frequently heard today. Jean-Michel Nectoux reports that the version performed in Paris's L'église de la Madeleine (1888) involved approximately sixty musicians including the choir of men and boys, and supported with a small ten-rank organ located behind the altar.[12] A larger orchestration was subsequently made to increase the likelihood of the composition's performance by traditional orchestras.

Fauré was, above all, a melodist and this trait pervades his *Requiem*, which contains one beautiful melody after another, like the simple "Pie Jesu" and the poignant Agnus Dei, warmly accompanied by violas, divided cellos, and double basses (ex. 5.4).

Example 5.4 Fauré, *Requiem*, op. 48, Agnus Dei, mm. 7–12

Fauré's earlier protestations notwithstanding, it may well be that this lyrical approach was a major factor in his omission of a separate movement for the *Dies irae*, the sequence text that has attracted composers from the Middle Ages on, including it as part of the "Libera me."

THE RISE OF THE AVANT-GARDE—*LES SIX*

The classicism of Fauré presented yet another style against which Debussy and Ravel rebelled. Inevitably, they too became "classicists" of a sort, abandoning the avant-garde community created largely by Jean Cocteau (1889–1963), author, artist-designer, filmmaker, and aesthetician. Cocteau, in turn, promoted Erik Satie as titular head of the musical avant-garde. Satie shared this role with Jean Cocteau, the entrepreneur and creator of ballet scenarios for Milhaud's compositions *Le Boeuf sur le toit* and *Le train bleu*, as well as texts for Honegger (*Antigone*), Stravinsky (*Oedipus Rex*), and Poulenc (*La voix humaine*). It was Cocteau that created the scenario for *Les Maries de la Tour Eiffel* (1920–21), which marked the public introduction of *Les Six* (Fig. 5.1). Together, they collaborated on *Parade* (1916–17), a work in which everything—from its inchoate scenario, use of multimedia, surrealist/cubist costumes and scenery to its futuristic noise-making mixture of ragtime and jazz—seemed contrived to offend someone, anyone. But none of Satie's other compositions (he wrote practically no choral music[13]) account for his role as mentor to the French composers collectively known as *Les Six*: Arthur Honegger (1892–1955), Darius Milhaud (1892–1974), Francis Poulenc (1899–1963), Germaine Tailleferre (1892–1983), Louis Durey (1888–1979), and Georges Auric (1899–1983).

Fig. 5.1 Les Six at the Eiffel Tower in 1921
l–r: Tailleferre, Poulenc, Honegger, Milhaud, Cocteau, Auric.

Only three of *Les Six* produced significant amounts of choral music: Honegger, Poulenc, and Milhaud. Arthur Honegger is chiefly known today for his oratorios *Jeanne d'Arc au bûcher* (1935) and *Le Roi David* (1921). *Le Roi David* began as incidental music for René Morax's play of the same name. In order to insure the life of his music life beyond this play, Honegger converted it into a kind of oratorio or, to use his designation, a *psaume symphonique*. Liberated from the play's supporting narrative, Honegger needed to add a narrator and expand the orchestration from the original pit band to a full symphony orchestra.[14]

The work consists of three parts that vary in length (Table 5.1). The list of movements illustrates the basic theatricality of Honegger's conception, especially instrumental sections like the fanfare and entrance music for Goliath (no. 3), and the instrumental underscore to the "Incantation" which involves the Witch of Endor and the ghost of Samuel (no. 12); Honegger labeled this section a "melodrama." The brevity of many of the movements is further evidence of the work's theatrical origins. Nonetheless, the longest movement is the 305 mm. of "The Dance before the Ark," (no. 16); of the rest, the next longest movement is no. 14, "The Lamentations at Gilboa" at just 72 mm.

Of the twenty vocal movements, six are solos for soprano, alto, and tenor; another five blend soloist(s) and chorus. The second and third movements present strikingly different aspects of Honegger's style. In *Cantique du Berger David*, a young shepherd sings a simple melody (based on E and C♯ minor) in ABA form. The accompaniment has multiple layers—oscillating, slow-moving chords in the bass, a palindromic, chromatic tenor line, and an instrumental descant comprising equally still chromatic lines moving in contrary motion (ex. 5.5).

Table 5.1 Honegger, *Le Roi David*, structure

Part 1:

1. Orchestral Introduction
2. *Cantique du berger David* (A)
3. *Psaume: Loué soit le Seigneur* (unison chorus)
3. Fanfare and *Entrée de Goliath* (repeat)
4. *Chant de Victoire* (satb)
5. *Cortège* (orchestra)
6. *Psaume: Ne crains rien* (T)
7. *Psaume: Ah! Si j'avais des ailes de colombe* (S)
8. *Cantique des Prophètes* (tb)
9. *Psaume: Pitié de moi, mon Dieu* (T)
10. *Le camp de Saül* (orchestra)
11. *Psaume: L'Éternel est ma lumiére infinie* (satb)
12. *Incantation* (Witch of Endor [spkr] and Samuel [spkr])
13. *Marche des Philistins* (orchestra)
14. *Lamentations de Guilboa* (S, A, and satb)

Part 2:

15. *Cantique de fête* (S and ssa)
16. *La danse devant l'Arche* (soli, satb, and dancers)

Part 3:

17. *Cantique: De mon coeur jaillit un cantique* (satb)
18. *Chante de la servante* (A)
19. *Psaume de pénitence* (satb)
20. *Psaume: Je fus conçu dans la pêche* (satb)
21. *Psaume: Je lève mes regards vers la montagnes* (T)
22. *La chanson d'Ephraïm* (S and ssa)
23. *Marche des Hébreux* (orchestra)
24. *Psaume: Je t'aimerai, Seigneur, d'un amour tendre* (satb)
25. *Psaume: Dans cet effroi* (satb)
26. *Couronnement de Salomon* (orchestra)
27. *La mort de David* (S and satb)

Example 5.5 a–b Honegger, *Le Roi David*, no. 2

a. mm. 2-6

b. mm. 1-6

The choral psalm, *Loué soit le Seigneur* (no. 3), is the work's simplest, most tonal piece. Honegger sets the psalm text to a vigorous melody sung by the unison chorus, accompanied by a neo-Baroque instrumental bass line and occasional trumpet scales that punctuate cadences.[15]

The "Alleluia," first heard at the end of "The Dance before the Ark," (no. 16) and again at the work's conclusion (ex. 5.6) is especially memorable.

Example 5.6 Honegger, *Le Roi David*, no. 27, mm. 46–51

This melody first appears in a soprano obbligato ("Angels"), then successively in the three upper choral voices. All present their melody as counterpoint to David's earlier melody for "And God said: One day shall dawn, Bringing a flower newly born," which bears a striking resemblance to the chorale "Wie schön leuchtet der Morgenstern." In both movements, Honegger employs a static accompaniment of flowing sixteenths that outline part of the pentatonic scale, which relies on enharmonic modulation to create new sonorities.

Honegger's other choral works are also large symphonic pieces like *Le Roi David*; he even christened *Jeanne d'Arc au bûcher* (1935) a "dramatic oratorio." Of his more conventional choral-orchestral works the best known is probably *Une cantate de Noël* (1953) for chorus, children's choir, and orchestra, a work of Bachian influence in its use of chorale-like melodies.

DARIUS MILHAUD (1892–1974)

While this composer's choral output is larger than that of any other member of *Les Six*, much of his music is either unknown or seldom performed today. Forty-three choral works have assigned opus numbers; fifteen of these require vocal soloists, chorus, and symphony orchestra. The *Service sacré*, op. 279 (1947); *Lekha Dodi*, op. 290 (1948); *Cantate de l'initiation (Bar Mitzvah Israël)*, op. 388 (1960); the Holocaust cantata *Le château de feu* op. 338 (1954); and *Ani maamin, un chant perdu et retrouvé*, op. 441 (1972) all employ Hebrew texts. Several other choral works also use biblical themes, for example, *Borechou–Schema Israël* (Bless Ye the Lord–O Hear, Israel) for cantor, chorus, and organ, op. 239 (1944). Other important larger works include the cantatas *Les miracles de la foi* (The miracles of faith, op. 314, 1952), *Cantate pour le louer le Seigneur* (op. 103, 1928), and the *Cantate de la guerre* (op. 213, 1940) for mixed chorus *a cappella*.

Perhaps Milhaud's most revolutionary choral writing occurs in the dramatic trilogy of operas based on Greek mythology (translated into French by Paul Claudel): *Agamemnon* (op. 14, 1913), *Les Choéphores* (op. 24, 1915–16), and *Les Euménides* (op. 41, 1917–23). In *Les Choéphores*, Milhaud constructs a series of three hair-raising movements for speech chorus and narrator (accompanied only by percussion including sirens), who recite the text rhythmically. This brief excerpt from the work's fourth movement, *Présages*, only hints at the power of dramatic expression that this seemingly simple music possesses (ex. 5.7).

Example 5.7 Milhaud, *Les Choéphores*, op. 24, mvt. 4, *Présages*, mm. 26–29

Given its origin early in the twentieth century, the dramatic, quasi-savage music of *Les Choéphores* promised that Milhaud was a progressive, visionary compositional force to be reckoned with. Milhaud's trilogy follows close on the heels of two other landmark works: Richard Strauss's opera *Elektra*, op. 58 (1906–8), and Igor Stravinsky's ballet *The Rite of Spring* (1913), both of which are sensual and violent. Both Stravinsky and Milhaud are intent on crafting musical presentations of ritual that are unrelentingly expressionistic.

Milhaud also composed an impressive array of smaller, mostly *a cappella* choral works; these include several choral cantatas based on the poetry of Paul Claudel, the most prominent of which is *Les Deux Cités*, op. 170 (1937). A different sort of work is *Les Momies d'Egypte*, op. 439 (1972), a twentieth-century revival of the madrigal comedy genre. Commissioned by the chamber choir of Graz Academy in Austria, this work brings back the tradition of Vecchi (*L'Amfiparnasso*) or Banchieri (*Il festino*), except that all of the characters are portrayed by the chorus. Although the majority of the text is French, there are some Italian words and character names such as Harlequin, Colombine, and Lépine (also known as *Scaramouche*) that clearly point to the *Commedia dell' arte* as Milhaud's source of inspiration. Considering the extreme difficulties of the vocal writing—angular melodic lines, rapid textual declamation, complex rhythms, dynamic extremes, and dissonant harmony—it is understandable why modern performances are rare. Also worthy of mention is Milhaud's setting of Psalm 121 (122), composed for and premiered by the Harvard Glee Club in 1922. This compelling setting of the Paul

Claudel's French-language version of the psalm, though relatively brief, powerfully combines modal melodies evocative of Jewish psalmody and a striking use of bitonality.

FRANCIS POULENC (1899–1963)

Chorally, Francis Poulenc's output is outstanding and includes works both sacred and secular, *a cappella* and accompanied. Poulenc's early preoccupation with secular music changed dramatically in 1936, when, after the death of a friend in an automobile accident, he re-embraced Roman Catholicism. The series of sacred music that ensued is one of the choral treasures of the century such as the motets for Lent (FP 97, 1938–89) and Christmas (FP 152, 1951–52).[16] As popular as Poulenc's music has proven to be, its style remains elusive and is notoriously difficult to perform well. The difficulty springs from the music's typically French textual inflection, even in melodies for Latin texts, as excerpts from the cantata *Un Soir de Neige* (FP 126, 1944) and his motet *Salve Regina* (FP 110, 1941) illustrate (ex. 5.8a, b).

Example 5.8 a–b Poulenc

These two melodies—one secular and one sacred—reveal the same basic approach. The melodic excerpt from the cantata's second movement, *La bonne neige*, demonstrates Poulenc's ability not just to realize the prosody of spoken French perfectly but also to create melodies that, like those of his colleague Arthur Honegger, move through a limited compass. The resulting meter changes are fundamentally different from those of Stravinsky in that they create neither a strong sense of crusic accent (i.e., the accent a downbeat receives) nor do they use that stress to emphasize text accent. The opening of *Salve Regina* reveals even less obvious congruence of downbeat and text accent. Had most composers wished to create an alignment of text and metric stress within the same melody, they might not have chosen single measures of 4/4 and 6/4. The second measure's downbeat would normally accent the first syllable of "Ma-ter," but Poulenc effectively neutralizes it by creating an agogic stress (dotted quarter) on the second syllable. The ascending pitches on "Regina" (m. 1), the stress on "-ter," and the ensuing streams of eighth notes re-create a French speaker's inflection of the Latin text, "rising" to the end of the second bar. The implicit meter of Poulenc's melody (2/4, 3/4, 5/4) creates another layer of ambiguity. The triadic design of the bass line matches the soprano perfectly, imbuing the passage with a stillness not unlike the gentle and gradual oscillations of a kaleidoscopic image.

Such ametrical, oscillating melodies abound in Poulenc's work, as example 5.9 from the Sanctus of his *Mass in G* (FP 89, 1937) shows.

Example 5.9 Poulenc, *Mass in G*, Sanctus, mm. 1–7

Poulenc's metric construction (4/4 + 3/4) mirrors also features agogic stress on the second beat of the 4/4 measures to create the same displacement and negation of any metrical accent seen in *Salve Regina*.

This passage also illustrates another of Poulenc's trademark devices—the repetition of small melodic units to create a larger formal shape. In the Sanctus, Poulenc alternates two contrasting melodies in an unpredictable sequence. Many of his compositions evolve by such juxtapositions, which, when repeated, create a larger formal span. An apt analogy is the art of mosaic, in which one assembles small bits and pieces of tile or glass to create a *Gestalt* best understood by stepping back and not closely examining its particulars. What Virgil Thomson wrote about Debussy's music could just as easily apply to Poulenc's: "But his profound originality lies in his concept of formal structure. Where he got it I do not know. It may have come out of Impressionist painting or Symbolist poetry. Certainly there is small precedent for it in music. It remains, nevertheless, his most radical gift to the art.... This formal pattern is a mosaic texture made up of tiny bits and pieces all fitted in together so tightly that they create a continuity. The structural lines of the composition are not harmonic, not in the bass, but rhythmic and melodic."[17] Compositional unity resides less in a single perception of cause and effect than in the simultaneity of many different interpretations. The author Roger Shattuck views such juxtaposition as a crucial element of twentieth-century formal processes.[18]

The Sanctus of Poulenc's *Mass in G* exemplifies a formal process, based on repetition of contrasting material without any connecting transition, which dates back to the *Litanies à la Vierge Noire* (FP 82, 1936). As the title implies, the *Litanies* imitates the call-and-response of a church litany where multiple petitions are followed by the same response, a process that creates both variety and unity. This cellular repetition points to another aspect of Poulenc's style—his frequent insertions of rests (often brief in duration)—seen in the opening measures of *Quem vidistis pastores, dicite* (ex. 5.10), the second of his four *Motets pour le temps de Noël*.

Example 5.10 Poulenc, *Quem vidistis pastores, dicite*, mm. 1–4

If taken literally, the rests in the soprano and tenor would fragment the line, creating small, isolated cells instead of Poulenc's more typical longer melodic arch. These embedded rests are remnants of a mosaic creation: the grout, still visible between the tiles, is nonetheless still part of the finished product. The rests are intended to facilitate the inflection of the sung line rather than create microdivisions within it.

Another Poulenc fingerprint is his penchant for creating awkward, often difficult voice leading. For example, the individual vocal lines of *La bonne neige* are difficult to sing because of the frequency with which awkward leaps appear in the voice parts. By simply playing the soprano melody with each of the other voices one discovers that all pairs are basically consonant, but none of them is without fault. This is particularly true of the soprano-bass pair with its direct and indirect parallelisms, and the dissonant intervals formed between the soprano and tenor. Even the basically consonant women's voices contain awkward voice leading, but correcting the passage to conform to traditional rules would no doubt result in some loss of color or nuance.

Poulenc composed five works for chorus and orchestra, the most popular of which is the *Gloria* (FP 177) for soprano, chorus, and large orchestra. Composed in the latter half of 1959 on commission from the Koussevitzky Foundation, the *Gloria*'s first performance was on January 20, 1961. Critics of the time praised the work, comparing it with some justification to Vivaldi's setting of the same text. A primary difference between these two settings is their respective divisions of the text: Vivaldi divides the text into twelve movements; Poulenc uses only six.

Poulenc's division of the text crowds more than half of the *Gloria*'s seventy-five words into the final two movements, while mvts. 1, 3, and 4 contain only a single sentence or one phrase. The traditional analytical strategy of noting key signature, meter, tempo, and the like is ineffectual here; Poulenc used multiple meters in every movement (nos. 2, 5 and 6), no key signature in three movements, and cast only one (mvt. 4) in a single key signature throughout.

Whoever sets the Gloria of the Mass faces the question of how to subdivide the text since its length is not conducive to a single through-composed movement. The approach also seems to vary depending on whether the Gloria is part of an entire Mass ordinary or a stand-alone composition. Poulenc uses six movements that contain varying amounts of text. The

Table 5.2 Poulenc, *Gloria*, form

Movement	Text	Scoring
1. *Gloria in excelsis Deo*	*Gloria in excelsis Deo . . . bonae voluntatis.*	satb, orchestra
2. *Laudamus te*	*Laudamus te . . . propter magnam gloriam tuam.*	S, satb, Orchestra
3. *Domine Deus*	*Domine Deus, Rex Coelestis, Deus Pater omnipotens.*	S, satb orchestra (pic, dbsn, br)
4. *Domine Fili unigenite*	*Domine Fili unigenite Jesu Christe.*	satb, orchestra
5. *Domine Deus Agnus Dei*	*Domine Deus, Agnus Dei . . . suscipe deprecationem nostram.*	S, satb, orchestra (dbsn, tbn, tba & timp)
6. *Qui sedes ad dexteram Patris*	*Qui sedes . . . in gloria Dei Patris. Amen.*	S, satb orchestra

first three movements shown in Table 5.2 ("Gloria," "Laudamus te," and "Domine Deus, Rex Coelestis") set small, syntactically defined text units. The same cannot be said of the final three movements. Movement 4 ("Domine Fili unigenite")—the second of three that begin with "Domine"—sets a single sentence. The fifth movement inexplicably combines the final Domine phrase ("Domine Deus, Agnus Dei") with the first two of the three sentences that begin with "Qui," leaving the third and final petition ("Qui sedes") to the beginning of the sixth movement, which also includes the three "Quoniam" phrases and the concluding "Cum sancto Spiritu . . . Amen." Poulenc's formal structure and his division of the text is based on a formal design with alternating tempi:

Maestoso	MM60
Très vif et joyeux	MM138–144
Très lent et calme	MM60
Très vite et Joyeux	MM112
Très lent	MM60
Maestoso	MM60

The first and last movements are both marked *Maestoso*. The four movements that lie between them form two pairs of fast and slow.

Despite the general critical approval accorded the Gloria, the "Laudamus te" movement (no. 2) has elicited criticism for its blithe, bustling, totally secular tone. Responding to such criticism, Poulenc remarked: "The second movement caused a scandal; I wonder why? I was simply thinking, in writing it, of the Gozzoli frescoes in which the angels stick out their tongues; I was thinking also of the serious Benedictines whom I saw playing soccer one day."[19] Whatever inspired it, this music, so utterly French and typical of Poulenc's early days, creates the naive, almost absurd juxtaposition Roger Shattuck poses as emblematic of the French avant-garde.

Keith Daniel views the third ("Domine Deus") and fifth ("Domine Deus, Agnus Dei") movements as the emotional pillars of the work, a residue of the profound effect composing *Dialogues des Carmélites* (1954–57) had upon Poulenc.[20] Both of these movements of the Gloria have slow tempi, reduced orchestration (absence of brass and extreme winds), and a dominant role for the soprano soloist. The appearance of the work's most reverential and otherworldly music here may explain Poulenc's nondoctrinaire division of the text; only by dividing it as he does is he able to begin two movements with the same words, "Domine Deus" (separated by the "Domine Fili unigenite," the work's shortest movement). Neither text suggests the particular kind of music that Poulenc composes; certainly, the choice of B minor to convey the sense of the text "Domine Deus, Rex coelestis, Deus pater omnipotens" is hardly traditional. Again, Daniel clearly believes this to be the case: "The stylistic source of this movement is unquestionably Act III, scene 3 in *Dialogues*, the moving scene in which the Second Prioress says goodbye to the Carmelite nuns. The text of this movement of the *Gloria* refers to the Son of God dying for our sins. An even stronger musical connection can be made between the main orchestral motif in this movement and a motif in the Sonata for clarinet, a piece Poulenc was composing during the last year of his life."[21] The specific themes to which Daniel alludes are presented in example 5.11.

Example 5.11 a–c Poulenc

a. *Gloria*, mvt. 5, mm. 54-5

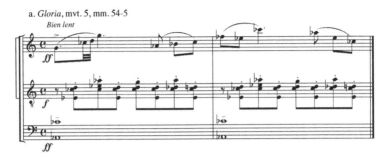

b. *Sonata for Clarinet*, mvt. 2, mm. 78-79

c. *Dialogues des Carmélites*, act 3, scene 3, mm. 54-55

Poulenc's *Gloria* is, in its own inimitable way, a convincing work that embraces the incongruous stylistic juxtapositions of its time.

MAURICE DURUFLÉ (1902–86)

The modernistic efforts of *Les Six* notwithstanding, the centrist classical language of Fauré and the École Niedermeier persisted, nowhere more clearly than in the music of Maurice Duruflé, whose choral output centers on two popular compositions rooted in Gregorian chant—the *Quatre motets sur des thèmes grégoriens* (op. 10) and his *Requiem* (op. 9). Since its composition, Duruflé's Requiem has elicited comparison with Fauré's, principally because both omit the traditional *Dies irae* sequence and assign the "Pie Jesu" to a mezzo-soprano soloist. Duruflé himself denied a connection, but these external similarities continue to suggest otherwise.[22] What most clearly distances Duruflé's *Requiem* from Fauré's is his use of Gregorian themes and a larger orchestra.

Following both liturgy and French tradition, Duruflé divides the Requiem text into nine movements.

Table 5.3 Duruflé, *Requiem*, op. 9

Movement	Mode	Tonality
Introit: Requiem Aeternam	6 (F Hypolydian)	F major/D minor
Kyrie	6 (F Hypolydian)	F major/D minor
Domine Jesu Christe	2 (Hypodorian)	F♯/F♯
Sanctus	Aeolian	D minor
Pie Jesu	Ionian	A♭
Agnus Dei	7 (Mixolydian)	G/G minor
Lux aeterna	8 (Hypomixolydian)	D minor/B♭
Libera me	1 (Dorian)	F♯ Dorian
In Paradisum	7 (Mixolydian)	F♯ Mixolydian

In Table 5.3 the numbers immediately to the right of each movement's title indicate the mode prescribed for that chant item in the *Liber Usualis*; the next column gives the tonal center used by Duruflé. The tonalities Duruflé uses (especially in the Introit, Kyrie, Agnus Dei, and "In Paradisum") reflect his contemporary approach to the integration of Gregorian chant into his Requiem; the traditional modes are often transposed to pitch centers not associated with them in Gregorian chant.

Duruflé was at that time composing a series of organ pieces based on these chants when his publisher, Durand et Cie., commissioned a choral Requiem. It was a simple matter for Duruflé to transform the organ preludes into a work for chorus, orchestra, and organ. Thus, each movement of the *Requiem* uses the Gregorian chant assigned to its text in the *Liber Usualis*.[23] Although the melodies are always modally correct, Duruflé treats them with a freedom consistent with a master improviser. In the Introit, for example, he assigns a rhythmic version of the plainsong to the unison male voices (accompanied by "free" women's vocal parts and the organ/orchestra). For the verse, "Te decet hymnus," Duruflé transposes the soprano melody up a third to A′ and then relocates the alto's version of the melody down a fourth on E′) at "exaudi orationem meam" (ex. 5.12). This transposition is also clearly evident in the pedal tones the organ plays in each section; for mm. 25–31, the organ sustains the pitch G′, which changes to D″ for mm. 33–37.

Example 5.12 Duruflé, *Requiem*, op. 9, Introit, mm. 24–31

Beginning in m. 42, Duruflé repeats the opening text of the Introit and its music, as prescribed by the liturgy. This time, however, the chant melody is in the orchestra/organ, freeing the voices to provide a descant that not only fits the previous harmony and melody but also creates a slightly different, more conclusive feel to the movement (mm. 42–59).

For the Kyrie, which is attached to the Introit, the voices imitate the head of the plainsong melody ahead of the entry of chant in augmentation in the orchestra/organ at m 10. The music of Christe eleison reveals no trace of the chant, but the return of Kyrie (m. 49) initiates vocal imitation of the descending fifth that opens the final part of the Kyrie chant. As before, Duruflé places the chant in augmentation in the orchestra. In general, Duruflé's treatment of the chant is closer to variation technique than a straightforward presentation à la cantus firmus. Here combination of traditional melody and modern harmonies establish this work as uniquely popular and accessible among the twentieth-century repertory for chorus and orchestra/organ.

Duruflé also composed a Messe "um jubilo," which requires unison male chorus, orchestra, and organ, op. 11 (1966). This work is less known and more rarely performed than his *Quatre motets sur des thèmes grégoriens* (*Ubi caritas, Tota pulchra es, Tu es Petrus,* and *Tantum ergo*), op. 10 (1960), and a setting of the Lord's Prayer (*Notre Père,* 1978), which is unique for its use of French text and absence of chant. The *Quatre motets* remain his most frequently performed compositions. Of these, *Ubi caritas* is the most popular, largely because of the colorful vocal sonorities Duruflé creates. The chant itself (*LU* 664–5) has only two melodic phrases. The first is used for the antiphon and vv. 1 and 2 of the text (ex. 5.13a); the second phrase sets vv. 3 and 4 (ex. 5.13b). Most performers and conductors believe that Duruflé used the entire chant; in reality he uses the first phrase for the antiphon and text lines 2, 5 (transposed), and 9. The melody used for lines 3 and 4 and 6–8 sounds Gregorian but is freely composed. Duruflé uses the chant's second phrase only as the alto part in his setting of the final "Amen." but Duruflé decides not to include it in his motet.

Example 5.13 a–b Duruflé, *Ubi caritas et amor,* op. 10, no. 1

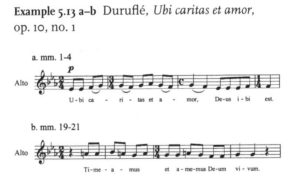

a. mm. 1-4

p

Alto

U - bi ca - ri - tas et a - mor,   De-us i - bi   est.

b. mm. 19-21

Alto

Ti-me - a - mus   et a - me-mus De-um   vi - vum.

Given the popular appeal of Duruflé's choral works, it is lamentable that he published only fourteen works during his lifetime. The relative paucity of this output is most likely attributable to his penchant for skillful improvisations, which resulted in many potential publications that were simply never written down.

OLIVIER MESSIAEN (1908–92)

One of the original and influential composers of the twentieth century, and perhaps the one who most clearly embodies the modernist spirit of *Les Six,* is Olivier Messiaen (Fig. 5.2). Messiaen pioneered the notion of integral serialism and coined the terms "modes of limited transposition" and "nonretrogradable rhythms." He used birdsong as a kind of melodic "musique con-crete," and Indian *talas* to create uniquely non-Western rhythms. Most importantly, like Satie, he became the mentor of younger composers like Pierre Boulez (1925–2016) and Karlheinz Stockhausen (1928–2007), who continued to develop his ideas.

Messiaen was, first and foremost, an organist and an important twentieth-century com-poser of organ music. His *Le Banquet céleste* (1926), *L'Ascension* (1933), *La Nativité du Seigneur* (1935), *Les corps glorieux* (1939), and *Messe de la Pentecôte* (1950) are staples of the organ repertory in which Messiaen continued to refine his musical language. The mature works written during and just after World War II include *Quatuor pour la fin du temps* (1941),[24] *Trois petites liturgies de la Présence Divine* (1944), *Vingt Regards sur l'Enfant-Jésus* (1944), *Harawi* (1945), and the *Turangalîla-Symphonie* (1946–48). The *Cinq rechants* (1948) and the "Rosetta stone" of integral serialism, *Modes de valeurs et d'intensités* (1949), are the logical conclusion of this evolutionary process.

Fig. 5.2 Olivier Messiaen (1940s)

With the exception of *O sacrum convivium*, Messiaen's choral music is infrequently discussed and performed possibly because it is inaccessible to all but the most accomplished choirs. When Marcel Couraud, the conductor of *Group vocal de France* attempted to commission a work, Messiaen rebuffed him, arguing that "anything I would write would be too difficult for your choir or any choir to perform."[25] Ultimately, he relented and composed *Cinq rechants* for them, but to call this a choral composition is misleading, since Messiaen scores it for twelve solo voices (SSSAAATTTBBB). The earlier *Trois petites liturgies de la Présence Divine* is only slightly more choral, requiring eighteen sopranos and chamber orchestra (including the precursor of the synthesizer, the *Ondes martenot*).

Messiaen's earliest choral work, *O sacrum convivium* (1937), is also his most traditional. This setting of the antiphon for the feast of Corpus Christi owes much to the style of Debussy and the great organist-composers of nineteenth- and early-twentieth-century France (most notably Marcel Dupré). Messiaen presents the text twice, creating a short bipartite musical form with a concluding coda.

These two text segments (mm. 1–16 and 17–26) share similar music, the first five measures reappearing at the beginning of the second text statement (mm. 1–5 = 17–21). This piece seems relatively simple because of Messiaen's relentless repetition of melody, harmony, rhythm, and homophonic texture. After texture, rhythm is the work's least variable element. Of thirty-five measures, twenty-six use one of two asymmetric rhythmic configurations. The first (m. 1, see ex. 5.14a) contains nine eighth notes arranged as 3 + 2 + 2 + 2, while its complement (m. 2, ex. 5.14a) deletes its final quarter note, resulting in a unit of 7/8 (3 + 2 + 2). These two cells appear in alternation in mm. 1–10, 17–20, and 23–26, as well as independently in mm. 11, 21, 22, and mm. 13, 28–30, and 34. Four of the nine remaining measures (mm. 14, 15, 31, 33) subtract the final quarter note of the 7/8 pattern; another (m. 12) may be understood either as a variant of m. 1 or an augmentation of m. 2. The other four measures (mm. 16, 31–32, and 35) contain an even number of eighth notes.

Despite a key signature of six sharps suggesting F♯ major, the work is not conventionally tonal. It opens with a major-major seventh chord on F♯, which Messiaen establishes as a tonic by constantly returning to it. The soprano's concluding oscillation between D♯ and G♯ suggests D♯ as an alternate tonic. The soprano melody of *O sacrum convivium* uses a scale that presages what Messiaen will later call "modes of limited transposition," meaning that if transposed, the scale's intervals yield the same pitches.[26] The most common of Messiaen's modes is the whole-tone scale (Mode 1); the next (Mode 2) is commonly known as the octatonic scale, a scale that alternates whole and half steps (ex. 5.13a, b).

Example 5.14 a–b Messiaen, *O sacrum convivium*

Minus the occasional appearance of A♯ and C𝄪, Messiaen's scale is Mixolydian mode transposed to D♯; the presence of A♯ creates an ascending octatonic pentachord (D♯–E♯–F♯–G♯–A), while the substitution of C𝄪 creates a descending pentachord that also exhibits octatonic qualities (D♯–C𝄪–B–A♯–G♯). Some form of the pitch A occurs sixteen times, twelve with the signed A♯ and four with A♮ (interestingly enough, always placed in close proximity to occurrences of the pitch, B♯ (C enharmonic).

The composition's two principal rhythmic cells are associated with specific melodic gestures. The 9/8 cell tends to use one of two related pitch sets: built on G♯, the first cell consists of the G♯, followed by a whole step, perfect fourth, and perfect fifth (G♯, A♯, C♯ and D♯). Example 5.15a contains two statements of this cell, the second a transposition of the first. The second set consists of either two tritones (ex. 5.15b) or a tritone and perfect fifth (ex. 5.15c). Since his melodic mode is nontransposable, Messiaen creates a periodic melody by repeating the same melody with varied conclusions (mm. 1–4 and 5–8) and sequential extensions.

Example 5.15 a–c Messiaen, *O sacrum convivium*

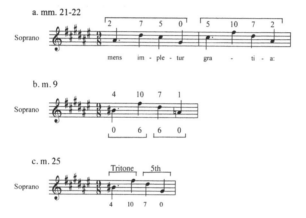

CINQ RECHANTS

Messiaen's celebrated and influential "choral" work is *Cinq rechants* (1948). Scored for twelve solo voices, it marks the advent of a new type of choral music, conceived for small, virtuosic vocal ensembles (one singer per part), and both the text and music of *Cinq rechants* exhibit important aspects of Messiaen's style. As the concluding member of a trilogy based on the legend of Tristan and Isolde (the song cycle *Harawi* [June 1945] and the *Turangalîla-Symphonie* [1948]), the five texts juxtapose aspects of sexual and mystical love. Messiaen's use of deeply imbedded symbolism and convoluted imagery is reminiscent of such landmark twentieth-century poets as T. S. Eliot, Ezra Pound, and e. e. cummings. Messiaen claimed that he had invented a language, basing it on ancient Peruvian and Eastern linguistic models as well as modern French; words constructed purely for their phonemic, onomatopoetic value (e.g., the text of the couplet of the third *Rechant*, which includes *cheu, cheu mayoma kapritama kalimoli sarisa*) appear in all five movements.[27] As the title indicates, all five movements use a *Rechant* (refrain), an apparent historical reference to the sixteenth-century French style known as *Vers mesurés à l'antique*.

Musically, this cycle employs the entire gamut of Messiaen's stylistic devices, including the previously mentioned "modes of limited transposition" and "nonretrogradable rhythms."[28] It also features such other signature devices as quotations of birdsongs as a source of melodic inspiration, and East Indian rhythms. The soprano solo that opens the first *Rechant* (ex. 5.16a) demonstrates yet another common device, additive rhythm; the first six notes increase arithmetically in sixteenth-note duration. He then follows this comparatively straightforward mathematical expansion by another expansion consisting of 1, 5, 6, and 16 sixteenth-notes.

Example 5.16 a–c Messiaen, *Cinq rechants*, no. 1

This same solo melody (ex. 5.16a) appears at the end of the movement, completing the frame within which its story unfolds. The first four measures of the refrain (ex. 5.16b) demonstrate the angularity and asymmetric rhythm that make this work so challenging.

In the first *Rechant*, we encounter Messiaen's "langue imaginaire ou pseudo-hindoue" combined with French. The contrived language is untranslatable and even the French text is altogether enigmatic (Table 5.4).

There is a kind of ferocious energy here, especially in the use of the fricatives (t, k) and the dissonant chords of maniacal laughter (ex. 5.16c). The pitch content of these chords is daunting: the six chords are two statements of three chords, in which the G″ of soprano 1 and the F′ of the alto are constants. Five other pitches—E, D♯, D♮, C♯ and A—appear in alternation with a second pitch collection.

Table 5.4 Messiaen, *Cinq rechants*, no. 1, text

Introduction:	*Hayo kapritama, la li la li la li la ssarèno*
Réchant:	*Les amoureux s'envolent*
	Brangien dans l'espace tu souffles
	Les amoureux s'envolent
	Vers les étoiles de la mort
	TKTK TKTK TKTK TKTK
	Ha, ha, ha, ha, ha, soif
	L'explorateur Orphée trouve son cœur dans la mort
Introduction:	No translation possible
Refrain:	The lovers fly off, Brangäne, you breathe into space,
	The lovers fly off, toward the stars of death.
	t k t k t k t k
	Ha, ha, ha, ha, ha, thirst.
	The explorer Orpheus finds his heart in death.

Thus the pitch class [C♯–D♯–E–F–G] is common to each chord. The total content of these three chords (G, F, E, D♯, D, C♯, C, B♭, A, G♯, F♯) contains eleven of the possible twelve chromatic pitches.

The text of the couplets introduce the characters Yseult (Isolde), Orphée (Orpheus), and Barbe Bleu(e) (Blue Beard). These texts present dark themes—separation, death, and the void of space. The references to darkness are mitigated by couplet's threefold reference to things starry—"star mirror," "star castle," and the "starry crystal bubble."[29] Messiaen presents his text in all three soprano parts. The first is as an oscillating ostinato, the pitch content of which is a tritone and enharmonic major third, D–A♭ and E♭–B. These are followed by three melodies, the first two built on the pairs of minor thirds heard at the outset of the *Rechant*—D′–F′ (S3) and C♯′–E (S2). The final melodic gesture is a transposition of three pitches from the conclusion of the *Rechant* (A♭′, C♯′′ and G′′) sung by S1 (ex. 5.17).

Example 5.17 Messiaen, *Cinq rechants*, no. 1, mm. 19–27

The sixteenth note used to set the final syllable of *é-toi-le* causes each melodic repetition to rotate with respect to the barline. To underscore the asymmetry of his construction, Messiaen divides the text and melody unequally among the three sopranos. In this couplet's nineteen measures (eighteen measures of 2/4 and one of 3/8), the sopranos sing the complete textual-musical unit twice complete and a partial, third statement (first four notes only).[30]

A similarly repetitive alto melody accompanies the soprano, distributing its melodic material among two of the three singers. The altos sing a single word ("hayomakapritama") to a melody comprising two related, yet different parts (ex. 5.18).

Example 5.18 Messiaen, *Cinq rechants*, no. 1, mm. 19–22

This short alto melody appears five times in the couplet vis-à-vis the two-plus statements of the soprano, a practice reminiscent of medieval isorhythmic motets.[31] Each melody has its own pitch content (*color*), unique rhythmic pattern (*talea*), and overlaps its partner in an asynchronous way.

For the second couplet, Messiaen repeats the soprano and alto parts but adds tenor and bass parts. The tenor part is unpitched, consisting entirely of a rhythmicization of the "t k t k" phonemes that appear in the *Rechant*. The bass part contains the only text ("Bluebeard, castle of the seventh door.") not set in the first couplet, as well as the words of the soprano's introductory phrase "hayomakapritama," sung by the altos. Like their female counterparts, the male voices repeat their text and music in overlapping fashion. The bass melody (divided into two parts: the French text sung by bass 3 and the invented word by bass 2) appears four times, while the tenor part has two complete and one partial statements of its percussive text. None of these entrances align vertically with the music of the women's voices. If one were to graph these four parts, it would become clear that Messiaen organizes the parts so that their melodies do not begin at the same time, thus insuring no simultaneity.

Messiaen's final stroke was the addition of a canon à 3 in the soprano above an otherwise literal repeat of the initial eight measures of the *Rechant*. Each of the sopranos sings the same ten-pitch melody starting an eighth note apart; each new melodic statement is marked with an asterisk (ex. 5.19).

Example 5.19 Messiaen, *Cinq rechants*, no. 1, mm. 71–6

This obbligato, a logical extension of the layered, asynchronous counterpoint of the couplets, is best understood as an intensification of the *Rechant*, more designed to create a sense of organic growth within the piece than to create a new harmonic paradigm.

The four remaining movements operate in similar ways. There are, however, two passages that deserve special mention. The first is the *Rechant* of the third movement, which consists of a soprano melody over a hummed accompaniment, a texture straight out of any one of Messiaen's organ compositions (ex. 5.20).

Example 5.20 Messiaen, *Cinq rechants*, no. 3, mm. 33–6

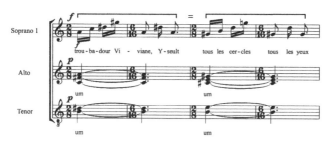

This dense, symbolist poetry, notable for its omission of connectives and descriptors, presents opposing concepts—openness/expansiveness, freedom/enclosed space, imprisonment/claustrophobia. Yseult and a new character, Vivien, are bound together within the circles of eyes (another common poetic thread).³² Concerning this image, Audrey Davidson has written, "Here, eyes are appropriately connected with circles, for by the act of *seeing* men and women are caught up in love, which for Messiaen was in part symbolized by the enclosed space of the circle."³³ Once again, Messiaen repeats a pair of phrases, the second of which is a transposition (down a semitone) of the first; when repeated, he alters the rhythm of the fourth note from a sixteenth to an eighth (to emphasize *rose*?). These melodies create circular patterns that may be a kind of tone painting. The sustained accompaniment chords are based on diminished-seventh chords (with added notes) that again imitate the color of Messiaen's organ music. The second notable passage is Messiaen's elaborate version of the third movement's *rechant*.³⁴ Here, a twelve-voice canon begins in the top soprano (descending through all voices); each entering part sings the same tortuous melody a whole tone lower than its predecessor (ex. 5.21).

Example 5.21 Messiaen, *Cinq rechants*, no. 3, mm. 86–88

Although Messiaen produced significant choral works after *Cinq rechants* (most notably the oratorio *La Transfiguration de Notre Seigneur Jésus-Christ*, 1965–69), none of his other compositions has had the impact of *Cinq rechants*, which introduced a new type of vocal ensemble music unique to the mid-twentieth century. Despite his reluctance to compose a choral work for Marcel Couraud, the work he eventually wrote redefined the boundaries of choral music. Works that followed Messaien's *Cinq rechants* adopted its scoring (one singer per part); these successors and the role they played in expanding the boundaries of choral composition will be discussed in chapter 9, "The Avant-Garde Aesthetic." For now, it is sufficient to acknowledge Messiaen as the rightful heir to the avant-garde spirit of composers like Satie, Debussy, and *Les Six*, and the part they all played in first creating and then healing the rupture between past traditions and new possibilities.

CONCLUSION

In *The Banquet Years*, Roger Shattuck chronicles France's celebration of *La belle époque*, even as its collapse spawned radical new forms of artistic expression. This uniquely Parisian event was Janus-like, looking back wistfully at the achievements of the dying era while it embraced the increasingly absurd experiments of the new century, experiments that Shattuck codified under the concepts of self-reflectiveness and stillness. This conundrum stemmed from the contradiction that Paris, one of Europe's oldest, most cultured cities, was an environment so absorbed by the continuous present that history had little cachet. The four French artists (Jarry, Rousseau, Satie, and Apollinaire) that Shattuck chose to study represented different disciplines and acknowledged different descriptive labels; they all vehemently refused to conform to any notion of what an artist was *supposed* to be other than their own strongly held personal identities and idiosyncrasies. Erik Satie deliberately changed his style the moment he suspected that his audience knew what to expect.[35]

This attitude of playful, even provocative artistic independence was shared by all composers at that time. No music resembled, much less imitated, the style of another, but despite their outward rejection of any sort of conformity, all of their music was utterly, if ineffably, French. Religious music was extremely important in the rebirth in France of a national musical identity following the relatively short Franco-Prussian War (1870–71). If proof of this assertion were needed, it lay in the distinguished tradition of French organists and the pioneering work of the *École Niedermeyer*, its successor, the *Schola Cantorum*, and the Benedictine monks of Solesmes. Religious sentiment offered the simplest way of separating these composers, even though their individual attitudes regarding church music followed no predictable evolutionary pattern. Debussy and Ravel were the least inclined toward religious music; they were counterbalanced by Fauré and Duruflé, for whom religion was a central aspect of their vocation. Poulenc, Milhaud, and Messiaen vacillated in their embrace of religious subjects. While Milhaud's Judaism inspired some of his larger choral works, it was, on balance, not a major influence. Poulenc's fervent return to Catholicism in 1936 clearly prompted the body of Latin sacred music that ensued. Messiaen's ardent Catholicism is more in evidence in his organ compositions than in his choral music, which, with the exceptions of *O sacrum convivium* and his oratorio, *La Transfiguration de Notre Seigneur Jésus-Christ*, tended toward a mystical secularism. None of these composers lived in an age that was particularly conducive to or respectful of traditional religious values, but such values embodied precisely the type of conformity to which artistic expression was fundamentally opposed.

6

Serialism and Choral Music
of the Twentieth Century

A seminal event in twentieth-century music was Arnold Schoenberg's (1874–1951) claim to have discovered a new method of composition, which, as he boasted to his student Josef Rufer, would "guarantee the supremacy of German music for the next hundred years."[1] Against what or whom did Schoenberg feel he had to defend the legacy of German music of the three Bs? The French avant-garde composers (discussed in chap. 5) were in large part responsible for some of these Schoenbergian assumptions.

The symbolist poet Stéphane Mallarmé was one of the early editors of the *Révue Wagnerienne*, a journal devoted to discussing Wagner's aesthetic. Martin Cooper points out that almost all French composers of the time made a pilgrimage to Bayreuth to experience firsthand the power of Wagner's music.[2] Ultimately the French were more intrigued with Wagner's philosophy than his music; in fact, the primary purpose of the techniques generated by French composers from Debussy on was to avoid being German.[3] France's defeat by Germany under Bismarck in the Franco-Prussian War (1870–71) prompted their search for alternative compositional techniques that were distinct from the German musical style. Schoenberg surely sensed this antipathy among the French and perhaps took it as his principal reason for revamping German music so as to help it regain its former prominence.[4]

ARNOLD SCHOENBERG AND ANTON WEBERN

There was a palpable sense among twentieth-century composers that they had to opt in or out of Schoenberg's new system. That is the point of Schoenberg's brief poem "Am Scheideweg" ("At the Crossroads"), which became one of the texts of the composer's *Drei Satiren*, op. 28:

> *Am Scheideweg*
>
> *Tonal oder atonal? Nun sag einmal in welchem Stall in diesem Fall die grössre Zahl, dass man sich halten kann am sichern Wall. Nur kein Schade!*
>
> ("Tonal or atonal? Just tell me in which category (stable), in this case, the greater number belongs, so that one can cling to the safe wall. Please, no regrets!")[5]

Very much tongue in cheek, Schoenberg assumes the part of every composer who wants to be modern but also performed. Even among trained musicians there is an understood equation that tonal means consonant and atonal means dissonant. While there are many pieces of atonal music that *are* dissonant, there are also pieces of consonant music that may be defined as atonal, if by that term we mean a piece that avoids the usual trappings of the tonal system—key signature, an understood hierarchy (tonic, dominant, subdominant, etc.) of pitch, harmony, cadences, and form based on the departure from and return to a major or minor key.

Schoenberg's quest is documented in a series of books (two by him and a third by his pupil Joseph Rufer). Schoenberg's personal manifestos were *Harmonielehre* ("The Teaching of Harmony," 1911) and *Stil und Gedanke* ("Style and Idea," 1950); Rufer's book, *Composition with Twelve Notes Related Only to One Another* (1954), became the Rosetta stone of pitch serialism. The first three chapters of Rufer's study review the historical precedents of Schoenberg's new method, now known as dodecaphony or twelve-tone technique. In fact, Schoenberg's technique is more than the mere appearance of all twelve chromatic pitches in some nonrepetitive sequence. He specifically referred to the term "atonal" as imprecise, preferring to label it as "pantonal."[6] The very same method finds validation in the music of J. S. Bach. The subject of the final fugue of Book 1 of the *Well-Tempered Clavier*, for example, uses all twelve pitches, yet no one would make the claim that this music is atonal in Schoenberg's sense of the term. Whereas Bach's inclusion of all twelve tones is designed to showcase his ability to make tonal counterpoint from a tortuous subject, as well as advocate for the use of a temperament that was a compromise between just intonation and other existing tuning schemes. Schoenberg's method pointedly equalizes all of these pitches to insure that there is no hierarchy as in tonal music. To accomplish this, the "rules" state that no pitch can be repeated until all twelve have been heard, lest such a repetition highlight that pitch and suggest a tonal centrism.

Schoenberg himself was quick to point out that his method was hardly new, as it grew out of his careful study of the music of those old three Bs—Bach, Beethoven, and Brahms—in addition to Mozart. And indeed, Schoenberg took Bach's contrapuntal prowess as the central tenet of his style. Alexander Ringer stated that Schoenberg's technique was unique in the history of musical precisely for its reliance on counterpoint to generate harmony and not the other way around. Evidence of his indebtedness is clear in the transcriptions that both Schoenberg and his disciple, Anton Webern, made of Bach's music;[7]

these were not mere modern arrangements like Mozart's re-orchestration of Handel or Mendelssohn's revival of the *St. Matthew Passion* but studies of Bach's contrapuntal process.

From Beethoven, Schoenberg borrowed the contrapuntal manipulating of motivic cells (as seen in Beethoven's late string quartets, for example); in Beethoven's transformational processes Schoenberg found the precedent for his creation of contrapuntal manipulations of a twelve-tone row, the prime, inversion, retrograde, retrograde inversion, and the like. Again, Rufer specifically mentions a hidden relationship between the antecedent and consequent phrases of the *Allegro* of Beethoven's String Quartet in F major, op. 135.[8] Following Beethoven, the tendency of nineteenth-century composers strayed farther and farther from the diatonic hierarchy of classical tonality; their increasing use of chromaticism to obscure the functional basis of tonality, even to obliterate the boundary between major and minor modes, may explain Schoenberg's denial in 1949 that he had created the twelve-tone method, for it was already there to be discovered.[9]

From Johannes Brahms, Schoenberg borrowed the idea of the developing variation. The repetition of themes and keys combined with periodic phrase structure was essential to tonal music's formal cohesion. The notion of variation served as an antidote to any predictability that ensued. "Repetition combined with variation allows the unit to create the manifold by procreating new shapes through 'developing variation.'" As an illustration Rufer cites the themes of Brahms's String Quartet in A minor (op. 51).[10] Furthermore, Brahms's conspicuous use of contrapuntal devices—canon, inversion, augmentation, and the like—in his choral music may well partly explain Schoenberg's own fascination with the idiom.

Schoenberg arrived only gradually at the rudiments that ultimately govern dodecaphonic composition. The compositions that precede the first thoroughly serial works (opp. 23–24) represent a style in flux, a style in which the wholesale abandonment of tonality is not a consideration. *Friede auf Erden*, op. 13, 1907, which he later described as an "illusion written when he still thought harmony among men conceivable," is still an arguably tonal work that fully embraces the Brahmsian notion of developing variation.[11] Despite its daunting vocal challenges, Schoenberg's setting of C. F. Meyer's poem for eight-part chorus is still nominally "tonal" as the presence of two key signatures, D minor and D major show. The implied ambivalence between major and minor mode illustrates another Brahmsian legacy assumed by Schoenberg. The simplest view of the work's formal scheme results from tracking the placement of the changes from one signature to the other in relation to the four eight-line stanzas of text.

Schoenberg divides the first stanza equally between D minor and D major; similarly; those two key signatures govern equal amounts of the remaining text, lines 9–20 under the signature of one flat and lines 21–32 under two sharps. But this information is itself an illusion because the music under these two signatures can rarely be described as conventionally in D (minor or major). Example 6.1 shows the first eight measures of the work.

The tenor maintains the diatonic limits of D minor save for the single appearance of an F♯ (m. 6) as a chromatic neighboring tone. Similarly, the soprano adds only two chromatic neighboring tones (C♯ and E♭) to D minor's standard collection of pitches. The alto and bass voices behave similarly. Yet in spite of the predominance of D minor's pitch content, the music doesn't actually sound like D minor. The reason for this is simple: the key signature doesn't represent the dominant feature of Schoenberg's vocal parts. Instead of voice parts that conform to D minor, we get voice parts that have their own separate contrapuntal and tonal logic. The soprano is the first to present the work's principal motive (m. 2), a diatonic melodic minor third starting on D. The bass follows suit in mm. 3 and 6 on the dominant. What we see are not melodic parts defined by tonal harmony, but separate contrapuntal lines that, by and large, respect the implied D-minor tonality but don't reinforce it. Harmony here is the product of melody, not the other way around (an idea related to medieval polyphony).

Example 6.1 Schoenberg, *Friede auf Erden*, op. 13, mm. 1–8
Used with kind permission of European American Music Distributors, LLC, sole U.S. and Canadian agent for Schott Music.

The set of melodies given in example 6.2 represent Schoenberg's application of the Brahmsian technique of developing variation. Each of these motives clearly derives from the soprano opening (bracketed portions in ex. 6.2), but riffs on it in increasingly chromatic and intervallically disjunct ways.

Example 6.2 a–g Schoenberg, *Friede auf Erden*, op. 13
Used with kind permission of European American Music Distributors, LLC, sole U.S. and Canadian agent for Schott Music.

Example 6.2 Continued

b. mm. 2-5

Soprano

pp

Da die Hir-ten ih-re Her-de lies - sen

c. mm. 31-33

Tenor

p

Seit die En-gel so ge - ra - ten,

d. mm. 53-55

Soprano

ppp

sang der Chor der Gei - ster za - gend,

e. mm. 100-102

Alto

p

Mäh - lich wird es sich ge - stal - ten,

f. mm. 43-45

Alto

f

hat der Streit auf wil-dem Pfer-de, der Ge-har - nisch-te voll-bracht

g. mm. 131-136

Tenor

f

des-sen hel - le Tu - ben dröh - - - nen,

Another subsidiary motive that figures prominently in the unfolding development of the piece is the figure first sung by soprano and bass in mm. 3–4.

A far more compelling example of Schoenberg's retention of the devices of tonality occurs at the first change of key signature (D minor to D major) in m. 11.

Example 6.3 Schoenberg, *Friede auf Erden*, op. 13, mm. 11–14
Used with kind permission of European American Music Distributors, LLC, sole U.S. and Canadian agent for Schott Music.

Bass

führ das himm - li - sche Ge - sind___

Between mm. 11 and 20 the choral basses sing the same ostinato-like melody (E–C♯–F♯–B) five times (ex. 6.3). This pattern is a standard cadential progression, but what key is it in? Schoenberg creates tonal ambivalence by allowing the same sequence of pitches to be understood in either E minor or B minor. This motive can be analyzed in either key, but, once again, the problem is that the resulting musical gestalt is neither of these tonalities; here the emphasis is less on the tonal foundation laid down by the bass part than on the melodic constructions that lie above it. The almost plodding regularity of the bass compared with the sinuous chromaticism and out-of-phase textual construction of the alto is shown in example 6.4.

Example 6.4 Schoenberg, *Friede auf Erden*, op. 13, mm. 11–20
Used with kind permission of European American Music Distributors, LLC,
sole U.S. and Canadian agent for Schott Music.

The relation of the alto and bass parts is emblematic of the texture as a whole. While the bass repeats its quasi-tonal ostinato, the alto moves above it producing a freely chromatic harmony, which is essentially consonant but transcends the boundary between tonality and atonality. Ironically, one could describe this passage using Roger Shattuck's term "still" because it lacks tonal direction, rather like the ever-changing design of a kaleidoscope.[12]

By contrast, Schoenberg's first setting of the refrain that ends three of the four verses ("Friede auf der Erden") seems more ordered and goal-oriented. Indeed, the soprano and alto duet at its beginning is a variant of the preceding bass ostinato, comprising thirds and sixths; the tenor and bass parts are a kind of lush remembrance of the parallel first-inversion triads of fauxbourdon. Schoenberg reprises this refrain (mm. 62–75 and mm. 137–48) in increasingly dense, abstruse harmonic constructions based on doubled thirds.

Seen from this perspective, the sprawling work shows clear signs of strophic developing variation. Consider the beginnings of the second (mm. 31–38) and fourth (mm. 100–113) verses; although each is different than the first, the thematic gestures and harmonies show clear connection to the first eleven measures of the composition. A comparison of the original motive (ex. 6.2a) and the opening of verse 2 (ex. 6.2b) validate Schoenberg's indebtedness to Brahms's idea of continuing variation. And we can hear the music for "Mählich wird es sich gestalten" (ex. 6.2d and ex. 6.5) as a recapitulation, albeit in the major rather than the minor mode.

Example 6.5 Schoenberg, *Friede auf Erden*, op. 13, mm. 100–03
Used with kind permission of European American
Music Distributors, LLC, sole U.S. and Canadian agent
for Schott Music.

Two other examples of melodic and harmonic variation conjure up visions of Brahms's use of canon to generate thematic development. First, notice the parallelism between Schoenberg's settings of comparable lines of stanzas 2 ("O wie viele blut'ge Tagen Hat der Streit auf wildem Pferde, Der Geharnischte vollbracht") and 3 ("Dass der Schwache nicht zum Raube Jeder frechen Mordgebärde Werde fallen allezeit"). Schoenberg realizes the violence of these texts, which stand in stark contrast with the illusion of *Friede auf Erden* by setting the alto line given in example 6.2e in canon against itself (mm. 43–46), creating a battle between rival declamations of the text. Schoenberg employs a less strict but no less compelling counterpoint based on a diminution of the soprano's motive from m. 2 to set the second text. The same imitative complex also appears in service of the text of v. 4: "Waffen schmieden ohne Fährde, Flammenschwerter für das Recht."[13] The coincidence of this text and music is effective yet ironic, for, unlike its predecessors, this text looks to humanity's salvation rather than its imminent doom.

The clearest Brahmsian reference appears at the conclusion of v. 2 (mm. 53–58). Here, Schoenberg adopts Brahms's characteristic voicing (SAATBB) deployed as antiphonal canons between the female and male voices (ex. 6.6).

Example 6.6 Schoenberg, *Friede auf Erden*, op. 13, mm. 53–58
Used with kind permission of European American Music Distributors, LLC, sole U.S. and Canadian agent for Schott Music.

To find the model for this homage, look at similar passages in the *Nachtwache* setting that opens Brahms's op. 104. Other examples of this same texture appear in the canonic variants of the "Friede" motive in mm. 43–44 and mm. 81–85.

Without question, *Friede auf Erden* is one of the landmark choral compositions of the twentieth century: it forms a bridge between the comparatively accessible choral repertory of the late Romantics (Brahms, Bruckner, Reger, Cornelius, and Wolf) and the emerging atonality of the pre–World War I period. If, as Schoenberg reportedly thought, it was an "illusion" that peace among mankind were still possible, it proved to be elusively difficult to sing, leading Schoenberg to orchestrate it in 1911; apparently he realized that performing this piece at all (not to mention staying in tune), required the support of a *colla parte* chamber orchestra. Schoenberg's attempt to use counterpoint to generate a new, nontonal harmonic language thus pays homage to his German musical heritage.

A similar perversion of tonality appears in a composition by Schoenberg's most famous disciple, Anton Webern (1883–1945). At roughly the same time Schoenberg was finishing his masterpiece, Webern writes a similarly experimental piece in which he attempts to marry contrapuntal rigor with consonant, tertian sonorities. Like Schoenberg's op. 13, Webern's setting of Stephan George's poem *Entflieht auf leichten Kähnen*, op. 2 (1908), turns the hallmark intervals of tonality—thirds and sixths—into a primer of derivative atonality. Like Schoenberg, Webern uses a tonal key signature (one sharp), but the music has little if anything to do with either G major or E minor tonalities (ex.6.7).

Example 6.7 Webern, *Entflieht auf leichten Kähnen*, op. 2, mm. 1–9
©1921, 1948 by Universal Edition A.G., Vienna © Renewed. All Rights Reserved.
Used by permission of European American Music Distributors, LLC, sole U.S.
and Canadian agent for Universal Edition A.G., Vienna

The thirds and sixths of both duets are consonant; example 6.7 shows that they are all freely chromatic, unrelated to one another or to a central tonality. To insure that he doesn't lapse into tonality, Webern has the male voices sing the same music as the female voices one measure later. By so doing, he asserts that counterpoint—not tonality—is the driving force of his composition. Ironically, the work ends a G-major triad that actually sounds dissonant because nothing in the preceding measures has prepared one to hear G major as confirmation of the key signature. *Entflieht* is that rare example of a composition that ends on major chord that sounds dissonant because it has nothing to do with the compositional logic of the piece.

But Schoenberg and Webern are best known for their advocacy and strict use of twelve-tone technique. Josef Rufer believes that this process provided both a new ordering for the pitch materials (absent the traditional frame of tonality) and a way of creating musical form not connected to the traditions of classicism; hence, the appellation of Schoenberg's circle as the "Second Viennese School."[14] Many would doubtless agree with Virgil Thomson's view that Schoenberg's twelve-tone technique is merely a set of rules insuring that one will not write "tonal" music.[15] But was it really as simple as avoiding tonality at all costs? If Schoenberg had simply tried to create a dissonant nontonal language, how could we explain the juxtaposition of the consonant imitative language of the *Three Folk Songs* (op. 49) with the dodecaphonic polyphony of *De Profundis* (op. 50b)? And if we assume that op. 49 is some senescent aberration, even atonal works like *De Profundis* are not totally devoid of tonal gestures.

Schoenberg composed Psalm 130 (*De Profundis*) at the request of the Polish conductor and musicologist Chemjo Vinaver, who wanted to include a Hebrew psalm-setting by Schoenberg for the anthology of Jewish music he was compiling for the Jewish Agency for Palestine.[16] Completed in 1950, Schoenberg dedicated *De Profundis* to the new State of Israel and asked Serge Koussevitzky, who had commissioned a new work for the first King David Festival, to accept this composition as his most fitting contribution.

Still, Schoenberg rejected using traditional Hebrew chants in his setting as Vinaver had suggested. He did adopt Vinaver's suggestion of using the call-and-response format traditionally associated with psalmody but did so in his own Schoenbergian unique way. Rather than restricting the "congregational" response at the end of each verse, Schoenberg introduced unpitched, rhythmic speech to simulate congregational participation and in a manner that places the unpitched element on a nearly equal footing with the sung psalm text. Twenty-five of the work's fifty-five measures contain purely sung music, which points up two tendencies: while Schoenberg begins each psalm verse with sung music, he introduces the spoken chants immediately (m. 2). This equivalence sets up a formal gradient in which the amount of pitched material increases in each successive verse, creating a textural crescendo.

As this facsimile (see Fig. 6.1) shows, Schoenberg scored *De Profundis* for six voices *a cappella*, re-creating the number and disposition of voices used so often by Brahms.[17] Over the opening melody, we see a rubric that will become a Schoenbergian fingerprint: the use of the symbol **H** to indicate the *Hauptstimme* ("leading voice"). This designation runs throughout the composition indicating the most important sung line. Schoenberg sets the eight verses of the psalm to a variety of textures. All six voices sing together in only thirteen of the composition measures (mm. 17, 26–27, 38–40, 42–44, 51–52, and 54–55). Clearly, Schoenberg reserves these for significant textual moments—the end of v. 3, the sung conclusion of v. 5, the end of v. 7, and the beginning and end of the final verse.

The absence of a key signature and the pitch content suggest dodecaphony, but although Schoenberg presents all twelve chromatic pitches in the first section (mm. 1–6), he does so as two hexachords, the pitches of which are separated by rests and "congregational" response. He also often constructs rows of two complementary hexachords, the second often being a transposition of the first (ex. 6.8). Here, the two are related by similar intervallic content (a tritone and two major thirds) arranged in two distinct shapes—asymmetrical (tritone, M3, M3) and symmetrical (M3, tritone, M3).

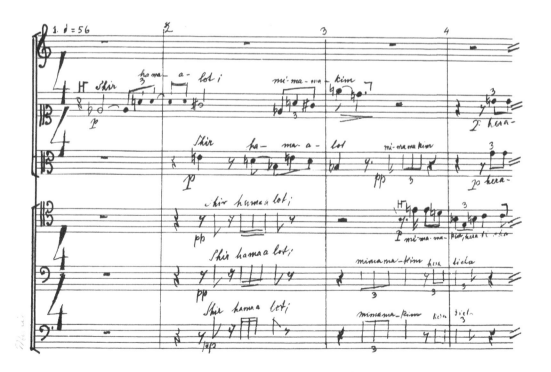

Fig. 6.1 Manuscript (facsimile) of Schoenberg's *De Profundis*, op. 50b

Example 6.8 Schoenberg, *De profundis*, op. 50b

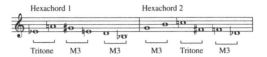

The following example (ex. 6.9) shows two duets resolving from a tritone to a major third, the equivalent of a V–I cadence in D♭ major (the dominant is incomplete). This measure (m. 7) also illustrates Schoenberg's reliance on canonic imitation to generate harmony.

Example 6.9 Schoenberg, *De profundis*, op. 50b, m. 7

Schoenberg associates this particular resolution with the word *Adonai* ("Lord"). This can hardly be a coincidence as he frequently uses the tritone–major-third progression when the word appears, which it does in every verse save the last. Perhaps, like J. S. Bach, Schoenberg equated imitative counterpoint with texts about God's justice and righteousness. If so, we have yet another manifestation of Schoenberg's belief that his new method, built on the cornerstones of traditional tonality, would guarantee the dominance of German musical heritage throughout the new century.

The canonic imitation seen in example 6.9 provides the briefest glimpse into a procedure that permeates the entire work. Schoenberg frequently creates duets that are canonic, such as the opening music of vv. 3 (mm. 13–15), 4 (mm. 18–19), 5 (mm. 23–26), and 6 (mm. 30–31).

Example 6.10 Schoenberg, *De profundis*, op. 50b, mm. 13–15

The last occurrence of this figure (mm. 30–31) shows Schoenberg breaking one of his own cardinal "rules" of dodecaphonic technique (ex. 6.10): no note is to be repeated before all twelve have sounded. But the text that opens v. 6, "Nafshi L'Adonai" prompts a series of oscillations where notes are repeated; the tenor's A–G♯–A–G♯–A is just one example. This counterpoint is visible; it is the contrapuntal juxtapositions that create the musical substance of the piece. It reminds us that Schoenberg himself was a painter and that one of his best friends was Wassily Kandinsky (1866–1944), the father of abstract painting. Like Kandinsky's canvases, Schoenberg's compositions are filled with beautifully shaped contrapuntal lines to the extent that the shapes overwhelm the expressive content of the work.

The work's dramatic conclusion offers a final example of Schoenberg's relentless contrapuntal logic. The melodic pitches of the first soprano and second bass create successive perfect fifths (A♭″–D♭, D″–G, B″ [s1]–E [b] and B♭ [b]–F″ [s1]) as a harmonic frame; the perfection of these intervals is trumped by the melodic tritones that appear between the inner pairs of voices (s2, a: D♯″–A′, E′–B♭′; t, b1: F♯′–C′, F′–B) and the dissonant sonorities they generate. Unlike Webern's *Entflieht*, there is no consonant (i.e., tertian) conclusion. The work's abrupt and seemingly incomplete ending perhaps symbolized the unfinished nature of both Schoenberg's spiritual journey and Israel's redemption.[18]

Comparatively speaking, Anton Webern's approach to serialism is stricter and more broadly applied than Schoenberg's. Webern was, of all of Schoenberg's pupils, the most ardent advocate and strict practitioner of pitch serialism. Webern's more severe style is evident in the three, large, dodecaphonic choral works he composed, all based on poems by Hildegard Jone (1891–1963): *Das Augenlicht*, op. 26, 1935; *Kantate I*, op. 29, 1938–39; *Kantate II*, op. 31, 1941–43. None of these works is often performed because the choral writing is both unidiomatic and very difficult.

Das Augenlicht is scored for mixed chorus and chamber orchestra (fl, cl, hn, sax, tpt, tbn, str, hp, mand, and perc). Webern consistently uses this unusual group of instruments in brief pointillist snippets that effectively obscure the contrapuntal intricacy of his multiple canons. The choral writing, which alternates between imitation (canon) and homophony, is unaccompanied (save for mm. 64–69). Unlike their instrumental counterparts, the voices present complete rows. The first choral passage presents the four basic (untransposed) row-forms as two duets: mm. 8–13, soprano and tenor; mm. 14–19: bass and alto. These canonic duets alternate with homophonic passages of increasing intensity, culminating in what Webern designates as the work's dynamic climax (*dynamischer Höhepunkt*), mm. 64–69 (ex. 6.11).[19]

Example 6.11 Webern, *Das Augenlicht*, op. 26, mvt. 1, mm. 64–69
© 1938 by Universal Edition A.G., English Version © 1956 Universal
Edition A.G. © Renewed. All Rights Reserved. Used by permission
of European American Music Distributors, LLC, sole U.S. and Canadian
agent for Universal Edition, A.G., Vienna.

In this climactic passage none of the choral voices presents a different row-form. Omission of any rows' pitch is rare in Webern's music, especially at climactic moments. The pitches in brackets are missing from the respective choral parts as we can see in the matrix. Four of these omissions may occur because the pitch is already present in another voice (the second and penultimate bass pitches and third alto and tenor pitches). But there is no such explanation for the omission of the final pitch of each part's row:

S	A#	B	D#	C	E	C#	D	F#	F	G#	G [A]
A	C#	C	[G#]	B	G	A#	A	F	F#	D#	E [D]
T	G#	G	[D#]	F#	D	F	E	C	C#	A#	B [A]
B	A	[G]	G#	F	F#	D	C#	E	C	D#	[B G#]

The first clue to solving this comes with the realization that the s/b and a/t pairs sing related row-forms. The alto and tenor sing retrograde forms, the pitches of which are a perfect fourth apart; each voice lacks its row's third and twelfth pitches. While the soprano and bass both use inversions, they differ in the way many pitches are missing (although their total is four, just like the alto/tenor pair). But it happens that the missing soprano pitch [A] is the first pitch of the bass, while the missing bass pitches [A#, B, and G] are pitches 1, 2, and 11 of the soprano. This discovery suggests that Webern used these particular rows because they are combinatorial, that is, the bass provides the missing soprano pitch [A] and the soprano supplying the bass's missing A#, B, and G.

For the three movements of *Kantate 1* (op. 29), Webern sets Jone's poem for soprano solo, mixed chorus, and a chamber orchestra that resembles the one used in op. 26. In the first movement, Webern sets these lines of poetry concerning life's beginning and end for chorus *a cappella*. He presents the text in three choral segments (mm. 14–22, 26–29, and 32–35) separated by brief instrumental interludes and framed by an instrumental prelude and postlude. Each section emphasizes one of the text's central themes—lightning, thunder, and peace. In mvts. 2 and 3 Webern uses the soprano soloist (joined by the chorus in mvt. 3) to create a formal design based on alternating textures. The second movement ("Kleiner Flügel Ahornsamen") was the first music Webern composed. Although he originally intended to open the cantata with the text of the current third movement, he changed his mind for "textual and musical reasons."[20]

The choral writing is daunting, a trait that results from Webern's deliberate use of compound intervals to create angular vocal lines. The sheer difficulty of these lines seems to preclude use of chorus. The vocal parts in mm. 14–21 contain nineteen different pitches instead of the expected twelve. The soprano's first twelve pitches form a row; furthermore, the intervals separating each successive pair of pitches reveals a symmetrical construction and a palindromic form that Webern likes to use in his rows. Even more astonishing is the discovery of a vertical symmetry based on the pitch content of each of the chords that occur in mm. 14–19. If we arrange the pitches of each chord in its most compact intervallic form, we discover that they too form a palindrome based on pitch-class sets (ex. 6.12).

In the example, the four vocal lines in the example present different symmetrical rows. Webern has arranged these lines as chords, the pitch content of which may be reduced to three separate and distinct groups of pitches. The pitch content of each chord forms a separate palindrome.

Such contrapuntally complex music, closely approaching the purity of mathematics, typifies much of Webern's music. The convoluted manipulation of row-forms, pointillist textures (both instrumental and vocal), and serialization of other structural components (timbre, dynamics, scoring, etc.) conspire to make Webern's music seemingly inimical to performance.[21]

Example 6.12 Webern, *Kantate I*, op. 29, mvt. 1, mm. 14–21

IGOR STRAVINSKY

Given the close working relationship with Igor Stravinsky (1882–1971) and Robert Craft's passionate advocacy of the music of Webern, Stravinsky's eventual adoption of twelve-tone technique in the 1950s seems inevitable (see Fig. 6.2). Even though Schoenberg and Stravinsky lived relatively close to one another in Southern California, they were never friends. Indeed, Stravinsky was the primary target of the third of Schoenberg's *Drei Satiren*, op. 28 (*Der neue Klassizismus*). Stravinsky waited until Schoenberg was dead to appropriate the method of composition so closely associated with him. Stravinsky's first exploration of row technique occurs in the canons of his *Cantata* (1952), the circumscribed intervallic series he uses in the *Septet* (1953), and *In Memoriam Dylan Thomas* (1954). Stravinsky's first wholesale adoption of Schoenberg's method is a choral work—*Canticum sacrum* (1955).[22] Composed for the city of Venice in honor of its patron saint, Mark, Stravinsky's cantata is scored for tenor and bass soloists, chorus, and a large orchestra. After the opening "Dedicatio," Stravinsky composes five musical movements, a representation of the five domes atop St. Mark's Cathedral, the city's most iconic landmark.

Stravinsky's repetition of the opening chorus ("Euntes in mundum") in retrograde as the closing movement ("Illi autem profecti") creates an audible and symbolic symmetry. The rationale for this musical relationship stems from the texts, both taken from the Gospel of Mark 16:15: the "Great Commission" ("Go ye into all the world and preach the gospel to every creature") and Mark 16:20: "And they went forth and preached everywhere, the Lord working with them and in them, and confirming the word with signs following." Thus, Stravinsky's use of retrograde for the final chorus represents the disciples' setting out to fulfill Christ's command. The two movements are built around a polytonal interplay of chords related by thirds—B minor and G minor—typical of Stravinsky. This harmonic language is essentially a continuation of that used in the *Symphony of Psalms* (1930, rev. 1948).

Canticum sacrum's two solo movements (2 and 4) for tenor and baritone, respectively, represent the next level of symmetry in the work's overall structural design. The tenor aria, "Surge aquilo," is Stravinsky's first composition to make exclusive use of a twelve-tone row. The solo tenor's initial melody is the prime version of Stravinsky's row (ex. 6.13a, b); it follows a harmonized presentation of the retrograde by harp and three contrabass soli. Stravinsky's use of pitch repetition is the first of many departures from the prescriptions of Schoenberg's technique.

Example 6.13 a–b Stravinsky: *Canticum sacrum*, mvt. 2

a. Row

b. mm. 2-4

Sur-ge a-qui-lo____ et   ve -   -   - ni, ve -   ni,____

The work's centerpiece is a cantata within a cantata; Stravinsky composes separate movements, each of which bears the title of one of three virtues—charity (*Caritas*), hope (*Spes*), and faith (*Fides*). Stravinsky ties the three movements together with a recurring organ ritornello and different brief orchestral introductions. The organ ritornello appears three times—on A in *Caritas*, on C in *Spes*, and on B in *Fides*. This solemn theme is a tone row that, as Eric W. White notes, is the retrograde inversion of the row used throughout the movement.[23] Stravinsky takes advantage of the fact that the ritornello's final pitch is one whole step lower than its starting pitch. By starting his final ritornello on B and ending on A, Stravinsky establishes A as the pitch with which the movement begins and ends. Stravinsky uses texture to differentiate the formal segments of mvt. 3. The central movement, *Spes*, has the clearest formal structure. After the organ (mm. 130–35) and instrumental (mm. 136–47) preludes, Stravinsky creates a rondo form (ABABA) based on the alternation of male solo voices (A) and the choral trebles (B). All three A sections use the same pitch content and rhythm, drawing their melody from two different rows, neither of which appears completely in a single voice. Conversely, the choral trebles sing different rows each time they appear. Despite these different choral rows, the accompaniment (oboes and tenor trombone 1) and its thematic material remain the same. The two outer movements feature a variety of rows sung contrapuntally. In *Caritas*, the voices sing various rows in canon, accompanied by bass trumpet. For *Fides*, Stravinsky assigns the row to the chorus in unison to reflect the steadfastness of faith.

Stravinsky composed several more choral works that use twelve-tone technique in Stravinsky's idiosyncratic way: *Threni, id'est Lamentationes Jeremiae Prophetae* (1957–58); *A Sermon, a Narrative and a Prayer* (1960–61); *Anthem: The Dove Descending Breaks the Air* (1962); *The Flood* (1961–62); and *Requiem Canticles* (1965–66). Of these, the simplest and best exemplar is *The Dove Descending*, a setting of text from the last of T. S. Eliot's *Four Quartets*. Eliot

Fig. 6.2 Igor Stravinsky (Pablo Picasso, 1917)

himself suggested this text to Stravinsky, who, at the time, was looking for a hymn text to set as his contribution to the new *English Hymnal*.[24]

Stravinsky dedicated the composition to Eliot, presenting the poet with the manuscript of the completed composition. This short, *a cappella* composition is pedagogically useful because Stravinsky restricts himself to just four rows—the prime, retrograde, inversion, and a retrograde inversion transposed six semitones from the original (ex. 6.14). These rows form the basis of four discrete musical sections defined by different vocal textures: A (s/a); B (satb); C (t/b), and B (satb).

Example 6.14 Stravinsky, *Anthem: The Dove Descending,* rows

The B sections are identical in scoring and music, concluding with two forms of the row—Retrograde (a/b) and retrograde inversion (s/t)—that allow the composition to end with a consonant, tertian sonority. Restricting himself to these four row-forms is yet another example of Stravinsky's penchant for elaborate pre-compositional planning; while this limitation simplifies analysis, it does little to facilitate aesthetic understanding or successful performance.

OTHER DODECAPHONIC COMPOSERS

Aside from Stravinsky, the list of other prominent composers of choral music who use twelve-tone technique to varying degrees includes George Rochberg (1918–2005), Ernst Krenek (1900–1991), Luigi Dallapiccola (1904–75), and Krzysztof Penderecki (b. 1933). Dallapiccola was the first to adopt Schoenberg's dodecaphonic style in his triptych *Canti di Prigionia* (1938–41) (see Fig. 6.3). These "Songs of Prisoners" were Dallapiccola's way of protesting Mussolini's adoption of Hitler's anti-Semitic policies (Dallapiccola's wife was a Jew). As a result of his own intellectual imprisonment, Dallapiccola set Latin prayers attributed to three famous prisoners of conscience—Mary Stuart, the sixth-century Roman philosopher Boethius, and the preacher-monk Girolamo Savonarola, who instigated protests against the Medici family in fifteenth-century Florence.[25] Dallapiccola composed the three movements separately, the first in July 1939, the second roughly a year later, and the last in October 1941.

Fig. 6.3 Luigi Dallapiccola

To unify these diverse texts Dallapiccola decided to include portions of the Gregorian sequence *Dies irae* in each movement; by so doing he sought to turn the persecution and death of three prisoners from different places and times into a more universal metaphor. In addition to varying the texture, pitch level, and instrumentation of each movement, Dallapiccola increased the amount of cantus firmus used to ratchet up the tension (ex. 6.15).[26]

Example 6.15 Dallapiccola, *Canti di Prigionia, Dies irae*

In the first *Canto*, Dallapiccola uses only the first phrase of the Gregorian sequence and limits its appearance to the instrumental introduction (mm. 1–25). Once the chorus begins singing in m. 26, the cantus firmus disappears. Dallapiccola seems to regard the archaic, modal diatonicism of the chant as a foil to his chromatic tone rows, creating a musical tension that mirrors the tense uncertainty of contemporaneous world events.

Dallapiccola's row for *Canto 1* resides in the series of piano tetrachords that accompany the first phrase of *Dies irae*. The intervallic construction of three tetrachords is reminiscent of the hexachordal symmetry found in Schoenberg's *De Profundis*. The intervallic separations of the pitches (number of semitones) of Dallapiccola's three tetrachords show that the first two are identical; the third tetrachord opens with two minor thirds, but the last two pitches are separated by a major third rather than the tritone found in the first two.

Analysis of twelve-tone music makes the reasonable, though not always accurate assumption that the first collection of pitches (linear or vertical) one hears is the primary thematic material. The collection of twelve pitches contained in the piano tetrachords duplicates two pitch classes—G and E, a redundancy that disqualifies them as the source of the tone row. The actual completion of Dallapiccola's twelve-note series appears not in piano 2 (m. 4) but in the piano 1 chord (m. 4): D–F–A♭–D♭. Therefore, the twelve-tone row is actually E–G–B♭–F♯–A–C–E♭–B–D–F–A♭–D♭. In the first *Canto*, Dallapiccola consistently uses only the first tetrachord in both prime and retrograde motion on a variety of pitches. In the twenty-five-measure introduction, this theme appears only in the instruments, but when the chorus begins singing (m. 26) Dallapiccola uses its distinctive contour as the basis of a point of imitation. Another clue that this movement is not a typical twelve-tone composition is the tetrachord's complete absence for considerable portions of the music (e.g., mm. 37–44).

At the beginning of the second *Canto*, Dallapiccola makes the pitches of his row explicit. Given the second movement's changes of tempo, meter, scoring and musical character, the appearance of what seems to be a new row is perfectly logical. However, analysis reveals that despite its fragmentation, the "new" row is not new but is in fact the retrograde of the row used in *Canto* 1. Armed with this information, it is easy to generate the complete serial matrix.

Like the gradual expansion of the *Dies irae* motive from movement to movement, Dallapiccola adds something new to his row: *Canto* 1 uses fragments of the row, *Canto* 2 begins with the entire retrograde, adding prime forms as early as the fifth measure. Dallapiccola injects another variation following the piano row (mm. 9–12) with a version (mm. 13–16) in which he reverses the order of the second and third pitches of each trichord.

In this same movement, Dallapiccola does something tonal that flies in the face of Schoenberg's attempted avoidance of his musical past. At the text "Felix qui potuit" (m. 184), Dallapiccola reprises, note for note, the music of the first 133 measures of the movement, effectively creating a large ternary form. Other aspects of the reprise are less literal than the row-forms, suggesting a modified or embellished return of A. The unison choral passage that begins *Canto* 3 apparently uses a new row, although its prominent fifth (the inversion of the fourth that began *Canto* 2) followed by two minor thirds suggest a connection between this row and its predecessor. But the change of the minor third from minor to major and the restriction of its presentation to the unison chorus dissolve any direct linkage. Following the choral row (mm. 2–4), the instruments play a harmonization of *Dies irae*, the bass line of which is the first tetrachord of row 1, used in both prime and inverted form. This template—alternating the unison choral row and the harmonized presentation of the sequence—marks the culmination of the thematic processes present in the work's opening measures.

Dallapiccola's use of twelve-tone materials represents his own personal appropriation of Schoenberg's formulation. While the choral writing tends to avoid the rows (*Canto* 3 being the exception), subtle uses of row elements appear in the choral parts of all three movements. In the first movement, the row's opening tetrachord (and *only* the opening tetrachord) becomes the basis for a point of imitation. By the time Dallapiccola wrote his opera, *Il Prigioniero* (1946–47) and the choral drama *Job* (1950), strict dodecaphony governs the choral parts as well as the instrumental parts.

The early career of the Austrian composer Ernst Krenek is marked by the influence of neoclassicism and American jazz, the latter evident in the opera *Jonny spielt auf* (1927), which launched his international reputation. As early as 1933, Krenek made extensive use of dodecaphony, adopting it as the exclusive language of his remaining compositional output. Following the annexation of Austria in 1938, Krenek immigrated to the United States and became an American citizen in 1945. His setting of the *Lamentations of Jeremiah*, op. 93 (1957), features a unique blending of twelve-tone procedure and Gregorian chant. In his preface to the score, Krenek provides invaluable insight into his compositional approach.[27] In recognition of liturgical precedent, Krenek sets off the Hebrew letters in a manner similar to the ornamented capitals of Renaissance manuscripts; more importantly, his primary theme reproduces the first four pitches of the Gregorian tone (ex. 6.16a).

Example 6.16 a–b Krenek, *Lamentatio Jeremiae Prophetae*, op. 93

Example 6.16 a–b Continued

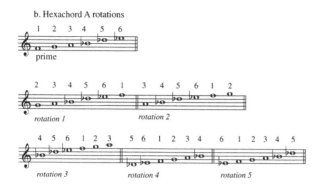

b. Hexachord A rotations

prime

rotation 1 · rotation 2

rotation 3 · rotation 4 · rotation 5

To complete the first hexachord, Krenek adds the pitches D♭ and E♭. He calls this Hexachord A. He orders the six missing pitches as an ascending scale—B, C, D, E, F♯, and G♯—to create the remainder of his row called Hexachord B. Instead of creating a traditional matrix based on this row, Krenek rotates both hexachords (ex. 6.16b), so that each new version of the two hexachords begins with the next pitch in the sequence; hence, the first rotation of Hexachord A (F–G–A–B♭–D♭–E♭) is G–A–B♭–D♭–E♭–F. He applies the same process to Hexachord B and then transposes both hexachords so that all six rotations of each begin on a single pitch— F (Hexachord A) and B (Hexachord B). He explains that the purpose of this arrangement "is to allow the use of the principle of composition by tone row, except that all twelve tones can be in play continuously while each, in accordance with the compositional purpose, can be chosen in various gradations of the six-pitch diatonic and the twelve-pitch chromatic series."[28] The resultant choral writing, while strictly ordered, is more consonant, expressive, and melodically accessible than most dodecaphonic choral music (ex. 6.17).

Example 6.17 Krenek, *Lamentatio Jeremiae Prophetae*, op. 93

The example shows the conclusion of the first lesson (*Lectio prima*). Despite his complex melodic manipulations and counterpoint, Krenek creates choral music that is quite beautiful but difficult to sing.

Krzysztof Penderecki ranks as an important twentieth-century exponent of twelve-tone technique. Known primarily for his innovative experiments in sonority and the new notational signs required to represent them, Penderecki's appropriation of Schoenberg's technique is just another in the large array of techniques he employs. His earliest choral use of row technique occurs in the second movement of *Aus den Psalmen Davids* (1959). In contrast to the percussion and quartal harmonies that dominate mvt. 1, mvt. 2 is a brief, *a cappella* setting of Psalm 30, which uses only two row-forms (prime and inversion) as well as their transposition by a perfect fourth. This simple application of serialism is most clearly visible in the first seven measures of the alto part (ex. 6.18).

Example 6.18 Penderecki, *Aus den Psalmen Davids*, mvt. 2, mm. 1–7
© 1976 by Schott Music. All Rights Reserved. Used by Permission of European American Music Distributors, LLC, sole U.S. and Canadian agent for Schott Music.

The bass inverts the first ten pitches of the alto's row, followed by the simultaneous entries of soprano and tenor. The soprano sings all twelve chromatic pitches, the tenor only five (repeating the last three of these in m. 8). From this point on, row usage is less predictable.

In his masterpiece, the *Passio et mors Domini Nostri Jesu Christi secundum Lucam* (*St. Luke Passion*, 1963), Penderecki makes a much greater use of rows; these occur most often in instrumental passages or solo melodies as a means of building chromatic clusters but not in the chorus. In their analysis of the work, Ray Robinson and Allen Winold document the diversity of the work's thematic material, which, among other melodic types, includes multiple twelve-tone rows derived in many cases from the BACH motive (B♭–A–C–B♮) motif.[29] Of the thirty-five motives Robinson and Winold cite, only two—cantus firmus 1 (CF-1) and the BACH row—use all twelve chromatic pitches; both utilize their pitches as a kind of cantus firmus.[30]

Example 6.19 Penderecki, *St. Luke Passion*, Rows
© 1960 by Schott Music, © Renewed. All Rights Reserved. Used by Permission of European American Music Distributors, LLC, sole U.S. and Canadian agent for Schott Music.

The first row (CF-1) follows Schoenberg's ideal, creating the second hexachord by transposing the first one a distance of six semitones (ex. 6.19a). Penderecki uses the opening intervals of the Polish hymn melody *Swięty Boże* (ascending semitone, ascending minor third, and descending semitone) to initiate his second hexachord.[31] The BACH row (ex, 6.19b) features three different arrangements of the BACH motive. Pitches 1–4 and 9–12 feature the motif in retrograde, beginning on E♭ and B♮ respectively;[32] the middle tetrachord uses the prime version starting on G (G–F♯–A–G♯).

Penderecki's use of pitch serialism rarely rises to the rigid application found in Schoenberg or Webern; at no point in the *St. Luke Passion* do multiple row-forms appear in the choral parts, either melodically or harmonically. The setting of Psalm 10, v. 1 closely resembles the row used in the second movement of *Aus den Psalmen Davids*.[33] Fifteen of the chorus's sixteen measures use only the four voices of chorus 1. The only complete statement of the row CF-1 appears as the alto's first eight pitches, the remaining pitches (9–12) follow in the bass. The remaining choral parts (save for the t/b reiteration of the BACH motive in mm. 13–15) use only partial row statements. Penderecki's use of twelve-tone rows is neither substantial (in terms of the vertical combination of multiple rows or melodic consistency) nor unique; he creates distinctive melodic curves with little apparent concern for the number of pitches they contain. All told, his row usage constitutes a fairly prescribed portion of his compositional palette.

BENJAMIN BRITTEN

A prominent composer who adapted the pitch-serialism method in a way that uniquely fitted his personal aesthetic is Benjamin Britten (1913–76), who uses aspects of twelve-tone technique in his *Cantata Academica* (op. 62, 1960), *Missa Brevis* (op. 63, 1959), and *War Requiem* (op. 66, 1963). In these works Britten's use of dodecaphony is purely melodic and typically harmonized by triads. His 1954 chamber opera *The Turn of the Screw*, op. 54, is built almost entirely around the twelve note "screw" theme. Only in his late opera *Death in Venice*, op. 88 (1973), does he give himself over wholly to twelve-tone procedure in both vocal and instrumental parts.

The *Cantata Academica* illustrates Britten's unique application of dodecaphony in a sustained and interesting way: the opening movement of the cantata's second part, *Tema seriale con fuga* ("Serial Theme with Fugue"), is a unison melody that includes all twelve chromatic pitches plus a concluding repetition of the opening pitch sung over a consonant triadic accompaniment (ex. 6.20).

Example 6.20 a–b Britten, *Cantata Academica*, op. 62, mvt. 8

a. mm. 2-5

b. mm. 11-12

After two identical presentations of this theme, Britten begins his fugue, the subject of which is clearly not a twelve-tone theme. Nonetheless, he presents this theme twelve times, starting each statement of the subject with the successive pitches of his row. He then caps off the movement with a contrapuntal tour de force in a stretto where each part presents recaps the twelve fugal entries starting on each successive quarter note beat. The ingenious part of this stretto is this compression of all twelve entries in such close proximity. Britten also extends the unifying presence of his serial theme by using each of its twelve pitches as the tonal center of the cantata's twelve movements.[34] Britten's use of serial technique in the *Missa Brevis* and *War Requiem* follows this model quite closely.

CONCLUSION

Although Schoenberg's belief that the twelve-tone technique would become the basis of modern music has had its advocates, the system he advocated failed to dominate the compositional landscape to the extent he envisioned. Nowhere has the style received a more tepid reception than among choral composers for the simple reason that, in choral singing, voice leading matters.

We return to the question posed by Schoenberg in his poem "Am Scheideweg." It appears that the great majority of people (whether composers, choral conductors, or audiences) have come to equate Schoenberg's opposition of tonal and atonal as code for consonant and dissonant, but history will show that his emphasis on counterpoint at the expense of sonority became one extreme of a musical spectrum. At the other extreme lay the inherently conservative nature of choral music. Music like Webern's, for example, may never become a staple of the choral repertory precisely because its voice leading (not to mention the level of harmonic dissonance) is ultimately unwieldy to choral singers and, in general, not worth the trouble. Most choral composers and conductors of the twentieth and twenty-first centuries have answered Schoenberg's query with an overwhelming vote for *tonal* even if they ultimately misunderstand the true nature of the categories being held in opposition. Recasting Schoenberg's question as "Consonant or Dissonant" advances neither our understanding of his motivation nor the transformative role that his method has had in the choral music of the twentieth century. As his *Drei Volkslieder*, op. 49, make abundantly clear, Schoenberg never envisioned a choice of consonance over dissonance but rather the affirmation of contrapuntal craft in the face of musical sentiment. The greatest legacy of serialism is to be found in the Hegelian synthesis it effected, enriching a choral music focused too much on sonority with new contrapuntal rigor.

7

Nationalism, Folk Song, and Identity

Music with a pronounced nationalistic flavor has been a presence in the concert halls of Western Europe since the eighteenth century. Interest in the music of a country other than one's own is present in the eighteenth- and nineteenth-century's fascination with "Turkish" (e.g., the *Rondo alla Turca* from Mozart's Piano Sonata in A major, KV 331, or the "Turkish March" in the Finale of Beethoven's Ninth Symphony), and "Gypsy" music (e.g., Schumann's *Zigeunerleben*, Brahms's *Zigeunerlieder*, or Liszt's *Hungarian Rhapsodies*, S. 244). At best, Western appropriation of such music retains little or no connection to its original cultural context. Although Chopin was Polish and the mazurka is a Polish dance, one is hard-pressed to see his mazurkas as overtly nationalistic. In this period, native elements are used more as novelty items than as serious representations of non-European cultures. Fascination with the exotic is part and parcel of romantic poetry, beginning as early as the French translations of the *One Thousand and One Nights* by Antoine Galland; the fascination of Western Europeans with these exotic tales persisted, eventually becoming the inspiration for Schumann's oratorio *Das Paradies und die Peri*, which is based on *Lalla Rookh*, a Persian-inspired tale by Thomas Moore published in 1817.

National music as exotic ornament is not the subject of this chapter, though. We will see how increasing local interest in and promotion of native culture for its own sake blossomed into a substantial body of choral repertory. This trend in countries with long-standing histories of music like France, Italy, and Germany can be traced back to movements of political unification.

That is not to deny the nationalist sentiment that spawned such works as Brahms's *Fest- und Gedenksprüche*, op. 109, *La Marseillaise*, or the chorus *Va pensiero* from Verdi's opera *Nabucco* (1841), which became something of a de facto national anthem for the Italian Risorgimento. But we will examine choral music that draws its textual and musical substance from the discovery and elevation of indigenous folk art to serious art music in countries such as England, Hungary, Russia, and Scandinavia. This folk art often arose as a response to what Glenn Watkins calls the "German hegemony."[1]

The first efforts at local musical training in many of these emerging countries took as their model the tradition of the German conservatory, a pedagogy immersed in the three Bs of German music. In chapter 6 we saw how Arnold Schoenberg attempted to ensure the continuance of this German dominance through his creation of a system of composition that would keep the German contrapuntal tradition at the center of modern music for the new century. Indeed, much of the nationalistic music of the early twentieth century took as its raison d'etre the provision of an active resistance to that German musical tradition. In *The English Musical Renaissance*, Frank Howes writes: "Germany, Italy, and France culturally hang together in spite of the wide stylistic and temperamental differences between them. But their tyranny in music, a tyranny of melodic and harmonic language based on key and a tyranny of structure and design as evolved in sonata form, was provoking revolt in Russia, in Scandinavia, in Hungary, in Bohemia, in Spain and finally in England."[2] The Franco-Prussian War (1870–71) initiated France's separation from the cultural axis Watkins describes, spilling over into the two world wars that dominated twentieth-century cultural history. Concurrent with French explorations of non-German alternatives are similar stirrings all over Europe—the music of Edvard Grieg (1843–1907), Jean Sibelius (1865–1957), and Carl Nielsen (1865–1931) in Scandinavia, and in Russia the "Mighty Russian Five": Mussorgsky, Borodin, Rimsky-Korsakov, Balakirev, and Cui.

ENGLAND

The renascence of English music in the twentieth century is still debated. What revival there was drew its impetus from the rediscovery of English folk song and the revival of polyphonic music from the Tudor and early Jacobean eras. The movement began in earnest with John Broadwood's publication of sixteen songs associated with harvest and other rural festivals in 1843. Fifty years later, his niece, Lucy, and J. A. Fuller-Maitland published *English Country Songs*, an expanded version of the earlier collection.[3] The Folk-Song Society was founded in 1898 to collect, preserve, and publish folk songs, ballads, and English tunes. This organization had as charter members such musical luminaries as John Stainer (1840–1901), Alexander Mackenzie (1847–1935), C. Hubert H. Parry (1848–1918), Charles V. Stanford (1852–1924), and Edward Elgar (1857–1934), later adding Percy Aldridge Grainger (1882–1961), whose folk-song research in Britain was concurrent with the work of Béla Bartók in Hungary.

But the prime architect of the folk song revival was Cecil Sharp (1859–1924), who despite a lack of professional musical training, pioneered what we now call ethnological fieldwork, collecting 3,000 English folk songs and another 1,700 tunes of English origin in the Appalachian Mountains of Virginia, North Carolina, Tennessee, West Virginia, and eastern Kentucky.[4] Editors and publishers, following Sharp's example, produced a steady stream of anthologies like *National English Airs* (1840) and *Popular Music of the Olden Time* (1859).

Sharp's efforts influenced the two composers who, more than any others, integrated folk song into the emerging English musical identity—Ralph Vaughan Williams (1872–1958) and Gustav Holst (1874–1934) (Fig. 7.1).

Vaughan Williams began collecting folk songs in East Anglia in 1903; his compositions *In the Fen Country* (1904) and three *Norfolk Rhapsodies* (1906) were the direct result of this activity. Concerning his own discovery of folk song, Vaughan Williams stated, "My intercourse with Sharp crystallized and confirmed what I already vaguely felt about folk-song and its relationship to the composer's art. With Sharp . . . (one) had to be either pro-folk-song or anti-folk-song and I came down heavily on the folk-song side."[5] Imogen Holst notes that her father undertook similar work at approximately the same time: "He had already begun to dream of a renaissance in English music; here [in the folk song] to his delight he found English music at its very best. Folk-songs finally brushed all trace of Wagner from his work. . . . He had the deepest admiration

Fig. 7.1 Gustav Holst with Edward Elgar (ca. 1921)

for Cecil Sharp . . . and felt that when the time came for the English musical history of the twentieth century to be written, Cecil Sharp's name would stand out above all others."[6]

The role of folk music hinged on the nature of its use. Vaughan Williams used two different approaches—straightforward arrangement (harmonization) of a melody, and the transformation of that melodic style into a new musical language. Hugh Ottaway and Alain Frogley describe his dilemma as one of "reconciling rounded lyrical structures with the demands of large-scale structures," a challenge made more difficult by his fondness for small-scale stanzaic tunes.[7] Vaughan Williams's arrangements led him to develop new principal methods of translating melody-based forms into larger musical designs.

Vaughan Williams became convinced that the folk song was capable of sustaining larger, more complex musical structures. His operas *Hugh the Drover* (1911) and *Sir John in Love* (1929) make conspicuous use of this genre. The first choral work to appropriate folk song was his popular *Fantasia on Christmas Carols* (1912), founded on traditional English Carols, together with fragments of other well-known carol tunes.

The first tune, "The Truth Sent From Above" (*Herefordshire*), is Hypoaeolian, although Vaughan Williams's harmonization often uses F♯, foreshadowing the E-major tonality of the second carol, "Come All You Worthy Gentlemen" (*Somerset*). Vaughan Williams sets "On Christmas Night" (*Sussex*) in G major, only to obscure that tonality by its combination with the final carol, "God Bless the Ruler of This House," which reuses the second tune and its key (*Somerset*). Wilfrid Mellers has suggested that the *Carol Fantasia* is "affecting precisely because it is not an exercise in anthropological lore or retrospective musical research but a modest re-vision of a life that had once seemed permanent."[8]

Vaughan Williams favored assimilation of folk song over direct quotation as the basis of his developing style. A typical by-product of this choice is the use of gapped, pentatonic melodies, a staple of folk songs. The hymn tune *Kingsfold* is an English folk song adapted by Vaughan Williams for use in the *English Hymnal* of 1906 and can be found in many hymnals throughout the United States and Britain.

Example 7.1 Kingsfold

The key signature suggests either G major or E minor; while both tonalities appear in the melody, the nearly complete avoidance of F♯ and C emphasizes the melody's pentatonic character. An inclination toward triads based on the third and sixth scale degrees as accompaniment adds to the modal feel of Vaughan William's harmonizations (ex. 7.1).

Vaughan Williams also composed pieces designated as "folk songs" the cycle *Five English Folk Songs* (1913) marks his earliest direct use of folk song. The five pieces included in this cycle are "The Dark-Eyed Sailor," "The Springtime of the Year," "Just as the Tide Was Flowing," "The Lover's Ghost," and "Wassail Song." It is interesting to compare the melody of *Kingsfold* (ex. 7.1) with his transcription of a Dorian folk melody for "Just as the Tide was Flowing" (ex. 7.2a) published in the 1906 issue of the *Journal of the Folk Song Society*.[9]

Example 7.2 a–b "Just as the Tide was Flowing"

a. Dorian Folk Song

b. Dorset Folk Song

These two pentatonic melodies are similar save for the latter's larger range. Compare the Dorset tune (ex. 7.2b) with the opening of Vaughan Williams's composition (ex. 7.3). Except for its transposition down a step and some minor modifications, his melody is virtually identical with the tune that George Gardiner published in July 1906.[10] Julian Onderdonk notes that contrary to the composer's self-proclaimed objectivity, frequent discrepancies between the transcription and its later use in compositions is par for the course, especially with arrangements.[11]

Like many folk songs, "Just as the Tide was Flowing" is strophic. Vaughan Williams sets the first four stanzas, omitting the rest due to variations in scansion. For the most part, he deploys the tune in the soprano or tenor voice. Harmonically, he favors tertian chordal accompaniments with a predilection for plagal cadences (D to A) suggested by the melodic cadences from F♯ to A (ex. 7.3).

Example 7.3 Vaughan Willliams, "Just as the Tide was Flowing," mm. 1–4

In addition to being strophic, many of these texts contain dialogue. "The Dark-Eyed Sailor," for example, involves two characters, William (the "dark-eyed sailor") and an unnamed young lady. The full chorus (as Narrator) sings the first two words of v. 2 ("Said William"), after which the tenors sing the tune (ex. 7.4).

Example 7.4 Vaughan Williams, "The Dark-Eyed Sailor," mm. 11–18

Later in the same verse, the chorus's "She said" precedes the women's voices singing "It's a dark-eyed sailor."

Gustav Holst published only two significant collections of folk songs, op. 36b (1916) and an unnumbered collection of twelve songs (1930–31). The *Six Choral Folk Songs* owe their existence to William G. Whittaker's fondness for Holst's arrangement of "This Have I Done for My True Love." When Whittaker asked Holst for permission to perform this "folk song," Holst replied that it was not a folk song, but he would arrange one for Whittaker's concert. On April 24, 1916, Holst sent Whittaker "I Sowed the Seeds of Love," confiding that he "had given up all hope of writing anything for yr. Concert when this 'came' all at once just 24 hours ago along with some ideas for arranging folk songs."[12] Holst dedicated the first three pieces to Whittaker, the last three to Charles Kennedy Scott and the Oriana Madrigal Society.[13] Five of the six melodies (including "Swansea Town," p. 85 in *Marrow Bones*) were transcribed and published by George B. Gardiner; the sixth ("I Love My Love") is based on "The Loyal Lover" published in *Songs of the West*.[14]

Holst's approach to "Swansea Town" is nearly identical to Vaughan Williams's in "Just as the Tide Was flowing": Holst transposes the melody to a more singable range and slightly modifies its melody. Like Vaughan Williams, Holst pays attention to the implied gender of the text using male voices to represent the anonymous sailor serenading "Nancy." In v. 2, Holst's simple, four-part harmonization avoids tonal progressions (e.g., V–I) in favor of inversions. The text of v. 3 leads to some obvious text painting—hummed chromatic lines and the alto's mournful octave ascent and descent to represent the howling winds of the storm. The concluding stanza resembles the second, except that the melody appears in the male voices accompanied by a descant (ssa) based on inverted parallel triads.

Both Holst and Vaughan Williams were active as choral conductors, which may explain the size of their choral output; alternatively, they simply may have conducted choirs to insure performances of their music. Both composers also participated prominently in major choral festivals. From 1920 to 1926 Vaughan Williams conducted the London Bach Choir (founded 1849); Holst, who had conducted the Hammersmith Socialist Choir in the late 1890s, created the Whitsuntide Singers in 1916 to perform his own music as well as compositions by Purcell, Weelkes, and other early English composers at annual music festivals. Vaughan Williams first set the poetry of Walt Whitman ("Toward the Unknown Region") for the Leeds Festival in 1907, followed by more Whitman texts in his *Sea Symphony* (1910). For the Gloucester Festival in 1910, Vaughan Williams produced a signature composition—the *Fantasia on a Theme of Thomas Tallis* for double string orchestra; this work uses as its theme the Phrygian melody composed by Thomas Tallis in 1562 ("The Third Tune") for the metrical psalm paraphrases of Archbishop Matthew Parker's Psalter.

The first choral manifestation of Tudor revivalism was Vaughan Williams's *Mass in G minor* (1922), inspired by the tireless advocacy of Richard Runciman Terry (organist-choirmaster at Westminster Cathedral) of the music of Tallis and Byrd and dedicated to Holst's Whitsuntide Singers. The opening melody of the Kyrie sets the tone for the entire work. Though nominally in G minor, the persistent presence of E♭s suggest Dorian mode. Similarly Tudor in style is the Kyrie's use of a point of imitation. The use of two major chords with roots a third apart generates cross relations like those commonly found in Tudor church music, as one finds in the opening harmonic progression of the Gloria. The Gloria and Credo feature double choir, a texture perhaps derived from the *Decani* and *Cantoris* divisions that form an essential aspect of Tudor practice. These terms indicate the ecclesiastic location: *decani*, the side of a cathedral where the dean sits, south side of a church; *cantoris*, the side of a cathedral where the precentor or music director and choir sit, north side of a church. A final historical allusion is Vaughan Williams's imitation of the planing first-inversion triads known as discant style in the Benedictus.

The closest parallel to Vaughan Williams's *Mass* is Holst's eight-part *Nunc Dimittis* (1915). Also composed for Richard R. Terry, the work was premiered in 1915 on Easter Sunday at Westminster Cathedral; after that, it lay forgotten until Imogen Holst reconstructed it for performance at the 1974 Aldeburgh Festival (the centenary of Holst's birth). Although Holst assigned a key signature of three sharps, the music is rarely in a key. Most striking are the abrupt juxtaposition of chords a whole step apart, prominent use of G naturals, and plagal cadences. Like Vaughan Williams's *Mass*, Holst uses the double-choir format but with even greater flexibility, as seen in the contrast between ensembles of high and low voices at "Lumen ad revelationem gentium."

Such references to the choral techniques of earlier times also appear in the larger works of both composers. The crown jewel of Holst's output is *The Hymn of Jesus*, op. 37 (1917), which directly followed his widely known composition of *The Planets*, op. 32 (1914–16). An earlier set of choral hymns (op. 26), based on texts from the *Rig Veda* that Holst had translated, is the choral ancestor of the *Hymn of Jesus*. Holst composed his *Choral Hymns from the Rig Veda* during a period of intense interest in subjects and texts drawn from Eastern culture. Richard Cappell commented that "So far as the spirit of the music went, the hymns might almost as well have belonged to prehistoric Gloucestershire as to the valley of the Indus. It was a misapprehension of twenty-five years ago to put the strangeness of the musical style down to Oriental influences."[15] Holst's specific musical techniques included use of asymmetrical meters (5/4, 7/4, etc.), unusual scales, cross rhythms, and canon to generate a new harmonic language. Perhaps most successful is the third set, scored for female voices and harp (1910); Holst dedicated them to Frank Duckworth and his all-female choir at Blackburn, who "were the first musical executants to take me seriously as a composer."[16] The "Hymn of the Travelers" (the fourth song in set 3) is an excellent representative of the collection as a whole (ex. 7.5).

Example 7.5 Holst, *Choral Hymns from the Rig Veda*, op. 26, no. 3, mvt. 4, mm. 1–5

A hypnotic Lydian (on D) tune cast in subtly varied versions of 5/4 meter is used to set all five verses of text; Holst injects variety by adding progressively added wordless countermelodies.

Dedicated to his friend Ralph Vaughan Williams, *The Hymn of Jesus* sets texts from the Apocryphal Acts of St. John (in the New Testament Apocryphal Books) translated from the original Greek by Holst. The text elaborates a verse from Matthew 26:30, "And when they had sung a hymn, they went out to the Mount of Olives." To this spare account, the apocryphal source adds considerable detail: "He commanded us to make as it were a ring, holding one another's hands, and Himself standing in the middle. He said: 'Respond Amen to me.' He began then to sing a hymn and to say: 'Glory to Thee, Father!' And we, going about in a ring, said 'Amen, Amen . . .' So then, my beloved, after this dance with us, the Lord went out: and we men gone astray or awakened out of sleep fled all ways."[17]

The work is scored for two mixed choruses, a treble semichorus (ssa) and a large orchestra.

Example 7.6 Holst, *The Hymn of Jesus*, op. 37, "Prelude," mm. 28–30

Example 7.7 Holst, *The Hymn of Jesus*, op. 37, "Hymn," mm. 69–70

Holst's orchestration is precise, guided by his experience as a professional trombonist. His prefatory notes even include a list of instruments that may be omitted if necessary. Compositionally, the work is strikingly progressive in several ways:

1. It uses plainsong as a prominent source of melodic themes (both instrumental and choral). In the "Prelude," Holst has the semichorus sing "Vexilla regis prodeunt" over an instrumental ostinato; neither part is metered, allowing the two layers to coexist without conflict.
2. Example 7.6 shows an early use of bitonality, its harmony compounded from triads (C major and F♯ major) the roots of which are a tritone apart.
3. Another typical Holst fingerprint is the repeating bass ostinato that supports the opening hymn. Over this same ostinato, occurs what may well be the first use of choral speech, indicated by specific rhythm notation without pitch (ex. 7.7).
4. The prominent use of 5/4 meter in the work's large central section ("Divine Grace is Dancing.") is strongly reminiscent of *The Planets*.
5. Like many twentieth-century composers, Holst avoids any key signature (and implication of tonality), the result being a constant flux of accidentals.

The larger choral works of Vaughan Williams are more popular and thus more often performed than Holst's. Especially well known are the *Fantasia on Christmas Carols, Five Mystical Songs, Serenade to Music,* and *Hodie*. The less familiar *A Sea Symphony* (Symphony No. 1) actually started out as a cycle of choral songs about the sea and modeled on a similar work by Charles Villiers Stanford.[18] Two other relatively unknown works of similar character and length are the oratorio *Sancta Civitas* (1923–25) and the cantata *Dona nobis pacem* (1936).

Vaughan Williams called *Sancta Civitas* an oratorio, although one is hard-pressed to discern why. Citing the maxim of William Blake that "to labour in knowledge is to build up Jerusalem," Wilfrid Mellers has argued that Vaughan Williams purposefully invoked the image of the New Jerusalem as an antidote to the tribulation afflicting England after World War I.[19] Indeed, the first work's premiere took place during the General Strike (1925) that threatened to paralyze England. Many commentators note that Vaughan Williams claimed this work as his favorite, perhaps because it was a personal exploration of the same mystical depths he found in Holst's *Hymn of Jesus*. Alternatively, this collation of biblical texts comes closer than any other to being a statement of his faith, an affirmative agnosticism that neither shied away from reality nor bathed in fatuous platitudes. A sense of Vaughan Williams, the man, is found in the quotation from Socrates (via Plato's *Phaedo*) that prefaces the score; having described the soul's journey after death, Socrates explains: "A man of sense will not insist that things are exactly as I have described them. But I think he will believe that something of the kind is true . . . and that it is worth while to stake everything on this belief."[20]

Sancta Civitas contains all the stylistic trappings associated with Vaughan Williams's music—parallel triadic harmonies, tonal ambivalence (created by the juxtaposition of unrelated triads), contrapuntal writing based on the pentatonic scale, a beautiful violin solo (reminiscent of those found in *The Lark Ascending* or *Serenade to Music*), and the somewhat overblown choral writing beloved and expected by English choral societies of the day. But there is also much that is novel, like the harmonies of the orchestral introduction; despite a key signature of one sharp, Vaughan Williams avoids both G major and E minor, emphasizing F♯ and B♭ in the bass, over which float chords comprising unrelated pentatonic collections (E, A, B, and D, E, A). The same music returns at the work's end.

In addition to a large orchestra, Vaughan Williams calls for three choruses—a large mixed chorus, a smaller semichorus (both divided antiphonally) and a so-called Distant Chorus of treble voices. The composer specifies that that particular choir (preferably consisting of male treble voices) literally *be* distant, and, if possible, invisible. This choir sings three times, always in A♭ major accompanied by a trumpet call. While the first two passages (m. 78 and m. 307) are brief and diatonic, the harmonic vocabulary of the third (ex. 7.8) expands to include neighboring chords in G♭ major/minor.

Example 7.8 Vaughan Williams, *Sancta Civitas*, mm. 492–97

The divided treble voices of the semichorus dominate the work's center, singing "Babylon the Great is fallen," not bombastically but as *pianissimo* chords that create a bitonal clash with the E♭ pedal of the orchestral basses. We expect such layered bitonality in Stravinsky but not in the Vaughan Williams of the 1920s. One of the more remarkable passages to appear in any of Vaughan Williams's choral music is his resolution of this bitonality by subtracting orchestral texture until only A♭ remains to provide an enharmonic pivot to E major for the text "For I saw a new heaven and a new earth" (Revelation 21.1).

If *Sancta Civitas* celebrates the hope for a new world order after World War I, *Dona nobis pacem* prays for peace amid the gathering certainty of a yet more terrible war in the late 1930s. Vaughan Williams assembled an eclectic selection of biblical and secular texts, which appealed for "inner and outer peace." Written amid the rise of National Socialism in Germany, the work sounds the tocsin of war. Vaughan Williams turns again to Whitman's poetry, specifically the collection titled *Drum Taps*, whose recollection of the American Civil War sets an appropriately martial tone in the first poem: "Beat, beat, drums! Blow, bugles, blow!" In response to this martial music comes a luminous setting of Whitman's "Reconciliation": "Word beautiful over all, beautiful as the sky, Beautiful that war and all its deeds of carnage must in time be utterly lost." Filled with hope, but tinged with the seeming inevitability of war, these words evoke one of Vaughan Williams's most beautiful melodies, sung first by a baritone soloist, then by the choral sopranos (ex. 7.9).

Example 7.9 Vaughan Williams, *Dona nobis pacem*, mvt. 3, mm. 22–34
© Oxford University Press 1936, Renewed in U.S.A., 1964. Used by permission. All rights reserved. Photocopying of this material is ILLEGAL.

A revised version of the 1908 setting of Whitman's poignant "Dirge for Two Veterans" follows. True to its title, this work features the persistent, muted rhythms of a funeral procession. The nine strophes of the poem fuel a musical procession that seems to start in the distance and grow nearer and nearer until the "strong dead march enwraps me" (using a rhythmic motive from the opening movement). The final movement begins with words "The Angel of Death ..." from John Bright's speech on the eve of the Crimean War in 1855, inciting the chorus to reply, "We looked for peace, but no good came; and for a time of health, and behold, trouble!" (Jeremiah 8:15). This despair gives way to more hopeful texts from Daniel 10:19 ("O Man, greatly beloved, fear not") and Haggai 2:9 ("The glory of this latter house shall be greater than the former ... and in this place will I give peace."), ushering in a procession that culminates "Glory to God in the highest and on earth peace, good will to men," set to music of Elgarian grandeur. Just like the angels who having sung words disappear leaving an uneasy quiet, Vaughan Williams diminishes the forces in each setting of "Dona nobis pacem," ultimately leaving only the plaint of the soprano soloist.

The Australian-born Percy Aldridge Grainger deserves mention as among the most ardent, if idiosyncratic, advocates of folk song. Long familiar in the American band world for his folk-inspired pieces (*Lincolnshire Posy*), Grainger is less well known as a composer of choral music, principally because his choral music often lacks text, as in his exquisitely tuneful arrangement of "Irish Tune from County Derby (Londonderry Air)." Recently, more of Grainger's music has become accessible in score and recordings, especially the multivolume *Grainger Edition* on the Chandos Label (1992–2002). The novelty and honesty of this little-known repertory make it an ideal source of piquancy for choral programs. Interestingly, Grainger largely disapproved of Vaughan Williams's treatment of folk song, believing that the words and music need always be kept together. According to Grainger, the music should never be used in isolation for that would deny the artistry of the singers who were the real "owners" of such music.[21]

HUNGARY

A pair of Hungarian composers—Zoltán Kodály (1882–1967) and Béla Bartók (1881–1945)—undertook the same type of ethnological fieldwork as had Sharp, Vaughan Williams, and Holst (See Fig. 7.2). For Kodály, the process began with his doctoral thesis, *A Magyar népdal strófa-szerkezete* (The Stanzaic Structure of Hungarian Folk Song, 1906). Driven by a shared interest in ethnic music, Bartók and Kodály undertook a systematic study of Hungarian folk song and produced "a complete collection of folk songs gathered with scholarly exactitude." Their transcriptions comprise a *Complete Edition of Hungarian Folk Songs*, published as *Transylvanian Hungarian Folk Songs*.[22]

ZOLTÁN KODÁLY

In the late 1920s, artistic differences ultimately led to the dissolution of the partnership between Bartók and Kodály. Bartók used ethnic melodies to create a new, personal harmonic language, while Kodály adhered more closely to traditional Western harmonies. Bartók's description of Kodály's music (1921) highlights their differences: "His music is not of the kind described nowadays as modern. It has nothing to do with the new atonal, bitonal and polytonal music—everything in it is based on the principle of tonal balance. His idiom is nevertheless new; he says things that have never been uttered before and demonstrates thereby that the tonal principal has not lost its raison d'être as yet."[23]

Kodály's *oeuvre* contains works as diverse as *Psalmus Hungaricus*, op. 13 (1923), the *Missa Brevis* (1942–44), and numerous *a cappella* compositions both sacred and secular. And

Fig. 7.2 Béla Bartók and Zoltán Kodály with members of the Hungarian Quartet

his choral output is larger than Bartók's, providing a more inclusive summary of his style. Despite its title, the *Psalmus Hungaricus* is not based on folk materials. Its genesis—the fiftieth anniversary of the unification of Pest, Buda, and Óbuda into the modern city of Budapest (1923)—is decidedly nationalistic, as is its use of a Hungarian paraphrase of the Psalm 55 by the sixteenth-century poet Mihály Kecskeméti Vég.[24] The success of its European premiere at the fourth ISCM Festival in Zurich (1926) and more than two hundred documented performances in Europe, Britain, and the United States suggest broad appeal.[25] Following the Zurich premiere, Edward Dent arranged a performance at Cambridge (March 1927) for which he provided an English singing translation. This performance also provided Kodály entrée to English composers (Elgar and Vaughan Williams) as well as various English choral festivals.[26]

Vég's text paraphrases Psalm 55 in seventeen strophes, the first of which is given here in Dent's translation: "When as King David / sore was afflicted, / By those he trusted / basely deserted / In his great anger / bitterly grieving, / Thus to Jehovah / he prayed within his heart."[27] Even this translation illustrates the original text's organization into lines containing a variable number of five-syllable lines with a concluding phrase of six syllables. The consistency of the text's format allows Kodály to create what is essentially a set of rhythmic/melodic variations. János Breuer believes that Kodály composed *Psalmus Hungaricus* straight through: "He sketched out the whole rondo form with three themes on a single music sheet (the recurring elements being an orchestral introduction, 'When as King David' and 'O hear the voice of my complaining')."[28]

Example 7.10 Kodály, *Psalmus Hungaricus*, op. 13, mm. 17–25
© 1926 by Universal Edition A.G., Vienna. All Rights Reserved. Used by permission of European American Music Distributors, LLC, solo U.S. and Canadian agent for Universal Edition, Vienna.

This ritornello melody (ex. 7.10) dominates the work, creating a ternary form:

A	B	A′
mm. 1–145	mm. 146–269	mm. 270–397
vv. 1–8	vv. 9–13	vv. 14–17

The second and third segments feature the same contrasts as the first—alternation of tenor solo and chorus, whose only appearance is a wordless wail over a truncated version of the orchestral introduction. In the final section the chorus returns to the prominence it enjoyed initially (the tenor soloist is absent for the final 127 measures); the concluding section also reasserts the principal melody (in varied form for vv. 14–17, returning to its initial shape in the final strophe). This overview emphasizes the multiple variants of the principal theme and their role in creating unification and variety. Although Kodály adheres to a basically tonal orientation, he manages at times to create an exotic, modernistic language similar to Bartók's. The clearest example of what later became Bartók's "night music" occurs at the conclusion of v. 13 (mm. 152–70), where the tenor soloist turns from prophetic vengeance to serene trust in God.

For Kodály's *Missa Brevis* (1942–44), the composer himself describes the early genesis of this work in a radio interview in 1944:

> During a lengthy stay in the country, I was asked, for want of someone bet-ter, to accompany a low mass—on a harmonium ... when a low Mass is cel-ebrated without the singing of any chorus or folk hymn, the organist plays solo throughout the Mass. This organ solo can be of two sorts: he either plays pieces he has selected in advance or improvises. In either case the music very rarely follows the passages of the Mass to express, as far as possible, the con-tents of the liturgical texts. I wanted something like this, and instead of an improvisation I sketched up the various movements; out of these there devel-oped, after a great many changes, the present form of the Mass.[29]

This "present form of the Mass" refers to its incarnation as a work for chorus and organ (1944), the form in which the work was premiered two days before the liberation of Budapest.[30] The informal performance was given by soloists of the Budapest Opera (who, like Kodály, were refugees in the basement of the Opera House); the composer played a harmonium found in a storage room.

In 1948, Kodály orchestrated the *Missa Brevis* for performance at the Three Choirs Festival in Worcester Cathedral, with the composer conducting. To the traditional five move-ments, Kodály added an *Introitus* for organ and a setting of the concluding "Ite, missa est" (for choir, organ, and solo organ). The *Introitus* functions as an overture and presents the main theme of the Kyrie in diminution (ex. 7.11a, b).

Example 7.11 a–b Kodály, *Missa Brevis*

Table 7.1 Kodály, *Missa Brevis, Gloria,* form

A	B	A′
Gloria in excelsis Deo . . . Domine Deus, Agnus Dei, Filius Patris	Qui tollis peccata mundi . . .	Quoniam tu solus Sanctus . . . Amen
mm. 1–39	mm. 40–77	mm. 78–111
2 sharps 4/4	3 sharps 3/4	3–2 sharps 4/4
Andante	Adagio	Tempo primo
D M–C♯ M	F♯ m–D♯ M	D♯ M–F♯ M–D

The "Ite, missa est" brings back the material first heard in the *Introitus.* Inside this frame lies another, the nearly exact return of the Kyrie motive in the Agnus Dei.[31]

Both the Gloria and Credo follow the nineteenth-century tradition of using tripartite form based on tempo (F–S–F), meter (4/4, 3/4, 4/4), and vocal texture (chorus, solo, chorus). Even Kodály's division of the text occurs at traditional places (see Table 7.1). The opening melody of the Gloria, though reminiscent of Hungarian folk song, is original. The opening of the Sanctus, featuring white notes (4/2) and imitative counterpoint, seems positively Caecilian in inspiration. At "Pleni sunt coeli," however, Kodály clearly references a Gregorian theme, followed by allusions to the Kyrie's melody at "Hosanna in excelsis."

Kodály's earliest *a cappella* chorus is a haunting setting of Gyulai Pál's poem *Este* ("Evening"), one of only four choral works that predate the *Psalmus Hungaricus.* Sections of the work's beginning, middle, and end feature a single vocal line (choral or solo) accompanied by a wordless chorus. The lush harmonies used here are more suggestive of German romanticism than of any folk-song influence. More obviously nationalistic is Kodály's cycle *Mátrai Képek* ("Matra Pictures," 1931), which contains no fewer than seven different folk songs.

BÉLA BARTÓK

If Kodály favored a consonant Western approach to harmonizing folk-song melody, Béla Bartók's path led to the creation of a new and distinctly personal musical language that epitomizes the gap between ethnic Hungarian/Romanian music and the Western tradition. Bartók's best-known choral work is the set of *Four Slovakian Folk Songs* (1917). The first of these pieces, the *Wedding Song from Poniky,* seems comparatively consonant and tertian. Bartok uses a modal melody, which resists reduction to any traditional, seven-note diatonic scale in order to create a modified strophic form (ex. 7.12).

Example 7.12 Bartók, *Wedding Song from Poniky,* mm. 1–9

The first quandary posed by this melody is its acceptance of two conflicting versions of the pitch class D (D♭ and D♮). The scale's lower tetrachord (E♭–F–G–A) is consistently Lydian, a modal construct more strongly associated with Slovakian melodies than Hungarian ones.[32] Depending on which form of D Bartók employs, the upper tetrachord vacillates between B♭ Dorian and Ionian. Another departure from Kodály's approach is his construction of cadences; to our tonal ears the melody ends on a half-cadence to the supertonic (F), a cadence that mirrors the first cadence to C (supertonic to B♭). Paired with the composition's contrasting initial and final harmonies (B♭ minor and F major), there is substantial tonal ambiguity. That said, Bartók's use of tertian chords (piano) to harmonize the melody and counterpoint in v. 2 creates a harmonic and textural variety not all that different from Kodály's. The textures used for the four strophes create a textural symmetry—unison (s), 2 part (s, a), à 4, and unison (sat). Bartók counters this symmetry by constantly changing his harmonization of the melody; although each verse is seemingly different, comparison of each verse's opening and closing harmonies reveals some similarities:

> Stanza 1:   B♭ minor—D minor
> Stanza 2:   B♭–F major
> Stanza 3:   G♭–D minor
> Stanza 4:   B♭–F major

The first and third stanzas end in D minor (approached from a diminished triad); the second and fourth close in F major, suggesting the conventional relationship of minor and relative major. Stanzas 2 and 4 begin with seventh chords built as different inversions of B♭ major (thus, D♮), while 1 and 3 assume the presence of D♭. The style of piano writing suggests yet a different pairing, the first two strophes (chordal accompaniment) against the final two (arpeggios). The piano introduction features an implied pentatonic scale on B♭ (the E♭ is omitted), the pitch that begins and ends the introduction and functions as the central pitch of the vocal melody.

The *Four Hungarian Folk Songs* (early 1930s) present a totally different approach to melody, harmony, form, and texture. The absence of piano accompaniment leads to frequent use of divisi, which, along with complex rhythms, sets this collection apart from its predecessor. The first setting of the four, titled (in English) "The Prisoner,"[33] is an old Hungarian folk song consisting of four six-syllable lines sung to a G-Dorian melody.[34]

Bartók sets only the first four stanzas of text, using rests to separate each verse. He relocates the Dorian melody to a new tonal center for each verse (3 flats, 2 flats, 1 flat, 3 flats). This modal transposition partially explains his changes of the melody's location (s, vv. 1 and 3, bar, v. 2, and the s and t alternately in v. 4). Bartók's vocal scoring sometimes reflects the gender of the speaker, but at other times he avoids such clear characterization. The first strophe (mm. 1–9) begins with women's voices, adding the first tenor in line 3 to identify the protagonist as the mother's son. Male voices dominate v. 2, but Bartók uses full texture (saattb) for the son's plea to his mother to secure his release. The change of voicing and tune location in the fourth strophe reflect the son's question (atbb, melody in tenor [above the alto]) and the mother's response (satb, melody in soprano). In addition, Bartók's setting creates a formal shape based on dynamics: v. 1 *p*; v. 2 *mp*; v. 3 *mf–f*; v. 4 *p*; Coda *pp*. Other interesting features are Bartók's gradual insertion of tones outside the mode (e.g., the appearance of G♭ and D♭ in v. 1) and melodic flourishes that suggest the improvisational nature of authentic folk performance (ex. 7.13).

Example 7.13 Bartók, *The Prisoner*, mm. 1–5

In v. 2 Bartók injects a harmonic style based on parallel sixths (ex. 7.14), which he expands to parallel triadic inversions in vv. 3 and 4, producing a denser harmonic language based on opposing harmonic layers in the female and male voices.

Example 7.14 Bartók, *The Prisoner*, mm. 22–27

Although clearly more challenging than the *Slovakian Folk Songs*, Bartók's basic approach—modal harmony combined with a linear melodic logic for each part—remains the same.

Despite its lofty position in Bartók's catalogue and relatively brief duration of about eighteen minutes, *Cantata Profana* (1930) remains the composer's least performed major work. Bartók had to wait four years for the work's premiere (by the BBC on May 25, 1934) and another two years for its premiere in Hungary (by the Budapest Philharmonic Society, conducted by Ernö Dohnányi). These delays and the paucity of contemporary performances stem from the difficulties of the choral and solo writing, difficulties made even more acute by the orchestra's completely independent, dissonant accompaniment.

It is the composition's text rather than its music that link it with folk song; this text is part of a body of Romanian songs, and Bartók writes of his text:

> The category "Christmas carols" (in Romanian, "colindas") is the most important. Their text is also extremely valuable and interesting, both from the standpoint of folklore and cultural history. However, we should not think of these songs in terms of the pious West European Christmas carols. The most important part of the text, perhaps one third, is not connected in any way with the Christian Christmas: instead of the Bethlehem story, they are about miraculous and victorious battles with a hitherto invincible lion (or stag); there is a legend about nine brothers who hunted so long in the depths of the forest that they were turned into stags; there is also a miracle story about how the Sun married his sister, the Moon. . . . In other words, all remnants of stories from pagan times![35]

Bartók saw the story of the nine hunters transformed into stags as a metaphor for urban civilization's increasing incursions into nature's realm. Taken literally, the story describes an ironic "escape" from the warmth of human companionship into the cold world of nature and the cosmos; metaphorically, however, the tale is one of triumph over a world that increasingly provides no protection from custom, compromise, or power and that, ultimately, humankind must rely only on its own innate abilities and moral values. The music that carries this story consists of three distinct, yet continuous movements:

1. *Molto moderato–Allegro molto–Molto moderato*: 198 measures (chorus and orchestra)
2. *Andante*: 215 measures (T, Bar, chorus and orchestra)
3. *Moderato*: 93 measures (chorus and orchestra)

Aside from these obvious divisions, typical formal markers do not apply. No change of tonal center demarcates the movements, their music being both nontonal and continuous. The tempos appear at the beginning of each movement (plus the important change to *Allegro molto* for the "Hunting Chorus") and impart a large-scale, rondo-like design based on alternating slow and fast tempi: the slow tempi imply narrative, the fast sections dramatic conflict. In reality, the tempi, carefully quantified by metronome markings, fluctuate constantly, and the analysis can not use the number of measures as an accurate gauge of form because the quantity of the measure is in a nearly constant state of flux. The most distinctive formal marker is the dominant presence of the tenor and baritone soloists in the

Table 7.2 Bartók, *Cantata Profana*, mvt. 2, formal symmetry

Instrumental introduction (8 mm.)
    t,b (8 mm.)
    s,a,t,b (then *divisi*) 25 mm.
        Aria T (53 mm.)
    s,a,t,b (7 mm.)
        Arioso Bar (5 mm.)
    a,t,t,b (7 mm.)
        Aria Bar (45 mm.)
    s,a,t,b (7 mm.)
        Aria T (20 mm.)
    T, B + ssaattbb (29 mm.)

middle movement and their absence in the outer movements. Bartók's decision to reduce the chorus's role to a narrative frame for a poignant dialogue creates the dramatic weighting of the work's form.

Bartók's well-documented sensitivity to symmetry begins with the ethnomusicological research that places him in contact with nature; his appreciation for the harmony and growth processes he found there are manifest not only in the overall textural symmetry but also in the internal balance between chorus and soloists in the critical second movement. Three seven-measure choral interludes simultaneously suggest a kind of rondo or concerto function and create a quasi-palindromic formal design.

This internal *scena* exists within a frame of choral and ensemble music—an introductory chorus of forty-one measures (including an eight-measure orchestral introduction) balanced by the twenty-nine-measure concluding ensemble. What Table 7.2 cannot convey is Bartók's use of different vocal styles and his use of strict imitation to create a tense buildup climax of the tale.

The second part of the cantata begins with eerie orchestral music generated by a duet in mirror inversion between the vla and vc 1, 2, and db (ex. 7.15).

Example 7.15 Bartók, *Cantata Profana*, mvt. 2, mm. 1–4

The seemingly random succession of pitches is anything but random, generated by Bartók's signature use of an octatonic scale (a symmetrical scale of alternating whole and half steps).[36] The implied tonal underpinning (F'–C'–F) provided by the bassoons and horns serves only to intensify the dissonance of the passage. The first choral entry, an imitative duet for bass and tenor, escalates into an eight-part texture founded on mirror inversion and the gradual reduction of the distance between entries that eventually produces entries harmonized in parallel fourths (ex. 7.16).

Example 7.16 Bartók, *Cantata Profana*, mvt. 2, mm. 33–35
©1934 by Universal Edition A. G., Wien/UE 10613 © Renewed All Rights Reserved. Used in the territory of the world excluding the U. S. by permission of European American Music Distributors LLC, agent for Universal Edition A.G., Wien.

The tempo increases and the orchestration thickens, building toward the entry of the tenor soloist, whose melody exhibits both metric fluctuation and a gradually rising tessitura. The music climaxes at m. 85 as the tenor ascends to C'', accompanied by string tremolos, a sustained fifth (G♯–D♯) in lower strings and bassoons, a four-part chord in the horns, canonic, pentatonic flourishes in the flutes and clarinets, and rapid harp *glissandi*.

Elliott Antokoletz points out that the authentic Romanian folk-song texts (*colindǎs*) throughout this work "are supported by ... diatonic and nondiatonic folk modes, which are transformed into several other diatonic modes, as well as octatonic and whole-tone collections, in support of the main idea of the story."[37] The strings open the cantata with such a nondiatonic, modal scale (ex. 7.17).

Example 7.17 Bartók, *Cantata Profana*, mvt. 1, mm. 1–5
©1934 by Universal Edition A. G., Wien/UE 10613 © Renewed All Rights Reserved.
Used in the territory of the world excluding the U. S. by permission of European American Music Distributors LLC, agent for Universal Edition A.G., Wien.

This scale contains both Dorian and whole-tone tetrachords, creating a scale that is partially octatonic. The Dorian tetrachord consists of whole step, half step, and whole step. The G♯ and A♯ of the whole-tone tetrachord extend the octatonic pattern (half step, whole step), but the A♯ breaks the pattern.

This very Bartókian scale can be viewed as a simplified demonstration of the mathematical construction known as the Fibonacci series, in which each number is the sum of the two immediately preceding numbers (e.g., 1, 1, 2, 3, 5, 8, etc.) Thus the distance from D to E is 2 semitones, from E to F one (2+1=3), from F to G two semitones (3+2=5), etc.[38] The web of interrelated melodies that spring from example 7.17 and return to conclude the composition suggest that Bartók constructed this collection of pitches to embody the purity of nature and the forest that nurtures the transformed stags. The dark, brooding music of the work's opening sets up a pattern commonly found in Western art—divergence (development) and return (recapitulation)—that Bartók re-creates despite his use of a nontonal musical language.

GYÖRGY LIGETI

The logical successor to Kodály and Bartók is György Ligeti (1923–2006), who in his maturity struggled to reconcile the contradiction implicit in the aesthetic of Kodály and the repressive politics of Communism. Publicly, Ligeti initially produced the kind of music the state required, but privately he explored new, adventurous sonic experiments. By the mid-1950s, the grip of Communism had relaxed enough to allow Ligeti to set two poems by Sándor Weöres for *a cappella* chorus: *Éjszaka* (Night) and *Reggel* (Morning). Of the two, *Reggel* is more indebted to folk music in its imitative opening and its soloistic imitation of rooster cries. Yet Ligeti manipulates these traditional folk music gestures to create new sonorities as the opening melody of *Éjszaka* demonstrates (ex. 7.18).

Example 7.18 Ligeti, *Éjszaka*, mm. 1–13

© 1973 by Schott Music © Renewed All Rights Reserved Used by permission of European American Music Distributors LLC, sole U.S. and Canadian agent for Schott Music.

Ligeti freely alternates two rhythmic cells (A and B) in creating a diatonic melody that, when sung in strict canon, gradually becomes more dense and dissonant. This cluster of sound reaches its apex in m. 27, where each chord contains all six pitches of the hexachord of white notes, C–A. After this development concludes (m. 42) Ligeti suddenly introduces a new sonority compounded from the black notes that he had previously avoided. (G♭, A♭, B♭, D♭, E♭). This pivot from white notes to black notes is the fulcrum by which he leverages a radical change of style.

RUSSIA

After the Italianate influence cultivated by Catherine the Great (1729–96), the quest for Russian identity produced the five composers known as the Russian Five—Mily Balakirev (1837–1910), Aleksandr Borodin (1833–87), César Cui (1835–1918), Modest Mussorgsky (1839–81), and Nikolai Rimsky-Korsakov (1844–1908). The nationalistic bent of these composers is more evident in their instrumental works and operas than in their small output of choral music.

Unlike areas such as Hungary, England, and the Baltic region, the secular choral music of Russian composers relies less on folk materials. Prior to the Bolshevik Revolution (October 1917), choral composition in Russia was largely the domain of court composers in St. Petersburg and, to a lesser extent, the composers who wrote music for the Moscow Synodal Choir, the group of singers who provided music for the Cathedral of the Dormition and the Church of the Twelve Apostles in the Kremlin.[39]

That said, the choral idiom is predominantly liturgical church music, which, ironically, becomes a principal expression of Russian nationalism within the secular society of Communism. The glorious tradition of Russian church music begins with Dmitri Bortniansky (1751–1825). Trained in Italy, Bortniansky returned to Russia to conduct the Imperial Chapel at the court of Prince Paul, the heir to the throne. Paul's accession to tsar in 1796 led to Bortniansky's promotion as director of the imperial musical establishment in 1801. Vladimir Morosan equates Bortniansky's sense of political acumen with that of Lully: "Thus, under Bortniansky's administration the Imperial Court Chapel gradually expanded its role from being merely the private choral establishment of the ruling monarch to that of an institution actively influencing, and eventually controlling, church choral singing in the entire Russian Empire."[40] The keys to Bortniansky's enormous success are his Italian compositional training, an innate sense of good singing, and a sincere reverence for the Russian tradition of liturgical music. His admixture of Western and Russian perspectives is clearly audible in his "Cherubic Hymn," disseminated in early twentieth-century America as a church anthem in English (based on Tchaikovsky's arrangement). Bortniansky's principal contribution to Russian choral music was his invention of a uniquely Russian genre—the choral concerto. Example 7.19 shows that stylistic genre in an excerpt from *Da voskresnet Boh* ("Let God Arise").

Example 7.19 Bortniansky, Choral Concerto 34, *Da voskresnet Boh*, mm. 25–33

Bortniansky's successors at the Imperial Chapel include Fyodor Lvov, Balakirev, Nicolai Rimsky-Korsakov, Anton Arensky, and Stepan Smolensky. Although by the late nineteenth century the Imperial Chapel Choir was in decline, it remained the pre-eminent Russian choral ensemble until the rapid social change in Russia after 1850 led to its demise. To fill this void choral singing was used as a way to promote cultural identity and improve literacy. As in Europe and especially England, this new social mission resulted in a flurry of public concerts. But the defining moment for Russian choral music was a court case. The director of the Imperial Chapel, Nikolai Bakhmetev, sought to block the publication of Tchaikovsky's *Liturgy*, op. 41, by legal maneuvering. But in 1880 Tchaikovsky emerged victorious, opening the door for a "new Russian choral school." For the first time, composers outside the Imperial Chapel establishment were able to compose and publish sacred music. The Moscow Synodal Choir's emergence from the shadow of the Imperial Chapel led to the creation of new choirs, the foremost of which was the ensemble founded in 1880 by Aleksandr Arkhangel'sky (1846–1924). Most of the Russian choral composers popular today in the West were the beneficiaries of this initiative. In addition to Arkhangel'sky, this group of composers included such familiar names as Pyotr Il'ich Tchaikovsky (1840–93), Mikhail Ippolitov-Ivanov (1859–1935), Pavel Grigor'evich Chesnokov (1877–1944), Aleksandr Grechaninov (1864–1956), and Sergey Rachmaninoff (1873–1943).

Following the example of Arkhangel'sky, the Moscow Synodal Choir began to give regular concerts in Moscow; they even toured outside Russia, most notably singing for the dedication of a church within the Russian embassy in Vienna in 1899.[41] The concert programs of the Moscow Synodal Choir in the years prior to World War I and the Bolshevik Revolution are dominated by this group of composers.[42] Two figures —Aleksandr Kastalsky, a composer and folklorist, and Sergey Taneyev, composer and music theorist—taught the new generation of Russian composers, but differences of personality resulted in two, very different traditions. Kastalsky, the Russian equivalent of Kódály, assimilated folk song and Orthodox music.

Central to his style was the idea of heterophony, that is, simultaneous yet different presentations of a melody in multiple voices. Because he primarily worked outside the Orthodox Church and fostered interest in the European contrapuntal tradition, Sergey Taneyev's career took a different path. His style is exemplified in a choral cycle that sets the poetry of Yakov Polonsky (op. 27).

The rise of new performing groups stimulated an astonishing growth in choral composition. The most prolific composer of the Moscow Synodal School was Pavel Chesnokov, who produced two settings of the Divine Liturgy, *All Night Vigil* and *Memorial Service*; several other liturgical settings; and 192 smaller sacred works. Choral conductors today know and regularly perform his anthem *Spaseniye sodelal* ("Salvation Is Created"). An early setting of the "Cherubic Hymn" from the Divine Liturgy, *Heruimskaya pesn* (1897), shows why we still find his style so attractive (ex. 7.20).

Example 7.20 Chesnokov, *Heruvimskaya pesn*, op. 7, no. 1, mm. 1–12

Paired thirds sung in octaves by the soprano and tenor over an alto and bass pedal is emblematic of his style.

Equally well known and often performed is the choral music of Aleksandr Grechaninov. Before the October Revolution, Grechaninov was absorbed in ethnographic work, arranging folk songs from all parts of the empire; he was also an active pedagogue, producing a considerable body of works for children. Grechaninov's discomfort with the new regime led to his emigration first to Paris in 1925 and then the United States in 1939. He became an American citizen in 1946. The bulk of his liturgical music, including three of his four settings of the Liturgy of St. John Chrysostom, opp. 13 (1897), 29 (1902), and 79 (1917–26), was written prior to his departure; it follows closely the traditional practice of sumptuous harmonizations of old Russian chant melodies. His most popular composition is the Vesper hymn, *Svete tikhiy* ("Gladsome Light"), which has long been a staple of collegiate choirs and church choirs.

For Western audiences, Sergey Rachmaninoff is the embodiment of Russian sacred choral music. His celebrity is somewhat ironic because Rachmaninoff is known, first and foremost, as a composer of instrumental music and because, as Vladimir Morosan points out, Rachmaninoff "did not concern himself with the liturgical minutiae of the service, such as litanies and responses."[43] Both of Rachmaninoff's major liturgical cycles—the *Liturgy of St. John Chrysostom* (*Liturgiya svyatovo Ioanna Zlatousta*, op. 31 [1910]) and his *All Night Vigil* (*Vsenoshchnoye bdeniye*, op. 37 [1915])—pre-date World War I and the Bolshevik Revolution. The first work contains settings of twenty texts from the central liturgy of the Russian Orthodox Church and is indebted to the earlier service by Tchaikovsky (1878). The popularity of the *All-Night Vigil*, a piece of formidable difficulty, is evident in the numerous recordings the work received.[44] Here, Rachmaninoff sets the fifteen "ordinary" texts sung polyphonically during the Vigil.

In his exemplary edition, Morosan notes that ten of these texts are based on chants taken from one of the principal orthodox traditions—Znamenny chant (nos. 8, 9, 12, 13, 14), Russian "Greek" chant (nos. 2, 15), and Kievan chants (nos. 4, 5). The five marked with an asterisk in Table 7.3 are freely composed. Of these, the beloved "Ave Maria" (*Bogoroditse Devo*) uses a "chant-like" melody of limited range (octave) and basically diatonic motion.

More conventional liturgically is *Blagoslovi, dushe moya, Ghospoda*, the text of which alternates fragments of vv. 1, 6, 10, and 24 of Psalm 103 with the refrain "Blagosloven yesi, Ghospodi" ("Bless the Lord, O my soul"). The chant refrain appears six times, each time using the same musical materials (a pedal point on C′, the chant melody, and Rachmaninoff's harmonization) distributed in slightly varied ways (ex. 7.21).

Table 7.3 Rachmaninoff, *All-Night Vigil*, op. 37

1. *Priidite, poklonimsia**	Come, Let us Worship God
2. *Blagoslovi, dushe moya, Ghospoda*	Bless the Lord, O My Soul
3. *Blazhen muzh**	Blessed is the Man
4. *Svete tikhiy*	Gladsome Light
5. *Nine otpushchayeshi*	Lord, Now Lettest Thou
6. *Bogoroditse Devo**	Rejoice, O Virgin
7. *Shesto psalmiye*	Six Psalms ("Lesser Doxology")
8. *Hvalite ímia Ghospodne*	Praise the Name of the Lord
9. *Blagosloven yesi, Ghospodi*	Blessed Art Thou, O Lord
10. *Voskreseniye Khristovo videvshe**	Having Beheld the Resurrection
11. *Velichit dusha moya Ghospoda**	My Soul Magnifies the Lord
12. *Slavosloviye velikoye*	The Great Doxology
13. *Tropar: Dnes spaseniye*	Troparion: "Today Salvation"
14. *Tropar: Voskres iz groba*	Troparion: "Thou Didst Rise"
15. *Vzbrannoy voyevode*	To Thee, Victorious Leader

Example 7.21 Rachmaninoff, *All-Night Vigil*, op. 37, no. 2

Rachmaninoff assigns the psalm verses to an alto soloist accompanied by male chorus; the varied placement of the pedal point and other materials in the refrain producing not only a rondo-like form but also a type of variation technique, which affects the form of the entire cycle. The "Allelulia" melody of no. 3 (*Blazhen muzh*) not only fulfills this formal function but reappears in the "Great Doxology" (no. 12), where two slightly different versions are heard—chant-like triplets in the alto and augmentation in the soprano (divided à 3).[45] The cycle's dramatic high point occurs in no. 9, whose Znamenny chant melody also appears in Rachmaninoff's *Symphonic Dances*, op. 45, composed twenty-three years later.

   Among Rachmaninoff's choral works was a choral symphony, *The Bells* (*Kolokola*, op. 35), for S, T, and Bar, chorus, and orchestra. From the Russian symbolist poet Konstantin Balmont's enhanced translation of Edgar Allan Poe's well-known poem, Rachmaninoff creates four symphonic movements. The chorus appears in all four movements, although it is limited to simpler music than that of the *All-Night Vigil*, perhaps in deference to the prominent roles of the orchestra and the three soloists. Nonetheless, one hears many of the same kinds of variation procedure and textural contrast found in the slightly later choral cycle. If the basis for including a discussion of Rachmaninoff's choral music in this chapter on nationalism is something of a stretch (given his apathy toward the church), we must admit that "The Bells" is even less relevant: it contains none of the Russian flavor of Rachmaninoff's Orthodox church music, being far more reminiscent of the colorful orchestral palette of the French Impressionists.

IGOR STRAVINSKY

Igor Stravinsky's use of Russian folklore in his early ballets (*The Firebird, Petrushka,* and *The Rite of Spring*) is well known. Less recognized are folk-based choral works like the *Four Russian Peasant Songs* (1917, rev. 1954) originally written for four women's voices and later revised for four equal voices and four French horns. By far the most significant expression of Stravinsky's Russian heritage, *Les Noces* ("The Wedding") is also his last; completed in 1917, this choral ballet underwent a series of experimental scorings before emerging in its final state in 1923. In that form, it became an archetypical twentieth-century work, scored for vocal soloists, mixed chorus, an orchestra of four pianos, and a large battery of pitched and nonpitched percussion instruments.[46] Stravinsky described the libretto as: "A suite of typical wedding episodes told through quotation of typical talk.... As a collection of clichés and quotations of typical wedding sayings it might be compared to one of those scenes in *Ulysses* in which the reader seems to be overhearing scraps of conversation without the connecting thread of discourse."[47] If the stories and remembrances of Russian folk weddings inform the text, the folk-song-like melodies, characterized by modality, limited range, predominantly stepwise motion, and ornamentation, are the musical bases of these wedding scenes. Stravinsky's primary melody involves the pitches B', D", and E", which prompts various possible classifications; the pentatonic is most obvious, followed by E Dorian (given the F♯ used as ornament and assuming an unseen C♯) or Dorian or Phrygian on B. To this vocal pitch collection, the piano accompaniment adds B♭ and F♮, creating bitonality (E Dorian versus B♭). Pitches added later hint at an octatonic collection (E, D♯, C♯, B, B♭, A♭, G, and F) that Stravinsky plays off against the opening melodic cell. The tonal drama of the work resides in the juxtaposition of these different approaches and their melodic and harmonic extensions. One of the many difficulties the work presents is the need to sing diatonic melodies within an alien rhythmic and harmonic context. The majority of Stravinsky's choral works are discussed in chapter 8.

NATIONALISM UNDER THE SOVIET REGIME

The nature of Russian nationalism changed drastically under the Communist regime of Joseph Stalin. One composer who managed to be both nationalistic and politically correct was Sergey Prokofiev (1891–1953).

SERGEY PROKOFIEV

Prior to the outbreak of World War II, Prokofiev's output was decidedly neoclassical; his compositional style was perfectly suited to that movement's preference for traditional instrumental forms. At times, his neoclassicism became explicit, as in his First Symphony (the "Classical Symphony," op. 25, 1916–17) and the First Violin Concerto, op. 19, from the same year. Both works are brief, cast in a luminous D-major tonality and beholden to Mozartean models. A later group of works that embody the spirit of eighteenth-century music includes his operas *Love for Three Oranges*, op. 33 (1919), and *Betrothal in a Monastery*, op. 86 (1940–41), the *Lt. Kijé Suite*, op. 60 (1934), and the ballet *Cinderella*, op. 87 (1940–44). Further evidence of Prokofiev's neoclassical bent are the numerous works in traditional forms—fifteen sonatas (ten for piano), nine concertos, and other chamber music, including two string quartets. His choral music consists exclusively of choral-orchestral compositions, the majority of which postdate Prokofiev's return to Russia in the late 1930s and thus adhere to the Communist Party line in ways both obvious and subtle. Prokofiev's cantata and a familiar choral work is *Alexander Nevsky*, op. 78 (1939), which began as a film score to accompany Sergei Eisenstein's movie of the same name (1938).

The movie and music are patently patriotic celebrations of Alexander Yaroslavich Nevsky's victory over invading Teutonic knights at Novgorod in 1242. The battle that took place on a frozen Lake Chud is the centerpiece of Eisenstein's epic film and, appropriately, the largest single part of Prokofiev's music. The result of this collaboration was so successful that in 1939 Prokofiev decided to extract music from the film score to create what he termed a "dramatic cantata." Although nominally a cantata (six of the seven movements have vocal parts), the work is predominantly orchestral. Prokofiev's vocal music is simple, frequently consisting of melodies doubled (in octaves) and harmonized (in thirds). Prokofiev reuses a patriotic melody from mvt. 2 in the finale (ex. 7.22); initially, he quotes it literally (with different words) but eventually transposes and slightly modifies the melody to create a grand climax.

Example 7.22 Prokofiev, *Alexander Nevsky*, op. 78, mvt. 2, mm. 5–13

What choral writing there is suffers from repetition. One of the few people not enthralled with the work at its premiere was Dmitri Shostakovich, who commented: "Despite a whole series of wonderful movements, I didn't like the work in its entirety.... It seemed to me in particular that many sections end before they get started."[48]

VELJO TORMIS

While composers in many countries set nationalistic texts and/or melodies, none is so thoroughly absorbed by and faithful to folk art than the Estonian Veljo Tormis (b. 1930). In 1930 Estonia was an independent state, but its autonomy was short-lived; in 1940 Estonia was subsumed into the Soviet Union. Consequently, Tormis's education (musical and otherwise) was both Estonian and Russian. Early musical training at the Tallinn Music School (1944–47) led to Tormis's enrollment in the Tallinn Conservatory as an organ student. Because of the institution's obvious ties to the Orthodox Church, the state-ordered termination of this course of study in 1948 turned Tormis toward choral conducting. In 1950 he enrolled at the Moscow Conservatory to study composition, returning to Tallinn in 1955 to embark on a teaching career. On a trip to Budapest (1962), Tormis encountered the music and philosophy of Kodály and Bartók, which in turn resulted in Tormis's first significant choral composition, *Looduspildid* ("Nature Pictures"), a series of four cycles for women's chorus.

The catalogue of Tormis's music occupies almost forty pages of Mimi Daitz's monograph on the composer.[49] Tormis burst upon the international scene after a performance devoted to him at the International Federation of Choral Music's 1990 World Symposium. Written summaries of his style are fairly numerous, but few are more succinct and to the point than the one Eve Tamm wrote for the English-language *Estonia Magazine*: "Sixty-two-year-old Veljo Tormis has had a monumental influence on Estonian music [of] this century. Almost single-handedly,

Tormis revived the use of an ancient and, at the time, mostly forgotten form of Estonian singing—the runic song. This eerie, chanting style of song frequently underlies Tormis's compositions to exceptional, almost supernatural effect. During the Singing Revolution of 1988, this folk-based singing style was even picked up by Estonia's top pop musicians to create some of the most memorable pro-independence rock."[50]

The composition that has consistently created the greatest sensation is *Raua Needmine* ("Curse upon Iron"). Composed in 1991, *Raua Needmine* is the first of Tormis's compositions to use text from the Finnish literary epic, the *Kalevala*. In this work, the ancient text becomes a warning for the potential abuses of technology.

The work's powerful impact comes from primal, visceral music, which takes its more powerful musical form in the central role of the Shamanistic drum. Like Stravinsky's *Les Noces* or Carl Orff's *Carmina Burana*, the music is simple and repetitive, and it is Tormis's enhanced repetition of ideas that accounts for most of the work's impact. To this text, Tormis adds new text, presumably of his own authorship.

Clearly, Tormis projects the past abuse of iron as a source of weapons into a late twentieth-century litany of potential destruction. He uses drones or pedal tones either pitched (voices) or unpitched (drum). Urve Lippus points to two principal melodies at work in this composition—the first is a "cursing" melody comprised of just two pitches (ex. 7.23); the second is a "telling" melody, which expands to three pitches (A, B♭, C).[51]

Example 7.23 Tormis, *Raua Needmine*, mm. 21–30

Lippus describes the work's first 111 measures as an "exposition" made up of three sections: an introduction (pedal point with "cursing" melody) and two episodes that retell the birth of iron ("Käisid kolme ilmaneitsit" ["Once there walked three nature spirits," m. 72] and *Soosi jooksis sooda mööda* ["A wolf then ran across the fen"], m. 107).[52] All of these themes descend from the melodic trichord of the "telling" song. Lippus sees the music beginning in m. 127 as a development that begins by transposing the motive chromatically every half measure, moving from A to C ("Nii kõneles suuri surma"), E♭' ("Kuulis kui tule nimeda"), and G♭. Tormis then returns to A and uses a typically Stravinskyan device that extends the melody's range past the octave (A) up to E♭. What follows is a thickening of the texture by splitting the unison E♭ into a dichord (F♭" and D♭"). Here he injects a new melody in 4/8 meter (ex. 7.24), which he treats canonically then combines with the first theme. And so goes his organic process of expansion and intensification that produces a stunning climax of both texture and dynamics.

Example 7.24 Tormis, *Raua Needmine*, mm. 222–24

The elegance of his system is its dependence on the simple three-note "telling" melody as the basis of the entire composition.

Although less dramatic than *Raua Needmine*, his other choral pieces provide more direct illustrations of Tormis's transformation of inherited folk materials into something both contemporary and timeless, artistically challenging yet immediately accessible. Such a work is *Unustatud Rahvad*, a large composition comprised of six separate choral cycles composed over a period of almost two decades (1970–89):

Liivlaste Pärandus	Livonian Heritage
Vadja Pulmalaulud	Votic Wedding Songs
Isuri Eepos	Izhorian Epic
Ingerimaa Õhtud	Ingrian Evenings
Vespa Rajad	Vespian Paths
Karjala Satus	Karelian Destiny

The cycle's long gestation results from breaks in the compositional process to gather new folk materials. The number of compositions in the first five parts of the cycles increase (5, 7, 9, 9, 14), which illustrates Tormis's learning curve, his gradual absorption, and his understanding of how to craft each new song and the techniques that derive from it into a set of interrelated compositions. The settings themselves are guileless, reflecting no apparent compositional artifice save for the artistic preservation of these Balto-Finnic "runic" songs. It is Tormis's genius to find a way to make such repetitive music constantly engaging.

Another series of cycles, *Eesti kalendrilaulud* (Estonian Calendar Songs, 1966–67),[53] contains multiple compositions based on the five important holidays that define the annual work cycle of Estonian farmers:

Mardilaulud	(St. Martin's Day, 11/9)
Kadrilaulud	(St. Catherine's Day, 11/29)
Vastalaulud	(Shrove Tuesday, movable)
Kiigelaulud	(Swing Songs, early summer)
Jáanilaulud	(St. John's Day, 6/24)

The nine songs of *Mardilaulud* and the three of *Vastalaulud* are scored for male chorus; the *Kadrilaulud* (four songs) and *Kiigelaulud* (six songs) use a women's chorus of six to eight parts. Only the final cycle, *Jáanilaulud*, is scored for mixed chorus (up to twelve parts). Tormis evidently did not conceive these pieces to be performed in their printed order. The final song of *Jáanilaulud*, *Jáanilaul* ("St. John's Song"), for instance, is often excerpted for separate performance, and this one chorus is an outstanding example of Tormis's ability to wring everything he can from folk song.

Tormis bases this entire composition on a hypnotic Aeolian melody, the two periods of which use the same pairs of phrases (ex. 7.25).

Example 7.25 Tormis, *Jáanlilaulud*, mm. 1–14

Its length (131 mm.) obviously requires considerable repetition of both text and melody. The basic design involves presentations of the melody that expand exponentially, incorporating increasingly dense triadic structures derived from the basic melody. Initially, these gestures are sporadic and short-lived, occurring in conjunction with the name of the saint.

Of his technique, Tormis writes: "I believe the runic songs to be the highest achievement and most original phenomenon of Estonian culture. But today, runic song has ceased to exist as a component part of the Estonian way of life. Through modern art forms, I try to expose the originality and meaning of runic song. Eternal is the great circle of life, eternal are the life events repeating in their own way with each passing age."[54]

CONCLUSION

All the music examined in this chapter shares a common desire: to create modern music that also acts as the conservator of a given people's distinctive ethnic heritage. Throughout the roughly one hundred years of music discussed here, the ways in which individual composers handle these materials vary widely, ranging from common "arrangements" that harmonize the original using traditional Western harmonies to those exceptional composers who accept the original not as something that needs to be "tamed" but as the source of a new, idiosyncratic musical language. In the first category are composers like Vaughan Williams, Kódaly, Prokofiev, and the Russian school of church music composers. In the second category are the innovative composers like Bartók, Ligeti, and Tormis, with the others falling at various points along the continuum. Regardless of how the inherited music is used, all of these composers attempt to confirm the validity of their unique cultural heritage. As our world shrinks due to technological innovation, we continue to see new traditions added to the mix without changing the fundamental dichotomy between Western tradition and new traditions from all corners of the globe.

8

Neoclassicism

The Revival of Historical Models in the Works of Stravinsky, Hindemith, and Others

Of all the "isms" of the twentieth century, none is more troublesome, none more persistent in the period from 1885 to 1935 than that of neoclassicism. It has been traditionally associated with the movement begun around 1920, from the time of Stravinsky's *Pulcinella* and *Octet*, in which the subject matter or the forms of the eighteenth century were overtly reinterpreted. For the world of music, the eighteenth century was the so-called classic century, and any neoclassicism would, by definition, relate to that era. In literature and the fine arts, though, the eighteenth century was already a neoclassic period, one that had witnessed the revival of interest in ancient Greece and Rome. Only a sparse Greco-Roman legacy had come down to the world of music, and in spite of a brilliant (if largely theoretically inspired) attempt at a revival in the late sixteenth century in Italy, the later and more common designation "classical" for the music of Haydn, Mozart, and their contemporaries had little to do with tapping the distant past for musical models. Instead, there was a general emphasis on proportion and balance as formal ideals and a mild revival of interest in classical subjects or texts. In Glenn Watkins's *Soundings*, the preface to the "Towards Neoclassicism" chapter lays out the fundamental problems this term poses.[1] Neoclassic music references the music of the eighteenth century, the so-called common practice period. The term describes music conceived with the balance, purity, objectivity, and logical construction of late-eighteenth-century music in mind; as such, it stands as the objective antipode to the subjectivity of nineteenth-century Romanticism. Neoclassical composers seek this balance in their use of the absolute classical forms (sonata, concerto, symphony, etc.) and in their emulation of composers of that era. Thus defined, neoclassicism was already in place by the mid-nineteenth century in France, Italy, and Germany, as such study was regarded as a necessary cure for the excesses of the romantic experiments. Thus, one finds classical trends in composers as diverse as Camille Saint-Saëns in France, Ferrucio Busoni, and Richard Strauss in Germany, and the *Generazione dell'Ottante* (generation of the 1880s) in Italy.

IGOR STRAVINSKY (1881–1971)

Neoclassicism is most closely associated with Stravinsky's music composed between 1920 and 1950. Stravinsky's neoclassical works begin with *Pulcinella* (1919–20) and end with *The Rake's Progress* (1948–51), all of which encompass symphonic genres (the *Symphony in C*, 1939–40), concerto form (*Concerto for Piano and Winds*, 1924), chamber works like the *Octet*, 1922–23), *Sonata for Piano*, 1924, *Concerto in D*, 1931, and the *Concerto in E♭* ("Dumbarton Oaks," 1937–38). Imbedded within this group of predominantly instrumental works are three choral works of major importance—the opera/oratorio *Oedipus Rex* (1926–27), the *Symphony of Psalms* (composed to honor the fiftieth anniversary of the Boston Symphony Orchestra in 1930), and the *Mass* for chorus, winds, and brass (1948).

In an article on *Oedipus Rex*, Wilfrid Mellers attributes the genesis of neoclassicism to Stravinsky's emigration to Western Europe after the twin catastrophes of World War I and the Bolshevik Revolution (1917) in Russia, which effectively denied him access to his native land. Mellers argues that Stravinsky was forced to abandon his Russian cultural roots in favor of the musical aesthetics of his adopted homeland.

> For him [Stravinsky], music has always been ritual, even though, as a modern man twice deracinated, he has lived in societies that have forgotten what ritual means. In early works like *The Rite of Spring* and *The Wedding* he was able, being a Russian, to re-invoke the ritual of a remote and primitive past. In so doing he was performing a negative and a positive act simultaneously: negative because the terror and the violence in the ritual seemed directly to parallel the death-struggle of our deracinated civilization which was then erupting in the first of the World Wars; positive because this primitive vitality served as a reminder of the instinctive passional life that modern man had lost.[2]

In *Pulcinella*, Stravinsky appropriates music supposedly written by Pergolesi as his first exercise in taking ownership of Western European music as his sine qua non.[3] Similarly, *Oedipus Rex* may be seen as a reworking of the dramatic music of Handel, especially the oratorios based on such classical subjects as Hercules and Semele. Therefore, *Oedipus Rex* is doubly neoclassical because it redresses Sophocles's famous play in modern garb (courtesy of Jean Cocteau) and relies on Latin to not just reflect the mythological roots of its story but also to assure a certain neutrality of text.

Fig. 8.1 Stage design for *Oedipus Rex* by Théodore Stravinsky

Stephen Walsh argues that labeling *Oedipus Rex* as neoclassical is a misnomer. What that piece offers "is neither new ('neo') nor classical; or rather its classical elements are not new, and its new elements are not classical."[4] Boris Asaf'yev is even more direct: "Certainly, the opera-oratorio *King Oedipus* (1926–27) is a synthesis of Stravinsky's latest and persistent efforts to create a new style that will be strictly practical and also neutral (that is, uncontaminated by national or subjective emotional connotations)—in short, a kind of musical esperanto."[5] Here we can understand that Oedipus Rex is "classical" textually in its use of a well-known Greek myth (recast into Latin) and "classical" musically in Stravinsky's unabashed use of tonal elements (Fig. 8.1).

Again, Mellers argues that Stravinsky uses specific tonal centers to represent emotional states and attributes.[6] This tonal symbolism is most obvious in the music Stravinsky crafts for Oedipus's realization of his fate (ex. 8.1).

Example 8.1 Stravinsky, *Oedipus Rex*, act 2, mm. 467–70

Stravinsky has Oedipus express his "light-bulb moment" as a descending B-minor arpeggio; Similarly, for the opening of Creon's aria "Respondit deus," Stravinsky chooses to use a C major arpeggio—the Enlightenment's musical embodiment of reason or, in this case, validation that Creon speaks for the gods (ex. 8.2).

Example 8.2 Stravinsky, *Oedipus Rex*, act 1, mm. 143–49

The tenet this C-major arpeggio represents (whether from heaven or Olympus) is confirmed by the chorus's salutation, "Vale Creo! Audimus!" ("Hail, Creon; we are listening!"); centered in G major (the dominant of C), it expresses the local population's hope that Creon speaks the truth and prepares us musically by expressing its hopes in the music's resolution to the tonic C major (ex. 8.3).

Example 8.3 Stravinsky, *Oedipus Rex*, act 1, mm. 139–42

Stravinsky's melodic language is largely diatonic, an Apollonian quality further reinforced by the use of sequence as a way of developing musical ideas. Stravinsky also appropriates another commonplace of classicism—patterned repetition—as a quasi-tonal way of expanding melodic ideas (ex. 8.4).

Example 8.4 Stravinsky, *Oedipus Rex*, act 2, mm. 325–28

In *The Unanswered Question*, Leonard Bernstein reveals his discovery of a striking similarity in *Oedipus Rex* between Jocasta's aria "Nonneerubescite, reges," the opening orchestral motive of that work, and the aria "Pietà ti prenda," sung by Aida in act 2 of Verdi's opera of the same name (ex. 8.5a,b,c).[7]

Example 8.5 a–c Stravinsky, *Oedipus Rex*

As striking as this apparent borrowing is, it hardly justifies calling the work neo-Verdian, even though Stravinsky was known to be an ardent admirer of Verdi's operas. Stephen Walsh remarks that "Stravinsky's opening rarely sounds specifically Verdian in the way Jocasta's aria later in the work does. This is partly because the modeling is not at the level of musical style but at the more general level of gesture and dramatic parallel. But it is also because Stravinsky typically mixes allusions in such a way as to confuse our sense of style, and because, finally, the temporal dynamic of his writing is crucially different from that of romantic Italian opera."[8]

Despite Stravinsky's imitations, allusions, and outright parodies, *Oedipus* transcends its borrowings. Whether one hears in Creon's music intimations of Handel, Mozart, Mendelssohn, or Meyerbeer, these characterizations all miss the fundamental point: no matter the diversity of its musical inspiration, this piece is ultimately and irrevocably Stravinsky.[9]

The second member of Stravinsky's neoclassical trilogy is the *Symphony of Psalms* (1930), a work that epitomizes Stravinsky's attention to detail and precompositional planning.

> The idea of writing a symphonic work of some length had been present in my mind for a long time.... My idea was that my symphony should be a work with great contrapuntal development, and for that it was necessary to increase the media at my disposal. I finally decided on a choral and instrumental ensemble in which the two elements should be on an equal footing, neither of them outweighing the other.... I sought for my words, since they were to be sung, among those which had been written for singing. And quite naturally my first idea was to have recourse to the Psalms.[10]

Stravinsky reveals himself as a meticulous composer who makes a priori decisions about his current work. His approach is simultaneously at odds with the romantic notion of the composer as inspired artist and attuned to the calculated appropriation of ideas and procedures as they fit into his larger scheme.[11]

The European premiere of Stravinsky's *Symphony of Psalms* took place, not in Boston but in Brussels on December 13, 1930, with Ernst Ansermet conducting the Orchestre de la Suisse Romande. The concert program initially listed the three symphonic movements as Prelude, Double Fugue, and Allegro symphonique; although these labels were later discarded, they offer insight into Stravinsky's conception of his symphony.[12] The implied connection of the first two movements as Prelude and Fugue aside, there is a geometric shape based on the durations of the three movements, each movement being roughly twice the length of its predecessor: mvt. 1 (ca. 3 minutes), mvt. 2 (ca. 6 minutes), mvt. 3 (ca. 12 minutes).

The orchestra itself was perplexed by Stravinsky's deliberate decision to avoid using the upper strings. The work's relatively brief duration for a work called "symphony" was also problematic; in order to achieve the expected length, it was decided that the work should be played twice, but Stravinsky himself never considered composing a traditional symphony, that is, "a succession of pieces varying in character."[13] His stated intention was to produce a work of "great contrapuntal development" in which the choral and instrumental ensembles were on an even footing. After making these preliminary decisions, Stravinsky chose his texts. As he had in *Oedipus Rex*, he chose Latin (texts from the Vulgate for Psalms 38, 39, and 150) to create a cultural distance between the work and its audience; in so doing, he lent credence to Roger Shattuck's notion that neoclassical art was "self-reflexive" and more concerned about the legitimacy of its own genesis than with fulfilling cultural norms.[14] Even given this neoclassical bent, Stravinsky's appropriation of the word "symphony" is potentially misleading. Like his later *Symphony in Three Movements* (1945), Stravinsky casts his Psalms in the pattern (fast–slow–fast) of the Italian sinfonia. The original titles suggest neither a symphonic conception nor the tonal plan of the typical classical symphony. Thus, the *Symphony of Psalms* is not in a key in the conventional sense as the first movement begins in E minor and ends in G major, a key that seems to function neatly as dominant to the second movement's tonality of C minor. From the outset, Stravinsky suggests a strong pull to E♭ (relative major of C minor), a tonal focus that persists well into the third movement.

The first movement begins with an astringent, symmetrically spaced E-minor triad that has come to typify Stravinsky (ex. 8.6).

Example 8.6 Stravinsky, *Symphony of Psalms*, mvt. 1, mm. 1–4

Stravinsky's excitement upon discovering this precisely spaced chord—E-minor triads at the top and bottom with two additional Gs, each a sixth away from the innermost member of the triad—has been explained by Walter Piston, speaking about another chord in another piece:

> In the course of a talk about *Oedipus Rex*, at one of these meetings, an observation that he made threw a bright light on a most important aspect of his artistic ideals. He said, "How happy I was when I discovered that chord!" Some of us were puzzled because the chord, known in common harmonic terms as a D-major triad, appeared neither new nor complex. But it became evident that Stravinsky regarded every chord as an individual sonority, having many attributes above and beyond the tones selected from a scale or altered this way and that.[15]

Stravinsky's reiteration of this chord establishes the first layer of formal design; we hear it as a special kind of tonic (not unlike the iconic opening of Debussy's *Prélude à l'après-midi d'un faun*) from which the subsequent music diverges and then returns. The first fourteen measures of orchestral music contain four statements of the chord separated by arpeggios. The chord sounds twice more in the opening movement, preceding the texts "Ne sileas" (m. 48) and "Quoniam advena" (m. 52), the conclusion of v. 13 and the opening of v. 14 respectively.

This boldly original chord and the unison arpeggiations of the dominant seventh chords of E♭ and C minor/C major respectively that follow it present the harmonic content of the entire work, analogous to the exposition in sonata-allegro form. Joseph N. Straus explains the harmonic flux of the first movement from E to G as movement along an axis comprised of two triads that share two common tones. Melodically, a Phrygian gesture (E–F–E) dominates the movement, seemingly predicting a final resolution to E. But Stravinsky denies this expectation, resolving from F upward to G rather than down to E. For Straus, though, this reversal of expectation confirms Stravinsky's modulation from one tonal axis (E–G–B) to the next (G–B–D).[16] The obvious problem with his interpretation is that this progression is linear, denying recapitulation of the opening material in its original tonal area. Such a deviation from eighteenth-century practice is one of the attributes that makes this work neoclassical. Stravinsky had no more interest in copying Haydn or Mozart's practice than their immediate successors did.

The Phrygian "Exaudi" theme first heard in the alto (m. 26) dominates the movement, but embraces slightly different accompaniments. Its first statement (m. 26) features three melodic strands: (1) an instrumental doubling of the alto melody (2) a variant of the introduction's arpeggiated melody, and (3) a B-minor ostinato in the second and fourth oboes. For its second appearance (m. 41), Stravinsky amplifies the minor thirds by adding an oscillating ostinato of minor thirds (F–A♭, E–G). A new vocal melody begins at m. 53, accompanied by now harmonic minor thirds and another typically Stravinsky device—successively longer repetitions of a scalar melody in the English horn and bassoons (ex. 8.7).

Example 8.7 Stravinsky, *Symphony of Psalms,* mvt. 1, mm. 53–55

The development of this new idea continues, culminating in the return of E minor in m. 65. Simultaneously, the orchestra plays music of the introduction (mm. 14–16) now in a much higher tessitura with two simultaneous rhythms (eighths and sixteenths). We hear what follows (m. 68) as a recapitulation of sorts in which the Phrygian "Exaudi" melody and two different versions of the ostinato thirds appear. Stravinsky continues to stretch the texture higher and lower, culminating in the logical, if aurally unexpected, resolution to G major.

The G-major conclusion of mvt. 1 is marked *Enchainez* ("Connect") to insure a direct connection to the vaguely familiar C-minor melody of his fugue subject (ex. 8.8).

Example 8.8 Stravinsky, *Symphony of Psalms,* mvt. 2, mm. 1–9

This subject should sound familiar because Stravinsky crafts it out of those same oscillating thirds that figured so prominently in the first movement. The only difference is that the formerly conjunct thirds are made more angular by the transposition of the third pitch up an octave. Imitated at the fifth and octave, the subject creates a four-voice exposition that transits a new triadic axis (C–E♭–G), allowing its combination with the new choral fugue theme ("Expectans expectavi") in E♭ (ex. 8.9).

Example 8.9 Stravinsky, *Symphony of Psalms,* mvt. 2, mm. 29–32

If the chorus's fugue theme is less memorable or durable than its instrumental predecessor, its emphasis of E♭ is critical, producing another triadic axis (C–E♭–G, E♭–G–B♭) affirmed by the unison chorus's concluding "et sperabunt in Domino" ("and will hope in the Lord"), a musical depiction of the steadfastness of faith.

The final instrumental chord of movement two (E♭–F–B♭) provides immediate connection to the opening of the final movement. The sustained E♭ is first harmonized as C minor (1st inversion), immediately followed by a dominant-seventh chord on F. In the second measure, horn and bassoon provide the expected tonic (B♭), culminating a compressed, quite tonal cadential progression. In the second measure, the chorus moves from F major to E♭, against which Stravinsky places another V–I cadence to C (minor). This bitonal harmonic construct validates the harmonic goals (E♭ and C) implied in the dominant-seventh chord arpeggios of mvt. 1 (ex. 8.10).

Example 8.10 Stravinsky, *Symphony of Psalms*, mvt. 3, mm. 1–8

Straus again explains that the third movement of *Symphony of Psalms* involves a second triadic axis, the center of which is C–E–G; this triad is overlapped by triads a minor third above (E♭–G–B♭) and below (A–C/C♯–E) its starting pitch. Regarding the composition as a whole, Stravinsky employs three related axes. The first two (mvts. 1 and 2) involve triads related to one another in the traditional relative minor/major configuration with no chromatic conflicts: E–G–B/G–B–D (mvt. 1), C–E♭–G/E♭–G–B♭ (mvt. 2). The third movement expands and complicates this same basic procedure by using three triads, the most important one being C–E–G; the other two traidic overlaps (E♭–G–B♭ and A–C♯–E) both introduce conflicting chromatics (E♭ vs. E and C♯ vs. C) that inject a new bitonal complexity to the concluding movement.[17]

Stravinsky's most cogent expression of E♭ as a tonality is a four-note ostinato (E♭, B♭, F, B♭) that accompanies the choral declaration (in 3/2): "Laudate eum in cymbalis bene sonantibus." ("Praise him on the loud-sounding cymbals"). With typical irony, Stravinsky sets this jubilant text to music (marked *sub. piano e ben cantabile*) that hardly moves (ex. 8.11).

Example 8.11 Stravinsky, *Symphony of Psalms*, mvt. 3, mm. 262–64

Stravinsky rotates the soprano's melody stepwise through the relatively restricted compass of a minor third, C″–E♭″. His homophonic choral writing benefits from its juxtaposition with the asymmetric ostinato, which requires three statements of its four-note pattern for its initial note (E♭) to land on a downbeat. This construction, so redolent of medieval isorhythm, accentuates the pivotal role that separate musical layers play in the music of Stravinsky and others. Layers of texture, harmony, and rhythm grudgingly coexist until one element eventually emerges as dominant. In the case of *Symphony of Psalms*, Stravinsky ultimately strips away the contesting tonal axes until only C major remains as the logical conclusion of the process he followed from the very beginnings of the work's conception.

The third and final member of Stravinsky's neoclassical triptych is his *Mass* (1948) for soloists, chorus of men and boys, and ten winds. This brief, austere work stands in direct contrast to the elaborate Masses of the late eighteenth and nineteenth centuries. Stravinsky deliberately avoids Mozartean style for this work, opting instead to set the venerable text in what he regards as a proper manner.[18] What emerges, even on first hearing, is a work whose incantational quality is clearly ritualistic, but its essence defies historical categories. Although not explicitly associated with the *Mass*, Stravinsky's most infamous musical pronouncement might well apply to it:

> For I consider that music is, by its very nature, essentially powerless to express anything at all, whether a feeling, an attitude of mind, a psychological mood, a phenomenon of nature, etc. . . . Expression has never been an inherent property of music. That is by no means the purpose of its existence. If, as is nearly always the case, music appears to express something, this is only an illusion and not a reality. It is simply an additional attribute which, by tacit and inveterate agreement, we have lent it, thrust upon it as a label, a convention—in short, an aspect which unconsciously or by force of habit, we have come to confuse with its essential being.[19]

Here, Stravinsky articulates a concern shared by all composers of his time—the need to distance his music from the past by relying on logically conceived structures that leave no room for intuitive, emotional music.[20] While his *Mass* (like his other neoclassical works) considers the text's meaning and accent, the structures he imposes on it are hardly expressive in the conventional sense. Edward Lundergan points out that Stravinsky's *Mass* exhibits a large-scale symmetry.

> The five movements of the *Mass* form a symmetrical plan on a large scale. The two outer movements, the Kyrie and the Agnus Dei, employ homophonic choral statements alternating with instrumental interludes, and share a complex tonal vocabulary including octatonic, diatonic, and modal scales. By contrast, the second and fourth movements, the Gloria and the Sanctus, incorporate florid solo lines in alternation with the chorus, in a more diatonically oriented idiom. In the Credo . . . the text is set to a static, syllabic, declamatory chant with a limited harmonic and rhythmic vocabulary . . . [in which] long stretches of text are set to a single repeated chord, evoking the "reciting tone" of Gregorian chant or the Orthodox liturgical chant that Stravinsky knew from his childhood in St. Petersburg.[21]

The fact that none of the movements of Stravinsky's *Mass* have key signatures is not indicative of any traditional system of harmony. Although Lundergan posits an overall symmetry for each movement, internal structures based on a collection of pitches also exist; unique to each movement, these scalar constructions are hardly tonal. The one historical precedent that Stravinsky retains is the use of the same music for both settings of the "Hosanna in excelsis." The version following the "Benedictus" includes five measures before the actual reprise of the nine measures of the first "Hosanna," but even these have a slightly different harmonic close than the original version.

Like his predecessors, Stravinsky acknowledges the tripartite textual structure of the Kyrie and Agnus Dei: in so doing, he creates a symmetrical frame for the entire *Mass* cycle. The Kyrie's ritornello opens (mm. 1, 6, and 10) and closes his Kyrie with accented statements of the pitches E♭ and C (ex. 8.12a).

Example 8.12 a–b Stravinsky, *Mass*

Example 8.12 a–b Continued

b. mm. 1-4

In the Agnus Dei, he repeats the same four-measure passage prior to each text presentation (ex. 8.12b); their absence during the choral passages texturally reinforces the tripartite design of the text.

Both the Gloria and Sanctus feature florid solo vocal writing that alternates with choral sections whose pitch contents are more diatonic than modal and exhibit a preference for sharps. The length and complex syntax of the Credo presents composers of Massses with severe challenges, and Stravinsky is no exception. Like composers from Machaut on, he opts for a declamatory texture that preserves text's accent and syntax. Each of the seventeen sentences that comprise the Credo generates distinct musical segments that vary in duration and meter. Aside from three consecutive sentences (mm. 4–6) in 6/8, Stravinsky adheres strictly to 2/4 meter. But neither this nor his retention of the text's threefold structure provide much illumination as to the movement's overall musical structure. Edward Lundergan suggests that structure principally resides in the various pitch aggregates Stravinsky uses at any given time. His analysis suggests that Stravinsky organizes his Credo around the pentatonic pitch-class set (G–A–B–D–E) using A as its center (E–G–A–B–D), a palindrome in which A is flanked by pairs of minor thirds (reminiscent of the *Symphony of Psalms*).[22]

The Credo, like the opening movement of the *Symphony of Psalms*, begins with the very Stravinskyan E-minor chord and ends in G major. This fact in no way suggests that the movement is tonal, even though the return of the opening E-minor harmony and syllabic declamation in m. 102 sound and feel like a recapitulation. Stravinsky's organization of the text is notably periodic in the sense that text statements often resemble one another. For example, mm. 13–19 sound like an upward transposition of the opening to F♯ and also share the same music as the following segment (mm. 20–25). Similarities of melody and final cadence suggest connection between mm. 26–33 and 34–43 and mm. 44–52 and 53–61. Both of the latter musical sentences conclude with chords that mix D and A major (the final chord of the choral parts in each case is an F♯-minor triad in first inversion). In the second bassoon part's chromatic descent from G to E (mm. 66–68), Lundergan perceives a musical representation of the incarnation mentioned in the preceding choral text (mm. 62–65).[23] The most strikingly different music of the entire movement is in the "Crucifixus" (mm. 71–79); the movement's ambiguity between F (E Phrygian) and F♯ (F♯ Dorian) seems to swing in the favor of F♮. In m. 72 Stravinsky introduces the B♭, the first flat heard in the movement to this point. Flats figure prominently into the music again in the setting of "Et iterum," which culminates in a chord based on E♭ (E♭, F, A♭, D). This relatively distant harmonic position sets up Stravinsky's "recapitulation" via a double Phrygian cadence in the third trombone. "Austere" is the word that best characterizes this movement and, indeed, the entire *Mass*; Stravinsky firmly controls all elements of the musical structure avoiding any possible lapse into music that might be taken as expressive.

PAUL HINDEMITH (1895–1963)

Stravinsky's neoclassicism has been viewed in opposition to Arnold Schoenberg's serialistic approach so that using this label to describe the music of other composers seems somewhat contrived. But Paul Hindemith is perhaps an even stronger candidate for the neoclassic label than Stravinsky. In a letter to Ernst Ansermet (dated August 14, 1922), Stravinsky had already recognized Hindemith as a kindred spirit: "I was unable to go to Salzburg, due to expenses and work . . . I have received a score from a young gentile German, full of talent, named Paul Hindemith. . . . This Hindemith is a sort of German Prokofiev, infinitely more sympathetic than all the others under Schoenberg."[24] Precisely what Stravinsky meant by Hindemith being "more sympathetic" remains unclear. One year later (1923), Darius Milhaud made an assertion that perhaps explains what Stravinsky was thinking: "Diatonicism and chromaticism are the two poles of musical expression. One can say that the Latins are diatonic and the Teutons chromatic. Here are to be found two different points; they are entirely opposed and their consequences are verified by history."[25]

Scott Messing argues that Milhaud's assertions are not validated historically as such starkly defined categories.[26] Nonetheless, it is possible that Stravinsky perceived Hindemith as a more preferable German option than Schoenberg. Hindemith's role in establishing a "new objectivity" (*neue Sachlichkeit*) in Germany to counter the intense subjectivity of expressionism lends credence to this assessment (Fig. 8.2).

From the outset, Hindemith distanced himself from more experimental, dissonant music by composing works for amateur orchestras and choruses of workers—music that became known as *Gebrauchsmusik* (useful or work-a-day music), a term Hindemith himself disowned.[27] He entered the

Fig. 8.2 Paul Hindemith (ca. 1944)

orbit of neoclassicism by becoming a strong advocate for the music of J. S. Bach in particular and earlier eras in general. The clearest manifestations of Hindemith's fascination with Bach are his *Ludus Tonalis* (1943), a sort of twentieth-century *Well-Tempered Clavier*, and the three organ sonatas that recall Bach's masterful trio sonatas. Hindemith's two-volume *The Craft of Musical Composition* (1937) was his attempt to encode a nontonal harmonic theory, which explained the increasingly complex language of contemporary music. Ultimately, Hindemith returned to the overtone series, constructing from its partials a continuum of intervallic relationships of varying degrees of stability (ex. 8.13).

Example 8.13 Hindemith, Series II

From this series, Hindemith extrapolated a theory of chordal quality based on the hierarchical stability and quality of various dyads. Although not accepted universally, Hindemith's system quantifies the consonance and dissonance of any intervallic combination without resorting to the rules of tonality.

Hindemith's body of choral music is impressive; some compositions earned a central place in the contemporary choral repertory, but unfortunately not the twenty-five compositions for men's and treble chorus. Hindemith's *Six Chansons* is undoubtedly the most popular *a cappella* choral work. This cycle of French poems by Rainer Maria Rilke (like Hindemith, Rilke was a German émigré) are the result of a commission tendered by Georges Haenni, the conductor of the Chanson Valaisienne chorus. Hindemith chose the six poems from a set of fifty-nine French poems that Rilke titled *Vergers* ("Orchards"), but Hindemith's ordering of the texts in no way conforms to Rilke's order (Table 8.1).

Hindemith's version creates a binary design (AABCCD) reminiscent of the bar form used by the medieval German Minnesingers and the later Meistersingers. Poems 1 2, 4, and 5 have common subjects (animals) and titles (*Printemps*). Any relationship between the third and sixth texts is less obvious. Perhaps poem 3 ("Since all is passing") marks the transition from the first pair to the second pair, the final poem serves as a paradigm for the larger poetic collection (*Verger*) from which all of the texts were taken.[28] Hindemith composed these six brief choruses in just four days, again typical of his compositional acumen. As twentieth-century music, they are remarkably conservative; not only is the harmonic language relatively consonant but there is a separate tonal center for each piece (Table 8.2).

Table 8.1 Hindemith, *Six Chansons*, poems

Choral Movement	Source
1. La Biche	*Vergers* no. 57
2. Un Cygne	*Vergers* no. 40
3. Puisque tout passe	*Vergers* no. 36
4. Printemps	*Vergers* no. 44 (Printemps 1)
5. En Hiver	*Vergers* no. 44 (Printemps 6)
6. Verger	*Vergers* no. 29 (Verger 3)

Table 8.2 Hindemith, *Six Chansons*, tonal centers

1."La biche"   2. "Un cygne"   3. "Puisque tout passe"   4. "Printemps"   5. "En hiver"   6. "Verger"

The lack of key signature in all six songs is typical of Hindemith, and the resulting flux of accidentals is one of his stylistic fingerprints. The tonal centers of nos.1, 2, 4, and 5 (A–E; A♭–E♭) reflect Hindemith's perception of their textual relatedness; the pieces that follow each pair (nos. 3 and 6) share G as a tonal center. The perfect fifth separating the tonal centers of the two pairs of mvts. 1–2 and 4–5 translates into a melodic gesture that permeates each separate composition (ex. 8.14a,b,c).

Example 8.14 a–c Hindemith, *Six Chansons*
© 1943 by Schott Music © Renewed All Rights Reserved Used by permission of European American Music Distributors LLC, sole US and Canadian agent for Schott Music.

Hindemith's accompanied choral works include two important works—*When Lilacs Last in the Dooryard Bloom'd: A Requiem "For Those We Love"* (1946), and *Apparebit repentina dies* (1947). In the Requiem, he transforms portions of Walt Whitman's "Memories of President Lincoln" into a "Requiem for Those We Love." Commissioned by Robert Shaw for the Collegiate Chorale of New York City, this uniquely twentieth-century work features mezzo-soprano and baritone soloists, mixed chorus, and a large orchestra. Hindemith dedicates the composition to the memory of Franklin D. Roosevelt and to those Americans who died in World War II. Whitman's deeply layered poem interweaves three important symbols—lilac blooms, the song of the hermit thrush, and the planet Venus. The reference to lilacs arose from the lavender blossoms that mourners heaped on Lincoln's coffin in the spring of 1865. The solitary lament of the hermit thrush, singing in the swamps, became Whitman's personal elegy to Lincoln. Finally, Venus, visible at the time of Lincoln's second inauguration and taken by many as a positive omen, became Whitman's symbol for the dreams for America that died with Lincoln.

Hindemith translates the twenty sections of Whitman's poem into a series of eleven vocal movements, preceded by an orchestral prelude (Table 8.3). The prelude begins with a plaintive theme, the pitches of which (A, C♯, F, E) sound over a C♯ pedal; the persistent use of this motto throughout the prelude and (transposed) in the work's concluding duet (mm. 89–94) create something like a tonal center for the entire work. From this pitch collection [C♯, A, F, E, and C♯], Hindemith derives tonal centers that each govern a portion of the work. The overture and first three vocal movements are grounded on C♯; they present two of the poem's three principal melodic images—the lilac theme (C♯–B–E–G) and the cuckoo-like thrush's song (G–E)—first heard simultaneously in m. 12, then repeated to close mvt. 1 (mm. 36–9) and open mvt. 2 (ex. 8.15a,b).

Table 8.3 Hindemith, *When Lilacs Last in the Dooryard Bloom'd: A Requiem "For Those We Love"*

Prelude

1. "When Lilacs Last in the Dooryard Bloom'd"
2. Arioso: "In the Swamp"
3. March: "Over the Breast of the Spring"
4. "O Western Orb"
5. Arioso: "Sing On, There in the Swamp"
6. Song: "O How Shall I Warble"
7. Introduction and Fugue: "Lo! Body and Soul"
8. "Sing On! You Gray-Brown Bird"
9. Death Carol: "Come, Lovely and Soothing Death"
10. "To the Tally of My Soul"
11. Finale: "Passing the Visions"

Example 8.15 a–b Hindemith, *When Lilacs Last in the Dooryard Bloom'd: A Requiem "For Those We Love"*, mvt. 1

Example 8.15 a–b Continued

b. no.1 (mm. 39) - no. 2 (mm. 1)

Movements 4–7 comprise a second formal unit centered on the pitch A. The images of the "western orb" and the "swamp bird's song" dominate the movements for solo baritone (mvt. 4) and mezzo-soprano (mvt. 5) respectively. In mvt. 6, the baritone voices the poet's personal musings on the tragedy of Lincoln's death. This second formal segment (mvts. 5–7) culminates in a rugged introduction and fugue that hymns the reunited Union (mvt. 7). At the outset of the third segment, Hindemith combines two poems—"Sing On! You Gray-Brown Bird" and the hymn "For Those We Love" in an interesting and characteristic way (ex. 8.16).

Example 8.16 Hindemith, *When Lilacs Last in the Dooryard Bloom'd*, mvt. 8, mm. 1–2

This brief excerpt features the prelude's pitch collection (C–E–A–F) as the initial pitches of a repeated string accompaniment. Above it, an English horn plays a melody that recollects the work's opening motif as pairs of minor thirds, which immediately sounds a half step higher in a near retrograde of the beginning. Hindemith reprises this two-measure ritornello to mark four critical points in the course of this extended movement (mm. 14–15, 22–23, 74–75, and 87–88). But what is truly fascinating is Hindemith's larger planning of the movement, which assumes a form familiar to us, most notably in the music of Handel and Mendelssohn. The duet that begins in m. 74 is a literal reprise of the opening mezzo-soprano solo and its accompaniment (mm. 1–23) to which Hindemith adds a male solo melody, effectively creating the textural form ABA+B.

In response to this threnody, the chorus sings the Death Carol, "Come, Lovely and Soothing Death" (mvt. 9); Hindemith, the neoclassicist, concludes this with a Bach-like chaconne bass that accompanies the chorus's presentation of the text "Approach, strong Deliveress!" The bass line consists of the pitch set F–E–B–F♯ (mm. 67–69) and mm. 142–56 are spelled enharmonically F–F♭–C♭–G♭); Hindemith uses this bass line twenty-nine times to undergird the choral homophony. The highlights of the final two movements (mvts. 10 and 11) both come at each movement's end: an off-stage military bugle playing "Taps" as an eerie descant to the orchestra's restatement of previously heard themes (mvt. 10) and the soloists' concluding intonation of "When Lilacs Last in the Dooryard Bloom'd" on a unison C♯, the same pitch with which the work began (mvt. 11).

A more accessible, more often-performed work is *Apparebit repentina dies*, which Hindemith composed the following year (1947) for a Symposium on Music Criticism held at Harvard University.[29] Scored for chorus and ten brass instruments, this stark composition sets an anonymous medieval Latin poem, the apocalyptic text of which features an alphabetic acrostic (twenty-four strophes each beginning with different consecutive letters of the Latin alphabet).[30] Each stanza is comprised of a double couplet with alternating lines of 8 and 7 but as a whole, there is no consistent rhyme scheme and what seems a daunting feat of musical genius becomes a little less intimidating when one carefully examines the work's structure.[31]

Table 8.4 presents a number of useful details concerning text distribution, creation of internal form based on motivic repetition and, to a lesser extent, tempo, texture and harmony; tempo but it fails to reveal the work's facile formal structure. The work's two principal themes appear in the first eight measures of the prelude.

Table 8.4 Hindemith, *Apparebit repentina dies*, mvt. 1, form

mm.	Scoring	Text line	Harmony	Musical equivalence
1–70	tpt 1,2, hn, tbn, tba	–	C F D G E♭ A♭	
71–98	satb tbn, tba	1	Phrygian (C–B, F–E)	
99–109	satb tpt 1,2, hn, tbn, tba	2	E minor	mm. 108–8 = mm. 95–7
110–41	satb tpt 1,2, hn, tbn, tba	3–4	mm. 1–4 transposed to E, G, B♭, G♭, D, C	mm. 110–13 = mm. 1–4 mm. 137–40 = mm. 1–4
142–85	satb tpt 1,2, hn, tbn, tba	5–6	C F D G E♭ A♭	mm. 142–85 = mm. 5–48
185–223	satb tpt 1,2, hn, tbn, tba	7	E7 – A♭	Br. mm. 187–9 = 191–3 Br. m. 208 = mm. 211–14

Example 8.17 a–b Hindemith, *Apparebit repentina dies*, Prelude
© 1947 Copyright Schott Music © Renewed. Used by permission
of European American Music Distributors, LLC, sole US and Canadian
for Schott Music.

Example 8.17a is a succession of perfect fifths/fourths: F–C'–D–G–D'♭–A♭, the second most stable interval according to *The Craft of Musical Composition*.[32] The second motive is an expansion of the first motive, and one that adds two additional pitches (as well as some repetitions). Hindemith uses the pitch content of the first (ex. 8.17a) and the rhythm of the second (ex. 8.17b) to create an instrumental fugue, complete with multiple expositions, episodes, a stretto (m. 33), and an augmented version as the final statement (mm. 63–69).

While the choral settings of vv. 1 and 2 (mm. 71–98 and 99–109) are as "free" as anything composed by Hindemith gets, the literal return of the first four measures in m. 110 sets up the expectation of a recapitulation. But the unison choral writing and transposed repetitions of that four-measure motive suggest something else. In mm. 137–40 the brass's restatement of mm. 1–4 ushers in a literal recapitulation of the brass fugue (mm. 5–48), over the top of which Hindemith constructs new choral parts to set the poem's line 5 (mm. 142–70) and line 6 (mm. 170–85). This is a contemporary application of the Baroque principle of *Choreinbau*, or choral inbuilding, in which voice parts are grafted onto an existing instrumental part. A new section, containing multiple presentations of the fugue subject by alto and bass, unfolds over fragments of the same theme. The first movement concludes with the same A♭ major chord that ended the prelude.

The final movement is a brief chorale à la Bach that underscores the true formal significance of Hindemith's opening motive. Within its fourteen measures (sung twice) Hindemith creates separate instrumental and choral layers. The instruments begin with a transposed, harmonized version of the work's opening four measures (ex. 8.18a) and close with a fragmented, unison statement of that same motive at original pitch (ex. 8.18b).

Example 8.18 a–b Hindemith, *Apparebit repentina dies*, mvt. 4
© 1947 Copyright Schott Music © Renewed. Used by permission of
European American Music Distributors, LLC, sole US and Canadian for
Schott Music.

Example 8.18 a–b Continued

b. mm. 7-14

The instrumental parts enharmonically bridge the conclusion of one choral phrase with the beginning of the next. The choral parts cannot be reduced to some version of this recurring theme, but the movement's final four bars do present a harmonization of it at the original pitch.

Hindemith uses texture and some cleverly disguised musical repetition to create the second movement's texture-driven presentation of the Last Judgment. The repetition Hindemith uses here is a literal restatement of the vocal line (mm. 23–43 = mm. 73–93) that is somewhat disguised by variation in the brass accompaniment.

Hindemith elevates repetition as a formal principle to new heights in the third movement's passacaglia (mm. 44–172). Like the passacaglia Bach uses for the "Crucifixus" of the Mass in B minor, Hindemith's theme is primarily melodic, appearing three times in the alto (mm.52–76) and bass (mm. 76–100), once in the soprano (mm. 116–25), and seven times instrumentally (mm. 100–116 and 126–68) (ex. 8.19).

Example 8.19 Hindemith, *Apparebit repentina dies*, mvt. 3, mm. 52–60

© 1947 Copyright Schott Music © Renewed. Used by permission of European American Music Distributors, LLC, sole US and Canadian for Schott Music.

While Hindemith retains the same rhythm and pitch in each statement, he varies the theme's location allowing precisely the kind of harmonic flexibility Bach denied himself. Hindemith most closely mimics Bach's approach when his theme is presented as the instrumental bass (mm. 126–33 and 142–68).

This work demonstrates Hindemith's creative use of musical repetition, a process that when deconstructed suggests a conscious recycling of material to forge relationships both within and between the separate movements. Concerning Hindemith's legendary prowess as a composer, Richard French states that "Hindemith took the gift of life seriously. For him talent had no reality and no value apart from the exercise of it. Ceaseless, serious, responsible exercise of talent was the distinctive characteristic of Hindemith alive, and what he required of himself he demanded of everyone else.... For Hindemith, then, a theology of expertise—his belief in the efficacy of technical skill—was a very natural view, and it is amusing that the view could be at once so modern and so fashionable and, at the same time, so roundly criticized."[33]

While Hindemith is the most obvious German neoclassical composer, Glenn Watkins cites Carl Orff, the early works of Ernst Krenek, and Kurt Weill as other exemplars of this new objectivity.[34] To these, one could reasonably add a group of church composers, headed by Hugo Distler (1908–42) and Ernst Pepping (1901–81), who consciously appropriate historical models to revitalize contemporary choral church music, and organ compositions. In his discussion of Krenek and Weill, Watkins focuses mainly on the influence of American jazz. As potent as this influence was, it was not historically grounded and had little effect on German choral music of that period.

Some of the best known choral works with a conscious sense of historicity are those of Carl Orff (1895–1982). These include *Carmina Burana* (1937) and its successor, *Catulli Carmina* (1943), written during the heyday of National Socialism. Judith Lynn Sebesta writes that the irregular form and scansion of the Latin poems Orff sets are quite different from the classical Latin poetry of Virgil or Catullus.[35] A curious blend of sacred and secular, these texts were written by the Goliards, essentially "medieval dropouts" whose disillusionment with contemporary religion and society revealed themselves in bitingly satirical, ribald, even heretical poetry. From this large, anonymous body of texts, Orff chose to set his songs (*Carmina*) for three principal soloists—soprano, tenor, and baritone—mixed chorus (with divisi), children's chorus, and large orchestra.[36]

Orff opens his composition by setting a poem concerning Fate, the power of which is portrayed as a rotating wheel (musically manifest in the literal repetition of the opening chorus at the end) that has turned full circle through a range of emotions and ideas. Orff groups the intervening texts into three large, titled parts: *Primo vere/Uf dem anger* (3–10); *In taberna* (11–14), and *Cour d'amour* (15–23). The first combines three Latin poems about spring and love with four German dance-songs drawn from a separate portion of the manuscript. *In taberna* depicts an increasingly drunken crowd, whose enjoyment of the pleasures of the flesh leads them to reject spiritual values. The title of the final scene, *Cour d'amour*, symbolizes medieval courtly love and casts the chorus as a "court" who observe love's progression from first flirtation to consummation.

The most familiar music is the opening chorus, "O Fortuna" (used in the sound track of more than a few hero-fantasy movies). Nonetheless, this chorus illustrates the essentials of Orff's style—simple, repetitive, declamatory music built to an immense climax over an accompanying ostinato. It is possible, even feasible, to link this music to the Stravinsky of *The Rite of Spring* and *Les Noces*—music noted for its primitive, primal power, reinforced by polymeter and polyrhythms.[37] Orff's modal melodies and his counterpoint's reliance on parallel motion further emphasize the medieval origins of the text. The music's static simplicity is reinforced by another anachronism—strophic settings based on minimal melodic material—as in the opening verse of "Tempus est iocundum" (ex. 8.20).

Example 8.20 Orff, *Carmina Burana*, no. 22, mm. 1–8

© 1937 by Schott Music © Renewed. Used by permission of European American Music Distributors, LLC, sole US and Canadian for Schott Music.

These eight measures alternate with six measures of contrasting music ("Oh, oh, oh, totus floreo") plus a one-measure choral reprise that links one stanza to the next. The simplicity of this music's form stems from Orff's regular alternation of tempo; all of the sections shown in example 8.20 are marked "quarter note = 144," slightly faster than the tempo of the B sections where quarter note = 120.

GERMAN CHURCH MUSIC IN THE TWENTIETH CENTURY

The renewal of Protestant worship in Germany began in the late nineteenth century and reached its full flower in the first half of the twentieth century. With the exception of Hugo Distler, the individual composers have remained relatively unknown. Their neoclassicism relied on the conscious use of historical forms (both musical and liturgical) in acknowledgment of their musical forebears, to which they added a new rhythmic vitality and contemporary harmony.

The church music revival in early twentieth-century Germany represents the confluence of many separate movements: liturgical reform (led principally by the theologians Karl Barth and Christhard Mahrenholz); an interest in older music (fostered by the Wandervogel and similar youth movements of the early 1900s); the publication of the various volumes of *Monuments of German Music* (*DDT, DTÖ, DTB,* etc.) were conceived of as musical and anthological extensions of the complete works projects of the nineteenth century; and, finally, the *Orgelbewegung* (organ reform movement) initiated by the musicologist Wilibald Gurlitt's construction of an organ in 1921 at the University of Freiburg based on Michael Praetorius's specifications (*Syntagma musicum,* II, 1619). Gurlitt's work spawned an interest among organ builders in the United States in organs with mechanical action (tracker organs) and polyphonic voicing.[38] In addition, the choral revival begins with composers of church music such as Kurt

Thomas (1904–73), Karl Straube (1873–1950), and Distler's teacher at the Leipzig Conservatory, Hermann Grabner (1886–1969).

Hugo Distler is perhaps the best-known member of this group. His earliest works—the double-choir, chorale motet *Herzlich Lieb hab ich dich, O Herr*, op. 2 (1931), and *Eine Deutsche Choralmesse*, op. 3 (1932)—drew inspiration from historical models. The *Choralmesse* blended Lutheran chorales with the text of the Latin Mass Ordinary. But in place of the Sanctus or its Lutheran equivalent (*Jesaiah dem Propheten, das geschah*), Distler set the words of institution (soloist) accompanied by the chorale "O Mensch bewein dein Sünde gross." Distler's apparent inspiration was Heinrich Schütz, whose *Zwölf Geistliche Gesänge*, op. 13, were republished in 1925 under the title *Die deutsche Messe*.[39] Similar works by Pepping (*Deutsche Choralmesse*, 1931), Wolfgang Fortner (*Ein deutsche Liedmesse* 1934), and Hans Friedrich Micheelsen (*Deutsche Messe*, 1953) followed Distler's lead.

Historical Lutheran hymnody was also the basis of motet collections like Distler's *Der Jahrkreis*, op. 5 (1933), *Drei kleine Choralmotteten*, op. 6, no. 2 (1933), and four of the nine motets (nos. 3–6) of his *Geistliche Chormusik*, op. 12 (after 1934). In *Der Jahrkreis*, Distler attempted "to meet the general need for simple de tempore music in the worship service," by composing fifty-two chorale motets for treble and mixed two- and three-part choirs.[40] By providing multiple settings to accommodate all verses of a hymn, he revived the seventeenth-century alternation of polyphony and congregational singing (*Alternatimpraxis*). His provision of instrumental ritornelli for some motets and use of SAB settings make the collection liturgically appropriate and musically accessible even to modest church choirs.

The best known of Distler's chorale motets is *Lobe den Herren*, op. 6, no. 2.[41] Settings for three and four voices provide both textural variety and the basis of a three-part (ABA) form based on the *da capo* of the four-part setting following the SAB verse. In the first setting, Distler places the chorale melody in the soprano (ex. 8.21), as opposed to the second setting in which he assigns it to the unison male voices. These two settings illustrate Distler's tendency to create rhythmic counterpoint based on an implicit conflict between the rhythm of the individual vocal lines and the motet's prevailing meter.

Example 8.21 Distler, *Lobe den Herren*, op. 6 no. 2, mm. 1–6

For his op. 4, the *Kleine Adventsmusik*, Distler creates a set of choral variations on the Advent chorale "Nun komm der Heiden Heiland." Composed for the *Abendmusiken* (evening music concerts) for the famed Marienkirche in Lübeck, where Franz Tunder and Dietrich Buxtehude were Kapellmeistern in the seventeenth century, Distler consciously emulates his predecessors both in his varied treatment of the hymn in the manner of a chorale partita and his use of modest vocal and instrumental forces.[42] Distler's repetition of the opening instrumental sonata as the concluding movement, and his use of the same music for vv. 1 and 7, create a double symmetric frame reminiscent of seventeenth-century German church music. Distler later composed two additional chorale cantatas as his op. 11—*Wo Gott zum Haus nit gibt sein Gunst* (1933) and *Nun danket all und bringet Ehr* (1941).

For his magnum opus, the *Geistliche Chormusik*, op. 12, Distler consciously borrowed the title of Heinrich Schütz's collection of German motets (1648). Like Schütz, Distler intended to provide music for the entire liturgical year, but this task was left unfulfilled at his early death. The textual bases for these motets are either chorales (3–6) or biblical texts (1, 2, 7–9). In *Wachet auf, ruft uns die Stimme*, Distler uses three different versions of the familiar Advent hymn. Aside from v. 1's greater length and the v. 2's use of vocal soloists, the three sections are similar in style. The large tripartite form of the whole derives from both meter (2/2–4/4–2/2) and tempo (fast–slow–fast).[43]

The five biblical motets are more stylistically diverse. *Singet dem Herrn ein neues Lied* evokes the memory of settings of the same text by both J. S. Bach and Heinrich Schütz.[44] And Distler's last two motets were conceived as the opening and closing choruses of an unfinished *St. John Passion*. Perhaps the most fascinating motet is *Der Totentanz* ("Dance of Death"), which takes its title from the stained-glass window in the Marienkirche that depicts Death interacting with people of varied ages and vocations. Intended for All Saint's Day, this fascinating work combines spoken drama, flute interludes based on a German hymn, and choral aphorisms in which Death confronts a variety of people. Example 8.22 typifies the brevity and sensitivity to text that characterizes the work as a whole.

Example 8.22 Distler, *Der Totentanz*, op. 12, no. 2, mvt. 13

In 1933 Distler composed a Passion (*Choralpassion*, op. 7) and a *Christmas Oratorio* (*Die Weihnachtsgeschichte*, op. 10), both of which use a set of chorale variations, a narrator (Evangelist), whose chant-like melodies are reminiscent of Schütz's Passions, and purely biblical texts.[45] In the epilogue to his *Choralpassion*, Distler recounted the "gripping impression" that the annual Good Friday performance of Schütz's *St. Matthew Passion* in Lübeck had on him. It was this performance that moved him to compose "a representation of the Passion story ... in raiment appropriate to the times ... but in the spirit of the early a cappella Passion as it culminated in Schütz, a form which uses to advantage every means to speak a folk-like, universally comprehensible, concise, and primitive as well as penetrating language."[46] To Schütz's basic format, Distler adds eight settings of the chorale "Jesu, deine Passion" interpolated at key points in the narrative.

The *Weihnachtsgeschichte* also has a Schützian template, except that Distler omits the Intermedii and their characteristic instrumentation, which were fundamental to Schütz's oratorio. As in the *Choralpassion*, Distler creates recitatives that are modern imitations of the pseudo-chant style that Schütz enlivened by use of rhetorical devices. The oratorio opens and closes with settings of biblical texts—"The people that walked in darkness" (Isaiah 9) and "For God so loved the world" (John 3:16–18). Chorale variations on "Es ist ein Ros' entsprungen" fulfill a formal function analogous to their role in the *Choralpassion*.

The principal differences between Distler and Ernst Pepping are Pepping's greater longevity and larger output. Like Distler, Pepping composed an early *Deutsche Choralmesse* (1928) and a chorale collection (*Choralbuch*, 1930–31) dedicated to Friedrich Blume.[47] Pepping's *Spandauer Chorbuch* (1934–38) fulfilled the same purpose as Distler's *Der Jahrkreis* but was far larger, extending to twenty volumes. For the Hochschule für Kirchenmusik in the Berlin suburb of Spandau, Pepping crafted nearly three hundred chorale arrangements for from two to six voices, which stands in for the twentieth-century's equivalent of Praetorius's *Musae Sioniae*. Pepping's hymn-based compositions for choir culminate in the *Neues Choralbuch* (1959), with seventy-six chorales arranged for three or four voice parts.

Beyond these chorale-based motets, Pepping produced a number of freely composed works. Foremost among these are the *Drei Evangelien-Motetten* (1937–38) for the worship services held at Spandau. Each motet is based on the Gospel lesson for a specific Sunday in the liturgical year (Epiphany 5, Trinity Sunday, and Trinity 20): *Gleichnis vom Unkraut zwischen dem Weizen* (Matthew 13:24–30); *Jesus und Nikodemus* (John 3:1–15); and *Gleichnis von der königliche Hochzeit* (Matthew 22:1–14). In *Jesus und Nikodemus*, Pepping imitates the sixteenth-century Gospel motet tradition, using a distinctive vocal scoring for the Evangelist (bass recitative), Nicodemus (tenor, bass duet), and Jesus (SATB choir). Despite its relative brevity and through-composed nature, Pepping's motet manages to recapture the text-driven musical settings of its Renaissance precursor, as the imitative setting "The wind blows where it will and you hear its rustling" (ex. 8.23) illustrates.

Example 8.23 Pepping: *Jesus und Nikodemus*, mm. 59–72

The largest and least known of Pepping's choral works is the *Passionsbericht des Matthäus* (1949–50) for *a cappella* double choir (8–10 voices). This imposing composition consists of two large parts (as in the Bach Passions) framed by an introduction and a finale, and divided by an Intermedium. For these three extraliturgical movements, Pepping uses both choruses simultaneously. Choir 1 functions as the Evangelist, while Choir 2 sings dramatic or reflective texts. The work typically favors homophonic texture for both choruses, enlivened through considerable variety of dynamics, meter, and rhythm. In the final section, "Golgotha," there is a notable exception to this pattern. Just as Choir 1 completes the text, "and led him away to be crucified" (using the BACH motive transposed to G♭), Choir 2 sings "crucifixus etiam pro nobis" (from the Credo) using a wedge-like fugue subject (ex. 8.24a). Initially immune to the rapid melismas and jagged contours of Choir 2's music, Choir 1 gradually begins to set aside its detached reportage in favor of the more expressive music of its partner (ex. 8.24b).

Example 8.24 a–b Pepping, *Passionsbericht des Matthäus, Golgotha*

CONCLUSION

All of the problems of etymology and propriety surrounding the use of neoclassicism suggest a fundamental problem—there is no clear, shared rationale that unites the composers. If Wilfred Mellers is correct in ascribing Stravinsky's neoclassicism to his involuntary separation from Russia and his subsequent decision to acquire the culture of his new homeland by imitating its significant musical and literary monuments, to what do we attribute Paul Hindemith's embrace of historical style as the basis for his modern music? Stravinsky perceived in Hindemith a kindred spirit, a "German Prokofiev," more sympathetic than Schoenberg's disciples. Stravinsky may suggest that the common bond he shared with Hindemith was a rejection of dodecaphony in favor of an array of forms and techniques rooted in the aesthetics of historical music. The music that grew from their individual visions of the new classicism was less compliant to a theory of form and harmony than the music of Haydn, Mozart, and their contemporaries to which it is compared.

Perhaps the basis for that comparison was less an agreement about the fundamental tenets of style than an affirmation of the enduring power of some sort of tonal formalism. If the essential factor in defining neoclassicism were adherence to historical processes, one would have to include Ligeti's conscious invocation of Ockeghem or Messiaen's appropriation of isorhythm and the structure of *vers mesurés* within the canon of neoclassical compositions. The obvious problem with such a syllogism is that neither Ligeti's nor Messiaen's music fits the unspoken criterion of consonance shared by the composers discussed in this chapter. If the reason for labeling a work "neoclassic" is an essentially conservative approach to harmony, then most of the composers examined later in chapter 10 "European Centrism" might more properly belong here, despite the lack of obvious use of historically based formal designs. In the end, the fundamental decision for composers of the first half of the twentieth century is precisely that formulated by Schoenberg—"tonal oder atonal." Compared to Stravinsky and Hindemith, the other composers surveyed here are clearly minor figures, discussed because their annexing of historical models and generally consonant harmonic language is more or less consistent with the approaches of Stravinsky and Hindemith. That neoclassicism did not play a larger role in choral composition may indeed be the result of the inherently conservative nature of the idiom itself.

9

The Avant-Garde Aesthetic

Webern died at the end of World War II; Schoenberg outlived him by a mere five years. The dominant personality to emerge from the aftermath of World War II was Olivier Messiaen, whose composition *Mode de valeurs et d'intensités* (1949) was the first composition to apply serialism to all musical parameters. Three years later Pierre Boulez published an article titled "Schoenberg is DEAD!" less acknowledging the obvious than espousing Webern's method as the only viable approach.[1]

PIERRE BOULEZ AND JOHN CAGE

Boulez began a dialogue with the American composer and aesthetic philosopher John Cage (1912–92) when Cage came to Paris on a Guggenheim Fellowship to study the music of Erik Satie. At Virgil Thomson's recommendation, Cage contacted Boulez and, at first, the two seemed to be kindred spirits, both interested in discovering new materials and methods of composition. But in reality their paths had already begun to diverge, Cage guided by Satie and Boulez by Webern (via Messiaen). Messiaen himself had begun to retreat from rigidly deterministic music, leaving it to Boulez to flesh out the full implications of *Mode de valeurs*. In 1952 Boulez offered his definition of integral serialism:

> We must expand the means of a technique already discovered: that technique having been, up to now, a destructive object, linked, for that very reasons, to

what it has wanted to destroy [tonality]. Our first determination will be to give it autonomy, and, furthermore, to link rhythmic structures to serial structures by common organizations, which will also include the other characteristics of sound: intensity, mode of attack, timbre. Then to enlarge that morphology into a coalescent rhetoric.[2]

In compositions like *Structures* (1952), which he considered serialism's equivalent of J. S. Bach's *Art of Fugue* and Boulez's own *Le Marteau sans Maître* ("Hammer without a Master," 1955), his nod to Schoenberg's *Pierrot Lunaire*, Boulez followed his own advice. He also offered encouragement to Karlheinz Stockhausen (1928–2007) and other European composers who fell under his spell at Darmstadt and Cologne.

At this same time, John Cage was moving in a direction that would effectively sever his connection with Boulez. In 1950 Cage met the young Christian Wolff, who gave him the *I Ching, Book of Changes* and a collection of ancient Chinese oracles translated by Richard Wilhelm. Having already experimented with Magic Squares (a game of numbers akin to Sudoku or Kakuro), Cage found an ideal modus operandi in *I Ching*'s advocacy of change. In 1951 he began composing *Music of Changes*; first, he created twenty-six musical gestures, then tossed three coins six times to determine the number and order of the gesture he would use. This elaborate and time-consuming process determined each and every pitch. Writing the nearly forty-minute-long *Music of Changes* required repeating this operation many times, as well as making complex calculations in an attempt to eliminate any subjectivity from the end result. Joan Peyser states that *Music of Changes* was, for Cage, the equivalent of Boulez's *Structures*.[3] Both Cage and Boulez sought to cleanse composition of any intuitive elements, but their approaches were so different as to place them at different ends of the spectrum of modern music in the 1950s.

Before exploring Cage's philosophy of chance music (aleatoricism), we need to look at the influence that Boulez's particular brand of serialism exerted on choral music after 1950. One piece of evidence is the composition Boulez wrote for Marcel Couraud and the French Radio Choir in 1952, *Cummings ist der Dichter* (1970). Scored for sixteen singers, twenty-four instruments, and two conductors, *Cummings ist der Dichter* was a reworking of material originally contained in his composition *Sequence* (1952). Concerning the new work, Gottwald writes:

> There are many contrasting elements in the music such as voice/instruments; melodic lines/single notes; pitch/noise; heterophony/organized chords; metric/ametric; certainty/uncertainty. These correspond to the contradictions inherent to the semantic/material aspect of Cummings' work. The composition mainly proceeds to mediate between the opposites after they have been introduced. Of course, this can even lead to the elimination of the contrasts, as one can infer from Boulez's mention of his occasional "orchestration of voices." Also, he did not limit himself to one single poem by Cummings, but chose four which are closely related in their semantic and material dispositions.[4]

After his break with Cage, Boulez turned his attention to two young composers, Henri Pousseur (1929–2009) and Karlheinz Stockhausen; this powerful trio dominated the Darmstadt Summer Courses (*Internationale Ferienkurse für Neue Musik*), founded in 1946 by Wolfgang Steinecke. The short list of composers who lectured at Darmstadt constitutes a veritable "who's who" of post–World War II serialism: Theodor Adorno, Wolfgang Fortner, Ernst Krenek, René Leibowitz, Olivier Messiaen, Edgard Varèse, Luigi Nono, David Tudor, Hermann Scherchen, Milton Babbitt,

Pierre Boulez, John Cage, Hans Werner Henze, György Ligeti, Bruno Maderna, Henri Pousseur, Karlheinz Stockhausen, and Iannis Xenakis.

KARLHEINZ STOCKHAUSEN (1928–2007)

Initially Boulez's protégé, Stockhausen began to distance himself from his mentor in the mid-1950s. Stockhausen's choral compositions are likely to be interesting more to theorists and historians of new music than to choral conductors. His body of choral music is quite limited.[5] Two early, comparably accessible works are *Chöre für Doris* (1950) and *Choral* (1950), both of which are uncharacteristically short and simple. Stockhausen constructs the melody in *Choral* from three row forms (prime, retrograde, and inversion) and centers the nonserial accompanying parts on the pitch D. *Chöre für Doris* sets three poems by Paul Verlaine ("Die Nachtigall," "Armer junger Hirt," and "Agnus Dei") translated into German by Georg von der Vring (1889–1968) and Rainer Maria Rilke (1875–1926).

What sets Stockhausen apart from Boulez is his aggressive interest in electronic music, something that led him to the newly formed *Studio für Elektronsiche Musik* at the *Nordwest deutscher Rundfunk* in Cologne in 1953. Stockhausen's fascination with electronic music grew in direct proportion to his frustration with the ability of classically trained musicians to deal with the complexities of new compositions. Poor performances of early works led both Boulez and Stockhausen to explore the emerging technology of synthesized sound production as an alternative to traditional performance. Eventually, this interest went beyond purely electronic sound to include manipulations of the human voice (both solo and ensemble); even though one might call works for the voice "choral," they are more accurately described as conceived for ensembles of specially trained solo singers. His earliest, most important work for such an ensemble is *Momente*, op. 13 (1962–64), scored for soprano, four choirs (three singers per part), and thirteen instrumentalists (two Hammond electric organs, four trumpets, four trombones, and three percussionists). The members of the vocal ensembles are also asked to play simple percussion instruments occasionally to enhance the "sound mass." Their vocal contributions are far more diverse with the use of traditional singing, extended vocal techniques (nontraditional vocal sounds), and nonvocal sounds such as hand claps, finger snaps, laughing, foot stomping, coughing, and knee slapping. Historically, "extended vocal techniques" have become the most significant of these experiments.

As distinct sound sources, which provide the unique array of textures and sounds required by increasingly precise and newly created notation, singers rarely sing complete words. Instead, they sing phonemes (often on random pitches), glissandi that vary in size and speed of execution, and a plethora of explicit directions that often seem to be a foreign language. One of Stockhausen's major contributions was the creation of new notational language capable of conveying this range of information. The title *Momente* also refers to his new formal process called "moment form."

> In the genesis of "Moment Forms" I tried to compose conditions and processes in which each moment is something personal and central, something which can exist by itself and also be related to its environment and to the work as a whole. Moments which are not geared to a beginning and inescapable end, which are just results of that which came before and a cause for that which follows, not particles of a certain measured time—but conditions in which the concentration cuts vertically into the here and now—in every "here and now"—and thus transgresses a horizontal view of time into a "timelessness," which I call eternity; an eternity which does not start at the end of time. But which is reachable in every moment.[6]

This statement reveals something important about Stockhausen's mental and aesthetic processes. For him, *Momente* is not rigidly deterministic but open to the spontaneous insertion of various forms and events. Such spontaneity represents the first crack in Stockhausen's rigid serial aesthetic; despite his contention that in *Momente* he contrives every possible permutation of the available sound mass, his score contains solid, vertical black lines indicating the possible interjection of musical remembrances from a previous moment (see ex. 9.1, which illustrates such a possibility with "Moment KM").[7]

Example 9.1 Stockhausen, *Momente, Km*

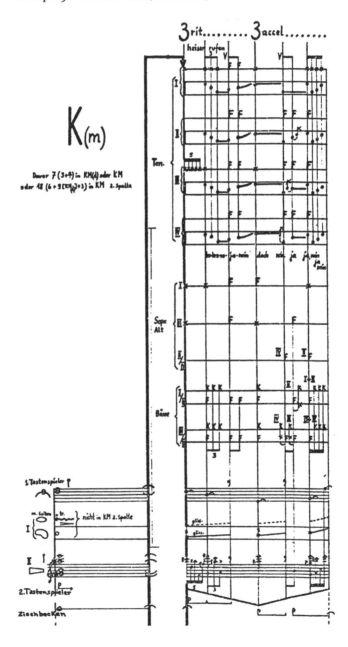

In this brief example, it is difficult to tell precisely what Stockhausen wants the chorus to do; suffice to say, their role is not typically choral. Only the fourth tenor has anything resembling a traditional text as the other voices all sing only rhythmicized consonants. Stockhausen discusses his process in "Speech and Music":

> In order to employ the most complex phonetic structure of speech in terms of serial composition, many different steps are necessary between the individual examples of a given phonetic system (in this case, German) so that regular timbre scales can be chosen from a continuum (for instance, steps from one vowel to another, from vowel to half-consonants, to consonants, etc.); this is only, if at all, possible with electronically produced sounds. This can be equally well formulated the other way round: in a selected scale of electronically produced sounds, single steps are replaced by sung speech-sounds. We only have a homogeneous sound-family if sung sounds sound at certain places like electronic sounds, electronic sounds like sung ones.[8]

Stockhausen experimented with electronic manipulations of speech as early as 1955/56 in *Gesang der Jünglinge*. That exploration continued in *Mikrophonie II* (1965), a vocal work based on two instrumental compositions using electronic manipulation of sound—*Mixture* (1964) for orchestra and ring modulators, and *Mikrophonie I* (1964). In *Mikrophonie II*, Stockhausen called for a larger group of performers than that in *Gesang der Jünglinge*—six sopranos and six basses arranged in four ensembles (3 S1, 3 S2, 3 B1, and 3 B2), Hammond electric organ, four microphones, four ring modulators, and a tape recorder (Fig. 9.1). Stockhausen also began to include theatrical effects, arranging the singers in a semicircle with their backs to the audience and facing the conductor (and a timekeeper), the organist, four speakers (each connected to a microphone placed in front of one of the vocal groups) and, once again, a tape recorder. These speakers broadcast the sounds made by the singers both in real time and as processed through the ring modulators. The tape recorder plays eight prerecorded excerpts (from *Gesang der Jünglinge*, *Carré*, and *Momente*) that create a series of "time windows."

In *Stimmung*, op. 24 (1968), Stockhausen dispenses with all external apparatuses save for amplification of the six singers. His focus is now on "harmonic" singing, each singer singing vowels in a manner calculated to produce certain overtones.[9] *Atmen gibt das Leben*, op. 24 (1974/1977), retreats even farther from electronic manipulation. The work's two segments are scored for *a cappella* chorus, to which Stockhausen adds a prerecorded accompaniment performed by orchestra, synthesizer, or organ. In the first choral portion, Stockhausen deconstructs the text "Atmen gibt das Leben, doch erst das Singen gibt die Gestalt" ("Breath gives life, but first singing gives the form"), creating a sonic re-creation of inhalation and exhalation. The second part is textually more complex, setting a collage drawn from Socrates, the Gospel of Thomas, and Meister Eckhart, as well as three haiku to manipulations of the first section's music.

Fig. 9.1 Stockhausen, premiere of *Mikrophonie II* (Stockhausen Archive)

Fig. 9.2 Géricault, *The Raft of the Medusa* (ca. 1819)

HANS WERNER HENZE (1926–2012)

Stockhausen's principal German disciple was Hans Werner Henze, a composer more notorious for his espousal of left-wing Marxist views than for his music. He did create a significant choral work, the oratorio *Das Floss der Medusa* ("The Raft of the Medusa"). Composed in 1968, this "oratorio volgare e militaire" drew its inspiration from Théodore Géricault's famous painting (1819) that depicted the tragic fate of a French colonial expedition to Senegal in 1816 (Fig. 9.2). Henze dedicated the work to the assassinated Cuban revolutionary Ernesto "Che" Guevara (1928–67). The Medusa incident provoked scandalous controversy, including allegations of cannibalism and the all-too-clear role race and class played in determining who survived.

Henze assigns the role of Jean Charles, a mulatto who, in Géricault's painting, waves a red cloth to attract a passing ship but dies before he can be rescued, to a baritone soloist; the two other principal characters are La Mort (S) and Charon (speaker). The chorus has two components, designated "The Living" (stage left) and "The Dying" (stage right), separated by the large orchestra (stage center). The libretto focuses on the immorality of those who avoided death by taking the only available longboats. The "many, too many" left behind to fend for themselves construct a makeshift raft towed by seven lifeboats. In mvt. 7 ("The Disembarkation"), Charon recounts that, "Seventeen men refuse to obey the order; they remain on the wreck. Nevertheless, when the lines are cast off, there are one hundred and fifty-four men aboard the raft, many standing up to their chests in water, and holding on to one another so as to avoid being swept off by the waves. They have put out their oars and set their course: seven spiders stretching out a hundred arms to lug an immense carcass, which, rolling adrift and pounded by the waves, drags after them."[10] Henze depicts the progressive loss of life by having the entire chorus begin the oratorio on the "Side of the Living"; as they die, they move to the "Side of the Dead." Henze doesn't specify the size of the chorus but occasionally includes comments in the score that provide clues. For example, the notes preceding Part 2 stipulate that the "Choir of the Living" has twenty-seven singers, divided into groups of fourteen ("The Living") and thirteen ("The Dying"). By mvt. 12, the "Chorus of the Dying" has eight parts, compared to only four in the "Chorus of the Living." Henze starts to notate the choral parts as *Sprechstimme* in mvt. 14 to indicate that even the living have lost the voices due to thirst. This long and unflinchingly atonal composition, although intensely dramatic, remains a daunting task for any group of performers brave enough to undertake its many challenges.

BRUNO MADERNA AND LUIGI NONO

Of the composers who attended the Darmstadt Summer Courses, two Italians—Bruno Maderna (1920–73) and Luigi Nono (1924–90, the future son-in-law of Arnold Schoenberg)—became Stockhausen's most ardent disciples. Nono would prove to be as controversial for his political extremism and his strong, public denunciation of Cage as for any of his (Nono's) music. His most important choral work, *Il canto sospeso* (1955–56), has nine movements based on excerpts from letters written by condemned members of the Italian anti-Fascist resistance in the mid-1970s (ex. 9.2). The notational complexity of Nono's score, visually reminiscent of Webern's pointillistic cantatas, explains the complaints that the chorus master for the Cologne premiere, Eigel Kruttge, conveyed to Nono on behalf of his exasperated chorus.[11]

Example 9.2 Nono, *Il canto sospeso*, mvt. 2, mm. 1–6

Stockhausen admits that "Nono set the text in a way which suggests that he wants to withdraw its meaning from the public sphere, where it does not belong. He does not allow the words to come across clearly, but hides them in a musical form which is so uncompromisingly strict that, when listening, one understands next to nothing."[12] While Nono disagreed with his mentor's analysis, the truth is that the choral writing is so daunting as to preclude wide acceptance or performance of the work.

Bruno Maderna's choral music comprises a minor part of his catalogue and suffers from the same flaws that plague his colleague. Maderna's works include two early compositions, an incomplete Requiem (before 1946), *Tre liriche greche* for soprano, chorus, and instruments (1948), and excerpts from an opera titled *Hyperion* (after Hölderlin, 1964).

LUCIANO BERIO (1925–2003)

Of the Italian modernists, the most prolific and successful was Luciano Berio. Giorgio Ghedini, his first composition teacher, loved the music of Stravinsky, so it comes as no surprise that Berio's first choral composition, *Magnificat* (1949), shows an unequivocal indebtedness to Stravinsky's *Symphony of Psalms*, a work that by 1949 had already become a monument of twentieth-century composition. Of the *Magnificat*, Berio writes:

> I never felt regretful of, or underprivileged by, living in a provincial town, but I felt injured and angry when, in 1945, with the end of fascism, I realized the extent and depth of cultural deprivation that fascism had imposed on me. That

same year (I was already twenty) I was for the first time in my life able to hear the music of Schoenberg, Milhaud, Bartók, Webern, etc.; that is, the real voices of my European heritage. These composers, as well as others, had previously been forbidden by fascist "cultural politics." The impact was, to say the least, traumatic, and it took me at least six years to recover from it. I believed, and still do, that the best way to deal with "traumatic experiences" is to cope with them to the end, and, if possible, to exorcise them on their own ground. These are the premises of *Magnificat*, written in 1949. It was one of my last exorcisms of the experiences and encounters of those years, and, I think, my last tribute to them.[13]

The orchestral introduction to mvt. 6 leaves no doubt concerning the impact that *Symphony of Psalms* made on Berio.

Example 9.3 a–b Berio, *Magnificat*, mvt. 6

a. mm. 1-4

b. mm. 241-244

The dry, accented piano chords (ex. 9.3a), the barking thirds of the horns, and an ostinato set against the metric regularity of these instruments are all vintage Stravinsky. Stravinsky's presence is also palpable in Berio's distributive, arrhythmic setting of the "Sicut locutus est" text in mvt. 6 (ex. 9.3b). Berio frames the work with duets for two sopranos, which are respectively followed and preceded by lengthy bitonal choruses that combine F major and A major, another Stravinsky fingerprint. In addition to these obvious homages, Berio's choral parts strongly resemble those of the Russian master.

Berio attended the Tanglewood Festival (courtesy of a grant from the Koussevitzky Foundation) where he studied composition with his fellow countryman Luigi Dallapiccola. Berio also attended the first American concert of electronic music at the Museum of Modern Art in New York on October 28, 1952).[14] Inspired, Berio returned to Milan where, with Maderna, he established the *Studio di Fonologia* as a division of Italian radio in 1955. Following Maderna's advice, Berio attended the Darmstadt Summer Course in 1956 and 1959). He also enjoyed a long-term, mutually beneficial relationship with the novelist and semiotician Umberto Eco (1932–2016); Eco's pioneering work in semiotics (the study of how the elements of a cultural art work acquire meaning) along with his passion for the works of James Joyce profoundly influenced Berio's development. Even if Berio's initial experiments with the atomicization of text stemmed from Stockhausen, Eco helped him shape his own unique approach to language.

A critical factor in his artistic growth was his marriage to the gifted American soprano Cathy Berberian. John Cage wrote *Aria* (1958) for her, and Berio heard the premiere during his second residency in Darmstadt (1959). David Osmond-Smith comments that "It was only once he felt able to marry the pleasures of rhetorical surprise and vocal agility to the intellectual discipline of articulatory phonetics, and to a sense of vocal line honed by many years of immersion in the Italian lyric traditions, that his own vocal style was to spring forth in its full complexity with *Circles*," settings of poetry by e. e. cummings, also written for Cathy Berberian.[15] Berio's work with Eco and his unique synthesis of these various strands of vocalism led to a series of breakthrough works in the 1960s—*Laborintus II* (1965), *Sequenza II* (1965–66), *Sequenza V* (1966), and *Sinfonia* (1968–69).

In the 1970s, Berio composed three important choral works—*Cries of London* (1973–74, rev. 1975), *Coro* (1974–76), and *A-Ronne* (1975). Of the three, only *Coro* is truly choral (the others specify vocal soloists). But even in *Coro*, Berio did not regard the forty voices the score calls for as a traditional chorus; he paired each singer with an instrument of similar range to create a unified ensemble sound. The ten sopranos are paired with four flutes, oboe, E♭ clarinet, trumpet, and three violins; similar treatment of the other voices produced forty distinctive vocal-instrumental duos. *Coro* is ostensibly based on folk music, although only one actual quotation (a Macedonian tune in episode 5) has been identified.[16] This seeming avoidance of real folk music voids Berio's claims regarding its use; on the other hand, it points us toward the textual collage that shapes his melodic gestures, modality, and rhythm. This collage includes texts drawn from Native American (Sioux, Navaho, Zuni), Peruvian, Polynesian, African, Persian, Yugoslavian, Italian, Israeli, and Chilean origins. Oddly, Berio chose to translate all of the texts into English, ignoring the linguistic nuances implicit in the original poetry, thus further distancing the work from any claims of ethnological authenticity. Berio sets this diverse array of texts as vocal solos tied together by his use of poetry from the Chilean poet Pablo Neruda's trilogy *Residencia en la Tierra*. Quotations from Neruda first appear as the even-numbered items of the first fourteen musical segments. The increase and decrease in the amount of Neruda's text that Berio uses creates an internal structure for this section of the work.

Table 9.1 shows the only words that appear in all seven segments: "Venid a ver" ("Come and see"). These three words constitute the entire text in episodes 2 and 4; Berio gradually adds additional text in episodes 6, 8, and 10 to complete the sentence ("Venid a ver la sangre por las calles" / "Come and see the blood in the streets") before reducing it to only the first five words in episodes 12 and 14. The climax of this mini formal arch is episode 8, where Berio adds

Table 9.1 Berio, *Coro*, Neruda fragments (episodes 1–14)

Episode	Text	Translation
2	*Venid a ver*	"Come and see"
4	*Venid a ver*	"Come and see"
6	*Venid a ver la sangre por las calles*	"Come and see the blood in the streets"
8	*Venid a ver la sangre por las calles*	"Come and see the blood in the streets"
	El día pálido se asoma	"The pallid day appears"
10	*Venid a ver la sangre por las calles*	"Come and see the blood in the streets"
12	*Venid a ver la sangre*	"Come and see the blood"
14	*Venid a ver la sangre*	"Come and see the blood"

another Neruda text ("El día pálido se asoma" / "The pallid day appears"). Berio reinforces his textual form by making several precompositional musical decisions:

> All twelve chromatic pitches appear in each event.
> Fluctuations in dynamics (from *fff* to *ppp*) and density are used to counter the resulting harmonic sameness.
> The lengths of these refrains, though irregular, clearly culminate in the eighth episode.

Example 9.4 is an extract from episode 4; Berio uses nonpitched, quasi-aleatoric gestures for the singers, real pitches appearing as clusters of instrumental color (Not shown).

Example 9.4 Berio, *Coro*, Episode 4
© Copyright 1976 by Universal Edition A.G., Vienna
© Renewed All Rights Reserved Used by permission
of European American Music Distributors LLC, sole US
and Canadian agent for Universal Edition A.G., Vienna.

Between episodes 14 and 21, Berio presents his "folk songs." Just prior to the last episode (21), he inserts more lines from Neruda. In episode 28, Berio adds four additional lines that appear no where else in the composition (see Table 9.2).

Berio's appropriation of seemingly random lines of Neruda's poetry and his deliberate delay in giving us the question that prompted their appearance effectively make any traditional understanding (causal or syntactic) of this text utterly impossible. Episode 28 is also interesting musically for it contains a melodic quote from his earlier work *Cries of London* (ex. 9.5).

Table 9.2 Berio, *Coro*, Neruda texts

Episode 28	Episode 28
El día . . . oscila rodeado	the day totters encircled
de seres y extension:	by things and extension
de cada ser viviente	by every living thing
hay algo en la atmósfera	with its trace in the atmosphere
Episode 30	Episode 30
El día pálido se asoma	The pallid day appears
con un desgarrador olor frío	with a cold, heart-breaking whiff
con sus fuerzas en gris	with its forces (clad) in grey
sin cascabeles,	without bells
goteando de alba	dispersing the dawn
por todas partes:	on all sides
con un alrededor de llanto . . .	with a boundary of weeping . . .
Preguntaréis por qué esta poesía	You will ask why this poem
no nos habla del sueño, de las hojas;	says nothing of dreaming, or of leaves;
de los grandes volcanes de su país natal?	or of the native land's great volcanoes?
Venid a ver la sangre por las calles.	Come and see the blood in the streets.
Pablo Neruda	Trans. Donald D. Walsh

Example 9.5 Berio, *Cries of London*, mvt. 1, mm. 1–7
© Copyright 1976 by Universal Edition (London) Ltd., London © Renewed.
All Rights Reserved. Used by permission of European American Music Distributors,
sole US and Canadian agent for Universal Edition (London) Ltd., London.

This composition was originally written to fulfill a commission tendered by the King's Singers, which explains its unique voicing (2 countertenors, 2 tenors, baritone, and bass). In 1975 Berio revised the work for the eight voices (SSAATTBB) of Swingle II, a new incarnation of the ensemble that had premiered Berio's *Sinfonia* in 1969.[17] Berio not only rescored the work but also rearranged its movements so that the melody quoted in *Coro* (see ex. 9.5) appears in the first, fourth, and fifth movements of *Cries of London* (Ex. 9.6).[18]

Example 9.6 a–b Berio, *Cries of London*
© Copyright 1976 by Universal Edition (London) Ltd., London © Renewed.
All Rights Reserved. Used by permission of European American Music Distributors,
sole US and Canadian agent for Universal Edition (London) Ltd., London.

a. mvt. 4, mm. 1-5

Example 9.6 a–b Continued

b. mvt. 5, mm. 1-7

Besides these quotations, Berio weaves this distinctive melodic contour into other movements (see mvt. 2, mm. 1–8; mvt. 6, mm. 41–44; and mvt. 7, mm. 50–51).

Written for one virtuoso ensemble and revised for another, *Cries of London* prefigures Berio's third choral work of the 1970s, *A-Ronne*. The text is a poem by Edoardo Sanguineti (1930–2010) that uses the old Italian alphabet (from A to Ronne = A–Z) both as a semiotic sign-post and a springboard for a collage of imagery and characters, which might well have appeared in James Joyce's *Ulysses* (1922). Berio scores the work for eight amplified singer-actors, once again recycling music from an earlier piece for electronic tape as their musical content.

IANNIS XENAKIS (1922–2001)

Nick Strimple summarizes Greek choral music in the twentieth century thus: "With one stag-gering exception, the composition of choral music in Greece during the twentieth century was dominated by attempts to come to terms with the specter of Greek folk music, either by integrat-ing it into the perceived mainstream of European art music or by celebrating it on its own terms. The exception was Iannis Xenakis."[19] The aftermath of World War II and Xenakis's Communist political leanings forced him to flee Greece for sanctuary in Paris; there, he found work in the studio of the iconic architect Le Corbusier, a position that led to his collaboration with Corbusier and Edgard Varèse on the Philips Pavilion at the 1958 World's Fair in Brussels (Fig. 9.3).

While in Paris, Xenakis tried to reconnect to mainstream music by taking composi-tion lessons from both Milhaud and Honegger, and auditing Messiaen's analysis course at the Paris Conservatoire (1950–52). An internship with Pierre Schaeffer's *Groupe de Recherches Musicales* (1954–62) led to experiments in the new field of electro-acoustic music, including some of the earliest examples of *musique concrète*, a concept that combined Xenakis's back-ground in engineering and architecture with music. Ultimately, these experiments led his to invention of stochastic music, that is, music generated by probability theory. Such "formal-ized music" (the title of his book *Formalized Music: Thought and Mathematics in Composition*, 1963) reflected the growing importance of the computer. In 1996 Xenakis created the *Equipe de Mathématique et Automatique Musicales* (EMAMu) to further the use of computers in musi-cal composition.[20]

Although Xenakis's concept of stochastic music appeared completely at odds with the choral idiom, he nevertheless wrote several pieces that are rarely, if ever, performed. Without question, his best-known work is *Nuits* (1967) for twelve solo singers (like Messiaen's *Cinq rechants*), the text of which consists entirely of phonemes derived from the Sumerian and Persian languages. His avoidance of actual words further distances this piece from the choral tradition; he compounds that distance by instructing the singers to sing "everywhere abso-lutely without vibrato" ("voix plates, rudes, à gorge déployée"). Prior to *Nuits*, Xenakis had focused on stringed instruments; unlike voices, those instruments never had problems with

Fig. 9.3 Le Corbusier's Philips Pavilion at Brussels World Expo '58

pitch accuracy and were able to sustain an absolute legato even during a glissando. The open-ing system of *Nuits* demonstrates Xenakis's attempt to reproduce the same effects using voices, a prospect made even more difficult by the high tessitura, loud dynamics, and liberal use of quarter-tone inflection (see ex. 9.7) by his variations on the traditional symbols for sharps and double sharps).

Example 9.7 Xenakis, *Nuits*, mm. 1–5
© Copyright 1969 Editions Salabert.

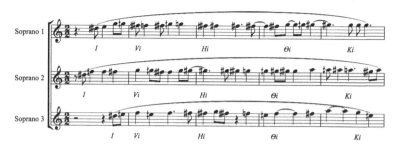

In fairness, this example is not representative of the entirety of the composition, but there are many (often abrupt) changes in dynamic, meter, rhythm, and vocal gesture.

Two later works by Xenakis owe their existence to commissions from professional groups that specialize in contemporary music. For James Wood and the New London Chamber Choir he wrote *Knephas* (1990), followed by *Sea Nymphs* (1994), which was commissioned to celebrate the seventieth anniversary of the BBC Singers. *Sea Nymphs*, scored for six of each voice type, sets a text comprised of phonemes derived from Shakespeare's *The Tempest*. The work begins with all the women's voices singing a complete chromatic cluster (F′ to E″), which continues to move as parallel, homophonic clusters.

GYÖRGY LIGETI

Of all those who attended the Darmstadt Summer Courses, György Ligeti (1923–2006) became the preeminent choral composer, an assessment based on the scope of his choral output and its influence on later composers. A native of Hungary, Ligeti had lived through two tyrannical governments—Nazi Germany and the Soviet Union. A thaw in Hungary's relations with Russia seemed to promise new freedom in 1956, but brutal Soviet repression forced Ligeti and his wife to flee, first to Vienna and then to Cologne. Here, Ligeti became familiar with monuments of twentieth-century music, to which Communist rule had denied him access. The composition of his orchestral work *Apparitions* (1958–59) and its successful premiere in Cologne in 1960 proved to be a turning point in Ligeti's career.

In Hungary, Ligeti needed to compose choral pieces with politically neutral texts. Composed in 1955, the early works *Éjszaka* ("Night") and *Reggel* ("Morning") set texts by his friend Sándor Weöres. These escaped censorship by claiming to be based, however loosely, on folk material; in reality these works are based mostly on Ligeti's imitation of a pentatonic theme in the opening of *Reggel*, and, later, a parody of a rooster's cry (kikeriki) in a polyphonically generated cluster technique (see ex. 9.8; note: the text of mm. 1–2 is repeated completely for each asterisked pitch.).

Example 9.8 Ligeti, *Reggel*, mm. 26–44
© Copyright 1973 by Schott Music © Renewed All Rights Reserved Used by permission of European American Music Distributors LLC, sole US and Canadian agent for Schott Music.

Example 9.8 gives only the series of pitches sung by the soprano (mm. 26–45); the first two measures show the rhythmicization of the text and each subsequent pitch denotes a new statement of that text and rhythm. The gradually expanding texture, rapid declamation, and relatively slow harmonic movement disguise Ligeti's use of a seven-voice canon at the unison. Ligeti uses the canonic entries of the voices to create increasingly dense pitch aggregates. All seven voice parts sing the first six pitches of this "melody" (the soprano's last three notes in ex. 9.8 are the first three pitches of a partial restatement of the opening). The first soprano's arrival on A″ (mm. 44–45) brings the passage to a precipitous halt. Beneath an inverted pedal on A (S/T), Ligeti returns to the opening theme, presented in augmentation as a series of descending fifths (F–B♭–E♭–A♭) that lead to a final cadence on D (see Table 9.3).

Table 9.3 Ligeti, *Reggel*, mm. 26–45, pitch aggregates

mm.	Voices	Pitches	Pitch-Class Sets
26–27	S1	E	0
28–29	S1	F♯	2
	S2	E	0
30–31	S1	A	5
	S2	F♯	2
	A	E	0
32–33	S1	G♯	4
	S2	A	5
	A	F♯	2
	B1	E	0
34–35	S1	C♯	9
	S2	G♯	4
	A	A	5
	B1	F♯	2
	B2	E	0
36–37	S1	B	7
	S2	C♯	9
	A	G♯	4
	B1	A	5
	B2	F♯	2
38–39	S1	D♯	11
	S2	B	7
	A	C♯	9
	B1	G♯	4
	B2	A	5
40–41	S1	E	0
	S2	D♯	11
	A	B	7
	B1	C♯	9
	B2	G♯	4
42–43	S1	F♯	2
	S2	E	0
	A	D♯	11
	B1	B	7
	B2	C♯	8

Table 9.3 Continued

mm.	Voices	Pitches	Pitch-Class Sets
44–45	S1	A	5
	S2	F♯	2
	A	E	0
	B1	D♯	11
	B2	B	7

The imitative middle passage of *Reggel* presaged the harmonic and formal processes Ligeti used in the 1960s—slowly moving, static clouds of sonority created by densely tangled canonic writing, which Ligeti called "micropolyphony," citing the music of Johannes Ockeghem as his inspiration. This technique first appeared in *Apparitions, Atmosphères* (1961), *Volumina* (1961–62), *Aventures* (1962), and *Nouvelles Aventures* (1962–65). In *Volumina*, for example, Ligeti notated immense clusters using a chiaroscuro-like range of shades from white (completely diatonic) to black (completely chromatic). He borrowed this technique from electronic music, where variations in sonic density were a principal generator of formal structure.

Lux Aeterna (1966), Ligeti's first choral work to use micropolyphony throughout, employed a sixteen-part chorus (four of each part). His use of traditional rhythmic notation in realizing his mensural canons underscored his indebtedness to Ockeghem. Like Ockeghem's *Missa Prolationum*, pairs of voices sing the same melody simultaneously in different meters, although these are not notated. In deference to the problems such dense, complex textures pose for choral singers, Ligeti wrote long melodies narrower in range than those of the earlier instrumental works; nonetheless, those melodies share those works' absence of metric or rhythmic synchronization. In form, *Lux Aeterna* consists of four interlocking canonic segments of roughly similar length.

After opening on a unison F, such clarity of pitch occurs only at various "gathering points" as each voice completes its line and sustains its final note while the other voices finish their canons allowing the complex harmony and counterpoint gradually to come back into focus. The first such point begins at m. 25, but it takes ten measures for all of the voices to arrive on A: the upper voices coalesce to A by m. 35, at which point the upper three bass parts sing a cluster (F♯', A', B'), which they access from the sustained A'. Given the range of these pitches, Ligeti instructs them to be sung "falsetto (quasi eco)" (ex. 9.9).

Example 9.9 a–b Ligeti, *Lux Aeterna*

Example 9.9 a–b Continued

b. mm. 87-90

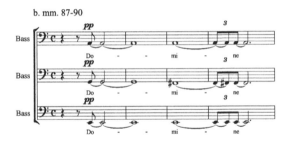

The tenors take the first bass's F♯′ as the starting pitch of a second canon on the text "Cum sanctis tuis" (m. 39). Beginning around m. 40, the basses join the tenor's canon, starting on D′; at m. 60, the male voices begin to coalesce to a dyad (B♭/C), from which a third canon emerges, starting on G. By m. 74, groups of three voices gather around two trichords, the first involving the soprano, tenor, and bass (D″, F, E♭), the second the altos (G′, B♭′, C′). The male voices gradually unify their pitch center, on E by m. 84. As he had done at the end of section 1, Ligeti makes this pitch the root of a [0,3,5] cluster in the bass, the resolution of which to D♯ in m. 90 provides an intervallic point of reference for a new alto canon on A♯. But the final actual beginning of fourth canon comes several measures later (m. 94) when all four soprano and four tenor parts enter simultaneously on high B♮. Ligeti uses these durational canons both to provide the composition's locomotion and create its formal shape; it is essential, therefore, that they not be overshadowed by the occasional respites from dissonance provided by the various "gathering points," the real purpose of which is to facilitate transitions from canon to the next.

One of the difficulties for performers is the amorphous nature of the canonic melodies and the seemingly random rates at which they unfold. Consider, for example the pitch content of the first canonic melody (ex. 9.10).

Example 9.10 Ligeti, *Lux Aeterna*, Canon 1, pitch content

By singing this melody, one can quickly discover that despite its atonality, it contains recognizably tonal melodic gestures (e.g., "do–ti–do" and "do–re–mi") within its otherwise random sequence of pitches. Near this melody's end, one even finds the pitch sequence F♭–E♭–G♭–F♮, the iconic BACH motif transposed a tritone. In fact, Ligeti uses this motive in the other canonic melodies not shown here.[21]

Another difficulty for the singer is Ligeti's persistent use of extreme tessituras (both high and low), which he stipulates must be sung very softly. His constant injunctions that the singers enter gently and imperceptibly multiplies the problem. The composer Ben Johnston opined that Ligeti was fascinated with Eastern culture and religion, specifically the *Tibetan Book of the Dead*.[22] Johnston sees Ligeti's restricted melodic and dynamic ranges, and the score's general lack of surface tension, as calculated efforts to produce the diffuse, flickering luminescence of devotional candles, an earthly manifestation of the *Lux Aeterna*, the Eternal Light (ex. 9.11).

Example 9.11 Ligeti, *Lux Aeterna*, mm. 4–6

The inherent conflict between the musical effect sought and the notation used to produce it ("How do I sing my entrance *ppp* when I have to enter on the second quintuplet of the beat?") cuts to the very heart of the conflict between the Boulez–Stockhausen camp and John Cage. While the first group tried to notate every aspect of the score as accurately as possible, Cage and his followers trended toward aleatoricism, relinquishing strict compositional control to chance and allowing the performers to become partners in the compositional process. The prioritization of intent (what the composer intends to happen musically) vis-à-vis performance (what actually happens in performance in response to the notation) increasingly forced mid-twentieth-century composers to make an exclusionary choice. This was especially evident in the choral idiom, where radical serialization and notational micromanagement collided head-on with the choral singer's innately conservative mentality and increasingly alienated those radically modernist composers from choral music, an idiom they increasingly came to regard as incapable of achieving their desires.

This musico-intellectual divide led to the formation of a quintessentially contemporary vocal ensemble, comprised of from six to sixteen solo singers. Such "self-conscious vocal ensembles" in which "the central occupation of ensemble members is best described not as the conveyance of a musical or dramatic text but rather as an exploration of the dynamics of the group itself; how each member of the group is both part of and separate from the group, how alliances are formed, modified, and abandoned with the group; how hostilities arise and how they are resolved" clearly represent the growing divide between traditional and modernist vocal ensembles.[23]

Although similar in style and device to *Lux Aeterna*, Ligeti's *Requiem* poses even more daunting challenges. In his choral works of the 1980s—the *Drei Phantasien nach Friedrich Hölderlin* (1983), the *Magyar Etüdök* (1983), and the *Nonsense Madrigals* (1988–93)—Ligeti increasingly distanced himself from the traditional chorus to embrace this new type of highly trained, virtuosic vocal ensemble. The *Hölderlin* choruses specify the increasingly typical "mixed choir of sixteen singers," but Ligeti's dedication of the work to Eric Ericson and the Swedish Radio Choir concedes two singers per part (the Swedish Radio Choir of that time had thirty-two singers). The *Nonsense Madrigals*, written especially for the King's Singers, are, like the original version of Berio's *Cries of London*, scored for the unique combination of six male voices. Like the *Hölderlin* choruses, Ligeti specifies up to sixteen parts arranged as two separate choirs for the *Magyar Etüdök* ("Hungarian Études") but with no indication from the composer regarding how many singers were to sing each part).

The first part of the *Magyar Etüdök* is a mirror canon for twelve voices arranged in two SSATTB choruses notated in different meters (6/4 and 2/2) but with the same tempo.[24] The result is a mensural canon like those found in *Lux Aeterna*. Two alto parts enter on D♭′ and E♭′ at a distance of three measures. The four remaining female voices (S1 and 2 of each choir) make their entries on successively higher pairs of pitches, F′ and G′ (S2) and A′ and B′ (S1). The six male voices also operate in pairs that descend by whole tones inverting the ascent of the women's voices (ex. 9.12).

Example 9.12 Ligeti, *Magyar Etüdök*, no. 1, mm. 1–8
© Copyright 1983 by Schott Music. All Rights Reserved. Used by permission of European American Music Distributors LLC, sole US and Canadian agent for Schott Music.

The second étude uses two different poetic texts. The first ("A'myak sora ül a réten") is initially sung in unison by the women of choir 1; their Bartók-like melody is shadowed by their counterparts in choir 2, who sustain selected pitches from the melody creating echo-like sound clusters. As early as m. 10, the altos of choir 2 beginning singing the second text ("Brekerex!" = "Brr [It's cold]"); this text playfully mimics Aristophanes's *The Frogs* and allows Ligeti to engage in some onomatopoetic tone painting. Beyond this simplistic description lies a complicated interaction that ignores traditional notions of text presentation or text intelligibility.

The final etude requires five equal vocal groups; the first four groups are gender specific, consisting of the majority of the basses, altos, soprano, and tenors (their actual order of entry) and the remaining singers of each section as the fifth ensemble. Each choir has its own text, music, and precise tempo (notated with five different metronome markings and requiring five subconductors). Ligeti distributes the text so that each group sings its part to its own melody, the variable lengths of which require different numbers of repetitions. For example, the basses sing a seven-measure tune eight times (the last statement is incomplete). Conversely, the altos (who enter next) sing a five-measure melody almost fourteen times. Since their tempo (quarter note = 160) is faster than the basses (quarter note = 90), their measures never coincide with those of the basses. Despite the same meter, the result is an asynchronous juxtaposition of five separate sound masses, all traveling at different speeds. Ligeti suggests the use of an electronic device, capable of displaying each tempo as a series of light pulses to synchronize the groups.

Despite the performance difficulties his music poses, Ligeti is one of the truly original choral composers of the twentieth century. He carefully avoids affiliation with any "school" dominated by a strong personality. If this independence makes his evolution difficult, his music is all the more interesting for it.

MAURICIO KAGEL AND HEINZ HOLLIGER

German composer Mauricio Kagel (1931–2008) and the Swiss Heinz Holliger (b. 1939) are important figures in modern serialism. Of the two, Kagel has demonstrated greater staying power, first bursting on the choral scene with his absurdist cantata, *Anagrama* (1957–58). Other choral works of note include: *Hallelujah* (1967) for sixteen-part choir (both solo and tutti, expandable); *Die Mutation* (1972) for mixed chorus, children's chorus, piano, and harpsichord; *Chorbuch* (1975–78) for choir (sixteen parts, up to forty-eight singers), piano, and harmonium; *sankt bach passion* (1981–85) for mezzo-soprano, tenor, and baritone, narrator, children's choir, mixed chorus, and orchestra (with organ), and *Schwarzes Madrigal* (1999) for choir, brass, and percussion.

The most accessible and intriguing of these works is *Chorbuch*, a collection of fifty-three Bach chorale settings, which Kagel transforms in interesting, quite innovative ways. The vocal parts are completely unrelated to the chorales, employing vocal techniques that range from the traditional (normal singing, *Sprechgesang*, semi-pitched speech, humming) to the realm of extended vocal techniques (whispering, quasi-tremolo, excessively wide vibrato, falsetto, use of highest/lowest register [both singing and speaking], and such instructions as "guttural, hysterical, nasal, babyish, with broken voice," and so forth).

Kagel first decided which phrases of Bach's chorale to assign to the piano and which to the harmonium.[25] Next, he transposed each chord of Bach's harmonization to a new pitch (determined by an unspecified, random process). We can see how this process works in Kagel's transformation of the chorale *Kommt her zu mir, spricht Gottes Sohn* (ex. 9.13a–c).

Example 9.13 a–c Kagel, *Chorbuch*, no. 34 (*Kommt her zu mir, spricht Gottes Sohn*)

Kagel's keyboard part retains Bach's chord positions and rhythms; however, his unpredictable transpositions create progressions in individual lines that are at odds with those of Bach's original.[26] For example, Kagel's opening chord is E minor instead of Bach's A minor; but whereas Bach retains that harmony, Kagel uses a C minor chord, a difference that changes the "bass" line from an octave (Bach) to a minor sixth in Kagel. The voice parts are another matter altogether. In the example, Kagel retained traditional notation of pitch and rhythm, but the relationship of the voices is completely new. Initially, the soprano and bass sing in parallel octaves, using the text of the second verse of Paul Gerhardt's hymn (1653) "Gott, Vater, sende deinen Geist."[27] The alto's first two phrases contain the iconic BACH motive (B♭–A–C–H/B♮) transposed up a tritone (E′, D♯′, F♯′, F♮′). While the tenor initially moves aimlessly between D♯, E, and F♯, the tenor line doubles the soprano line in parallel sixths at the outset of the second phrase, displacing the bass as the soprano's partner. While these vocal parts have notated pitch, rhythm, and text, the vocal scoring of other chorales is far less conventional. Any harmonic correspondence between the voices and the keyboard part disappears after the first pitch.

The *sankt bach passion* is Kagel's most ambitious, if obscure, work. Kagel began composing it in 1981 with a deadline of 1985 (the tercentenary of Bach's birth) from the *Berliner Festwochen* for the premiere, which Kagel conducted. The work's stylistic roots lay in *Chorbuch* and two earlier works—*Ludwig van* (1969–70) and *Die Mutation*, which used the A-minor prelude from Book 2 of the *Well-Tempered Clavier* as its thematic basis. In both works, Kagel appropriated the music of Bach and Beethoven as *musique trouve* ("found music"), which he then transformed into something totally new.

The text of the *sankt bach passion* is drawn from documents that tell the story of Bach's life. The libretto traces Bach's life in the same way that the biblical Passion narratives recount the death of Jesus of Nazareth. Bach is both the subject of this ersatz work and the victim of a symbolic crucifixion, "Hanging for decades on the cross of officials who hindered his work as a composer."[28] Because the score has not been widely distributed, this lack of access makes a more informed discussion of the work impossible; nevertheless, the sheer emotional impact of this music is palpable, consistent with the experience of listening to any one of Bach's Passion settings.

Principally known as a concert oboist and conductor, Heinz Holliger is also a highly regarded modernist composer. His output of choral works is surprisingly large but nearly unknown. His major works include *Dona Nobis Pacem* (1968–69; three related cycles on poems by Friedrich Hölderlin: *Die Jahreszeiten* (1975–79); the *Scardanelli-Zyklus* (1975–91), and *Gesänge der Frühe* (1987); and a set of three *haiku* settings for the Hilliard ensemble, *Jisei I, II*, and *III* (1988–92). *Die Jahreszeiten* is a piece for twelve solo voices, the text of which is a deconstruction (à la Kagel's *Anagrama*) of the work's title. In some respects, it resembles Holliger's earlier, aleatoric composition, *Psalm,* in which Holliger deconstructs Paul Celan's poem into phonemes using the full array of postserial modernist techniques. Not one single pitch is notated, the vocal parts consisting of rhythms, diagrams of a certain gesture to be performed, and instructions about dynamics, articulation, and vocal production. Duration is notated by vertical lines drawn through the boxes that contain each singer's part; these lines indicate either a specific duration (e.g., ten seconds) or the number of metric pulses. Holliger specifies form four to eight singers per part, including the following note at the end of the printed score: "PSALM is a piece of music which is close to the threshold of audibility. Voices should be used (as unobtrusively as possible) only in those places where are specifically required. The use of 2–4 microphones to provide the choir with very slight amplification is possible. The loudspeakers should then be placed slightly behind the singers, directed upwards if possible."[29] What may not be clear, but which is essential to understand, is that the great majority of this composition consists of the sounds produced by singers that are just on the threshold of audibility and phonation. Hence, the otherwise odd instruct that "voices" are to be used only where "specifically required." For the majority of the piece, however, there is no traditional vocal sound: the sonic spectrum ranges from breathing in and out (and thus on the "threshold of audibility") up to (but rarely becoming) actual singing.

The three *Hölderlin* cycles draw their texts from that poet's cycle of twelve poems titled *Die Jahreszeiten* ("The Seasons"). The second work, *Scardanelli-Zyklus*, is a conflation of these three choruses, the flute composition *(t)air(e)*, and *10 Übungen zu Scardanelli*, a work for chamber ensemble. *Gesänge der Frühe* uses chorus, tape, and orchestra to realize a composition based on Robert Schumann's piano piece of the same name, alluding to the madness of both Hölderlin and Schumann.

OTHER MODERNIST CHORAL COMPOSERS

The American composer Pauline Oliveros (b. 1932) began exploring electronic and tape composition in the 1960s. She expanded her compositional format to include meditative practices gleaned from her study of Native American and Eastern cultures. The choral work for which she is best known is *Sound Patterns* (1961), a piece similar to the music of Holliger in some ways.[30] Like Holliger, Oliveros eschews specific pitch notation, although she notates meter and tempo quite precisely. In this, her signature choral work, there is no text per se, the language of the composition comprising phonemic bits and vocal effects (whispering, glissandi, lip-popping, tongue-clucking, snapping fingers in front of open mouth, use of the hands as a mute, etc.). Oliveros does include pitched sounds using usual notation; however, she leaves the actual choice of pitch to the singer, indicating only relative range (low, medium, high) by placement of the gesture with two lines of pitch demarcation. She specifically states that multiple singers should not sing the same pitch for a given event, preferring instead a cluster of indeterminate density.

The infamous villain of Stanley Kubrick's *2001: A Space Odyssey* (1968) is HAL, a computer constructed at the University of Illinois. While this is fiction, it does document the university's importance for modern music. In 1958 Lejaren Hiller and James Beauchamp founded the University of Illinois Experimental Music Studio, a unique facility that attracted many major composers. The opening of this facility followed the beginning of a Festival of Contemporary Arts, jointly sponsored by the School of Music and the College of Fine and Applied Arts. From 1955 to 1971, month-long festivals were held that attracted such notables as Harry Partch, John Cage, Elliott Carter, and Milton Babbitt. The climactic musical event of this series was the premiere of John Cage and Lejaren Hiller's composition *HPSCHD* in 1969. The project had its roots in a commission Cage received for a work for harpsichord. The final result featured seven harpsichords and up to fifty-one tapes, created by using fifty-one different divisions of the octave, while the harpsichords played random inventions based on a composition by Mozart. This multimedia event, held in the university's sports arena, attracted seven thousand people and lasted for four hours.[31]

Salvatore Martirano (1927–95) studied with Bernard Rogers at the Eastman School of Music and with Luigi Dallapiccola in Florence (1952–54) prior to a residence at the American Academy in Rome (1956–59). An important and controversial work was *L.'s G. A.*, a multimedia piece of musical theater, which was widely performed during the Vietnam War era. Martirano's choral output is somewhat small but includes two important compositions: an *a capella* setting of T. S. Eliot's "O O O O that Shakespeherian Rag" (from *The Waste Land*) and a beautifully crafted setting of the Latin Mass ordinary (1974).

Ben Johnston's (b. 1926) primary compositional interest was in just intonation and microtonal music. In 1974, he too composed a *Mass for Mixed Chorus*, accompanied by organ or four trombones, double bass, and drums. While the music can be performed using equal temperament, Johnston conceived it being sung with just intonation, which explains the alternative scoring for organ or four trombones. The organ he had in mind was the Scalatron electronic organ built by Motorola, which could be programmed to use any temperament. In lieu of that instrument, Johnston allowed a quartet of trombones, because they could adjust their pitch to match the microtonal intervals of the choir. Superficially simple, the work's contemporaneity depended on the piquant colors and dissonance that emerge only when the musical intervals are tuned "dead on." In 1981 Johnston wrote his most sophisticated choral composition, *Sonnets of Desolation*, using the poetry of Gerard Manley Hopkins, for the New Swingle Singers.

Edwin London (1929–2013) joined the Illinois faculty in 1973. In 1975 he formed a choral ensemble, Ineluctable Modality, dedicated to the performance of new music. Several of the titles of his choral music—*Psalm of These Days* (1986); *Geistliche Musik or Advent-sure on OK Chorales* (1975); *The Polonius Platitudes* (for male chorus and balloons, 1973); *Sacred Hair* (1974) for mixed chorus, organs, and hair combs; and *Wounded Byrd Song* (1976) show his sense of humor. The last work takes William Byrd's consort song "Wounded I am" as its basic content, subjecting it to performance by six choruses that enter separately and sing at different tempi, all accompanied by an organ drone. London's simplification of the modernist aesthetic allows any chorus to make complex sounds without having to deal with the impediments of complex modernist notation.

Two British practitioners of serial modernism, Harrison Birtwistle (b. 1934) and Brian Ferneyhough (b. 1943), deserve mention. Birtwistle attended the Royal Manchester College of Music where, with Alexander Goehr, Peter Maxwell Davies, and other student composers, he formed the Manchester New Music Group. Influenced by Boulez, Stockhausen, and their disciples, Birtwistle manages to transcend this stylistic niche to become a more mainstream composer in the mold of Stravinsky, Webern, and Varèse. In his vocal music Birtwistle is more interested in and better represented by operatic rather than choral works. Nonetheless, one of his earliest choral pieces, *Narration: A Description of the Passing of a Year*, for chorus and organ (1963), uses a medieval text that he later used in his operatic work *Gawain* (1990–91).[32] *Narration*, an *a cappella* choral piece, uses the text of fourteenth-century romance "Sir Gawain and the Green Knight."[33] This work consists of discrete sections that vary in length and scoring. Similar in style (though much briefer) is the motet *Carmen Paschale* ("Easter Song"), commissioned by the BBC for the 1965 Aldeburgh Festival. Here, Birtwistle uses a ninth-century hymn by Sedulius Scottus as the text. This motet turns relatively vocal lines into an aurally complex *Gestalt*. Examination of this and other of Birtwistle's composition reveals a fondness for tritones in his melodic constructions (ex. 9.14).

Example 9.14 Birtwistle, *Carmen Paschale*, mm. 1–14
© Copyright 1965 by Universal Edition (London) Ltd., London
© All Rights Reserved. Used by permission of European American Music Distributors, sole US and Canadian agent for Universal Edition (London) Ltd., London

Brian Ferneyhough is much less likely than Birtwistle to use such traditional formal designs. Ferneyhough is that relative rarity, a composer who is largely self-taught and independent of the academic centers that are home to the most ardent modernists. After brief tenures at the Birmingham School of Music and the Royal Academy of Music, Ferneyhough managed to secure funding for private study in Holland, Switzerland, and Germany. Active in the Darmstadt Summer Courses from 1984 to 1994, Ferneyhough went on to teach at the *Institut de Recherche et Coordination Acoustique/Musique* (IRCAM) in Paris. The severity of his compositional style—including significant use of microtonality, notoriously complex, irrational rhythm, and "texture types"—makes Ferneyhough less than cordial to the choral idiom. His only significant choral work is an early (1969) *Missa Brevis*, a performance of which at the Royan (France) Festival in 1974 provided significant international momentum to his career. This early work (score for three mixed choruses) poses nearly insuperable rhythmic problems, raising the question of how truly choral the work is. The apparent rationale for the designation *brevis* was Ferneyhough's omission of the Credo; except for the Gloria, the movements are brief but extremely dense. The opening measures of the Agnus Dei (ex. 9.15) show the complexity of the larger work.

Example 9.15 Ferneyhough, *Missa Brevis*, Agnus Dei

In the example we can see the following techniques:

> Each part of choir 1 employs a central pitch, embellished by other pitches notated in smaller font, indicating that they are approximate in pitch and rhythm. The four principal pitches are B♭–D–E♭ and E♮. The composer indicates that this gesture (enclosed

in a box) is to be performed four times at various tempos and dynamic levels. The tempo increases from eighth note = 56 to eighth note = 72, while the dynamics create an arch shape, *pp* to *mf* (third statement) to *pp* by the end.

The voice parts in choirs 2 and 3 use more pitches than those of choir 1. The reference pitches of choir 1 appear in the corresponding vocal parts of choir 3, surrounded by other pitches that vary in number with each part (s [5], a [4], t [13], and b [5]). The tenor part is a palindrome (E′–G#′–A′–G#′–E′), while both the soprano and bass begin and end with the same pitches.

Like choir 1, choir 3 performs its material four times at varying tempi and dynamics. Unlike choir 1, however, all of choir 3's pitches are printed in the same font (indicating equal importance). Choir 3 shows a much more pronounced use of rhythms based on complex arithmetic ratios.

Choir 2 begins after both choirs 1 and 3. Unlike them, choir 2 presents a complete text (Agnus Dei). There is no indication that this material is to be performed more than once; indeed, choir 2 begins after and finishes before choirs 1 and 3.

Each of choir 2's vocal parts has six pitches that are performed as chords. On closer inspection, what seem to be random collections are actually quite deliberately structured. The soprano and bass present the same hexachord a tritone apart, while up to the final pitch, the alto and tenor sing the same melodic contour (a semitone apart). These melodic similarities are ultimately less significant than the resulting vertical sonorities, which form a pitch palindrome in the manner of Webern (Table 9.4).

Table 9.4 Ferneyhough, *Missa Brevis*, Agnus Dei, mm. 4–6. Choir 2 pitch aggregates

S	B′	G#″	F#″	D#″	F″	Db″
A	D#′	G′	A′	C″	Bb′	D′
T	E	F#	G#	B	A	F′
B	FF	D	C	AA	BB	Eb
	[0,4,5,6]	[0,4,5,6]	[0,2,3,6]	[0,2,3,6]	[0,4,5,6]	[0,4,5,6]

Despite this apparent similarity to Webern, Ferneyhough does not use hexachords to construct complete, independent twelve-tone melodic or harmonic structures. Such niceties aside, the music presents the choral singer with numerous problems—how do I find my pitch, how do I execute such complex rhythms, how does the music fit together, and how will I know if it is "right"? Such dilemmas epitomize the "un-peaceful coexistence" of postmodern serialism and the choral tradition.

The arcane methods, dissonant sonorities, and abstruse rhythms of modernist composers may seem inimical to traditional choirs. Messiaen's reply to Marcel Couraud's request that he a compose a piece for the French Radio Choir ("Anything I would want to write, you could not perform!") or even Hindemith's caustic response to those who questioned his absence from the premiere of his *When Lilacs Last in the Dooryard Bloomed: A Requiem "For Those We Love"* ("Do you think that this performance can measure up to the one I have already imagined?") express the antipathy that the most modern contemporary composers have had for the choral ensemble. The choral music of the composers discussed here is rarely performed; indeed, if they write for vocal ensembles at all, such composers favor a self-conscious vocal ensemble. What then is the rationale for including these composers in a historical survey of Western Choral Music? The contribution of the avant-garde is to be measured less by the number of performances the music has received than by looking to those composers who have found ingenious ways to translate its forbidding extremes into a more accessible, user-friendly language.

The first technique to consider is the creative use of aleatoricism in which multiple groups perform a single piece of traditional music in nonaligned layers, and which may achieve the dense, blurred harmonies that the modernists labor so mightily to notate precisely. Edwin Fissinger's *In Paradisum* (1991), Ed London's *Wounded Byrd Song*, and Knut Nystedt's *Immortal Bach* all involve getting singers to forget their disciplines regarding coordination of sound and perform as individuals blissfully ignorant of what their fellow singers are doing. Another approach is to use graphic notation, the very imprecision of which is open to different interpretations in order to achieve a similarly disjunct aural result. A composer who has made a reputation by so doing is R. Murray Schafer (b. 1933). Nick Strimple summarizes Schafer's accomplishment as "the free and intuitive use of virtually every technique to come in vogue during the middle third of the century."[34] An example of Schafer's combination of music education and sonic exploration is his composition for "youth choir," *Epitaph for Moonlight*.[35] By ingeniously using modest means, Schafer has given young singers the permission and opportunity to explore modern musical sonorities while simultaneously honing their interval-recognition skills. Rather than deconstructing an existing text for *Epitaph for Moonlight*, Schafer challenged the young singers to invent an imaginative vocabulary of sound words that connote moonlight: Noorwahm, Nuyuyul, Shimonöel, Sheelesk, Shalowa, Ooslooful, Lunious, Malloma, Maunklinde, Shiverglowa, Sloofulp, and Neshmoor!

This interactive strategy also involves the choir in the creation of music that is theirs in a singularly important way; they "own" the piece in a uniquely personal way and tend not to view it as a daunting exercise. Schafer takes their words and creates a series of sonic events depicted not with traditional notation but with graphic designs, which, in and of themselves, encourage a de facto aleatoricism, and simple musical processes, which remove the possible stigma of being either right or wrong. Among his techniques is a division of the choir into sixteen parts to sing "fans" of sustained sound built first around a descending chromatic scale and, later, a descending whole-tone scale that begin on notes described as "medium high" and "high-ish" respectively. The entire choir starts in unison and cascades downward sustaining each designated pitch to create a cluster (ex. 9.16).

Example 9.16 Schafer, *Epitaph for Moonlight*

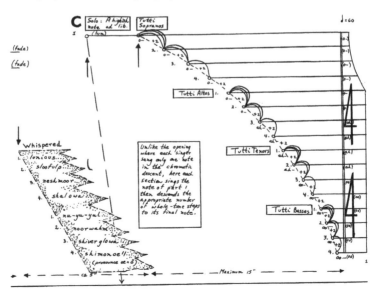

From such sustained clusters Schafer orchestrates new events according to a visual interpretation of time (not unlike what Witold Lutosławski calls "controlled aleatoricism.")[36] In the
first such event, soloists within each pitch subgroup execute *crescendi* and *diminuendi* on their
pitches using a magic word of their choice. These improvisations take place with a time span
of approximately thirty seconds, the precision (or lack thereof) of their placement determined
entirely by each singer's visualization of where their event falls within the allotted duration.
Following the whole-tone fan, Schafer sculpts the sound mass by cutting away parts of the
design the way one cuts paper dolls from folded paper. Subsequent events include a melody
notated by numbering the distance of each new note from the last (in semitones) and direction
by plus and minus signs. Schafer has not only made a satisfying composition filled with challenging games and intriguing sonorities but also created one of the more creative examples of
applied music education. He replicates these techniques in other pieces (*Miniwanka, Gamelan,*
etc.) that vary in dimension and difficulty of the challenges posed. More recent examples of
limited aleatoricism occur in pieces by Eric Whitacre (see chap. 11, this volume) like *Cloudburst*
(1992) and *Five Hebrew Love Songs* (1996).

The dialogue between modernism and tradition has produced a wide array of compro-
mises between complexity and accessibility. One of the more creative responses to this dialogue
is the choral music of the Russian Alfred Schnittke (1934–98), music that makes few concessions
to choral commercialism. Schnittke has openly acknowledged his indebtedness to the polystylis-
tic syntheses of his visionary Russian contemporary, Sofia Gubaidulina (b. 1931), whom he has
described as trying to be both old and new at the same time: "One can compose with the help of a
modern musical language by borrowing elements from an archaic mode or the reverse: by using
the old idiom but with the logic of contemporary development."[37] Most of Schnittke's choral works
date from later in his career; these include his Requiem (1975) for soloists, chorus, and instrumental ensemble, two choral symphonies (Second Symphony, "St. Florian," 1979, and the Fourth
Symphony, 1984), the Faust cantata, *Seid nüchtern und wachet* (1983), the *Concerto for Choir* (1984–
85), *Lux Aeterna* (his contribution to the collaborative "Requiem of Reconciliation" commissioned
by Helmut Rilling to commemorate the fiftieth anniversary of the end of World War II), and, finally,
what many consider his most moving work, the *Twelve Penitential Psalms* (*Stichi Pochajannye,* 1988).

The texts Schnittke uses to commemorate the one-thousandth anniversary of the bap-
tism of Grand Prince Vladimir in 988 and the Christianization of Russia) are not biblical psalms
but are penitential poems, a specific subgroup of the larger literary genre of "spiritual poems."
Whereas spiritual poems are written or oral poetic texts that originate in Orthodox monasteries
or as secular imitations of monastic texts and draw from a wide range of apocryphal and patris-
tic texts, these penitential psalms emphasize the popular understanding of historical religious
events. According to the German musicologist Uwe Schweikert, Schnittke found his texts in a
1986 collection of Old Russian literature from the sixteenth century.[38] He chose eleven anonymous poems that speak to various aspects of Russian Christianity. The text of psalm 6 ("When
they beheld the ship that suddenly came") recounts the murder in 1015 of Prince Vladimir's two
sons Boris and Glebo (the first Christian martyrs in Russia) by their elder brother, Svyatopik.
Schnittke likely chose their martyrdom as a historical metaphor for all those who have suffered
and died for their faith. An alternate theory suggests that Schnittke intended his psalms to assert
the centrality of religion in the so-called godless Russian Communist state or, alternatively, to
plead for mercy on the Russian people who tacitly allowed this regime to flourish.

Like their texts, each of the twelve musical movements is unique.[39] Schnittke's
music certainly sounds modern; even so, auditors will easily hear the evocations of traditional Russian Orthodox church music such as the use of pedals tones in eight of the twelve

movements; these run the gamut from a single pitch (no. 1) to sustained fifths (usually in the bass part) to the multiple pedals that comprise 80 percent of the ninth psalm in *Twelve Penitential Psalms*. Ultimately, the entire final movement (no. 12) unfolds over a sustained pedal on D.

A second such reference is Schnittke's use of thick choral textures involving considerable use of *divisi*, especially in the male voices. This texture is evident in the first movement's three bass parts and remains a textural constant throughout the entire composition. Schnittke routinely uses eight voice parts, adding additional parts for added drama (see ex. 9.17).

Example 9.17 Schnittke, *Psalms of Penitence*, no. 5, mm. 49–2
© Copyright 1995 by M. P. Belaieff, Frankfurt, Germany All Rights Reserved.
Used by Permission of European American Music Distributors LLC,
sole US and Canadian agent for M. P. Belaieff, Frankfurt, Germany.

This passage also reveals other features of Schnittke's style, such as his use of triads in root position that lack any apparent functional relationship. Example 9.17 also shows Schnittke's preference for syllabic homophony, but hardly any of these psalms would qualify as melismatic, save for the final movement, which is textless.

Despite generic references to Orthodox chant, Schnittke's melodies are typically chromatic and tend to utilize inflected rotation around central pitches. Svetlana Kalashnikova cites a theme from Schnittke's Fourth Symphony to illustrate this centralization of pitch in melodic constructions.[40] This particular theme consists of four groups of contiguous pitches:

1.   C♯   D   E♭
2.   F♯   G   A♭
3.   B   C   D♭
4.   E   F   G♭

The pitches in the middle column provide the central focus of Schnittke's melody; they are flanked on either side by lower and upper chromatic neighboring tones. The pitches of each column, read from top to bottom, form perfect fourths or fifths (e.g., C♯, F♯, B, E). Had Schnittke so desired, he could have created a complete chromatic scale by adding one more transpositions of this pattern to A.

A typical example of his melodic technique is evident in the canon between soprano and tenor (ex. 9.18) in the sixth psalm.

Example 9.18 Schnittke, *Psalms of Penitence*, no. 6, mm. 17–25

Over an alto/bass bitonal pedal, the sopranos and tenors sing a canon that is strict as to pitch but flexible as to duration. Their melody features chromatic inflections of central pitches a third apart: G–B♭; B–D, and D–F (see asterisked pitches in ex. 9.18).

Few movements better depict the stylistic extremes that Schnittke negotiates with unerring instinct and logic than the fourth of the *Twelve Penitential Psalms* ("My soul, why are you in a state of sin?"). The movement opens with a simple, diatonic duet for soprano and alto (ex. 9.19a), which he expands to three (mm. 11–16), four (mm. 17–19), five, six, and finally seven voices at the climactic D-minor cadence in m. 24. Following a brief reprise of the opening duet, the texture continues its growth, expanding from five to eight parts in the span of just four measures (mm. 28–31). Here, the music reaches its most extreme tessitura (F″ in the soprano and FF in the second bass). Without warning, Schnittke unexpectedly injects chromaticism as the texture expands to fourteen parts (ex. 9.19b). Having reached this dramatic apogee, texture and dynamics quickly dissipate in a series of unrelated triads, finally ending on a widely voiced G-major chord (ex. 9.19c).

Example 9.19 a–c Schnittke, *Psalms of Penitence*, no. 4

Even more compelling than the final sorority is the compositional logic that makes this conclusion seemingly inevitable.

The examples drawn from this exquisite composition by Alfred Schnittke reveal a common dilemma in trying to discuss such recently composed music. Although these examples (esp. ex. 9.19b) are evidence of how daunting the work is to perform, very little if any of the writing they contain justifies classifying Schnittke as an avant-garde extremist in the Boulez-Stockhausen mold. Schnittke notates both pitch and rhythm conventionally, and although they are not tonal, these psalms contain many moments of consonance, most vividly seen in Schnittke's propensity for ending movements with full triads, the pitches of which are spread across multiple octaves. Of the twelve movements, seven (nos. 2, 4, 5, 6, 7, 8, 9, and 11) end with triads (mostly minor), and the composition's final sonority is a D-minor triad with a flattened second degree. The commonplace of these triadic endings is a natural consequence of Schnittke's reliance on pedal points and the overtones they generate. In turn, these pedals are direct descendants of similar textures and sonorities found throughout the vast repertory of Russian liturgical music. The principal modernism and difficulty encountered in this composition result from Schnittke's serpentine melodies, which frequently coil back on themselves using different configurations of whole and half steps. As difficult as these chromatic melodies (and occasional clusters moving in parallel motion) are to execute, there is never the sense that Schnittke uses them simply to be modern. Rather, they are his chosen means to the end of his profound and uniquely personal musical language.

CONCLUSION

Much of the music discussed in this chapter may never be performed by choirs other than those whose sole function is the presentation of such music, and there are indeed many such choirs and choruses that specialize in new music. For traditional choruses, though, a composer's decision to use extremely radical approaches to harmony, pitch, rhythm, and text presents specific demands and a lack of enjoyment that do not generally justify the effort. Indeed, most of this music was never conceived with a traditional chorus in mind. From Messiaen on, many composers assume performance by specialist vocal ensembles comprised of highly trained singers performing one to a part. There is a similar trend in both major symphonic and operatic repertory. Most young composers lack the resources or reputation necessary to garner the support necessary to mount works that make such demands on performers. This is especially true for the traditional choral singer, who, unlike his instrumental counterpart, is typically less interested in (and often less equipped to handle) such extreme music. That said, there is scarcely a composer in the twentieth and early twenty-first century who has not benefited from the experimental works of the modernist school. Willingness to question all of the basic assumptions about what constitutes music has forcibly moved choral composing outside its comfort zone—the assiduous rehearsal of music that embraces the safe, time-honored notions of what music is or should be. As the nineteenth-century German philosopher G. W. F. Hegel posited, change comes from the dialogue between radically different points of view. In the best-case scenario, such a synthesis requires compromise. In the realm of choral music, this has meant translating the forbiddingly difficult language of the avant-garde into a language we all can, to some extent, access or understand. Such dialogue does not mean the "dumbing down" of music (or any other aspect of modern culture); rather, it has to do with a creative response that preserves the best aspects of what is controversial and discarding what is merely pretentious.

10

European Centrism

The first five chapters of this volume have focused on twentieth-century compositional developments driven by various aesthetic systems—impressionism, expressionism, serialism, nationalism, and neoclassicism. The importance of this approach stems from the belief—commonly held by composers in the twentieth century—that tonality was no longer viable. Composers and various music groups sought out new modes of expression, the purpose of which was a conscious disavowal of preexisting conventions. Largely organized according to geography, this chapter focuses on choral composers who resisted the new procedures of the avant-garde and whose music resists the modernism described in earlier chapters. First, we turn to a group of Italian composers born in the 1880s and thus collectively known as the *Generazione dell'Ottante*.

These composers were interested generally in creating a modern compositional language that differed from that of Verdi. The principal members of the *Generazione dell'Ottanta* were Ottorino Respighi (1879–1936), Gian Francesco Malipiero (1882–1973), Ildebrando Pizzetti (1880–1968), Alfredo Casella (1883–1947), and Goffredo Petrassi (1904–2003). Casella wrote almost no choral music, and Respighi, despite his popular series of orchestral landscapes, composed only two choral works—a cantata, *La Primavera* (1923), and a Christmas cantata-musical play, *Lauda per la Natività del Signore* (1933). Gian Francesco Malipiero, best known today for his edition of Claudio Monteverdi's works, remains a virtual unknown in the field of choral composition. This neglect is particularly unfortunate since Malipiero was one of only three composers (along with Aaron Copland and Paul Hindemith) commissioned to write a choral work, the "pastoral cantata" *La Terra* for chorus and chamber orchestra (1946), to be performed as part of the Harvard Symposium on Music Criticism in 1947.

ITALY

ILDEBRANDO PIZZETTI

This group's two most celebrated members are Ildebrando Pizzetti and Goffredo Petrassi. Pizzetti's choral style is indebted to his teacher, Giovanni Tebaldini, a pioneer in Italian musicology and director of the Parma Conservatory. Pizzetti eventually succeeded Tebaldini as the director of the Milan Conservatory before moving to Rome to teach at the Academy of Saint Cecilia in 1936. His choral works tend to use melodic, chant-derived lyricism and expressive counterpoint, which can be seen clearly in his most important work, the *Messa di Requiem* (1922). Unlike Verdi and other earlier Requiem composers, Pizzetti's setting of the *Dies irae* takes the form of motet-like modules of similar lengths, which suggest possible musical relationships:

1. vv. 1–2 and 13–14 (10 mm.)
2. vv. 3–6 and 15 (9 mm.)
3. vv. 7 and 12 (17 mm.)
4. vv. 8 and 17 (12 mm.)
5. vv. 10 and 19 (8 mm.)
6. vv. 11, 16, and 20 (11 mm.), and
7. v. 18 and the "Amen" (5 mm.)

The first grouping (vv. 1–2 and 13–14) shows the closest musical correlation, marking the initiation of complete cycles of the Gregorian melodies. Pizzetti uses these for vv.1–6 and 13–16; aside from references to the distinctive opening motive, he virtually ignores the sequence's melody in vv.7–12.

Example 10.1 a–b *Messa di Requiem*, Dies irae

The first part of example 10.1 is the Gregorian chant melody of *Dies irae*; the second portion shows Pizzetti's rhythmicization of its first phrase. Pizzetti distributes the chant throughout the work in such a way that it becomes a determinant of form. He uses the complete Gregorian melody for vv.1–6 and 13–16 and, aside from references to the distinctive opening motive, he virtually ignores it in vv.7–12. This fact suggests a tripartite form based on the chant melody's presence or absence.

Pizzetti composed two countermelodies to accompany the chant. The first (ex. 10.2a) happens at the very beginning of the composition and returns in m. 124 as a literal recapitulation of the opening music to set vv. 13–16 of the sequence. The second countermelody (ex. 10.2b) first appears in his setting of v. 7, underscoring the developmental nature of mm. 51–124.

Example 10.2 a–b Pizzetti, *Messa di Requiem*, Dies irae

Combining the use of these themes with the harmonic centers of the various textual-musical modules suggests a design similar to the traditional sonata-allegro form:

Exposition	Development	Recapitulation
mm. 1–51	51–124	124–192

Pizzetti reinforces this design by reprising the music of the "development" (mm. 51–124), originally heard in the dominant (A) of D, the chant melody's modal center.

Another significant work by Pizzetti is the *Tre composizioni corali* (1944). The texts of these include a poem from Gabriele d'Annunzio's play *Alcione* (*Cade la sera*, 1942) and two biblical texts: "Ululate quia prope est dies Domini" (1943) from Isaiah 13:6 and "Recordare, Domine, quid acciderit nobis" (1943) from Lamentations 5:1–3, 15–17, 19–21. Pizzetti uses pedal points and imitative counterpoint to a degree not found in his other choral compositions of this period. His triadic melodies and harmonies produce conservative, accessible music as this excerpt from the end of *Recordare, Domine* demonstrates (ex. 10.3).

Example 10.3 Pizzetti, *Recordare, Domine*, mm. 97–100

Pizzetti's later *Due composizioni corali* (1961) sets poetry by Sappho (translated into Italian by Manara Valgimigli).[1] Although he appends the rubric "6 voci sole" to his score, this designation more likely reflects his awareness that, historically, madrigals were intended for soloists rather than an endorsement of soloistic performance. Certainly, the part-writing in no way prohibits choral performance. Like the Arcadian texts of many Renaissance madrigals, the Italian text of *Il giardino di Afrodite* abounds with nature references:

> *Un boschetto di meli; Sugli altari bruciano incensi, Mormora fresca l'acqua tra i rami tacitamente, Tutto il luogo è ombroso di rose, Stormiscono le fronde, e ne discende molle sopore.*

> (A little grove of apples; on the altars they are burning incense, Fresh waters murmur among the silent branches, The entire place is shadowed in roses, the leaves rustle and upon them descends a vapid drowsiness.)[2]

GOFFREDO PETRASSI

Although younger than the other members of the *Generazione dell'Ottanta* and nearly an exact contemporary of Luigi Dallapiccola, Goffredo Petrassi is typically included in the *Generazione*. Unlike Dallapiccola, who eventually embraced serialism, Petrassi's background as a chorister imbued him with the traditions of the "Palestrina School."[3] As Enzo Restagno notes: "Petrassi was not concerned as to whether he should be a tonal, neoclassical or twelve-tone composer: he had no belief in the certainty of any definitive approach, but only in the certainty of the struggle and torment of life, and his musical language is the diary of these uncertainties. Disinclined to express emotions directly, Petrassi found himself in the peculiar position of presenting his own intellectual struggle as an abstract drama."[4]

A cursory examination of Petrassi's works list reveals how important choral music was throughout his career. Sacred texts prevail, the only secular works being the early *Coro dei Morti* (1940–41) and two compositions, *Nonsense* (1952) and *Sesto non-senso* (1964), that set poetry by the English poet Edward Lear (1812–88). The *Coro dei Morti* are "dramatic madrigals" for male voices, 3 pf, br, perc, and 3 dbs, the soundscape of which is reminiscent of Stravinsky or Dallapiccolla. Thanks to Eric Ericson's landmark recording *Five Centuries of European Choral Music*, choral conductors today are most likely to know Petrassi's first setting of Lear's "nonsense" poems.[5] These whimsical pieces feature *ostinati* prominently. In "There was a Young Lady" (no. 1), Petrassi assigns the basses a seven-pitch ostinato, which they sing eleven times at irregularly spaced intervals (ex. 10.4a). The upper three parts are homogeneous, all using either parallel or inverted motion (ex.10.4b).

Example 10.4 a–b Petrassi, *Nonsense*, mvt. 1

a. mvt. 1, mm. 1-2

Example 10.4 a–b Continued

For "There was an Old Man of Cape Horn" (no. 3), Petrassi took his musical cues from both Lear's poem and its accompanying drawing (Fig. 10.1).[6]

THE COMPLETE NONSENSE BOOK

There was an Old Man of Cape Horn,
Who wished he had never been born;
So he sat on a Chair till he died of despair,
That dolorous Man of Cape Horn.

[111]

Fig. 10.1 Edward Lear, illustration from A *Book of Nonsense* (1846), no. 57

Once again, Petrassi uses an ostinato (s, t, b) to portray the protagonist's despair and eventual boredom. This four-note ostinato consists of different combinations of consecutive fifths used in nearly continuous rotation and accompany an alto melody comprised entirely of seventh-chord arpeggios.

Petrassi's appreciation of Lear's "nonsensical" humor is most evident in the brief interlude for three male soloists following the old man's demise (ex. 10.5). They present a three-part harmonization of *Dies irae* to which the sopranos respond with a barely stifled yawn of boredom.

Example 10.5 Petrassi, *Nonsense*, mvt. 3, mm. 28–31

EASTERN EUROPE

CZECH REPUBLIC

Western awareness of the choral music composed in the nineteenth century in the countries that lie between the Italo-German axis and Russia remains sparse. Both Bedřich Smetana (1824–84) and Antonín Dvořák (1841–1904) were born in Czechoslovakia, but the orchestral and instrumental music of Dvořák may be the better known in the West. Smetana, often considered the founder of Czech music, concentrated on the composition of operas and orchestral music. Outside the use of chorus in his operas, Smetana's choral output consists of just eight works for male voices, women's chorus, and a cantata with orchestra. Dvořák, on the other hand, is known for his incorporation of Bohemian, American, Native American folk melodies, and other nationalistic influences, all of which become fingerprints of his style. The successful European premiere of Dvořák's *Stabat Mater*, op. 58 (Prague, 1880), with performances in London (1883) and Worcester (1884), led to commissions from the Birmingham Festival (*The Spectre's Bride*, 1885) and the Leeds Triennial Festival (the oratorio *St. Ludmila*, 1887). His three-year residence (1892–95) in the United States as composer-in-residence and director of the National Conservatory of Music in New York City reawakened an interest in folk melodies and dance rhythms. Dvořák's contributions to choral music include a setting of the *Te Deum*, op. 103 (1892), a *Mass in D*, op. 86 (1887), his *Requiem*, op. 89 (1890), and a cantata titled *The American Flag*, op. 102 (1892). Dvořák's delightful *a cappella* collection "Songs of Nature" (*V Přírodě*), op. 63 (1882), still merits performance today.

Like Smetana, Leoš Janáček (1854–1928) was known more for his operas (*Jenůfa*, *The Cunning Little Vixen*, and *From the House of the Dead*) and scenic orchestral music (*Taras Bulba*) than for strictly choral music. Janáček produced a sizable but largely unknown body of nationalistic male-chorus music, as well as several choral-orchestral works of moderate length, the most interesting of which is the five-movement cantata *Amarus* (1896–97, 1901). His *Glagolitic Mass* (*Mša glagolskáya*, 1926–27), for SATB, double chorus, organ, and orchestra, may be his most well-known choral work. Uniquely Czech, Janáček's Mass retains the ancient Slavonic texts implied by the word "Glagolitic." Derived from the Russian "glagol" ("verb"), the title acknowledges the Greek origin of the Slavonic alphabet used by the Russian monks who Christianized Moravia. In his *Glagolitic Mass*, Janáček casts the eight movements (three of which are instrumental) into three, clearly audible sections; in fact, Paul Wingfield finds no fewer than fifty-one different motives used to flesh out these musical sections.[7] Janáček utilizes his own kind of thematic transformation (a potential Lisztian influence?) to create a dynamic musical form built on a colorful, if somewhat conservative, harmonic language. Janáček's prominent use of the orchestra (especially brass and timpani), reliance on the higher solo voices (soprano and tenor), and predilection for parallel thirds constitute the uniquely Eastern European basis of his music.

Another important Czech composer of the early twentieth century is Bohuslav Martinů (1890–1959), whose choral output includes works for chorus and orchestra (e.g., the oratorio *Gilgameš*, 1955, H. 351, after the ancient Assyrian "Epic of Gilgamesh"), several cantatas, and ten publications of secular *a cappella* music, including two sets of "madrigals" to Moravian texts for mixed chorus. His masterpiece is the *Field Mass* (*Polní Mše*, H. 279, 1939), which, like Benjamin Britten's *War Requiem*, combines antiwar poetry with liturgical texts and makes conspicuous use of martial music.[8] The work's designation as a "Mass" is somewhat misleading, as Brian Large notes:

> The *Field Mass* is not a setting of the liturgy, but a collection of texts by Jiří Mucha and passages from Bohemian folk poetry interspersed with lines from the Psalms and phrases from the Common [Ordinary] of the Mass. Designed for performance out of doors, the *Mass* was intended to unite soldiers at the front with compatriots at home. Preference is given, therefore, to brass and wind instruments and strings are omitted altogether. An impressive percussion section, bells and hand bells of the type used at the altar during Mass (the so-called sistrum) and the crotola, an instrument tuned to two notes a perfect fifth apart, piano, harmonium, solo baritone and male chorus complete the forces.
>
> The work's unique character resulted from its text, scoring and pure, unbridled patriotism. Martinů quoted motives from native Moravian folk music as musical reminders of just what was at stake in the war. The work's limited instrumental palette (in keeping with a "mass" intended for the battlefield) and Martinů's rich, sonorous writing for male voices serve the text's simple desperation. Most moving is "a deeply felt apostrophe to the fatherland ... in which Martinů, with charmingly observant music, recalls the sweet, holy place of his childhood and muses on the mourning boom of the funeral bell that used to sound from the Polička Church.[9]

A native of northern Bohemia, Petr Eben (1929–2007) was profoundly affected by World War II, especially his internment in the Buchenwald concentration camp because his father was a Jew. This, coupled with the strictures placed on artists under the Communist regime after the war, limited the amount and type of choral music he was allowed to write. Despite his painful experiences, Eben remained fundamentally optimistic, a quality exemplified by his oratorio, *Apologia Sokratus* (1967). The libretto consists of excerpts from Plato's *Apology of Socrates* and based on Socrates's speech at the trial that led to his execution. These become movements sung in the original Greek by a baritone soloist (Socrates), mixed chorus, and children's chorus, all accompanied by a large orchestra. The three movements—"Concerning Honor," "Concerning Evil," and "Concerning Death"—allow Eben to use his fascination with intervallic counterpoint to create themes that exemplify the focus of each movement. But Eben gives the work a less than subtle religious conclusion, departing from Socrates's Greek to end with Alleluias, set to a Gregorian-like theme. Within his large and varied output of choral music are a ballet for chorus and instruments in 1983 (*Curses and Blessings*), and the brief *Praeger Te Deum* (1989) for chorus and brass/percussion (or organ) that proclaimed the fall of Communism.

HUNGARY

Franz Liszt, the dominant representative of Hungarian music in the nineteenth century (1811–86), enjoyed enormous popularity in Western Europe as a virtuoso composer and performer of works for the piano. In the twentieth century, the major Hungarian composers were Zoltán Kodály and Béla Bartók (see chap. 7). Their legacy continues in the choral music of Lajos Bárdos (1899–1986) and, more recently, György Orbán (b. 1947). A colleague of Kodály, Bárdos's choral music reflects his mentor's love of folk song and concern with practicality. But Bárdos is most important for his role in founding Hungarian choirs, the most notable of which is the Palestrina Chorus of Budapest, to whom Orbán later dedicated a number of compositions. A professor of composition at the Liszt Academy in Budapest, Orbán's music owes its popularity to an eclectic blending of musical traditions. His output of Latin sacred music, all of which postdates the demise of the Communist regime in Hungary in 1989, is indeed significant. His most important sacred works are twelve settings of the Mass ordinary, no two of which are alike. The series begins with a work composed in 1989 to fulfill a commission tendered in the early 1980s by András Déri, a chorister at the church Pasarét in Budapest. Only half of the Masses (nos. 1, 2, 4–6, and 9) have been published; the rights for the remaining manuscripts reside with Hinshaw Music. Orbán has also composed nearly seventy smaller sacred works, most of which are *a cappella*. To these could be added another forty works in Hungarian for mixed chorus and nine more for equal voices, only one of which, *Fülemüle* ("Nightingale," 1996), has been published.

Orbán's most popular composition is *Daemon irrepit callidus*, a "motet" based on anonymous Latin verse. Interesting harmonies and driving rhythms are the primary appeal of this piece. Orbán's melodic writing mixes harmonic minor (D) and major (E♭) scales. One senses his affinity for (or perhaps evocation of) Carl Orff, although Orbán's work is shorter and less dependent on repetition than Orff's. The conclusion of the work (ex. 10.6) reveals a use of melodic tritones (s/b) to convey the devilish spirit of the piece.

Example 10.6 Orbán, *Daemon irrepit callidus*, mm. 43–49

POLAND

Twentieth-century choral music in Poland begins with Karol Szymanowski (1882–1937). Best known for his Polish setting of the *Stabat Mater*, op. 53, Szymanowski synthesized traditional and progressive elements in a manner similar to Janáček and Martinů. Richard Zielinski's article "Karol Szymanowski (1882–1937): The Father of Contemporary Polish Music" states that "In the *Stabat Mater*, he combined old and new elements of Polish music within a religious framework. Moreover, rather than the Latin text, Szymanowski used a modern Polish translation by Józef Jankowski."[10] Not only did Szymanowski establish the precedent (taken up by Penderecki) of using vernacular Polish in lieu of the traditional Latin, but he also lent a dignity and legitimacy to musical expressions of religious sentiment in Poland that not even Communism could eradicate. (The choral works of Krzysztof Penderecki and Henryk Górecki, both of whom were born in 1933, are dealt with more fully in chap. 13.) Poland, like the former Eastern European countries that formed the Soviet Bloc, gained its independence in 1989, and for that reason, there is an entire generation or more of Polish choral composers who remain largely unknown in the West.[11]

SWITZERLAND

ERNEST BLOCH

Switzerland's tradition of political neutrality may also account for the stylistic centrism of two native composers, Ernest Bloch (1880–1959) and Frank Martin (1890–1974). The isolation that assured Switzerland's survival also forced Bloch to further his musical education in Brussels, Frankfurt, Munich, and Paris. When a proposed American tour (as conductor for a touring dance troupe) collapsed in 1916, Bloch found a teaching position at the Mannes College of Music in New York (1917–20), followed by stints as founding director of the Cleveland Institute of Music (1920–25) and director of the San Francisco Conservatory (1925–30). An anticipated return home in the early 1930s was derailed by the rising tide of anti-Semitism in Europe, precipitating his return to the United States to teach at the University of California at Berkeley in 1940.

David Kushner argues that a series of Bloch's early works, including cycles of psalms for soprano and orchestra (1912–14) and baritone and orchestra (1914), the "Israel" Symphony for five soloists and orchestra (1912–16), and the popular rhapsody for cello and orchestra, *Schelomo* (1915–16), comprise a "Jewish Cycle."[12] Bloch's landmark choral work, *Avodath an Hakodesh* ("Sacred Service"), is of later origin (1930–33). Commissioned by Temple Emanu-El in San Francisco, Bloch scores his liturgy for baritone cantor, several incidental soloists, mixed chorus, and a large orchestra. With one exception, Bloch divides the work's five principal movements into a number of liturgically defined parts. Following tradition, Bloch's *Service* music is largely responsorial, invoking a call-and-response interplay between the cantor and the chorus. In some cases, Bloch uses Hebrew liturgical chant melodies, most notably in his setting of "Tzur Yisrael" from the *Sacred Service* (ex. 10.7), which he learned from Cantor Reuben Ronder of Temple Emanu-El.

Example 10.7 Bloch, *Sacred Service*, mvt. 1, mm. 223–29

Bloch's choral writing was, for its time, remarkably simple, avoiding extremes of range, rhythm, and texture. Alexander Ringer, a German musicologist, believed that especially the imitation prelude of Bloch's well-known "Silent Devotion and Response," mvt. 3, is a conscious imitation of Palestrina (ex. 10.8).[13]

Example 10.8 Bloch, *Sacred Service*, mvt. 3, mm. 17–31

FRANK MARTIN

Although Martin showed an early interest in and talent for composition, he initially acquiesced to his parents' wish that he not study music, but as a student at the University of Geneva, he secretly studied both piano and composition. Compositions from the 1920s show a "linear, consciously archaic style, restricted to modal melody and perfect triads and evading the tonal gravitation of Classical and Romantic harmony."[14] His *Mass for Double Chorus* (1922–26) illustrates this historical style-consciousness in its scoring; his use of double choir reflects his admiration of J. S. Bach, while its chronology tends to link it with Vaughan Williams's *Mass in G minor* (also for double choir *a cappella*). Like Vaughan Williams, Martin demonstrates a penchant for modal melody and harmony seen in the theme of the *Kyrie* (ex. 10.9).

Example 10.9 Martin, *Mass for Double Chorus*, Kyrie, mm. 1-5

Even when he transposes it to create harmonic variety and dynamic growth, the melody retains its Aeolian profile, as the soprano entries of both choirs (mm. 9, 13, 14, and 16) confirm.

Bernhard Billeter suggests that Martin's unique personal style is best understood as extended tonality, that is, the persistent use of triads outside a central key.[15] While the individual movements rarely begin and end in the same key, triads figure prominently in Martin's harmonic planning on both local and global levels. Aeolian mode dominates the opening of the *Kyrie* (mm. 1–36), closing on its "dominant," E major. The ensuing music retains Martin's modal theme but presents it in diminution (ex. 10.10).[16]

Example 10.10 Martin, *Mass for Double Chorus*, Kyrie, mm. 37–47

Martin often uses one of the choirs as a harmonic "pedal," a constant that defines the ebb and flow of the other choir's music as either consonant or dissonant. Martin uses this device in the Gloria (mm. 58–84), the Credo (mm. 30–39), the Sanctus (mm. 1–20), and most clearly in the Agnus Dei. Here, Choir 1 sings the text as a unison melody that interacts with the repeated, ostinato-like chords of Choir 2 to create unexpected and striking harmonies (ex. 10.11).

Later works such as: *Cantate pour le temps de Noël* (1929–30), *Le Vin herbé* (1938–41), *In terra pax* (1944), *Golgotha* (1945–48), *Le Mystère de la Nativité* (1957–59), *Pilate* (1964), and *Requiem* (1971–72) tend toward oratorio. Of these, *Golgotha*, a Passion written without any apparent external impetus is interesting for its blending of the traditional Protestant Passion with the theology of St. Augustine. Its initial shouts of "Père!" (ex. 10.12) are strongly reminiscent of the opening chorus, "Herr! Herr," of Bach's *St. John Passion* (BWV 245). A nod to Bach's *St. Matthew Passion* appears in the opening alto aria of Part 2 (ex. 10.13); its lack of a conventional bass line invites comparison with the soprano aria "Aus Liebe will mein Heiland sterben."[17]

Example 10.11 Martin, *Mass for Double Chorus*, Agnus Dei, mm. 16–23

Example 10.12 Martin, *Golgotha*, mvt. 1, mm. 1–3

Example 10.13 Martin, *Golgotha*, mvt. 6, mm. 1–8

The foremost smaller choral work by Martin are the *Songs of Ariel* (1950), which Martin dedicated "to Felix de Nobel and his marvelous 'Netherlands Chamber Choir.'"[18] The texts of these five songs are drawn from Shakespeare's *The Tempest*:

1. "Come unto these yellow sands" (act 1, scene 2)
2. "Full fathom five thy father lies" (act 1, scene 2)
3. "Before you can say 'come and go'" (act 4, scene 1)
4. "You are three men of sin" (act 3, scene 3)
5. "Where the bee sucks, there suck I" (act 5, scene 1)

While Martin uses a sixteen-part chorus to generate complex texture and harmony, he clearly seems to have envisioned these "Songs" as choral pieces because the voice-leading is so clear. In his setting of "Full fathom five" Martin creates a vivid picture of the ocean's mysterious depths by crafting an oscillating ostinato for women's voices based on imitation of diminished pentachords on F♯ minor and C minor that sound over a tenor and bass 1 line that hints at F♯ major (ex. 10.14).

Example 10.14 Martin, *Songs of Ariel*, no. 2, mm. 1–6
© Copyright 1949 by Universal Edition A.G., Vienna © Renewed.
All Rights Reserved. Used by permission of European American
Music Distributors LLC, sole US and Canadian agent for
Universal Edition A.G., Vienna.

As he did in the Kyrie of the *Mass for Double Chorus* (see exx. 10.9 and 10.10), Martin retains the gesture's basic shape but manipulates it through different tonal regions to create a climax on the words "But doth suffer a sea change / into something rich and strange" (ex. 10.15).

Example 10.15 Martin, *Songs of Ariel*, no. 2, mm. 19–24

© Copyright 1949 by Universal Edition A.G., Vienna © Renewed. All Rights Reserved. Used by permission of European American Music Distributors LLC, sole US and Canadian agent for Universal Edition A.G., Vienna.

This series of triads (G#–G–E–A#//D#–D–B–F) belong to no single key; their cohesion lies in their sequential relationship, the second tetrad (mm. 21–24) being an upward transposition of the first (mm. 19–21). The same process shapes the melodies of the first and second tenor and soprano parts into two antiphonal statements anchored to the minor thirds of two interlocking diminished triads (E′–C#–A# and D′–F–Ab), creating chords that, while tertian, are indeed "rich and strange."

Despite their charm, the technical and textural demands of Martin's choral works exceed the grasp of all but the most accomplished choirs. That caveat noted, Martin must be regarded as one of the more creative composers of choral music at a time when composers either ignored the genre as hopelessly old fashioned or reduced it to worn-out harmonic clichés.

CHORAL MUSIC IN SCANDINAVIA AND THE BALTIC STATES

From the 1960s to the late 1980s the choral music of Scandinavian composers generated considerable interest and performance in the United States. Arguably, this interest stemmed from America's discovery of Eric Ericson (1918–2013) and the Swedish Radio Choir (a tradition sustained by this group and the other fine ensembles that have spun off from it).[19] Another major influence was the tenure of the Norwegian Dag Hammarskjöld (1905–61) as Secretary-General of the United Nations (1953–61), which overlapped Ericson's ascent. Hammarskjöld's cool yet assertive diplomacy and his posthumously discovered series of personal reflections and meditations *Markings* (*Vägmärken*, 1963) projected those qualities of Scandinavian society that the West found so appealing in this critical period of world history.

Fig. 10.2 Dag Hammarskjöld at the United Nations

SWEDEN

Ericson's legendary career as conductor of the Swedish Radio Choir began in 1952 and ended with his mandatory retirement in 1983.[20] The popularity of Swedish music in America was largely the result of the creation of Walton Music Corporation by the American choral conductor

Norman Luboff and his wife Gunilla Marcus, which made this Scandinavian repertory commercially available. Frank Pooler (1926–2013), the renowned choir director at Long Beach State College in California, was also an ardent advocate of this same choral repertory. Their combined efforts received additional impetus from the Swedish Radio Choir and the Tapiola Children's Choir, founded and conducted by Erkki Pohjola. This extraordinary children's choir popularized the adventurous compositions of such 1930's composers as Arnë Mellnäs and Folke Rabe. Performances by these ensembles encouraged American conductors to program the new repertory. To their amazement and delight they found that their choirs reveled in the challenges such works posed and their success in performing music they had previously thought inaccessible.

A Swedish composer who enjoyed great popularity in the 1970s and '80s was Eskil Hemberg (1938–2004). One of his best-known choral compositions capitalized on the popularity of Hammarskjöld's book *Markings*; Hemberg's choral suite *Signposts*, op. 15 (1968), draws its texts from Hammarskjöld's publication and is dedicated him. At first glance, Hemberg's use of extended vocal techniques and graphic notation seem to suggest anything but traditional style. But Hemberg's modernist devices were common in the late 1960s as a kind of contemporary text painting, employed sparingly to achieve a specific sound. The appeal of Hemberg and his colleagues was their ability to translate techniques borrowed from the avant-garde into modern sonorities that traditional choirs could perform. Consider Hemberg's idiosyncratic notation of the evocative text "how thou dost set them in *slippery* places" (author's emphasis) (ex. 10.16):

Example 10.16 Hemberg, *Signposts*, no. 2, mm. 14–27

* Sound like that made when on loses footing on the ice

Hemberg juxtaposes modern and traditional styles in an even more dramatic way in his *Messa d'oggi*, op. 23 (1968–70), which was assembled over time from three separate pieces. The first three movements, "Omaggio a Salvatore Quasimodo," were composed in 1968 for performance at a World Church Meeting held in Uppsala, Sweden. In the Kyrie, Hemberg surrounds the tenor cantus firmus with an array of nonpitched vocal sounds, framed by even more modernistic settings of two more poems by Quasimodo (*Ed è subito sera* and *Amen per la Domenica in albis*). When Torsten Nilsson commissioned a new work for a Stockholm church (*Oscarskyrkan*), Hemberg composed a Gloria and another "psalm" from Hammarskjöld's book to complete his Mass. The Kyrie–Gloria pair constitute a Lutheran *missa brevis*, which perhaps prompted Hemberg's quotations of short excerpts from the Gloria of a Mass traditionally ascribed to Dietrich Buxtehude. Fragments of Buxtehude's music, sung by five solo voices, interrupt the setting of the Gloria text sung by a sixteen-part choir to a series of whole-tone clusters. Hemberg varies the number and combination of voices used to create a formal structure based on textural density. The Gloria concludes with all sixteen parts singing an additive "fan" (ex. 10.17) that starts from a simple dyad (E♭' for the men's voices and F' for the women's voices) and expands outward by whole step in both directions.

Example 10.17 Hemberg, *Messa d'oggi*, op. 23, Gloria

A significant composer of this "younger generation" of Swedish composers is Sven-David Sandström (b. 1942). A student of Lidholm, Nørgård, and Ligeti at the Royal College of Music in Stockholm, Sandström taught composition there from 1985 to 1995. Until the successful premiere of his *Requiem, "De ur alla minnen fallna"* ("Mute, the bereaved speak") in 1979,

Sandström was known primarily as an instrumental composer. *Agnus Dei* (1980) for eight-part chorus *a cappella*, dedicated to Eric Ericson and the Swedish Radio Choir, shows the work's fundamental concept that involves paired inversion of the parts from the inside out (S1 and B2, S2 and B1, etc.); these parts sing essentially the same scalar melody but at different speeds. As the piece unfolds, Sandström creates longer, larger waves of sound that extend vocal ranges, dynamics, and tempi culminating in a dramatic, dissonant chord (m. 41). Within three measures, Sandström effects a drastic *diminuendo* and *ritardando* arriving at a densely packed cluster containing seven pitches (D, C♯, B♭, A, G♯, F♯, and E♭) arranged as overlapping major thirds in the women's parts (A′–C″♯, D′–F♯′, and E♭′–G′) and two minor thirds and a diminished third in the men's voices (F♯–A, G–B♭, and C♯′–E♭′).[21] From this sonority, the music begins to gradually coalesce to the three remaining pitches (G, A, B♭). The progression's logic seems to dictate a unison ending on A, but the composer resolves the cluster to a luminous, most unexpected F-major triad instead.

Other choral works by Sandström include a setting of William Blake's poem *The Tyger* (1978), *Es ist genug* (a long choral work dedicated to Eric Ericson), and his "completion" of Henry Purcell's anthem *Hear my prayer, O Lord*.[22] In "Süssmayr-like" fashion, Sandström finishes what Purcell ostensibly left unfinished, eschewing any attempt to re-create Purcell's style, opting instead for a massive development based on the word "crying" (using the traditional semitone "sigh" motive as his principal theme), which is unmistakably and unapologetically modern. More recently, Sandström has garnered attention for his textual reinterpretation of Handel's *Messiah* (2009).

Sandström served on the faculty of Indiana University's Jacobs School of Music from 1999 to 2008, a post to which he returned for a three-year stint in September 2014. The most recent example of Sandström's revisionist historical composition is a *St. Matthew Passion*, which received its premiere by the Berlin Philharmonic, Philharmonischer Chor Berlin, and Staatskapelle Halle in February 2014.

NORWAY

Norway's contributions to contemporary choral music are represented by Egil Hovland (1924–2013) and Knut Nystedt (1915–2014). Hovland is known for dramatic choral works like *Saul* and *Jerusalem*, and his lyric *Missa Misericordiae* (1973). His intensely dramatic setting of *Saul* for narrator, choir, and organ uses controlled aleatoricism; the women's and men's voices randomly intone the unison phrase "Saul, breathing threats and murder against the disciples of his Lord." Following a succession of slightly varied textures, Hovland generates an extended choral development of the text "Why do you persecute me?" that ends with this haunting accusation (ex. 10.18).

Example 10.18 Hovland, *Saul*, mm. 71–75

Despite its brevity, Hovland's utterly simple yet profound setting of John 1:14 (*The Glory of the Father*), is one of his best.

Knut Nystedt compiled a catalogue of choral compositions that ran the gamut from conservative early works like the *Three Motets* (1958) and *Seven Last Words* (1961) to compositions like *De Profundis*, op. 54 (1961), in which we see the influence of Ligeti and Penderecki. Typically Scandinavian in its synthesis of old and new, Nystedt's *De Profundis* progresses from traditionally notated whole-tone clusters to experimental, graphic notation reminiscent of Ligeti (ex. 10.19).[23]

Example 10.19 a–b Nystedt, *De Profundis*

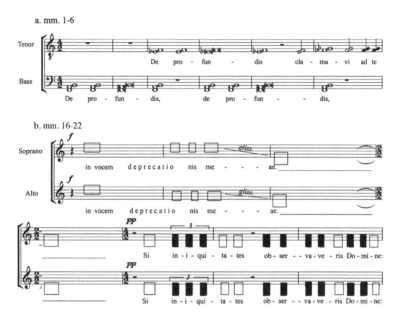

Nystedt's experimental phase was short-lived, giving way to more conventional compositions like *O Crux* (1977) and *Veni* (1978). In *O Crux*, Nystedt sets a hymn text of Venantius Fortunatus (530–609) using music that is declamatory, static, and more reliant on changes in timbre than changes in harmony (ex. 10.20).

One of Nystedt's most interesting works is his *Immortal Bach*, a transformation of J. S. Bach's aria *Komm, süsser Tod*, BWV 478, from G. C. Schemelli's 1736 *Musicalisches Gesangbuch*. Here, Nystedt achieves a modernistic reading of Bach's chorale by employing a simple type of aleatoricism in which Bach's original music is sung by subchoirs, whose members sing their individual lines asynchronously, creating layers of dissonance that only resolve as each voice completes its line and sustains its last note as a gathering chord.

Trond Kverno (b. 1945) and Ola Gjeilo (b. 1978) are members of the younger group of Norwegian composers. Unlike many of the prominent composers of the twentieth century, Kverno has focused on liturgical choral music. He joined the faculty of the Oslo Conservatory as a teacher of music theory in 1974. In 1991 he became a professor of church music at the conservatory, still focusing his teaching on composition and related subjects. His body of choral music is dominated by a ninety-minute *St. Matthew Passion* (1986), which requires eleven vocal soloists and double chorus *a cappella*. His later religious music has tended toward Latin liturgical texts: a *Stabat mater* (1991), the Marian antiphon

Salve Regina, and a *Symbolum Nicenum,* both composed in 1996. His interest in Latin texts reflects the influence of Kverno's own ordination as a priest in the Old Catholic Church of Norway in 1996. The work most likely known in the United States is his set of diverse variations on the text and music of the Marian antiphon, *Ave Maris Stella* (1976) and his *Corpus Christi Carol* (1992).

Example 10.20 Nystedt, *O Crux,* mm. 62–67

The new star of Norwegian choral composition is Ola Gjeilo. He moved to New York in 2001 to study composition at the Juilliard School. Many of his choral pieces are recorded by the Phoenix Chorale on their *Northern Lights* CD, which won a Grammy Award in 2009. Gjeilo's breakthrough composition was a setting of the traditional Maundy Thursday text *Ubi caritas* (1999), to which he added a derivative sequel in 2007. Gjeilo also has a substantial interest in film scores, and much of the music on the *Northern Lights* CD bears that out in two respects: (1) the choral writing is an example of voices treated as instruments, and (2) this music reveals a composer for whom text has seemingly little importance. While its sonorities provide a visceral thrill to singers, there is no audible connection between what the words mean and the music they supposedly inspire.

DENMARK

At the outset of the twentieth century, Denmark's leading composer was Carl Nielsen (1865–1931). Although his primary focus was instrumental music, Nielsen's choral output is substantial. His eleven cantatas are clearly occasional and based on folk themes that might not translate well outside of Denmark (e.g., his cantata for the Lorens Frølich Festival). Nielsen's largest choral work is *Hymnus Amoris* (op. 12, CNW 100, 1896–97) for mixed chorus, children's choir, soloists (S, S, T, Bar, B) and orchestra.[24] The majority of Nielsen's approximately ninety *a cappella* choral works are secular, drawing on Danish texts and tremes. His collection of psalm settings, *Tre Motetter* (op. 55, 1929), contains settings of Psalm 37 (38), 9 (attb), Psalm 22 (23), 1–2 (satb) and Psalm 30 (31), 22 (ssatb), all of which have Latin texts.[25]

The Danish composer Bernhard Lewkovitch (b. 1927) deserves wider recognition. A contemporary of Egil Hovland, Lewkovitch began his career as a composer of Roman Catholic church music. In 1952, he published three Latin Psalms (*Tre Salmi*, op. 9), a Mass (op. 10), and three liturgical motets (op. 11). Lewkovitch's contrapuntal mastery is evident in the opening of the second of his *Tre Salmi, De profundis* (Psalm 130) (see ex. 10.21).

Example 10.21 Lewkovitch, *De profundis*, op. 9, no. 2

Later in the 1950s Lewkovitch embarked on an extensive study of Stravinsky's choral music, which ultimately led him to the refined, modal harmonic language of the *Tre Madrigali di Torquato Tasso*, op. 13 (1954–55).[26] In the second, *All' Aurora*, Lewkovitch sets a text ("Ecco mormorar l'onde") that Monteverdi included in Book 2 of his *Madrigali* (1591). Lewkovitch invokes Monteverdi by using predominantly declamatory writing, modal melody and harmony, and a simple modular construction. The composition's Lydian flavor is best seen in a cadence that appears throughout the work (ex. 10.22a).

Example 10.22 a–b Lewkovitch, *Tre Madrigali di Torquato Tasso*, op. 13, no. 2

a. m. 14

Example 10.22 Continued

b. mm. 15-23

In example 10.22b, Stravinsky's influence on Lewkovitch takes the form of different scales and repetitive patterns that define each voice part (s = C major; a = D major; t = A minor; b = D minor).

Lewkovitch's articles on Stravinsky's early dodecaphonic music, published in the journal *Dansk musiktidsskrift* (1959–60), led to his adoption of a similar style in *Cantica sacra* (1959), *Improperia* (1961), and *Il cantico delle creature* (1962–63). Lewkovitch eventually grew disenchanted with Stravinsky's dodecaphonic style and returned to the modal church music of his early period. The series of blended compositions that follow, include a *Pater Noster* (1983) for chorus and six wind instruments (2 cls, 2 hns, 2 bsns), *Via Stenonis* (1987) for tenor, chorus, and brass quintet; and *Three Passion Motets* "ad honorem Tomás Luis de Victoria," for chorus, clarinet, horn, and bassoon (1996).[27]

Other notable contemporary Danish choral composers are Bo Nilsson (b. 1937) and Bo Holten (b. 1948). Holten is more well known due to his various roles as conductor of the Danish choral ensembles Ars Nova and Musica ficta; the Flemish Radio Choir in Brussels until 2012, and guest conductor of the BBC Singers since 1991. His BBC Singers recordings include performances of the choral music of Arvo Pärt and Veljo Tormis; Holten himself has composed works to mark the seventieth and seventy-fifth anniversaries of the group's founding. His first composition, "Rain, Rush, and Rosy Bush," sets texts by Hans Christian Andersen for four soloists and eight-part choir. Holten employs the same texture for the second commission, a large cycle titled *The Marriage of Heaven and Hell* (1992–95) based on the poetry of William Blake.

FINLAND

Finland is well represented by two choral composers, Joonas Kokkonen (1921–96) and Einojuhani Rautavaara (b. 1928). Kokkonen, regarded by many as the heir apparent to Sibelius, produced four symphonies, a cello concerto (1969), and a considerable body of keyboard and chamber music (including three string quartets). Chorally, his major work was a *Requiem* (1981) composed in memory of his wife, Maija. This nine-movement work, commissioned by the Helsinki Philharmonic and Akateeminen Laulu Choir is scored for solo soprano and baritone, large chorus, and orchestra.[28]

Rautavaara, who was also a protégé of Sibelius, used his teacher's recommendation to study with Copland, Persichetti, and Sessions at Tanglewood (1955). While Rautavaara's choral works of the 1970s resembled those of Nystedt and Lewkovitch, they employed a wider range of media and style than either of his Norwegian contemporaries. Like his more famous Estonian contemporaries, Veljo Tormis (chap. 7) and Arvo Pärt (chap. 13), Rautavaara's setting of texts from the Finnish national epic, the *Kalevala*, and the Orthodox liturgy (two settings of the Vigil liturgy in 1991/92) reveal nationalistic tendencies. His most popular choral work remains the *Lorca-sarja*, op. 72 (1973), a choral suite based on four poems by Federico García Lorca: *Canción de jinete* (*Ratsylaulu*), *El Grito* (*Huuto*), *La luna asoma* (*Kuu nousee*), and *Malagueña*.

In *Lorca-sarja*, Rautavaara showed himself to be a gifted dramatist and musical draftsman. We see his flair for the dramatic in the graphic *glissandi* in *El Grito* and his architectural sensibility in the use of the pitch E as the common tone and unifying ground of all four movements. The bass part of *Canción de jinete* consists entirely of the word "Córdoba" sung to one pitch (E) and rhythm. The single-mindedness of this ostinato is closely matched by the twenty-one bass statements of *La muerte entra y sale de la taberna* in the final movement's thirty-two measures. Fourteen of these statements are on E, the remainder divided between A and D (the next pitches in the circle of fifths). Rautavaara arranges these twenty-one statements so as to create a binary formal design (ex. 10.23a–b).

Example 10.23 a–b Rautavaara, *Lorca-sarja*, op. 72

a. mvt. 1, mm. 1-8

b. mvt. 4, mm. 1-5

His fixation with E provides a foundation over which Rautavaara arrays opposing choral textures. In the first movement, the tenor, while clearly allied with the text and rhythm of the bass, cycles through a collection of pitches (E–F♯–G–A♭–B♭–C–D♭) that show an affinity for the octatonic scale.[29] Against the ostinato in mvt. 4, he deploys the three upper voices singing a succession of first-inversion triads. The bass's departure from E occasions a realignment in which the tenors join the basses' rhythm (singing E) while the women's parts continue with first-inversion triads. The return to E by the bass line assumes the role of dominant to the tenors' recitation on A.

The final four bass statements on A (ex. 10.24) are doubled at the octave by the altos as the tenor and soprano reach their highest range and dynamic.

Example 10.24 Rautavaara, *Lorca-sarja*, op. 72, mvt. 4, mm. 27–31

If *Lorca-sarja* represents the populist side of Rautavaara's output, his setting of *Die Erste Elegie*, the first of Rainer Maria Rilke's *Duino Elegies*, shows what his imagination can produce when loosed from the fetters of practicality. Rautavaara composed this piece in 1993 on commission from *Europa Cantat*.[30] While more than twice the length (nearly nine minutes) of the entire *Lorca-sarja* (*Lorca Suite*), the differences between the two works are more one of degree than of style. Like *Lorca-sarja*, Die Erste Elegie relies heavily on the consecutive juxtaposition of unexpected triadic sonorities to create surprisingly lush and unexpected harmonies. In the opening measures of *Die Erste Elegie*, the women's parts begin with a D-minor 6/4 chord pulsed as eighth notes; after the first two beats, Rautavaara changes one pitch in each successive beat creating a constantly evolving series of harmonies (ex. 10.25). Against this pulsed accompaniment, the tenors and then the basses sing melodies of a dramatic scope and virtuosity not found in *Lorca-sarja*.

The remainder of the work tends to be less dramatic, relying more on the pulsing, kaleidoscopic harmonies than on the disjunct melodic lines. As in the *Lorca-sarja*, Rautavaara relies on extended pedal points (like the D♯ bass pedal that occupies nineteen of the work's final twenty-one measures) to create coherence and formal structure. Of this work, Rautavaara writes, "The basic pitch material of *Die Erste Elegie* is derived from four triads that, taken together, form a twelve-tone row. The way that this material is applied, however, stands in considerable contrast to methods typically used for atonal music. In consequence, the tone of this work is mellow—poetic, yet expressive—even at its most dramatic moments."[31] This revelation of twelve-tone content in triads is surprising because the work, being harmonically dense, does not present the level of dissonance typically associated with dodecaphonic writing.

Example 10.25 Rautavaara, *Die Erste Elegie*, mm. 1–6

What comes as something of a surprise to all but the most dedicated admirers of contemporary Scandinavian choral music is Rautavaara's output of sacred choral music. Rautavaara acknowledges this, noting that, "As a composer, I have always been interested in metaphysical and religious topics and texts."[32] He began composing sacred works early in his career (1955), a preoccupation that continues to the present. His significant choral works include an *Ave Maria* (1957), the *Missa Duodecanonica* (1963), Psalms 23 and 130 (1968, rev. 1971), *Credo* (1972), *Marjatan Jouluvirsi* ("Marjatta's Christmas Hymn," 1995), *Canticum Mariae Virginis* (1978), *Magnificat* (1979), *Rakkaus ei koskaan häviä* ("Charity never faileth," ssa, 1983), and, most significant, his *Vigilia* (*All-Night Vigil*, 1971, 1972, 1996.).

The *Magnificat* (1979) marks a compositional turning point as it contains Rautavaara's first construction of a texture based on two levels of activity—an inner "field of sound" produced by the constant intertwining of separate vocal lines, and a dialogue involving the outermost voices (soprano and bass). The culmination of his new style is the Vigilia in honor of St. John the Baptist, which contains settings of the texts for Vespers and Matins as separate halves of a larger composition. Both segments contain multiple liturgical (Orthodox) texts that require vocal soloists and a large *a cappella* choir that nearly always has some *divisi*. Like Rachmaninoff's vaunted *All-Night Vigil*, op. 37, Rautavaara relies on thick textures with extremely low bass parts. Still present are ostinatos reminiscent of the *Lorca-sarja*, as this excerpt from the third movement of the *Vigilia*, "Avuksihuutopsalmi" ("Psalm of Invocation"), illustrates (ex. 10.26).[33]

Example 10.26 Rautavaara, *Vigilia*, "Avuksihuutopsalmi"

Jaakko Mäntyjärvi (b. 1963), a singer-composer who has described himself as an eclectic traditionalist, is currently enjoying enormous popularity. His published choral compositions include attractive, if somewhat quirky, choral works like *Pseudo-Yoik* (1994), *El Hambo* (1997), and the *Four Shakespeare Songs* (1984). At the other end of the emotional spectrum is his moving lament *Canticum Calamitatis Maritimae* (1997), dedicated to those who perished in the sinking of the ferryboat *Estonia* in 1994; this composition won third prize in a European competition for cathedral choirs. The work's contemporary language (aleatoricism, frequent meter changes, choral speech, etc.) is tempered by his melodic reliance on chant-like recitation and triadic harmony. Mäntyjärvi is a product of the famous Tapiola Children's Choir, which he served as deputy conductor from 1998 to 2004.

BALTIC STATES

The history of contemporary choral music in these countries has only recently come onto the worldwide stage, a development due largely to the success of two Estonians, Arvo Pärt (b. 1935) and Veljo Tormis (b. 1930). Tormis's music is covered in chapter 7, and Pärt's will be examined in chapter 13. Despite a strong tradition of choral singing in these Baltic countries, their geographical proximity to Russia has been a critical factor in the development of choral music. Amid the general chaos that resulted from World War I and the specific turmoil brought on by the Bolshevik Revolution in 1917, Latvia, Lithuania, and Estonia declared independence from Russia in 1918, and within the following year they set up national conservatories independent of Russian influence. This window of independence lasted until the end of World War II when these countries were once again subsumed into the Soviet Union. Whatever distinctive national traits choral music had developed during those twenty-five years of autonomy were rooted out by the new political reality. As with other countries in the Soviet Bloc (e.g., Hungary, Czechoslovakia, Albania, Yugoslavia, and Poland), the various indigenous cultures could be expressed only in ways that were politically acceptable to Soviet Russia. The *realpolitik* tended to create two separate and distinct layers of compositional activity, the better known being the more recent one that followed the breakup of the Soviet Union.

The older generations of composers in each of these countries, while virtually unknown today, were critical to the survival of the Baltic choral tradition. In Latvia, the two most important figures were Jāzeps Vītols (1863–1948) and Alfrēds Kalniņš (1879–1951). Vītols studied with Nicolai Rimsky-Korsakov at the St. Petersburg Conservatory; in 1901 he joined the faculty there, where his students included Sergey Prokofiev and Nikolai Myaskovsky. In 1918 Vītols returned to Latvia and founded the national conservatory that today bears his name. His position as conductor of the Latvian National Opera earned him the title "father of Latvian opera." His largely ethnocentric body of choral music (about one hundred choral songs) remains popular among Latvian choirs. Alfrēds Kalniņš was also active in opera, his most famous work being the four-act opera *Baņuta* (1920). His catalogue contains a sizable component of choral music including nearly two hundred choral songs and six cantatas, the most popular of which is *Jūra* ("The Sea").

Among the more prominent contemporary Latvian composers are Ēriks Ešenvalds (b. 1977), Rihards Dubra (b. 1964), Maije Einfelde (b. 1939), and Uģis Prauliņš (b. 1957). Ešenvalds's tenure as a member of the Latvian National Choir has given him an important understanding of the choral instrument. His most substantive work thus far, *Passion and Resurrection* (2005), reveals awareness of Pärt's music and the innovative layering of old and new in recordings by Paul Hillier like *Morimur* (2001) and *Officium* (1994). In *Passion and Resurrection*, Ešenvalds overlays a solo quartet performance of Cristóbal de Morales's setting of *Parce mihi, Domine* ("Spare me, O God") with independent string writing that interacts with the vocal music to produce atmospheric dissonances. A similar use of layered strata of sound, rhythmic ostinatos, syllabic declamation, and an omnipresent concern with thick, beautiful choral sonorities may be heard in the music of Dubra and Einfelde.[34]

LITHUANIA

The principal member of the Lithuanian old guard is Mikalojus Konstantinas Čiurlionis (1875–1911). Čiurlionis, who studied at the Warsaw Institute of Music and also at the Leipzig Conservatory, was also an accomplished painter, whose paintings show an affinity for German

Symbolism. During his brief life, he produced a number of compositions, many of which were destroyed or lost during World War II; thus, the precise size of his choral output remains uncertain. He is known to have composed a cantata, *De Profundis*, as his graduation piece for the Warsaw Institute. He also wrote a substantive body of choral songs, which embodies the folk idiom.

Of the modern Lithuanian composers, Vytautas Miškinis (b. 1954) enjoys great popularity. His choral roots begin at age seven when he joined the famous Ąžuoliukas Boys Choir. He later became its accompanist and the assistant to its founder, Hermanas Perelšteinas, whom he succeeded in 1979. Since 1985 he has served as director of the choir at the Lithuanian Academy of Music and Theater in Vilnius. His choral output (currently estimated at nearly seven hundred compositions) is published by such prominent houses as Editio Ferramontana, Carus Verlag, and Schott.[35] Many of the same attributes found in Ešenvalds's music are evident in Miškinis's—layers of rhythm, often offset from one another, against which unfold engaging melodies and a stream of thick, essentially consonant harmonies punctuated by occasional colorful clusters. Miškinis shows a preference for Latin liturgical texts in his choral compositions: *Ave Maria* (1988), *Pater noster* (1994), *O sacrum convivium* (2000), *Tenebrae factae sunt* (1995), *Seven O Antiphons* (1995–2003), and *O magnum mysterium* (2008). That said, the music that he crafts to realize these texts seems more suited to the concert hall than the church. As appealing as his sonorities are and as interesting as his use of contemporary rhythms may be, this is not music to be consumed in large quantities lest the intriguing sonorities inevitably begin to be undermined by a lack of contrapuntal and formal rigor.

ESTONIA

Estonia has been and continues to be the dominant Baltic country chorally, based largely on the conducting career of Tõnu Kaljuste (b. 1953), who is to Finland what Eric Ericson was to Sweden, and the huge international success of Tormis and Pärt, whose works represent the secular and sacred sides of contemporary Estonian choral music. In the late nineteenth century, the primary composer was Rudolf Tobias (1873–1918), who represented a link to the German rather than the Russian tradition. He taught in Berlin from 1912 to 1918 and his landmark oratorio, *Des Jona Sendung* ("Jonah's Mission," 1909), continues the German Romantic oratorio tradition. The central links to the modern Estonian tradition were Mart Saar (1882–1963) and Cyrillus Kreek (1889–1962), both of whom studied at the St. Petersburg Conservatory. In such iconic works as *Talvine õhtu* ("A Winter's Evening," 1915) and *Maga, maga Matsikenne* ("Sleep, Little Mats," 1922), Kreek created models of large-scale choral/orchestral works for succeeding generations to emulate. Like Bartók in Hungary, Kreek actively pursued ethnomusicological field work, transcribing folk melodies from various parts of Estonia. To these native melodies he applied a coloristic harmony with modal/tonal roots and the exceptional use of counterpoint. Among the leading Estonian choral composers (other than Tormis and Pärt) are Lepo Sumera (1950–2000), his student Erkki-Sven Tüür (b. 1959), Toivo Tulev (b. 1958), and Urmas Sisask (b. 1960). Sisask has produced works for male, female, and mixed choruses (*a capella* and accompanied).[36]

CONCLUSION

This chapter covers a large and disparate group of European choral composers who remained staunchly committed to a traditional approach to choral composition. While not unaffected by the experiments taking place around them, these composers continued to use conventional notation of rhythm and pitch, a choir in the traditional, inherited sense of the term, and voice-leading that, if not tonal, was nonetheless accessible. Within each subset of composers are individuals who strayed from this generally conservative path at times, but their music favored consonance over dissonance, traditional methods of text-setting over "extended" vocal techniques, and rhythms that adopted the text's word stress. This chapter cannot be thought of as all-inclusive; any number of composers from the countries surveyed here have been omitted because their compositional output did not rise to the same level of significance as those that were mentioned. Indeed, there are composers throughout Europe who have consciously decided to function creatively within the conservative choral tradition either because they were intent on commercial success or because conditions dictated such a relatively conservative approach.

11

The American Experience

THE FIRST NEW ENGLAND SCHOOL

The foundations of American choral music were laid down by the earliest white settlers who came seeking religious freedom. They often expressed their faith by singing, initiating a long-standing American tradition still nourished today. The history of American choral composition began with the so-called First New England School, those itinerant "Singing Masters" who moved from town to town teaching music and singing—based on their own original tunes—along with rudimentary knowledge of theory and pedagogy. Of this group, William Billings (1746–1800) remains the best-known figure. He was a musician and a peddler, and teaching music supplemented his more stable income as a tanner. His *New England Psalm-Singer, or, American Chorister* (Boston, 1770) and *The Singing Master's Assistant* (1778) were important pedagogical and repertorial resources as well as repositories of psalms, hymns, and original compositions like the popular canon *When Jesus Wept*.

The *Singing Master's Assistant* marked the first appearance in print of a "fuguing tune," a genre in which poetic psalm paraphrases were set for four-part chorus, with the main melody in the tenor. Typically, these pieces opened homophonically and featured a quicker central section with imitative vocal entries; Billing's anthem "Creation" followed this formula, setting Isaac Watts's versification of Psalm 139 first homophonically, then using imitation for the words "Strange that a harp of thousand strings should stay in tune so long." In his preface to *The Continental Harmony* (1794), Billings summarized the fundamental task of any composition: "The grand difficulty in composition is to preserve the air [melody] through each part separately and yet cause them to harmonize with each other at the same time."[1] Example 11.1a–c shows that the simple tenor melodies found in the first thirty measures of "Creation" suggest a through-composed approach. The tenor's melodic dominance remains intact in the fugal portion, as the other parts do not imitate it literally. Both components are tightly bound to the key's primary chords, limiting Billings's ability to create variety in the form of either melodic sequence (mm. 36–44) or duet texture (mm. 45–50).

Example 11.1 a–c Billings, *Creation*

a. mm. 1-15

b. mm. 32-35

c. mm. 45-50

Craig Timberlake notes that melismatic passages in this soprano-tenor duet (ex. 11.1c) are typical of late Billings; their primary function here depicts the final word "long."[2] Typically, these parts double one another at the octave creating a thicker, distinctive vocal texture.

The series of lessons preceding the music of *The Continental Harmony* provides essential information about notation ("Musical Characters"), solfege, the character of keys, and what Billings called the "moods of time."[3] These indicate both the music's time (meter) and tempo (in a manner not unlike the Renaissance notion of *tactus*). In "Creation," Billings uses three meters—3/2, 3/4, and C-slash. From Billings's comments, we can deduce that he expected movement from 3/2 to 3/4 to produce a proportional increase in tempo from half = 60 (3/2) to quarter = 80 (3/4).

If Billings was the foremost of the Yankee tunesmiths, he certainly was not the only one. Different groups of composer-teachers pursued this vocation: some, like Oliver Holden (1765–1844), Samuel Holyoke (1762–1820), Jacob Kimball (1761–1826), and Supply

Belcher (1751–1836, dubbed the "Handell [*sic*] of Maine"[4]) were city dwellers who imitated contemporary European music, castigating Billings and his rural brethren as unschooled. The group that included Abraham Wood (1752–1804), Justin Morgan (1747–98, who gained fame as a horse breeder), and Stephen Jenks (1772–1856) were more itinerant, picking up musical idioms from the various churches and tent meetings they encountered. Between these two extremes lay Billings and his less well-known compatriots Daniel Read of New Haven (1757–1836) and Timothy Swan (1758–1842); Swan was exceptional in that he also composed secular music.[5]

Outside of New England, significant musical enclaves began to show up in areas settled by German and Moravian immigrants; most active of these were the Moravian establishments in Bethlehem, Pennsylvania, and Winston-Salem, North Carolina. Composers in Pennsylvania included Johannes Herbst (1735–1812), John Antes (1740–1811), and Johann Friedrich Peter (1746–1813). The relative isolation of these religious communities prevented wider dissemination of any composer's music. An exception to this regional isolation was Charleston, South Carolina, which attracted the talented organist-composer Carl Theodore Pachelbel (1690–1750), the son of Johann Pachelbel.

Charleston's status reflected the growing importance of cosmopolitan cultural centers that looked to Europe for models. The growth of such urban centers in the early nineteenth century gradually rendered the itinerant composers of the First New England School obsolete. The dominant American composer of this period was Lowell Mason (1792–1872), known as "the founder of American school music education." Mason's forte was the composition of hymn tunes, but he also published arrangements in hymn style of acknowledged European masters.[6] In 1827 Mason became president of Boston's Handel and Haydn Society, a position that ensured his reputation as the leading hymn-tune composer of his day.

If Mason's innovative hymns displaced the fuguing tunes and straightforward anthems of the Yankee tunesmiths, that movement soon found new life in America's expansion to the south and west. The foundation of the First New England School had been its connection with religious revivalism. That same fervor, transplanted to the fertile soil of the South, produced a new generation of composers, many of whom relied on the shape-note system of musical notation. William Little and William Smith's *Easy Instructor or A New Method of Teaching Sacred Harmony* (1798) was the first tutorial to utilize this method.[7] Smith and Little (and imitators like Andrew Law) replaced the traditional seven-tone solfeggio system with one comprised of two similar tetrachords—*fa sol la fa* and *fa sol la mi* (see Table 11.1). The simplicity of this system rendered the approaches of Billings and his contemporaries obsolete.

Table 11.1 Smith and Little, shape-note system

Diatonic solfege	do	re	mi	fa	sol	la	ti	do
Pitch	C	D	E	F	G	A	B	C
Shape-note solfege	fa	sol	la	fa	fa	sol	la	mi
Shape-note symbols	Δ	O	□	Δ	Δ	O	□	◊

The new system not only reduced the number of syllables but also used a differently shaped note-head to represent each pitch. The more intricate hymns of Mason and the older Yankee reper-tory essentially drove shape-note singing away from New England to the south and west, where this method was ideally suited to the improvisational nature of the music of the Appalachians, the Deep South, and the frontier territories. Shape-note music began to appear in collections like William Walker's *The Sacred Harp* (1844) and B. F. White's *The Southern Harmony* (1835).[8] The hymn "Amazing Grace" (tune, *New Britain*) first appeared as a three-part, STB, shape-note setting in *Southern Harmony*; the version seen in Example 11.2 shows the addition of an alto part by S. M. Denson (1854–1936) for the book's revision, titled *The Original Sacred Harp*, in 1911.[9]

Example 11.2 *Amazing Grace*

In the late twentieth and early twenty-first centuries there has been a revival of shape-note singing in church choirs and in community choruses, largely in the rural South, although singing groups in New England now specialize in performing this music. Aside from unique musical notation, the Sacred Harp "sing-ins" of the South shared such cultural traits as fixed seat-ing arrangements, lack of formal musical training, socialization, and the pivotal roles of leader and the "keyer."[10] The popularity of this style of singing stems as much from the fervent religiosity and natural style of singing of its participants as its notational novelty as Buell Cobb describes:

> Staunch Sacred Harp singers from rural Georgia to Texas have not been drawn
> to various fads of music, secular or sacred, because they cannot respond deeply
> to a music so diluted. Instead they follow a need that other kinds of music
> and fellowship do not satisfy. And for this, on warm Saturdays or Sundays in
> the year, they drive for distances, sometimes across state, to meet at country
> churches or occasionally a county courthouse. Here at a kind of democratic
> songfest, in a ritual much older than any of the participants, they re-create
> from the tune book *The Sacred Harp* harmonized melodies that are for them
> the purest sounds they have ever heard. Even they are aware, it might be
> admitted, of the frayed voices in their midst. But they make no pretensions to
> angels' song. They speak with pride of "earthly tones."[11]

There is something about the purity of untrained voices, the scrupulous attention to intonation, and the independence of the melodic lines that connect the modern practice both stylistically and spiritually to nineteenth-century traditions, which may have kept the tradition alive, a contemporary vision of "heavenly music."

These groups joined with the growing body of revival songs and their more rural counterpart, gospel hymns, to popularize composers like William Bradbury (1816–68), Ira D. Sankey (1840–1908), and Philip Bliss (1838–76). The mid-nineteenth century was also the heyday of minstrelsy; ensembles like the Christy Minstrels toured the country giving shows that blended many different forms of musical entertainment. Perhaps the most famous composer of minstrel and dialect songs was Stephen Collins Foster (1826–64), composer of such classics as "Jeanie with the Light Brown Hair," "My Old Kentucky Home," "Oh Susanna," "De Camptown Races," and "Old Folks at Home." His tuneful catchy melodies never brought fame or riches to Foster; he died at the age of thirty-eight, an impoverished alcoholic, in New York City.

THE SECOND NEW ENGLAND SCHOOL

Increased attention to and interest in European music pushed aside the pedagogically conceived music of the First New England School. Philharmonic Societies began to appear in cosmopolitan centers like Boston, New York, Philadelphia, and Washington, all founded on the belief that American composers should emulate the styles and trends of their European forerunners. The emergence of Horatio Parker (1863–1919) and John Knowles Paine (1839–1906) created what Gilbert Chase dubbed the "Second New England School."[12] Paine studied in Berlin, became the chapel organist at Harvard University in 1862, and was that institution's first professor of music. His choral works, largely forgotten today, included a *Mass in D*, op. 10 (1867), the oratorio *St. Peter*, op. 20 (1872), a *Centennial Hymn*, op. 27 (1876, with text by the poet John Greenleaf Whittier), and the cantata *Realm of Fancy*, op. 36 (1882, text by John Keats). Stylistically, Paine emulated Mendelssohn, although he tried to keep abreast of modern developments, even acknowledging the influence of Liszt and Wagner. His influence led to a group of Harvard-educated composers in Boston that included Arthur Foote (1853–1937), George Chadwick (1854–1931), Horatio Parker, Amy Marcy Cheney Beach (1867–1944), and Daniel Gregory Mason (1873–1953), the grandson of Lowell Mason.

Amy Beach is an interesting yet overlooked composer of choral music. She began as a successful concert pianist who debuted with the Boston Symphony Orchestra on October 24, 1883. Her husband, Dr. Henry Harris Aubrey Beach, a prominent physician and surgeon, forbade her to appear publicly under her own name (Cheney). Thereafter, Mrs. H. H. A. Beach turned to the composition of symphonic and chamber music, pieces for piano, and chorus and piano. Her choral compositions include the *Festival Jubilate*, op. 17, composed and performed for the dedication of the Women's Building of the World Columbian Exposition in Chicago (May 1, 1893); an enormously long *Mass in E♭*, op. 5 (1890), for soloists, chorus, and orchestra; and a setting of St. Francis of Assisi's "Canticle of the Sun," op. 123 (1924).[13] Conductors of women's choirs need to look closely at Beach's twenty works for women's chorus (à 4) and piano, especially the *Three Flower Songs*, op. 31 (1896), *Three Shakespeare Choruses*, op. 39 (1897), and a setting (op. 66, 1908) of Oliver Wendell Holmes's famous poem "The Chambered Nautilus" for women and chamber orchestra. In an age of European consciousness, Beach's model was Johannes Brahms, whose close relationship between words and music, pianistic style, use of modal harmony and modulation to keys related to the tonic by thirds are all evident in her compositions.

Horatio Parker, after studying for four years in Munich with Josef Rheinberger, returned to the United States and took on a series of prestigious church jobs. In 1894 he became chair of the Music Department at Yale University, a position he held until his death in 1919. Parker was also the founder and first conductor of the New Haven Symphony Orchestra and its choral society. His extensive catalogue of choral music included part songs, oratorios, cantatas, and smaller liturgical pieces. Of his ten large choral works, the only ones performed these days are *Hora novissima*, op. 10 (1893), and several of his sacred anthems (see http://www.allmusic. com/artist/horatio-parker-mn0002181201).

Hora novissima defines the American compositional conscience at the end of the nineteenth century: it was as Germanic in its syntax and correct in its form as Parker could make it. It shares something of a mystical (as well as musical) connection with Elgar's *The Dream of Gerontius*, at that time the most popular English oratorio (see chap. 1). Both works are their composer's major contribution to the musical history of their respective countries. Parker's text—a complex poem about the afterlife by the twelfth-century poet Bernard de Morlaix of Cluny—bears a striking resemblance to the text by Cardinal Newman that Elgar used in *Gerontius*. Parker divides this long poem into two parts, which, unlike Elgar's work, has separate movements. The music is harmonically and formally Romantic in design but includes the use of such abstract textures as fugue and the return of a theme from the opening chorus as countermelody to the principal vocal theme in mvt. 10.

CHARLES IVES

Fig. 11.1 Charles Edward Ives

From 1894 to 1898 Charles Ives (1874–1954) was Horatio Parker's student at Yale University. It is not surprising that one of Ives's first large compositions, the cantata *The Celestial Country*, resembled Parker's *Hora novissima* in its text choice and formal disposition. Composition of *The Celestial Country* began in 1898 (Ives's last year at Yale) and was completed in 1899 during his tenure as organist at Central Presbyterian Church in New York. Although Ives's cantata is little more than half the length of Parker's oratorio, it mirrors Parker's alternation of music for chorus, solo quartet, and arias (Table 11.2).

Table 11.2 A comparison of Parker's *Hora novissima* and Ives's *The Celestial Country*

Parker	Ives
Part 1:	
1. Introduction and Chorus	1. Prelude, Trio, and Chorus
2. Quartet	3. Quartet
3. Aria (Bass)	2. Aria (Baritone)
4. Chorus	
5. Aria (Soprano)	
6. Chorus	
	4. Intermezzo for String Quartet
Part 2:	
7. Solo (Tenor)	6. Aria (Tenor)
8. Double Chorus	5. Double Chorus
9. Solo (Alto)	
10. Chorus *a cappella*	
11. Quartet and Chorus	7. Chorale and Finale

The table shows that a number of movement titles in Ives's work (chorus, bass solo, quartet, double chorus *a cappella*, and quartet and chorus) correspond to ones used by Parker. Musical differences between the two works may be traced to the different prosody of the texts, and the size and ability of the forces that premiered each work.[14] Parker scored his oratorio for a full orchestra, while Ives made do with string quartet, organ, and two horns. But the real point is that *The Celestial Country* appropriated Parker's style even though Ives didn't complete that work until after he had left Yale and Parker's tutelage. That separation may explain the short bitonal instrumental pieces that precede mvts. 1, 2, 4 and 7 but have no precedents in either Parker's style or Ives's texted music. Conversely, Gayle Sherwood points out musical similarities between the two works, the most obvious being the alternating 4/4 and 3/4 meters (ex. 11.3a–b).[15]

Example 11.3 a–b Comparison of Parker's *Horissima Nova* and Ives's *The Celestial Country*

a. Horatio Parker, *Hora novissima*, mvt. 3, mm. 33-40

Pa - tri - a   splen-di- da,   Ter - ra-que   flo-ri- da,   Li - be - ra   spi- nis,   li - be - ra   spi-nis.

Example 11.3 a–b Continued

b. Charles Ives, *The Celestial Country*, mvt. 3, mm. 60-65

According to Sherwood's revised chronology of Ives's early choral works, 1898 also saw the genesis of Ives's *Psalm 67*.[16] Here Ives consistently notates the soprano and alto parts in C major, while the tenor and bass are in G minor. This use of bitonality is neither as striking nor as early as the polytonal interlude that appears between Variations 2 and 3 of his organ piece *Variations on "America"* (1891); here, Ives places the familiar melody in canon in the keys of F major and D♭ major.[17] *Psalm 67* also illustrates another facet of Ives's style in his use of quasi-Anglican chant (ex. 11.4), found both here and in *Psalm 90*.

Example 11.4 Ives, *Psalm 67*, conclusion

Following *Psalm 67*, Ives composed settings of Psalms 24, 25, 54, 100, 14, and 135; in these works he systematically explored a variety of innovative compositional procedures. In *Psalm 24*, Ives's melodies comprise intervals of gradually increasing size (ex. 11.5). The opening soprano melody (inverted by the bass) begins with semitones (with octave displacement), followed by major seconds, thirds, fourths (ex. 11.5), tritones, and so forth.

Example 11.5 Ives, *Psalm 24*, mm. 25–27

In the early 1900s, Ives composed his most adventurous choral work, the *Harvest Home Chorales* (1902–15), in which he sets hymn texts by George Burgess, John Hampton Gurney, and Henry Alford for mixed choir, brass ensemble (four trumpets, three trombones, tuba), and organ. The characteristic Ives fingerprints found in these pieces include organ pedal points, chant, and dissonant harmony created by parallel triads played against a sustained chord, as in this passage from the first *Chorale* (ex. 11.6).

Example 11.6 Ives, *Harvest Home Chorales*, no. 1, mm. 1–4

Ives's premier choral composition is his *Psalm 90* (1923–24), scored for SATB chorus (with extensive *divisi* and occasional brief solo passages), organ, and bells (four parts). Ives's formal approach parses the psalm text into four characteristic moods, the musical gestures of which became the work's introduction (ex. 11.7).[18]

Example 11.7 Ives, *Psalm 90*, mm. 1–5

1. The Eternities
2. Creation
3. God's Wrath against Sin
4. Prayer and Humility
5. Rejoicing in beauty and work

Later appearances of these typical Ivesian sonorities coincided with the return of similar textual ideas. For example, mention (direct or implied) of God's anger summons the polychord heard in m. 2. After the introduction, the same motive appears five more times (mm. 20–23, 36–38, 51–53, 76–79, and 104) either as a single chord or in sequentially moving blocks.[19] In his setting of the ninth verse ("For all our days are passed away in thy wrath"), Ives replaced the expected "anger" chord with a fascinating compositional device by subdividing the male and female voices into eleven and ten parts respectively, all starting on C'. These two groups fan out in contrary motion to create a dense, sustained whole-tone cluster of twenty-one pitches; the expansion is matched by a similar contraction of the texture back to C'. Perhaps prompted by the text's reference to our "passing" years, Ives mirrors this pitch wedge with a durational one. The verse begins with a duration of nine sixteenths, shrinking by one sixteenth with each new chord. This acceleration is then matched by a complementary deceleration as each chord adds back a sixteenth note with each new chord (ex. 11. 8).[20]

Example 11.8 Ives, *Psalm 90*, mm. 60–65

The resulting durational palindrome constituted what probably was the earliest use of additive rhythm. Such advanced, abstract concepts confound any sense of stylistic evolution as they happen without apparent precedent within a limited time span. Awareness of such innovative techniques confirms Ives as an American original, impossible to duplicate.

His unique aesthetic and style found no real successor, although fellow New Englanders like Henry Cowell (1897–1965) and Henry Brant (1913–2008) preserved something of his uncompromising spirit of invention. While neither composer is well known today in choral circles, Brant's use of spatially conceived music and improvisation (best seen in his 1983 work, *Meteor Farm*) continued Ives's experiments and led to an influence on John Cage.

Henry Cowell is best known for his radical experiments involving the use of the overtone series (and geometrically shaped note-heads to represent that series) to determine rhythm, melodically and rhythmically dissonant counterpoint, and extended polychords/clusters.[21] His most famous innovation is what he called "string piano" in which the piano's strings are strummed or plucked (e.g., *Aeolian Harp*, no. 370, ca. 1923, and *The Banshee*, no. 405, 1925[22]). Cowell founded the New Music Society of California in 1925; that organization put on concerts of challenging contemporary music by American and European composers until its demise in 1936.[23] It was followed in 1928 by the creation of the Pan-American Association of Composers with Cowell, Edgard Varèse, and Carlos Salzédo (1885–1961) at the forefront.[24] Such radical modernism seems inimical to choral music; in fact, Cowell's modernism moderated during his unexpected and unfortunate imprisonment in San Quentin in 1936 following his trial for being a subversive and homosexual. Sentenced to fifteen years, he served only four years due to intense lobbying on his behalf by Charles Seeger (the father of Pete Seeger) and Percy Grainger, into whose custody Cowell was released in 1940. Alan Rich notes that, after his release, his music "seemed to abandon the old experimental stance, as though Cowell imagined that his points along that line had already been made. The music became simpler, the rhythms more straightforward, the harmonies no longer forbidding."[25] The great majority of Cowell's published choral works come after his release from prison, and one can hear a new lyrical warmth in such works as "Luther's Carol for his Son" (no. 723, TTBB, 1948) and the cantata ... *if He please* (no. 818, 1956).[26]

American composers born in the 1890s—Walter Piston (1894–1976), Virgil Thomson (1896–1989), Roger Sessions (1896–1985), Roy Harris (1898–1979), Leo Sowerby (1895–1968), and Aaron Copland (1900–1990)—succumbed to the allure of European culture; all were drawn to the Paris of Cocteau and *Les Six*, and especially to the American Conservatory at Fontainebleau. There they studied with Nadia Boulanger (1887–1979), the most famous and influential teacher of composition, a world-renowned organist, and the first woman to conduct the Boston and the New York Philharmonic orchestras.

AARON COPLAND

Best known for such iconic American works as *Appalachian Spring, Rodeo, Billy the Kid, Fanfare for the Common Man, A Lincoln Portrait*, and his film score for *Our Town*, Copland's choral works include *Lark* (1939), *Las Agachadas* (1942), *In the Beginning* (1947), the popular choral arrangements (by Irving Fine) of his *Old American Songs*, and the choruses (*Stomp your foot!* and *The Promise of Living*) from his opera *The Tender Land* (1954). Copland embraced a wide variety of styles ranging from jazz to serialism, but his uncanny ability to capture an essentially American sound assured his place in the musical history of the twentieth century. Although not a serious collector of folk songs like Holst, Vaughan Williams, Kodály, and others, Copland's more popular choral music (e.g., the songs "Ching-a-ring chaw," "At the River," "Long time ago," and "The Promise of Living") presents the essence of folk art in a unique way. But it is his *a cappella* cantata for mezzo-soprano soloist and mixed chorus, *In the Beginning*, that continues to inspire curiosity and interest among discerning choral conductors.

For a "Symposium on Music Criticism" held at Harvard University (May 1–3, 1947), three choral works were premiered: Aaron Copland's *In the Beginning*, Paul Hindemith's *Apparebit Repentina Dies* (see chap. 8), and G. F. Malipiero's *La Terra* (poetry by Vergil, for chorus and organ), as well as new chamber works by Arnold Schoenberg, Walter Piston, and Bohuslav Martinů. The Harvard music professor A. Tillman Merritt (1902–98) asked Copland to write "a composition … for *a cappella* chorus on a text drawn from Hebrew literature, either sacred or secular."[27] Copland responded by setting parts of the two conflicting creation stories in Genesis (1:26–27 and 2:5–7). In his review in the *New York Herald Tribune*, the Harvard alumnus and symposium presenter Virgil Thomson wrote that "Copland's is the least ambitious expressively.… It is modest and thin of substance."[28] Several weeks later, Francis Perkins reviewed a second performance at Carnegie Hall in the *Herald Tribune*, noting that Copland's work "gives the impression of appealing clarity and simplicity, but is somewhat handicapped by insufficient variety of pace."[29] Harold Taubman's review in the *New York Times* that same day was somewhat more positive: "His writing has simplicity and tenderness without the pathos such a theme might invite."[30] And Nicholas Temperley's reaction to a Cambridge performance in 1964 was decidedly negative: "It is a curious work; the musical ideas are interesting, but there is a complete lack of any atmosphere of awe at the tremendous event described by the words."[31] While these reviews accurately represent initial critical reaction, they don't account for the continued popularity of *In the Beginning*. Some regard it as a masterpiece, others question whether the effort required to perform it successfully is ultimately justified. Perhaps Copland found the prospect of writing a choral piece of such length daunting. That said, Copland approached his formidable task by dividing the thirty-eight verses of text into seven sections (Table 11.3). With the exception of Day 6, each day contains roughly comparable amounts of text and music.

Copland's most obvious formal device is his use of a formulaic textual/musical refrain to mark the end of each day. Each uses a primary major triad for recitation and a chord of inflection, which contains a chromatic cross relation. In the case of Day 3 (ex. 11.9) we find a D-major "recitation" chord and an inflection consisting of a B♭ major 6/4 chord (F–B♭–D) with an added raised fourth (E).

Table 11.3 Copland, *In the Beginning*, Text distribution

Day	Text	No. of Verses	Location mm.	Length in mm.
1	Gen 1:1–5	5	1–42	42
2	Gen 1:6–8	3	43–74	30
3	Gen 1:9–13	5	74–131	57
4	Gen 1:14–18	5	132–72	41
5	Gen 1:19–23	5	172–211	39
6	Gen 1:24–31	8	211–325	115
"8"	Gen 2:1–7	7	327–89	63

Example 11.9 Copland, *In the Beginning*, mm 129–31

Beyond the form-giving refrains, there are several significant motives, the first of which is a three-note cell (ex 11.10a) that appears throughout the work. The disjunct contour of the second motive (ex. 11.10b), associated with the words "And it was so" obscures its reliance on two interlocking minor thirds, a microcosm of Copland's harmonic process.

Example 11.10 a–b Copland, *In the Beginning*

Copland also uses imitation of varying degrees of strictness, sometimes approaching canon, as another important generative device. In example 11.11, Copland creates a canon at the fourth between the soprano and alto, which he then harmonizes by successive entries in the tenor and bass (transposed up a whole step from the women's pitches); by making small changes in individual voice parts he maintains the illusion of canon while creating interesting harmonies.

Example 11.11 Copland, *In the Beginning*, mm. 52–57

Copland's persistent, flexible use of triadic arpeggios makes his music sound uniquely American and populist, and contributes to an overall sense of formal cohesion. That said, performances of this rather lengthy, daunting work are best undertaken by elite choirs and an equally strong mezzo-soprano soloist. Copland includes an optional piano reduction to be used "At the conductor's discretion" in performance, which tacitly testifies to the difficulties of executing the work *a cappella*.

Walter Piston is less important as a composer of choral music than as a teacher (Fig. 11.2). His textbooks *Harmony, Counterpoint,* and *Orchestration* still set the standard of music theory relied upon by generations of music students throughout the United States and England. A list of his students at Harvard comprises a who's who of significant twentieth-century American composers, including Leroy Anderson, Leonard Bernstein, Samuel Adler, Gail Kubik, Irving Fine, Daniel Pinkham, and Elliott Carter.[32] The diversity of style and personality represented by this group attests to Piston's ability to give his students both a sense of discipline and the permission not to be slavish imitators of his own style.

A second generation of Nadia Boulanger pupils includes Ross Lee Finney (1906–97), Louise Talma (1906–96), and Elliott Carter (1908–2012). While none is primarily known for choral music, all have contributed some notable pieces to the repertoire. In addition to his studies with Boulanger, Finney studied with Alban Berg and Roger Sessions. After concurrent teaching posts at Smith College and Mount Holyoke College, he joined the faculty of the University of Michigan in 1948. Both his extended work *Pilgrim Psalms* (1945) and

Fig. 11.2 Walter Piston

a neglected cycle of secular pieces, the *Spherical Madrigals* (1947), set seventeenth-century English poems about spheres and circles. Louise Talma taught at Hunter College in New York and produced a discrete body of choral music crowned by *Let's Touch the Sky* (1952), a choral suite of settings of poems by e. e. cummings for SATB chorus and three woodwinds.[33] Elliot Carter was the most significant member of this group, although instrumental music did more to establish his reputation than his several choral works, which include an oratorio (*The Bridge*, 1937), a few pieces for men's chorus (*Tarantella*, 1936, and *The Defense of Corinth*, 1942), and a small but impressive group of *a cappella* choral pieces—*Madrigal Book* (1937), *Heart Not so Heavy as Mine* (poem by Emily Dickinson, 1939), and *Musicians Wrestle Everywhere* (1945).[34] Of these, Carter's setting of Dickinson's poem is a particularly compelling blend of rigorous counterpoint and expressive music. Within Carter's elaborate artifice, one can perceive the natural inflection of someone reading the poem aloud. Carter parlays the emblematic melodic thirds of his opening into an ostinato-like theme into which he inserts fragments of melody that gradually disclose more of the poetic text and Dickinson's vision of fragments ("a careless snatch, a ballad") overheard by someone too distracted by her own pain to respond.

Leo Sowerby (1895–1968) served as organist-choirmaster at the Episcopal Cathedral of St. James in Chicago from 1927 to 1962. He was also the founding director of the College of Church Musicians (CCM) at the Washington National Cathedral (1962–68). He is remembered as the leading composer of American Episcopal church music; his output includes more than 120 anthems, many settings of the Anglican canticles and Communion services, and a number of rarely performed cantatas.

Of the composers born at the turn of the century, Howard Hanson (1896–1981) was an influential voice. He was best known for his long tenure as director of the Eastman School of Music (1924–64) and the role he played as president of the National Association of Schools of Music (NASM) in instituting the doctoral degree in music performance (DMA). Although his compositional output was primarily symphonic, Hanson composed several larger choral works with orchestral accompaniment: *The Lament for Beowulf* (1926), the wordless *Heroic Elegy* (for the Beethoven centennial in 1927), *Three Songs from "Drum Taps"* (1935), *Hymn for the Pioneers* (1938), and *The Song of Democracy* (1957). The unabashed neo-Romantic lyricism of his music ensured its accessibility and popularity.

RANDALL THOMPSON

Randall Thompson (1899–1984) was the giant of this generation of composers. In contrast to Hanson and others, Thompson seemed completely at home in the choral idiom, possessing an unfailing instinct for writing vocally grateful and expressive music. His large-scale works for chorus and orchestra include *Odes of Horace* (male voices, 1924), *Rosemary* (women's voices, 1929), *Americana* (1932), *Tarantella* (male voices, 1937), *The Testament of Freedom* (1943), *Ode to the Virginian Voyage* (1956–57), *Frostiana* (1959), *The Passion According to St. Luke* (1964–65), *A Psalm of Thanksgiving* (1966–67), *The Place of the Blest* (1969), and *A Concord Cantata* (1975). He is justly famous for his numerous octavos, which remain popular with choirs and amateur choruses to this day. Four compositions in particular—the ubiquitous and vastly singable *Alleluia* (1940), *The Peaceable Kingdom* (1936), *The Last Words of David* (1949), and *Frostiana* (1958–59)—continue to endear him to generations of singers.

The Peaceable Kingdom is an eight-movement choral cantata, which takes its title from a painting (one of more than sixty versions of the same subject and with the same title) by the Quaker pastor Edward Hicks (1780–1849). Hick's many paintings depict text from Isaiah 11:6–9, which, in its most common formulation, tells of the wolf lying down with the lamb. Thompson's assemblage of texts has less to do with such implied tranquility than with the judgment of those who "forsake the Lord." Indeed, the few textual references to the peacefulness or faithfulness (mvts. 1, 6, and 8) are far outnumbered by texts and music that are full of gloom and doom.

Thompson highlights this dichotomy tonally in mvt. 1 by placing the first two texts—v. 10 ("Say ye to the righteous") and v. 11 ("Woe unto the wicked)—in the related yet contrasting tonalities of D major and B minor. The final reference to those "who forsake the Lord" appears at the opening of mvt. 6 as a melody in B♭, a tritone removed from the E-minor conclusion of the preceding movement ("The Paper Reeds by the Brook"). Here Thompson illustrates the general uneasiness of the cycle by opposing triads in the three upper voices against the bass line, which moves in contrary motion (ex. 11.12) and admits no resolution.

Example 11.12 Thompson, *The Peaceable Kingdom*, mvt. 5, mm. 4–12

If the scope of Thompson's cantata *Frostiana* is similar to *Peaceable Kingdom*, its mood is totally different. *Frostiana*, commissioned by the town of Amherst, Massachusetts, to commemorate the bicentennial of that city, was first performed on October 18, 1959, with the composer conducting. Also present at the premiere was Robert Frost, the author of the seven poems that Thompson set to music and the source of the cantata's title (Table 11.4).

The formal design of *Frostiana* relies primarily on the alternation of different vocal textures. While traditional keys, meter, and tempo are used for each movement, the tonalities reveal no discernible pattern (save for the implied V–I relation between mvts. 4 and 5). Thompson's use of both the major and minor modes of F (mvts. 2 and 6) and G (mvts. 7 and 3) as the tonal centers of consecutive movement pairs provides the work's only hint of modernism.

The musical charm and aptness of text setting make selection of a single movement as representative of Thompson's style difficult. The framing movements for mixed chorus set different moods—the first tentative, the last unshakably affirmative. In "The Road Not Taken," Thompson adhered to the poem's strophic design, while the music of "Choose Something Like a Star" is as continuous as its text. The music emerges from the composer's reading of the poem, a reading that ignored the boundaries suggested by rhyme or punctuation. The composition's distinctive gesture is an octave leap in the soprano, emblematic of the title's "star" (ex. 11.13).

Table 11.4 Thompson, *Frostiana*, texts and structure

Movement	Text	Key/Meter	Vocal Scoring
1.	"The Road Not Taken"	D minor 4/4 *Andante moderato*	SATB
2.	"The Pasture"	F minor 6/8 *Lento pastorale*	TBB
3.	"Come In"	G minor 4/4 *Lento*	SSA
4.	"The Telephone"	A 4/4 *Allegretto scherzoso*	SSA/TBB
5.	"A Girl's Garden"	D minor 4/4 *Allegro con brio*	SSA
6.	"Stopping by Woods on a Snowy Evening"	F minor 4/4 *Lento assai*	TBB
7.	"Choose Something Like a Star"	G 4/4 *Larghetto*	SATB

Example 11.13 Thompson, *Frostiana*, mvt. 7, mm. 4–6

Thompson repeats this gesture five times in the soprano, and as such it hovers star-like over the lower voices as an inverted pedal. He masterfully inserts the motive twice later in the piano part—at the height of the composition's harmonic development (mm. 43–45) and at the work's conclusion (mm. 94–95). All of these statements pictorialize the title of Frost's poem ("Choose Something Like a Star"); they also reference Frost's allusions to John Keat's sonnet "Bright Star, would I were stedfast [sic] as thou art/ . . . / Like nature's patient, sleepless eremite."[35]

Jean Berger (1909–2002), a contemporary of Thompson, taught at Middlebury College in Vermont, the University of Illinois at Urbana-Champaign, and at the University of Colorado.[36] His most significant composition was his *a cappella* setting of Jorge de Lima's *Salmo* published with both the original Portuguese and an English text in 1941 as *Brazilian Psalm*. Due to the extreme difficulty of the music, the concluding "Alleluia" was published separately and achieved wide popularity in the 1950s and 1960s. In addition to "A Rose Touched by the Sun's Warm Rays," "Speak to One Another," and the charmingly quirky *Five Canzonets*, which are still performed by church and college choruses, his "The Eyes of All Wait Upon Thee" remains his most popular work, principally on the strength of its piquant yet accessible harmonies. In general, Berger's sizable body of secular choral music remains less well known than his sacred music.

American composers from the second decade of the century include William Schuman (1910–92), Samuel Barber (1910–81), Gian Carlo Menotti (1911–2007), and Norman Dello Joio (1913–2008). Schuman assumed two important posts during his long career: director of publication for G. Schirmer in 1944, and president of the Juilliard School from 1945 to 1962. His popular choral composition *Carols of Death* (1958) comprises settings of three poems by Walt Whitman, "The Last Invocation," "The Unknown Region," and "To All, To Each." Their harmonic language harks back to that of Hindemith (no key signature, many accidentals). Of particular interest is Schuman's practical adaptation of the contemporary technique known as *Klangfarbenmelodie* ("Tone Color Melody") in "The Unknown Region." For most of the composition, each vocal part sings a single pitch (creating the pitch-class set F#–G#–A#–C#); the resulting rhythmic canon (at three-measure intervals) with its unsynchronized text presentations compensates for the lack of harmonic change.[37]

SAMUEL BARBER

The importance of Barber's output is greater than its relatively small size, producing a body of choral compositions in both small and larger scale including his setting of Stephen Spender's poem *A Stopwatch and an Ordnance Map*, op. 15 (1940), for male chorus and three timpani; the triptych *Reincarnations*, op. 16 (1937–40); an arrangement of a solo song, op. 13, no. 3, *Sure on This Shining Night* (1961); and two *a cappella* choruses—*Twelfth Night* and *To Be Sung on the Water*—published as his op. 42 (1968). Barber's choral-orchestral works, *Prayers of Kierkegaard*, op. 30 (SATB chorus and orchestra, 1951),[38] and Pablo Neruda's sensuous poem *The Lovers*, op. 43 (baritone solo, chorus, and orchestra, 1971), are unjustly neglected works, while *A Stopwatch and an Ordnance Map* is one of the truly outstanding twentieth-century compositions for male chorus. Barber arranged his best-known composition, the *Adagio for Strings* (itself an alternative version of the slow movement of his String Quartet in B minor, op. 11, 1935–36) for mixed chorus by adding the Agnus Dei text in 1967.

Barber's most popular choral pieces are the three poems collectively known as *Reincarnations*. Barber's interest in Celtic poetry was pronounced. By the time *Reincarnations* was published, he had demonstrated a clear affinity for and thorough knowledge of poetry of the British Isles. The Easter Uprising (1916) in Dublin inspired James Stephens to write these poems, modeled on the songs of Irish authors from the seventeenth to the nineteenth centuries. All three of the *Reincarnations* are scored for SATB chorus *a cappella*. The first piece, "Mary Hynes," has two parts, each based on a distinct melody (ex. 11.14a–b). The poem's nearly exclusive use of monosyllabic words, and Barber's declamatory choral writing and tempo combine to make the first section sound somewhat frenetic. The conclusion, cast as an unaccompanied fugue, is followed by more pastoral, relaxed music. Barber's concluding fivefold setting of the single word "airily" is a marvel of structural logic and expressive text setting (ex. 11.14b).

"Anthony O'Daly," the second song in the *Reincarnations* and the last to be composed (December 1940), presents the starkest possible musical contrast. This poem draws heavily on images of nature; stars, fish, dew flowers, and trees all of which lament the passing of Anthony O'Daly. The principal musical idea in this dirge is a drone, heard initially in the bass, then later in the unison women's voices (ex. 11.15a–b).

Example 11.14 a–b Barber, *Reincarnations*, "Mary Hynes," op. 16, no. 1

a. mm. 1-5

Example 11.14 a–b Continued

b. mm. 38-50

Example 11.15 a–b Barber, *Reincarnations*, "Anthony O'Daly," op. 16, no. 2

a. mm. 1-5

This ominous, unbalanced five-beat ostinato serves as the platform over which Barber presents a straightforward 3/4 melody in the soprano (mm. 1–7), and then as a tenor and alto canon.

"The Coolin" is a five-stanza poem with interlocking rhyme: abab/bcbc/dede/ebeb/abab. From these five stanzas Barber produces an ABA design. The first musical segment (mm. 1–25) sets the first three stanzas while the other two stanzas each become separate musical sections (v. 4, mm. 26–31; v. 5, mm. 32–38). In many respects, "The Coolin" is the simplest piece of *Reincarnations*; its deceptive simplicity and direct, honest expression make it the most popular work of the three (ex. 11.16).

Example 11.16 Barber, *Reincarnations*, "The Coolin," op. 16, no. 3, mm. 32–35

LEONARD BERNSTEIN

The American composers born later in the second decade of the twentieth century—Alan Hovhaness (1911–2000), Irving Fine (1914–62), Lou Harrison (1917–2003), Leonard Bernstein (1918–90), and George Rochberg (1918–2005)—are as diverse as the country itself. Of these, the standout is the conductor-composer Leonard Bernstein, whose choral works include the *Chichester Psalms* (1965); *The Lark* (1955), which consists of choruses originally written for Lillian Hellman's translation of Jean Anouilh's play (*L'Alouette*) and later rearranged as a *Missa Brevis* in 1988; choral arrangements of excerpts from Bernstein's opera *Candide* (1956); his *Mass: A Theatre Piece for Singers, Players, and Dancers* (1971), commissioned for the opening of the Kennedy Center for the Performing Arts; and numerous arrangements of memorable tunes from *West Side Story*. Bernstein's adept blending of multiple musical styles (and theological precepts) makes his *Mass* unique: in it he demonstrates a populist facility with twelve-tone technique in the work's Kyrie, a feat also accomplished in his musical *Candide* (1956) and his "Kaddish" Symphony (1963).

Bernstein's *Chichester Psalms* was commissioned by Rev. Walter Hussey, dean of Chichester Cathedral, Sussex, for the 1965 music festival that featured the combined choirs of Chichester, Winchester, and Salisbury Cathedral. Hussey had earlier demonstrated his support for contemporary art when he commissioned works by W. H. Auden, Henry Moore, and Benjamin Britten to celebrate the fiftieth anniversary of St. Matthew's Church, Northampton, in 1943.[39] Indeed, Bernstein only received the commission for his *Chichester Psalms* in 1965 because Britten turned down this request from Hussey for a new work.[40] In addition to the *Chichester Psalms*, Hussey also commissioned several stained-glass windows by Marc Chagall for the festival.

Given its English destination, Bernstein chose to score *Chichester Psalms* for boy soprano (or countertenor), solo quartet, choir, and orchestra; Bernstein set the six psalm texts in Hebrew (sans English translation), relying on the tonal and rhythmic attributes of the Hebrew language. The Hebrew psalms are arranged by pairs in three movements, each movement containing one complete psalm and verses from another:

> Mvt. 1. Introduction: Ps 108:2/v. 3 in Hebrew (*Urah hánevel*); Ps 100 (*Hariu l'Adonai kol haarets*).
> Mvt. 2. Ps 23 (*Adonai roi lo ehsar*); Ps 2:1–4 (*Lamah rag'shu goyim*); Ps 23 continued.
> Mvt. 3. Ps 131 (*Adonai, Lo gavah libi*); Finale: Ps 133:1 (*Hineh mah tov*); Amen.

The work's formal cohesion is the result of Bernstein's decision to reprise the distinctive opening melody (*Urah, hánevel!*) in both the orchestral prelude and final chorale of the third movement (ex. 11.17a, b, c).

Example 11.17 a–c Bernstein, *Chichester Psalms*

Example 11.17 a–c Continued

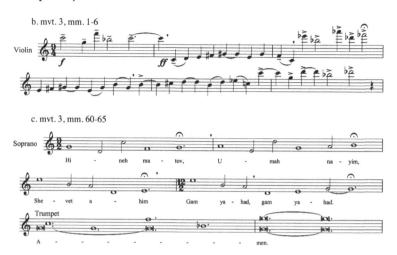

b. mvt. 3, mm. 1-6

c. mvt. 3, mm. 60-65

The music is typical Bernstein—bold, theatrical rhythms driven by a substantial amount of indispensable percussion and the lush, lyric melodicism of a Broadway musical. Although the work was commissioned for an English Cathedral choir, the first performance took place on July 15, 1965, with Bernstein conducting the New York Philharmonic. On July 31, the British premiere took place in Chichester Cathedral, with cathedral organist John Birch conducting the combined festival choirs and orchestra. This work proved so popular that Bernstein also crafted a version scored for organ, harp, and one percussionist; it has been the author's experience, however, that even this version needs as many percussionists as one can muster for the vigorous rhythmic texture.

Best known for his choral arrangements of Copland's *Old American Songs*, Irving Fine was a talented composer in his own right, creating such distinctive works as the *Three Choral Settings from Alice in Wonderland* (1942), *The Choral New Yorker* (1944), and *The Hour Glass Suite* (1949), all of which are still periodically performed.[41] George Rochberg's only significant contribution to choral music is his setting of three psalms (Pss 23, 43, and 150). Like Bernstein, Rochberg uses Hebrew texts, but his learned, serialistic style has proven less enduring than Bernstein's unabashed lyricism.[42]

A highly prolific American composer, Alan Hovhaness produced fifty-three works for chorus and instrumental ensemble and another nineteen *a cappella* works. Choral works actually assigned opus numbers by Hovhaness range from as early as op. 4 (*Missa Brevis*, 1935) to op. 433 (*How Lovely Are Thy Dwellings*, n.d.). His first stylistic influence was the church music of his native Armenia; later he absorbed the melodic and tonal structures of Indian, Finnish, and Asian music into his ever-changing sound palette. Although most of his works are instrumental (including sixty-seven symphonies), all are imbued with a mystical quality (e.g., the *Prayer of St. Gregory* for trumpet and strings, op. 62b).[43] His accompanied choral works range from the short and simple (e.g., *From the End of the Earth*, op. 187 [1951, rev. 1960]) to the large and complex (*Symphonia Sacra*, op. 389 [1985] scored for SATB, S and Bar. solos, flute, horn, trumpet, timpani, chimes, harp, and strings). In addition to a generally mystical quality, his choral music shows a particular fondness for modes and considerable contrapuntal expertise.

Like Hovhaness, Lou Harrison was obsessed with the search for new tonal resources, an endeavor nurtured by Henry Cowell and Charles Ives.[44] It was in Cowell's class on "Music of the Peoples of the World" at San Francisco State College in 1936 that Harrison first encountered non-Western music. In 1942 Harrison moved to Los Angeles to study with Arnold Schoenberg; never a devotee of Schoenberg's method, Harrison often recounted Schoenberg's advice: "'Thin out! Less. Thin. Thinner. Less and only the essentials!'"[45]

Harrison moved to New York in 1943, where he won the respect of Virgil Thomson, who hired him as assistant music critic at the *New York Herald Tribune*.[46] It was Thomson who gave Harrison a copy of *Genesis of a Music* (1947) by Harry Partch (1901–74), a self-taught composer and instrument inventor. Inspired by Partch's microtonal approach, Harrison began to explore composition based on just intonation, which differs from the standard equal temperament by preserving whole-number ratios between frequencies (in fourths, fifths, and octaves), which in turn creates unequal scale steps.[47] As a result of such tuning, a trip through the circle of perfect fifths would not bring one back to the same C on which one began. In other words, the purity of intonation undermines the artificial equality that underlies music composed in the Common Practice Period. Harrison discusses the essence of his approach to composition in his own book *Music Primer* (1971):

1. Compose rhythm and Tune—these are the important things. The Song and Dance conjoin at cadences and bow the form.
2. Melodicles [Harrison's word] are your life. The tune begins in tiny ways, and grows almost organically, cell within each other cell.
3. Know and use your numbers. Ratios are your analogues and aids. The interval is just or not at all, and the rhythm true.
4. Make Form.
5. Do not forget to grace your melody. Study grace as such.[48]

Harrison's most representative choral work is *La Koro Sutro*, composed in 1972 for the International Congress of Esperantists. David Brunner describes the work as "a large scale setting of the *Heart Sutra*, in seven *paragrafos* (movements) with prelude and epilogue."[49] Harrison scored the work for SATB, reed organ, harp, gamelan, and a wide range of traditional and Eastern percussion instruments. The gamelan Harrison prescribes is an American hybrid, tuned in just intonation to D to allow the blending of Eastern and Western elements. Although Harrison called for a chorus of one hundred singers, the simple choral writing uses lucid unison passages; what polyphony there is stems from an organum-like doubling of the principal melodic line.

VINCENT PERSICHETTI

Another important composer born in the century's second decade is Vincent Persichetti (1915–87), who received his initial musical education and practical experience as a church organist in his hometown of Philadelphia. On completing his degree at the Curtis Institute of Music there, he joined the compositional faculty where he remained until he was asked to join the faculty of the Juilliard School of Music in 1947. Persichetti's style is characterized by sparse counterpoint, distinctive rhythms, and nontonal harmony, which despite considerable chromatic inflection, exhibits a discernible tonal center. Persichetti's extensive choral output includes both sacred and secular works. He was particularly fascinated with the poetry of e. e. cummings, as is evident in the numerous works that use this distinctive poetry (opp. 33, 46, 94, 98, 103, 129, and 157). Another Persichetti fingerprint is a fondness for two-part choral writing, which permits multiple performance combinations. These pieces frequently involve the piano, less as accompaniment than as equal partner in the presentation of thematic material. His choral and piano writing are equally idiomatic—spare, rhythmic, and eschewing the thick textures used by earlier composers in favor of a consistently lean, essentials-only texture that defines the musical style of the 1950s (ex. 11.18).

Example 11.18 Persichetti, *dominic has a doll*, op. 98, no.1, mm. 25–32

The piano alternately punctuates and fills out the choral texture, often presenting material that the chorus will ultimately sing. This same array of techniques is present in all of Persichetti's settings of texts by cummings, indicating a close stylistic connection between the poetry and Persichetti's music.

Persichetti's *Mass*, op. 84 (1960), for mixed chorus, offers a different stylistic perspective. Here, he abandons the percussive rhythms of the piano in favor of an *a cappella* chorus singing a chant-like theme to open the Kyrie (ex. 11.19).

Example 11.19 Persichetti, *Mass*, op. 84, Kyrie, mm. 1–6

Similar melodies appear throughout the work, sometimes metered (as in the imitative opening of the Gloria), sometimes in the a-metric (no particular metric organization) style of the Kyrie and Credo. The absence of percussive rhythms and harmonic cues of the piano prompt a more contrapuntal approach and carefully planned harmonic connections. Even so, the two-part writing found in the cummings settings is still evident, notably in the conclusion of the Credo (mm. 121–28).

Among other works by Persichetti are several seasonal cantatas for women's voices: *Spring Cantata*, op. 94 (1964); *Winter Cantata*, op. 97, with flute and marimba (1964); two cantatas with texts by Whitman, *Celebrations*, op. 103 (1966), for mixed voices and winds, and *The Pleiades*, op. 107 (1967), with trumpet and strings; and *Flower Songs*, op. 157 (1983), in which he again turns to the poetry of e. e. cummings.

DANIEL PINKHAM

Another protégé of Nadia Boulanger, Daniel Pinkham (1923–2006) also studied with Walter Piston and Aaron Copland at Harvard and with Paul Hindemith, Arthur Honegger, and Samuel Barber at Tanglewood. Pinkham taught at various colleges and universities before becoming a fixture at the New England Conservatory in the Department of Musicology and music director at King's Chapel in Boston. Well grounded in keyboard (harpsichord, organ) and choral conducting (named composer of the year in 1990 by the American Guild of Organists and in 1996 the recipient of the Alfred Nash Patterson Foundation Lifetime Achievement Award for contributions to the choral arts), Pinkham's vast output spans symphonies, concertos, chamber music, cantatas, SATB anthems, organ sonatas, and other significant additions to the repertoire. Although he produced cantatas for all the major festivals of the church year, the *Christmas Cantata* (1957) is likely his most popular work. This three-movement cantata features exciting and idiomatic brass writing, vital declamatory settings of the Latin texts, and styles ranging from the jazziness of the first movement to a mystical style to conjure the atmosphere of the *O magnum mysterium* movement. Of his nearly seventy extended choral works with some kind of accompaniment, the *Christmas Cantata* is his most oft-performed work.

The *Easter Cantata* features brass and a large battery of percussion, while the *Wedding Cantata*, originally conceived for keyboard, exists in a later version scored for two horns, celesta, and strings. Here, Pinkham's settings of texts from the Song of Solomon include a canonic setting of "Many waters cannot quench love," the rollicking chorus "Awake, O North Wind," and the expressive "Set me as a seal" with which the cantata closes. Three compositions from the early to mid 1970s (*To Troubled Friends*, *Daniel in the Lions' Den*, and *Fanfares*) represent the short-lived popularity of pieces accompanied by synthesized music on electromagnetic tape.[50]

Pinkham's *Songs of Peaceful Departure* deserve mention because of the relative scarcity of choral works with acoustic guitar accompaniment. This set of pieces, commissioned by Leonard Van Camp and the Concert Chorale of the University of Southern Illinois at Edwardsville, reveal a populist component of Pinkham's compositional style. The three epigrammatic movements ("All Flesh Is Grass," "Lord, Make Me to Know Mine End," and "Lord, Thou Hast Put Gladness in My Heart") show that saying something harmonically rich and musically accessible is possible even with stringent economy of means and duration.

The generation of composers born in the 1920s includes Lukas Foss (1922–2009), Ned Rorem (b. 1923), Kirke Mechem (b. 1925), and Dominick Argento (b. 1927). All have written significant quantities of well-crafted choral music. Foss emigrated from Germany to the

United States in 1937 and enrolled at the Curtis Institute of Music in Philadelphia; he also studied during the summers with Serge Koussevitzky at Tanglewood (1939–43) and with Paul Hindemith at Yale from 1939 to 1940. Foss's appointment as Schoenberg's successor as head of the composition department at the University of California, Los Angeles in 1953 was a major career event. Foss also served as the music director of three important American orchestras—the Buffalo Symphony (1963–70), Milwaukee Orchestra (1981–86), and the Brooklyn Philharmonic (1971–90). Chorally, he is known primarily for two cantatas: his setting of texts by Carl Sandburg in *The Prairie* (1941), and the later *American Cantata* (1976) in which Foss sets his own poetry with additional verses by Arieh Sachs. *The Prairie* is a work of the composer's youth, completed when he was nineteen and premiered three years later by the Collegiate Chorale conducted by Robert Shaw. This work bears the indelible imprint of Hindemith in its use of spare, rhythmic counterpoint, frequent metric changes, and a process-driven melodic design. The following brief excerpt from *The Prairie* could easily be mistaken for a composition by Hindemith (ex. 11.20).[51]

Example 11.20 Foss, *The Prairie*, mvt. 7, mm. 36–42

Although *The Prairie* (1943) is more modernistic, his *American Cantata* (1976) is notably dependent on so-called "found" music and texts. In his preface to this work, Foss notes that all texts are quotations and that there are numerous musical quotations as well, including seven folk songs in mvt. 4 (a Scherzo titled "Money").[52] Modernist elements include a limited use of aleatoricism, electric guitars, and an eclectic array of textures and timbres. If *The Prairie* is reminiscent of Hindemith, the blend of musical jargons in *American Cantata* recalls Bernstein in its use of spirituals, folk tunes, and rock 'n' roll. Foss's cantata for chorus and organ (1950) *Behold, I Build an House!* combines a virtuoso piano/organ part with exuberant choral polyphony. Foss quoted in the *New York Times* in 1997 this take on his music from the 1980s: "The whole point now is that I can be just as crazy tonally as I was before atonally. Crazy in the sense of unexpected."[53]

NED ROREM

Born in Richmond, Indiana, Ned Rorem matriculated at Northwestern University in 1940. Two years later, the offer of a scholarship took him to the Curtis Institute in Philadelphia, where he studied for only one year. In 1943, he moved to New York to become Virgil Thomson's secretary and typist, absorbing much from this literate American music critic and composer. He eventually received both baccalaureate and MA degrees from the Juilliard School. In 1949, Rorem moved to Paris to study with Arthur Honegger, where he resided until 1958. In Paris, Rorem gained access to the circle of artists that included Poulenc, Cocteau, and Auric. The influence of Thomson and the French avant-garde informed Rorem's own artistic process and led to a chronicling of the contemporary scene, which is startlingly candid—even cutting—yet urbane and witty. In addition to his primary legacy of more than four hundred songs, Rorem has composed a surprisingly large amount of diatonic, accessible choral music. Some of these compositions are for *a cappella* chorus and include *From an Unknown Past* (1951) and *Missa Brevis* (1973), but the majority require orchestral accompaniment (as is the case in *Little Prayers* (1973), *An American Oratorio* (1983), and *Swords and Ploughshares* (1990).

Rorem's songs and choral cycles reveal a flair for finding interesting poems and creating settings that reveal more than the words themselves. Three of his larger works—*The Poet's Requiem* (1954–55), *An American Oratorio*, and *A Whitman Cantata* (both 1983)—illustrate this particular talent. In the foreword to *An American Oratorio*, Rorem speaks openly about his process: "A fair share of the craft—or the art, if you prefer—of making a song lies in pre-musical choices. Where will I find the poem? Does it really need to be set? The composer's chief question is not 'From whence sonic notions?' . . . but 'From whence the texts?' "[54]

Commissioned by Robert Page and the Mendelssohn Choir of Pittsburgh, *An American Oratorio* consists of "twelve movements based on texts by eight nineteenth-century American authors." Concerning his choice of authors, Rorem admits his choice of nineteenth-century American poetry was a way of psychically withdrawing from contemporary politics in the 1980s. Although Rorem calls this work an oratorio, none of the historical traits associated with this genre are evident. The music is alternately contemporary (but in a 1950-ish way) and lyrical, some of the better choral writing appearing in contemplative movements like "War is kind." An overall formal scheme is evident in the musical continuity of the last three movements and the three successive settings of poetry by Stephen Crane (mvts. 7–9). The work opens with a homophonic choral hymn, the text of which includes the well-known quote from Emma Lazarus's "The New Colossus" inscribed on the base of the Statue of Liberty:

> "Keep ancient lands, your storied pomp!" cries she
> With silent lips. "Give me your tired, your poor,
> Your huddled masses yearning to breathe free,
> The wretched refuse of your teeming shore,
> Send these, the homeless, tempest-tost to me,
> I lift my lamp beside the golden door!"[55]

Rorem also produced a quantity of church music. For anyone who has read his prose diaries, such religious devotion may come as something of a surprise. Obviously liturgical works such as the *Prayers and Responses for Chorus* (1969), two sets of Canticles (1971, 1972), *Seven Motets for the Church Year* (1986), and *Three Hymn Anthems* (1955) all reveal close ties to the composer's Anglican bent. A particularly grateful and accessible composition is *Sing My Soul His Wondrous Love* (1955), in which Rorem's lovely melody is surrounded in each statement with just enough harmonic variety to keep the singers alert and interested.

AFRICAN AMERICAN SPIRITUALS

What was once referred to as the "Negro spiritual" has morphed into one of the most recognizable of American choral genres. Along with jazz and what Roy Harris termed "autogenetic" music, the spiritual grew from African-influenced rhythms and melodies into songs of community, faith, and coded defiance. Originally monophonic work songs to ease the tedium and grinding labor, the call-and-response (or lining) format of these songs incorporated biblical themes, especially those from Exodus, and often contained hidden messages. For example, the words in "Swing Low, Sweet Chariot," Wade in the Water," and "The Gospel Train" held instructions to runaway slaves that the coast was clear; "Follow the Drinking Gourd" (referring to the Big Dipper) was a coded map whose lyrics describe how to transit the Underground Railroad.[56]

> The spirituals are a library of sorts. By studying them, it is possible to gain a wealth of information and insight into the historical, social, and religious development of African slaves and their descendants who have journeyed within the United States over the decades and centuries. Negro spirituals have had their home in cotton fields, work camps, churches, meeting rooms, and recital halls. They contributed to the birth of various types of popular music such as gospel, jazz, and blues, to the financial support of Black colleges and other institutions, to the folklore of social struggles including the civil rights movement, and to the uplift of outstanding African American musicians and singers worldwide. The opera community is historically linked to the promotion of such artists. Clearly, what gives Negro spiritual songs their power is the way in which they invite the human voice to add contour, rhythm, texture, melody, tempo, variation, and emotional depth to words. The African American experience resonates within and all through them. They have been preserved over time, and developed/redeveloped both in a distinctive choral form and in a characteristic style arranged for performance by the non-amplified solo voice with piano accompaniment.[57]

Encouraged to sing by plantation-owners who grew nervous if their slaves were quiet, the spiritual, firmly grounded in Old and New Testament texts, gained a foothold in African American homes and churches. The songs of slavery first met the public in concerts given by the Fisk Jubilee Singers from Fisk University in Nashville. Fisk, incorporated in 1867, was the first university to offer a liberal arts curriculum to African Americans. Their pioneering efforts were continued in choirs conducted by such iconic composer/arrangers as Harry T. Burleigh (1866–1949), R. Nathaniel Dett (1882–1943), Hall Johnson (1888–1970), William L. Dawson (1899–1990), John Wesley Work III (1901–67), and Leonard De Paur (1915–98).[58] In recent years concert audiences have delighted in the proliferation of this music beyond African American choirs, due to the efforts of such music educators, conductors, and composers as Jester Hairston (1901–2000), Albert J. McNeil (b. 1924), Lena McLin (b. 1928), Brazeal Dennard (1929–2010), Wendell Whalum (1931–87), André Thomas (b. 1952), and Moses Hogan (1957–2003). Each in his or her own way has made this remarkable music available to choirs of all ages, genders, and races. Of these, the most important and best-known is undoubtedly Moses Hogan, whose masterful arrangements live on, in large part due to his editorship of the *Oxford Book of Spirituals* (Oxford University Press, 2002). The newest generation of African American arrangers includes David Morrow (b. 1959), Stacey V. Gibbs (b. 1962), Rollo Dilworth (b. 1970), Jeffrey L. Ames (b. 1969), and Victor C. Johnson (b. 1978). What began as a unique artistic reaction of a disenfranchised people to discrimination and abuse has grown into a considerably significant musical genre and one that is uniquely American. There has also been a tendency to view the spiritual as a bang-up ending of a concert or as an encore, but this agenda needs some serious rethinking lest it lend impetus to the notion that the spiritual is one-dimensional music appropriated to insure a standing ovation.

One extremely talented African American composer, Adolphus Hailstork (b. 1941), who expressly downplays his role as an "arranger of spirituals," a position that goes against tradition. He has arranged some spirituals for choir, but his compositional output is comprehensive, including works for symphony orchestra, band, chamber ensemble, keyboard, opera, solo song, and choral music not derived from spirituals. His larger works for chorus and orchestra include the cantata *I Will Lift up Mine Eyes* (1989), *Serenade* ("To Hearts which Near Each Other Move," 2001), *Songs of Innocence* (2000), and *Whitman's Journey* (2005). All of these compositions transcend the implicit restrictions of being regarded as merely an arranger of spirituals.

AMERICANISM

A substantial number of choral composers have made significant contributions that are often based on market-driven niches. A comprehensive list is impossible to include here because of the proliferation of composers, publishing houses, and availability of scores both in print and online. However, Nick Strimple's *Choral Music in the Twentieth Century* (Milwaukee, WI: Amadeus Press, 2005) contributes some very useful categories (e.g., the Education Market, the Church Market, Jewish Composers) to which I would add yet an additional category, the Children's Choir. The virtue of these categories is that they allow large numbers of composers to be grouped according to their primary areas of compositional contribution.[59]

Of Morten Lauridsen (b. 1943), Strimple states that his choral music has "eclipsed Randall Thompson as the most frequently performed American choral composer." Lauridsen's use of close, clustered harmonies, counterpoint (especially in the *Madrigali* and *Chansons des Roses*) and sense of mystical serenity have brought his works to the forefront of those twenty-first-century American composers whose music has become popular. The wide appeal and spiritual tonalities have rightly placed many of his works (the quasi-requiem *Lux Aeterna*, *O Magnum Mysterium* and *Three Nocturnes*) at the top of "popular classical" choral music charts. Donald Grantham (b. 1947, *Five Emily Dickinson Songs*), Gwyneth Walker (b. 1947), Stephen Paulus (1949–2014, *Pilgrim's Hymn, The Old Church*), and Eric Whitacre (b. 1970, *Water Night, Cloudburst, little tree, Sleep, Leonardo Dreams of His Flying Machine*) are all important among the growing list of contemporary choral composers, many of whose works are choral octavos, but in some cases (e.g., many of the Lauridsen compositions) individual pieces are available both separately and as parts of larger sets.

To this far from comprehensive list, we need to mention three composers, all born in 1938: John Harbison, William Bolcom (*Songs of Innocence* and *The Mask*), and John Corigliano (*Fern Hill*). Harbison is currently the Active Artistic Director for Emmanuel Music in Boston and holds the position of Institute Professor, the highest academic distinction for resident faculty at MIT. His choral works include twenty-two *a cappella* pieces and thirteen works with orchestra/ensemble. The most famous of these are *The Flight into Egypt: Sacred Ricercar* (1986), for which he was awarded a Pulitzer Prize in 1987, and the movement he contributed to the *Requiem of Reconciliation* (1995), "Juste judex" (SATB chorus, alto and bass soli, chamber orchestra). His most recent work is the cantata *The Supper at Emmaus* (2013), scored for SATB chorus and soloists, and chamber orchestra; the premiere took place May 10, 2014, at the New England Conservatory of Music in Boston.[60] William Bolcom, a student of Darius Milhaud at Mills College and later Milhaud and Messiaen at the Paris Conservatoire, enjoyed a long and celebrated tenure at the University of Michigan from 1973 to 2008). His latest works include *Four Piedmont Choruses* (SATB chorus, piano, 2007); *Lady Liberty* (SATB chorus, piano, 2008) and *A*

Song for St. Cecilia's Day (SATB/organ, 2008). Bolcom's dramatic atonality coupled with what he described as a breakdown of distinctions between popular and serious music are evident in all of his works. John Corigliano, a protégé of Samuel Barber, now teaches at the Juilliard School of Music; His many awards include the first composer-in-residence at the Chicago Symphony Orchestra (1987), the Grawemeyer Award for Music Composition (University of Louisville, 1991), and two Grammy Awards for Best Classical Contemporary Composition (1992, 1995), in addition to a Pulitzer Prize (2001). His oratorio *A Dylan Thomas Trilogy* (SATB chorus/soloists, orchestra, 1979/1999), *Salute for Chorus (with kazoos)* (SATB chorus, brass, and percussion 2005), and *Psalm 8* (SATB chorus with organ, 1976), illustrate Corigliano's innovative and theatrical stylistic maneuvers; he employs a wide range of unique musical ideas and materials, all of which are often more harmonically complex than not. In terms modern performance, his most popular work remains the cantata-length setting of Dylan Thomas's poem *Fern Hill* (1960) for chorus and chamber orchestra.

A new group of younger composers, generally classified as postmodernists, includes David Lang (b. 1957) and Ted Hearne (b. 1982). Currently chair of the composition department at Yale, Lang won a Pulitzer Prize in 2008 for his *Little Match Girl Passion* (2007). The work retells the Hans Christian Andersen tale as seen through the lens of Bach's *St. Matthew Passion*. It exists in a version for solo voices and chorus with percussion. The music is almost unbearably spare and, for that reason, quite intense; but for anyone who treasures the Bach *Passions*, the lack of emotion and narrative contrast may be off-putting. It is difficult to imagine a traditional mixed chorus being able to achieve the clarity and precision needed for this work to be successful. There is a litany-like quality to the narrative sections of this work, and this fingerprint also appears in other of Lang's choral works (especially *for love is strong* [2007], his setting of a concatenation of texts from the Song of Songs). His most intriguing and successful work is *again (after ecclesiastes)*, written for Kristina Boerger and the Cerddorion Vocal Ensemble (2005). Ted Hearne, a native of Chicago, is currently a faculty member at the University of Southern California. In some ways, he, like Lang, is historically influenced, although his range of styles is wider and less predictable. A work like *Partition* (composed for Jeffrey Douma and the Yale Glee Club in honor of their 150th anniversary, 2010) presents an array of different musical styles and texts, which might have been unthinkable in the not-so-distant past. In this piece, there is a mix of Edward Said's poetry to long lists of street names and businesses encountered within a one-mile route in New Haven. Both Lang and Hearne question to what extent their music is practical for contemporary, non-specialist choirs. Only with time will we be able to tell whether they become defining choral works of the early twenty-first century.

CONCLUSION

The contemporary American choral experience is certainly one of plenty and pluralism, reflected in the arrangements of traditional songs for every imaginable voicing or age group. In this chapter, some composers are either omitted or not discussed in any detail despite their being fairly prolific. The nature of history requires such winnowing and filtering of repertory to separate what is genuinely important and innovative from the enormous quantity of music whose importance is extremely localized either geographically or stylistically.

Our untrammeled access to literally anything from any time, place, or culture should not be confused with what future readers will hopefully recognize as the landmark choral works of this era. That canon already includes the choral music of Ives, Bernstein, Persichetti,

Thompson, Pinkham, Rorem, and the like. There are indeed quite a few contemporary composers whose music is so often heard at choral concerts today—whether performed during professional music conventions, all-state honor choirs conducted by the current stars of the profession, choral competitions held at theme parks across the country, reading sessions sponsored by music publishers, seasonal concerts held at local colleges, community colleges, high schools, and middle schools, or worship services at local churches or synagogues. The issue here is not availability of new works but rather their quality as defined by contemporary audiences. What will insure the future of choral music is, again, not the amount of music that is published or performed but what that body of music has to say about what we value culturally and aesthetically. And this explains the great disparity between the total amount of music composed during any historical period and what becomes a necessary part of the process of choral music history.

12

The British Isles

While choral music was an integral part of nineteenth-century British musical life, the relatively negative Continental estimation of Victorian music cried out for a new beginning to escape from the belief that England was *Das Land ohne Musik*, "the land without music."[1] The concept of such a revitalization first surfaced in Frank Howes's book *The English Musical Renaissance*.[2] In the vacuum created by the death of Felix Mendelssohn in 1847, England's musical establishment responded by seeking other Continental composers/conductors to fill the void, most notably Charles Gounod.[3] Howes declared that the revival of English music was instigated by C. Hubert H. Parry (1848–1918) and brought to fruition by Charles V. Stanford (1852–1924), Edward Elgar (1857–1934), a group of late Romantics headed by Frederick Delius (1862–1934), and the pioneering work of Ralph Vaughan Williams (1872–1958) and Gustav Holst (1874–1934) (see chap. 7). Hugh Wood, for example, questions the validity of this assessment: "In spite of Dunstable, in spite of Purcell, Handel, Elgar, nobody can get it into their heads that *Das Land ohne Musik* was only a slogan invented around 1917 by a German professor as a piece of war propaganda."[4]

But in the 1880s, a new musical messiah was not easy to identify. Ironically, the composers whose music enjoyed the greatest popular success (most notably Sir Arthur Sullivan [1842–1900]) did not conform to the ideals espoused by the founders of the so-called English Musical Renaissance, primarily George Grove (1820–1900) and J. A. Fuller-Maitland (1856–1936).[5] The composers most able to effect that renascence—Delius, Elgar, Stanford, and Frank Bridge (1879–1941)—all shared a grounding in and appreciation of contemporary continental (i.e., Germanic) compositional technique, which allowed them to transcend the notion of all English music as pastoral and pretty.

THE ENGLISH MUSICAL RENAISSANCE

Table 12.1 List of representative twentieth- and twenty-first century British choral music composers

Charles Villiers Stanford (1852–1924)	Bernard Rands (b. 1934)
Herbert Howells (1892–1983)	Jonathan Harvey (1939–2012)
Gerald Finzi (1901–56)	John Tavener (1944–2013)
Edmund Rubbra (1901–86)	John Rutter (b. 1945)
William Walton (1902–83)	Giles Swayne (b. 1946)
Lennox Berkeley (1903–89)	Paul Patterson (b. 1947)
Michael Tippett (1905–98)	Judith Weir (b. 1954)
Elisabeth Lutyens (1906–83)	Bob Chilcott (b. 1955)
Elizabeth Maconchy (1907–94)	Jonathan Dove (b. 1959)
Benjamin Britten (1913–76)	James MacMillan (b. 1959)
Thea Musgrave (b. 1928)	Gabriel Jackson (b. 1962)
Alun Hoddinott (1929–2008)	Thomas Adès (b. 1971)
Kenneth Leighton (1929–88)	Paul Mealor (b. 1975)
Peter Maxwell Davies (1934–2016)	Tarik O'Regan (b. 1978)
Harrison Birtwistle (b. 1934)	
William Mathias (1934–92)	

FREDERICK DELIUS

British born to German immigrant parents and a longtime resident of France and Norway, Delius hardly seems ideally suited to revitalize English composition. At least initially, Delius's large body of choral music was dominated by two works with a Germanic bias, *Sea Drift* (1903–4) and *A Mass of Life* (1904–5). *Sea Drift* reflects the early twentieth-century English fascination with Walt Whitman; it received its premiere in Germany, as did *A Mass of Life* (1906), which draws its text from the writings of Friedrich Nietzsche (1844–1900). In the second and third decades of the century Delius's music began to take on a more typically English flavor. He was championed by Sir Thomas Beecham (1879–1961), who conducted the English premiere of *A Mass of Life* in London (1909) and included several of Delius's orchestral works on his well-attended public concerts. In the 1920s Delius created such visionary *a cappella* choral works as "To be sung of a summer night on the water" (1917) and "The splendour falls on castle walls" (1923, Tennyson). Both were written for and premiered by C. K. Scott and the Oriana Madrigal Society; performance by this ensemble and less rigorous sonorities helped bolster Delius's choral reputation despite the lack of enthusiasm generated by his Requiem (soprano, baritone, double chorus, and orchestra) of 1913–16. Chromatic lyricism and memorable melodies are emblematic of such orchestral pieces as *On Hearing the First Cuckoo in Spring*, *North Country Sketches*, and *Brigg Fair: An English Rhapsody*. Unfortunately, for all of his innovation, Delius's works tend to sound alike.

Edward Elgar's oratorios and part songs have been discussed in chapters 1 and 2, respectively. His most demonstrably English choral work, the dramatic cantata *Caractacus*, op. 35 (1898), retells the defeat of the presumed first English king by the Romans in 51 CE For his cantata, Elgar relied on a libretto by H. A. Ackworth, which emphasized the magnanimity of the English warrior even in defeat, a celebration of the Victorian notion of the "Pax Brittanica."[6] Elgar's Germanic inclinations were furthered by the fact that his agent with Novello, A. J. Jaeger (1860–1909), was a German émigré.[7]

Charles Villiers Stanford is often referred to as "the English Brahms." According to an unattributed article in the *Musical Times* of 1898, Stanford actually met Brahms at the Schumann Festival in Bonn in the autumn of 1873 and Brahms "became his idol."[8] Stanford later studied with Carl Reinecke in Leipzig (1875–76) and Friedrich Kiel in Berlin (1877). Hans von Bülow's performances of Stanford's early opera, *Savonarola* and the Symphony No. 1 in F major (the "Irish" symphony) were better received in Germany than in England.[9] Indeed, Stanford's instrumental compositions are the truer measure of his indebtedness to Brahms. His most important choral works include the *Three Motets*, op. 38 (1905), and the Anglican Services in A (1880), F (1889), and C (1909), which are, according to Nicholas Temperley, outstanding examples of the genre.[10] But Stanford's most important legacy is the impressive list of composers who studied with him at the Royal College of Music: Arthur Bliss, Gustav Holst, Herbert Howells, John Ireland, Ralph Vaughan Williams, and Frank Bridge.[11]

Frank Bridge wrote a mere handful of choral works, all of which, save *A Prayer* (1916), are pieces rarely heard today.[12] His greatest significance is that he was Benjamin Britten's first and foremost composition teacher, a pivotal relationship that began in 1927 and continued in various ways until Bridge's death in 1941.[13] It may well have been Frank Bridge who was responsible for Britten's awareness of and wish to study with Alban Berg.[14] Britten's *Phantasy Quartet*, op. 2 (1932), for oboe and strings owes more than its title to Bridge's *Phantasy Quartet* (1905). Between the wars, Bridge was "the only senior figure who had faced up to the most advanced continental developments and proved that an English composer of integrity could emerge from the experience not only unscathed, but immeasurably enriched."[15] He communicated this fascination with technique to his most famous pupil.

Given the number of well-known twentieth-century English choral composers listed in Table 12.1, this chapter will first focus on four acknowledged masters: Herbert Howells, Benjamin Britten, William Walton, and Michael Tippett; following these, we turn to representative composers born in each of the following decades: Kenneth Leighton, Peter Maxwell Davies, John Tavener, and James MacMillan.

HERBERT HOWELLS

Herbert Howells entered the Royal College of Music in 1912, studying composition with Charles Villiers Stanford and counterpoint with Charles Wood. For a time, he assisted Richard R. Terry (director of music at Westminster Cathedral, the mother church of Roman Catholics in England and Wales, from 1921–44) with transcribing and editing Tudor music manuscripts, an activity that led to a teaching position for Howells at the RCM. Howells remained on that faculty for most of his life. The tragic death of his young son, Michael, in 1935 prompted his composition of a Requiem for *a cappella* chorus, which lay neglected until its publication in 1980. In the meantime, this work became the substrate of another, larger work, the *Hymnus Paradisi* (1938); Howells also withheld this work until Vaughan Williams and others persuaded him to allow its performance as part of Three Choirs Festival in 1950. The work's successful premiere provided Howells entrée to the choral festival circuit, resulting in such choral-orchestral works as the *Missa Sabrinensis* (1954) and *Stabat Mater* (1963–65).

Table 12.2 Howells, *Requiem* and *Hymnus Paradisi*, textual comparison

Requiem	*Hymnus Paradisi*
1. "Salvator mundi" ("O Saviour of the World")	1. "Preludio"
2. "Psalm 23"	2. "Requiem aeternam"
3. "Requiem aeternam I"	3. "The Lord is my shepherd" (Ps. 23)
4. "Psalm 121"	4. *Sanctus:* "I will lift up mine eyes"
5. "Requiem aeternam II"	5. "I heard a voice from heaven"
6. "I heard a voice from heaven"	6. "Holy is the true light"

Publication of the *Requiem* in 1980 not only added another composition to Howells's catalogue, but also revealed the derivative nature of *Hymnus Paradisi* (see Table 12.2).

The most obvious difference between the two works is Howells's replacement of the *Requiem*'s first movement ("Salvator mundi") with an orchestral prelude based on themes drawn from the second and third movements of the *Requiem*. While both settings of Psalm 23 are melodically similar, the *Hymnus Paradisi* version is extended by the addition of soprano and tenor solos. The clearest example of auto-parody is Howells's setting of the text "Yea, though I walk through the valley of the shadow of death, I will fear no evil." He retains the *Requiem*'s unison melody intact (ex. 12.1a) as the soprano and tenor parts of *Hymnus Paradisi* to which he adds new alto/bass counterpoint and orchestral accompaniment (ex. 12.1b).

Example 12.1a Howells, *Requiem*, mvt. 2, mm. 9–11

Example 12.1b Howells, *Hymnus Paradisi*, mvt. 3, mm. 34–41

The second movement of *Hymnus Paradisi* melds the *Requiem*'s two settings of "Requiem aeternam" into an extended essay for soloists and orchestra. The first thirty-four measures are a literal restatement of the *Requiem*'s third movement (Choir 2); since in the *Requiem*, choir 1 doesn't sing until m. 13, Howells composed new material for it. Quotations from the *Requiem*'s fifth movement (Requiem aeternam II) focus on the words "et lux perpetua"; once again, the *Hymnus Paradisi* version is more expansive, concluding with a literal quotation of Requiem aeternam I's final melody.

The Sanctus "I will lift up mine eyes" of *Hymnus Paradisi* is entirely new. Howells's combination of the *Requiem*'s setting of Psalm 121 with the Sanctus allows him to unleash a broader palette of orchestral and soloistic music than would likely have been possible had these texts been set separately. The sparse orchestration Howells uses for the version of "I heard a voice from heaven" in *Hymnus Paradisi* leads to the closest correspondence between the two works. The final movement of *Hymnus Paradisi*, "Holy is the true light," sets a text from the Salisbury Diurnal (trans. G. H. Palmer) to music totally unrelated to the 1936 *Requiem*. It is somewhat ironic that, while the *Requiem* has become a popular, often performed work, the composition that superseded it remains a neglected masterpiece.

Howells's enduring legacy is the enormous body of music he composed for the Collegiate Churches of England, an activity that occupied him from the mid-1940s until his death.[16] Many of these anthems remain in the repertory of many cathedral choirs; these include the *Three Carol Anthems*—"A Spotless Rose" (1919), "Here Is the Little Door" (1918)—and "Sing Lullaby" (1918) and *Four Anthems*—"O Pray for the Peace of Jerusalem," "Like as the Hart," "Let God Arise," and "Great Is the Lord"—for choir and organ (1941). More demanding and rewarding is the setting of Prudentius's Latin hymn *Hymnus circa exequias defuncti* (translated by Helen Waddell as "Take him, earth, for cherishing"), which Howells composed in 1964 to commemorate the death of John F. Kennedy. But the real measure of Howells's greatness lies in the impressive series of canticles composed between 1944 and 1991 for major Anglican cathedrals in England.

Regarded by many as the epitome of the Anglican Cathedral tradition, Howells was hardly your average church music composer. Christopher Palmer attributes the primacy of his cathedral music not only to his love of Tudor church music (especially Tallis) but also to the inspiring grandeur of cathedral architecture: "Howells saw his spirituality—and realized his musicality—in terms of three As—Architecture, Acoustic, and Association. He was first moved by Gloucester, he said, to start attempting the 'nearly-impossible translation of the frozen poetry of Architecture into the living immemorial sounds of voices in consort.' "[17]

A tendency to begin the Magnificat with treble voices and the Nunc Dimittis with male voices may reflect the gender of the biblical singers of these canticles. Howells's first Evening Service, composed for King's College, Cambridge (*Collegium Regale*, 1944), remains his best known. Especially praiseworthy is the tenor solo that opens the Nunc Dimittis (ex. 12.2).

Example 12.2 Howells, *Collegium Regale*, Nunc Dimittis, mm. 1–15

The range of the tenor solo, its ambivalent use of both E♭ and E♮, and consistent use of Tudor-like clashes (false relations) between F♮ and F♯ (the leading tone of work's essentially G-minor tonality) affirm that, like Vaughan Williams in his *Mass in G minor*, Howells sees modality as a viable alternative to tonality. Howells subsequently abandons the use of flats to create the luminescent grandeur of the "light" that is to lighten the Gentiles.

BENJAMIN BRITTEN

The first composer to embody the goals of the English musical renaissance was Benjamin Britten. Musically precocious, he studied piano and viola, and created some one hundred compositions by the age of fourteen. He began formal composition lessons with Frank Bridge in 1927 and remained an advocate of Bridge's music even after the composer's death in 1941. From 1930 to 1933 Britten studied composition at the Royal College of Music with John Ireland and Ralph Vaughn Williams; but he developed a disdain for their music, finding greater inspiration in Bridge and such continental masters as Gustav Mahler and Alban Berg (1885–1935), neither of whom were highly esteemed in Britain. Of the composers of the Second Viennese School, it was Berg who most intrigued the young Britten, so much so that he wanted to go to Vienna to study with Berg, a proposal ultimately vetoed by his parents and the hierarchy of the Royal College of Music.[18] Instead, Britten took a job writing music for the General Post Office's Film Unit, an invaluable experience that taught him how to craft abstract music to order from spare and ordinary materials; this position also afforded him entrée to a group of liberal intellectuals led by W. H. Auden and Christopher Isherwood, an experience that forced him to confront questions of politics, personal values, and his own sexuality.

Britten's first published choral work, *A Hymn to the Virgin* (1930), for chorus and semi-chorus *a cappella* is the first of a series of works inspired by English medieval texts. The text (a macaronic, strophic hymn) is from the *Oxford Book of English Verse*, a book he received as a prize for musical accomplishment at Gresham School in the summer of 1930.[19] When Winthrop Rogers published the work in 1934, the text's medieval spellings were modernized (see Table 12.3).

The first choral work to which Britten assigned an opus number is the formidable, if seldom-heard, choral variations, *A Boy Was Born*, op. 3 (1933–34). Early on, Britten began to compile thematically-related poems to use in some future work. Some of these mini-anthologies came to nothing, like the eight poems he tentatively labeled "A Poet's Dream" (1928) or the series of poems projected as a "Sea Symphony"; evidence of these appears on a microfilm catalogued as A30 at the Britten-Pears Library in Aldeburgh. Whether some of these "little anthologies" became compositions (even compositions quite unrelated to his original plan), this practice of collection and saving various texts explains the eclectic textual collage used in op. 3 (see Table 12.4).

Table 12.3 Britten, *A Hymn to the Virgin*, textual comparison

Original Text	Published Text
Of on that is so fayr and bryght	*Of one that is so fair and bright*
Velut maris stella.	*Velut maris stella.*
Bryter than the day is light,	*Brighter than the day is light,*
Parens et puella	*Parens et puella:*
Ic crie to the, thou see to me,	*I cry to thee, thou see to me,*
Lev'dy preye thi sone for me	*Lady, pray thy Son for me,*
Tampia,	*Tampia,*
That ic mote cum to the, Maria.	*That I might come to thee, Maria.*

Table 12.4 Britten, *A Boy Was Born*, op. 3, texts

1. Theme: *A Boy was born*	*Oxford Book of Carols* (184–85)
2. Var. 1: *Lullay, Jesu*	*Ancient English Christmas Carols,* E. Rickert, 74–76 (vs.1, 2, 3, 7, 8)
3. Var. 2: *Herod*	E. Rickert, Anon.
4. Var. 3: *Jesu, as Thou art our Saviour*	Rickert, Anon., 176–77 (vv. 3–5)
5. Var. 4: *The Three Kings*	Rickert, 110, Anon. (vv. 3, 7, 8, 11)
6. Var. 5: *In the bleak mid-winter*	Christina G. Rossetti (Rickert, Appendix II, 293)
	Anon., Rickert, 193
7. Var. 6: *Noel!*	Anon., *Good day, good day* (Rickert, 219), Thomas Tusser (1558); Anon.; *Oxford Book of Carols* (364), Francis Quarles

The musical theme of this set of choral variations consists of the pitches D'–E'–G'E', which forms the pitch-class set [0,2,5]. Britten's prominent use of this motive starting on various pitches and inverted provides a reminder of Britten's familiarity with and admiration for the Second Viennese School technique (Schoenberg, Berg, and Webern) (ex. 12.3).

Example 12.3 Britten, *A Boy Was Born*, op. 3, mm. 1–14

Britten uses this cell to produce music that despite allusion to pentatonicism is markedly different from the major/minor modalism of Vaughan Williams. Unlike traditional sets of theme and variations, Britten introduces new material as the musical foreground for each new variation; the original theme lurks, *Leitmotiv*-like, as a subordinate presence. The contrapuntal craftmanship displayed here underscores what Christopher Mark and Peter Evans describe as a masterful economy of content and formal control. These techniques (in such instrumental works as the *Phantasy Quartet* of 1932) mark a major stylistic advance over Britten's earlier choral works.[20]

Infrequent performance of the work are attributable to its length, complexity, and vocal scoring (SSAATTBB, boy's chorus). Two SATB movements (the theme itself and Variation 3: *Jesu, as Thou art my Saviour*) were published separately precisely because of their relative accessibility. In the haunting setting of Christina Rosetti's well-known poem "In the Bleak Mid-winter" (Var. 5), the divisi women's voices sing a static, piquant setting of the poem, against which the boy trebles sing "Lully, lully, the falcon hath bourne my make away," an anonymous fifteenth-century poem. Such juxtaposition of different textual strata is, again, typical of Britten's music. Philip Rupprecht points out that "Timbral contrast between older and younger 'high' voices defines the opposition of speakers and linguistic registers—while the women paint a landscape without figures ['snow on snow'], the boys sing of a child borne away by a falcon."[21]

The two choral works for which Britten is best known—*Hymn to St. Cecilia* (op. 27) and *A Ceremony of Carols* (op. 28)—continue his penchant for blending ancient and modern texts with elements of ritual ("hymn" and "ceremony"). Both were composed during the composer's return to England aboard the container ship MS *Axel Johnson* in 1942, following a three-year residence in the United States (1939–42) that coincided with the beginning of World War II.[22]

The text of the *Hymn to St. Cecilia* consists of three poems that W. H. Auden wrote as a birthday present for Britten (born, rather auspiciously, on November 22, the feast day of St. Cecilia); the poems were first published in the December 1941 issue of *Harper's Bazaar*.[23] The text of the poem remains somewhat of an enigma, but it is clear that Auden's gift (a prodigious feat of rhyme, rhythm, and imagery) to Britten (whose persona he invokes throughout the poem) produces music of a rarefied, thoroughly personal aesthetic space.[24] The most conspicuous aspect of the composition's structure is a refrain, "Blessed Cecilia, appear in visions to all musicians, appear and inspire / Translated Daughter, come down and startle Composing mortals with immortal fire." Auden closes each of the three "hymns" with these words; Britten follows suit, setting each appearance to the same melody (ex. 12.4).

Example 12.4 Britten, *Hymn to St. Cecilia*, op. 27, refrain

Another recurring device is the ground bass, a technique closely associated with the first *Orpheus Brittanicus*, Henry Purcell, whom Britten regarded as his direct musical ancestor.[25] Ostinati appear in all three movements of the *Hymn*: the tenor/bass theme that opens the work, the alto/bass cantus firmus in mvt. 2, and, in its most Purcellian garb, the principal musical basis for the second half of the final movement (ex. 12.5a,b,c).

Example 12.5 a–c Britten, *Hymn to St. Cecilia*, op. 27

Example 12.5 a–c Continued

Britten's other compositional project on his return trip to England was the well-known *A Ceremony of Carols*. During a layover in Nova Scotia, Britten picked up a copy of the *English Galaxy of Shorter Poems*, from which he selected the texts of this work.[26] In his personal copy, he marked poems slated for inclusion in the cycle with a penciled X. To emphasize the work's ceremonial nature, Britten framed the composition with the Gregorian antiphon *Hodie Christus natus est* as a processional and recessional.[27] Perhaps the difficulties encountered in the premiere of *A Boy Was Born* still haunted him; this *Ceremony*, while textually similar, is far more accessible in its scoring (harp and treble voices) and harmonic language.[28]

The setting of Robert Southwell's poem "This little Babe" is outstanding for its ingenious canonic writing and vibrant harp rhythms. Britten sets the strophic text to a 3/4 melody that rhythmically emphasizes the second "beat." This motif appears successively in unison, in canon à 2, and then in a canon à 3: all three voices sing the melody at the same pitch in stretto at the quarter note. A final harmonized statement brings the movement to a splendid, hemiola-laced close (ex. 12.6).

Example 12.6 Britten, *A Ceremony of Carols*, op. 28, mvt. 6, mm. 36–44

Table 12.5 Britten, *Rejoice in the Lamb*, op. 30, mvt. 2, text

A 4–8	**OMITTED**
A9	Let Nimrod, the mighty hunter, bind a leopard to the altar and consecrate his spear to the Lord.
A10	Let Ishmael dedicate a Tyger, and give praise for the liberty in which the Lord has let him at large.
A11	Let Balaam appear with an Ass, and bless the Lord, his people, and his creatures for a reward eternal.
A12	**OMITTED**
A13	Let Daniel come forth with a Lion, and praise God with all his might through faith in Christ Jesus.
A14-17	**OMITTED**
A18	Let Ithamar minister with a Chamois, and bless the name of Him, which clotheth the naked.
A19-66	**OMITTED**
A67	Let Jakim with the Satyr bless God in the dance.
A41	Let David bless with the Bear—The beginning of victory to the Lord, to the Lord the perfection of excellence. Hallelujah from the heart of God, and from the hand of the artist inimitable, and from the echo of the heavenly harp in sweetness magnifical and mighty. [Hallelujah!]

The cantata *Rejoice in the Lamb*, op. 30, remains one of Britten's most enduring compositions. In 1943, Britten accepted the Reverend Walter Hussey's commission to write an anthem for soloists, choir, and organ to mark the fiftieth anniversary of St. Matthew's Church, Northampton. Britten enlisted the help of Sir Edward Sackville-West to create a libretto from the sprawling, seemingly inchoate poem, *Jubilate Agno* ("Rejoice in the Lamb"), by Christopher Smart (1722–71).[29] Although the resulting text reads as if it were a series of discrete poems, it is actually an artificial construct. Only the first three lines of the poem appear successively in both Britten's cantata and Smart's poem; Table 12.5 documents the omissions of the second movement.

The version of Smart's poem that Britten set is not continuous; all the lines in the second section ("Let Nimrod, the mighty hunter") conjoin the names of obscure Old Testament personalities with animals, the significance of which only Smart in his wisdom and/or madness knew; as a text, this is the product of choices made by Britten and Sir Edward Sackville-West.[30] The edited text often rearranges lines of a poem that is far too long to set in its entirety. The chosen lines do, however, suggest a polymetric scheme, prompting the hypothesis that the omitted lines did not allow for the regular alternation of asymmetric and symmetric meters, which are a major structural component of the chorus (ex. 12.7).

Example 12.7 Britten, *Rejoice in the Lamb*, op. 30, mm. 19–25

In this brief excerpt, Britten uses 7/8 (grouped as 2+2+3) for the first phrase, changing to 6/8 for "bind a Leopard to the altar." Britten expands this pairing of asymmetrical and symmetrical meters (underscored by dynamic shifts) throughout the movement, culminating in another Purcellian setting of "Hallelujah from the heart of God."

Three additional representative works deserve comment—*Saint Nicolas*, op. 42 (1948); the *War Requiem*, op. 66 (1961–62); and Britten's final choral opus, *Sacred and Profane*, op. 91 (1975). Like *Rejoice in the Lamb*, *Saint Nicolas* is a cantata, scored for tenor and treble soloists, mixed chorus (comprised of the combined choirs of three schools for boys), a treble chorus (located in the balcony), two pianos, strings, percussion, and organ. Britten composed the work to celebrate the centenary of Lancing College, Sussex, the public school that Peter Pears had attended. The text, created for Britten by the British librettist Eric Crozier, retells the life story of the original St. Nicolas, bishop of Myra. In Britten's hands, Crozier's text becomes nine movements that synopsize the saint's life. As Britten's first composition intended for amateur performers, *Saint Nicolas* anticipates aspects of the later, more well-known *Noye's Fludde* (op. 59, 1957–58). In both works, Britten strove for a simplicity that would make the work accessible to young singers, yet maintain a level of musical sophistication. The scoring of both works is similarly limited to instrumental and vocal forces that are readily available. As in *Noye's Fludde*, Britten includes the audience in the singing of familiar hymns at pivotal moments in the narrative. Appropriately, Nicolas's appointment as bishop concludes with the hymn "All people that on earth do dwell" (*Old Hundredth*) in true Anglican tradition. After Nicolas's death, the choir and congregation sing "God moves in a mysterious way" (*London New*) as a valedictory to his courage. Juxtaposed against this solemn hymnody is a jaunty march that accompanies the liturgical procession celebrating the rescue of three resurrected boys, who were about to be eaten by diners at a local inn ("Nicolas and the Pickled Boys," mvt. 7). What makes this movement so charming is its simplicity—the mixed choir sings in thirds (doubled by the strings) over a persistent FF♯–BB ostinato. These passages alternate with contrasting music for the girls chorus in 6/8 meter, their simple melody contrasting with the ostinato bass that stubbornly continues in the original tempo and meter (4/4). Britten transforms this simple textural template into a rondo-like form that is interrupted by the intervention of Saint Nicolas. The movement concludes with a serenely simple "alleluia" sung by all the vocal forces first separately, then together.

Noye's Fludde, based on the thirteenth- to fourteenth-century Chester miracle cycle, also uses congregational hymns to underscore high points in the narrative: "Lord Jesus, think on me" (Southwell) opens the opera; the well-known naval hymn "Eternal Father, strong to save" (Melita) is heard during the great storm that precedes the flood; at the sign of the rainbow the choir sings "Lord we thanke thee through thy mighte" followed by the concluding number in which choir and congregation join in "The spacious firmament on high" (sung to the well-known tune Tallis canon).

Britten's War Requiem is a landmark of twentieth-century music. During World War II, the British city of Coventry was heavily bombed, resulting in the near total destruction of its cathedral (Fig. 12.1). To celebrate the completion and consecration of the new cathedral, the city commissioned Britten to compose a large work for soloists, chorus and orchestra. Departing from tradition, the new cathedral was to be situated on a north-south axis, rather than east-west, so as to intersect the shell of its predecessor, left standing as both memorial and warning. The south end of the new edifice is constructed entirely of glass (on which etched angels symbolize the cathedral's patron—St. Michael), allowing the remains of the original cathedral to be seen from within the new.

Britten's acceptance of this commission put the composition of Curlew River (op. 71, 1964) on hold. But, as Philip Rupprecht points out, both works invoke ritual: "Equally, in the late fifties, the paired genesis of Curlew River and the War Requiem underscores the intricate and mutually complementary balance struck, in each work, between an extant ritual and some outside force of symbolism. Thus, the Buddhist Nō play becomes a 'Christian' work almost at the same time as the Coventry Mass is transformed by the interpolation of English texts, into a composite symbol, far more skeptical in tone than the sacred liturgy embedded within."[31] These symbolic elements of ritual are manifestations of Britten's lifelong fascination with "hymns" (starting with A Hymn to the Virgin, Hymn to St. Cecilia, the choral hymns to St. Peter (op. 56a, 1955) and St. Columba (1962), and "ceremony" (A Ceremony of Carols).

The War Requiem's text is as significant an artistic accomplishment as the music it elicits. Inspired by the cathedral's commitment to a ministry of reconciliation and pacifism, Britten fashioned a powerful synthesis of antiwar poetry by Wilfred Owen (1893–1918) and the Latin Requiem Mass. This textual dualism led to a multidimensional musical composition that requires three separate and distinct musical ensembles. The main one involves the soprano soloist, large chorus, and full orchestra. To these forces, along with the second—a spatially distant choir of boy trebles accompanied by a portative organ—Britten entrusts the Requiem's Latin texts. Finally, Britten set Owen's poems for tenor and baritone soloists and a small chamber orchestra, reminiscent of the operas he crafted for the English Opera Group in the 1950s.[32]

His selection (and occasional editing) of Owen's poems and his juxtaposition of them with the traditional Latin Requiem texts offer profound insights into Britten's artistic vision. He positions the poems so that they become both a linguistic gloss on and a transformational exegesis of the Requiem text. The resulting textual construction is then the generative force of the music. The complex made up of the Latin Introit and Kyrie and Owen's "Anthem for Doom'd Youth" is one example of Britten's inspired compilation.

Fig. 12.1 Coventry Cathedral reduced to rubble by German air raids (November 14, 1940)

The tritone, C–F♯, is central to the work's tonal architecture. This difficult interval sounds in the orchestral bells throughout the choral portions of the opening movement, forming the total pitch content of the choir (prior to the concluding Kyrie chorale). This primary interval resonates throughout the tenor solo in the harp's ostinato (C–G♭, enharmonically F♯) and the melodic profile of many of the tenor's phrases. The closing chorale consists entirely of parallel tritones (and perfect fifths) in contrary motion (ex. 12.8).

Example 12.8 Britten, *War Requiem*, op. 66, Kyrie, mm. 165–74

In tonal practice, the C–F♯ tritone resolves either inward (to D♭/F) or outward (to B/G), but such traditional resolution was as impossible for Britten as attaining peace had proven to be for those his music memorializes. Britten uses this chorale (and the variations of it that conclude the *Dies irae* and *In Paradisum*) to reinforce the C–F♯ tritone as the movement's "tonic;" but its final resolution takes an unexpected turn, F♯ resolving downward to F♮ while retaining the C as part of an F-major triad.

The first appearance of the boy choir comes at the text "Te decet hymnus." Mozart and Verdi have led us to expect some change of style here, and Britten does not disappoint. The music the boys sing, despite its dodecaphonic feel, is a series of perfect intervals reminiscent of Hindemith. The two voice parts interface, the melody of the first traversing from C to F♯, the second inverting that motion. Typical of other instances where Britten adapts twelve-tone procedure to his own ends, these tonally ambiguous melodies are harmonized (in the left hand of the organ part) with simple triads (see ex. 12.9).[33] Simultaneously, the violins of the orchestra teeter back and forth from C to F♯, connecting the boys' music to that of the chorus, all the while asserting the primacy of the tritone (ex. 12.9).

Example 12.9 Britten, *War Requiem*, op. 66, "Te decet hymnus," mm. 29–36

The final component of the *War Requiem*'s opening movement is Owen's poem "Anthem for doom'd youth" for tenor and chamber orchestra. Why did Britten place this particular poem here? Owen's words provide the composer with prompts for a series of musical cross references. The first line of text, "What passing bells for these who die as cattle," is the likely source of the ominous tolling of orchestral bells that dominates the Introit. Similarly, Owen's "for these who die as cattle" glosses the final line of the Introit's verse, "ad te omnis caro veniet" ("To you all flesh must come"). Both Owen and Britten saw the flood of healthy young men into the war as a meta-phorical slaughter akin to a stockyard. Perhaps it was this image that led Britten to transform the Introit from a liturgical procession of the clergy into a procession of wounded veterans, portrayed musically in the orchestra's angular melody and quintuplet rhythms.[34]

The onset of Owen's poem is marked by a new key signature (five flats) and quicker tempo at m. 77. It is certainly not a coincidence that this new scale (Bb minor) diatonically contains the pitches for the harp's tritone glissando (C″–Gb″). Britten's experience as a film composer shows in his portrayal of "The shrill, demented choirs of wailing shells" as whistling flute and clarinet melis-mas (m.83). Britten's sensitivity to the expressive power of words prompt him to give a foretaste of the martial fanfares of the Dies irae in response to the line, "And bugles calling for them" (ex. 12.10).

Example 12.10 Britten, *War Requiem*, op. 66, Introit, mm. 111–116

Another musical correlation driven by text is Britten's re-use of the first music the trebles sing ("Te decet hymnus," m. 29) to set Owen's "Not in the hands of boys." We hear their angular melody first in the orchestra (m. 123) and then in the tenor (m. 126). But the *pièce de résistance* of his musical "recapitulation" is the augmentation of that melody to set the poem's final line. The chamber orchestra fades away (upward despite the image of the "lowering of blinds"), replaced by the somber tolling of the bells' ominous tritone that heralds the choral setting of Kyrie eleison.

Britten exploits the separate elements of text, space, and music throughout the work, their varied interactions creating the work's formal design. Early commentators like Malcolm Boyd pointed out the many similarities between Britten's Requiem and its most famous prede-cessor, the Manzoni Requiem by Giuseppe Verdi.[35] This appropriation is clearest in the *Dies irae*, where Britten borrowed Verdi's key (G minor), his heavy orchestration with "off-beat" drum strokes, brass fanfares that culminate at "Tuba mirum," the nonliturgical reprise of the opening music following "Confutatis maledictis" (in Britten's case delayed by the interpolation of Owen verse "Be slowly lifted up") and, finally, setting the "Lachrymosa" for the soprano and choir in Bb minor. Despite these obvious borrowings, Britten manages to create a distinctive work, the pro-found musical and dramatic logic that renders such similarities superficial. In the final analysis, Britten's Requiem is original in its inclusion of the Owen poems, which suggests that the *War Requiem* is less a Latin Requiem with some added text than an Owen "cycle" (akin to Mahler's *Das Lied von der Erde*) that tropes the timeless Latin text and provides it with new meaning.

There are certainly more familiar *a cappella* choral works by Britten than *Sacred and Profane* (Eight Medieval Lyrics), op. 91,[36] but its position as Britten's last published choral composition pro-vides a compelling rationale for closer examination.With this publication, Britten comes full circle, returning to his first use of medieval English texts. Winthrop Rogers, the publisher of *A Hymn to the*

Virgin, quite reasonably insisted on modernizing the spellings for the text, which Britten had, at one time during the composition of this work, used. By 1975 Britten's status allowed him to retain the original spellings in *Sacred and Profane*.[37] The texts of three of the eight compositions are unquestionably religiously oriented: "sacred" (1, 5, and 7), leaving the other four as "profane," or secular.

1. *St. Godrick's hymn* "Sainte Marye Virgine" (mid-twelfth century)
2. *I mon waxe wod* "Fowles in the frith" (late thirteenth century)
3. *Lenten is come* "Lenten is come with love to toune" (late thirteenth/early fourteenth century)
4. *The long night* "Mirie it is, while sumer ilast" (earlier thirteenth century)
5. *Yif ic of luve can* "Whanne ic se on Rode" (earlier fourteenth century)
6. *Carol* "Maiden in the mor lay" (early fourteenth century)
7. *Ye that pasen by* "Ye that pasen by the weiye" (mid-fourteenth century)
8. *A death* "Wanne mine eyhen misten" (thirteenth century)

Labeling movements as either sacred or secular is, nonetheless, dangerous given the remoteness of the language and the ambiguity of textual reference (e.g., *St. Godric's Hymn* or *Lenten is come*, in which the first word has nothing to do with Lent, simply meaning "Spring").

Rather unusually for Britten specifically or the period in general, the key signatures are accurate predictors of each movement's tonal center. Those movements with no signature (1, 2, and 7) center on C major or A minor; the same is true for those with two sharps (3 and 4, both on D, and 5 on B minor), two flats (6, G minor) and one sharp (8, E minor). Viewed in sequence, these tonal centers (C–A minor–D/A mixolydian–G minor/major–B minor–G minor–A minor/E Mixolydian–E minor/major) create no discernible pattern. If, however, they are rearranged as a sequence of thirds (A–C–E–G–B/B♭) they provide insight into Britten's harmonic and melodic language. For example, this preference for melodic thirds is clearly visible in prominent themes of the eight movements (see bracketed notes in ex. 12.11a–g).[38]

Example 12.11 a–g Britten, *Sacred and Profane*, op. 91

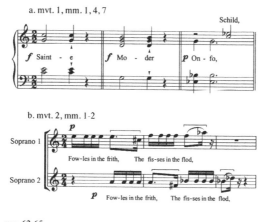

Example 12.11 a–g Continued

d. mvt. 5, mm. 1-7

e. mvt. 6, mm. 30-34

f. mvt. 7, mm. 1-3

g. mvt. 8, mm. 17-19

The soprano's canonic ostinato in mvt. 2 (ex. 12.11b) is built on two minor thirds (E″–C♯″ and F″–A♭″); minor thirds also figure prominently in the melody of the final movement and its sequential development (ex. 12.11g). In his last opera, *Death in Venice*, op. 88 (1973), Britten explicitly uses twelve-tone rows, so the presence of tertian themes and larger tonal structures here are as unsettling as the juxtaposition presented by Schoenberg's harmonically conventional *Drei Volkslieder* (op. 49) and dodecaphonic op. 50 (*De Profundis, Dreimal tausend Jahre*), especially since both of these works are choral. Britten offers no explanation for this stylistic dichotomy, but beyond the distinction between opera and *a cappella* choral music, a possible answer may lie in his championing of the musical amateur. When he received the Aspen Award in 1964, Britten made the following statement: "I certainly write music for human beings—directly and deliberately. I consider their voices, the range, the power, the subtlety, and the color potentialities of them. I consider the instruments they play—their most expressive and suitable individual sonorities, and where I may be said to have invented an instrument (such as the Slung Mugs of *Noye's Fludde*) I have borne in mind the pleasure the young performers will have in playing it. I also take note of the *human* circumstances of music, of its environment and conventions."[39] Perhaps Britten's artistic creed explains his fascination with the choral idiom's essential conservatism and uniquely social dimension.

WILLIAM WALTON AND MICHAEL TIPPETT

The choral works of William Walton and Michael Tippett might seem to fall short of the high level that Britten attained. While Walton's dramatic cantata *Belshazzar's Feast* (1930–31) and

Tippett's oratorio *A Child of Our Time* (1939–41) are important choral works of the mid-twentieth century, neither compares favorably with similar works by Britten. Walton's splashy retelling of the Babylonian captivity and King Nebuchadnezzar's demise is pure film music; Tippett's oratorio, written in response to the assassination of Ernst vom Rath (Paris, 1938) and the ensuing pogrom (*Kristallnacht*), is its complete antithesis, a brooding, philosophical work steeped in Tippett's somewhat amateurish fascination with the pyschoanalytical theory of Carl Jung. The opposite characters of these two works may also have something to do with when they were written—Walton's written in a time of seeming prosperity and carefree living, while Tippett's was filled with the foreboding of World War II.

Walton's choral output favors large, lavishly scored works like *Belshazzar's Feast* (for eight-part chorus, soloists, and orchestra). He uses this large array of forces to maximize dynamic and coloristic contrasts (much like the film scores he composed for Sir Laurence Olivier's versions of Shakespeare's *Henry V* (1944), *Hamlet* (1948), and *Richard III* (1955), and the MGM epic *Battle of Britain* (1969). Nowhere is Walton's penchant for pictorialism more evident than in the battery of percussion he uses to portray the gods of wood, brass, and ivory in *Belshazzar*. Walton's early career was defined by *Façade*, music he composed in 1922 to accompany the recitation of poetry by Dame Edith Sitwell (1887–1964), who was his patroness. *Façade's* premiere on June 12, 1923, provoked an uproar and effectively earned Walton the reputation of being a modernist composer—and this after the riot that accompanied Stravinsky's 1913 *Rite of Spring*. Although he went on to extract orchestral suites from this music (1926 and 1938), no vestige of *Façade* remains in such later choral works as the *Te Deum* for the coronation of Queen Elizabeth II (1952) and the *Gloria* for double chorus, soloists, and orchestra (1961). Though lacking soloists and orchestra, Walton's *Missa Brevis* (1966), *Jubilate Deo* (1971–72), and *Magnificat and Nunc Dimittis* (1974, rev. 1976) demonstrate a continued fascination with opulent choral scoring. His most popular choral works, *A Litany* (1916, rev. 1930) and *Set me as a Seal upon Thine Heart* (1938), are four-part, *a cappella* anthems—calm, soothing music, utterly lacking in pretense or bluster (ex. 12.12).

Example 12.12 Walton, *A Litany*, mm. 1–12
© Oxford University Press 1936. Renewed in USA 1964.

Michael Tippett's oratorio *A Child of our Time* is unique in its synthesis of Jungian psychology and the composer's own pacifism into a nonargumentative, yet morally persuasive work. Concerning the evolution of the oratorio's text, Ian Kemp writes:

> After having planned the broad shape and character of his work Tippett asked
> T. S. Eliot to write the text. Eliot was a natural choice for Tippett, since he

both greatly admired the poet's work and also had reason to expect that Eliot would find the writing of an oratorio text congenial. Eliot obviously understood that the text writer would be in a subordinate position, for he asked that his part be spelt out for him. He wanted a precise scheme of musical numbers and the quantity and quality of the words to go with them. Tippett then prepared a careful typescript of what at the time was headed "Sketch for a Modern Oratorio." Eliot considered the "sketch" for some weeks, and then advised Tippett to write it, adding, "Anything I add to it will stand out a mile as so much better poetry."[40]

Choral conductors are most familiar with the "Five Negro Spirituals" from *A Child of Our Time*, which are published separately.[41] These spirituals frame the narrative of Tippett's modern "Passion play" and provide an element of universality (Fig. 12.2). Tippett's source for these songs was *The Book of American Negro Spirituals*, collected by two African American songwriters, James Weldon Johnson and John Rosamond Johnson, both more famous for their ragtime hits.[42] James Johnson edited the collection and wrote a lengthy introduction detailing the history of the music; his brother, John, created the musical arrangements (both vocal solo with piano and choral). Respecting this appropriated cultural music, Tippett's arrangements scrupulously retain the melodic and rhythmic contour, as well as the keys, of Johnson's arrangements. In fact, Tippett uses these original keys as "found" music to shape the oratorio's harmonic frame. More broadly, Tippett perceived the spirituals as another expression of the general European appreciation of American jazz. For this reason, he instructed the spirituals be sung with a strong underlying pulse and slightly "swung." From their melodic language Tippett extracted the minor third as a fundamental shape (especially prominent as the interval between the dominant and the flat seventh). This characteristic melodic inflection is evident in the spiritual "Nobody knows the trouble I see, Lord" (ex. 12.13).

Example 12.13 Tippett, *A Child of Our Time*, mvt. 16, mm. 1–8
© 1949 by Universal Edition A.G., Vienna © Renewed All Rights Reserved
Used by permission of European American Music Distributors LLC, sole US and Canadian agent for Universal Edition A.G., Vienna.

Fig. 12.2 Scene from Michael Tippett's *A Child of Our Time* (2005)

The example does not contain Tippett's orchestral accompaniment. Performed *a cappella* and removed from the larger context of the oratorio, the spirituals present the conductor with the question of how rigidly to interpret Tippett's arrangements. Accompanied within the oratorio, they function like the chorales in Bach's Passions, providing dramatic culmination for the music that precedes them and serving as points of reflection before the oratorio's narrative continues.

Like the oratorios of Handel that Tippett acknowledged as his model, *A Child of Our Time* has three parts, which function much like the three parts of *Messiah*—prophecy and preparation; narrative drama, metaphysical meditation. Parts 1 and 2 end with spirituals; the other three sections delineate the unfolding drama of part 2 (see Table 12.6). The three scenes of part 2 contain seventeen musically continuous movements (nos. 9–25). Except for mvt. 23, this continuity is obvious in the score; however, Tippett adds the rubric "segue" (end of mvts. 15, 17, and 20) to ensure the logical connection of one movement with its successor.

Given that the spirituals are more likely to be performed separately, the question logically arises as to how their detachment from their original context changes them (if at all). These five spirituals are totally unlike the dynamic arrangements of a gospel song, spiritual, or popular hymn that often close choral concerts; any attempt to "correct" the style of Tippett's arrangements is unwise. Even though the composer himself sanctioned their separate performance, thoughtful musicians must seek a way to imbue them with the psychic distance of a dramatic soliloquy, sung less to communicate explicitly than to express the internal emotions of those involved in the drama.

Tippett's choral output includes several other large works and approximately eighteen smaller choral works. In the first category are two large, oratorio-like works—*The Vision of Saint Augustine* (1965) for baritone, chorus, and orchestra; and *The Mask of Time* (1985) for

Table 12.6 Tippett, *A Child of our Time*, part 2

9. Chorus	*A Star rises in mid winter*
10. Narrator (B)	*And a time came*
11. Double Chorus of Persecutors and Persecuted	*Away with them!*
12. Narrator (B)	*Where they could, they fled*
13. Chorus of the Self-righteous	*We cannot have them in our Empire!*
14. Narrator (B):	*And the boy's mother wrote a letter, saying:*
15. Scena: Solo Quartet	*O my son/Mother, ah Mother!* (*segue*)
16. A Spiritual: Chorus and soli	*Nobody knows the trouble I see*
17. Scena: Duet (Bass and Alto)	*The boy becomes desperate* (*segue*)
18. Narrator (B)	*They took a terrible vengeance.*
19. Chorus: The Terror	*Burn down their houses!*
Narrator (B)	*Men were ashamed of what was done* (*segue*)
20. A Spiritual of Anger (B, chorus)	*Go down, Moses!*
21. The Boy sings in his Prison (T)	*My dreams are all shattered*
22. The Mother (S)	*What have I done to you, my son?*
23. Alto	*The dark forces rise like a flood.*
25. A Spiritual:	*O by and by*

soprano, mezzo, tenor, and baritone solo, chorus and orchestra. Both employ the more modernist style Tippett adopted in the 1960s (influenced by Igor Stravinsky). Among the smaller choral works are *Two Madrigals* (1942) for unaccompanied mixed chorus, a somewhat academic motet for eight-part choir, *Plebs angelica* (1944), and several popular Christmas carols, notably *What Cheer?* (1961). His early madrigal *The Windhover* (1942) is an excellent example of his attention to text; there, Gerard Manley Hopkins's poem about a falcon in flight provides Tippett with an opportunity to explore text painting to an extent not typical of his choral style. More generally, *The Windhover* reflects the composer's interest in early music during his brief tenure as director of music at Morley College in London (1940–42). Somewhat more accessible are the *Four Songs from the British Isles* (1956).[43] In the first of these, "Early One Morning," Tippett revisits a tune first used in his *Suite in D for the Birthday of Prince Charles* (1948). Tippett presents that tune in all four verses (just as Vaughan Williams does in his own arrangement of "Early One Morning"), and thus he seems more interested in lending the simple melody an element of erudition in the form of idiosyncratic accompaniments that accompany each new strophe.

KENNETH LEIGHTON

The career of this mid-century composer parallels Britten's in several ways: like Britten, Leighton won the Royal College of Music's coveted Mendelssohn Scholarship, which he used to study with Goffredo Petrassi in Rome. Leighton's assemblage of an eclectic, thematically related group of poems in his *Symphony No. 2, Sinfonia Mistica* is reminiscent of Britten's *Spring Symphony*. Unlike Britten, though, Leighton began his career as a chorister at Wakefield Cathedral, eventually moving to numerous academic posts including at the University of Edinburgh from 1955 to 1968, Oxford University (1968–1970), then back to Edinburgh (1970–88).

Leighton, again like Britten, produced choral music throughout his life; between 1960 and 1979 he published at least one new choral piece a year. There was an early hiatus in the 1930s and 1940s that Leighton attributed to a period of intense stylistic experimentation. Those decades were "a question of building up tension and not relaxing it until the very end. Now I'm trying to write music that is more static, but perhaps more varied and relaxed, with greater emphasis on color and harmony. The best way of putting it is I want to write simpler music."[44] This retrospective assessment came at a time when Leighton was less involved with stylistic experimentation than of stylistic consolidation.

Crucifixus pro nobis, op. 38 (1971), is one of Leighton's finest and most representative compositions. The text of his cantata is poetry by two seventeenth-century mystical poets—Patrick Cary (ca. 1624–1657) and Phineas Fletcher (1581–1650). The scoring is basic—tenor (or soprano) solo, chorus (with *divisi*), and organ. The first three movements set poems by Cary ("Christ in the Cradle," "Christ in the Garden," and "Christ in his Passion"); Fletcher's popular hymn "Drop, drop, slow tears" (from "A Litany") concludes the work. Typical of Leighton's mature style are the prominence of melodic semitones and tritones (often, like Britten, implying Lydian mode) and astringent harmonies produced by the contrapuntal interaction of the two melodic lines (see ex. 12.14a).

Example 12.14 a–b Leighton, *Crucifixus pro nobis*, op. 38, mvt. 1

Leighton's melodic writing is strongly diatonic, moving predominantly in stepwise motion but using leaps for emphasis, as in the tenor's first extended solo passage (ex. 12.14b).[45]

The climactic moment of mvt. 2 (mm. 123–29) is an excellent example of how Leighton uses counterpoint to generate harmony. Example 12.14 points out the Lydian frame that produces the harmony. The passage cited below (ex. 12.15) begins with a dissonant chord (D♭–G–A♭) grounded in D♭ Lydian mode and made even more intense by Leighton's use of an organ polychord built on the clash between F♭ major and D♭ major with the explicit cross relation of F♭ against F♮.

Example 12.15 Leighton, *Crucifixus pro nobis*, op. 38, mvt. 2, mm. 123–29

Leighton's contrapuntal craftsmanship is evident in the elegant yet simple design of each voice's descent: the bass's Lydian descent (A♭–G–F–E♭–D♭); the near canonic relationship of the tenor and soprano; and the chorus's piquant final sonority that juxtaposes the choral bass's sustained D♭ against a C-major chord in the upper three voices, thus creating both another tritone [D♭–G] and a semitone [D♭–C]).[46]

There are some thirty-five choral anthems by Kenneth Leighton, most of which are short; the most impressive is a setting of a medieval Easter text "Solus ad victimam" (Peter Abelard, 1079–1142) for chorus and organ. Other extended works with instrumental accompaniment include *The Light Invisible* (1958) for tenor, eight-part choir, and full orchestra; *Columba mea* (1977) for baritone, chorus, strings, and piano; and *The World's Desire* (1984) for chorus and organ. The conductor Paul Spicer offers this evaluation of Leighton's work: "Perhaps Leighton's misfortune was to be born at a time when musical experimentation was at its height. Thus, his rather conservative style made even his serial compositions a search for lyrical possibilities. He was also to some extent a formulaic composer whose mannerisms were often transposed from work to work and detractors would find reliance on certain notational figures and rhythmic cells tiresome. But this very insistence on his developed style was part of what makes the unique experience of Leighton's music."[47]

PETER MAXWELL DAVIES

This composer's stylistic metamorphoses ranged from serialism to arrangements of medieval carols for schoolchildren, then to expressionist music as theater in the 1960s to reworking music of the past involving the use of magic squares and isorhythm. First trained at the University of Manchester alongside Alexander Goehr and Harrison Birtwistle, Davies, like Leighton, studied in Rome with Petrassi (1957–58). In Rome, he became fascinated with Gregorian chant and constantly sought out opportunities to hear it. He returned to England in 1959 to become the director of music at Cirencester Grammar School, not the typical career path for a serialist composer. Davies flourished there because he refused to regard children as inferior musical performers, choosing instead, like Britten, to find innovative ways to engage them musically without "dumbing down" his own process. In 1962 Davies left Cirencester for Princeton University to study with Milton Babbitt and Roger Sessions. The turning point in his life was his decision in 1971 to settle in Orkney, a move that attached him to that barren, unique landscape as Britten was similarly attached to East Anglia. Like Britten and Pears, Davies also established a festival, in his case the St. Magnus Festival, in 1977 to showcase local artists and musicians.

Scanning Davies's output one finds titles that deliberately or not have titles that reference historical choral music when the works are not choral at all. His *Missa super L'Homme armé* (1968–71), despite the plethora of Renaissance Mass cycles based on that famous melody, is a work for speaker/singer and instrumental ensemble, reminiscent of his *Eight Songs for a Mad King* (1969). That work, scored for baritone and several unusual instruments (bird whistle, didgeridoo, crow, dulcimer, etc.), is based on tunes that King George III supposedly played on a mechanical organ. Similarly, his *Tenebrae super Gesualdo* (1972) has three purely instrumental movements, before concluding with an arrangement of Gesualdo's *Tenebrae factae sunt* for mezzo-soprano and guitar. Another ambiguous title is his *Grand Oratorio: The Meaning of Life*, op. 170 (2000); again, despite allusions to choral music, this work is scored for barbershop quartet and percussion.

The poetry of George Mackay Brown, a Scotsman and fellow Orkney resident, had an enormous impact on Davies's choral music. John Warnaby states that "the stark lands and seascapes of Orkney, the stability of a relatively traditional community, and its history and mythology as mediated through the poetry and fiction of George Mackay Brown began to have a lasting impact on Davies's creative imagination."[48] Typical of their collaboration is the set of choral songs *Westerlings* (1977). The texts deal with the sea voyage that brought the first Norse settlers to the Orkneys in the eighth century. Written for the quincentenary of Uppsala University (1977), four of the nine movements of Maxwell Davies's cycle are titled "Seascape." Warnaby believes that Davies's association with Mackay Brown led to a "more detached style" with "less emphasis on innovation or experimentation."[49]

Example 12.16 Davies, *Westerlings*, Song 2, mm. 1–13

The opening of the first piece, "Oarsmen, we drive a golden whale," hardly seems to de-emphasize experimentation; in fact, the copious use of tritones (e.g., t/b, mm. 2–3) and simultaneous cross relations (s/b, m. 13) seems to preclude choral performance (ex. 12.16). We find the same style in Davies's *Five Motets* (1959); written while still at Circencester, they were withheld due to their difficulty. Davies calls for three ensembles—one solo and two choral—that "should be spaced as far apart as is practical so that real antiphonality is achieved."[50] In 1962, he added *colla parte* instrumental doublings of the two choral ensembles in tacit recognition of the work's difficulty. Davies also specified that the solo ensemble (accompanied by string quartet and double bass) should be flanked on either side by the choirs, which are doubled by brass and organ (to the left) and woodwinds and organ (to the right).

Davies's choral output is extensive but highly variable in terms of accessibility. Some larger works (e.g., *Job*, op. 183, 1997, and *The Three Kings*, op. 172, 1995) are dissonant enough that they are hard to listen to and, therefore, unlikely to be performed. Conversely, the *Two Latin Motets*, op. 235 (2003), appear more daunting visually than the sound of the fine recording made by Martin Baker and the choir of Westminster Cathedral would suggest.[51] Both motets are based on Gregorian chants for Pentecost (*Dum complerentur* and *Veni Sancte Spiritus*). In the first, the simplest and most recognizable version of the chant melody does not appear until mm. 57–63. This unison version confirms the initial impression that while the opening two verses contain audible snippets of the chant, the music's heterophonic harmonic texture obscures the actual chant melody. The construction of each individual voice is quite logical; Davies writes consonant vocal pairs (s/a, t/b), which, heard separately, are consonant but become dissonant when combined. *Veni Sancte Spiritus* is, on the whole, simpler both texturally and harmonically. Unlike *Dum complerentur*, Davies opens with the chant sung in unison, followed immediately by a harmonized version that juxtaposes the chant with an augmented inversion of itself.

A work that is exceptional for both its simplicity and beauty, is Davies's *Missa parvula*, op. 233 (2002). Composed for the treble voices of Westminster Cathedral, this work is strikingly consonant. The unison vocal melodies sound vaguely modal; even the organ accompaniment lacks the asperity often found in other choral works. Davies also composed a larger *Mass* for SATB choir and two organs, op. 226 (2002), which is denser and more complex than the *Missa parvula*. This mass is based on the same two chants used in the *Two Latin Motets*, op. 235. The second organ creates greater density of sound and, in the Credo, depicts the "flames of fire" referred to in the Pentecost motet texts. Davies employs contrapuntal techniques associated with medieval and serial music to generate harmonic textures from the chant melodies. Roderic Dunnett sums up Davies's style by pointing out that "Effectively, everything in a piece of Maxwell Davies's music relates to itself, or to a countermelody set at odds and colliding with it ... the practices which Maxwell Davies's music engages ... are not random, but systematic, in such a way as to bring to the surface, or 'incarnate' material from the deepest levels of the human psyche."[52] In this way, Davies, like Britten, uses counterpoint to generate all of the musical texture, though Britten's music is rarely so dense or dissonant.

JOHN TAVENER

Standing six feet, six inches tall with a "luminously thin figure, flowing hair and other-worldly stare," John Tavener was a striking musical personality. In the 1960s, he was the closest thing English classical music had to a "rock star."[53] Ringo Starr initially heard a tape of Tavener's cantata *The Whale* (1968), and John Lennon authorized a recording of it on the Beatles' Apple label.[54] Despite this recognition from Britain's most famous musical figures, the work did not garner critical praise. His *Celtic Requiem* (1969) fared no better but did manage to attract the attention of Benjamin Britten, whose recommendation led the Royal Opera to tender a commission, which never materialized because of management's concerns about its viability.[55] His major choral work of the 1960s was a fifty-minute-long choral meditation on texts by the Spanish mystic St. John of the Cross, *Ultimos Ritos* (1972). Its fifth movement reuses an earlier work, *Coplas* (1970) for four soloists, four choruses, and electronic tape. *Ultimos Ritos* documents Tavener's eclectic mixture of pitch serialism, durational canons, and recorded music as *musique concrète*. The four SATB choirs, arranged in the shape of a cross, sing different voicings of a diminished-seventh chord from the Crucifixus of J. S. Bach's B-minor Mass. To further distance his music from Bach's, Tavener increases the duration of each new chord by a half note (see ex. 12.17a). Simultaneously, four soloists sing the Spanish text "Coplas del mismo hecas sobre un éxtasis de alta contemplación" ("Stanzas concerning an ecstasy experienced in high contemplation"), which provide the composition's title. Tavener distributes the text syllabically, each syllable one quarter note longer than its predecessor (see ex. 12.17b).

Example 12.17 a–b Tavener, *Coplas*

a. mm. 17-51

b. mm. 17-55

Example 18 shows the twelve-tone melody that Tavener uses in three different versions: the prime, an I2 inversion on E, and a new row that randomly reorders the pitch content of this inversion.

Example 12.18 a–c Tavener, *Coplas*

a.

Example 12.18 a–c Continued

Taped fragments of a performance of Bach's *Crucifixus* appear seven times. Each appearance (save the last) consists of four-measure segments of Bach's chorus (mm. 1–4, 9–12, 17–20, 25–28, 33–36, 41–44, and 49–53). For the deleted measures of Bach's original, Tavener substitutes an equal number of measures of rest.

Tavener's popularity as a choral composer comes mostly from his settings of William Blake's poem "The Lamb" (1982) and "Song for Athene" (text by Mother Thekla, 1993). The performance of "Song for Athene" for the funeral of Princess Diana in 1997 elevated Tavener's music to new heights of popularity and legitimacy. Both compositions are typical of the choral music Tavener wrote following his conversion to the Eastern Orthodox Church in 1977, an event that transformed him into what some have called a "holy minimalist."[56] The serial techniques Tavener claimed to have renounced at his conversion survive in his elegantly simple setting of Blake's "The Lamb." He builds the entire piece from two related melodies. The first is a simple G-major melody (ex. 12.19a), which the sopranos sing twice (mm. 1–2); the second starts with the first four pitches of the first, adding three chromatically altered pitches (E'♭, F'♮, A'♭) (ex. 12.19b). Tavener immediately repeats the melody in retrograde motion to create the palindrome marked by arrows in example 12.19a.

Example 12.19 a-c Tavener, *The Lamb*

Tavener creates an accompanying alto part that uses a mirror inversion of both soprano melodies (ex. 12.19c). For the final four lines of text, the soprano and alto sing melody A four times (the alto harmonizing the soprano in thirds); after three identical statements, Tavener stops the piece by augmenting the harmonized melody. The tenor and bass join in for these final four lines, harmonizing the soprano/alto duet with somewhat conventional tonal harmony. Tavener repeats the same music for the second verse; in this version, the men sing all ten lines of text. For the first six, they sing in octave pairs with their female analogs (s = t, a = b); the final four lines are the same as verse one.

Mirror inversion also plays a significant role in "Song for Athene" and the second of the *Two Hymns for the Mother of God* (1985). Both works also feature pedal points (mimicking the *ison* drone of Byzantine music) and melodic doubling in thirds (much like the medieval English polyphonic style known as *gymel*). Reflecting the musical traditions of his Orthodox faith, Tavener harmonizes this principal melody using the parallel triads closely associated with the Russian church music of the late nineteenth and early twentieth centuries (ex. 12.20).

Example 12.20 Tavener, *Hymn for the Dormition of the Mother of God*, no. 2

This simple, accessible, and quite expressive style has generated a considerable following for both the composer and his work.

Many of the titles of Tavener's postconversion music are evidence of a profound change of content and the strong influence of Mother Thekla (1918–2011), the Russian-born abbess of the Orthodox monastery near Whitby in North Yorkshire: *Funeral Ikos* and *The Great Canon of St. Andrew of Crete* (1981), *Ikon of Light* (1984), a *Vigil Service* (1984), *The Tyger* (William Blake, 1987), *Akathist of Thanksgiving* (1986-87), *Resurrection* (1989), *The Annunciation* (1992), *The Apocalypse* (1993), *Fall and Resurrection* (2000), and *The Veil of the Temple* (2003). Tavener considered this last work (scored for four choruses, several orchestras, and soloists, utilizing texts from a number of religious traditions) to be his supreme achievement. A work that more likely will survive the test of time and which distances Tavener from the label of "holy minimalism" is *A Village Wedding* (1992), written for the Hilliard Ensemble in 1992 and premiered in the United States by the professional male ensemble, Chanticleer, in 1995. Here, Tavener depicts a Greek wedding using a poetic description by Angelos Sikeliano and words from the Orthodox wedding ceremony.

JAMES MACMILLAN

In 1987, upon completion of his various degrees in music from the University of Glasgow and the University of Durham, James MacMillan (b. 1959) returned to his native Scotland. This event, coupled with his fervent Roman Catholicism, triggered the development of a new, distinctly personal style. His first successes—*Búsqueda* (1988), *The Confession of Isobel Gowdie*

(1990), and the percussion concerto *Veni, Veni Emmanuel* (1992), composed for Dame Evelyn Glennie—were purely instrumental; thereafter, MacMillan found that choral music's unique requirement—words—provided a more effective platform for his belief in social justice, especially the Liberation theology that dominated South American Catholicism. This theme dominates his cantata *Cantos Sagrados* ("Sacred Songs") for chorus and organ (1989). His texts are English translations of poems by Ariel Dorfman (mvts. 1 and 3) and Ana Maria Mendoza (mvt. 2), each of which is combined with a Latin liturgical text.

1. "Identity," Ariel Dorfman (Edie Grossman, tr.), *Libera animas*
2. "Virgin of Guadalupe," Ana Maria Mendoza (Gilbert Markus, tr.), *Salve Mater, coeli porta*
3. "Sun Stone," Ariel Dorfman (Edie Grossman, tr.), *Et incarnatus est*

In mvt. 1, MacMillan portrays the shock of villagers finding a corpse floating in the river by using an antiphonal, almost *Sprechstimme* texture to represent their animated, furtive questions (ex. 12.21).

Example 12.21 MacMillan, *Cantos Sagrados*, mvt. 1, mm. 1–6

MacMillan also uses conflicting tonal layers to depict the different opinions expressed by the people of the village.

In the second movement, "Virgin of Guadalupe," MacMillan sets Mendoza's poem as the modern equivalent of a fourteenth-century motet, complete with polytextuality and isorhythm. These two features define the different layers that generate the music's form. The sopranos sing Mendoza's poem as one layer, the second layer is the alto, tenor, and bass singing the Marian sequence *Salve Mater coeli porta*.[57] The third layer is the organ's clusters that begin without warning in m. 46. While dissonant, the pitch content of these chords is ultimately less important than their rhythmic function.

MacMillan provides each textual layer with its own unique music. The first sopranos sing a simple, folk-song-like tune, harmonized simply by the second sopranos (ex. 12.22).

Example 12.22 MacMillan, *Cantos Sagrados*, mvt. 2, mm. 5–11

The first soprano's melody demonstrates MacMillan's blending of old and new techniques. In mm. 1–58, the first sopranos sing five musical segments articulated by rests. The regularity of their length and rhythmic pattern is strongly reminiscent of medieval isorhythm. Each segment's melody consists of fourteen separate pitches (a medieval *color*?) sung twice (see ex. 12.22). The varying lengths of each pitch is dependent on the amount of text. The pitch content of the second soprano part, while far more flexible, is limited to the pitches of a diatonic hexachord on G' (G', A', B', C", D", E").

While the three lower voices all sing the same words, MacMillan uses different melodic shapes to separate the alto/tenor pair from the bass. The former sing two different chord progressions (marked A and B in ex. 12.23; although notated in 4/2 meter, the rhythmic durations suggest 3/2 meter. The basses sing four pitches (D, AA, GG, AA) using a separate repetitive rhythmic pattern (numbered in ex. 12.23). The final sonic layer is the organ's persistent chord, a nine-pitch cluster anchored on FF, which not only forms another layer but allows MacMillan to create a proportional relationship between the initial half-note triplets (mm. 46–59) and the quarter-note pattern that dominates the middle section.

The most significant of MacMillan's premillennial choral works is his *Seven Last Words from the Cross*, a work commissioned by the BBC to accompany a series of seven short films shown during Holy Week (1994). In addition to the inevitable comparison his setting would generate with its predecessors (Schütz, Haydn, Dubois, and others), MacMillan was faced with a larger problem of creating movements of the requisite length from such relatively brief texts. "When I realized I had committed myself to making a forty-five-minute piece around seven sentences, I was horrified! Then I began to think. Some of them could be done on their own, a starkly repetitive setting maybe, but there was also scope for amplification. So I found words from the service of Tenebrae, the Good Friday liturgy, that could act either as a reflection on the word or as a direct counterpart—like the versicle *Ecce lignum crucis* (Behold the wood of the Cross)."[58]

Example 12.23 MacMillan, *Cantos Sagrados*, mvt. 2, mm. 4–13

MacMillan adds additional text in movements 1, 3, 5, and 6 (see Table 12.7). He draws these texts, whether Latin or English, from the *Liber Usualis* that provides both the wanted length and the basis for musical contrast. The first movement begins with the first of the seven words, "Father forgive them;" the added text and the music it engenders create a sharply differentiated layer of counterpoint. Conversely, the added Latin Adoration of the Cross (*Ecce lignum crucis*) dominates the third movement. Here, MacMillan uses the contrasting text and music to create three alternating sections. In each, the Latin antiphon is sung by highly virtuosic pairs of solo voices (B, T, and A) over pedal tones. Following a cleansing measure of rest, MacMillan sets the response (*Venite adoremus*) to an achingly beautiful, Pucciniesque musical refrain, in which a solo violin plays the text's original Gregorian melody. The choral component of each refrain expands in density (two basses, all four male voices and, finally, a six-part texture A, A, T, T, B, B) and is demonstrably more rhythmically active. That all three statements are exactly the same length—seventeen measures of solo music, followed by the eleven measure refrain and a final measure of rest—again suggests use of isorhythm. After completing this process (m. 87), MacMillan reverses the order of presentation; an intensified version of the refrain's string accompaniment precedes the words from the Gospel of Luke 23:43 ("Verily I say unto you, today thou shalt be with me in paradise") sung by two high soprano soloists accompanied by violins.

The short biblical text of mvt. 5 ("I thirst") is heard as bare, parallel fifths that alternate whispered declamations of text from the *Improperia* ("Reproaches")—"Ego te potavi aqua salutis de petra; et tu me potasti felle et aceto" ("I gave you saving water to drink from the rock; you gave me bitter gall")—simulating someone whose mouth is so dry they can barely speak. The following movement takes a similar tack, setting the Good Friday Responsory, "My eyes were blind with weeping" (soprano) over a reprise of the poignant sorrow cadence first heard in mvt. 1.

Table 12.7 MacMillan, *The Seven Last Words from the Cross*, texts

Seven Last Words	Additional Text(s)
1. "Father, forgive them for they know not what they do." (Lk 23:34)	*Hosanna Filio David, benedictus qui venit in nomine Domini, Rex Israel, Hosanna in excelsis.* <div align="right">Mt 21:9</div><div align="right">*LU*, 578</div>"The life that I held dear I delivered into the hands of the unrighteous and my inheritance has become for me like a lion in the forest. My enemies spoke out against me, 'Come gather together and hasten to devour him'. They placed me in a wasteland of desolation, and all the earth mourned for me. For there was no one who would acknowledge me or give me help. Men rose up against me and spared not my life."<div align="right">Tenebrae responsory, *LU*, 681–82</div>
2. "Woman, Behold thy Son! Son, Behold thy Mother!" (Jn 19:26–27)	NONE
3. "Verily, I say unto thee; today thou shalt be with me in Paradise" (Lk 23:42)	*Ecce lignum crucis in quo salus mundi depedit: Venite adoremus.*<div align="right">*LU*, 704</div>
4. "Eli, Eli, lama sabachthani" (Mt 27:46)	NONE
5. "I thirst" (Jn 19:28)	*Ego te potavi aqua salutis de petra: et tu me potasti felle et aceto.*<div align="right">*Improperia*, *LU*, 707–8</div>
6. It is finished (Jn 19:30)	"My eyes were blind with weeping, for he that consoled me is far from me; Consider, all you people, is there any sorrow like my sorrow? All you who pass along this way take heed and consider if there is any sorrow like mine."<div align="right">Good Friday Tenebrae Responsory *LU*, 688</div>
7. "Father, into Thy hands I commend my Spirit" (Lk 23:46)	NONE

The return of this distinctive music is reminiscent of Britten's pervasive use of the C–F♯ tritone to unify his *War Requiem*. The "Sorrow Cadence" is an example of auto parody; MacMillan used it earlier in an instrumental composition, *Tuireadh* (1991), where its traditional Scottish keening served a similar function (ex. 12.24).[59]

Example 12.24 MacMillan, *Seven Last Words from the Cross*, "Sorrow" cadence"

Mantra-like repetitions of this cadence open and conclude the *Seven Last Words*. Simply playing this figure will reveal the affective transcendence of the music based on it.

Had MacMillan written no other choral music but these two works, his place in this historical narrative would have been assured. The varied body of choral works written in the new century demonstrate both a devotion to the choral idiom and care to provide music for choirs of different levels of ability. His distinctive blend of Scottish nationalism, transformed medievalism, and sincere Catholic belief continues to produce music that is vital, visionary, and prophetically relevant. His liturgical music, composed for the major cathedrals of England and Scotland, has made him the heir apparent to Herbert Howells. His *Magnificat* and *Nunc Dimittis*, commissioned by the BBC (*Magnificat*) and Winchester Cathedral (*Nunc Dimittis*) show the possible future trajectory of liturgical music. The *Magnificat* was heard at the first choral evensong of the new millennium; on Wednesday, January 5, 2000, the composer conducted the combined choirs of Wells Cathedral and St. John's College, Cambridge, and the BBC Philharmonic Orchestra in the work's premiere. The *Nunc dimittis* (and the organ version of the *Magnificat*) were premiered by that cathedral's choir (Philip Scriven, organ) conducted by David Hill on July 15, 2000.[60]

As is fairly common in setting this pair of canticles, MacMillan sets the Lesser Benediction of both to the same music. The extremely loud and dissonant organ chord that begins each may come as something of a shock. But this dissonance is not gratuitous but becomes a musical gesture used to create a formal alternation of organ (dissonance) and choir (consonance). Despite opening bitonal vocal pairs (C major [S/A] vs. D♭ major [T/B]) the choral writing is accessible—fundamentally homophonic and ultimately consonant; MacMillan's inclusion of a piquant cross relation (F♯ vs. F♮) in the final chord is understandable as a sonority familiarly found in the church music of Tallis and Byrd.

The practicality of the choral writing in these canticles prefigures the *Strathclyde Motets* (2005–10), two volumes of Latin liturgical motets written for Alan Tavener (unrelated to John) and the Strathclyde University Chamber Choir. At the opposite end of the spectrum of difficulty are such *a cappella* works as *Màiri* (1994), which the BBC commissioned to celebrate the seventieth anniversary of the BBC Singers, and other commissioned works for double choir: *Christus vincit* (1994), *Laudi alla Vergine Maria* (2004), the *Tenebrae Responsories* (2006), *Sun Dogs* (2006), and *fiat mihi* (2007).

Nonetheless, the most significant choral works of the new millennium are Passion-related compositions like the *St. John Passion* (2008). In interviews given to publicize its premiere, MacMillan states that, as early as his composition of the *Seven Last Words* in 1993, he knew that he would compose other Passion-based works, of which his *St. John* is the first.[61] Though longer and more sumptuously scored than the *Seven Last Words*, the *St. John Passion's* use of added Latin liturgical texts and a purely orchestral conclusion strongly suggest that the two are related. The added texts, all drawn from Catholic liturgical sources, function meditatively, like the chorales in J. S. Bach's Passions. While acknowledging the looming shadow of Bach's compositions and shared devices (the use of the bass voice for Jesus, of specific instruments associated with Jesus's words—here a string trio and trombone choir, which underscores the Johannine Gospel's emphasis on the kingship of Jesus—not to mention his deft insertion of a phrase of the Passion chorale to conclude mvt. 7, "Jesus and his mother"), MacMillan asserts a personal "sense of ownership over the Passions because, after all, Catholic passions by Lassus, Palestrina, and Victoria existed well before Bach."[62] Like Bach, MacMillan creates music of extreme drama, reliant upon conventions that lay claim to a certain degree of universality. Indeed, the work's dominant impression, even on first hearing, is MacMillan's ability to craft a compelling audible thread of dramatic reference that relies on recognition of specific gestures (e.g., the association of Pilate with wood blocks, different vocal timbres for other characters, and allusion to music of his own and by other composers, especially his appropriation of the dramatic percussion rhythm of Aaron Copland's *Fanfare for the Common Man.*

CONCLUSION

Even if the British themselves had doubts about the quality of their choral music, Americans have come to regard the English sound and level of performance as an ideal worthy of emulation. Beginning with Elgar, Stanford, and Parry, sustained by major contributions from Holst, Vaughan Williams, Finzi, and Howells, British choral music arguably reached its first high-water mark in the works of Tippett, Walton, and, especially, Benjamin Britten, whose *War Requiem* will stand as one of the greatest choral works of the twentieth century. Britten is the first English *contemporary* composer to realize the goals and ideals put forward as part of the English musical renaissance.

Britten marked something of a turning point for English music; his operas generally marked acceptance of a British composer as an equal player on the world stage. Inevitably, those who followed him have proven unable to match his deft assimilation of tradition and modernity, his contrapuntal prowess, or his penchant for creating striking and effective dramatic images. Lacking his focus, they have tended to separate into diverse camps. Some composers—most notably John Rutter and Bob Chilcott—have closely hewn to music that is commercially viable; modernists like Maxwell Davies, Birtwistle, Ferneyhough, and, to some extent, Tavener have succumbed to creating works that can be performed only by select, professional ensembles like the BBC Singers or recording-driven ensembles like Polyphony, London Sinfonietta Voices, or the New London Chamber Choir. That John Rutter is a gifted composer is beyond question; the huge success of pieces like "What Sweeter Music" and his *Gloria* (to name the two best-known examples), as well as his numerous useful anthologies of choral music and recordings, assure his place in any history of English choral music. The tradition continues in a diverse array of composers that includes John Gardner, William Mathias, Jonathan Dove, Gabriel Jackson, Tarik O'Regan, and Paul Mealor, assuring that Great Britain will continue to be a source of singable, consumable choral music well into the twenty-first century.

The only composer who may approach Benjamin Britten's lofty perch is James MacMillan, who continues to compose a stylistically diverse group of choral works that demonstrate facility over a wide range of difficulty without sacrificing his unique personal voice. While future histories of choral music will necessarily deal with composers of the stature of Britten and MacMillan, the ability of others to withstand the winnowing process of time is less certain. Yet, the vitality and diversity of choral singing in the British Isles augurs well for the future, leading one to ask who will be the John Eliot Gardner, Andrew Parrott, Paul Hillier, Harry Christophers (among others) of future decades?

13

The New Simplicities

Debussy resented "Impressionism." Schoenberg preferred "pantonal" to "atonal" or "twelve-tone" or "Expressionist." Too bad for them.

Edward Strickland, *American Composers: Dialogues on Contemporary Music*

Late-twentieth-century [music] transmission, in a word, was "horizontal." All musics past and present, nearby and far away, were, thanks to recording and communications technology, simultaneously and equally accessible to any musician in the world. The way in which this horizontal transmission supplanted the "vertical" transmission of styles in chronological single file (the assumption of which all historicist thinking depends) was the genuine musical revolution of the late twentieth century, the full implications of which will be realized only in the twenty-first and beyond.

Richard Taruskin, *OHWM* 5

A truly valid twentieth-century music would be "a music that is essentially percussive and pulse-generated rather than melodic and phrase-generated."

John Adams on Steve Reich,
New Grove Dictionary of American Music, 4

If the title of chapter 9 ("The Avant-Garde Aesthetic") doesn't cause you to skip it entirely, the music discussed there might have made you wonder why music so clearly inaccessible to many choirs is included there. The simple answer is, like Mount Everest, it's there, it exists. The more complicated answer is that such forbidding stuff must have caused a similar reaction among those who first encountered it. The composers discussed in chapter 10 ("European Centrism") largely ignored the nascent avant-garde, preferring to hew more closely to the safety of tradition. To varying degrees the composers discussed in chapters 11 ("The American Experience") and 12 ("The British Isles") adapted most of modernism's arcane technical procedures to suit their individual needs. This chapter presents another response to the question that faced all twentieth-century choral composers, namely, how does one write choral music and still feel modern or relevant? Indeed, the notion of "contemporary" music as something unique and distinctly different is a recent development. Before the nineteenth century discovered historical music (starting with Mendelssohn's famed revival of Bach's *St. Matthew Passion* in 1829), all music that was performed was contemporary and very often written by the conductor.

In post–World War II Europe, leading composers (Boulez, Henze, Stockhausen, and Berio) embraced the "integral serialism" more or less invented by Olivier Messiaen. In the United States, composers in search of a way forward coalesced around John Cage (1912–92), the poster child of indeterminacy. Both the serial modernists and the chance-music camps sought to eliminate entirely the artist's personality and ego from the process of creation (Fig. 13.1). Although the specifics of their methods varied greatly, the end result was more or less the same. In 1940

Fig. 13.1 John Cage (1972)

Cage expanded on Henry Cowell's advancements in pianistic technique, creating the "prepared piano," in which garden-variety items available at the local hardware store transformed the piano into even more of a percussion instrument. Cage sought to emancipate his music from any preconceived notions of what music is. In the late 1940s Cage found in Zen Buddhism a way to banish rational control by emptying one's mind. Shortly thereafter, he received a copy of the ancient Chinese manual *I Ching* ("Book of Changes"). This book advocated tossing three coins or six sticks multiple times to generate a random sequence of figures, which Cage adapted to represent the various parameters of music. As Richard Taruskin explains: "The predetermination of the relationships between the divination charts and the musical results was precisely the sort of music-producing algorithm that Boulez and Stockhausen and their Darmstadt colleagues had been seeking via the multiple application of the twelve-tone serial principle."[1] While Cage's output of choral music was small and without imitators, he did manage to lay the groundwork for one of the two major principles to be discussed in this chapter—aleatoricism or "chance music."[2]

WITOLD LUTOSŁAWSKI (1913–94)

One of Poland's outstanding twentieth-century composers, Witold Lutosławski's (1913–1994) significance transcended Poland's borders. Like so many other composers who lived in Soviet Bloc countries, Lutosławski's early music (*Symphonic Variations* [1938], *Symphony 1* [1947], *Overture for Strings* [1949], *Little Suite* [1950], and *Concerto for Orchestra* (1954]) reflected the nationalistic, folkloric trends promulgated by the Soviet Union. Apart from fragments of a Requiem written as his diploma composition in 1937, scarcely any published choral music exists, aside from his masterpiece, *Trois poèmes d'Henri Michaux* (1961–63).[3]

In 1956, Hungary staged a short-lived revolt against Communist control, a bid for independence that was ruthlessly suppressed by the Russians. But this brief window that allowed composers like György Ligeti to escape to the West closed quickly. Władysław Gomułka, the de facto leader of Poland's Communist Party from 1956 to 1972, made unilateral internal reforms designed to stave off the resulting restrictions imposed on artists elsewhere in the Soviet Bloc. His success encouraged Lutosławski to stay in Warsaw where, along with the composers Tadeusz Baird and Kazimierz Serocki, he helped organize the Warsaw Autumn Festival of Contemporary Music. The inaugural festival took place in September 1956 as a way of countering Western claims of Soviet censorship. The first and, for a long time, only festival of contemporary music in the Soviet Bloc countries used openness to modernist Western music as a public relations ploy. The plot worked, providing Polish composers unique access (within the Communist world) to the music of Schoenberg, Webern, Berg, Varèse, Bartók, and Stravinsky and, later, compositions by Pierre Boulez, Luigi Nono, Bruno Maderna, and John Cage.[4] It also served as the vehicle for the premiere of numerous works by Lutosławski, Górecki, and Penderecki.

Lutosławski's *Trois poèmes d'Henri Michaux* (1961–63) is scored for chorus and orchestra, each of which has its own conductor. It demonstrates what Lutosławski was to call "limited aleatoricism," a wonderfully simple technique in which singers perform their individual parts by visualizing them—based not on levels of rhythmic notation or meter but on the placement of notes within the composition's only unifying device, a timeline in which 2.5 centimeters of space in the score equals a specific time duration. To describe his new approach, Lutosławski invoked Werner Meyer-Eppler's definition of aleatoricism: "One calls aleatoric those events the courses of which are well defined in broad outlines, but whose details depend on chance."[5] This technique appears primarily in choral writing; while the orchestral parts are metered, the simultaneous use of 1/2, 3/4, 5/8 precludes conducting in the normal sense. Lutosławski indicates that in the first two movements, the conductor's gesture (indicated with ↓) indicates a duration of one second (MM 60, visually 2.5 centimeters). The chorus is tacet for the first eighteen measures, and when they do enter (m. 19), none of the parts has a meter sign. The orchestra continues on at "tempo," overlapping with the chorus for an additional ten seconds. Example 13.1 shows the task facing the singers—executing their parts independent of any external control.

Example 13.1 Lutosławski, *Trois Poèmes d' Henri Michaux*, mvt. 1 ("Pensée")
Copyright © 1963, Carl Fischer, LLC on behalf of Theodore Presser and Polskie Wydawnictwo Muzyczne. Used by permission.

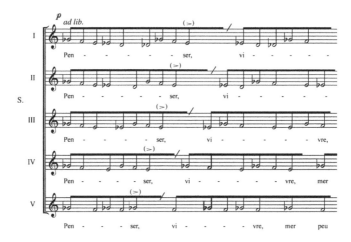

The top four soprano parts sing a durational canon comprised of six pitches.[6] Each part sings this "melody" at different speeds and in variable quantities indicated by vertical slashes. Left to chance is how accurately the singer(s) can execute their part; the element of chance increases incrementally as more than one singer takes each part.

Although the title page calls "for a twenty-part choir," Lutosławski really envisions twenty *soloists*; he does, however, suggest doubling or even tripling the number of singers per part when the work is performed in larger halls. To further complicate the issue, Lutosławski marks the first choral entrance "tutti" (implying that, at some point, only soloists will sing). The conclusion of this first choral event follows a two-second caesura (marked by a fermata); when the soprano and alto parts resume, Lutosławski marks these parts "soli," suggesting that now there is but one singer per part. The use of this term implies that variation in the number of singers performing the choral parts becomes an element of form. In this new section, the conductor cues the beginning of each new event based on elapsed time rather than meter. For example, beginning at m. 29, the solo soprano and alto parts sing for approximately fifteen seconds, followed by the entry of the male voices at m. 30 (ten seconds). The next cue signals the end of the women's singing (m. 31). Five seconds later (m. 32), the basses begin to sing a new text, while the tenors continue free, asynchronous repetitions of their music. Such extensions occur throughout the work, routinely marked by wavy lines, which indicate that "Each of the singers repeats his phrase till the conductor's next signal."[7]

The relative simplicity of Lutosławski's approach springs from his willingness to surrender absolute control over certain of the composition's parameters; by so doing, he intended to "restore ... the pleasure which the performer should feel with the performance of a work."[8] While the aural results may not differ substantially from those achieved by Stockhausen, Berio, and others, he simplified the singer's task by leaving specific details of execution to chance.[9]

This twelve-minute work's three movements each set a poem by Henri Michaux (1899–1984) and retains the poem's original title—"Pensée," "Le grand combat," and "Repos dans le Malheur." But Lutosławski's process of selecting what texts to use is decidedly not the path taken by earlier composers: "I chose these three poems *after* [my emphasis] I had already made a general outline of the entire work. The texts of the chosen poems then influenced the detailed development of the musical form. The verse, its sense and construction, and even particular words had to exert an influence on the music of my composition. This was, moreover, as I had intended. If I had proceeded otherwise, if the words of the text were to be merely one more sound-element of the music, this would be a misuse of the poetry and artistically false, and at any rate it would be a wrong approach."[10]

Even though Lutosławski fails to provide any rationale for his poetic choices, he does acknowledge distinct textual qualities. "Pensée" ponders the nature of thought using diverse imagery, while "Repos dans le Malheur" speaks of resignation to fate by projecting total collapse. Conversely, the middle poem, "Le grand combat," conjures images of an angry mob, screaming their encouragement to the combatants, anxious to see if "enlightenment" ("Le grand secret") will emerge from the carnage. This movement is also exceptional in that its vocal parts lack the specific pitch notation used by Lutosławski in the movements that frame it. Lutosławski affirms a symmetrical tripartite form for the entire work based on text and realized by his use of notated pitch and the same type of durational canon in the outer movements, a claim slightly diminished by the third movement's comparative brevity and considerably reduced orchestral palette (primarily harp and piano).

KRZYSZTOF PENDERECKI

The notation Lutosławski uses in *Trois Poèmes* becomes an accurate predictor of the significance of his work for the newly emerging school of Polish composers, the most famous of whom is Krzysztof Penderecki (b. 1933) (Fig. 13.2). Penderecki managed to parlay Poland's artistic tolerance into recognition in prestigious Western centers of new music, most notably the Donaueschingen Festival of New Music. It was for this festival that Penderecki composed *Anaklasis* (1960), the success of which led to such similar, sonority-driven works as *Polymorphia* (1961), *Fluorescencje* (1962), *De natura sonoris* (1966), and, the most successful, *Threnody to the Victims of Hiroshima* (1961) for fifty-two solo strings. Penderecki realized that Lutosławski's methods were much more practical than those used by Ligeti and the Darmstadt composers. Instead of conventional notation and tempo, Penderecki adopted Lutosławski's use of duration; his most conspicuous borrowing was Lutosławski's use of blank space rather than measures of rests for instruments or voices not performing at any given moment.

It is somewhat ironic that Penderecki's first significant choral work, the *Passio et Mors Domini Jesu Christi Secundum Lucam* (*St. Luke Passion*, 1963–66), appears in this chapter about "The New Simplicities." Nothing about the music it contains is simple, but its appropriation of Lutosławski's simplified notation in the choral parts justify its inclusion here. In the work's eighth measure, Penderecki distributes the four words "Crux ave spes unica" ("Hail to the cross, our only hope") among four different voices.[11] Seven measures later, Penderecki uses the symbol ~ to indicate—for the first time—asynchronous rhythmic performance in the choral parts. Although Lutosławski completely avoids traditional metric notation in the choral parts of his *Trois Poèmes*, Penderecki retains traditional metric notation in the choral parts (even when a measure's length is not defined by a conventional meter sign, as in m. 15). He also borrows Lutosławski's use of slanted lines to indicate gradual glissandi, straight lines for sustained pitches, creating his own version of visualized rhythmic distribution (mvt. 9, m. 62).[12]

Penderecki's *St. Luke Passion* is, ultimately, far more indebted to the two Passion settings by J. S. Bach than to the notational innovations of Lutosławski (Fig. 31.2). The similarities between the two composers' Passions are both generic and specific: *generic* in their common use of hymn text and melodies, "turba" choruses, additional texts beyond the Gospel narrative, and alternation of narrative and contemplative elements; *specific* in using a bass voice for the role of Jesus, an evangelist (a speaking part in Penderecki), bipartite division of the text, distinct vocal genres such as chorus, aria, chorale/hymn, and use of Bach's musical monogram (B♭–A–C–H[B♮]).

That noted, the differences separating the two composers are far more numerous, especially regarding text; while Bach limited himself to the gospel narrative, free poetic texts, and hymn texts, Penderecki includes Hebrew Bible texts (Psalms 5, 10, 15, 16, 22, 31, and 56) Latin liturgical texts (e.g., the refrain "Jerusalem, Jerusalem, Dominum" sung at the conclusion of

Fig. 13.2 Penderecki conducting (1989)

Table 13.1 Penderecki, *St. Luke Passion*

Part 1:		
1. *O Crux, Ave*	Chorus	*Vexilla Regis*
2. *Et egressus ibat*	Narration	Lk 22:39–44
3. Aria: *Deus Meus*	Aria (B)	Ps 22:1–2, Ps 5:1
4. *Domine, quis habitabit*	Aria (S)	Ps 15:1, 4–8; Ps 16:9
5. *Adhuc eo loquente*	Narration	Lk 22:47–53
6. *Jerusalem*	Chorus	Lamentations of Jeremiah
7. *Ut quid Domini*	Chorus	Ps 10:1
8. *Comprehendentes*	Narration	Lk 22:54–62
9. *Judica me*	Aria (B)	Ps 43:1
10. *Et viri qui tenebat illum*	Narration	Lk 22:63–71
11. *Jerusalem*	Aria (S)	Lamentations of Jeremiah
12. *Miserere*	Chorus	Ps 56:1
13. *Et surgens omnis*	Narration	Lk 23:1–22
Part 2:		
14. *In pulverum mortis*	Psalm	Ps 22:15
15. *Et baiulans*	Narration	Jn 19:17 (*Via Crucis*)
16. *Popule meus*	Passacaglia	*Improperia*
17. *Ibi crucifixerunt eum*	Narrative	Lk 23:33
18. *Crux fidelis*	Aria/Chorus	Antiphons (*Pange Lingua*)
19. *Dividentes vero vestimenta*	Narration	Lk 23:34*
20. *In pulverum mortis*	Chorus	Ps 22:15–19
21. *Et stabat populus*	Narration	Lk 23:35–37
22. *Unus autem de his*	Narration	Lk 23:39–43*
23. *Stabant autem juxta crucem*	Narration	Jn 19:25–27*
24. *Stabat Mater*	Triple Chorus	Sequence, vv. 1, 5, 9–10, 19, 20
25. *Erat autem fere hora sexta*	Narration	Ll 23:44–46*, Jn 19:30*
26. Instrumental interlude		
27. *In te Domine speravi*	Chorus	Ps 31:1–2, 5

* Settings of Seven Last Words

settings of the Lamentations, the hymns *Vexilla regis prodeunt* and *Pange lingua*, the *Improperia* ["Reproaches"], and six strophes of the sequence *Stabat mater*) (See Table 13.1). Penderecki shapes this collage of texts into twenty-seven movements that comprise the work's two large formal divisions.

Penderecki omits sixty verses of Luke's account: forty of Luke 22's seventy-one verses and twenty of Luke 23's fifty-six verses. Penderecki's decision to end Part 1 with the first twenty-two verses of Luke 23 is similarly unorthodox. And he replaces Luke's eight-verse description of the procession to Calvary (Luke 23:23–32) with a single verse from John 19:17: ("So they took Jesus; and carrying the cross … he went out to what is called The Place of the Skull, which in Hebrew is called Golgotha"). Penderecki again borrows John's account of the interaction between Jesus, his mother, and John, the disciple (19:25–27) as the necessary pretext for including his earlier *Stabat Mater* (1962). After the *Stabat Mater*'s surprisingly triumphant conclusion, Penderecki sets the final two of the Seven Last Words—"Into your hands I commend my Spirit" (found only in Luke) and "It is finished." (John 19:30).[13]

In such an extended work with multiple texts and an experimental musical style, formal cohesion is bound to be an issue. In their descriptive analysis of the Passion, Allen Winold and Ray Robinson present thirty-five themes used by Penderecki; these consist of twelve-tone rows (both compete and fragmentary) and other less extensive melodies.[14] The most prominent theme is the musical spelling of Bach's name, which appears (in retrograde form) in the organ part in m. 6 of the first movement. The first choral use of this distinctive motive comes two measures later in the distributive setting of "Crux ave spes unica" and again near the work's conclusion (mvt. 27, mm. 22–24) to achieve a measure of formal closure. The BACH motif shares intervallic similarities with another motive drawn from the Polish hymn *Święty Boże* (also known as the Trisagion: "Holy God, Holy Mighty . . ."). This shared intervallic content (two descending semitones framing a minor third) underlies many of the themes that Robinson and Winold identify. Although this motive's appearances in the Passion are too numerous to catalogue, its appearance as the imitative theme of mvt. 12 (an *a cappella* setting of Psalm 56:2) is interesting and significant.

The most important aspect of Penderecki's formal design is his inclusion of his earlier *Stabat Mater* for three *a cappella* choirs (1962) as mvt. 24 of the Passion. Like Verdi in his Requiem, Penderecki uses the earlier composition not only to generate this movement but also mines it for many of the motives he uses elsewhere. Next, Robinson and Winold identify a distinctive cadence, which they call the "Domine chord." This cadence features both semitone ascent and descent to different pairs of pitches. The semitone resolution of these chords can be seen as either an extension of the "sigh" motif or the use of that same interval in the BACH motif (see ex. 13.2).[15]

Example 13.2 Penderecki, *St. Luke Passion*, mvt. 3, m. 12
© 1967 by Schott Music. © Renewed. All rights reserved. Used by permission of European American Music Distributors LLC, sole US and Canadian agent for Schott Music.

This distinctive cadence appears five times in Part 1 of the passion and three times in Part 2. Although Penderecki's placement of these cadences elude us, they become a recognizable, audible formal gesture. As shown in example 13.2, all but one (mvt. 7, m. 15) involves a cadence to one of three different pairs of pitches (E–G, E–C♯, or B–D). Of the three, the cadences to E and G are important because of their location (they comprise the work's first three and final two use of this cadence) and because Penderecki uses their pitches as the work's opening (G) and closing (E) tonal centers.[16]

Of the other motives that Robinson and Winold list, one stands out as structurally significant: cluster chords constructed as sets of perfect fourths a semitone apart.[17] Not surprisingly, the prototype for this gesture appears in the *Stabat Mater* (ex. 13.3a).

Example 13.3 a–d Penderecki, *St. Luke Passion*

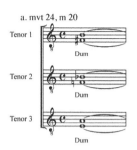

a. mvt 24, m 20

b, mvt. 1, m. 6

c. mvt. 13, m. 66

Example 13.3 a–d Continued

d. mvt. 20, mm. 9-11

The first entrance of the three divisi tenor parts in m. 20 of mvt. 24 is a stack of perfect fourths built on E, F, and F♯. Example 13.3b shows the first use of this construction in m. 6 of mvt. 1; example 13.3c ends Part 1; setting the crowd's demand that Jesus be crucified ("Crucifige") by altering the perfect fourths to tritones. Example 13.3d (from mvt. 20) uses the same harmonic construction built over an alto/bass pedal on D, the tonal center of the *Stabat Mater*.

The *St. Luke Passion* is an astonishing accomplishment, considering that it comes just eight years after the completion of Penderecki's musical studies and the composition of just twenty works. It stands as a landmark of twentieth-century choral music primarily because of its comparison with the Bach Passions. It was closely followed by equally challenging works like *Dies irae* (1967), *Utrenja* (1969–71), *Cosmogony* (1970), and *Canticum Canticorum Salomonis* (1970–73). What justifies Penderecki's inclusion in this chapter is less these early experimental works than later works like his *Magnificat* (1973–74), which use a much simpler style. Concerning the *Magnificat*'s pivotal role, Penderecki writes: "But *Magnificat* is also the last piece where I used a very complicated polyphonic technique; here you find 48 different voices. This makes the piece almost impossible to perform. You need fifty rehearsals to prepare the piece."[18] Financial considerations, the most powerful incentive of all, led Penderecki to create a new, simpler style less beholden to the creative imperatives of the 1960s. Some commentators label this new, simpler style neo-Romantic (a label that the composer does not reject), but, in the end, financial concerns drove Penderecki to embrace a style less beholden to the modernistic imperative that drove his compositions of the 1960s.

Principal examples of his simpler style are *Agnus Dei*, SSAATTBB *a cappella* (1981); *Pieśń Cherubinów* (*Cherubic Hymn*), SSAATTBB *a cappella* (1987); and, most noticeably, *Credo* (1998). Despite its lack of a conventional key signature, *Agnus Dei* exhibits the tonal properties of F minor, embroidered with remnants of the gestures found in the *St. Luke Passion* (notably the dissonant cluster setting of the word *peccata*, ["sins"] at mm. 71–73). Despite such allusions to his more experimental music, the harmonic style of the *Cherubic Hymn* implies traditional harmony notated conventionally (see ex. 13.4).

Example 13.4 Penderecki, *Pieśń Cherubinów*, mm. 11–23

A similar blending of old and new appears in *Credo*, a fifty-minute-plus, multimovement composition for boys choir, large chorus, five vocal soloists, and orchestra. Helmut Rilling, to whom the work is dedicated, conducted the premiere at the Oregon Bach Festival on July 11, 1998. Penderecki divides the text into five large "movements" or sections that exhibit a degree of symmetry. The first ("Credo in unum Deum") and fifth ("Et in Spiritum Sanctum") movements set roughly the same amount of the Latin Mass text and use a theme (see ex. 13.5) derived from one of the traditional Gregorian intonations associated with this text.

Example 13.5 Penderecki, *Credo*, mm. 1–3

The second ("Qui propter nos homines / Et incarnatus") and fourth ("Et resurrexit") movements also contain similar amounts of Mass text, which leaves the third movement ("Crucifixus etiam pro nobis") to stand as the centerpiece of an arch form. And it is here that Penderecki inserts the majority of the liturgical texts drawn from sources other than the Mass. The most important of these are two verses of the "Pange lingua . . . lauream certaminis" ("Sing loud the conflict, O my tongue").[19] Used liturgically, this hymn directly precedes the second added text, "Populus meus, quid fecisti tibi?" ("My people, what have you done to me?") from the *Improperia*. Penderecki also uses two traditional Polish Lenten hymns and the first line of the chorale *Aus tiefer Not schrei' ich zu dir* ("Out of the depths I cry to you").

The *Crucifixus* was the first section that Penderecki composed (December 1996), and from it springs the distinctive chromatic theme first sung by the boys choir (mvt. 3, m. 77). This theme (ex. 13.6) finds its way into the second (mm. 11–15) and fourth mm. 304–8) movements as well, underscoring the centrality of the *Crucifixus*.

Example 13.6 a–b Penderecki, *Credo*

a. mvt. 2, mm. 11-15

b. mvt. 4, mm. 304-08

We have already discussed the prominent role that semitones play in the *St. Luke Passion*—the "sigh" motive, the "Domine" chord, the BACH motive (with its two consecutive "sighs", B♭–A / C–B♮), along with Penderecki's extension of this gesture into multiple twelve-tone rows. In his monograph on Penderecki's life and works, Wolfram Schwinger re-emphasizes the importance of this procedure across Penderecki's output.[20] The extension of this motif into themes that dominate his *Credo* strongly suggests that the role of the semitone is indeed the critical link throughout Penderecki's music, in this statement from the composer himself:

> I now see only one stream of development in my music from the beginning until now. Starting with the *Psalms of David*, which was my first step as a composer, and where I discovered the elements of my own musical language for the first time, until the two most recent pieces [*Seven Gates of Jerusalem* and *Hymn to the Holy Daniel*]. Even in the melodic approach and the structure of, for example, *Seven Gates*, you will find elements of the Psalms I wrote as a student in 1958. Of course, there have been periods where I have been fascinated by the avant-garde or fascinated by the late-romantic music. . . . Elements of romantic music were present in my works during the 1980s. But this is only for a short period. Then I went away from what I did and looked for something else. . . . Since *The Awakening of Jacob* (1974) . . . I have sought a synthesis

between the avant-garde style of my earlier works and a more expressive [romantic] musical language. This synthesis was achieved in the opera *The Black Mask*. I believe that the same musical elements are present in my works from the 1950s until now.[21]

It remains the task of future scholars to determine which of these two assessments is the more accurate. Suffice to say that the *St. Luke Passion* is indisputably one of the landmark choral compositions of the twentieth century, even if practical considerations eventually led Penderecki to simplify its lofty artistic aims.

It is necessary here to acknowledge the transition that has taken place from the aleatoricism practiced by John Cage, adapted by Lutosławski, and used by Penderecki to its more selective use, which is most typically found in choral music as an episode that provides a modernist contrast to the otherwise traditional style. If a purely indeterministic choral music exists, the complexity of the requisite decision-making processes has prevented its wholesale adoption by choral composers. Choirs are creatures of habit, taught to abhor chance occurrences, discrepancies of intonation, balance, or rhythmic unity. While they may tolerate brief periods of randomness, they require a largely stable, traditional notational environment. This possibly explains why Penderecki's *Credo* is more consonant and accessible than the *St. Luke Passion*, notwithstanding those echoes of his experimental style like the unpitched *Sprechgesang* in mvt. 4 (mm. 186–99) or the carefully controlled emergence of a cluster chord from the mumbled unison litany (*in remissionem peccatorum*) in mvt. 5 (mm. 56–63). Similarly, Lutosławski and Penderecki's notational innovations have become accepted, even unremarkable features of the contemporary choral score.

HENRYK GÓRECKI

After Penderecki, the next important contemporary Polish composer is Henryk Górecki (1933–2010). His choral output is smaller and less well known than Penderecki's, but has garnered more frequent performance due its fusion of New Age mysticism and contemporary folk/popular music into a music more easily accessed by contemporary audiences. Górecki was largely unknown outside of Poland until a 1992 recording of his Third Symphony (1976) suddenly appeared on the best-seller lists in the UK, other European countries, and, eventually, in the United States. Górecki's relatively small output of choral music has generated considerable popularity in the West, but it stirred up political controversy in Poland for not only defying the prohibitions against sacred music but also for being closely associated with *Solidarność* (Solidarity), a free-trade unionist movement that began in 1980 at the shipyards in Gdańsk. Under the leadership of Lech Wałęsa (and further emboldened by the 1978 election of a Polish cardinal, Karol Józef Wojtyła, as Pope John Paul II), Solidarity promoted the Catholic church's teaching on social justice, a stance that emboldened Górecki (and possible also Penderecki) to create such openly Catholic works as *Amen*, op. 35 (1975), *Beatus vir*, op. 38 (1979), *Miserere*, op. 44 (1981), and *Totus tuus*, op. 60 (1987).

While both *Beatus vir* and *Totus tuus* were dedicated to the pope, *Miserere* is dedicated to the city of Bydgoszcz, where some of the fiercest clashes between Solidarity and the Communist regime took place. Górecki specifies a chorus of "at least 120 voices" for this *a cappella* work that begins with a chant-like, whole-note melody sung by the second basses (ex. 13.7).

Example 13.7 Górecki, *Miserere*, op. 44, mm. 1–40

The work's restricted vocal range, repetitions of material, pauses between statements, and slow tempo (which grows even slower as the work progresses) act together to create an impression of timelessness, a quality that helped establish Górecki as a guru of the New Age aesthetic and, despite his protests to the contrary, a minimalist.

Each successive section of the work adds a new voice that embellishes (or, more accurately, reminisces about) the music that preceded it. Thus the music grows, organically, from the bottom up, building texturally and dynamically to a dramatic male voice tutti at the end of the fourth segment. In sections 5 through 8, Górecki adds the four female voices in similar fashion; despite this continued textural and harmonic growth, the music remains tranquil until the sudden eight-part tutti marked *ff* that scales heights of vocal tessitura not even hinted at in the preceding music. After thirty measures of loud, slow, sustained singing, the insistent dynamic begins to relax, only to be rebuilt in section 10. Finally, the chorus begins a long, slow descent marked *Lento–Tranquillissimo, cantabilissimo, dolcissimo–Blagalnie* ("Imploringly"), in which the singers finally seek God's mercy. Given these demands of dynamic and stamina, one understands why Górecki stipulated performance by 120 singers, why this piece was regarded as a defiant political statement, and why this seemingly simple work is so difficult to perform.

MINIMALISM

The ascension of Górecki to the triumvirate of "holy minimalists" (with Arvo Pärt and John Tavener) provides a neat segue into a discussion of the compositional technique broadly identified as minimalism.[22] As an aesthetic concept, minimalism first appears in painting and sculpture of the 1960s. Its application to music is slightly problematic in that there is no single defining characteristic broadly applicable to the composers whose music bears that label. As Keith Potter points out, minimalism was generically seen as "an antidote to Modernism, as represented by both the total serialism of Boulez and Stockhausen and the indeterminacy of Cage."[23] Stylistic details were less important and consistent than a general simplicity. The musicologist Richard Taruskin suggested that a more appropriate description might be "pattern and process music," referring to

Steve Reich's 1968 essay "Music as a Gradual Process."[24] The lineage of such music is generally regarded as completely American, led by four composers born within fourteen months of one another—La Monte Young (b. 1935), Terry Riley (b. 1935), Steve Reich (b. 1936), and Philip Glass (b. 1937). Their music reduces all the musical parameters to the bare minimum; other commonly encountered features are pieces of considerable length that unfold slowly in a kaleidoscopic way and rely on constant pulsation of a chosen rhythmic unit. Young and Riley are virtually unknown in the choral arena, whereas Reich and Glass have used the chorus in many interesting ways. Each has produced at least one significant work. Of the two, Philip Glass is the more successful commercially; this is due, in large measure, to his scores for such films as *The Thin Blue Line* (1988), *The Truman Show* (in collaboration with Burkhard Dallwitz, 1998), *The Hours* (2002), and Woody Allen's *Cassandra's Dream* (2007). In addition to a handful of little-known, mostly early choral works, Glass's two symphonies (Symphony No. 5, "Choral," 1999, and Symphony No. 7, "Toltec," 2004) and the symphonic portrait *Itaipú* (1999) feature the chorus. His most important work is the 1976 opera *Einstein on the Beach*, written in collaboration with the director Robert Wilson; considered at the time the model for opera in an age of technology, *Einstein*'s choral component is neither vital nor easily extracted from the larger flow of the opera.

STEVE REICH

The music of Steve Reich is strongly influenced by Glass; both distinguish themselves from Young and Riley in their commitment to composition rather than improvisation and in a fascination with harmony as a central formal construct.[25] Reich's education included undergraduate degrees from Cornell and graduate study at the Juilliard School, but it was his exposure to non-Western music in addition to study with Milhaud and Berio at Mills College in 1963 that would prove most pivotal to his development. His early success came in such phased music works as *Drumming* (1970–71) and *Clapping Music* (1972). In these pieces, Reich creates musical form by deploying a simple rhythmic idea; as the work progresses, one group of performers gradually goes out of phase rhythmically with the other. This gradual shifting from synchronous to asynchronous performance results in a musical ebb and flow that is audible, interesting, and the basis of a rudimentary musical form. *Music for 18 Musicians* (1974–76) synthesized the experiments conducted in the music of the 1960s and pointed a new way forward through its contrapuntal treatment of four amplified voices and sixteen instrumentalists. *Tehillim* (1981)—ecstatic, mesmerizing music that expands on the techniques used in *Music for 18 Musicians*—has four amplified female solo voices (high soprano [no. 4], two lyric sopranos [nos. 1 and 2] and alto [no. 3]) sing the Hebrew texts from Psalms 34, 19, 18, and 150. Each text is a separate movement, although Reich organizes them into movement pairs. While repetition remains the most important musical principal, one can discern separate layers of rhythm, harmony, text, and melody that interact with one another in ways not all that dissimilar from the earlier phased music. For example, the text of mvt. 4 consists of six lines repeated in various ways but always in the same order:

a.	*Hallelúhu batóf umachól*	"Hallelujah! Praise Him with drum and dance"
b.	*Hallelúhu baminím vaugáv*	"Hallelujah! Praise Him with strings and winds"
c.	*Hallelúhu batziltzláy shamáh*	"Hallelujah! Praise Him with sounding cymbals"
d.	*Hallelúhu batziltzláy taruáh.*	"Hallelujah! Praise Him with clanging cymbals"
e.	*Kol hanshamá tahaláil Yah,*	"Let all that breathes praise the Eternal"
f.	*Hallelúhu*	"Hallelujah!"[26]

The text, repeated many times throughout the movement's 309-measure length, always follows the sequence: a–b–c–d–e–f–e–f. This text repetition is nothing extraordinary; but it becomes more interesting when it is this regular and plays against other equally regular layers that don't match up with it one to one. Take, for example, vocal texture. Reich opens the movement (mm. 1–30) with a homophonic setting of the entire text for voices 2 and 3. For the next 140 measures, Reich reuses this melodic material using canon for first two (nos. 1 and 2, mm. 31–61) and then four voices (mm. 62–169). Beginning at rehearsal letter O (m. 170), Reich restates the first thirty measures of music in augmentation, a coda that sounds like a recapitulation but ultimately isn't. In the harmonic accompaniment provided by the strings, Reich sets up a cycle of chords based on the roots CC–BB♭–GG–AA–BB♭–GG–BB♭–DD. Despite the constantly changing meter, the chords follow this sequence of roots and each root's extended tertian harmonic content until the change of key signature (one flat to one sharp in m. 133).

Many of these same characteristics are evident in Reich's most substantive choral work, *The Desert Music* (1982–84).[27] The work was jointly commissioned by West German Radio (Cologne) and the Brooklyn Academy of Music; ensembles of these entities/institutions gave the European and American premieres. The work's title and Reich's primary text source comes from a collection of poems by William Carlos Williams, *The Desert Music and Other Poems* (1954). Concerning his choice of texts, Reich explicitly notes that "There are no complete poems used and the arrangement of parts is my own. This arrangement was my first compositional activity and the form of the piece into a large arch follows the text."[28] He also notes that the work's five movements create a large arch (A–B–C–B–A); the outer movements (A) are both fast and use the same harmonic cycle (A), while movements 2 and 4 set the same text in moderate tempo using another shared harmonic cycle (B). The central movement is itself an arch (C–B–C) based on Reich's use of the same tempo and text for the flanking sections (C), while the middle section reuses the same moderate tempo of mvts. 2 and 4. The work as a whole is a palindrome based on repeated tempi and, to a lesser extent, shared harmonic cycles. Despite more variety of harmony in the internal movements, the symmetry established by tempo and harmony is clear evidence of the composer's interest in constructive formalism.

Reich's first use of a cycle of chords shows up in *Music for 18 Musicians* and, less consistently, in *Tehillim. The Desert Music* begins with a five-chord cycle (harmonic cycle A), which first unfolds in mm. 5–26 (ex. 13.8).

Example 13.8 Reich, *The Desert Music*, mvt. 1, harmonic cycle A

As was the case in *Tehillim*, each chord of this cycle is an extended tertian sonority played and sung to a rhythm of pulsed eighth-notes, which the chorus sings on a single syllable ("De"). The root of each new chord derives from the pitch content of the preceding chord, which juxtaposes two unrelated triads. Reich repeats this same sequence of five chords three times to form the first movement's opening section. After a considerable absence (mm. 92–153), this harmonic cycle returns twice—mm. 154–98, where it combines with the new figure developed in its absence, and mm. 219–51, where it functions as a recapitulatory coda.

The new, contrasting figure mentioned above first appears m. 98; it takes the form of a syncopated ostinato (performed by the principal violins 1 and 2, and doubled by synthesizer 2), which has three distinct segments. Reich gradually inserts two other versions of the ostinato, each beginning with a different segment of the theme than the first (ex. 13.9).

Example 13.9 Reich, *The Desert Music*, mvt. 1, event 2, mm. 115–16

Reich calculates this event's close canonic construction (again reminiscent of *Tehillim*) to produce a complete, dense rhythmic/harmonic saturation. Once this new instrumental ostinato is established, the chorus sings Williams's poetic text for the first time. Like everything else, the chorus presents the text in increments that gradually increase in numbers of words and pitches (ex. 13.10).

Example 13.10 Reich, *The Desert Music*, mvt. 1, mm. 126–27

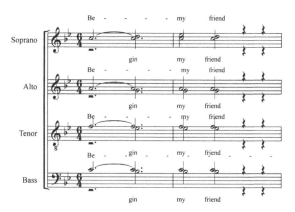

Despite commonly held beliefs that minimalism is numbingly repetitive and lacks any real structural design, these two compositions by Reich show that this is not the case. While pulsed rhythms form the prominent surface layer, evidence of careful compositional planning at both the macro- and microstructural layers tempers the extent to which these works can be considered purely minimalistic. Reich uses harmonic cycles (a kind of nonfunctional progression of chords), often with a flexibility that approaches intuition and contradicts the minimalist notion that a predictable process drives the composition.[29] Reich's use of sophisticated contrapuntal devices (most notably, canon) likely occurs because "no other Western technique comes as close to meeting the definition of a musical process; canons . . . determine all the note-to-note details and the overall form simultaneously."[30] Conversely, it is the dominant surface layer of pulsed rhythms that constitutes the most audible impression of minimalism.

ARVO PÄRT

Of the trio of composers dubbed "holy minimalists," Arvo Pärt (b. 1935) may be the most religious. His early career went largely unheralded in the West due to the strictures placed on all the Baltic countries under Communist rule. Like so many of his contemporaries, Pärt gravitated toward twelve-tone composition because that was the dominant style in the late 1950s. Given this orientation, early works like *Nekrolog*, op. 5 (1960), *Perpetuum mobile*, op. 10 (1963) and Symphony No. 1, "Polyphonic," (1963) are instrumental. But these serial works already manifest the rigorous precompositional organization and use of patterning that show up in the later minimalistic works. For Pärt 1964 was a pivotal year; among the works from that year, three—*Diagrams* (op. 11), *Quintettino*, and *Collage sur B-A-C-H*—incorporate the Bach cipher not merely as a motive but also as the generative force behind their twelve-tone rows. Of these three works, *Collage* stands out because it not only uses the BACH theme but also adds neo-Baroque elements of form (the three movements are titled Toccata, Sarabande, and Ricercar) as well as literally quoting from the Sarabande from Bach's *Sixth English Suite in D minor* (BWV 811). That year also marks the appearance of *Solfeggio*, a work for *a cappella* chorus that uses a seven-pitch "row" (the C-major scale) sung ten times to the syllables of the tonic sol-fa system.

These works presage the pivotal choral work of Pärt's compositional output, the *Credo* (1968) for piano, choir, and full orchestra. This work was in fact an act of political defiance (it provoked a huge scandal and was performed only because of a breakdown in bureaucratic oversight) and a trigger for a prolonged silence during which Pärt reevaluated his life and style of composition. In many ways, *Credo* became the culmination of the decade-long dialogue between serialism and historical music, especially the music of Bach.[31] Its bold political resistance took the form of Pärt's blatantly Christian texts: *Credo in Jesum Christum* and excerpts from the Latin version of the Gospel of Matthew (5:38–39) decrying violence.[32]

Pärt's inner conflict between serialism and tonality led him to create a dialogue between Bach's iconic *Prelude in C major* (BWV 846) and increasingly loud and dissonant music based on a tone row that bears a remarkable resemblance to the row Benjamin Britten used as the thematic core of his opera *The Turn of the Screw* (1959).[33] The *Credo* falls into three parts, the first and last of which are dominated by Bach's prelude (the non-arpeggiated form of its original draft becomes the choral parts of ex. 13.11). The middle section features a strident, dodecaphonic dialogue between chorus and orchestra, and it is this which provides another example of Pärt's patterned expansion of material.

In the end, Bach and C major are triumphant, but for Pärt the conflict exposed in this work led to nearly a decade of silence and artistic reevaluation, from which emerged the *tintinnabuli* style (a two-part texture evoking the sound of bells, a prominent sonic element in Eastern Orthodox ritual) that is such an integral part of his choral composition. Paul Hillier says it best: "With *Credo*, Pärt had written himself into a cul-de-sac: he had reached a position of complete despair, in which the composition of music appeared to be the most futile of gestures, and he lacked the musical faith and will-power to write even a single note. It was from this creative death that there arose in him a search for an entirely new way to proceed."[34]

Example 13.11 Pärt, *Credo*, mm. 23–31

Pärt's period of silence included divorce and remarriage (1972), joining the Russian Orthodox Church, his discovery of chant, and his emigration from his native Estonia to Berlin (1980) (Fig. 13.3) . His reemergence as a composer in 1976 yielded a spate of works that contain the first consistent use of the tintinnabular style, which became his signature technique.[35] This period of creativity continued into 1977 with the release of his most popular and oft-performed works—*Fratres*, *Cantus*, and *Tabula Rasa*. The codification of the tintinnabular style culminates in his first major choral work, *Passio Domini Nostri Jesu Christi Secundum Johannem* (1982).[36] Scored for tenor and bass solo, SATB solo quartet, SATB chorus, organ, oboe, violin, and cello, *Passio* sets John's seventy-verse Passion account with no repetitions, interruptions, or insertion of non-Gospel text. A high degree of precompositional planning is immediately evident and is maintained consistently throughout the work's duration. This planning led to his division of the text into 173 segments based on changes of speaker. The beginning of each new verse of biblical text is labeled in the score, and the conclusion of each verse is separated from its follower by an instrumental echo or a measure of rest. Pärt assigned the roles of Jesus and Pilate to bass and tenor respectively, each with organ accompaniment. And instead of using the traditional tenor soloist for the evangelist, Pärt assigns that role to quartets of vocal and instrumental soloists, which appear in many combinations; the choir (with or without accompaniment) take the roles of all minor characters as well as the traditional crowd choruses. The work's musical shape (meter, bar lines, etc.) derives strictly from the text. The work's overall form is traditional, essentially copying the three-part structure (Exordium, Passion, Conclusion) used in the dramatic Passions of the Renaissance.

Fig. 13.3 Arvo Pärt in his studio (Berlin, 1990)

The level of precompositional planning regarding the use of rhythm to elucidate each character or group is seemingly at odds with the minimalist aesthetic. For example, Pärt assigns different durational units to the evangelist (quarter note), the turba and Pilate (half note), and Jesus (whole note).[37] There is an elaborate series of rules that determine whether opening and closing notes of a phrase are short (one unit), medium (two units), or long (three units). In the evangelist's first entry (ex. 13.12), the quarter note is the fundamental rhythmic unit. Pärt then lengthens the first syllable of the words "hortus" (m. 25, "garden") and "ipse" (m. 30, "this") to medium length (half note) since these are the closing words of a phrase. His determination of the length of any given measure is directly tied to the number of syllables (syllable = unit pulse) in the word it contains.

Example 13.12 Pärt, *Passio*, mm. 23–35

This brief excerpt also shows the basic, two-part contrapuntal construction of Pärt's tintinnabuli style; the evangelist's part is melodic (M) while the accompanying cello part is tintinnabular (T). When the oboe joins the concluding phrase, it inverts the vocal melodic line. This example also demonstrates how Pärt's harmonic and melodic vocabulary is governed by specific tonal areas. In this case, the evangelist's melody centers on the pitch A; its triad (A minor) dictates the pitch content of the tintinnabular cello part.[38]

Example 13.13 is more elaborate, containing a turba chorus (with organ accompaniment) and the evangelist's lead-in to Pilate's response to the crowd's call for Jesus's crucifixion.

Example 13.13 Pärt, *Passio*, mm.779–87

The chorus and evangelist parts both demonstrate the familiar M and T functions of Pärt's style (even if not specifically labeled as such in Pärt's score or this example). As shown in example 13.13, the alto and bass lines of each ensemble are melodic, comprised of diatonic lines that begin on the pitch B and move in contrary motion. The alto and bass voices of the evangelist end on A while the alto and bass voices of the turba chorus end on B. This difference of pitch orientation is part of Pärt's larger and more complex organizational scheme. Paul Hillier notes that the melodic and harmonic vocabulary of this entire piece is circumscribed by a series of overlapping perfect fifths: D–A–E–B. The evangelist's part centers on the pitch A in both its melodic (A/B) and contrapuntal (S/T) aspects; the melodic voices of the chorus (A/B) take B as their initial and final pitch. The T voices of both ensembles arpeggiate different triads, A minor for the evangelist and E major for the chorus. Further, each pair of voices (M and T) are inversions of one another. Hillier's analysis of the work's basic structure reveals even more layers of preplanned structural differentiation.[39]

The notation in this example is strikingly similar to that commonly found in Penderecki. The metric notation of the chorus (half note) and the evangelist (quarter note) follow the scheme described earlier. Given these multiple layers of formal planning, how truly minimalistic is *Passio*? Pärt does not use the pulsed rhythms or the phased structure associated with Steve Reich. Conversely, it has the requisite length (seventy-five minutes) and reliance on process. But the most minimal element in Pärt's Passion is drama. Its piquant, unpredictable harmonies have a certain charm and tranquil clarity reminiscent of Górecki, even if Pärt never extends a given sonority or range to anything approaching the extremes of dynamic or duration of his Polish contemporary. Individual listeners will vary in their reaction to this Passion; some will appreciate its tranquility and kaleidoscopic changes of color, while others may find its lack of drama and sonic variety an obstacle.

After *Passio*, Pärt continued to mine the tintinnabular style in an impressive series of choral works in Latin, German, English, and Church Slavonic. Notable among these are *Magnificat* and *Miserere* (1989), *Berliner Messe* and *The Beatitudes* (1990), and the slight but charming setting of *Bogoróditsye Djévo* written for Stephen Cleobury and the Choir of King's College, Cambridge. While Pärt persists in this style, changes of detail begin to appear. For example, in the *Magnificat* (1989), the solid bar lines and ubiquitous meter changes of *Passio* are gone, although measures are still determined by one word and the number of syllables it contains. In *The Beatitudes* (1991), Pärt abandons this principle, setting an entire text phrase as one "measure" followed by a so-called Grand Pause of unspecified duration. Then, in the two English-texted anthems composed to commemorate the 350th anniversary of the Karlstad diocese (1997)—*The Woman with the Alabaster Box* and *Tribute to Caesar*—Pärt reverts to his earlier use of solid bar lines and measures that contain a single word. This reversal suggests that Pärt's stylistic evolution, at least in terms of metrical notation, is not rigidly deterministic but subject to change.

Over time, Pärt makes adjustments to the contrapuntal system used in *Passio*. Michael Chikinda points to two fundamental changes in the evolution of Pärt's style:

1. In post-1990 works, the clear delineation between M and T voices present in *Passio* begins to disappear, most notably in the clear separation between how M and T voices are constructed.
2. There is an increased emphasis on chromatically inflected intervals (especially augmented seconds and neighbor tones) in the M voices; this new melodic variety tends to produce more stagnant T lines.[40]

Tribute to Caesar contains examples of Pärt's new, freer approach to the assignment of T and M voices. After opening with the divisi tenors singing parallel thirds over a divided bass of just two chords in A minor (mm. 1–7), Pärt transfers the tenor's melodic thirds to the soprano and alto (now starting on C' and E') (ex. 13.14).

Example 13.14 Pärt, *Tribute to Caesar*, mm. 8–11

The bass continues its monotone accompaniment (AA–E) until m. 11, at which point it becomes a typical T voice, singing an arpeggiated A-minor triad. But, the tenor part is the most interesting line because it functions as both an M and T voice. After starting as a T voice (m. 8), it becomes an M voice (mm. 9–10), singing an inversion of the soprano's melody, before resuming its T function in m. 10. The entire opening section (mm. 1–11) illustrates Chikinda's point that Pärt is beginning to mix "stagnant" and normal T lines, as well blurring the distinction between these roles in any given voice.[41]

Regarding Pärt's emphasis on the augmented second, consider the baritone solo (*Vox Christi*) that begins in m. 74 (ex. 13.15).

Example 13.15 Pärt, *Tribute to Caesar*, mm. 74–80

The baritone solo line is a diatonic scalar construction, save for Pärt's consistent use of G♯. In mm. 74–78, the melody consists of two statements of an A harmonic-minor scale, the end of the first overlapping the beginning of the second. But Pärt omits the one pitch (E in m. 77, either octave) that would have made the second scale complete. Perhaps he does this so that the second setting of "Caesar" begins with G♯ like its predecessor. Given the number of syllables, this coincidence occurs only because that pitch is omitted. The melody that concludes the example (mm. 79–80) is totally different: it starts and ends on the pitch B, otherwise preserving the diatonic collection of A-harmonic-minor. We hear it as a kind of E major in second inversion that closes with a Phrygian cadence to B.

Another innovation is Pärt's new approach to creating measures; gone is the old approach (one word per measure), replaced by the greater flexibility seen in example 13.15. After three measures each defined by a single two-syllable word ("Render / therefore / unto"), he sets "Caesar the things which are . . . " as a single measure of six quarter notes. Had the phrase been set using the formula of *Passio*, there would have been six measures("Caesar / the / things / which / are / Caesar's"), the middle four containing a single quarter note. Pärt does the same thing for the next phrase, setting "unto God the things that are God's" as an 11/4 measure comprised entirely of quarter notes until the concluding whole note.

Pärt uses a traditional T structure in the soprano and alto (D minor). In the first five measures, the soprano and alto sing new pitches on every other quarter note (regardless of how that sonority relates to the pitch of the baritone). This harmonic pair of T voices in D minor creates a kind of bitonality with the A harmonic minor→E 6/4 melody of the baritone. Only five of their eleven chords (marked with as asterisk in the example) are consonant with the pitches of the baritone, and these all occur in the first phrase. Pärt might have employed this tonal dichotomy as a metaphor for the differences between tribute to Caesar and reverence for God.

If we map the location of M and T voices in *Tribute to Caesar*, we find irregularities that might never have happened in *Passio*. Similarly, while the static T voices alternate between pitches a fifth apart (like *Passio*), Pärt alternates them to create a rondo-like harmonic form (**A–E**, E–B, **A–E**, D–A, **A–E**). Thus, in *Tribute to Caesar*, the assignment of M and T functions to pairs of voices is much freer than in *Passio*.

All the features enumerated in *Tribute to Caesar* are consistent with the more flexible approach taken by Pärt in the tintinnabular works composed in the 1990s and after. Whereas the strictness of application of compositional principles in *Passio* suggests a composer in transition from a serial background, the departures from those strictures in later works seems more intuitive than process-driven. In general, the danger of the seeming simplicity and verticality of Pärt's music is a loss of linear phrasing. Paul Hillier's perceptive remarks about the optimal style of singing in this music—a de-emphasis of vibrato—and the need to guard against undue focus on the music's vertical alignment are wise and essential to the creation of Pärt's unique sonic environment.[42]

JOHN ADAMS

Born a decade after Glass and Reich, John Adams (b. 1947) is heir to aspects of minimalism that he uses as a stylistic choice, not an obligation. The elements of pulsed rhythm, harmonic stasis, and patterned repetition are all evident in his first major choral-orchestral work, *Harmonium*, commissioned (at the suggestion of Edo de Waart, at that time the conductor of the San Francisco Symphony) to celebrate the orchestra's inaugural season in its new home, the Laura M. Davies Symphony Hall, in 1981. While Adams creates three numbered movements, *Harmonium* really has only two parts—the setting of Donne's "Negative Love" and the arrangements of two poems by Emily Dickinson ("Because I could not stop for death" and "Wild Nights"), which are performed as a seamless pair. In his prefatory note, Adams writes that *Harmonium* began "as a simple, totally-formed mental image: that of a single tone emerging out of a vast, empty space and, by means of a gentle unfolding, evolving into a rich, pulsating fabric of sound."[43] While this description is accurate and explains essential aspects of the minimalist aesthetic, the dimensions and scoring of the work (large orchestra, mixed chorus *divisi*) are anything but. Herein lies a fundamental problem: to many contemporary musicians, critics, and audiences, the term "minimalism" often implies that such music is insubstantial and lacking in contrast.

Given its length, sumptuous scoring, and constant parade of tempo and key changes, *Harmonium* in no way conforms to that expectation. Indeed, there are ten changes of tempo and seventeen different key signatures in its first movement alone, facts that do not help the listener or the analyst understand how the music works nor assess how "minimalistic" it is. The tempo generally accelerates gradually (from MM 126 to MM 184) through nearly the first five hundred measures, only to return to the initial tempo at the end. Similarly, changes of key signature seem more a matter of notational convenience than formal significance. Neither piece of information seems dependent on the syntax of Donne's poem (as would surely have been the case in a pre-twentieth-century composer) nor do they identify any significant formal design. Adams's vast canvas (for this music is indeed more painted than composed, a conclusion that may constitute its closest link to minimalism) is at once filled with enormous intricacy of detail and yet simple enough to comprehend in its essence. The masterful orchestration and the interaction of so many layers of sonority and rhythm combine to produce a magical gestalt that is certainly more than the sum of its parts.

As in traditional minimalist music, the rate at which harmony changes (or harmonic rhythm) is extremely slow in Adams's *Harmonium*. The first movement retains the pitch D in varying degrees of concentration for its first 178 measures (despite three changes of key signature). Adams says that with such slowing down of harmonic rhythm, "modulation took on a new and exciting meaning . . . that when properly handled [it] could accomplish the effect of a kind of cosmic gear shifting. A successful performance of any one of these pieces should give the feeling of travelling—sometimes soaring, sometimes crawling, but nonetheless always moving forward over vast stretches of imaginary terrain."[44] He acknowledges two very different kinds of harmonic change: (1) the kind of glacial movement in which very subtle changes are introduced over a lengthy time span, and (2) a sudden change of harmony or "juxtaposition" that produces abrupt transitions.[45] This second type of procedure explains the six, abrupt changes from E♭ major to E minor that occur between mm. 239 and 310. These tonal juxtapositions coincide with the final three lines of stanza 1 of Donne's poem ("My love, though silly, is more brave . . .") creating a module filled with changes of tempo, key, simpler texture, and new melodies. The end of this passage is both the climax of one section and a transition to the next (ex. 13.16).

Example 13.16 Adams, *Harmonium*, mvt. 1, mm. 308–11 (choral parts only)

The choral parts form two harmonic layers; the female voices sing a first-inversion E-minor triad, which may be heard as a resolution to the opening E♭ major, while the male voices sing a first-inversion dominant-seventh chord on E, a harmonic extension of the E♭–E alternation that holds two versions of G (G♮ and G♯) in tension. The final chord shows yet another sudden shift as both pairs of voices shift to a polychord comprised of an F-minor seventh (T/B) and what is presumably (though ambiguously) a first-inversion E♭ major triad (S/A).

An even more explicit use of pitch and rhythm layers occurs shortly before the final tempo increase (m. 428) and near a climax where Adams sets the opening lines of the poem's second stanza (ex. 13.17).[46]

Example 13.17 Adams, *Harmonium*, mvt. 1, mm. 415–17

This example shows how cleverly Adams overlaps simple gestures moving at different speeds. The simplest level is the simultaneous presence of E minor (A) and F♯ minor (S), a dialogue made more interesting by casting the soprano and alto in different meters (6/4 [S] and 3/2 [A]), a device used throughout their material. The two viola parts are in the midst of expanding the length and pitch content of an arpeggio fashioned from the pitch content of the women's voices.

The pattern begins in m. 409 (not shown) as a three-pitch canon (G′–B′–E″) played one quarter-note beat apart. In the example, the violas play a seven-note figure (F♯′–G′–B′–C♯″–E–F♯″) seen in its entirety in viola 1. Above the voice parts, the piano and synthesizer play inversions of a four-note pattern drawn from the bitonal chord of the voices. The four trumpets present similar figures (based on E minor and F♯ minor) in pairs reminiscent of Pärt's tintinnabuli. Similarly, the flutes play a close canon in F♯ while the piccolos play a countermelody resembling that of the trumpets. Such a complex layering of essentially consonant pitches moving at different speeds is one way Adams creates the lustrous, shimmering surface that is a signature of his style.

Following *Harmonium*, Adams and the librettist/director Peter Sellars (b. 1957) began an unprecedented string of successful collaborations that included the operas *Nixon in China* (1987), *The Death of Klinghoffer* (1991), *Doctor Atomic* (2005), and *The Flowering Tree* (2006), all of which treat controversial subjects using the modernist perspective of contemporary political reality for which Sellars is famous. Adams and Sellars also collaborated on a pair of "oratorios," *El Niño* (2000) and *The Gospel of the Other Mary* (2013). Each work is dramatic in its own unique way and both feature the chorus prominently. Of the operas, the choral extracts from *The Death of Klinghoffer* are the most interesting and accessible. The opera tells the story of an American Jew, Leon Klinghoffer, killed by four Palestinian commandos who took over the cruise liner *Achille Lauro* in 1984. In a manner resembling medieval Passion plays, Adams uses the chorus as nondramatic commentary representing the nations of Israel and Palestine, as well as oppositions within the natural world. Save for "Hagar and the Angel," the choruses are arranged as opposing pairs: "Song of the Exiled Palestinians" and "Song of the Exiled Jews"; "Night" and "Day"; and "Ocean" and "Desert." Sellars's staging not only involves the chorus but also uses video to create a separate, compelling narrative that blurs the distinction between opera and oratorio.

El Niño was co-commissioned by the San Francisco Symphony (as a choral-orchestral work) and the Théâtre du Châtelet (as an opera) to usher in the new millennium.[47] This opera/oratorio in two acts contains twenty-four movements (eleven in Part 1 and thirteen in Part 2); the division between the two acts occurs directly following the birth of Jesus and the appearance of the star over Bethlehem. The Adams/Sellars text is typically "multicultural." In addition to the principal text source (Mt 1:18 to 2:1–13), the text includes passages from the Hebrew Bible, apocryphal gospels, and Hildegard of Bingen. Adams broadens the story by including, as did Britten in his *War Requiem*, poetic commentary from Sor Juana Inés de la Cruz (seventeenth century), Gabriela Mistral (early twentieth century), and Rosario Castellanos (mid-twentieth century), all of which provide a contemporary, cross-cultural perspective, balanced by *The Play of the Annunciation* from the Wakefield Mystery Plays (fifteenth century) and an adaptation of Martin Luther's gloss on "Joseph's Dream."[48] Using the Christmas birth narrative allows Adams to indulge in an allusion to Handel's *Messiah*, most evident in Adams's riff on Handel's recitative setting of "Thus saith the Lord . . . and I will shake all nations" (Haggai 2:6–7, 9) in no. 8, "Shake the Heavens."[49]

Although traditional elements of minimalism are present, *El Niño* differs notably from *Harmonium* in its use of lyrical melodies, that musical element least typical of minimalist works. Both *El Niño* and its sister work, *The Gospel of the Other Mary*, share a triadic musical language, enhanced by the extended triads associated with jazz. In this regard, the chorus "For with God no thing shall be impossible" (no. 4) is most interesting. Adams uses three-part *divisi* of the female and male choral voices to create a hocket-like texture based on closely related triads (e.g., D major and B minor). This particular texture also appears in *The Gospel of the Other*

Mary, along with an unexpected trio of countertenors, who function much like a Baroque evangelist. The latter work retells the story of Christ's Passion, using the same forces and array of textual elements as *El Niño*.

Adams's *On the Transmigration of Souls*, a work commissioned by the New York Philharmonic, commemorates the victims of 9/11. It is doubtful that anyone other than John Adams could have written such a threnody without indulging in over-sentimentality. In this ethereal work, Adams makes several departures from the traditional impression of minimalism as "process" music: he uses a piano and violin ensemble intentionally tuned a quarter-tone higher than the notated pitch, which creates an eerie musical tension. Then there is his allusion to the solo trumpet that figures so prominently in Charles Ives's *The Unanswered Question* (1906, rev. 1930–35). Adams chose to use the recorded comments of observers, the ambient noises of the city, and a solemn recitation of the names of those who died that day as part of this sound collage lasting more than twenty-five minutes. The final product is both respectful of its subject and true to the unique artistic perspective of the New York Philharmonic.[50]

CONCLUSION

By now, the discerning reader will have discovered the conundrum that lies at the center of this chapter—a major disconnect between its title, "The New Simplicities," and the reality that the great majority of the music surveyed within it isn't all that simple. The entire chapter cries out for some clarification of the word "simple"—simple in comparison to what? Save for the pure lucidity of some of Pärt's music, how is it possible to view the works of Penderecki, Lutosławski, Reich, and Adams as simple? The existential dilemma that faces any serious composer in the first half of the twentieth century can be summed up in Arnold Schoenberg's poem "Am Scheideweg" ("At the Crossroads"); its opening line couches the modern composer's dilemma as "Tonal oder atonal?"—"consonant or dissonant."[51] At that particular time, many composers understood the dilemma of how to write modern music and NOT use the system of tonal harmony that formed the basis for all of the important music that came before. What Schoenberg advocated, what led him to boast to Josef Rufer that he had discovered a compositional system that would guarantee the continued preeminence of German music well into the future, was the radical notion that counterpoint must generate harmony, not vice versa. To avoid the historical imperative of tonality meant devising a system where intellectual process replaced romantic intuition. Virgil Thomson hit the nail on the head when he described Schoenberg's elaborate system as nothing more than a set of rules designed to insure that he didn't lapse back into tonality.[52] Pitch serialism inevitably led to integral serialism, meaning the application of the precompositional rules formerly applied only to pitch to every parameter of music (dynamics, timbre, rhythm, etc.). The modernistic music described in chapter 9 on the avant-garde aesthetic became the target of aleatoric/chance music and minimalism, their relative simplicity broadly seen as remedies to its extremity. Their solutions restore intuition by requiring the composer to surrender complete control of the musical object either by embracing an element of chance or by accepting the inability of performers to perfectly realize their notated intent. Richard Taruskin argues that composers like György Ligeti embraced electronic music because "the composer of electronic music realizes the actual sounding of the composition in the act of creating it, so that there is no need for performers, publishers, or any social mediation at all."[53] Witold Lutosławski's concession to such imperfection was to embrace it, requiring the performers to visualize their parts intuitively. For choral musicians, however, such notation is only marginally simpler to interpret and execute than the abstruse rhythms and pitches associated with composers like Berio, Stockhausen, Boulez, and their disciples.

The increasing gap between composer prescription and the ability of less virtuosic performers to realize it has led to the phenomenon of "choral" music being written for groups of professional specialists who typically perform one singer per part, the antithesis of traditional choral performance. Even the sheer number of decisions required by the indeterminacy practiced by Cage and his disciples proved too cumbersome to be used in choral music; consequently, there is little, if any, purely aleatoric choral music, although there are brief sections of it in otherwise quite ordinary choral music as a kind of contemporary tokenism.

While minimalism poses choral singers far fewer notational problems, choruses were initially not the ensemble of choice for its practitioners. The prominent use of phased construction in minimalist music would have proven daunting for choral ensembles who spend most of their rehearsal time trying to coordinate their parts rather than making subtle departures from and returns to a constant rhythmic pulse. The great popularity of Arvo Pärt's choral music lies in its retention of traditional notation; even choirs of average ability are able to successfully surmount its challenges—intonation, unpredictable shifts of meter, and too much attention to vertical alignment at the expense of linear phrasing.

The works of Reich and Adams have a level of complexity that seemingly contradicts the original intent of minimalism. One saving grace is that for the most part, neither composer exercises his penchant for close canonic writing in the choral parts. The choruses tend to use largely homophonic textures with predominantly syllabic text declamation. Even when Adams's choruses are contrapuntal (e.g., the opening chorus of *El Niño*), imitation is restricted to vocal pairs that repeat each other. Conversely, Adams likes writing unrelated triadic harmonies, which are made even more difficult by abrupt changes of range (e.g., the "Cheers" chorus from *Nixon in China*). Still, he demonstrates an awareness of what the chorus's capabilities are; compared to the vocal writing of *Harmonium*, his postmillennial choral works possess a distinct melodic lyricism that is both idiomatic and eloquent. His melodic gifts distance him still farther from the original minimalists, for whom melody was at best an afterthought.

Anyone actively involved in the world of choral music realizes that there is another layer of simplicity; it takes the form of the seemingly unending stream of choral octavos that, DNA-like, seem to replicate each year. That these are important and useful in filling our immediate performance needs is undeniable, yet only a handful of them likely will figure in a future history of today's music. Indeed, the choral octavo may be the most obvious antidote to avant-garde music, embracing a simplicity and adherence to musical tradition that exceeds either chance music or minimalism. At present, this river of mainstream music has spread out to become a vast but shallow estuary. In the history of choral music, never has more music been so readily available in printed and electronic formats, and in recordings that range from commercial perfection to whatever people are willing to post online. At the same time, the divide between art music and accessible choral music has never been wider, with no immediate sign of consolidation. Choral conductors have increasingly felt the need to fill their programs with diverse, multicultural music of all genres (sacred or secular) and whatever language; the new benchmark of inclusive contemporaneity has supplanted the focus on mastery of the canon of historical music that previous generations agreed on as the measure of a choir's quality. What began as the creation of small, specialist groups who could and did perform the most contemporary music (regardless of its musical or linguistic difficulties) has expanded to include what formerly comprised the earlier music of the historical canon. Live performances of historical music outside of the choral societies for which many of these works were created are increasingly rare. The seeming perfection of performance made possible by quantum leaps in recording technology has had the chilling effect of reinforcing the belief of many conductors that "my choir couldn't possibly perform that music with such perfection, so why bother?" While excellent school and church choirs do exist, they are the exception rather than the rule; their place in social choral singing has been ceded to choirs that draw from a much larger demographic than any single local institution can support (and we see this most acutely in the area of children's choirs). And a perhaps unexpected by-product of this sea change in choral performance is a decline in the literacy (musical and otherwise) of many school and amateur choirs. Why, amid all of this diverse bounty and seeming prosperity, do we find ourselves in an "Unknown Region," quite unsure of our future destination?

There is no question that the instant access to entertainment has been both a blessing and a curse. Immediate access to an unlimited supply of performances of any kind of music has changed our cultivation of musical taste as well as our interest in or ability to interact knowledgably with the printed score. The Internet has even encouraged celebrity composers (notably Eric Whitacre) to create virtual choirs that allow individuals anywhere in the world to participate in a "choral experience," which is far less discriminating and, for that reason, far less satisfying given the inherently social interaction that is fundamental to choral music. Similarly, composers in any region of the world, no matter how geographically isolated, can now assess what is commercially popular and marketable, focusing on what is currently in fashion. The result is a disturbingly monochromatic array of music that, while filled with pretty sounds, is bereft of contrapuntal rigor, less attentive to the meaning of the text, and therefore more likely to result in quantity than variety of individual utterance. As has always been the case in history, technological progress, while seemingly of limitless benefit in the short run, has a downside that inevitably takes longer to recognize and makes us less aware of what we have lost. Because of our proximity to these rapidly evolving developments, we run the risk of making the same mistake made by French musicians of the early fifteenth century concerning the new popularity of the *contenance angloise*. In 1476 Johannes Tinctoris summed up a French reaction to the wildly popular style of English composers: "Nor can the English, who are popularly said to shout while the French sing, stand comparison with them. For the French contrive music in the newest manner for the new times, while the English continue to use one and the same style of composition, which shows a wretched poverty of invention."[54] And this led him to conclude a year later that "music written more than forty years ago is not worth hearing."[55] Do we, like Tinctoris, engage in a polemic about what is beautiful (tonal) and what is not (atonal), without the essential perspective that only time can provide? Such a discussion runs the risk that one point of view will find itself on the wrong side of history. And here, at the end of our survey of Western choral music, we stop, not because everything has been said but because—at this point—we lack the perspective of history to guide us.

Notes

CHAPTER 1

1. Howard E. Smither, *A History of the Oratorio*, vol. 3, *The Oratorio in the Classical Era* (Chapel Hill: University of North Carolina Press, 1987), 319–87, 257–89, 245–61, 302–15.

2. Johann Gottfried Walther, *Musikalische Lexikon, oder Musikalische Bibliothek* (Leipzig: W. Deer, 1732), 451–52, quoted in Bruce MacIntyre, *Haydn: The Creation*, Monuments of Western Music (New York: Schirmer Books, 1998), 14.

3. Smither, *Oratorio*, 3:98–114.

4. Georg Griesinger, *Biographische Notizen über Joseph Haydn* (Leipzig: Breitkopf & Härtel, 1810), quoted in MacIntyre, *Haydn: Creation*, 17.

5. Ibid., 165.

6. See Nicholas Temperley, *Haydn: The Creation*, Cambridge Music Handbooks (Cambridge: Cambridge University Press, 1991) and MacIntyre, *Haydn: Creation*, as well as the extensive Haydn biography by H. C. Robbins-Landon, *Haydn: Chronicle and Work*, vol. 4, *Haydn: The Years of Creation, 1796–1800* (Bloomington: Indiana University Press, 1977).

7. The entire letter is given in Smither, *Oratorio*, 3:490.

8. See Landon, *Haydn: Chronicle*, 4:449–50, and Smither (*Oratorio*, 3:491, n. 66).

9. This subject is treated in considerable detail in Peter Brown's book *Performing Haydn's "The Creation": Reconstructing the Earliest Renditions* (Bloomington: Indiana University Press, 1986). Nicholas Temperley has also contributed much toward a definitive understanding of this complex issue in his article "New Light on the Libretto of *The Creation*," in *Music in Eighteenth-Century England*, ed. Christopher Hogwood and Richard Luckett (Cambridge: Cambridge University Press, 1982), 189–211. See also Temperley's edition of *The Creation*, in which the original English text is restored. (New York: C. F. Peters, 1998).

10. Temperley, "New Light on the Libretto of *The Creation*," 196.

11. An alto soloist is required for the closing chorus of Part 3.

12. Temperley, *Haydn: The Creation*, 13.

13. Even in Part 3, when Gabriel becomes Eve and Raphael becomes Adam, the tenor is still referred to as Uriel.

14. Haydn had used this same unusual juxtaposition of tonal centers in his *Missa in tempore belli* ("Paukenmesse"), composed just prior to *The Creation* in 1796. The predominant C-major tonalities of the *Missa*'s Gloria and Credo give way to contrasting slow movements in A major (Gloria) and C minor (Credo).

15. MacIntyre, *Haydn: Creation*, 68.

16. MacIntyre notes the continuing scholarly debate about this anomaly. Some believe that the change of key center is merely fortuitous or practical, while others perceive programmatic intent.

17. It might be coincidental that Mozart's famed "Dissonance" Quartet (K. 465), one of six dedicated to Haydn (and given to Haydn on the occasion of Mozart's initiation into Freemasonry), is also in C and begins with a harmonically dense slow introduction (thus its nickname), which resolves to C major at the outset of the allegro.

18. The fact that Raphael (the bass) sings first may be Haydn's acknowledgement of the tradition in Passion music that the bass voice is the *Vox Christi* (or, in this case, the *Vox Dei*).

19. Walter Horst, "Gottfried van Swieten's handschriftliche Textbücher zu *Schöpfung* und *Jahreszeiten*." *Haydn-Studien* 1, no. 4 (1967): 261, quoted in MacIntyre, *Haydn: Creation*, 81.

20. C. G. Stellan Mörner, *Haydn-Studien* 1/1, 1969, 28, trans. H. C. Robbins-Landon, in *Haydn: Chronicle and Works*, 4:318.

21. MacIntyre, *Haydn: Creation*, 121–24.

22. Giorgio Pestelli, *The Age of Mozart and Beethoven* (Cambridge: Cambridge University Press, 1984), 125 and 126.

23. Percy A. Scholes, *The Mirror of Music, 1844–1944: A Century of Musical Life in Britain as reflected in the pages of the "Musical Times,"* 2 vols. (London: Novello and Oxford University Press, 1947).

24. Richard Taruskin, *Music in the Nineteenth Century*, OHWM (Oxford: Oxford University Press, 2005), 172.

25. Julius Schubring, ed., *Briefwechsel zwischen Felix Mendelssohn Bartholdy und Julius Schubring, zugleich ein Beitrag zur Geschichte und Theorie des Oratoriums* (Leipzig: Dunder and Humblot, 1892); repr. Walluf bei Wiesbaden: M. Sändig, 1973, 16–104.

26. Michael Märker, ed., "Preface (1997)" to *Paulus* (Wiesbaden: Breitkopf & Härtel, 1998).

27. Mendelssohn, *Paulus*, ed. Michael Märker, 78–79 (mm. 16–18, 21–23, and 25–27).

28. "Diese Rezitativ muss anfangs sehr ruhig, dann immer crescendo und vom Allegro molto an mit voller Kraft vorgetragen werden" ("Initially, this recitative should be very calm, then crescendo little by little, and from the *Allegro molto* on be executed with full power").

29. That same question has even greater relevance in a work like the "Reformation" Symphony (Symphony No. 5, op. 107).

30. There is a fascinating (and probably coincidental) similarity between this motive and the principal melody of Schubert's song *Der Tod und das Mädchen*.

31. See Arntrud Kurzhals-Reuter, *Die Oratorien von Felix Mendelssohn-Bartholdy: Untersuchungen zur Quellenlage, Entstehung, Gestaltung und Überlieferung*, Mainzer Studien zur Musikwissenschaft, vol. 12 (Tutzing: Hans Schneider, 1978), 184.

32. If so intended, the citation of the curse motive in the jubilant concluding chorus might indicate another Bach reference, the concluding chorus of the *Weihnachtsoratorium* (BWV 248) being a jubilant chorale fantasia on the Passion chorale *O Haupt voll Blut und Wunden*.

33. E major is also involved in a piece of tonal planning that validates this entire speculative system. The opening chorus of despair ("Help, Lord!") holds a highly dramatic moment. For the first thirty-four measures the chorus has been lamenting the lack of food and water. In m. 35, after a rest in all parts, the people dare to ask, "Will then the Lord be no more God in Zion?" Their initially timid questioning of God's existence in the larger scheme of things is sung in E major.

34. "Neue Oratorien," *Gesammelte Schriften über Musik und Musiker* (1854), cited in John Daverio, *Robert Schumann: Herald of a "New Poetic Age"* (New York: Oxford University Press, 1997), 267.

35. These were entered under the heading "Texts suitable for concert pieces" and included "Paradies und die Peri," "Der falsche Prophet," and "Das Rosenfest/Das Licht des Harems," in Daverio, *Robert Schumann*, 271.

36. Robert Schumann, *Tagebücher*, vol. 2, *1836–1854*, ed. Gerd Neuhaus (Leipzig: VEB Deutscher Verlag für Musik, 1987), 270, quoted in Daverio, *Robert Schumann*, 272.

37. Robert Schumann, Letter of May 5, 1843, in *Briefe, Neue Folge*, ed. Gustav Jansen 2nd ed. (Leipzig: Breitkopf and Härtel, 1904), 226–27, quoted in Daverio, *Robert Schumann*, 272.

38. *Tagebücher* 2, 260, quoted in Daverio, *Robert Schumann*, 273, 265–66.

39. Ibid., 275.

40. Schumann, *Briefe, Neue Folge*, 228, quoted in ibid, 276.

41. Carl Dahlhaus, "Zur Problematic zur Musikgattungen im 19. Jahrhundert," in *Gattungen der Musik in Einzeldarstellen: Gedenkschrift Leo Schrade* (Bern: Francke Verlag, 1973), cited in Daverio, *Robert Schumann*, 275.

42. This trend is manifested in numerous ways, ranging from the use of ersatz Turkish music by Mozart and Beethoven, the interest in Gypsies as representatives of a "free" people, and, in more traditional poetry, a fascination with the Orient, as in Goethe's *West-Östlicher Divan* (1819) and Friedrich Schlegel's *Über die Sprache und Freiheit der Inder* (1819).

43. Daverio, *Robert Schumann*, 277.

44. Such use of a unifying network of motives is most obvious in the operatic experiments of Richard Wagner.

45. Another manifestation of Schumann's fascination with Loewe (and this oratorio specifically) is seen in his Schumann's unrealized plan to write an oratorio on the life of Martin Luther.

46. Daverio, *Robert Schumann*, 278.

47. Rita Gerencsér cites this letter in her preface to the Eulenburg octavo edition, no. 10171 (Zurich: Eulenberg, 1979).

48. Daverio, *Robert Schumann*, 282.

49. Ibid., 281.

50. This "postlude" is reminiscent of the important piano postludes in Schumann's song cycles like *Dichterliebe*.

51. This chorus calls to mind the fugue that concludes the sixth movement of Brahms's *Ein Deutsches Requiem*.

52. Peter Raabe, *Liszts Schaffen* (Stuttgart: Colla, 1931), 144.

53. The myth/legend/hagiology relates that at the age of four, Elizabeth was betrothed to Ludwig, the future Landgrave of Thuringia. She moved to Wartburg castle near Eisenach, the ancestral home of Thuringian rulers. She became known and revered as a helper to the poor and displaced. In 1855, six frescoes by Moritz von Schwind depicting major events in St. Elizabeth's life were installed in the Wartburg.

54. Here, the term "choral books" refers to collections of Gregorian chant (*choralbücher*).

55. Raabe, *Liszts Schaffen*, 146.

56. For a useful overview of this work, see David Friddle, "Franz Liszt's Oratorio *Christus*," *Choral Journal* 46, no. 5 (2005): 89–99.

57. Percy M. Young, *Elgar, Newman, and The Dream of Gerontius: In the Tradition of English Catholicism* (Brookfield, VT: Ashgate, 1995), 116.

58. Ibid., 119.

59. *Observer* (London), October 7, 1900, quoted in ibid., 120.

60. Charles Edward McGuire, *Elgar's Oratorios: The Creation of an Epic Narrative* (Burlington, VT: Ashgate, 2002), 134.

61. Ibid., 135.

62. Percy Young, *Elgar, O.M.: A Study of a Musician*, rev. ed. (London: White Lion, 1973), 312.

63. McGuire, *Elgar's Oratorios*, 147.

64. Ibid., 147–48.

65. Ibid., 148–53.

66. Ernst Newman, *Elgar*, Music of the Masters Series, 3rd ed. (London: Bodley Head, 1922), 58–62.

67. McGuire, *Elgar's Oratorios*, 165.

68. Alfred Einstein, *Music in the Romantic Era* (New York: Norton, 1975), 36.

CHAPTER 2

1. Einstein, *Music in the Romantic Era*, 36.
2. Franz Gehring, "Liedertafel," in *NG2*, 10:848.
3. The original version was the one for mezzo-soprano, male chorus, and piano. It was composed as a birthday present for the daughter of Schubert's poet friend, Grillparzer. When Schubert realized that the piece was to be sung outside the door of a young female, he recast it for women's chorus. Either version works well.
4. For example, Clifford Bartlett's anthology, *Madrigals and Partsongs* (Oxford: Oxford University Press, 2001) contains no pieces by Schumann.
5. Daverio, *Robert Schumann*.
6. Ibid., 388.
7. To this list can be added three relatively less well-known works: the *Spanisches Liederspiel*, op. 74, the *Spanisches Liebeslieder*, op. 138, and *Minnespiel*, op. 101, a collection of Rückert's poems.
8. Originally, the eight compositions were arranged in this order (using their current numerical placement): 5, 4, 2, 1, 6, 7, 8, 3.
9. "The rose stands, pearly gray, covered with dew; but as the sun shone upon them, the pearls turned to rubies" (author's translation).
10. *Waldmädchen* (op. 69/2) is expressly marked for solo voices, and the piano part is obligatory.
11. This generic title also may suggest the intended use of these songs. After choral concerts, Mendelssohn often invited the chorus to his house for a party, during which this music was available to small groups to sing as they wandered the grounds.
12. Henderson, "The German Part Song," 166.
13. Hunting music for horns figures prominently in four Haydn symphonies (nos. 6, 31, 92, 93) and in his opera *La fedeltá premiata* (1781) and in Mozart's Symphony no. 40. For more detail on this subject, see Josef Pöschel, *Jagdmusik, Kontinuität und Entwicklung in der europäischer Geschichte* (Tutzing: Hans Schneider, 1997).
14. Prompted by a new love interest, the contralto Hermine Spies, Brahms also published this piece as a solo song (op. 94).
15. See Jan Swafford, *Johannes Brahms: A Biography* (New York: Vintage Books, 1999), 483–84.
16. Siegfried Kross, *Die Chorwerke Johannes Brahms* (Berlin: Max Hesses Verlag, 1958), 422.
17. Max Kalbeck is also among the earliest of Brahms's biographers, producing a four-volume study of the composer that was published between 1904 and 1914.
18. Kross, *Chorwerke*, 423.
19. For a discussion of Bruckner's compositions for male chorus, see Andrea Harrandt, "Bruckner and the Liedertafel Tradition." *Choral Journal* 37, no. 5 (1996), 15–21.
20. Angela Pachovsky and Anton Reinthaler, eds., *Anton Bruckner Sämtliche Werke*, vol. 23, pt., 2, *Weltliche Chorwerke* (Wien: Musikwissenschaftlicher Verlag, 2001), 47–48, 121–24. This music is identical with the setting of the poem "Nachruf" that precedes it in the edition.
21. Ibid., 77–89, 62–69, 109–16, and 174–86.
22. James Deaville, "Peter Cornelius," in *NG* 2, 6:477, and *Cornelius Werke*, 2:194.
23. *Max Reger Sämtliche Werke*, vol. 27, *Chorwerke a cappella*, ed. Hermann Grabner (Wiesbaden: Breitkopf & Härtel, 1961), 115–17.
24. Gerd Neuhaus, ed., *Clara Schumann, Drei gemischten Chöre, 1848* (Wiesbaden: Breitkopf & Härtel, 1989).
25. See Fanny M. Hensel, *Gartenlieder*, op. 3, *Quartett für vier gemischten Stimmen a cappella* (Kassel: Furore Verlag, 1977).

26. See the discussion of S. S. Wesley's sacred music in vol. 1, chap. 14.

27. *Musical World* 1 (1836): 8.

28. See the study of Joseph Novello and his time in Scholes, *Mirror of Music.*

29. *Athenaeum* 770 (1842): 685; *Musical World* 17 (1842): 211–12.

30. *Musical World* 32 (1864): 403.

31. Two useful anthologies are *English Pastoral Partsongs Selected by Paul Spicer* (Oxford: Oxford University Press, 1994), and *300 Years of English Part Songs: Glees, Rounds, Catches, Partsongs, 1600–1900*, ed. Paul Hillier (London: Faber Music, 1983).

32. *Musical Times* 40 (1899): 400.

33. Paul Rodmell, *Charles Villiers Stanford*, Music in Nineteenth-Century Britain (Burlington, VT: Ashgate, 2002), 261.

34. Ibid.

35. C. H. H. Parry, *Style in Musical Art* (Oxford: Clarendon Press, 1900), 12.

36. Letter from Elgar to August Jaeger, April 26, 1908. See Percy Young, ed., *Letters to Nimrod* (London: Dennis Dobson, 1965), 272.

CHAPTER 3

1. See Joseph Kerman, "A Few Canonic Variations," *Critical Inquiry* 10 (1983): 112, cited in Steven Paul Scher, "Hoffmann, Weber, Wagner: The Birth of Romantic Opera from the Spirit of Literature?" in *The Romantic Tradition: German Literature and Music in the Nineteenth Century*, ed. Gerald Chapple, Frederick Hall, and Hans Schulte (Lanham, MD: University Press of America, 1992), 240.

2. For a vocal score, see *Opera Choruses*, ed. John Rutter (Oxford: Oxford University Press, 1995), 167–72.

3. Paolo Fabri, "Metrical and Formal Organization," in *The History of Italian Opera*, vol. 6, *Opera in Theory and Practice, Image and Myth*, ed. Lorenzo Bianconi and Giorgio Pestelli (Chicago: University of Chicago Press, 2003), 184.

4. Philip Gossett, "Becoming a Citizen: The Chorus in *Risorgimento* Opera," *Cambridge Opera Journal* 2, no. 1 (1990): 44.

5. Hervé Lacombe, *The Keys to French Opera in the Nineteenth Century* (Berkeley: University of California Press, 2001), 135.

6. From an 1817 pamphlet, portions reprinted in Adalbert Behr and Alfred Hoffmann, *Das Schauspielhaus in Berlin* (Berlin: Verlag für Bauwesen, 1984), 34, cited in Karin Pendle and Stephen Wilkins, "Paradise Found: The Salle le Peletier and French Grand Opera," chap. 7, in *Opera in Context: Essays on Historical Staging from the Late Renaissance to the Time of Puccini*, ed. Mark A. Radice (Portland, OR: Amadeus Press, 1998), 173.

7. Richard Wagner, "Reminiscences of Auber" ("Erinnerungen an Auber"), in *Richard Wagner's Prose Works*, trans. William Ashton Ellis (London, 1896; repr., New York: Broude Brothers, 1966), 5:35–55, quoted in Lacombe, *French Opera*, 239.

8. Rutter, *Opera Choruses*, 167–72.

9. Anselm Gerhard, "Rossini and the Revolution," in *The Urbanization of Opera: Music Theater in Paris in the Nineteenth Century*, trans. Mary Whittall (Chicago: University of Chicago Press, 1998).

10. Nestor Roqueplan, *Les Coulisses de l'Opéra*, 38, quoted in Gerhard, "Rossini," 84.

11. Richard Osborne, *Rossini: His Life and Works*, 2nd ed. (Oxford, New York: Oxford University Press, 2007), 32.

12. Ibid., 111.

13. Ibid., 114

14. Mary Ann Smart, "Verdi, Italian Romanticism and the Risorgimento," in *The Cambridge Companion to Verdi*, ed. Scott L. Balthazar (Cambridge: Cambridge University Press, 2004), 33. Also, see Gossett's "Becoming a Citizen," 53–56, for a discussion of the problems regarding music and text in *Nabucco*.

15. Markus Engelhardt, "'Something's Been Done to Make Room for Choruses': Choral Conception and Construction in *Luisa Miller*," in *Verdi's Middle Period: 1849–1859*, ed. Martin Chusid (Chicago: University of Chicago Press, 1997), 198.

16. David Brown, *Mussorgsky: His Life and Works* (Oxford: Oxford University Press, 2002), 141.

17. For a detailed examination of this topic, see Vladimir Morosan, "Folk and Chant Elements in Mussorgsky's Choral Writing," in *Mussorgsky in Memoriam, 1881–1891*, ed. Malcolm H. Brown (Ann Arbor, MI: UMI Press, 1982), 95–133.

18. Morosan, "Folk and Chant Elements in Mussorgsky's Choral Writing," 104–5.

19. Caryl Emerson and Robert Oldani, *Modest Mussorgsky and "Boris Godunov": Myths, Realities, Reconsiderations* (Cambridge: Cambridge University Press, 1992), cited in Brown, *Mussorgsky*, 152, n. 10.

20. Joachim Köhler, *Richard Wagner: The Last of the Titans*, trans. Stewart Spencer (New Haven, CT: Yale University Press, 2004), 147. Originally published as *Der Letzte der Titanen–Richard Wagners Leben und Werk* (Munich: Claasen Verlag, 2001).

21. Rutter, *Opera Choruses*, 359–63.

22. Ibid., 353–58.

23. Köhler (*Richard Wagner*, 608) notes that Wagner had arranged the various "Grail" choruses on three separate levels in the *Frauenkirche* for the 1843 performance of *Das Liebesmahl*, but these choruses were entirely male.

24. Cosima Wagner, *Tagebücher*, vol. 2, ed. Martin Gregor-Dellin and Dietrich Mack (Munich and Zurich: Piper, 1977), 556; *Cosima Wagner's Diaries*, trans. Geoffrey Skelton (New York: Harcourt Brace Jovanovich, 1980), 498–99, quoted in Katherine R. Syer, "Wagner's Shaping of the Grail Scene of Act I," in *A Companion to Wagner's Parsifal*, ed. William Kinderman and Katherine R. Syer (Rochester, NY: Camden House, 2005), 208.

25. Dieter Borchmeyer, "Goethes FAUST musikalisch betrachtet," in *Eine Art Symbolik fürs Ohr: Johann Wolfgang von Goethe; Lyrik und Musik*, Heidelberger Beiträge zur deutschen Literatur, vol. 12, ed. Hermann Jung (Frankfurt am Main: Peter Lang, 2002), 87.

26. Wolfgang Marx, "Faust und die Musik" (1995), notes to the recording of Schumann's *Szenen aus Goethes Faust* (Sony Classical, 1995, S2K 66 308DD).

27. Daniel Albright, *Berlioz's Semi-Operas: "Roméo et Juliette" and "La damnation de Faust"* (Rochester, NY: University of Rochester Press, 2001), 110.

28. For a discussion of Berlioz's *Roméo et Juliette*, see chap. 4, this volume.

29. Felix Mendelssohn, *Letters from Italy and Switzerland*, trans. Lady Wallace (1865: repr., Freeport, NY: Books for Libraries Press, 1970), 115.

30. The overture to *Walpurgisnacht* is approximately the same length as Mendelssohn's typical concert overtures, three of which (*Meerstille und Glückliche Fahrt*, *Die Hebriden*, and *Das Märchen von der schönen Melusine*) are contemporary with the premiere of the cantata.

31. Marx, "Faust und die Musik."

32. Robert Schumann, "Neue Bahnen," *Neue Zeitschrift für Musik*, October 28, 1853, cited in Daniel Beller-McKenna, *Brahms and the German Spirit* (Cambridge, MA: Harvard University Press, 2004), 40.

33. Peter Horst Neumann, "Anmerkungen zu Robert Schumanns *Szene aus Goethes* Faust," in *Eine Art Symbolic fürs Ohr: Johann Wolfgang von Goethe; Lyrik und Musik*, 103.

34. I refer to such rubrics as "Mittlere Region" (*Pater Seraphicus*) or the description of the angelic choir (no. 4) as "schwebend in der höheren Atmosphäre, Faustens Unsterbliches tragend" ("soaring in the higher regions, bearing the immortal soul of Faust").

35. Arnfried Edler, *Robert Schumann und seine Zeit* (Laaber, 1982), 255. My translation of a quote in Hermann Jung's article "Wozu Musik zu solch vollendeter Poesie? Robert Schumann und seine *Szenen aus Goethes* Faust," in *Eine Art Symbolik fürs Ohr*, 114.

36. See also chap. 1, this volume.

37. Berthold Litzmann, ed., *Clara Schumann–Johannes Brahms, Briefe*, 2 vols. (Leipzig: Breitkopf & Härtel, 1927, repr. Hildersheim, 1971), 1:601, quoted in Siegfried Kross, *Johannes Brahms: Versuch einer kritischen Dokumentar-Biographie*, 2 vols. (Bonn: Bouvier Verlag, 1997), 2:552.

38. Johannes Brahms, *Briefwechsel*, ed. Deutschen Brahms-Gesellschaft, 16 vols. (Berlin: 1907–22, Tutzing, 1974), 6:12, quoted in Kross, *Johannes Brahms*, 1:409–10.

39. J. Bradford Robinson, ed., *Johannes Brahms: Rinaldo*, op. 50 (Munich: MPH Press, 2004).

40. Swafford, *Johannes Brahms*, 350.

41. Ibid., 351

42. The significance of the change from C minor to C major at this point should not be overlooked, especially in light of the recurrence of the same change of mode that occurs in the last movement of Brahms's Symphony 1 in C minor, op. 68.

43. In this case, the *Triumphlied* uses biblical texts to celebrate the Prussian victory over the French in the Franco-Prussian war (1870–71).

44. Johannes Brahms and Theodore Billroth, *Johannes Brahms and Theodor Billroth: Letters from a Musical Friendship*, trans. and ed. Hans Barkan (Norman: University of Oklahoma Press, 1957), 121–22; letter from August 3, 1882, Vienna, quoted in Swafford, *Johannes Brahms*, 477.

45. Brahms and Billroth, *Letters*, 124–25, letter from August 10, 1882, quoted in Swafford.

46. Kross, *Johannes Brahms*, 2:873.

CHAPTER 4

1. J. A. Scheibe's criticism of J. S. Bach's music as "too instrumental" in his "Critischer Musikus" is perhaps the first indication that the instrumental vernacular is beginning to surpass, even replace, the vocal idiom as the predominant musical language. For a fuller discussion of Scheibe's contentious editorializing, see Philipp Spitta, *Johann Sebastian Bach: His Work and Influence on the Music of Germany, 1685–1750*, trans. A. Fuller-Maitland and Clara Bell (London: Novello and Co.; New York, H. W. Gray Co., 1899; repr. 1951, New York: Dover Publications), 2:645–47.

2. For a discussion of the evolution of this textual connection to Schiller's ode, see Elliot Forbes's *Thayer's Life of Beethoven*, rev. ed. (Princeton: Princeton University Press, 1967), 2:891–94.

3. The original 1785 version of Schiller's *An die Freude* contained 108 lines of poetry comprising alternating lines of eight and seven syllables. From this, Beethoven used thirty-four lines, changing one word in line 6 and replacing Schiller's line 7 with a text of his own devising.

4. It was for this same occasion that Mendelssohn wrote a "hymn," *Gutenberg, der deutsche Mann*, which provided the melody currently associated with the Christmas carol "Hark, the Herald Angels Sing."

5. This is the case in an early G. Schirmer vocal score (no. 5187, New York: n.d.).

6. As the first movement to actually cadence, it provided the audience with its first opportunity to applaud, a fact that may partially explain the popular reception this movement received.

7. Julian Rushton, *Berlioz: Roméo et Juliette* (Cambridge: Cambridge University Press, 1994).

8. This was the view proposed by Auguste Morel, *Le Constitutionel, Journal du Commerce, Politique et Literature*, November 28, 1839, quoted in Rushton, *Roméo et Juliette*, 80, "With the ball scene, the garden scene, the Queen Mab scherzo, and the finale, one has a complete symphony, cut virtually according to the pattern of Beethoven's Choral [Symphony]."

9. Rushton, *Roméo et Juliette*, 80–86.

10. Albright, *Berlioz's Semi-Operas*, 49.

11. Hector Berlioz, *New Edition of the Complete Works*, vol. 18, *Roméo et Juliette*, ed. D. Kern Holoman (Kassel: Bärenreiter, 1990), 239.

12. The use of treble voices, supported by an onomatopoeic children's choir, is dictated by the title of the song, *Armer Kinder Betterlied* ("Poor Children's Begging Song").

13. These programs are printed as app. 2 to Edward E. Reilly's discussion of the symphony ("*Todtenfeier* and the Second Symphony"), in *The Mahler Companion*, ed. Donald Mitchell and Andrew Nicholson (New York: Oxford University Press, 1999), 123–25.

14. Ibid., 88. Friedrich Gottfried Klopstock (1724–1803) was a German poet.

15. Gustav Mahler, score of *Symphonie II, Revidierte Fassung*, Philharmonie Partituren no. 395 (Vienna: Universal Edition, © 1897, 1925), 186.

16. The opening line of *Urlicht: O Röschen rot!* ("O Small Red Rose") refers to the Virgin Mary. Reilly also cites a variant of the poem that contains explicit links to the Last Judgment (which Mahler also invokes through his use of the theme of *Dies irae*). Reilly, "*Todtenfeier* and the Second Symphony," 113.

17. Ibid., 120–21.

18. Aptly named, given the Berliozian dimensions of the vocal (SSSAATB, B soli, two mixed choirs and a children's choir), and orchestral forces (fl [4], pic, [2] ob [4] eh, cl. in E♭, cl [3], bcl, bsn [4], dbsn, hn [8], tpts [4] tbn [4], tba, str, cel, pf, harm, man, perc, and offstage brass.

19. Considerable discussion and analysis suggests that the second part of the symphony is, in fact, a conflation of the Scherzo, Adagio, and Finale of a typical four-movement symphony. Mahler gives his movements four descriptive titles—*Hymne Veni Creator, Scherzo, Adagio Caritas*, and *Hymne: die Geburt des Eros*. For a full discussion, see Paul Bekker, *Gustav Mahlers Sinfonien* (Berlin: Schuster & Loeffler, 1921; repr. 1969), 273. Subsequently, Donald Mitchell argues (on the basis of a sketch first described by Alfred Rosenzweig in June 1933) that the titles were actually *Veni Creator, Caritas, Weihnachtspiele mit dem Kindlein/Scherzo*, and *Schöpfung durch Eros/Hymne*. See Donald Mitchell, *Gustav Mahler: Songs and Symphonies of Life and Death; Interpretations and Annotation* (Berkeley: University of California Press, 1985), 529.

20. Alma Mahler, *Gustav Mahler: Memories and Letters*, trans. Basil Creighton (Seattle: University of Washington Press, 1968), 90–91, quoted in Mitchell, *Gustav Mahler*, 523–24.

21. In the original draft of movements, Mahler (perhaps coincidentally) used the French spelling (*Hymne*) for the first and last movements, as did Berlioz in his setting of the *Te Deum*.

22. At least this is not the version found in the *Kyrie seu Ordinarium Missal* (1927), which otherwise closely accords with Mahler's version of the text.

23. These two insertions are found in mvt. 2 between mm. 540–80 and 1208–37, which correspond to mm. 131–68 and m. 46 in the first movement.

24. At m. 775 Mahler inserts the rubric "Mater gloriosa schwebt einher."

25. Mitchell, *Gustav Mahler*, 583–84.

26. The list includes the American composers Paul Hindemith, Roger Sessions, William Schumann, and Ned Rorem, to name only a few.

27. Walt Whitman, *Complete Poetry and Collected Prose* (New York: Literary Classics of the United States, 1982), 341–50, 400–403, and 531–40.

28. Michael Short, *Gustav Holst: The Man and his Music* (Oxford: Oxford University Press, 1990), 218.

29. Harold Edgar Briggs, ed., *The Complete Poetry and Selected Prose of John Keats* (New York: Modern Library, 1951), 64–161, 294–95, 250–52, 180–81, 9–10, and 64–141 respectively.

30. A letter to Serge Koussevitzky (dated January 12, 1947) contains a reference to the symphony, inferring that it was initially conceived with Latin texts in mind, although no evidence of any specific text choices exists. See Benjamin Britten, *Letters from a Life: The Selected Letters of Benjamin Britten*, vol. 3, *1946–51*, ed. Donald Mitchell, Philip Reed, and Mervyn Cooke (London: Faber and Faber, 2004), 546–47.

31. Jack Gottlieb, "Bernstein: The Symphonies," notes to the DGG recording of Bernstein's symphonies (Hamburg: DG 445 245-2), 7.

32. Quoted in Manashir Yakubov, "Notes on Shostakovich's Symphony in B♭, Opus 113," (England: Olympia Recordings, OCD 132, 1988), iii.

33. David Osmond-Smith, *Berio*, Oxford Studies of Composers, no. 20 (Oxford: Oxford University Press, 1991), 66.

34. Berio had composed a composition titled *Omaggio à Joyce* (1958) in which he deconstructed the author's text and reduced it to a phonemic analysis of the original that explored the relationship of words as sound and words as meaning.

35. Charles Rosen, *The Classical Style: Haydn, Mozart, Beethoven* (New York: Norton, 1971), pt. 6, chap. 3, "Church Music," 367.

CHAPTER 5

1. Roger Shattuck, *The Banquet Years: The Origins of the Avant-Garde in France; 1885 to World War I* (New York: Vintage Books, 1955), 31–35 (author's paraphrase).

2. Ibid., 36.

3. A selection of Charles D'Orléans's poetry appears in the anthology *Medieval Song: An Anthology of Hymns and Lyrics*, trans. and ed. James Wilhelm (New York: E. P. Dutton, 1971), 279–86, 362.

4. Claude Debussy, *Debussy on Music: The Critical Writings of the Great French Composer Claude Debussy*, ed. François Lesure, trans. and ed. Richard Langham Smith (New York: A. A. Knopf, 1977), quoted in Scott Messing, *Neoclassicism in Music: From the Genesis of the Concept Through the Schoenberg/Stravinsky Polemic*, Studies in Musicology 101 (Ann Arbor, MI: UMI Research Press, 1988), 54.

5. Specifically, see mm. 22–23 of *Nicolette* and the "la-la-la" refrain of *Ronde*.

6. The poem was written in English and translated into French for Debussy by Gabriel Sarrazin.

7. Martin Cooper, *French Music: From the Death of Berlioz to the Death of Fauré* (London; New York: Oxford University Press, 1951).

8. Richard Taruskin, *Music in the Nineteenth Century*, vol. 3, *OHWM* (Oxford: Oxford University Press, 2005), 781.

9. John Rutter traces the text to a collection by Racine titled *Hymnes traduites du bréviaire romain*; John Rutter, ed., *European Sacred Music*. Oxford Choral Classics (Oxford: Oxford University Press, 1996), 370.

10. Foreword to Jean-Michel Nectoux and Roger Delage's edition of Fauré's *Requiem* (Paris: Hammele, 1994), x.

11. Ibid., xi.

12. Ibid.

13. There are, nonetheless, choral passages in Satie's *Messe des pauvres* (1888), and the symphonic drama *Socrate* (1917–18), scored for soprano and chamber orchestra, is one of his masterpieces.

14. In this sense, the work is oratorio-like, since the distinguishing characteristic of the earliest oratorios was the presence of a narrator (albeit one who sang).
15. There are only ten measures of chorus, after which the orchestra plays a truncated version of the choral melody.
16. Carl B. Schmidt, *The Music of Francis Poulenc (1899–1963): A Catalogue* (Oxford: Clarendon Press: Oxford University Press, 1995).
17. Virgil Thomson, *Music Reviewed, 1940–1954* (New York: Vintage Books, 1967), 249.
18. Shattuck, *Banquet Years*, 332.
19. Jean Roy, *Francis Poulenc: L'Homme et son oeuvre* (Paris: Seghers, 1964), 144.
20. Keith W. Daniel, "Poulenc's Choral Works with Orchestra" in *Francis Poulenc: Music, Art and Literature*, ed. Sidney Buckland and Myriam Chimènes, 48–86 (Aldershot: Ashgate, 1999).
21. Ibid., 68–69.
22. Duruflé's denial of influence appears in a letter, dated November 8, 1971, cited in Jeffrey Reynolds, "On Clouds of Incense," in *Maurice Duruflé, 1902–1986: The Last Impressionist*, ed. Ronald Ebrecht (Lanham, MD: Scarecrow Press, 2002), 170.
23. *Liber Usualis* (Tournai, New York: Desclée Co., 1961).
24. Sometimes referred to as the "Quartet for the end of meter." See Roger Nichols, *Messiaen*, Oxford Studies of Composers 13 (Oxford: Oxford University Press, 1986), 29.
25. Marcel Couraud in a lecture at the University of Illinois in 1978.
26. This concept, along with other mainstays of Messiaen's style, is defined in his autodidactic book, *The Technique of My Musical Language*, trans. John Satterfield, 2 vols. (Paris: A. Leduc, 1956).
27. Messiaen said "I composed *Cinq Rechants* on a poem written partly in French, but mainly in a new language sometimes resembling Sanskrit and sometimes Quechua, the ancient Peruvian language." Olivier Messiaen, *Music and Color: Conversations with Claude Samuel*, trans. E. Thomas Glasgow (Portland, OR: Amadeus Press, 1994), 129.
28. Messiaen did indeed use these terms in his book *Technique de mon language musical* [The technique of my musical language] (Paris: A. Leduc, 1944).
29. The French texts are "Miroir d'étoile," "Château d'étoile," and "Bulle de cristal d'étoile cristal."
30. This connection is possible because of the similarity between the couplet's final syllable ("é-toi-le") and the opening word of the *Rechant*.
31. This reference to isorhythm is a more subtle example on Messiaen's part of his obvious historical reference to the *vers mesuré* chansons of LeJeune and other members of *Les Pléiades*.
32. Messiaen's *Turangalîla-Symphonie* refers to three great feminine magicians—Yseult, Vivien, and Ligeia.
33. Audrey Ekdahl Davidson, *Olivier Messiaen and the Tristan Myth* (Westport, CT: Praeger, 2001), 121–22.
34. Ibid., 122.
35. Shattuck, *Banquet Years*, 168–69.

CHAPTER 6

1. Joseph Rufer, *Composition with Twelve Notes Related Only to One Another*, trans. Humphrey Searle (London: Barrie and Rockliff, 1954). The German original was published in 1952 by Max Hesse Verlag in Berlin.
2. Martin Cooper, *French Music*, 55–59.
3. At about this same time conservatories all over Europe were established following the German model, enshrined around Bach, Beethoven, and Brahms.
4. Such an anti-German sentiment may also be seen in the rise of Nationalism in composers like Sibelius (Finland), Grieg (Norway), the "mighty Russian Five" (Mussorgsky, Rimsky-Korsakov, Borodin, Balakirev, and Cui).

5. Arnold Schoenberg, *Drei Satiren*, in *Complete Works of Arnold Schoenberg* (Mainz: B. Schott's Söhne, 1980), vol. 19, 68–69.
6. Taruskin writes that "Schoenberg objected to the word because its connotations were purely negative: merely to say what something is not is a far cry from saying what it is," in *Music in the Early Twentieth Century*, Oxford History of Western Music (Oxford: Oxford University Press, 2010), 312.
7. Schoenberg orchestrated several Bach chorale preludes and the Prelude and Fugue in E♭ (BWV 522). Webern made a serialistic transcription of the *Ricercare à 6* from the *Musical Offering* (BWV 1079); these two transcriptions became the models for Stravinsky's arrangement of Bach's canonic variations on *Vom Himmel Hoch* (BWV 769) for chorus and orchestra (1956), and Berio's orchestration (2001) of *Contrapunctus 19* from *Art of Fugue* (BWV 1080).
8. Rufer, *Composition with Twelve Tones*, 12.
9. Ibid., 20–21.
10. Ibid., 26, 30.
11. O. W. Neighbour, "Schoenberg, Arnold," Grove Music Online, ed. L. Macy, available at http://80-www.grovemusic.com. Proxy2.library.uiuc.edu, accessed February 16, 2005.
12. See chap. 5, this volume.
13. The English singing translation by Fagge, while poetically faithful to the era in which it was done, is not a literal translation of Conrad Mayer's text.
14. Rufer, *Composition with Twelve Tones*, 79.
15. Virgil Thomson, *Music Reviewed (1934–1948)*, 248.
16. Chemjo Vinaver, *Anthology of Jewish Music: Sacred Chants and Religious Folk Song of the Eastern European Jews* (New York: Edward B. Marks, 1955), 203–14.
17. Although Schoenberg labels the voices S1, S2, A, T, B1, and B2, the clefs used for the two soprano parts are different (G clef for S1 and C1 for S2), clearly indicating that the second soprano is lower than the first. Moreover, the second soprano most often operates in conjunction with the alto part.
18. Alex Ringer's book, *Arnold Schoenberg: The Composer as Jew* (Oxford: Oxford University Press, 1990), contains an in-depth discussion of the role Schoenberg's faith played in his compositions.
19. Letter to Hildegarde Jone, dated October 15, 1935, in Anton Webern, *Letters to Hildegarde Jone and Josef Humplik*, ed. Josef Polnauer, trans. Cornelius Cardew (Bryn Mawr, PA: Theodore Presser, 1967), 31.
20. Kathryn Bailey, *The Twelve-Tone Music of Anton Webern: Old Forms in a New Language* (Cambridge: Cambridge University Press, 1991), 286, 292.
21. Webern's famous orchestration of the *Ricercare à 6* from J. S. Bach's *Musical Offering* is similar in its use of serialized instrumentation to reveal motivic relationships not heard in a traditional performance.
22. Some commentators view the first serial work as the ballet *Agon*; although begun before the *Canticum sacrum*, this ballet was not completed until 1957.
23. Eric Walter White, *Stravinsky: The Composer and His Works*, 2nd. ed. (London: Faber, 1979), 486–87.
24. Ibid., 516.
25. The notion of freedom and imprisonment are a recurrent theme in Dallapiccola's output. This obsession goes back to the internment of his family in Austria and the privations that resulted from this "imprisonment." The imposition of these anti-Semitic policies forced Dallapiccola's family to move continuously, ultimately resulting in his wife's decision to live apart from the family to spare them further hardship.
26. Dallapiccola heard Stravinsky's *Les Noces* for the first time in 1927. While the orchestration of the *Canti* seems indebted to Stravinsky's composition, Richard F. Goldman sees more influence from Varese's *Ionisation* than from Stravinsky. Richard F. Goldman, "Current Chronicle: New York," *Musical Quarterly* 37, no. 3 (1951): 405–10.

27. Ernst Krenek, preface to *Lamentatio Jeremiae Prophetae* (Kassel: Bärenreiter Verlag, 1957, *Ausgabe* 3648).

28. Ibid.

29. Ray Robinson and Allen Winold have compiled a complete list of all themes used in *A Study of Penderecki's St. Luke Passion* (Celle: Moeck Verlag, 1983).

30. In table 1 of Robinson's study, these rows appear as no. 2 and no. 27.

31. This motive appears as no.16 in the same table, starting a half step higher.

32. The starting pitches of these two versions are a tritone apart, the same process Penderecki uses to generate the second hexachord of CF-1.

33. Like its predecessor this movement is a short, *a cappella* psalm setting with in a fairly transparent texture.

34. Given Britten's early and continued admiration for Alban Berg (with whom he wanted to study but his parents did not allow him to do so), it is tempting to see this entire composition as homage to the Viennese composer, especially in the application of these variation principles, which are reminiscent of some of Berg's processes, especially in his masterpiece *Wozzeck*.

CHAPTER 7

1. Glenn Watkins, *Soundings: Music in the Twentieth Century* (Belmont, CA: Wadsworth Group, 1995), 394.

2. Frank Howes, *The English Musical Renaissance* (New York: Stein and Day, 1966), 69.

3. *English Country Songs: Words and Music*, ed. Lucy E. Broadwood and J. A. Fuller Maitland (London: Leadenhall Press; New York: C. Scribner's Sons, 1893).

4. Howes, *English Musical Renaissance*, 80.

5. Ibid., 231. Howes quotes a statement made by the composer contained in Hubert Foss, *Ralph Vaughan Williams: A Study* (London: Harrap, 1950).

6. Ibid., 232. The quote itself is from Imogen Holst's book, *Gustav Holst: A Biography* (London: Oxford University Press, 1938).

7. Hugh Ottaway and Alain Frogley, "Vaughan Williams, Ralph," in *NG2*, 26:355.

8. Wilfrid Mellers, *Vaughan Williams and the Vision of Albion* (London: Barrie and Jenkins, 1989), 28.

9. Ralph Vaughan Williams, "'Just as the Tide was Flowing,' (Dorian melody) as sung by Mr. Harper at King's Lynn, January 14, 1905," *Journal of the Folk Song Society* 2, no. 8 (1906): 173. In 1905 and 1906 the composer collected and transcribed folk melodies from the fishermen and laborers in the small fishing village of King's Lynn. The tune *King's Lynn* (from the folk song "Young Henry the Poacher") is now a staple in English and American hymnals and not to be confused with the *Kingsfold* tune.

10. Frank Purslow, ed., *Marrow Bones: English Folk Songs from the Hammond and Gardiner Mss* (London: EFDS Publications Ltd., 1965), 48.

11. Julian Onderdonk, "Vaughan Williams's Folksong Transcriptions: A Case of Idealization?" in *Vaughan Williams Studies*, ed. Alain Frogley (Cambridge: Cambridge University Press, 1996), 118–38.

12. *G. Holst: Letters to W. G. Whittaker*, ed. Michael Short (Glasgow: University of Glasgow Press, 1974), 7, letter from April 24, 1916, quoted in Michael Short, *Gustav Holst* (Oxford: Oxford University Press, 1990), 136.

13. Ibid., 137.

14. The collection *Songs of the West: Folk Songs of Devon and Cornwall* is the work of Sabine Baring Gould, H. F. Sheppard, and F. W. Bissell, ed. Cecil Sharpe (London: Methuen and Co. [n.d.]). "The Loyal Lover" is no. 92 (188).

15. Richard Capell, "Death Comes to Satyavan," *Radio Times* 49, no. 629, October 18, 1935, 15, quoted in Short, *Gustav Holst*, 79.

16. *Gustav Holst: Letters to W. G. Whittaker*, 4, letter from March 6, 1916, quoted in Short, *Gustav Holst*, 89.

17. Edward J. Dent, "The Hymn of Jesus," *Athenaeum* 4462 (April 2): 455, quoted in Short, *Gustav Holst*, 147.

18. This work is discussed separately in chap. 4, "Choral Symphony from Beethoven to Berio."

19. Mellers, *Vaughan Williams*, 135.

20. Alain Frogley, liner notes to the recording of *Sancta Civitas* by the London Symphony Orchestra and Chorus, conducted by Richard Hickox (recorded 1992, EMI Records CDC 7 54788 2, 1993), 2.

21. Percy Grainger to Cyril Scott, April 11, 1955, held by the Grainger Museum, University of Melbourne, Australia.

22. Cited in the editor's preface to Béla Bartók, *The Hungarian Folk Song*, ed. Benjamin Suchoff, trans. M. D. Calvocoressi, with annotations by Zoltán Kodály, in New York Bartók Archive Studies in Musicology, no. 13 (Albany: SUNY Press, 1981), xxii, xxix.

23. Quoted in László Eősze, Mícheál Houlahan, and Philip Tacka, "Kodály, Zoltán," *NG2*, 13:719.

24. For the same event, Bartók composed the *Dance Suite*.

25. János Breuer, *A Guide to Kodály* (Budapest: Corvina Books, 1990).

26. Breuer's *A Guide to Kodály* (76–79) provides a complete account of the performances of Kodály in England during his visits.

27. This English text was made by Dent for the 1927 Cambridge performance. A persistent problem in performing the music of Kodály and Bartók is that the only published editions have English and/or German text, not the original Hungarian; thus, it is impossible to know the original rhythmic configuration of the text.

28. Breuer, *A Guide to Kodály*, 82.

29. Ibid., 174–75.

30. In May and June 1966 Kodály revised and corrected the original "Organ Mass," the new and final version of the work now titled *Organoedia ad missam lectam*.

31. Breuer, *A Guide to Kodály*, 174, 178–79. Kodály's *Missa Brevis* exhibits a cyclic structure similar to Beethoven's *Mass in C*, a work Kodály conducted in 1930.

32. Elliott Antokoletz, *The Music of Béla Bartók: A Study of Tonality and Progression in Twentieth-Century Music* (Berkeley: University of California Press, 1984), 27.

33. Ironically, the published version of these pieces contains English and German texts but not the original Hungarian. The English translations are by Nancy Bush, the wife of the English composer Alan Bush, emphasizing the central role that England played in the choral music of both Bartók and Kodály.

34. Béla Bartók, *Hungarian Folk Song*, no. 33a, 227.

35. András Batta, liner notes for Hungaroton recording (HCD 12759-2, 1981), 4.

36. This scale is Messiaen's second Mode of Limited Transposition.

37. Antokoletz, *Music of Béla Bartók*, 241.

38. Bartók's fascination with this mathematical expression of natural symmetry is most famously employed in his *Music for Strings, Percussion, and Celesta* (1936).

39. See Vladimir Morosan, *Choral Music in Pre-Revolutionary Russia* (Ann Arbor: UMI Research Press, 1986).

40. Ibid., 71.

41. Ibid., 105, 112, 113.

42. Ibid., 106–11.

43. Sergei Rachmaninoff, *All-Night Vigil*, op. 37, ed. V. Morosan and A. Ruggieri, Monuments of Russian Sacred Music, series 9, vol. 2 (Madison, CT: Musica Russica, 1992), v.

44. Among the recordings of this work are those by Robert Shaw (Telarc, 80172, 1990); Andrei Roudenko (Northeastern Records, NR 256-CD, 1992); Stephen Cleobury, King's College (EMI Classics, 56752, 1999); St. Petersburg Chamber Choir (Russian Season, 1998); Paul Hillier (Harmonia Mundi, 2005); Tonu Kaljuste, Swedish Radio Choir (EMI 45124 and Virgin Classics, 7243 5 61845 2 7); Matthew Best (Hyperion, 66460); and David Hill (BBC MM97 DDD, 2000, BBC).

45. Geoffrey Norris, *Rachmaninoff*, Master Musicians Series (London: Oxford University Press, 1993), 150–51.

46. The orchestration is suggestive of such successors as George Antheil's *Ballet Méchanique* (1923–25) and Edgard Varèse's *Ionisation* (1929–31).

47. Peter van den Toorn, *The Music of Igor Stravinsky* (New Haven, CT: Yale University Press, 1983), 155–77, quoted in Watkins, *Soundings*, 228.

48. Julian Haycock, notes to EMI recording of "Alexander Nevsky" (London: EMI Records Ltd., 1999), no. 7243 5 73353 2 4.

49. Mimi S. Daitz, *Ancient Song Recovered: The Life and Music of Veljo Tormis* (Hillsdale, NY: Pendragon Press, 2004), 288–325.

50. Eve Tarm, "Singing Freedom" introduction and interview with Tormis, *Estonia Magazine* 1, no. 3 (1992): 16.

51. Urve Lippius, "Magnum Opus: Veljo Tormis, 'Curse Upon Iron'—Analytical Study," trans. Velve Luuk and Urve Lippius, in *Teater Muusika, Kino* 2 (1985): 20–29

52. Translation by Eero Vihman, taken from the recording of the work by the BBC Singers, Bo Holton, conductor, Collins Classics (Lambourne Productions, 1996), Disc no. 14722.

53. "Calendar Songs" is the term Tormis himself decided on in 1993 to classify such compositions. See Daitz, *Ancient Song Recovered*, 173.

54. Veljo Tormis, notes to the recording *Forgotten Peoples* (Munich: ECM Records, 1992), CD ECM 1459–1460.

CHAPTER 8

1. Watkins, *Soundings*, 308.

2. Wilfrid Mellers, "Stravinsky's Oedipus as 20th-Century Hero," in *Stravinsky: A New Appraisal of His Work*, ed. Paul Henry Lang (New York: Norton, 1963), 34.

3. At that point in music history, there was a considerable body of music incorrectly attributed to Pergolesi because of his enormous reputation. Stravinsky and choreographer Leonid Massine unearthed some music at the Naples Conservatory that, although attributed to Pergolesi, was probably composed by a number of his contemporaries.

4. Stephen Walsh, *Stravinsky: Oedipus Rex* (Cambridge: Cambridge University Press, 1993), 23.

5. Boris Asaf'yev, *A Book About Stravinsky*, trans. Richard F. French (Ann Arbor: U.M.I. Press, 1982), 263. Asaf'yev's book was originally published in St. Petersburg in 1929.

6. Mellers, "Stravinsky's Oedipus Rex as 20th-Century Hero," 43.

7. Leonard Bernstein, *The Unanswered Question* (Cambridge, MA: Harvard University Press, 1976), 410–11.

8. Walsh, *Stravinsky: Oedipus Rex*, 35.

9. Igor Stravinsky and Robert Craft, *Dialogues and A Diary* (London: Faber and Faber, 1968), 25.

10. Igor Stravinsky, *An Autobiography* (New York: Simon and Schuster, 1936; Norton, 1962), 161–62.

11. I have long thought that Stravinsky's greatest nightmare was that, left to his own intuition, he would have become another Tchaikovsky. Such planning was one way of making sure that he never had that lapse.

12. Prelude and Fugue would seem to suggest that the label neo-Baroque is more appropriate than neoclassical. In the 1930s, the Baroque period had not achieved the status is now has, so neoclassicism included any music of the "Common Practice Period.

13. Peter S. Hansen, *An Introduction to Twentieth Century Music*, 3rd. ed. (Boston: Allyn and Bacon, 1971), 162.

14. Roger Shattuck, *The Banquet Years*, 327.

15. Walter Piston, "Stravinsky's Rediscoveries," in *Stravinsky in the Theatre*, ed. Minna Lederman (New York: Pellegrini & Cudahy, 1949), 130–31.

16. Joseph N. Straus, "Stravinsky's Tonal Axis," *Journal of Music Theory* 26, no. 2 (1982): 268.

17. Ibid., 279.

18. Perhaps the most successful performance of Stravinsky's *Mass* would take place in a liturgical setting; with the exception of the Kyrie-Gloria succession, the movements come at the proper place in the Mass liturgy and gain significant clarity and power from their severance from each other.

19. Stravinsky, quoted in Peter S. Hansen, *Twentieth-Century Music*, 151.

20. Schoenberg devised a method of composition that virtually eliminated the possibility of reverting to tonal music. Paul Hindemith was another system builder, producing *The Craft of Musical Composition* as an *apologia* for his iconic style. The same motivation is evident in the book written by Olivier Messiaen, *Technique de mon langage musical* (Paris: A. Leduc, 1944) and the many similar books written by contemporary composers explaining why they composed they way they did.

21. Edward Lundergan, "Modal Symmetry and Textual Symbolism in the Credo of the Stravinsky Mass," *Choral Journal* 45, no. 8 (2005): 9.

22. Ibid.

23. Ibid.

24. Stravinsky to Ernst Ansermet, *Revue musicale de Suisse-romande* 33, no. 5 (1980): 215, quoted in Messing, *Neoclassicism in Music*, 124–25.

25. Darius Milhaud, "The Evolution of Modern Music in Paris and in Vienna," *North American Review* (1923): 544–54, quoted in Messing, 124.

26. Ibid.

27. Nonetheless, there is an element of *Gebrauchsmusik* that is critical to valuing Hindemith's contribution to contemporary music, namely his concern with providing serious music for nearly every imaginable instrument and level of performer. To that end, Hindemith's sonatas and concertos have become staples in the repertory of every principal orchestral instrument.

28. For a more substantive discussion of the texts, see Alwes, "Paul Hindemith's *Six Chansons*: Genesis and Analysis," *Choral Journal*, 36, no. 2 (1995): 35–39.

29. It was for this same symposium that Aaron Copland composed his large choral work, "In the Beginning."

30. The source of Hindemith's text is *The Anthology* of *Medieval Latin Verse*, ed. Stephen Gaselee (London: Macmillan, 1925).

31. The sole exception to this pattern is the combination of the lines beginning with U and V to form a single couplet.

32. Paul Hindemith, *The Craft of Musical Composition*, 2 vols. (London: Schott, 1937–40; English translation 1942 by Associated Music Publishers, Inc., New York).

33. Richard French, "Hindemith's *Mass* (1963): An Introduction," in *Words and Music: The Scholar's View; A Medley of Problems and Solutions Compiled in Honor of A. Tillman Merritt by Sundry Hands*, ed. Laurence Berman (Cambridge, MA: Harvard Department of Music, 1972), 84–85.

34. Watkins, *Soundings*, 286–307.

35. Judith Lynn Sebesta, *Carmina Burana: Cantiones profanes* (Chicago: Bolchazy-Carducci Publishers, 1985), 3.

36. In 1956 Orff published a version with a reduced scoring—two pianos, timpani, and percussion—to facilitate performances in schools and in music societies that have no orchestra.

37. This is especially true in the purely instrumental music (e.g., *Uf dem anger*), but also shows up occasionally in vocal movements such as the introduction to no. 10, *Were diu werlt alle min*.

38. The twentieth-century organ builders Walter Holtkamp, Robert Noehren, Hermann Schlicker, Rudolph von Beckerath, Phares Steiner, and John Brombaugh were among the first in the United States to build tracker instruments, and firms such as Létourno, Fisk, and Maier are among those who build new organs to this musical standard throughout the world. See www.apoba.com and Lawrence I. Phelps, "A Short History of the Organ Revival," *Church Music* 67, no. 1 (1967).

39. Friedrich Blume et al., eds., *Protestant Church Music: A History* (New York: Norton, 1974), 422.

40. In the Bärenreiter publication (Kassel: 1966, no. 676), there is an index at the end of the collection, indicating how the collection follows the various feasts of the liturgical year.

41. The other two motets are *Es ist das Heil uns kommen her* and *Komm heiliger Geist*.

42. A narrator reads lessons appropriate to the Advent season between the musical movements.

43. Distler does not provide metronome markings, but the rubrics for each movement establish their basic speed: v. 1 uses "measured quick half notes" and v. 3 says much the same thing ("Swinging half notes, but not hurried"); in contrast, the middle movement is in 4/4 with "peacefully moving quarter notes."

44. The similarity between Distler and Schütz lies in their use of tone painting, especially for the words "mit Trompeten" ("with trumpets")—Schütz uses triadic arpeggios, while Distler sets the syllable "Trom-" to *two* syllables, almost as if were being tongued.

45. Although it lies outside the criteria for including Distler in this chapter, one of the most successful compositions during his lifetime was the *Mörike-Chorliederbuch*, op. 19, 3 vols. (1938–39).

46. Distler, epilogue to *Choralpassion*, op. 7, in Blume et al., *Protestant Church Music*, 454.

47. Adam Adrio, "Renewal and Rejuvenation," in Blume et al., *Protestant Church Music*, 420.

CHAPTER 9

1. Pierre Boulez, "Schoenberg is DEAD!" *Score* (London), no. 6 (May 1952): 18–22. See also *Stocktakings from an Apprenticeship*, ed. Paule Thévenin, trans. Stephen Walsh, with an introduction by Robert Piencikowski (Oxford: Clarendon Press), 209–14.

2. Extract from Boulez's article "Eventuellement" *La Revue Musicale*, 1952, quoted in Joan Peyser, *To Boulez and Beyond: Music in Europe since "The Rite of Spring"* (New York: Billboard Books, 1999), 182.

3. Peyser, *Boulez and Beyond*, 183.

4. Clytus Gottwald, notes to the recording "atelier schola cantorum 3," Bayer-Records: Cadenza (CAD 800 893, 1993).

5. A complete list of Stockhausen's works is available at http://www.stockhausen.org (Stockhausen Foundation for Music).

6. Karl-Heinz Stockhausen, *Texte zur elektronischen und instrumetan, len Musik*, ed. Dieter Schnabel, 2 vols. (Köln: M. Dumont Schauberg Verlag, 1963–64), 250.

7. Ibid.

8. Karlheinz Stockhausen, "Music and Speech," *die Reihe*, no. 6. The journal was originally edited by Stockhausen and Herbert Elmert, and published by U. E. Wien (1955–62). An English edition

under the same title was published by Theodore Presser (1957–68) (Bryn Mawr: Theodore Presser Co., 1964, in association with Universal A.G. Wien, 1960), 58.

9. A recent, more user-friendly example of this technique may be found in Sarah Hopkins's "Past Life Melodies" (Morton Music, 1992).

10. Henze, *Das Floss der Medusa* (Mainz: B. Schott's Söhne, Edition 6719, 1977), 80.

11. The letter is quoted in the preface to the Eulenburg score (# 8029, 1995), vi.

12. Karlheinz Stockhausen, "Sprache und Musik," Darmstadter Beiträge zur Neuen Musik, no. 1 (1958), 65–74, quoted in Christopher Flamm's prefatory notes to the Eulenburg edition, trans. Angela Davies (London: Eulenburg, 1995, EE8029), vii.

13. Luciano Berio, "Composer's Note," to full score of *Magnificat* (New York: Belwin-Mills, 1971, # EL 2289).

14. David Osmond-Smith, "Berio, Luciano," NG2, 3:351.

15. Ibid. 352.

16. David Osmond-Smith, *Berio*, Oxford Studies of Composers, no. 24 (Oxford: Oxford University Press, 1991), 82.

17. Swingle II was formed by Ward Swingle (1927–2015) after the 1973 demise of the original, French-based group (the "Swingle Singers"), which was co-founded by Swingle and Christiane Le Grand in 1962–63. The group, an octet of English singers with an expanded repertory, toured and recorded until 1985. For more on the composition *Sinfonia*, see chap. 4, "Choral Symphony from Beethoven to Berio."

18. These numbers represent movements of the revised version; in its earlier incarnation for the King's Singers, Berio used a different ordering.

19. Nick Strimple, *Choral Music in the Twentieth Century* (Portland, OR: Amadeus Press, 2002), 174.

20. In 1972 this society was renamed the *Centre d'Études de Mathématique et Automatique Musicales* (CEMAMu).

21. In canon 3, the last note resolves up a semitone rather than down (that is, B♭, A, C, C♯). In the fourth canon, the motif appears at the opening of the melody in retrograde.

22. Ben Johnston, conversation with the author, 1980.

23. Laurie C. Matheson, "The Self-Conscious Vocal Ensemble in Selected Twentieth-Century Vocal Works." (DMA diss., University of Illinois at Urbana-Champaign, 1998), 1.

24. This work is yet another allusion to Ockeghem's *Missa Prolationum*, which also features mensural canons in which different parts sing the same melody simultaneously in simple and compound meters.

25. Originally, he envisioned a single performer to play both but decided, on grounds of practicality, to go with two players.

26. This chorale appears in Bach's cantata *Wer mich liebet, der wird mein Wort halten* (BWV 74). The chorale itself is in open score in Riemenschneider's collection of Bach chorales (G. Schirmer, 1939), 38.

27. See *Neue Bach Ausgabe*, Series I/13 (*Kantaten zum 1. Pfingsttag*), Dietrich Kilian, ed., *Kritischer Bericht* (Kassel: Bärenreiter Verlag), 100.

28. Mauricio Kagel, Liner notes, "About the 'st. bach passion,' a conversation with Werner Klüppelholz" (recorded 1985: Mauricio Kagel Edition, vol. 8, France, Montaigne, Auvidis: MO 782044, 1996).

29. Heinz Holliger, *PSALM für gemischten Chor* (B. Schott's Söhne, Mainz, Edition 6487, n.d.).

30. Pauline Oliveros, *Sound Patterns* (Hackensack, NJ: Joseph Boonin, 1984, B 111).

31. Ann L. Silverberg. *A Sympathy with Sounds* (Urbana: University of Illinois School of Music, 1995), 73.

32. Harrison Birtwistle's score *Narration: A Description of the Passing of a Year* (London: Universal Edition, 1964), UE 14157 L.

33. *Sir Gawain and the Green Knight*, trans. Brian Stone (Harmondsworth: Penguin Classics, 1959).

34. Strimple, *Choral Music in the Twentieth Century*, 279.

35. R. Murray Schafer, "Epitaph for Moonlight," Berandol Music Ltd. (Scarborough, ONT, 1969).

36. See chap. 13, this volume.

37. Schnittke, quoted in Uwe Schweikhert, "Psalms of Somber Grief: Alfred Schnittke's Twelve Psalms of Repentance," liner notes to Schnittke's *Psalms of Repentance* (Swedish Radio Choir, Tõnu Kaljuste, conductor, ECM Records, ECM New Series, 1583, 1999).

38. The title of the publication is *Pamyatniki Literatury Drevni Rus': Vtoraya Polovina XVI. Veka* (Monuments of Literature of Ancient Rus': Second Half of the Sixteenth Century), ed. Dmitry Likhachev and Lev Dmitriev (Moscow: Khudozhestvennaya Literatur, 1986), 560–63.

39. Only eleven movements are texted. The twelfth psalm is sung *bocca chiusa* (hummed) as though it were a prayer for forgiveness of sins that had not been specifically named.

40. Svetlana Kalashnikova, "Universal'nost'–i Lakonizm? Paradosky i Tainy Tzukovysotnogo Pis'ma Al'freda Shnitke" (Universalism and Laconisism? Paradoxes and Mysteries of Pitch Construction in Alfred Schnittke), *Muzykal'naya Akademiya* (Music Academy), no. 2 (1999): 84–90.

CHAPTER 10

1. Published by Ricordi of Milan (1989), Edition 130337.

2. Translation by Dr. Rachel Jensen.

3. For a discussion of Dallapiccolla's most significant choral composition, the *Canti di Prigionia*, see chap. 20, "Serialism and Choral Music of the Twentieth Century."

4. Enzo Restagno, "Petrassi, Goffredo," *NG2*, 19:500.

5. Eric Ericson, "Five Centuries of European Choral Music," (His Master's Voice, IC 153 29916–153 29919), 1971. A more recent performance can be found at www.tubeid.net, featuring the Kings Singers, 2015.

6. Edward Lear, *The Complete Book of Nonsense*, ed. Holbrook Jackson (New York: Dover Publications, 1951).

7. Paul Wingfield, *Janáček: Glagolitic Mass*, Cambridge Classical Music Handbook Series (Cambridge: Cambridge University Press, 1992), 67–71.

8. H. Halbreich, *Bohuslav Martinů: Werkverzeichnis, Documentation und Biographie* (Zurich: Atlantis Verlag, 1968).

9. Brian Large, *Martinů* (New York: Holmes & Meier Publishers, 1975), 78.

10. Richard Zielinski, "Karol Szymanowski (1882–1937): The Father of Contemporary Polish Music," *Choral Journal* 46, no. 3 (2005): 9.

11. Our knowledge of Eastern European music before 1989 awaits scholarly discovery. There is a body of music and a number of performing ensembles that have only recently surfaced, for example, *Mystic Chants / la voix Bulgare*, 1999, and the *Mystery of the Bulgarian Voice*, 2006, see www.YouTube.com/watch?v=IZ4LCejQg8o.

12. David Kushner, *Ernst Bloch: A Guide to Research*. Garland Composer Resources Manuals, no. 14 (New York: Garland, 1968), 12.

13. Alexander Ringer, personal communication, 1994.

14. Bernhard Billeter, "Martin, Frank," *NG2*, 15:908.

15. Ibid., 909.

16. With added F$\sharp$ and C$\sharp$ as color tones.

17. Part 2 of Bach's *St. Matthew Passion* also opens with an aria for alto and chorus, *Ach, nun ist mein Jesus hin.*

18. Like Petrassi, Martin's *Mass* and the *Songs of Ariel* owe their prominence, again, to the land-mark recordings of Eric Ericson—*Five Centuries of European Choral Music* (*Mass*) and *Virtuose Chormusik* (*Ariel*), EMI IC 165-30796//99 (1978); see also Frank Martin, *Messe pour Double Choeur*, RIAS-Kammerchor, Harmonium Mundi S.A. 2004.

19. It would be remiss of me not to mention the influential role played by Tapiola Children's Choir, a group that did much to further Scandinavian choral composition and the growth of American children's choirs. Over the forty-five years of its existence, the choir has evolved into a well-known entity for contemporary and Scandinavian music. See www.allmusic.com/artist/tapiola-childrens-choir-mn.

20. Richard Sparks, *The Swedish Choral Miracle: Swedish a Cappella Music since 1945* (Pittsboro, NC: Blue Fire Productions, 1999).

21. An alternative view of this collection posits three perfect intervals (D–G, C♯–F♯ and B♭–E♭) and the single pitch (A) which may be an extension of the first interval (A–D–G).

22. As noted in vol. 1, chap. 9, a number of scholars, including Peter Holman, the author of the *NG2* article on Purcell, as well as a respected monograph titled *Henry Purcell* (Oxford Studies of Composers, Oxford: Oxford University Press, 1994) believe that Purcell intended this eight-part chorus to be part of an unfinished larger work.

23. The use of black and void notation in both examples indicates a traditional type of rhythmic notation (black = quarter note; white = half note) rather than Ligeti's use of varying amounts of coloration to represent the range of pitch density (white = diatonic cluster; black = chromatic cluster).

24. For a catalogue of Nielsen's works (CNW), see the website of the Danish Centre for Music Publication, available at www.kb.dk/dcm.

25. For a complete list, see the website of the Carl Nielsen Society (www.carlnielsen.dk).

26. Bernhard Lewkovitch, *Tre Madrigali di Torquato Tasso* (Copenhagen: Wilhelm Hansen, 1955).

27. Highly recommended is the recording of many of Lewkovitch's choral works by the Jyske Kammerchor (Mogens Dahl, conductor) titled "Apollo's Art" (Copenhagen: Da Capo Records, 2000).

28. Kokkonen's *Requiem* is published by Fennica Gehrmann. For more information on his life and works, see Edward Kurkowski, *The Music of Joonas Kokkonen* (Farnham: Ashgate, 2004).

29. Soloists, drawn from both sections, present fragments of the poetic text to the same descending trichord (B♭, A, G).

30. Composer's Note to *Die erste Elegie* (Espoo, Finland: Fazer Music, 1994).

31. Ibid.

32. Einojuhani Rautavaara, *Sacred Works for Mixed Chorus*, liner notes (Helsinki: Ondine Inc. ODE 935–32, 1999).

33. Rautavaara, *Vigilia* (Helsinki: Edition Fazer, 1998).

34. For examples of the music of Rihards Dubra and Einfelde, see the Hyperion recording (CDA67799, 2009) of the Choir of Royal Holloway, conducted by Rupert Gough. Music by Maija Einfelde appears on a recording by Stephen Layton (with the Choir of Trinity College, Cambridge) titled *Baltic Exchange* (London: Hyperion CDA67747, 2010). Readers can also find noncommercial recordings on YouTube; while the recordings may vary widely in quality, this source has the virtue of being instantly accessible and free.

35. For a recent list of Miškinis's compositions, see Nikolaus B. Cummins's monograph, *The Unaccompanied Choral Works of Vytautas Miškinis with Texts by Rabindranath Tagore: A Resource Guide* (Baton Rouge: Louisiana State University, 2012).

36. For a list of Sisask's works, see the Estonian Music Information Centre, available at www.emic.ee.

CHAPTER 11

1. Richard Crawford, "Psalmody (ii), North America" *NG2*, 20:482.
2. William Billings, *Creation*, American Choral Music for Church and Concert, ed. Craig Timberlake (Orleans, MA: Paraclete Press, 1992).
3. All contained in the facsimile edition of *The Continental Harmony* (1794), ed. Hans Nathan (Cambridge, MA: Harvard University Press, 1961). Nathan is also the editor of *The Complete Works of William Billings*, 4 vols. (Boston: American Musicological Society and The Colonial Society of Massachusetts; Charlottesville: University Press of Virginia, 1977–90).
4. Richard Crawford and Nym Cooke, "Supply Belcher," *NG2*, 3:162.
5. The compositions of many of these composers appear in *Music of the New American Nation*, ed. Karl Kroeger, vols. 36–37, *Early American Anthems* (New York: Garland Press, 2000). Kroeger also edited selected music by Samuel Holyoke and Jacob Kimball (vol. 12, 1998), and two Vermont composers (Elisha West and Justin Morgan, vol. 7, 1997) for the same series, as well as the music of Daniel Read (vol. 24, 1995) in *Recent Researches in American Music* (Madison, WI: A-R Editions, 1995).
6. Carol A. Pemberton, *Lowell Mason: His Life and Work* (Ann Arbor: UMI Research Press, 1985).
7. William Little and William Smith's *Easy Instructor or A New Method of Teaching Sacred Harmony* (Hopewell near Trenton, NJ: William Smith & Co., 1798, pub. 1803).
8. William Walker's *Southern Harmony* sold more than 600,000 copies in editions spanning the period from 1835 to 1854. See Robert Stevenson, *Protestant Church Music in America: A Short Survey of Men and Movements from 1564 to the Present* (New York: Norton, 1966), 90.
9. *NG2*, vol. 7, s.v. "Denson, Seaborn M."
10. For an extensive discussion of the history and tradition of the Sacred Harp movement and Americanism in music, see Buell E. Cobb Jr., *The Sacred Harp: A Tradition and its Music* (Athens: University of Georgia Press, 1989), and Richard Taruskin, *Music in the Twentieth Century*, "Twentieth-Century Americanism," Oxford History of Western Music, 657–59.
11. Cobb, *Sacred Harp*, 1–2. For an excellent documentary about sacred harp singing, see *Awake, My Soul: The Story of the Sacred Harp*, directed by Matt Hinton and Jennifer Brooks (Atlanta: Awake Productions, 2006).
12. Gilbert Chase, *America's Music from the Pilgrims to the Present*, 3rd ed. (Urbana: University of Illinois Press, 1987). This terms was actually coined by Chase in the original publication (New York: McGraw-Hill, 1955). The term took hold and was subsequently used by H. Wiley Hitchcock, *Music in the United States: A Historical Introduction* (Englewood Cliffs, NJ: Prentice Hall, 1969), 130–38. For more recent discussions of this period, see Joseph Horowitz, *Classical Music in America* (New York: Norton, 2005) and Wilfrid Mellers, *Music in a New Found Land* (Oxford: Oxford University Press, 1987).
13. For a critical score, see *Recent Researches in American Music*, vol. 57, ed. Betty Buchanan (Madison, WI: A-R Editions, 2006).
14. In her article, "'Buds the infant mind': Charles Ives's *The Celestial Country* and American Protestant Choral Traditions," *19th-Century Music* 23, no. 2 (1999): 163–89, Gayle Sherwood indicates that the Haydn and Handel Society chorus consisted of more than three hundred singers, while the choir at Central Presbyterian Church that premiered *The Celestial Country* consisted of seventeen singers (four of whom were paid soloists), 175.
15. Ibid., 179, 166.

16. Ibid., 172–73. The same table also appears and receives a more thorough discussion in Sherwood's article "Redating Ives's Choral Sources," in *Ives Studies*, ed. Philip Lambert (Cambridge: Cambridge University Press, 1997), 77–101.

17. Philip Lambert, *The Music of Charles Ives* (New Haven, CT: Yale University Press, 1997), 27.

18. Chester L. Alwes, "Formal Structure as Guide to Rehearsal Strategy in 'Psalm 90' by Charles E. Ives," *Choral Journal* 25, no. 8 (1985): 21–25.

19. Ibid., 22.

20. Lambert, *Music of Charles Ives*, 60–61.

21. Henry Cowell, *New Musical Resources* (New York: Knopf, 1930). Annotated versions of this book have been published by Joscelyn Godwin (New York: Something Else Press, 1969) and David Nicholls (Cambridge: Cambridge University Press, 1996).

22. The numbers assigned to Cowell's music come from William Lichtenwanger's *The Music of Henry Cowell: A Descriptive Catalog* (Brooklyn, NY: Institute for Studies in American Music, Conservatory of Music, Brooklyn College of the City University of New York, 1968).

23. Alan Rich. *American Pioneers: Ives to Cage and Beyond* (London: Phaidon Press, 1995), 119.

24. Ibid., 88.

25. Ibid., 136.

26. Henry Cowell, . . . *if He please* (William Strickland, Norske Solistkor, New York: Composers Recordings) CRI165, 1963, commissioned by the New York Oratorio Society.

27. A. Tilmann Merritt (Cambridge, MA) to Aaron Copland (New York, NY), April 29, 1946. Library of Congress, Aaron Copland Collection, Box 403, Folder 8.

28. Virgil Thomson, "Music: Choral Commissions," *New York Herald Tribune*, May 3, 1947.

29. Francis Perkins, "Collegiate Chorale: Shaw Conducts Concert at Carnegie Hall," *New York Herald Tribune*, Tuesday, May 20, 1947.

30. Harold Taubman, "Shaw and Chorale Give 2 New Works," *New York Times*, May 20, 1947.

31. Nicholas Temperley, "Copland Work Lacks Awe," *Cambridge News*, February 1, 1964.

32. For an examination of these teacher/pupil relationships see Howard Pollack, *Harvard Composers: Walter Piston and his Students from Elliot Carter to Frederic Rzewski* (Metuchen, NJ: Scarecrow Press, 1992).

33. The first of these pieces is printed in Ray Robinson, ed. *Choral Music: A Norton Historical Anthology* (New York: Norton, 1978), 954–67.

34. Ibid., 972–84.

35. Keats's sonnet appears in *John Keats: Complete Poems*, ed. Jack Sillinger (Cambridge, MA: Belknap Press, 1982), 247. It is tempting to believe that Thompson's use of the inverted D″ pedal in the soprano as a "steadfast" musical gesture is another, equally knowledgeable reference to Keats.

36. Born Artur Schloßberg in Germany, he moved to Paris in 1933 to escape the Nazis and changed his name to Jean Berger; he lived and taught in South America and in 1941 moved to the United States.

37. The distribution of these pitches varies; in the first section, the pitches occur in the sequence G♯ (B), A♯ (T), F♯ (A) and C♯ (S); in the second (mm. 94–118) the sequence of vocal entries and pitches are altered to F♯ (S), C♯ (A), G♯ (T), and A♯ (B).

38. The *Prayers of Kierkegaard* came into existence as part of the groundbreaking Louisville Orchestra's Contemporary Music Project, receiving its premiere by that orchestra in 1954, with conductor Robert Whitney and the choral forces of the Southern Baptist Theological Seminary's School of Church Music.

39. Britten's contribution was the cantata *Rejoice in the Lamb*, op. 30 (see chap. 12 for a discussion of this work).

40. Britten, *Letters from a Life*, vol. 2, 1939–45, eds. Donald Mitchell and Philip Reed, 1139.

41. See YouTube SATB version of "The Lobster Quadrille" (from *Alice in Wonderland*)by the University of Michigan Chamber Choir (www.music.umich.edu/mediashowcase) and an SSA version by Flow Women's Voices (www.YouTube.com/watch?v=_TtGMD27CWA).

42. Rochberg's *Psalms for Mixed Chorus* is published by Theodore Presser (Bryn Mawr, PA: 1956).

43. For a complete listing of Hovhaness's choral works, see http://www.hovhaness.com/hovhaness-vocal-works.html.

44. There is a 2004 documentary film by Eva Soltes about Harrison's music, *Lou Harrison: A World of Music*. See www.louharrisondocumentary.com.

45. Heidi Von Gunden, *The Music of Lou Harrison* (Metuchen, NJ: Scarecrow Press, 1995), 59.

46. Rich, *American Pioneers*, 194.

47. Equal temperament, on the other hand, divides an octave into equal-sized scale steps.

48. Lou Harrison, *Music Primer: Various Items About Music to 1970* (New York: C. F. Peters, 1971), 48.

49. Brunner, "Choral Music of Lou Harrison," 162.

50. Showing one of these pieces to students elicited mystified exclamations, "It says you need a stop-watch!" Personal experience confirms that, unfortunately, the coordination this provided was far from precise.

51. Lukas Foss, *The Prairie* (New York: G. Schirmer, 1944, no. 40798), 96.

52. Lukas Foss, "Composer's Preface," *American Cantata* (New York: Amberson Music, 1977).

53. Allan Kovinn, "Lukas Foss, Composer at Home in Many Stylistic Currents, Dies at 86," available at www. nytimes.com/2009/02/02/arts/music/02foss.html?.

54. Ned Rorem, foreword to *An American Oratorio* (New York: Boosey and Hawkes, 1984).

55. *Emma Lazarus: Selected Poems and Other Writings*, ed. Gregory Eiselein (Orchard Park, NY: Broadview Literary Press, 2002), 233.

56. See www.authentichistory.com/1600-1859/3-spirituals.

57. See www.negrospiritual.org/why-negro-spiritual.

58. For more in-depth information, see André J. Thomas (b. 1952), *Way Over in Beulah Lan'* (Dayton, OH: Heritage Music Press, 2007).

59. A useful survey of contemporary American composers appears in Strimple's *Choral Music in the Twentieth Century* , 216–74.

60. The *Requiem of Reconciliation* is a collaborative work for chorus and orchestra (somewhat like the *Messa per Rossini* to which Verdi contributed). *Reconciliation* commemorates the fiftieth anniversary of the end of World War II and contains the works of fourteen composers whose countries were involved in the war. The composers who contributed music include Luciano Berio, Friedrich Cerha, Paul-Heinz Dittrich, Marek Kopolent, John Harbison, Arne Nordheim, Bernard Rands, Marc-André Dalbavie, Judith Weir, Krzysztof Penderecki, Wolfgang Rihm, Alfred Schnittke, Joyi Yuasa, and György Kurtág.

CHAPTER 12

1. Oskar A. H. Schmitz, *Das Land ohne Musik: Englische Gesellschaftsprobleme* (Munich: 1914). See also Ruth A. Solie, "No 'Land without Music' after All," available at www.jstor.org/stable/25958664; and Andrew Blake, *The Land without Music: Music, Culture, and Society in Twentieth-Century Britain* (Manchester: Manchester University Press, 1998).

2. Frank Howes, *The English Musical Renaissance* (New York: Stein and Day, 1966). See also Peter Pirie, *The English Musical Renaissance* (London: Gollancz, 1979), and Michael Trend, *The Music Makers: The English Musical Renaissance from Elgar to Britten* (London: Weidenfeld and Nicholson, 1985).

3. See Chester L. Alwes, "Choral Music in the Culture of the Nineteenth Century," in *The Cambridge Companion to Choral Music*, ed. André de Quadros (Cambridge: Cambridge University Press, 2012), 32.

4. Hugh Wood. "Frank Bridge and the Land without Music," *Tempo* 121 (June 1977): 9.

5. For more on this, see Meirion Hughes and Robert Stradling, *The English Musical Renaissance 1840–1940: Constructing a National Music*, 2nd ed. (Manchester: Manchester University Press, 2001), 215–50.

6. Ackworth also fashioned Henry Wadsworth's epic poem, "The Saga of St. Olaf" into the libretto for Elgar's *Scenes from the Saga of St. Olaf*, op. 30 (1896).

7. August Johannes Jaeger emigrated to England from Düsseldorf in 1878 and joined Novello and Co. in 1890. He corresponded with both Parry and Elgar; his close relationship with Elgar led to him being the subject of the "Nimrod" movement of the *Enigma Variations*.

8. Charles Villiers Stanford.*The Musical Times and Singing Class Circular (1844–1903)*, vol. 39, no.670, 789. Available at http://searchproquest.com/docview/774403?accountid=14553.

9. Ibid., 791.

10. *The Blackwell History of Music in Britain*, vol. 5, *The Romantic Age, 1800–1914*, ed. Nicholas Temperley (Oxford: Blackwell Reference, 1988), 205.

11. Jeremy Dibble. "Stanford, Sir Charles Villiers," *Grove Music Online, Oxford Music Online*. Oxford University Press, available at http://www.oxfordmusiconline.com/subscriber/article/grove/music/26549 (accessed Feb. 23, 2015).

12. Anthony Payne, "The Music of Frank Bridge: The Early Years," *Tempo* 106 (September 1973): 25. Payne's article on "The Last Years" appears in the same journal (no. 107, December 1973), 11–18.

13. Britten, *Letters from a Life (1913–1976)*, vol. 1, *1923–1939*, ed. Donald Mitchell and Philip Reed, 100.

14. In an interview with Murray Schafer in 1963, Britten expressed his belief that it was Frank Bridge who suggested that he "leave England and experience a different musical climate," Britten, *Letters from a Life*, vol.1, 394. Anthony Payne (*Tempo* 107, 12) lends further credence to this belief, noting Bridge's high opinion of Berg and the striking similarity between Bridge's Third String Quartet (1927) and the harmonic practices of the Second Viennese School.

15. Anthony Payne, Lewis Foreman, and John Bishop, *The Music of Frank Bridge* (London: Thames Publishing in conjunction with the RCM Frank Bridge Trust, 1976), 51.

16. Collegiate churches are those institutions endowed for a chapter of canons (usually presided over by a dean) but lacking designation as the seat of authority for a bishop.

17. Christopher Palmer, *Herbert Howells: A Centenary Celebration* (London: Thames Publishing, 1992), 146. The text he quotes is taken from *Music for the Church*, an article in the Southern Cathedrals Festival program book (Winchester, 1966), 11.

18. Britten, *Letters from a Life*, vol. 1, 394.

19. Ibid., 128.

20. Christopher Mark, *Early Benjamin Britten: A Study of Stylistic and Technical Evolution* (New York: Garland Press, 1995); Peter Evans, *The Music of Benjamin Britten* (Oxford: Oxford University Press, 1996).

21. Philip Rupprecht, *Britten's Musical Language* (Cambridge: Cambridge University Press, 2001), 191.

22. Britten, *Letters from a Life*, vol. 2, 1026.

23. Ibid., 939.

24. To take one of the more obvious and controversial references, the second stanza of part 3 begins "O dear white children," followed in lines 5 and 6 by "O hang the head, Impetuous child with the tremendous brain." A letter from Edward Sackville-West (an unsuccessful suitor) to Britten is addressed, "My dear white child," a reference to Britten's pale complexion. Certainly Auden,

whose intellectual brilliance dominated Britten in the 1930s, thought of Britten as immensely intelligent and talented, though largely unaware of his gifts (and sexual orientation); thus, "hang the head" (in shame for unacknowledged feelings and potential), "Impetuous child" (Auden clearly regarded himself as Britten's mentor and surrogate father), and "with the tremendous brain" (referring to Britten's latent genius).

25. Britten, like Purcell, was renowned for his facility and genius in setting the English language. Indeed, Britten fancied himself the second *Orpheus Brittanicus*. Purcell's fingerprint ground bass (*basso ostinato*) is exemplified in Dido's lament (*Dido and Aeneas*) and "Sound the Trumpet" from the duet "Come, Come Ye Sons of Art" from *Birthday Ode for Queen Mary* (1694), and in many of Purcell's instrumental works.

26. *The English Galaxy of Shorter Poems, Chosen and Edited by Gerald Bullett* (New York: Macmillan Co., 1934). This volume is kept in the Britten-Pears Library at Aldeburgh.

27. *LU*, 413.

28. There is a published version of the *Ceremony of Carols* for mixed voices and also for each individual movement, but the original scoring is more successful for concerts.

29. For the complete text of the poem and interesting commentary, see *The Complete Poetical Works of Christopher Smart*, vol. 1, *Jubilate Agno*, ed. Katrina Williamson (Oxford: Clarendon Press, 1980).

30. Britten, *Letters from a Life*, vol. 2, 1157.

31. Rupprecht, *Britten's Musical Language*, 189–203.

32. The English tenor Peter Pears (Britten's life partner) and the German baritone Dietrich Fischer-Dieskau sang the solo parts in the premiere in 1962. Surely it is no accident that the soloists represent the two warring countries and, in their final duet, individual English and German soldiers.

33. Specifically in the Benedictus of the *Missa Brevis* and the *Tema Seriale* movement of the *Cantata Academica* (see chap. 6).

34. The mostly unison orchestral music consists of quintuplets (i.e., five sixteenth notes per beat); this asymmetrical rhythm suggests that the *Requiem*'s Introit is less a procession of the clergy than a procession of wounded veterans dragging a wounded or useless leg.

35. See Malcom Boyd, "Britten, Verdi, and the *Requiem*," *Tempo* 86 (1968): 2–6.

36. For example, the popular *Flower Songs* (op. 47, 1950) or the suite of Choral Dances extracted from the second act of Britten's opera *Gloriana* (op. 53), composed to celebrate the coronation of Queen Elizabeth II in 1953.

37. *Medieval English Lyrics: A Critical Anthology* (London: Faber and Faber, 1963), ed. R. T. Davies. Davies authored the modern English "translations" that appear in the score. The same anthology served as the source of the "Corpus Christi Carol" in *A Boy Was Born*, op. 3 (1932–33).

38. A similar phenomenon occurs in Britten's *Spring Symphony*, op. 44 (see chap. 4).

39. Benjamin Britten, "On Winning the First Aspen Award," in *Contemporary Composers on Contemporary Music*, ed. Elliott Schwarz and Barney Childs (New York: Da Capo Press, 1978 [1967]), 116–17.

40. Ian Kemp, *Tippett: The Composer and His Music* (London: Eulenburg Books, 1984), 152–53.

41. Michael Tippett, "Five Negro Spirituals" from *A Child of our Time* (Mainz: Schott, 1958, Edition 10585).

42. James Weldon Johnson and John R. Johnson, *The Book of American Negro Spirituals* (New York: Viking Press, 1925).

43. Michael Tippett, *Four Songs from the British Isles:* "Early One Morning" (Mainz: Schott, 1957, no. 11346).

44. Martin Dreyer, "Yorkshire Composers 6," *Month in Yorkshire*, November 1979, 5, quoted in Bruce Gladstone, "A Style Analysis of the Choral Music of Kenneth Leighton," (DMA diss., University of Illinois at Urbana-Champaign, 1999), 52.
45. Ibid., 13–31.
46. For an excellent survey of Leighton's sacred choral music, see the CD by The Finzi Singers, Paul Spicer, conductor, with Andrew Lumsden, organ (Colchester: Chandos, 1997).
47. Spicer's complete seventy-fifth anniversary tribute is available at www.musicweb-international. com/Leighton?index.htm.
48. John Warnaby, "Davies, Peter Maxwell," *NG2*, 7:63.
49. Ibid.
50. Composer's Notes, *Five Motets*, Boosey and Hawkes (1966), B&H 19336. For a discussion of these motets, see Anthony Payne's article, "Peter Maxwell Davies's Five Motets," *Tempo* 72 (Spring 1965): 7–11.
51. *Peter Maxwell Davies: Mass, Missa parvula and Other Sacred Works* (London: Hyperion Records CDA67454, 2004). Liner notes by Roderic Dunnett.
52. Ibid.
53. Tom Service. "John Tavener Dies at 69; The Veil Falls for the Final Time," obituary in the *Guardian* (UK), November 12, 2013, available at www.theguardian.com/music/2013/mov/12/ john-tavener-british-composer-dies.
54. Obituary in the *Telegraph* (London) (11/12/2013), available at www.telegraph.co.uk/news/obituaries/culture-obituaries/music-obituaries/1044987/Sir-John-Tavener-obituary.html.
55. Michael J. Stewart, "Sir John Tavener obituary," available at www.theguardian.com/music/2013/ nov/12/john-tavener.
56. www.npr.org/ . . ./remembering-holy-minimalist-composer-john-tavener (November 12, 2013).
57. Guido Maria Dreves, ed., *Analecta Hymnica Medii Aevi*, vol. 9, *Sequentiae Ineditae: Liturgischen Prosen des Mittelalters* (Leipzig: O. R. Reisland, 1890), 74.
58. Stephen Johnson, "Harnessing Extremes," *Gramophone* 72 (May 1995), 17.
59. The title is the Gaelic word for "lament for the dead." The composition that bears that name was commissioned by the BBC for the Allegri String Quartet and the clarinetist James Campbell to commemorate the explosion of the North Sea oil rig, *Piper Alpha*, in 1988. This work is dedicated to those 167 victims and their families.
60. Notes to the Boosey and Hawkes score (© 1999).
61. Recorded by Sir Colin Davis, the London Symphony Orchestra and Chorus, and baritone Christopher Maltman (LSO0671). Subsequently, MacMillan has written a post-Passion narrative, "Since It Was the Day of Preparation" (2012) and a *St. Luke Passion* (2013).
62. James MacMillan, interviewed by LSO, London, available at http://lso.co.uk/macmillan.

CHAPTER 13

1. Richard Taruskin, *OHWM*, 5:55.
2. The Latin root of the word is *alea*, meaning "dice" (as in Julius Caesar's declaration when he crossed the Rhine River to subdue the Gauls in 49 BCE: *Alea jacta est* ("The die is cast").
3. This information drawn from the Polish Music Center's website, available at www.usc.edu/dept/ polish_music/VEPM/lutos/lu-wrk-f.html, (accessed April 18, 2015). The score is published by Polskie Wydawnichtwo Muzyczne (Warsaw: 1969).
4. See Culture.pl/en/article/warsaw-autumn-international-festival-of-contemporary-music (accessed, April 18, 2015).

5. Witold Lutosławski, "About the Element of Chance in Music," in *Three Aspects of New Music*, ed. G. Ligeti (Stockholm: Nordiska Musikförlaget, 1986), 47; quoted in Istvan Anhalt, *Alternative Voices: Essays on Contemporary Vocal and Choral Composition* (Toronto: University of Toronto Press, 1984), 86.

6. Note the similarities and differences between this composition and Ligeti's *Lux aeterna* (see also chap. 9).

7. Lutosławski, *Trois poèmes d'Henri Michaux*, Polskie Wydawnichtwo Muzyczne (Warsaw: 1969), notes. Since Lutosławski intends there to be two separate conductors (for orchestra and choir), there are two different versions of the score—one for each conductor. Thus, all of the notes relative to performance and the actual music notated apply only to the ensemble that that particular conductor will serve. The events of the other ensemble are merely cued in.

8. Notes to Ergo Recording 60019; quoted in Watkins, *Soundings*, 620.

9. For an in-depth examination and analysis of Lutosławski's sketches, see Martina Homma, "Witold Lutosławski's *Trois poèmes d'Henri Michaux*: The Sketches and the Work," *Polish Music Journal* 3, no. 2 (Winter 2000), trans. Michael Kubicki; available at www.usc.edu/dept/polish/PMJ/issue/3.2.00/homma.html.

10. Anhalt, *Alternative Voices*, 98.

11. Penderecki uses the same sign again in mm. 47–48.

12. Another notation Penderecki borrows from Lutosławski is the use of a blackened box to indicate a complete chromatic cluster, the boundaries of which are defined by how much of the staff the box occupies.

13. Two of the seven last words, "My God, my God, why have you forsaken me" cites Psalm 22:1, and "I thirst" is dramatically irrelevant.

14. Ray Robinson and Allen Winold, *A Study of Penderecki's St. Luke Passion* (Celle: Moeck Verlag, 1983).

15. Ibid, 115.

16. For an interesting discussion of tonal remnants in Penderecki's *St. Luke Passion*, see Dominic DiOrio's article, "Embedded Tonality in Penderecki's St. Luke Passion," *Choral Scholar* 3, no. 1 (Spring 2013): 1–16, available at www.ncco/org/tcs/issues/vol.3/no.1/diorio/TCS_DiOrio_Penderecki.pdf.

17. Robinson and Winold, *Study*, 66–67.

18. Krzysztof Penderecki, *Labyrinth of Time: Five Addresses for the End of the Millennium* (Chapel Hill, NC: Hinshaw Music, 1998), 76.

19. This hymn by Venantius Fortunatus (ca. 503–609) is often confused with Thomas Aquinas's *Pange lingua gloriosi. Corporis mysterium*. Fortunatus's hymn is traditionally sung during the ritual of the Adoration of the Cross on Good Friday. Positioned just prior to the *Improperia* (Reproaches), the hymn's eighth verse comes first liturgically. *The Catholic Encyclopedia: An International Work of Reference*, 15 vols, ed. Charles G. Habermann, Edward A. Pace, Condé B. Pallen, Thomas J. Shahan, John J. Wynne (New York: Robert Appleton Co./Encyclopedia Press, Inc., 1907–12), vol. 11, 442.

20. Wolfram Schwinger, *Krzysztof Penderecki: His Life and Work; Encounters, Biography and Musical Commentary*, trans. William Mann (London: Schott, 1989), 203–5.

21. Penderecki, *Labyrinth of Time*, 71–2.

22. The moniker "holy minimalist" has been widely applied to these particular composers because of their use of minimalist techniques in the service of sacred music. The origin of this label may trace to an article by Mark Swed that appeared in the *Los Angeles Times* on January 8, 1995, available at www.articles.latimes.com/1995-01-08/entertainment/ca-17655_1_composer-john-tavener. The term has persevered, being mentioned in NPR's announcement of John Tavener's

death in 2013, available at www.npr.org/sections/deceptvecadence/2013/11/12/244788638/remembering-holy-minimalist-composer-john-tavener.

23. Keith Potter, "Minimalism," *NG2*, 16:717.

24. Taruskin, *OHWM*, 5:351; Steve Reich, "Music as a Gradual Process," in *Writings about Music, 1965–2000*, ed. with an introduction by Paul Hillier (Oxford: Oxford University Press, 2002), 9–11.

25. For a thorough discussion of Reich's harmonic tendencies prior to 1985, see Jonathan Bernard, "Tonal Traditions in American Art Music since 1960," in *The Cambridge Companion to American Music*, ed. David Nicholls (Cambridge: Cambridge University Press, 1998), 555–59.

26. The transliteration of the Hebrew text and the English translation are taken from the score (rev. version 1994 by Hendon Music Inc., a Boosey and Hawkes Company. HPS 1189).

27. *The Desert Music* is nominally choral. While the score looks like a typical SATB chorus (with divisi), the "performance placement diagram" included in the score clearly shows nine groups of three singers (sop. 1, sop. 1a, sop. 2, alto 1 & 2, tenor 1 & 2, and bass 1 & 2) clustered around a microphone (New York: Hendon Music, HPS 983, 1985). Reich later created a chamber version that reduced the number of singers to ten.

28. Reich, *The Desert Music*, "Note by the Composer."

29. In his article "Process vs. Intuition in the Recent Works of Steve Reich and John Adam," *American Music* 8, no. 3 (1990): 249, K. Robert Schwarz points out that Reich treats the harmonic cycle in mvt. 3 of *The Desert Music* with considerable freedom, preserving the majority of the harmonic content intact, but substituting new bass pitches that are a tritone remove from the original pitch.

30. Ibid., 250.

31. See Peter Quinn's article, "Out with the Old and in with the New: Arvo Pärt's 'Credo.'" *Tempo* 211 (January 2000): 16–20.

32. This text consists of two parts: "Audivistis dictum: oculum pro oculo, dentem pro dente" ("You have heard it said: An eye for an eye and a tooth for a tooth") and "Autem ego vobis dico: non esse resistendum injuriae" ("But I say unto you: Do not resist evil"). From the liner notes to Deutsche Gramophone recording CD 471 769-2 DG (2003).

33. Lyn Henderson, "A Solitary Genius: The Establishment of Pärt's Technique," *Musical Times* 149, no. 1904 (2008): 87.

34. Paul Hillier, *Arvo Pärt*, Oxford Studies of Composers (New York: Oxford University Press, 1997), 64.

35. For a comprehensive summary of the technique, see ibid., 86–97.

36. The work is often referred to as simply *Passio* (Universal Edition, Wien 1982, 1985, UE 17 568).

37. Hillier, *Arvo Pärt*, 126.

38. Ibid., 93. For another discussion of this technique, see John Roeder, "Transformational Aspects of Arvo Pärt's Tintinnabuli Music," *Journal of Music Theory* 55, no. 1 (2011): 1–41.

39. Hillier, *Arvo Pärt*, 126–39.

40. Michael Chikinda, "Pärt's Evolving Tintinnabuli Style," *Perspectives of New Music* 49, no. 1 (2011): 182–206.

41. Ibid., 184.

42. Paul Hillier, *Arvo Pärt: Collected Choral Works: Complete Scores* (Vienna/London/New York: Universal Publishing Musikverlags GmbH, 1999), 7.

43. John Adams, notes to the full score of *Harmonium* (New York: Associated Music Publishers, 1984), HL 50480015.

44. Ibid.

45. Shattuck, *The Banquet Years*, 332.

46. The tempo change in m. 428 also coincides with the return of the phonemic syllables with which the movement begins. While these appear initially only in the male voices, they leak over into the female voices twenty measures later.

47. Other sponsors included the Lincoln Center for the Performing Arts, the Barbican Centre in London, and the BBC.

48. Taruskin, *OHWM* 5:524.

49. Michael Steinberg, "A Nativity for a New Century," liner notes to the recording of *El Niño* (New York: Nonesuch Records, CD 79634-2, 2000), 15.

50. More information on this work is available at www.npr.org/sections/deceptivecadence/2011/09/10/140341459/john-adams-memory-space-on-the-transmigration-of-souls.

51. See chap. 6.

52. Virgil Thomson, *Music Reviewed*, 248.

53. Taruskin, *OHWM*, 5:51.

54. Oliver Strunk, ed., *Source Readings in Music History*, rev. ed., general ed. Leo Treitler (New York: Norton, 1998), 195.

55. Leeman L. Perkins, *Music in the Age of the Renaissance* (New York: Norton, 1999), 46.

Bibliography, Volume 2

Adams, Byron, and Robin Wells, eds. *Vaughan Williams Essays*. Farnham: Ashgate, 2011.

Adrio, Adam. "Renewal and Rejuvenation." In *Protestant Church Music*, edited by Friedrich Blume, 405–506. New York: Norton, 1974.

Albright, Daniel. *Berlioz's Semi-Operas: "Roméo et Juliette" and "La damnation de Faust"*. Rochester: University of Rochester Press, 2001.

Alwes, Chester L. "Choral Music in the Culture of the Nineteenth Century." In *The Cambridge Companion to Choral Music*, edited by André de Quadros, 27–42. New York: Cambridge University Press, 2012.

Alwes, Chester L. "Formal Structure as Guide to Rehearsal Strategy in *Psalm 90* by Charles E. Ives." *Choral Journal* 25, no. 8 (1985): 21–25.

Alwes, Chester L. "Paul Hindemith's 'Six Chansons: Genesis and Analysis.'" *Choral Journal* 36, no. 2 (1995): 35–39.

Alwes, Chester L. "Words and Music: Benjamin Britten's 'Evening Primrose.'" *Choral Journal* 45, no. 1 (2004): 27–33.

Anhalt, István. *Alternative Voices: Essays on Contemporary Vocal and Choral Composition*. Toronto: University of Toronto Press, 1984.

Antokoletz, Elliott. *The Music of Béla Bartók: A Study of Tonality and Progression in Twentieth-Century Music*. Berkeley: University of California Press, 1984.

Asaf'yev, Boris. *A Book about Stravinsky*. Translated by Richard F. French. Russian Music Studies, no. 5. Ann Arbor, MI: UMI Research Press, 1982.

Bailey, Kathryn. *The Twelve-Note Music of Anton Webern: Old Forms in a New Language*. Music in the Twentieth Century. Cambridge: Cambridge University Press, 1991.

Balthazar, Scott L., ed. *The Cambridge Companion to Verdi*. Cambridge: Cambridge University Press, 2004.

Baring-Gould, Sabine, H. F. Sheppard, and F. W. Bissett. *Songs of the West: Folk Songs of Devon and Cornwall*. Edited by Cecil Sharpe. London: Methuen, n.d.

Bartók, Béla. *Hungarian Folksongs: Complete Edition*, vol. 1. Compiled by Béla Bartók. Commissioned by the Hungarian Academy of Sciences 1934–1940. Edited by Sándor Kovács and Ferenc Sebö. Budapest: Akadémiai Kiadó, 1993.

Bartók, Béla. *The Hungarian Folk Song*. Edited by Benjamin Suchoff. Translated by M. D. Calvocoressi. New York Bartók Archive Studies in Musicology, no. 13. Albany: SUNY Press, 1981.

Bayley, Amanda, ed. *Cambridge Companion to Béla Bartók*. Cambridge: Cambridge University Press, 2001.

Bekker, Paul. *Gustav Mahlers Sinfonien*. Berlin: Schuster & Loeffler, 1921. Reprint, 1969.

Beller-McKenna, Daniel. *Brahms and the German Spirit*. Cambridge, MA: Harvard University Press, 2004.

Berlioz, Hector. *Memoirs of Hector Berlioz: From 1803 to 1865; Comprising his Travels In Germany, Italy, Russia, and England*. Translated by Ernest Newman. London, 1932. Reprint, New York: Dover, 1966.

Bernard, Jonathan W. "Minimalism, Postminimalism, and the Resurgence of Tonality in Recent American Music." *American Music* 21, no. 1 (2003): 112–33.

Bernstein, Leonard. *The Unanswered Question: Six Talks at Harvard*. Cambridge, MA: Harvard University Press, 1976.

Bianconi, Lorenzo, and Giorgio Pestelli, eds. *The History of Italian Opera*, part 2, *Systems*, vol. 6 in *Opera in Theory and Practice, Image and Myth*. Translated from the Italian by Kenneth Chalmers and from the German by Mary Whittall. Chicago: University of Chicago Press, 2003.

Billeter, Bernhard. "Martin, Frank." *New Grove Dictionary of Music and Musicians* (hereafter *NG2*). Edited by Stanley Sadie and John Tyrrell, 15:908–12. London: Macmillan, 2001.

Billings, William. *The Continental Harmony*. Edited by Hans Nathan. The John Harvard Library. Cambridge, MA: Belknap Press of Harvard University, 1961.

Blume, Friedrich, Ludwig Finscher, Georg Feder, Adam Adrio, Walter Blankenburg, Torben Schousboe, Robert Stevenson, and Watkins Shaw. *Protestant Church Music: A History*. Foreword by Paul Henry Lang. New York: Norton, 1974.

Bobbitt, Richard. "Hindemith's Twelve-Tone Scale." *Music Review* 26, no. 2 (1965): 104–17.

Borchmeyer, Dieter. "Goethes *FAUST* musikalisch betrachtet." In *Eine Art Symbolik fürs Ohr: Johann Wolfgang von Goethe; Lyrik und Musik*. Heidelberger Beiträge zur deutschen Literatur, Vol. 12. Edited by Hermann Jung. Frankfurt am Main: Peter Lang, 2002.

Boulez, Pierre. "Schoenberg is DEAD!" *Score* 6 (1952): 18–22.

Boulez, Pierre. *Stocktakings from an Apprenticeship*. Collected and edited by Paule Thévenin. Translated from the French by Stephen Walsh, with an introduction by Robert Piencikowski. Oxford: Clarendon Press, 1991.

Boyd, Malcolm. "Britten, Verdi and the Requiem." *Tempo* 86 (1968): 2–6.

Brahms, Johannes, and Theodor Billroth. *Johannes Brahms and Theodor Billroth: Letters from a Musical Friendship*. Translated and edited by Hans Barkan. Norman: University of Oklahoma Press, 1957.

Breuer, János. *A Guide to Kodály*. Budapest: Corvina Books, 1990.

Briggs, Harold Edgar, ed. *The Complete Poetry and Selected Prose of John Keats*. Modern Library of the World's Best Books. New York: Modern Library, 1951.

Britten, Benjamin. "On Winning the First Aspen Award." In *Contemporary Composers On Contemporary Music*, edited by Elliot Schwarz and Barney Childs. New York: Da Capo Press, 1978.

Britten, Benjamin. *Letters from a Life: The Selected Letters of Benjamin Britten*. Edited by Donald Mitchell, Philip Reed, and Mervyn Cooke. 6 vols. London: Faber and Faber, 1991–2012.

Broadwood, Lucy E., and J. A. Fuller-Maitland. *English Country Songs: Words and Music*. New York: Charles Scribner's Sons, 1893.

Brown, David. *Mussorgsky: His Life and Works*. Master Musicians Series. Oxford: Oxford University Press, 2002.

Brown, Malcolm H., ed. *Mussorgsky in Memoriam, 1881–1891*. Ann Arbor, MI: UMI Press, 1982.

Brown, Peter. *Performing Haydn's "The Creation": Reconstructing the Earliest Renditions*. Bloomington: Indiana University Press, 1986.

Bullett, Gerald. *The English Galaxy of Shorter Poems Chosen and Edited by Gerald Bullett*. New York: Macmillan, 1934.

Cazden, Norman. "Hindemith and Nature." *Music Review* 15, no. 4 (1954): 288–306.

Chapple, Gerald, Frederick Hall, and Hans Schulte. *The Romantic Tradition: German Literature and Music in the Nineteenth Century*. Lanham, MD: University Press of America, 1992.

"Charles Villiers Stanford." *Musical Times and Singing Class Circular* 39, no. 670 (1898): 785–793.

Chikinda, Michael. "Pärt's Evolving Tintinnabuli Style." *Perspectives of New Music* 49, no. 1 (2011): 182–206.

Chusid, Martin, ed. *Verdi's Middle Period: 1849–1859; Source Studies, Analysis, and Performance Practice*. Chicago: University of Chicago Press, 1997.

Cobb, Buell E., Jr. *The Sacred Harp: A Tradition and its Music*. Athens: University of Georgia Press, 1989.

Cooper, Martin. *French Music: From the Death of Berlioz to the Death of Fauré*. London: Oxford University Press, 1951.

Crawford, Richard. "Psalmody (ii), II: North America." *NG2*, 20:480–83. London: Macmillan, 2001.

Daitz, Mimi S. *Ancient Song Recovered: The Life and Music of Veljo Tormis*. Dimension and Diversity Series, no. 3. Hillsdale, NY: Pendragon Press, 2004.

Daniel, Keith W. "Poulenc's Choral Works with Orchestra." In *Francis Poulenc: Music, Art and Literature*, edited by Sidney Buckland and Myriam Chimènes. Aldershot: Ashgate, 1999.

Daverio, John. *Robert Schumann: Herald of a "New Poetic Age."* New York: Oxford University Press, 1997.

Davies, R. T., ed. *Medieval English Lyrics: A Critical Anthology*. London: Faber and Faber, 1963.

Davidson, Audrey Ekdahl. *Olivier Messiaen and the Tristan Myth*. Westport, CT: Praeger, 2001.

Deaville, James. "Cornelius, (Carl August) Peter." *NG2*, 6:475–79. London: Macmillan, 2001.

Dibble, Jeremy. "Stanford, Sir Charles Villiers." *NG2*, 24:278–85. London: Macmillan, 2001.

DiOrio, Dominick. "Embedded Tonality in Penderecki's St. Luke Passion." *Choral Scholar* 3, no. 1 (2013): 1–16.

Dunlop, Carolyn C. *The Russian Court Chapel Choir, 1796–1917*. Music Archive Productions. Series F, 19th century; vol. 1. Amsterdam: Harwood Academic Publishers, 2000.

Ebrecht, Ronald. *Maurice Duruflé, 1902–1986: The Last Impressionist*. Lanham, MD: Scarecrow Press, 2002.

Edelman, Marsha Bryan. *Discovering Jewish Music*. Philadelphia: Jewish Publications Society, 2003.

Eden, Myrna G. *Energy and Individuality in the Art of Anna Huntington, Sculptor, and Amy Beach, Composer*. Composers of North America, no. 2. London: Scarecrow Press, 1987.

Edler, Arnfried. *Robert Schumann und seine Zeit*. Grosse Komponisten und ihre Zeit. Laaber, 1982.

Einstein, Alfred. *Mozart: His Character, His Work*. Translated by Arthur Mendel and Nathan Broder. New York: Oxford University Press, 1945.

Einstein, Alfred. *Music in the Romantic Era*. New York: Norton, 1975.

Emerson, Caryl, and Robert Oldani. *Modest Mussorgsky and "Boris Godunov": Myths, Realities, Reconsiderations*. Cambridge: Cambridge University Press, 1992.

Engelhardt, Markus. "'Something's Been Done to Make Room for Choruses': Choral Conception and Construction in *Luisa Miller*." In *Verdi's Middle Period: 1849–1859; Source Studies, Analysis, and Performance Practice*, edited by Martin Chusid, 197–206. Chicago: University of Chicago Press, 1997.

Eösze, Lázló, Mícheál Houlahan, and Philip Tacka. "Kodály, Zoltán." *NG2*, 13:716–26. London: Macmillan, 2001.

Evans, Peter. *The Music of Benjamin Britten*. Oxford: Oxford University Press, 1996.

Fabri, Paolo. "Metrical and Formal Organization." In *The History of Italian Opera*. Vol. 6, *Opera in Theory and Practice, Image and Myth*. Edited by Lorenzo Bianconi and Giorgio Pestelli. Translated from the Italian by Kenneth Chalmers and from the German by Mary Whittall. Chicago: University of Chicago Press, 2003.

Feder, Georg. "Decline and Restoration." In *Protestant Church Music*, edited by Friedrich Blume. New York: Norton, 1974.

Floros, Constantin. *Gustav Mahler: The Symphonies*. Translated by Vernon Wicker. Portland, OR: Amadeus Press, 1993.

Forbes, Elliot. *Thayer's Life of Beethoven*, 2 vols. Rev. ed. Princeton: Princeton University Press, 1967.

Frazier, James E. *Maurice Duruflé: The Man and His Music*. Eastman Studies in Music. Rochester, NY: University of Rochester Press, 2007.

Frogley, Alain. Liner notes to the London Symphony Orchestra and Chorus's recording of Ralph Vaughan Williams's *Sancta Civitas* and *Dona Nobis Pacem*. London: EMI Classics, 1993 (CDC 7 54788 2), 2.

Garden, Edward. "Alexander Kastalsky (1856–1926)." Available at http://musicarussica.com/Kastalsky, accessed August 30, 2015.

Garden, Edward. "Taneyev, Aleksandr Sergeyevich (1850–1918)." Available at http://www.grovemusiconline.com, accessed August 30, 2015.

Gardiner, George. *Marrow Bones: English Folk Songs from the Hammond and Gardiner MSS.* London: EFDS Publications, 1974.

French, Richard F. "Hindemith's Mass 1963: An Introduction." In *Words and Music: The Scholar's View; A Medley of Problems and Solutions Compiled in Honor of A. Tillman Merritt by Sundry Hands,* edited by Laurence Berman. Cambridge, MA: Harvard University Department of Music, 1972.

Friddle, David. "Franz Liszt's Oratorio *Christus.*" *Choral Journal* 46, no. 5 (2005): 89–99.

Gehring, Franz. "Liedertafel." *Grove Dictionary of Music and Musicians* (hereafter *NG*). Edited by Stanley Sadie, 10:848. London: Macmillan, 1980.

Geiringer, Karl. *Haydn: A Creative Life in Music.* 3rd. rev. ed. Berkeley: University of California Press, 1982.

Gerhard, Anselm. "Rossini and the Revolution." In *The Urbanization of Opera: Music Theater in Paris in the Nineteenth Century,* translated by Mary Whittall. Chicago: University of Chicago Press, 1998.

Gillies, Malcolm. "Béla Bartók." *NG2,* 2:808–18. London: Macmillan, 2001.

Goldman, Richard F. "Current Chronicle: New York." *Musical Quarterly* 37, no. 3 (1951): 405–10.

Gossett, Philip. "Becoming a Citizen: The Chorus in *Risorgimento* Opera." *Cambridge Opera Journal* 2, no. 1 (1990): 41–64.

Gossett, Philip. "Rossini, Gioachino." *NG,* 16:226–51. London: Macmillan, 1980.

Griesinger, Georg. *Biographische Notizen über Joseph Haydn.* Leipzig: Breitkopf & Härtel, 1810.

Halbreich, Harry. *Bohuslav Martinů: Werkverzeichnis, Documentation und Biographie.* Zurich: Atlantis Verlag, 1968.

Hansen, Peter S. *An Introduction to Twentieth Century Music.* 3rd ed. Boston: Allyn and Bacon, 1971.

Harrandt, Andrea. "Bruckner and the Liedertafel Tradition." *Choral Journal* 37, no. 5 (1996): 15–21.

Harrison, Lou. *Music Primer: Various Items about Music to 1970.* New York: C. F. Peters, 1971.

Heinzheimer, Hans, and Paul Stefan. *25 Jahre Neue Musik: Jahrbuch 1926 der Universal Edition.* Buchschmuck von Carry Hauser. Vienna: Universal Edition A.G., [nd], no. 8500.

Henderson, Lyn. "A Solitary Genius: The Establishment of Pärt's Technique (1958–68)." *Musical Times* 149 (2008): 81–88.

Hillier, Paul. *Arvo Pärt.* Oxford Studies of Composers. New York: Oxford University Press, 1997.

Hindemith, Paul. *The Craft of Musical Composition.* 2 vols. Translated by Arthur Mendel. 4th ed. New York: Associated Music Publishers, 1942.

Hitchcock, H. Wiley *Music in the United States: A Historical Introduction.* Englewood Cliffs, NJ: Prentice-Hall, 1969.

Hogwood, Christopher, and Richard Luckett, eds. *Music in Eighteenth-Century England.* Cambridge: Cambridge University Press, 1982.

Holst, Imogen. *Collected Facsimile Edition of Autograph Manuscripts of the Published Works of Gustav Holst.* Vol. 4, *First Choral Symphony, op. 41.* London: Faber Music, 1974.

Holst, Imogen. *A Thematic Catalogue of Gustav Holst's Music.* London: Faber Music, 1974.

Howes, Frank. *The English Musical Renaissance.* New York: Stein and Day, 1966.

Irmen, Hans-Josef. *Gabriel Josef Rheinberger als Antipode des Cäcilianismus.* Studien zur Musikgeschichte des 19. Jahrhunderts. Bd. 22. Regensburg: G. Bosse, 1970.

Johnson, James Weldon, and John Rosamund Johnson. *The Book of American Negro Spirituals.* New York: Viking Press, 1925.

Jung, Hermann. "Wozu Musik zu solch vollendeter Poesie? Robert Schumann und seine *Szenen aus Goethes* Faust." In *Eine Art Symbolic fürs Ohr: Johann Wolfgang von Goethe; Lyrik und Musik.* Heidelberger Beiträge zur deutschen Literatur, Band 12. Edited by Hermann Jung. Frankfurt am Main: Peter Lang, 2002.

Köhler, Joachim. *Richard Wagner: The Last of the Titans.* Translated by Stewart Spencer. New Haven, CT: Yale University Press, 2004. Originally published as *Der Letzte der Titanen–Richard Wagners Leben und Werk.* Munich: Claasen Verlag, 2001.

Krones, Hartmut, ed. *Arnold Schoenberg in seinen Schriften: Verzeichniz–Fragen–Editorisches.*Vol. 3, Schriften des Wissenschaftszentrum Arnold Schoenberg. Vienna: Böhlau Verlag, 2011.

Kross, Siegfried. *Die Chorwerke von Johannes Brahms.* Berlin: Max Hesses Verlag, 1958.

Kross, Siegfried. "The Choral Music of Johannes Brahms." *American Choral Review* 25, no. 4 (1983): 1–30.

Kross, Siegfried. *Johannes Brahms: Versuch einer kritischen Dokumentar-Biographie.* 2 vols. Bonn: Bouvier Verlag, 1997.

Kurzhals-Reuter, Arntrud. *Die Oratorien Felix Mendelssohn-Bartholdys: Untersuchungen zur Quellenlage, Entstehung, Gestaltung und Überlieferung.* Mainzer Studien zur Musikwissenschaft, vol. 12. Tutzing: Hans Schneider, 1978.

Kushner, David. *Ernst Bloch: A Guide to Research.* Garland Reference Library of the Humanities. Vol. 796, Garland Composer Resource Manuals. New York: Garland Press, 1988.

Lacombe, Hervé. *The Keys to French Opera in the Nineteenth Century.* Berkeley: University of California Press, 2001.

Lambert, Philip. *The Music of Charles Ives.* Composers of the Twentieth Century. Edited by Allen Forte. Ann Arbor, MI: Edwards Brothers, 1997.

Landau, Victor. "Hindemith the System Builder: A Critique of his Theory of Harmony." *Music Review* 22, no. 2 (1961): 136–51.

Lang, Paul Henry. *Music in Western Civilization.* New York: Norton, 1941.

Large, Brian. *Martinů.* New York: Holmes and Meier Publishers, 1975.

Lazarus, Emma. "The New Colossus." In *Emma Lazarus: Selected Poems and Other Writings,* edited by Gregory Eiselein. Orchard Park, NY: Broadview Literary Press, 2002.

Lichtenwanger, William. *The Music of Henry Cowell: A Descriptive Catalog.* Institute for Studies in American Music, Conservatory of Music, Brooklyn College of the City University of New York, 1968.

Likhachev, Dmitri, and Lev Dmitriev, eds. *Pamyatniki Literatury Drevni Rus': Vtoraya Polovina XVI. Veka* [Monuments of ancient Russian literature: Second half of the sixteenth century], 560–63. Moscow: Khudozhestvennaya Literatur, 1986.

Little, William, and William Smith. *The Easy Instructor, or, A new method of teaching sacred harmony. Containing, I. The rudiments of music on an improved plan. . . . A choice selection of psalm tunes and anthems, from the most celebrated authors, with a number composed in Europe and America, entirely new, suited to all the metres sung in the different churches of the United States.* Hopewell, near Trenton, NJ: William Smith, 1803. New ed. Albany, NY: Websters and Skinner and Daniel Steele, n.d. [1809].

Litzmann, Berthold, ed. *Clara Schumann–Johannes Brahms Briefe.* 2 vols. Leipzig: Breitkopf & Härtel, 1927. Reprint, Hildesheim, 1971.

Long, Kenneth R. *The Music of the English Church.* London: Hodder and Stoughton, 1972.

Lundergan, Edward. "Modal Symmetry and Textual Symbolism in the Credo of the Stravinsky Mass." *Choral Journal* 45, no. 8 (2005): 9–15.

MacIntyre, Bruce C. *Haydn: The Creation.* Monuments of Western Music. New York: Schirmer Books, 1998.

Mahler, Alma. *Gustav Mahler: Memories and Letters.* Translated by Basil Creighton. Seattle: University of Washington Press, 1968.

McGuire, Charles Edward. *Elgar's Oratorios: The Creation of an Epic Narrative.* Burlington, VT: Ashgate, 2002.

Mellers, Wilfrid. "Stravinsky's Oedipus as 20th-Century Hero." In *Stravinsky: A New Appraisal of His Work,* edited by Paul Henry Lang. New York: Norton, 1963.

Mellers, Wilfrid. *Vaughan Williams and the Vision of Albion*. London: Barrie and Jenkins, 1989.

Mendelssohn, Felix. *Letters from Italy and Switzerland*. Translated by Lady Wallace. 1865. Reprint. Freeport, NY: Books for Libraries Press, 1970.

Messiaen, Olivier. *Music and Color: Conversations with Claude Samuel*. Translated by E. Thomas Glasgow. Portland, OR: Amadeus Press, 1994.

Messiaen, Olivier. *The Technique of My Musical Language*. Translated by John Satterfield. 2 vols. Paris: A. Leduc, 1956.

Messing, Scott. *Neoclassicism in Music: From the Genesis of the Concept through the Schoenberg/Stravinsky Polemic*. Studies in Musicology 101. Ann Arbor, MI: UMI Research Press, 1988.

Mintz, Donald. "Mendelssohn's 'Elijah' Reconsidered." *Studies in Romanticism* 3, no. 1 (1963): 1–9.

Mintz, Donald. "Schumann as Interpreter of Goethe's 'Faust.'" *Journal of the American Musicological Society* 14, no. 2 (1961): 235–56.

Mitchell, Donald. *Gustav Mahler: Songs and Symphonies of Life and Death; Interpretations and Annotations*. Berkeley: University of California Press, 1985.

Mitchell, Donald, and Andrew Nicholson, eds. *The Mahler Companion*. New York: Oxford University Press, 1999.

Moody, Ivan. "Górecki: The Path to the 'Miserere.'" *Musical Times* 133 (1992): 283–84.

Morosan, Vladimir. *Choral Performance in Pre-Revolutionary Russia*. Russian Music Studies, No. 17. Ann Arbor, MI: UMI Research Press, 1986.

Morosan, Vladimir. "Folk and Chant Elements in Musorgsky's Choral Writing." In *Musorgsky in Memoriam, 1881–1891*, edited by Malcolm H. Brown. Ann Arbor, MI: UMI Press, 1982.

Neighbour, O. W. "Schoenberg, Arnold," *NG2*, 22:577–604. London: Macmillan, 2001.

Neruda, Pablo. *España en el Corazón*. "Residence on Earth" ("Residençia en la tierra"). Translated by Donald D. Walsh. New Direction Books. New York: New Directions, 1973.

New Grove Dictionary of American Music. Edited by Charles Hiroshi Garrett. 2nd edition. New York: Oxford University Press, 2013.

Neumann, Peter Horst. "Anmerkungen zu Robert Schumanns *Szenen aus Goethes* Faust." In *Eine Art Symbolic fürs Ohr: Johann Wolfgang von Goethe; Lyrik und Musik*, edited by Hermann Jung. Heidelberger Beiträge zur deutschen Literatur, Band 12. Frankfurt am Main: Peter Lang, 2002.

Newman, Ernest. *Elgar*. Music of the Masters Series, 3rd ed. London: John Lane, Bodley Head, 1922.

Nicholls, David. *American Experimental Music, 1890–1940*. Cambridge: Cambridge University Press, 1990.

Nichols, Roger. *Messiaen*. Oxford Studies of Composers 13. Oxford: Oxford University Press, 1986.

Norris, Geoffrey. *Rachmaninoff*. Master Musician Series. London: Oxford University Press, 1993.

Onderdonk, Julian. "Vaughan Williams's Folksong Transcriptions: A Case of Idealization?" In *Vaughan Williams Studies*, edited by Alain Frogley. Cambridge: Cambridge University Press, 1996.

Osmond-Smith, David. *Berio*. Oxford Studies of Composers 20. Oxford: Oxford University Press, 1991.

Osmond-Smith, David. "Berio, Luciano." *NG2*, 3:350–58. London: Macmillan, 2001.

Owen, Wilfred. *The Complete Poems and Fragments*. 2 vols. Edited by John Stallworthy. London: Chatto and Windus, 1983.

Palmer, Christopher. *Herbert Howells: A Centenary Celebration*. London: Thames Publishing, 1992.

Parry, C. Hubert H. *Style in Musical Art*. Oxford: Clarendon Press, 1900.

Payne, Anthony. "The Music of Frank Bridge: (1) The Early Years." *Tempo* 106 (1973): 18–25.

Payne, Anthony. "The Music of Frank Bridge: (2) The Late Years." *Tempo* 107 (1973): 11–18.

Payne, Anthony. "Peter Maxwell Davies's Five Motets." *Tempo* 72 (1965): 7–11.

Penderecki, Krzysztof. *Labyrinth of Time: Five Addresses for the End of the Millennium*. Chapel Hill, NC: Hinshaw Music, 1998.

Pendle, Karin, and Stephen Wilkins. "Paradise Found: The Salle le Peletier and French Grand Opera." Chap. 7 in *Opera in Context: Essays on Historical Staging from the Late Renaissance to the Time of Puccini*. Edited by Mark A. Radice. Portland, OR: Amadeus Press, 1998.

Pestelli, Giorgio. *The Age of Mozart and Beethoven*. Cambridge: Cambridge University Press, 1984.

Peyser, Joan. *To Boulez and Beyond: Music in Europe Since the "Rite of Spring."* New York: Billboard Books, 1999.

Phillips-Matz, Mary Jane. *Verdi: A Biography*. Oxford: Oxford University Press, 1993.

Pirie, Peter. *The English Musical Renaissance*. London: Gollancz, 1979.

Piston, Walter. "Stravinsky's Rediscoveries." In *Stravinsky in the Theatre*, edited by Minna Lederman. New York: Pellegrini and Cudahy, 1949.

Pöschl, Josef. *Jagdmusik: Kontinuität und Entwicklung in der europäischer Geschichte*. Tutzing: Hans Schneider, 1997.

Purslow, Frank, ed. *Marrow Bones: English Folk Songs from the Hammond and Gardiner Mss.* London: EFDS Publications, 1965.

Raabe, Peter. *Franz Liszt*. 2 vols. Stuttgart: Colla, 1931.

Randel, Don Michael, ed. *The Harvard Dictionary of Music*. 4th ed. Cambridge, MA: Belknap Press of Harvard University Press, 2003.

Reilly, Edward R. "*Todtenfeier* and the Second Symphony." In *The Mahler Companion*, edited by Donald Mitchell and Andrew Nicholson. New York: Oxford University Press, 1999.

Restagno, Enzo. "Petrassi, Goffredo." *NG2*, 19:499–503. London: Macmillan, 2001.

Rich, Alan. *American Pioneers: Ives to Cage and Beyond*. London: Phaidon Press, 1995.

Rilke, Rainer Maria. *Sämtliche Werke*. Zweiter Band. Edited by the Rilke Archive. Wiesbaden: Breitkopf & Härtel, 1957.

Ringer, Alexander L. *Arnold Schoenberg: The Composer as Jew*. New York: Oxford University Press, 1990.

Robbins-Landon, H. C. *Haydn: Chronicle and Work*. Vol. 4, *Haydn: The Years of Creation, 1796–1800*. Bloomington: Indiana University Press, 1977.

Robinson, Ray. *Choral Music: A Norton Historical Anthology*. New York: Norton, 1978.

Robinson, Ray, and Allen Winold. *A Study of the Penderecki St. Luke Passion*. Celle: Moeck Verlag, 1983.

Rodmell, Paul. *Charles Villiers Stanford*. Music in Nineteenth-Century Britain. Burlington, VT: Ashgate, 2002.

Roeder, John. "Transformational Aspects of Arvo Pärt's Tintinnabuli Music." *Journal of Music Theory* 55, no. 1 (2011): 1–41.

Roy, Jean. *Francis Poulenc: L'homme et son oeuvre*. Paris: Seghers, 1964.

Rufer, Joseph. *Composition with Twelve Notes Related Only to One Another*. Translated by Humphrey Searle. London: Barrie and Rockliff, 1954.

Rupprecht, Philip. *Britten's Musical Language*. Cambridge: Cambridge University Press, 2001.

Rushton, Julian. *Berlioz: Roméo et Juliette*. Cambridge Music Handbooks. Cambridge: Cambridge University Press, 1994.

Rushton, Julian. *The Music of Berlioz*. Oxford: Oxford University Press, 2001.

Sachs, Joel. *Henry Cowell: A Man Made of Music*. New York: Oxford University Press, 2012.

Scher, Steven Paul. "Hoffmann, Weber, Wagner: The Birth of Romantic Opera from the Spirit of Literature?" In *The Romantic Tradition: German Literature and Music in the Nineteenth Century*, edited by Gerald Chapple, Frederick Hall, and Hans Schulte. Lanham, MD: University Press of America, 1992.

Schmidt, Carl B. *The Music of Francis Poulenc (1899–1963): A Catalogue*. Oxford: Clarendon Press; New York: Oxford University Press, 1995.

Schmitz, Oskar A. H. *Das Land ohne Musik: Englische Gesellschaftsprobleme*. Munich, 1914.

Schneider, David E. *Bartók, Hungary and the Renewal of Tradition: Case Studies in the Intersection of Modernity and Nationality*. Berkeley: University of California Press, 2006.

Schnittke, Alfred. *A Schnittke Reader*. Edited by Alexander Ivashkin. Translated by John Goodliffe. Russian Music Studies. Bloomington: Indiana University Press, 2002.

Scholes, Percy. *The Mirror of Music, 1844–1944: A Century of Musical Life in Britain as Reflected in the Pages of the "Musical Times."* 2 vols. London: Novello; Oxford University Press, 1947.

Schubring, Julius, ed. *Briefwechsel zwischen Felix Mendelssohn Bartholdy und Julius Schubring, zugleich ein Beitrag zur Geschichte und Theorie des Oratoriums*. Leipzig: Dunder and Humbolt, 1892. Reprint, Walluf bei Wiesbaden: M. Sändig, 1973.

Schumann, Robert. *Tagebücher*. Vol. 2, 1836–1854. Edited by Gerd Neuhaus. Leipzig: VEB Deutscher Verlag für Musik, 1987.

Schwarz, K. Robert. "Process vs. Intuition in the Music of Steve Reich and John Adams." *American Music* 8, no. 3 (1990): 245–73.

Schwinger, Wolfram. *Krzysztof Penderecki: His Life and Work; Encounters, Biography and Musical Commentary*. Translated by William Mann. London: Schott, 1989.

Sebesta, Judith Lynn. *Carmina Burana: Cantiones profanes*. Chicago: Bolchazy-Carducci Publishers, 1985.

Service, Tom. "John Tavener Dies at 69; The Veil Falls for the Final Time." Obituary in *The Guardian*. November 12, 2013. Available at www.theguardian.com/music/2013/nov/12/john-tavener-british-copmposer-dies.

Shattuck, Roger. *The Banquet Years: The Origins of the Avant-Garde in France; 1885 to World War I*. New York: Vintage Books, 1955.

Sherlaw Johnson, Robert. *Messiaen*. Berkeley: University of California Press, 1975.

Sherwood, Gayle. "'Buds the Infant Mind': Charles Ives's *The Celestial Country* and American Protestant Choral Traditions." *Nineteenth-Century Music* 23, no. 2 (1999): 163–89.

Sherwood, Gayle. "Redating Ives's Choral Sources." In *Ives Studies*, edited by Philip Lambert. Cambridge: Cambridge University Press, 1997.

Short, Michael. *Gustav Holst: The Man and his Music*. Oxford: Oxford University Press, 1990.

Sichardt, Martina. "Schönberg, Arnold." *Die Musik in Geschichte und Gegenwart: Allgemeine Enzyklopädie begründet von Friedrich Blume*. Zweite neubearbeitete Ausgabe, ed. Ludwig Finscher. Personenteil, Vol. 14, "Ric–Schön." Kassel: Bärenreiter Verlag, 2005.

Siegel, Linda. *Music in German Romantic Literature: A Collection of Essays, Reviews, and Stories*. Novato, CA: Elra Publications, 1983.

Silverberg, Ann L. *A Sympathy with Sounds: A Brief History of the University of Illinois School of Music to Celebrate Its Centennial 1995*. Urbana: University of Illinois School of Music, 1995.

Smart, Mary Ann. "Verdi, Italian Romanticism and the Risorgimento." In *The Cambridge Companion to Verdi*, edited by Scott L. Balthazar. Cambridge: Cambridge University Press, 2004.

Smith, Joan Allen. *Schoenberg and His Circle: A Viennese Portrait*. New York: Schirmer Books, 1986.

Smither, Howard E. *A History of the Oratorio*. Vol. 3, *The Oratorio in the Classical Era*. Chapel Hill: University of North Carolina Press, 1987.

Somfai, Lázló. *Béla Bartók: Composition, Concepts and Autograph Sources*. Berkeley: University of California Press, 1996.

Stevenson, Robert. *Protestant Church Music in America: A Short Survey of Men and Movements from 1564 to the Present*. New York: Norton, 1966.

Stewart, Michael J. "Sir John Tavener obituary." Available at www.theguardian.com/music/2013/nov/12/john-tavener.

Straus, Joseph N. "Stravinsky's Tonal Axis." *Journal of Music Theory* 25–26, no. 2 (1981–82): 260–90.

Stravinsky, Igor. *An Autobiography*. New York: Simon and Schuster, 1936. Reprint, New York: Norton, 1962.

Stravinsky, Igor, and Robert Craft. *Dialogues and A Diary*. London: Faber and Faber, 1968.

Strickland, Edward. *American Composers: Dialogues on Contemporary Music*. Bloomington: Indiana University Press, 1991.

Strimple, Nick. *Choral Music in the Twentieth Century*. Portland, OR: Amadeus Press, 2002.

Stuckenschmidt, Hans Heinz. *Schoenberg: His Life, World and Works*. Translated by Humphrey Searle. London: John Calder, 1977.

Swafford, Jan. *Johannes Brahms: A Biography*. New York: Vintage Books, 1999.

Syer, Katherine R. "Wagner's Shaping of the Grail Scene of Act I." In *A Companion to Wagner's Parsifal*, edited by William Kinderman and Katherine R. Syer, 177–214. Rochester, NY: Camden House, 2005.

Taruskin, Richard. *The Oxford History of Western Music*. 5 vols. Vol. 4. "Music in the Early Twentieth Century"; Vol. 5. "Music in the Late Twentieth Century." New York: Oxford University Press, 2005.

Temperley, Nicholas. *Haydn: The Creation*. Cambridge Music Handbooks. Cambridge: Cambridge University Press, 1991.

Temperley, Nicholas. "New Light on the Libretto of *The Creation*." In *Music in Eighteenth-Century England*, edited by Christopher Hogwood and Richard Luckett, 189–211. Cambridge: Cambridge University Press, 1983.

Thomas, André. *Way Over in Beulah Lan': Understanding and Performing the Negro Spiritual*. Dayton, OH: Heritage Music Press, 2007.

Thomson, Virgil. *Music Reviewed, 1940–1954*. New York: Vintage Books, 1957.

Thomson, William. *Schoenberg's Error*. Studies in the Criticism and Theory of Music. Philadelphia: University of Pennsylvania Press, 1991.

Trend, Michael. *The Music Makers: The English Musical Renaissance from Elgar to Britten*. London: Weidenfeld and Nicholson, 1985.

Van den Toorn, Peter C. *The Music of Igor Stravinsky*. Composers of the Twentieth Century. New Haven, CT: Yale University Press, 1983.

Vaughan Williams, Ralph. *National Music and Other Essays*. Oxford: Oxford University Press, 1967.

Vinaver, Chemjo. *Anthology of Jewish Music: Sacred Chants and Religious Folk Songs of the Eastern European Jews*. New York: Edwards B. Marks, 1955.

Von Gunden, Heidi. *The Music of Ben Johnston*. Metuchen, NJ: Scarecrow Press, 1986.

Von Gunden, Heidi. *The Music of Lou Harrison*. Metuchen, NJ: Scarecrow Press, 1995.

Von Gunden, Heidi. *The Music of Pauline Oliveros*. Metuchen, NJ: Scarecrow Press, 1983.

Wagner, Cosima. *Cosima Wagner's Diaries*. Translated by Geoffrey Skelton. New York: Harcourt Brace Jovanovich, 1980.

Wagner, Cosima. *Tagebücher*, vol. 2. Edited by Martin Gregor-Dellin and Dietrich Mack. Munich and Zurich: Piper, 1977.

Wagner, Richard. "Reminiscences of Auber" ("Erinnerungen an Auber"). In *Richard Wagner's Prose Works*. Vol. 5, *Actors and Singers*. Translated by William Ashton Ellis. London, 1896. Reprint, New York: Broude Brothers, 1966.

Walsh, Stephen. *Stravinsky: Oedipus Rex*. Cambridge Music Handbooks. Cambridge: Cambridge University Press, 1993.

Walter, Horst. "Gottfried van Swieten's handschriftliche Textbücher zu *Schöpfung* und *Jahreszeiten*." *Haydn-Studien* 1, no. 4 (1967).

Warnaby, John. "Davies, Peter Maxwell." *NG2*, 7:63–72. London: Macmillan, 2001.

Watkins, Glenn. *Soundings: Music in the Twentieth Century*. Belmont, CA: Wadsworth Group, 1995.

Webern, Anton. *Letters to Hildegard Jone and Josef Humplik*. Edited by Josef Polnauer. Translated by Cornelius Cardew. Bryn Mawr, PA: Theodore Presser, 1967.

Weller, Philip. "Messiaen, the *Cinq Rechants* and 'Spiritual Violence.'" In *Messiaen Perspectives 1: Sources and Influences*, edited by Christopher Dingle and Robert Fallon, 279–312. Farnham: Ashgate, 2013.

White, Eric Walter. *Stravinsky: The Composer and his Works*. 2nd ed. Berkeley: University of California Press, 1979.

Whitman, Walt. *Complete Poetry and Collected Prose*. Library of America. New York: Literary Classics of the United States. Distributed by Viking Press, 1982.

Whittall, Arnold. *Musical Composition in the Twentieth Century*. Oxford: Oxford University Press, 1999.

Williamson, Karina. *The Complete Poetical Works of Christopher Smart*. Vol. 1. *Jubilate Agno*. Oxford English Texts. Oxford: Clarendon Press, 1980.

Wingfield, Paul. *Janáček: Glagolitic Mass*. Cambridge Classical Music Handbook Series. Cambridge: Cambridge University Press, 1992.

Wood, Hugh. "Frank Bridge and the Land without Music." *Tempo* 121 (1977): 7–11.

Wörner, Karl H. *Stockhausen: Life and Work*. Translated and edited by Bill Hopkins. Berkeley: University of California Press, 1973.

Xenakis, Iannis. *Formalized Music: Thought and Mathematics in Composition*. Bloomington: Indiana University Press, 1971.

Young, Percy M. *Elgar, Newman, and The Dream of Gerontius: In the Tradition of English Catholicism*. Brookfield, VT: Ashgate, 1995.

Young, Percy M. *Elgar, O.M.: A Study of a Musician*. Rev. ed. London: White Lion Publishers, 1973.

Young, Percy M., ed. *Letters to Nimrod*. London: Dennis Dobson, 1965.

Zielinski, Richard. "Karol Szymanowski (1882–1937): The Father of Contemporary Polish Music." *Choral Journal* 46, no. 3 (2005): 9–24.

SCORES OF SELECTED WORKS

Adams, John. *El Niño*. Piano reduction by John McGinn. New York: Hendon Music; Boosey & Hawkes, distributed by Hal Leonard (HL 48021216), 2000.

Adams, John. *Harmonium*. New York: Associated Music Publishers (G. Schirmer), 1984.

Adams, John. *On the Transmigration of Souls*. New York: Hendon Music: Boosey & Hawkes; Milwaukee, WI: Distributed by Hal Leonard (HL 48019451), 2009.

Bartlett, Clifford J., ed. *Madrigals and Partsongs*. Oxford: Oxford University Press, 2001.

Bartók, Béla. *Cantata Profana*. Vienna: Universal Edition; New York: Boosey & Hawkes, 1955.

Berlioz, Hector. *New Edition of the Complete Works*, Hugh Macdonald, general ed. Vol. 18: *La Damnation de Faust*, op. 24. Edited by Julian Rushton. Kassel: Bärenreiter (5448), 1979.

Berlioz, Hector. *New Edition of the Complete Works*, Hugh Macdonald, general ed. Vol. 8 a–b. *Roméo et Juliette*, op. 17. Edited by D. Kern Holoman. Kassel: Bärenreiter (5458), 1990.

Berio, Luciano. *Coro*. Milan: Universal Edition, 1976.

Berio, Luciano. *Cries of London*. Milan: Universal Edition, 1976.

Berio, Luciano. *Magnificat*. New York: Belwin Mills (EL 2289), 1971.

Berio, Luciano. *Sinfonia*. London: Universal Edition, no. 13f 783mi, 1969.

Bernstein, Leonard. *Chichester Psalms*. New York: Amberson Enterprises. Boosey & Hawkes.

Bernstein, Leonard. *Kaddish: Symphony No. 3*. New York: Amberson Enterprises; G. Schirmer (48031), 1980.

Bloch, Ernst. *Avodath Hakodesh (Sacred Service)*. New York: Broude Brothers. Summy-Birchard Music, assigned to Broude Bothers, 1962, 1972.

Brahms, Johannes. *Rinaldo, op. 50.* Edited by J. Bradford Robinson. Munich: Musikproduction Höfflich, 2004.

Bruckner, Anton. *Sämtliche Werke*, vol. 23, pt. 2, *Weltliche Chorwerke.* Edited by Angela Pachovsky and Anton Reinthaler. Vienna: Musikwissenschaftlicher Verlag, 2001.

Cornelius, Peter. *Musikalische Werke: Erste Gesamtausgabe im Auftrage seiner Familie herausgegeben von Max Hasse.* 5 vols. Vol. 2, "Mehrstimmige Lieder und Gesänge." Leipzig: Breitkopf & Härtel, 1905–06, Reprint, Westmead: Gregg International, 1971.

Dallapiccolla, Luigi. *Canti di Prigionia.* Milan: Carisch, 1941.

Debussy, Claude. *Le Martyre de Saint Sébastien.* Munich: Musikproduction Höfflich, 2008.

Elgar, Edward. *The Dream of Gerontius*, op. 38. Mineola, NY: Dover Publications, 2002.

Elgar, Edward. *Four Unaccompanied Part-Songs*, op. 53. Borough Green: Novello, 1978.

Fauré, Gabriel. *Requiem in D minor*, op. 48. New York: Dover Publications, c2000.

Ferneyhough, Brian. *Missa Brevis.* Hinrichsen Edition, 1969 (C. F. Peters, 7125).

Hindemith, Paul. *Apparebit Repentina Dies.* London: Schott, 1947.

Hindemith, Paul. *When Lilacs Last in the Dooryard Bloom'd: A Requiem "For Those We Love."* New York: Associated Music Publishers, 1948; Mainz: B. Schott's Söhne (Edition Schott 3800).

Holst, Gustav. "First Choral Symphony, op. 41." *Gustav Holst Collected Facsimile Edition.* Edited by Imogen Holst and Colin Matthews. Vol. 4. London: Faber Music, 1983.

Holst, Gustav. *Hymn of Jesus*, op. 37. London: Stainer & Bell, 1919.

Honegger, Arthur. *King David (Le Roi David).* English version by Edward Agate. Lausanne: Foetisch Freres, 1925, 1962.

Ives, Charles Edward. The Celestial Country (*Tenebris vitae in lucem coeli*). Edited by John Kirkpatrick. New York: Peer International Corporation (PIC 2254-90), 1971, 1973.

Janáček, Leoš. *Glagolitic Mass (Mša glagolskáya).* Vienna: Universal Edition (No. 9544), 1928, 1956.

Kagel, Mauricio. *Chorbuch.* Frankfurt; New York: H. Litolff's Verlag/C. F. Peters, 1993.

Kodály, Zoltán. *Psalmus Hungaricus.* Vienna: Universal Edition (UE 7550 8463), 1928.

Krenek, Ernst. *Lamentatio Jeremiae prophetae*, op. 93. Kassel: Bärenreiter Verlag (BA 3648), 1957.

Ligeti, György. *Lux Aeterna.* Frankfurt: H. Litolff's Verlag; New York: C. F. Peters, 1968.

Ligeti, György. *Magyar Etüdök.* Schott Kammerchor Reihe (SKR 20006). Mainz: B. Schott's Söhne, 1983.

Lutosławski, Witold. *Trois poèmes d'Henri Michaux.* Krakow: Polskie Mydawn. Muzyczne [1965, 1963].

Mahler, Gustav. *Symphonie II, Reverdierte Fassung.* Philharmonie Partituren 395. Vienna: Universal Edition, 1897, 1925.

Mahler, Gustav. *Symphonie No. 8.* Mineola, NY: Dover Publications, 1989.

MacMillan, James. *Cantos Sagrados.* London: Boosey & Hawkes, 1992.

MacMillan, James. *Seven Last Words from the Cross.* Boosey & Hawkes (HPS 1360), 2003.

Martin, Frank. *Golgotha; oratorio en deux parties . . . d'apres les Evangiles et des textes de Saint Augustin.* Vienna: Universal Edition (UE 11949], 1953.

Mendelssohn, Felix. *Die erste Walpurgisnacht*, op. 60. New York. Edwin F. Kalmus, n.d.

Mendelssohn, Felix. *Paulus*, op. 36. Edited by Michael Märker. Wiesbaden: Breitkopf & Härtel, 1998.

Messiaen, Olivier. *Cinq rechants.* Paris: Rouart Lerolle; Salabert, 1949.

Milhaud, Darius. *Les Choéphores.* French translation by Paul Claudel. Paris: Heugel (H 30244), 1947.

Nono, Luigi. *Il Canto Sospeso.* Edited by Christopher Flamm. London: Eulenburg (EE8029), 1955, 1957, 1995.

Pärt, Arvo. *Adam's Curse.* Vienna: Universal Edition (UE 34741), 2010.

Pärt, Arvo. *Collected Choral Works: Complete Scores.* Edited by Paul Hillier. Hamburg: UE Publishing Musikverlags, GmbH., 1999.

Pärt, Arvo. *Credo* (1968). Vienna: Universal Edition (UE 33344), 1982, 2006.

Pärt, Arvo. *Passio Domini nostri Jesu Christi secundum Johannem.* Vienna: Universal Edition (UE 17568), 1985.

Penderecki, Krzysztof. *Agnus Dei.* Mainz: B. Schott's Söhne (Schott Kammerchor Reihe 20002), 1983.

Penderecki, Krzysztof. *Credo.* Piano score by Claus-D. Ludwig. Mainz: B. Schott's Söhne, 1998.

Penderecki, Krzysztof. *Pieśń Cherubinów (Cherubinischer Lobgesang).* Mainz: B. Schott's Söhne (SKR 20020), 1987.

Penderecki, Krzysztof. *Passio et mors Domini Nostri Jesum Christum secundum Lucam.* Masterpieces of Polish 20th Century Music. Krakow: Polskie Wydawn. Muzyczne (PWM 5677), 2000.

Penderecki, Krzysztof. *Stabat Mater.* Warszawa: Polskie Wydawn. Muzyczne, 1963.

Pepping, Ernst. *Passionsbericht nach Matthäus.* Kassel: Bärenreiter (BA 2276), 1960.

Pizzetti, Ildebrando. *Messa di Requiem.* Milan: G. Ricordi, 1923, 1966.

Poulenc, Francis. *Dialogues des Carmélites.* New York: G. Ricordi, 1959.

Poulenc, Francis. *Figure humaine.* Paris: Rouart Lerolle et Cie. (Editions Salabert), 1945.

Poulenc, Francis. *Gloria.* New rev. ed. Paris: Salabert, 1959, 1960.

Poulenc, Francis. *Sonata for Clarinet in B-flat and piano.* 4th ed. London: J. W. Chester, ca. 1963.

Prokofiev, Sergei. *Alexander Nevsky,* op. 78. Edited by Harold Sheldon. English text by A. Steiger. New York: MLA Music, 1966.

Rachmaninoff, Sergei. *All-night Vigil,* op. 37. Edited by Vladimir Morosan and Alexandra Ruggieri. Monuments of Russian Sacred Music. Series 9, vol. 2. 2nd ed., rev. and corr. Madison, CT: Musica Russica, 1992.

Rautavaara, Einojuhani. *"Suite" de Lorca (Lorca-sarja),* op. 72. Helsinki: Edition Fazer, 1976.

Reger, Max. *Sämtliche Werke.* Vol. 27: *Chorwerke a cappella.* Edited by Hermann Grabner. Wiesbaden: Breitkopf & Härtel, 1961.

Reich, Steve. *The Desert Music.* New York: Hendon Music (983), 1985.

Reich, Steve. *Tehillim.* New York: Hendon Music (1189), 1994.

Rossini, Gioachino. *Edizione Critica delle Opere di Gioachino Rossini: Sezzione Prima–Opere Teatrali.* Vol. 39, "Guillaume Tell," Edited by M. Elizabeth C. Bartlett. Fondazione Rossini Pesaro. Milan: G. Ricordi, 1992.

Rutter, John, ed. *European Sacred Music.* London: Oxford University Press, 1996.

Rutter, John, and Clifford Bartlett, eds. *Opera Choruses.* London: Oxford University Press, 1995.

Schnittke, Alfred. *Zwölf Bussverse (= 12 Stikhi pokaiannye).* Frankfurt: M. P. Belaieff, 1995.

Schoenberg, Arnold. *Sämtliche Werke, Abteilung V: Chorwerke, Reihe A. Bd. 19: De Profundis,* op. 50b. Edited by Josef Rufer and Christian Martin Schmidt. Kassel: Bärenreiter, 1975.

Schoenberg, Arnold. *Friede auf Erden,* op. 13. Mainz: B. Schott's Söhne (SKR 19008), 1995.

Schumann, Robert. *Szenen aus Goethes Fausts,* WoO 3. Leipzig: Breitkopf & Härtel (1895), Munich: Musikproduktion Höflich, 2005.

Schumann, Robert. *Das Paradies und die Peri.* Edited by Rita Gerencsér. Zurich: Eulenburg, 1979.

Stockhausen, Karlheinz. *Mikrophonie II.* London: Universal Edition (UE 15140E), 1974.

Stockhausen, Karlheinz. *Momente.* Kürten, Germany: Stockhausen Verlag, 1993.

Stravinsky, Igor. *Canticum Sacrum ad honorem Sancti Marci nominis.* London: Boosey & Hawkes (8168), 1956.

Stravinsky, Igor. *Mass.* London: Boosey & Hawkes (16501), 1948.

Stravinsky, Igor. *Oedipus Rex.* Rev. ed., 1948. London: Boosey & Hawkes (16497), 1949.

Stravinsky, Igor. *Symphony of Psalms.* Piano score by Soulima Stravinsky. Rev. ed., New York: Boosey & Hawkes, 1948.

Tavener, John. *Coplas.* London: J. & W. Chester, 1971.

Tormis, Veljo. *Raua Needmine.* Helsinki: Warner/Chappell Music Finland; Fennica Gehrmann, 2007.

Vaughan Williams, Ralph. *Dona nobis pacem.* Vocal Score. London: Oxford University Press, 1936.

Wagner, Richard. *Sämtliche Werke in Verbindung mit dem Bayerische Akademie der Schönen Künste, München herausgegeben von Carl Dahlhaus.* Vol. 4, 1–4. "Der fliegende Holländer; Romantische Oper in drei Aufzügen (Urfassung, 1841)." Mainz: B. Schott's Söhne; Vienna: Universal Edition, 1983. Vol. 14, 1–3. "Parsifal: Ein Bühnenfestspiele, Erster Aufzug." Mainz: B. Schott's Söhne; Vienna: Universal Edition. 1972.

Xenakis, Iannis. *Knephas.* Paris: Salabert, 1993.

Xenakis, Iannis. *Nuits.* Ed. Patrick Butin. Paris: Salabert, 1969.

Xenakis, Iannis. *Sea Nymphes.* Paris: Salabert (EAS 19220), 1994.

Permissions

2.8 *Der Wassermann*, Op. 91, No. 3 by Robert Schumann. © Breitkopf und Haertel. Reprinted by Gregg International Publishers, Ltd., 1968. Public Domain. 2.9 *Die Nachtigall*, Op. 59, No. 4 by Felix Mendelssohn. © Breitkopf und Haertel. Reprinted by Gregg International Publishers, Ltd., 1967. Public Domain. 2.10 *Fruehzeitiger Fruehling*, Op. 59, No. 2 by Felix Mendelssohn. © Breitkopf und Haertel. Reprinted by Gregg International Publishers, Ltd., 1967. Public Domain. 2.11 *Der Jaeger Abschied*, Op. 50, No. 2 by Felix Mendelssohn. © Breitkopf und Haertel. Reprinted by Gregg International Publishers, Ltd., 1968. Public Domain. 2.12 *Vineta*, Op. 42, No. 2 by Johannes Brahms. © Breitkopf und Haertel (1926–7). Reprinted by J. W. Edwards, 1949. Public Domain. 2.13 *Waldesnacht*, Op. 62, No. 3 by Johannes Brahms. © Breitkopf und Haertel (1926–7). Reprinted by J. W. Edwards, 1949. Public Domain. 2.14 *Der Bucklichte Fiedler*, Op. 93a, No. 1 by Johannes Brahms. © Breitkopf und Haertel (1926–7). Reprinted by J. W. Edwards, 1949. Public Domain. 2.15–16 *O süsser Mai*, Op. 93a, No. 4 by Johannes Brahms. © Breitkopf und Haertel (1926–7). Reprinted by J. W. Edwards, 1949. Public Domain. 2.17–18 *Nachtwache* I, Op. 104, No. 1 by Johannes Brahms. Clifford Bartlett, ed. *Madrigals and Partsongs* © Oxford University Press 2001. Used by permission. All rights reserved. Photocopying this copyright material is ILLEGAL. 2.19 *Der Abend*, Op. 64, No. 2 by Johannes Brahms. © Breitkopf und Haertel (1926–7). Reprinted by J. W. Edwards, 1949. Public Domain. 2.20 *Troesterin Musik* by Anton Bruckner. Public Domain. 2.21 *Grablied*, Op. 9, No. 4 by Peter Cornelius. © Breitkopf und Haertel. Reprinted by Gregg International Publishers, Ltd. (1971). Public Domain. 2.22 *Liebeslied*, Op. 20, No. 4 by Peter Cornelius. © Breitkopf und Haertel. Reprinted by Gregg International Publishers, Ltd., (1971). Public Domain. 2.23 *Über Die Berge*, Op. 38, No. 3 by Max Reger. © 1961 by Breitkopf und Haertel. Used by permission. 2.24 *The Blue Bird*, Op. 119, No. 3 by Charles Villiers Stanford. Clifford Bartlett, ed. *Madrigals and Partsongs* © Oxford University Press 2001. Used by permission. All rights reserved. Photocopying this copyright material is ILLEGAL. 2.25 *Music, When Soft Voices Die* by C. Hubert H. Parry. Clifford Bartlett, ed. *Madrigals and Partsongs* © Oxford University Press 2001. Used by permission. All rights reserved. Photocopying this copyright material is ILLEGAL. 2.26 *There Is Sweet Music* from *Four Part Songs*, Op. 53. Music by Edward Elgar (1847–1934). Words by Alfred, Lord Tennyson (1809–92). © Novello & Company Limited. All rights reserved. Reprinted by permission. 2.27 *Deep In My Soul* from *Four Part Songs*, Op. 53. Music by Edward Elgar (1847–1934). Words by Lord Byron (1788–92). © Novello & Company Limited. All rights reserved. Reprinted by permission. 2.28 *Owls* from *Four Part Songs*, Op. 53. Music by Edward Elgar (1847–1934). Words by Alfred Lord Tennyson (1809–92). © 1908 Novello & Company Limited. All rights reserved. Reprinted by permission.

CHAPTER 3

3.1–2 *Guillaume Tell*. Music by Gioachino Rossini. Copyright by Fondazione Rossini-Pesaro (Italy). Reproduced by kind permission. 3.3–7 John Rutter, ed. *Opera Choruses* © Oxford University Press 1995. Used by permission. All rights reserved. Photocopying of this copyright material is ILLEGAL. 3.8 *Richard Wagner: Sämtliche Werke in Verbindung mit dem Bayerische Akademie der Schönen Kuenste, München*; Band 4: 1–4, edited by Carl Dahlhaus. Mainz: B. Schott's Söhne, 1983. Used with permission. 3.9 *Richard Wagner: Sämtliche Werke in Verbindung mit dem Bayerische Akademie der Schönen Künste, München*; Band 14, 1–3, edited by Carl Dahlhaus. Mainz: B. Schott's Söhne, 1972. Used with permission. 3.10 *La Damnation De Faust*, Op. 24 by Hector Berlioz. © Breitkopf und Haertel, 1900. Public Domain. 3.11–14 *Die Erste Walpurgisnacht*, Op.

60 by Felix Mendelssohn. © Breitkopf und Haertel. Reprinted by Gregg International Press Limited (1967). Public Domain. 3.15 *Szenen Aus Goethes Faust*, WoO 3 by Robert Schumann. © Breitkopf und Haertel. Reprinted by Gregg International Press Limited (1973). Public Domain. 3.16 *Alto Rhapsodie*, Op. 53 by Johannes Brahms. © Breitkopf und Haertel. Reprinted by J. W. Edwards (1949). Public Domain. 3.17–18 *Gesang Der Parzen*, Op. 89 by Johannes Brahms. © Breitkopf und Haertel. Reprinted by J. W. Edwards (1949). Public Domain.

CHAPTER 4

4.1 Symphony No. 9 in D Minor, Op. 125 by Ludwig van Beethoven. *Beethoven Werke*; Edition Breitkopf. Used by permission. 4.2–3 Symphony No. 2 in B♭ Major, Op. 52, "Lobgesang" by Felix Mendelssohn. © Breitkopf und Haertel. Reprinted by Gregg International Press Limited (1967). Public Domain. 4.4 *Roméo et Juliette*, Op. 17. Music by Hector Berlioz. Breitkopf und Haertel, 1900–07. Public Domain. 4.5–6 Symphony No. 2 in D Minor. Music by Gustav Mahler. © 1917 by Universal Edition Vienna, London © Renewed Used by permission of European American Music Distributors, LLC, US and Canadian agent for Universal Edition, Vienna. 4.7–10 Symphony in E♭ Major ("Symphony of a Thousand"). Music by Gustav Mahler. © 1992 Dover Publications. Used by permission. 4.11a *Hymn To The Dawn*, Op. 26, No. 3. Music by Gustav Holst. © 1920 J. W. Chester. Used with the kind permission of Stainer & Bell, Ltd. 4.11b *Ode To Death*, Op. 38. Music by Gustav Holst (1874–1934). Words by Walt Whitman (1819–1892). © 1922 Novello & Company Limited. All rights reserved. Used by permission. 4.11c *Nunc Dimittis*. Music by Gustav Holst (1874–1934). © 1919 Novello & Company Limited. All rights reserved. Reprinted by permission. 4.11d, 4.12, 4.13a, 4.14 *First Choral Symphony*, Op. 41. Music by Gustav Holst. By permission G. and I. Holst, Ltd. 4.13b *The Planets*, Op. 32, "Mercury" by Gustav Holst. Public Domain. 4.15 *Spring Symphony*, Op. 44 by Benjamin Britten. © 1949 Hawkes & Son (London) Ltd. Reprinted by permission. Boosey & Hawkes Inc., sole agent. All rights reserved. International Copyright Secured. Reprinted by permission. 4.16–17 *Kaddish Symphony* by Leonard Bernstein. © Copyright 1963, 1965, 1977, 1980. Copyright assigned to Amberson Holdings LLC, Leonard Bernstein Music Publishing Co., LLC, Publisher.

CHAPTER 5

5.1–2 Clifford Bartlett, ed. *Madrigals and Partsongs* © Oxford University Press 2001. Used by permission. All rights reserved. Photocopying of this material is ILLEGAL. 5.3 John Rutter, ed. – © Oxford University Press 1996 Used by permission. All rights reserved. Photocopying this copyright material is ILLEGAL. 5.4 With the kind authorization of Hamelle, Paris. 5.5–6 Foetsche Freres, Lausanne. Used with permission. 5.7 *Les Choéphores* by Darius Milhaud. © Heugel et Cie 1947. (H. 30244) Reprinted with kind permission of Heugel et Cie. 5.8a *La Bonne Neige* (extrait de *Un soir de neige*) © Universal Musical Publishing Ricordi. Used with the kind authorization Les Editions Durand & Salabert. 5.8b *Salve Regina*, mm. 1–2 © Editions Salabert. Used with the kind authorization Les Editions Durand & Salabert." 5.11a. Gloria © 1960 Editions Salabert. Used with the kind authorization Les Editions Durand & Salabert. 5.11b. Sonata for Clarinet © 1963 Chester Music Limited. All rights reserved. International Copyright Secured. Reprinted by permission. 5.11c. *Dialogues Des Carmelites* (Extrait) © Universal Musical Publishing Ricordi. Used with the kind authorization Les Editions Durand & Salabert. 5.12 Requiem (op. 9) © 1968 Editions Salabert. Used with the kind authorization Les Editions Durand & Salabert. 5.13 *Ubi*

Caritas et Amor (extrait de *4 Motets*) © 1960, Editions Salabert. Used with the kind authorization Les Editions Durand & Salabert. 5.14–15 *O Sacrum Convivium* © 1937 Editions Durand. Used with the kind authorization Les Editions Durand & Salabert. 5.16–21 *Cinq rechants* by Olivier Messiaen. © 1949 Editions Salabert. Used with the kind authorization Les Editions Durand & Salabert.

CHAPTER 6

6.1–6 *Friede auf Erden*, Op. 13 by Arnold Schoenberg. Used with kind permission of European American Music Distributors, LLC, sole US and Canadian agent for Schott Music. 6.7 *Entflieht auf leichten Kaehnen*, Op. 2 by Anton Webern. ©1921, 1948 by Universal Edition A.G., Vienna © Renewed. All rights reserved. Used by permission of European American Music Distributors, LLC, sole US and Canadian agent for Universal Edition A.G., Vienna. 6.8–10 *De Profundis*, Op. 50B by Arnold Schoenberg. © Belmont Music. Reprinted by permission. 6.11 *Das Augenlicht*, Op. 36 by Anton Webern. © 1938 by Universal Edition A.G., English Version © 1956 Universal Edition A.G. © Renewed. All rights reserved. Used by permission of European American Music Distributors, LLC, sole US and Canadian agent for Universal Edition, A.G., Vienna. 6.12 *Kantate* I, Op. 29 by Anton Webern. © 1929 by Universal Edition A.G., © Renewed. All rights reserved. Used by permission of European American Music Distributors, LLC, sole US and Canadian agent for Universal Edition, A.G., Vienna. 6.13 *Canticum Sacrum* by Igor Stravinsky. © 1956 by Hawkes & Son (London), Ltd. US copyright renewed. Reprinted by permission. 6.14 *The Dove Descending Breaks the Air* by Igor Stravinsky. © 1962 by Boosey & Hawkes Music Publishers Limited. US Copyright renewed. Reprinted by permission. 6.15 *Canti di Prigionia* by Luigi Dallapiccola. Milano: Carisch, © 1939. Public Domain. 6.16–17 *Lamentatio Jeremiae Prophetae*, Op. 93. Bärenreiter Verlag, Kassel. Used with permission. 6.18 *Aus den Psalmen Davids* by Krysztof Penderecki. © 1976 by Schott Music. All rights reserved. Used by permission of European American Music Distributors, LLC, sole US and Canadian agent for Schott Music. 6.19 *St. Luke Passion* by Krysztof Penderecki © 1960 by Schott Music, © Renewed. All rights reserved. Used by permission of European American Music Distributors, LLC, sole US and Canadian agent for Schott Music. 6.20 *Cantata Academica*, Op. 62 by Benjamin Britten. © 1959 Boosey & Co. Ltd. Reprinted by permission.

CHAPTER 7

7.1 Public Domain. 7.2 Public Domain. 7.3 *Just as the Tide Was Flowing* Music by Ralph Vaughn Williams. © Copyright 1913 Stainer & Bell. Used by kind permission. 7.4 *The Dark-Eyed Sailor* Music by Ralph Vaughan Williams. © Copyright 1913 Stainer & Bell. Used by kind permission. 7.5 *Hymns from the Rig Veda*, Op. 26, No. 3. Music by Gustav Holst. © 1920 J. & W. Chester. Used by permission. 7.6–7 *Hymn to Jesus*, Op. 37. Music by Gustav Holst. Used by kind permission of Stainer & Bell, Ltd. London, England. 7.8 *Sancta Civitas* Music by Ralph Vaughan Williams. © Copyright 1925 by Ralph Vaughan Williams. Exclusively licensed to and reproduced by J. Curwen & Sons Limited for the World (ex British Reversionary Territories including but not limited to the United Kingdom, Eire, Canada, Australia, New Zealand, Israel, South Africa, British African and Caribbean Territories, Hong Kong, Malaysia, Pakistan, Singapore). All rights reserved. International Copyright Secured. 7.9 R. Vaughan Williams *Dona nobis pacem* © Oxford University Press 1936, Renewed in USA., 1964. Used by permission.

7.10 *Psalmus Hungaricus*, Op. 13 by Zoltán Kodály. © 1926 by Universal Edition A.G., Vienna. All rights reserved. Used by permission of European American Music Distributors, LLC, solo US and Canadian agent for Universal Edition, Vienna. 7.11 *Missa Brevis* by Zoltán Kodály. © Copyright 1947 by Boosey and Hawkes Music Publisher, Inc. Copyright renewed. Boosey & Hawkes, Inc., sole licensee. For the world except Hungary. Reprinted by permission. 7.12 *Four Slovak Folksongs* by Béla Bartók. © Copyright 1924 by Hawkes & Son (London) Ltd., Reprinted by permission. 7.13–14 *The Prisoner* from *Four Hungarian Folksongs* by Béla Bartók. © Copyright 1932 by Hawkes & Son (London) Ltd. Reprinted by permission. 7.15–17 *Cantata Profana* by Béla Bartók. ©1934 by Universal Edition A. G., Wien/UE 10613 © Renewed All rights reserved. Used in the territory of the world excluding the U. S. by permission of European American Music Distributors LLC, agent for Universal Edition A.G., Wien. 7.18 *Éjszaka* by György Ligeti. © 1973 by Schott Music © Renewed All rights reserved Used by permission of European American Music Distributors LLC, sole US and Canadian agent for Schott Music. 7.19 *Concerto 34: Da Vokresnnet Boh* by Dmitri Bortniansky. © Copyright 2005 by Musica Russica Incorporated. Used with permission. All rights reserved. 7.20 *Heruvimskaya Pesn*, Op. 7.1 by Pavel Chesnokov. © 1991 by Musica Russica Incorporated. Used by permission. 7.21 *All-Night Vigil*, Op. 37 by Sergey Rachmaninoff. © 1992 by Musica Russica Incorporated. Reprinted by permission. All rights reserved. 7.22 *Alexander Nevsky*, Op. 78 by Sergey Prokofiev. Copyright © 1941 (Renewed) by G. Schirmer, Inc. (ASCAP) International Copyright Secured. All rights reserved. Used by permission. 7.23–24 *Raua Needmine* by Veljo Tormis. © 1972. Revised, 1991. Fennica Gehrmann Oy, Helsinki. Used with permission. 7.25 *Eesti Kalendrilaulud 5: Jaanilaulud* by Veljo Tormis. © Copyright 2007. Fennica Gehrman Oy, Helsinki. Used with permission.

CHAPTER *8*

8.1–5 *Oedipus Rex* by Igor Stravinsky. © Copyright 1927 by Hawkes & Son (London) Ltd. Revised version © 1949, 1950 by Hawkes & Son (London) Ltd. US Copyright renewed, Reprinted by permission. 8.6–11 *Symphony of Psalms* by Igor Stravinsky. © Copyright 1930 by Hawkes & Son (London), Ltd. Revised version © Copyright 1948 by Hawkes & Son (London) Ltd. US copyright renewed. Reprinted by permission. 8.12 *Mass* by Igor Stravinsky. © Copyright 1948 by Hawkes & Son (London) Ltd. Reprinted by permission. 8.13 *The Craft of Musical Composition* by Paul Hindemith, 2 vols. 4th Edition. © 1942 Associated Music Publishers. Public Domain. 8.14 *Six Chansons* by Paul Hindemith. © 1943 by Schott Music © Renewed All rights reserved Used by permission of European American Music Distributors LLC, sole US and Canadian agent for Schott Music. 8.15–18 *Requiem* by Paul Hindemith. © Copyright 1946 by Schott Music © Renewed. All rights reserved. Used by permission of European American Music Distributors, LLC, sole US and Canadian for Schott Music. 8.19 *Apparebit Repentina Dies* by Paul Hindemith. © 1947 Copyright Schott Music © Renewed. Used by permission of European American Music Distributors, LLC, sole US and Canadian for Schott Music. 8.20 *Carmina Burana* by Carl Orff. © 1937 by Schott Music © Renewed. Used by permission of European American Music Distributors, LLC, sole US and Canadian for Schott Music. 8.21 *Lobe den Herren*, Op. 6, No. 2 by Hugo Distler. © Copyright 1967-68 by Bärenreiter Verlag, Kassel. Used with permission. 8.22 *Der Totentanz*, Op. 12, No. 2 by Hugo Distler. © Copyright 1953 by Bärenreiter Verlag, Kassel. Used with permission. 8.23 *Jesus Und Nikodemus* by Ernst Pepping. © Copyright 1938 by Schott Music © Renewed All rights reserved Used by permission of European American

CHAPTER 9

CHAPTER 10

10.12–13 *Golgotha* Music by Frank Martin. © Copyright 1949 by Universal Edition A.G., Vienna © Renewed. All rights reserved. Used by permission of European American Music Distributors LLC, sole US and Canadian agent for Universal Edition A.G., Vienna. 10.14–15 *Songs of Ariel* Music by Frank Martin. © Copyright 1949 by Universal Edition A.G., Vienna © Renewed. All rights reserved. Used by permission of European American Music Distributors LLC, sole US and Canadian agent for Universal Edition A.G., Vienna. 10.16 *Signposts* Music by Eskil Hemberg. © 1969 Walton Music Corp. Used by permission. 10.17 *Messa d'oggi* Music by Eskil Hemberg. © 1972 Walton Music Corp. Used by permission. 10.18 *Saul* Music by Egil Hovland. © 1972 Walton Music Corp. Used by permission. 10.19 *De Profundis* Music by Knut Nystedt. Copyright © 1966 (Renewed) by Associated Music Publishers, Inc. (BMI) International Copyright Secured. All rights reserved. Used by permission. 10.20 *O Crux* Music by Knut Nystedt. Copyright © 1978 Hinshaw Music. Chapel Hill, NC International Copyright Secured. All rights reserved. Used by permission. 10.21 *De Profundis*, Op. 9, No. 2 Music by Bernhard Lewkovitch. Copyright © 1952 Edition Wilhelm Hansen AS, Copenhagen. International Copyright Secured. All rights reserved. Reprinted with permission. 10.22 *Tre Madrigali di Torquato Tasso*, Op. 13 Music by Bernhard Lewkovitch. Copyright © Wilhelm Hansen AS. Used with permission. 10.23-24 *Suite de Lorca* Music by Einojuhani Rautavaara. © Copyright 1976 Fennica Gehrman Oy, Helsinki. Printed with permission. 10.25 *Die erste Elegie* Music by Einojuhani Rautavaara © Copyright 1994 Fennica Gehrmann Oy, Helsinki. Printed with permission. 10.26 *Vigilia* ("Psalm of Invocation") Music by Einojuhani Rautavaara. © Copyright 2008. Fennica Gehrmann Oy, Helsinki. Printed with permission.

CHAPTER 11

11.1–3a Public Domain. 11.3b "Celestial Country" by Charles Ives/ Copyright © 1971, 1973 by Peer International Corporation/ Copyright Renewed/ All rights reserved/ Used by permission. 11.4 *Psalm 67* Music by Charles Ives. Copyright © 1939 (Renewed) by Associated Music Publishers, Inc. (BMI) International Copyright Secured. All rights reserved. Reprinted by permission. (A-274). 11.5 *Psalm 24* by Charles Ives. Copyright 1955. Carl Fischer, LLC. On behalf of Theodore Presser Co. Used with permission. 11.6 *Harvest Home Chorales* by Charles Ives. Copyright 1949. Carl Fischer, LLC. On behalf of Theodore Presser Co. Used with permission. 11.7–8 *Psalm 90* by Charles Ives. Copyright 1970. Merion Music. Carl Fischer, LLC. On behalf of Theodore Presser Co. Used with permission. 11.9–11 *In the Beginning* by Aaron Copland. © Copyright 1947 by The Aaron Copland Fund for Music, Inc. Copyright renewed. Boosey & Hawkes, Inc., sole licensee. Reprinted by permission. 11.12 *The Peaceable Kingdom* by Randall Thompson. © Copyright 1936 by E. C. Schirmer Music Co. Used with permission. 11.13 "Choose Something Like A Star" (from *Frostiana*) by Randall Thompson. © Copyright 1962 (c. 1960), E. C. Schirmer Music Co. Used with permission. 11.14–16 *Reincarnations*, Op. 16 by Samuel Barber. Copyright © 1942 (Renewed) by G. Schirmer, Inc. (ASCAP) International Copyright Secured. All rights reserved. Reprinted by permission. 11.17 *Chichester Psalms* by Leonard Bernstein. © 1965 by Amberson Holdings LLC, Publisher Boosey & Hawkes Inc., sole agent. All rights reserved. International copyright secured. Reprinted by permission. 11.18 "Dominic has a Doll" Op. 98, No. 1 by Vincent Persichetti. Carl Fischer, LLC. On behalf of Theodore Presser Co. Used with permission. 11.19 *Mass*, Op. 84, "Kyrie" by Vincent Persichetti. Copyright 1961. Carl Fischer, LLC. On behalf of Theodore Presser Co. Used with permission. 11.20 *The Prairie* Music by Lukas Foss. Copyright

CHAPTER 12

CHAPTER 13

Index

Notes

Page numbers for examples from musical scores are in *italics* and are followed by the letter *e*.
Page numbers for figures (images) are in *italics* and are followed by the letter *f*.
Page numbers for tables are in *italics* and are followed by the letter *t*.

Printed in the USA/Agawam, MA
December 2, 2021

785532.028